THE LEGAL

& ETHICAL

ENVIRONMENT

OF BUSINESS

THE LEGAL

& ETHICAL

ENVIRONMENT

OF BUSINESS

EDWIN W. TUCKER, B.A., M.A., J.D., LL.M., S.J.D.

Professor of Business Law
School of Business Administration
The University of Connecticut

JAN W. HENKEL, B.S., M.B.A., J.D.
Professor of Legal Studies
Terry College of Business
University of Georgia

IRWIN
Homewood, IL 60430
Boston, MA 02116

Sponsoring editor: Craig Beytien
Project editor: Rebecca Dodson
Production manager: Diane Palmer
Designer: Jeanne Rivera
Art coordinator: Mark Malloy
Compositor: Better Graphics, Inc.
Typeface: 10/12 Cheltenham Light
Printer: Von Hoffman Press, Inc.

Library of Congress Cataloging-in-Publication Data
Tucker, Edwin Wallace, 1927-
    The legal and ethical environment of business / Edwin W. Tucker,
Jan W. Henkel.
      p.   cm.
    Includes index.
    ISBN 0-256-09154-4
    1. Industrial laws and legislation—United States. 2. Trade
regulation—United States. 3. Commercial law—United States.
4. Business ethics—United States. 5. Industry—Social aspects—
United States. I. Henkel, Jan. W. II. Title.
KF1600.T83 1992
346.73′07—dc20
[347.3067]   91-11602

Printed in the United States of America
1 2 3 4 5 6 7 8 9 0 VH 8 7 6 5 4 3 2 1

To Gladys and Audrey for their patience, understanding, and thoughtfulness

Preface

Teaching in a Dynamic Environment

In the course of performing their duties, judges, legislators, and public officials are often challenged to scrutinize and evaluate established legal principles. When in doubt as to the suitability of such principles, they are prone to consider whether the principles should continue to be followed. If convinced that a change is called for, and if they have the power to bring it about, they are likely to replace the principles that they find unacceptable.

Professional Inquiry

The inquiries of professors who teach law in the context of business behavior do not end with the study or application of past and present legal principles. These professors must look beyond the law and probe the restraints on business behavior that exist apart from the law, such as contemporary ethical standards and the voluntarily adopted restraints of firms and business persons. They must do this if they are to help their students to fully appreciate the full breadth of the domestic and global parameters within which firms and businesspersons are expected to satisfy an enormous variety of demands.

Blending Law and Ethics

Because both law and ethics are directed at how business is conducted, both are considered in every chapter after Chapter 1, in which ethical constraints on business behavior are introduced and extensively examined. Chapters 2 through 20 deal with law and ethics either concurrently or in tandem. Among the ways in which this is done is through cases in which the court takes both legal and ethical principles into account to arrive at a decision; immediately after each court case, the pos-ing of questions on both legal issues and ethical issues; the presentation and examination of legal principles and ethical standards alongside each other; and the examination of related ethical concerns in a portion of chapters that are primarily devoted to the study of a particular array of legal principles.

Interlacing of Domestic and International Law

In light of the increasing trend in business toward multinational development, the impact of the law of other nations on the transaction of business in the global economy is treated in a manner similar to the treatment of ethics. A single chapter, Chapter 20, is entirely devoted to transnational trade. However, other chapters also deal with international business. This is done to avoid the segregation of legal rules that are directed at global trade from those that are directed at domestic business arrangements, with the unfortunate result that foreign law is likely to be overlooked. "Law Abroad" sections illustrate how a legal issue is treated by the legal systems of the European Community, Germany, Japan, and other countries. This alerts students to the fact that firms and business executives must take both domestic and foreign law into account when they do business abroad.

Judicial Reasoning

An understanding of judicial reasoning is essential if one is to fully grasp how courts go about the judging process. To impart such an understanding, a portion of Chapter 3 is devoted to this subject. Many of the court decisions included in the text are edited in such a way so as to include crucial aspects of the judge's reasoning. As a result, in a number of instances the length of the court's decision that appears in the text is more extensive than the length of edited cases commonly found in texts that do not use court cases for this purpose. This "beyond the bare bones" approach offers students an opportunity to gain insights into judicial reasoning that would otherwise be denied them. In addition, each chapter contains hypothetical cases. These cases are described in the same way as one would describe the facts of actual cases. The questions that follow the hypothetical cases challenge students to carefully analyze the facts, consider the legal principles with which they are familiar, and offer their views as to the principle or principles that should be used to resolve the controversy. The legal principles are discussed in the textual material that follows.

Students are invited to test their understanding of judicial reasoning by the questions posed in Chapters 2 through 20 and by the Review Questions & Problems that appear at the close of these chapters. The Review Questions & Problems allow students not only to draw on materials dealt with in the given chapter but also to step out on their own and go beyond the principles that they have already studied. This dual-purpose format beckons them to apply what they have learned and to think creatively. In those instances in which they must work without having already been exposed to the relevant legal principles, they are asked to act as if they were judges who have been called on to make new law in order to resolve disputes. This mind-broadening task should enhance students' awareness of the judicial process and their appreciation of judicial reasoning.

Historical Perspective

Legal constraints are sometimes best understood if they are examined in light of what has gone before. In such instances a brief historical statement precedes the examination of the present legal standard.

Book Structure

To promote ease of presentation and facilitate study, the text is divided into 20 chapters and the following nine parts:

Part 1, "Introduction to Business Ethics, Legal Philosophies, and the Judicial and Legislative Process," examines business ethics and corporate social responsibility. It also considers the functions of law, justice, legal philosophies, and the judicial and legislative process.

Part 2, "Litigation, Alternate Dispute Resolution, and the Administrative Process," comprises chapters on court procedure, various forms of alternate dispute resolution, and the function and operation of administrative agencies.

Part 3, "Business Crimes, Business Torts, and Contracts," covers business crimes, business torts, and the essentials and enforceability of contracts.

Part 4, "Constitutional Law," examines the restrictions that the Constitution places on governmental regulation of business.

Part 5, "Corporate Law," deals with the legal parameters within which corporations must operate.

Part 6, "Employment Law," focuses on employer-employee relations, unlawful employer discrimination, and union-management relations.

Part 7, "Consumerism and Environmental Regulation," examines the various ways in which law protects consumers and the legal rules that government uses to safeguard the environment.

Part 8, "Securities Law and Antitrust Policy," considers securities laws as well as policies designed to protect competition.

Part 9, "International Business," examines legal principles that have to do with transnational trade.

Ease of Study

The following features are intended to smooth the way for students to appreciate the materials covered in the text:

Chapter Overviews: Commentary at the start of each chapter signals what is to follow.

Margin Definitions: Terms in the text that warrant prompt explanation are defined in the margin.

Linkage of Law and Ethics: Questions on legal issues and ethical issues follow each of the court cases in Chapters 2 through 20.

Hypothetical Cases and Questions: Hypothetical cases and questions that call for creative thinking are specifically identified as such.

EDWIN W. TUCKER
JAN W. HENKEL

Acknowledgments

Together the authors have taught undergraduate and graduate college students for almost 50 years. During that time we have had the privilege of teaching thousands of students. This book reflects many of their questions and concerns. Without their contributions we would not have been able to include the broad variety of questions and the responses to those concerns that will ease the task of the students who use this text. Our discussions with business executives at executive seminars and in other settings have assured that this book includes "real world" materials. Our exchanges of ideas with teachers in foreign universities have especially sensitized us to the importance of foreign law. Time and again, our sponsoring editor, Craig Beytien, helped us to steer clear of tempting pitfalls and prompted us to find a better route. Ceaselessly, our project editor Becky Dodson lent her uniquely comforting assistance to dispel potential roadblocks so as to leave us free to proceed with the tasks at hand. We are extremely grateful to Gene Zucker for the care and attention that he paid to our manuscript and for his many thoughtful and provoking comments and suggestions. The astute analyses of statistical data provided by Pamela A. Tucker and Leonard B. Sanders were particulary helpful. Special thanks go to Marc Lampe, University of San Diego, for his contribution in the area of alternate dispute resolution. We wish to thank the following professors who read the entire manuscript and provided us with their extremely helpful reviews:

Don Evans—Stephen F. Austin State University

Myron Erickson—University of Missouri-Columbia

Thomas L. Gossman—Western Michigan University

Harold Hotelling—University of Kentucky-Lexington

Eric Richards—Indiana University

John R. Carrell—North Texas State University

Jeffrey Randall Pittman—Arkansas State University

Roscoe Shain—Austin Peay State University

Marsha E. Hass—College of Charleston

John Houlihan—University of Southern Maine

Mary L. MacNabb—University of Nevada-Las Vegas

Susan E. Grady—University of Massachusetts-Amherst

John M. Norwood—University of Arkansas

Ann R. Henry—University of Arkansas

Adley Shulman—Humboldt State University

Janice Loutzenhiser—California State University-San Bernardino

Contents in Brief

Contents

APPENDIXES

PART

1

INTRODUCTION TO BUSINESS ETHICS, LEGAL PHILOSOPHIES, AND THE JUDICIAL AND LEGISLATIVE PROCESS

1. Business Ethics, Corporate Social Responsibility, and the Legal Environment of Business

2. Functions of Law, Justice, and Legal Philosophy

3. The Judicial and Legislative Process

1

CHAPTER

1

Business Ethics, Corporate Social Responsibility, and the Legal Environment of Business

In the 1980s many firms and individuals were possessed by unrestrained greed. They sought to make untold amounts of money in a very short time, giving little attention to how they acquired their wealth. By the beginning of the 1990s, some of the foremost financial winners of the 80s were losers, loathed by those whom they had cheated. A number of persons who had acquired celebrity status and wealth during the "anything goes" 80s were by 1990 convicted felons, defendants in criminal cases, or targets of investigation for possible criminal wrongdoing. Others were either in the throes of bankruptcy or no longer in business.

In the wake of what occurred in the 1980s, a challenge arose to measure the worth of businesses and businesspersons by their behavior. Are they ethical? Do they obey the law? Are they fulfilling their compact with society to act responsibly?

This chapter presents various views of ethical conduct. It also examines the demands of corporate social responsibility, introduces the legal environment of business, illustrates codes of ethics, and considers ways in which business may help resolve matters of public concern.

ETHICS, ACCOUNTABILITY, AND LAW

Ethics
standards of worthy conduct

Standards of worthy conduct are commonly spoken of as **ethics.** The term *business ethics* may refer both to how businesses and businesspersons *do* behave and to how they *should* behave. In matters of public concern, society expects business to behave with a sense of "corporate social responsibility" or "enterprise accountability." A study of corporate social responsibility focuses on the ways in which businesses respond to this expectation. The legal constraints within which business must operate are the "legal environment of business." Unlike the constraints on behavior imposed by ethics and social responsibility, these constraints are enforceable through courts or through other governmental bodies that are commonly referred to as "administrative agencies."

Generally, the demands of business ethics, corporate social responsibility, and the legal environment of business are consistent. For example, it is generally ethical for firms to fulfill their lawful contractual obligations. In most instances they do so. Not to do so would ordinarily be regarded as socially irresponsible. When lawful agreements are not honored, courts ordinarily enforce them.

At times business behavior that some regard as unethical or as socially irresponsible may be lawful. One may consider it unethical and socially irresponsible for a seller not to allow an absentminded buyer to cancel an exorbitantly overpriced purchase. Traditionally, however, at the seller's insistence a court would enforce the contract for such a purchase. But widespread misgivings about the blanket enforceability of consumer purchase agreements led to legislation which allows consumers to cancel various sorts of such agreements.

WHY BE ETHICAL, RESPONSIBLE, AND OBEDIENT TO THE LAW

A firm's success is often influenced by how well its actions measure up against ethical standards and by whether it conducts its affairs in a socially responsible way and obeys the law. A firm may succeed because its executives and employees take pride in the fact that it behaves ethically, meets its social obligations, and complies with the law. Thus most business executives believe that "ethics is good business." This view reflects the fact that other businesses, businesspersons, and customers are likely to avoid or discontinue dealings with firms that are unethical, socially irresponsible, or break the law.

Widespread unethical, socially irresponsible, or illegal types of business activity lead to general anxiety about business behavior. The public's confidence in business and businesspeople declines. Business transactions are marked by suspicion, apprehension, and concern. In response to the public's demands, legislators enact new laws to curb the objectionable forms of business conduct.

The current law of insider trading is an example of how legislation has been used to fill gaps in business ethics. Five decades ago it was common for a potential investor who knew a director or officer of a firm to solicit inside information about the firm's plans and its probable future profitability before purchasing its stock. Profiting from the use of such information was then regarded as both ethical and lawful. Today, few if any persons believe such behavior is ethical. As we shall see in Chapter 17, it is illegal.

VARIOUS IDEAS OF ETHICAL BEHAVIOR

There is practically universal agreement that certain acts are unethical. Few people would regard unprovoked killing as acceptable conduct. Generally, however, there is room for disagreement among individuals and groups as to whether a particular act is or is not ethical. For instance, a society that places a high value on individual success is far more likely to view as ethical actions intended solely to promote personal gain than is a society that regards promotion of the general welfare as the primary value.

Table 1-1 identifies various views of ethical behavior that have been advanced from the time of the ancient Greek philosophers to the present.

Early Greek Philosophers

In speaking of ethics, about 2,500 years ago, Socrates expressed the belief that proper behavior contributes to individual happiness. To find contentment, persons should pursue the truth, make their souls "as good as possible," and acquire

---

Views of Ethics TABLE 1-1

Early Greek philosophers	Socrates: Truth; good; self-awareness Plato: Praiseworthy conduct Aristotle: Doing the right thing; self-control
Theological doctrine	Religious commands as ethical behavior
Self-centered values	Psychological realism Ethical egoism Pragmatic ethics
Concern for others	Utilitarian ethics Expectancy ethics Ethical relativism Ethics of fairness Preventive ethics
Inflexible or flexible standards	A priori ethics Situation ethics
Conglomerative values	Intuitive ethics Cultural relativism

knowledge of the "true good." He summoned each individual to "know thyself." A brief time later Plato characterized ethical behavior as praiseworthy action. Shortly thereafter Aristotle asserted that it is ethical to do what is "right" and "good." To be ethical, persons must control their desires.

Theological Doctrine

Religious Commands as Ethical Behavior

Many ethical standards have their origins in theological doctrine. Time and again, it is said that a person who does not lie, cheat, or steal is ethical. This simple and concise measure of ethical behavior originated in the Judeo-Christian principles of the Old and New testaments, particularly in the Ten Commandments and the Golden Rule.

Self-Centered Values

Psychological Realism

Psychological realism
views action in one's best interest as ethical if it is acceptable to other group members

According to the view of ethics commonly referred to as **psychological realism,** it is ethical for individuals to act in their own best interests so long as such behavior is generally acceptable to other group members. Under this objective standard, if, for personal gain, most of a firm's financial executives generally inflate the firm's or their own accomplishments, it would be ethical for the other financial executives and for employees in the financial division to do the same. This view of ethics is fraught with danger. A chief executive officer or board of directors that sanctions psychological realism invites irresponsible and illegal behavior by firm executives and employees.

Ethical Egoism

Ethical egoism
views behavior motivated by self-interest as ethical

Like psychological realism, the ethical standard known as **ethical egoism** approves of behavior motivated merely by an individual's desire for personal gain. But this model of proper behavior does not require an objective test to decide whether the individual's action is ethical. How others would behave in comparable circumstances is irrelevant. Everyone is free to decide how to advance his or her own interests. As strange as it may seem, under this subjective measuring rod, it is ethical for corporate executives to award themselves bonuses, salaries, and perquisites hideously in excess of their contributions. No consideration need be given to the effect of doing this on the company's other officers, employees, stockholders, creditors, or customers, or on society as a whole. Because individual choice is the sole limitation that ethical egoism places on the pursuit of personal gain, only external restraints, such as a firm's code of ethics and the law, can check the relentless pursuit of self-interest.

Pragmatic Ethics

Pragmatic ethics
views behavior that produces desired results as ethical

The view of ethics that pays special attention to means and ends and emphasizes behavior that promotes the efficient attainment of goals is known as **pragmatic ethics.** For example, when a company officer directs that equipment that is costly to operate be replaced with a more efficient substitute, he or she is practicing pragmatic ethics.

MAKING WAY FOR NEW RESIDENTS

Hypothetical Case

Walwort, once a thriving city, suffered a long period of economic decline. However, its economy began to improve when several corporations established home offices, two commercial banks opened branch offices, and a number of professional and business people bought or rented homes in its northern section.

The so-called old section of Walwort, adjacent to the newly prospering northern section, was a primarily residential area most of whose inhabitants lived in poorly tended three- or four-family dwellings seven or eight decades old. Many of its inhabitants could barely get by on their meager earnings. A significant number received public welfare assistance.

Valient, Inc. was the largest construction firm in Walwort. At a meeting of its board of directors, Jim Quick, its chief executive officer, presented a plan to develop the old section. The plan contained several key provisions.

Valient would join forces with several investors and other builders. The joint venture, to be known as Wal Associates, would ultimately purchase several thousand acres of land in the old section. To impel the section's present residents to move and thereby keep acquisition costs to a minimum, the initial purchases would include the small local retail firms with which most of the residents did business.

The joint venture would retain a lobbyist whose prime task would be to persuade the appropriate planning and zoning commissions to approve the construction of a government, commercial, and arts complex in the old section. Nearby, Wal Associates would build luxury condominiums, office buildings, and a mall with shops that would serve the new residents and businesses.

Wal Associates would employ a small real estate firm, already located in the old section, to make all of its building and land purchases. No seller would be informed that the firm was working on Wal's behalf. As soon as possible, the buildings purchased would be razed.

Charlotte Reed, one of Valient's directors, insisted that it would be unethical for Valient to put the plan into effect. She asked: "What will happen to the displaced residents? Where will the poorest ones get shelter?" She charged that the plan was nothing more than a "grab for dollars, an irresponsible scheme." Jim Quick promptly responded. "Look," he said, "Walwort needs to be rejuvenated. Someone must do it. Valient is a publicly owned corporation. There are hundreds of stockholders. They have the right to get dividends, good dividends. This plan is a money-maker."

Do you agree with Charlotte Reed or with Jim Quick? Why?

Concern for Others

Utilitarian Ethics

One view of ethics that is obviously incompatible with psychological realism and ethical egoism is known as **utilitarian ethics.** This view gauges a person's conduct by its value to others and by whether it satisfies the interests, wants, and needs of most persons. Under this standard, conduct is ethical if it promotes the greatest happiness for the greatest number of people.

An advocate of utilitarian ethics would approve the sale of a drug that benefits

Utilitarian ethics
views conduct that brings the greatest happiness to the greatest number of persons as ethical

thousands and thousands of the persons for whom it is prescribed but is harmful to a score or so. He or she would condemn as unethical the sale of musical instruments that bring pleasure to only a small number of avid high-decibel music fans but permanently impair the hearing of most people.

Expectancy Ethics and Ethical Relativism

Two intimately related visions of ethical conduct are expectancy ethics and ethical relativism. **Expectancy ethics** is based on a social contract. The terms of this unwritten agreement are commonly understood, silently assented to, and observed by most members of society. For example, when two strangers pass on the street, they are confident that they will not collide with each other. A customer who deals with a department store does not expect to be deceived, to receive a package that lacks the purchased item, to pay more than the ticket price, or to receive incorrect change. If any of these things occur, the store is guilty of unethical conduct.

Expectancy ethics views action that satisfies commonly held expectations as ethical

Ethical relativism evaluates conduct in terms of how persons or businesses are expected to behave because of the activity in which they are engaged. For example, a customer expects different behavior from a bank or a bank officer than from a marketing executive. Those who entrust their assets to a bank expect the bank to invest the assets in a way that is most advantageous to the customer, not in a way that enables the bank to garner undisclosed profits at the customer's expense. Customers do not expect such treatment from a marketing executive. It is unethical for a bank officer not to disclose that the bank stands to gain if the customer follows its advice and buys a piece of land that the bank owns but has been unable to sell. It is not unethical for a marketing executive to promote the sale of a firm's product and make no mention of the fact that the product has been selling poorly and the firm seeks to get rid of the remaining inventory of that product.

Ethical relativism views conduct anticipated by other group's members as ethical

Ethics of Fairness

The view that ethical conduct must be just, honest, upright, and decent is known as the **ethics of fairness.** To decide whether conduct is fair, the entire setting in which it took place must be considered. More often than not, one determines what conduct is fair by responding to the query "Is such conduct unfair?" For example, a firm advertises that certain goods are being offered for sale at 25 percent off, but it never charges the supposed usual price and the advertisement contains photographs of goods that are not on sale. Clearly, such conduct is unfair and there can be no doubt that the firm is guilty of unethical business behavior.

Ethics of fairness views upright behavior as ethical

Preventive Ethics

A business may behave in ways that are not only socially responsible but are also likely to reduce the chances that it will be subjected to undesirable effects, such as being sued or being found guilty of a crime because of the misconduct of its executives or employees. To avoid such effects, the business may establish procedures that are commonly called **preventive ethics.**

The programs of automobile manufacturers to immediately recall vehicles with defects that can cause physical injury are observances of preventive ethics, as are

Preventive ethics views action taken to shield others from harm as ethical

the procedures of drug companies to assure that persons are promptly advised to return drugs discovered to be dangerous.

Inflexible or Flexible Standards

A Priori Ethics

One way to test whether behavior is ethical is to see whether it satisfies an established body of commands that declare what conduct is and is not acceptable. This approach is known as **a priori ethics.** Ordinarily, such a command is spoken of as an "imperative." Conduct that does not offend any imperative is ethical. Conduct that violates an imperative is unethical.

A priori ethics views behavior that satisfies established standards of conduct as ethical

     Truthfulness is a common imperative. Suppose that the chairperson of a firm's board of directors asked one of the firm's junior executives whether she will carry out the board's new policy and deal sternly with any supplier that does not exactly fulfill the terms of a purchasing agreement. Because doing this would at times require her to violate her own values and perhaps the law, the executive knew that she would not do so. Yet a truthful reply might jeopardize her job. She answered, "Yes, I will." Because she violated the imperative of truthfulness, an adherent of the a priori view of ethics would accuse her of unethical behavior.

Situation Ethics

Unlike a priori ethics, **situation ethics** rejects robotic obedience to a set of imperatives. It holds that under particular circumstances an individual may violate an established norm of conduct and still behave ethically. For example, it contends that in some circumstances lying may be acceptable.

Situation ethics considers circumstances in determining whether one's conduct is ethical

□□□□

Because Robert Long, the chief executive officer of Bell, Inc., was regarded as a financial wizard, Bell had always been able to obtain loans from lenders even when its financial condition was poor. When Mark Masson, Bell's president, learned that Long had suffered a massive heart attack and that his survival was in doubt, he called an emergency meeting of the firm's board of directors. At the meeting he accurately reported that the firm's financial condition was superb and that even if it repaid all of its outstanding loans immediately, it would continue to be in excellent financial condition. Masson reminded the board members that a number of borrowing agreements contained a clause requiring the firm to notify the lender immediately after any of its key personnel left or became seriously ill. If this happened, the lender had the option of demanding repayment within 10 days after receipt of notification. At Masson's urging, the board voted not to inform any lender of Long's condition. When reporters sought to confirm a rumor that Long was gravely ill, Masson assured them that he was simply on a "well-earned vacation, far away from telephones."

    Was it unethical for Masson to persuade the board of directors to agree not to inform Bell's lenders that Long had suffered a massive heart attack? Why?

□□□□

Foes of situation ethics contend that it is unacceptable to consider circumstances in evaluating behavior. They insist that abandoning imperatives and simply paying attention to self-interest is never acceptable. Defenders of situation ethics contend that through the use of objective criteria and reliance on an individual's sense of right and wrong, situation ethics effectively determines whether business conduct is ethical. To decide whether particular behavior is proper, they would ask such questions as these: Would a body of objective, reasonable individuals fairly conclude that because of the circumstances what was done was ethical? Would the individual who behaved in this way feel comfortable when reading a newspaper account of what was done?

Conglomerative Values

Intuitive Ethics

Intuitive ethics
uses personal perceptions of right or wrong to evaluate behavior

People may rely on their own sense of what is right or wrong not only to decide how they should behave but also to evaluate the behavior of others. This is **intuitive ethics.** A person's intuitive ethics is likely to be shaped by characteristics of one or more of the previously mentioned value systems. For instance, a person who says "My conscience just would not let me do this" may be saying nothing more than "I cannot do this because it is not in my own best interest," or "My religious training has taught me that doing this would be wrong," or "Doing this would not be fair."

Cultural relativism
view that varying standards of conduct among societies must be considered in evaluating behavior

Cultural Relativism

The globalization of business invites attention to cultural relativism. Like ethical relativism, this view of ethics denies the existence of universally approved standards of acceptable behavior. **Cultural relativism** takes into account differences in perceptions of right and wrong conduct among societies. Conduct that one society views as appropriate behavior may be perceived as unethical by another society. For example, in some nations bribery of public officials is so commonplace that paying off a tax collector to reduce one's tax bill is not regarded as unethical. This is not true in the United States, where aside from being unlawful, such conduct is generally denounced as unethical.

PICKER INTERNATIONAL, INC. v. VARIAN ASSOCIATES INC.
U.S. COURT OF APPEALS, FEDERAL CIRCUIT
869 F.2d 578(1989)

The law firms of McDougall, Hersh & Scott (MH&S) and Jones, Day, Reavis & Pogue (Jones Day) merged. MH&S had had an attorney-client relationship with Varian Associates, Inc. (Varian) and Jones Day had had a long standing attorney-client relationship with Picker International, Inc. (Picker). MH&S had represented Varian in two lawsuits, one of which was *Genus v. Varian.* The other was a lawsuit brought by Picker against Varian in which Picker had been represented by Jones

Day. MH&S, in a pre-merger letter, had asked Varian to consent to a screening process so that the law firm resulting from the merger could continue to represent Picker in the litigation against Varian, but keep Varian as a client in the *Genus* case as well as other matters. Varian had rejected the offer that the combined firm represent Picker. MH&S had then advised Varian that it was compelled by the Model Code of Professional Responsibility, which prescribes ethical standards for members of the legal profession, to "cease . . . representation of Varian in all matters," including the ongoing *Genus* case. Varian insisted that without MH&S's lawyers it would not be suitably represented in the *Genus* lawsuit. This problem was resolved by onetime MH&S attorneys who were now with the merged firm agreeing as individuals, but not as firm members, to represent Varian in *Genus*. Varian then asked the court in which the *Picker v. Varian* case was pending to disqualify the merged firm from representing Picker. Varian's request was granted on the ground that Disciplinary Rule (DR) 5-105(B) of the Model Code requires that a lawyer "not continue multiple employment if the exercise of his independent professional judgment in behalf of a client will be or is likely to be adversely affected by his representation of another client, or if it would be likely to involve him in representing differing interests." Picker appealed.

MICHEL, CIRCUIT JUDGE

[The] MH&S planned merger with Jones Day would certainly result in the merged firm taking a position adverse to a present client, Varian, because the merged firm, if it followed the wishes of its merged predecessors, wanted to continue to represent [Picker in its lawsuit against] Varian.

An attorney may represent multiple clients with inconsistent interests only if "it is obvious that he can adequately represent the interest of each *and if each consents* to the representation after full disclosure of the possible effect of such representation on the exercise of his independent professional judgment on behalf of each."

Having failed to obtain Varian's consent to the overlapping representation, [the new firm] attempted to legitimatize the continuing representation of Picker by trying to withdraw its representation of Varian in all outstanding matters. However, [MH&S's] unilateral attempt to terminate Varian as a client was not complete and thus could not resolve the conflict problem posed by the impending merger. [The merged firm's] actions have therefore violated DR 5-105.

The propriety of an attorney's conduct under DR 5-105(B) is " 'measured not so much against the similarities in litigation, as against the duty of undivided loyalty which an attorney owes to each of his clients.' " Since clients of the same firm with conflicting or differing interests are protected by the obvious conditions of DR 5-105, and since Varian never gave its consent to the newly merged [firm representing] Picker in the [lawsuit] against Varian, [the firm's] continuing representation of Picker violated the undivided loyalty that it owed to Varian.

We recognize that conflicts of interest between clients arising under DR 5-105 may increase as mergers between law firms become more common. To allow the merged firm to pick and choose which clients will survive the merger would violate the duty of undivided loyalty that the firms owe each of their clients.

[T]he decision of [the trial court] disqualifying [the merged firm] as counsel for Picker is

Affirmed.

Ethical Issues

1. Is the merged firm's insistence on representing both Varian and Picker an example of ethical egoism or expectancy ethics? Why?

2. Was Varian's insistence that members of the merged law firm who had represented it prior to the merger continue to represent it in the *Genus* case consistent with Plato's and Aristotle's view of ethical behavior? Why?

Hypothetical Case

CHANGING FIRM PRACTICES

At the beginning of 1982, Carlton National Bank and Security Bank were the two largest commercial banks in Midland and its suburbs. In 1983 Security acquired Columbia Trust, a highly profitable commercial bank. At the March 1984 meeting of Carlton's board of directors, the bank's chief economist informed the directors that during the preceding nine months, Carlton had suffered a 10 percent loss of market share and that she would not be surprised if within a year it lost its status as the second-largest bank in the Midland area.

Paula Lane, the vice chairman of Carlton's board, spoke next. She said: "We must formulate a plan that takes no prisoners. We must win this war. Let's not leave this room until we have such a plan." Following a 12-hour discussion, at times heated, the directors decided that Carlton would (1) meet—and whenever possible, beat—Security's customer service fees, (2) reduce its operating costs by every means possible, and (3) eliminate at least 20 percent of its 40 officer positions and at least 20 percent of its other positions. Carlton's best interests would be taken into account to decide which officers and employees would be discharged. The tasks that had been performed by terminated personnel would be reassigned to retained personnel.

The plan was immediately implemented in a variety of ways, including a 15 percent reduction in the fees charged for most customer services, a ¼ percent increase in the interest paid on savings accounts, a ¼ percent reduction in the interest charged borrowers, and installation of 50 automatic teller machines. There was no charge for using these machines to deposit or withdraw funds. Customers were encouraged to use them. Customers who, instead of dealing with a teller, used the machines solely for three consecutive months would have $20 added to their savings accounts. New customers could obtain credit cards without charge for a 12-month period. Carlton opened a small, limited-service branch in each of the two most deprived areas of Midland. Carlton's chief executive officer, who conceded that neither of the branches would be profitable, defended this action on the ground that it was the "right thing to do."

Within a year Carlton's board of directors was informed that Carlton had more than regained the market share it had lost following Security's acquisition. Shortly thereafter Carlton instituted a number of operational changes. It imposed a 75-cent charge per transaction for customer use of an automatic teller machine, increased customer service fees by 15 percent, initiated a $35 annual charge for credit cards, paid the same interest rate on savings accounts and charged the same interest rate on loans as Security, and closed the two branches that it had opened in the deprived sections of Midland.

Was Carlton's behavior ethical? Why?

BUSINESS ETHICS

Business Ethics the Same as General Ethics

One way to assess the ethics of business behavior is to use the same measuring rods that are employed to assess the ethics of nonbusiness behavior. This approach is based on the premise that no unique considerations are required to decide whether business behavior is ethical. To be ethical, one must behave in the same manner whether he or she is dealing with a business transaction, a family matter, or some sort of social activity involving friends or neighbors. Ethics is ethics.

Business Ethics Different from General Ethics

Those who do not agree that ethics is ethics so far as business behavior is concerned would insist that to evaluate a firm's behavior, attention must be given to the fact that a business—whether individually owned, a partnership, a joint venture, or a corporation—is organized and operated to make a profit. To evaluate a firm's behavior under this vision of business ethics, attention must be given to the consideration that the firm gives to competitiveness and profitability as well as the ethical standards that appear in Table 1-1.

Under this profit-directed measuring rod of worthy conduct, the makeup of a company's mix of competitiveness and profitability and of its behavior with regard to each of the categories of valued conduct found in Table 1-1 would determine its score when it is tested on its ethics. For example, a company's behavior would be rated high if its management emphasized its self-interest, yet also practiced preventive ethics; dealt fairly with its suppliers, customers, and employees; contributed to programs that promoted the public interest; met the demands of utilitarian ethics; did not use situation ethics to support a pricing policy that cheated customers; adhered to a priori standards that called for treating customers honestly; and in general did what was commonly regarded as the right thing to do. On the other hand, a company's behavior would be rated low if its executives and employees were driven solely by a desire to advance its self-interest, recklessly deceived those with whom it did business, and paid no or far too little attention to any of the general ethical considerations contained in Table 1-1.

Bottom-Line Ethics

When a company evaluates its executives and employees *solely* in terms of whether and how much they contribute to its profits, the company is practicing **bottom-line ethics**. The key standards of bottom-line ethics are listed in Table 1-2.

Businesses and businesspersons that are obsessed by a quest for gain and conduct themselves in ways designed solely to produce the highest possible profit would receive high marks under these standards. For example, if a company's management judges performance solely on the basis of ethical egoism, it would exclusively value self-interest and would give no attention to any other standard of ethical behavior, such as fairness, utilitarian ethics, or preventive ethics. It would

Bottom-line ethics
view that behavior is acceptable only if it contributes to a company's profits

TABLE 1–2   **Key Standards of Bottom-Line Ethics**

Ethical egoism	Cost control
Competitiveness	Profit enhancement
Improvement of products and services	Team players
Elimination of unproductive activities and persons	Sense of mission
	Getting the job done

applaud shameless acquisitiveness, abusive greed, and the avid pursuit of company success. The harm that others might suffer on account of the arrogant ambition of company executives to produce profits would not be a factor in deciding its policies or practices.

Among the business practices generated by bottom-line ethics are competitiveness; the improvement of existing products and services and the introduction of new ones; the elimination or sale of unprofitable lines or divisions; the formulation and implementation of means to increase productivity, cut costs, and expand profit margins; the promotion of cooperation among executives and employees through emphasis on the value of being a "team player"; the encouragement of a sense of mission and "getting the job done" regardless of the obstacles; the continuous quest for an increase in quarterly and annual profits; and the termination of chief executive officers, other company officials, and employees whose performance levels do not meet company goals.

Unless a firm blindly engages only in practices that directly, exclusively, and immediately promote the firm's best interests, bottom-line ethics does not preclude behavior beneficial to those with whom the firm does business or are affected by how it behaves. Abiding by other than simply self-interest ethics, a firm, as well as its executives and employees, can behave in ways that are not only compatible with bottom-line ethics but may actually promote its profitability. A perceptive advocate of bottom-line ethics is likely to conclude that if this ethical standard displaces all other ethical standards, in time an organization's bottom line may actually suffer. Pursued in its rawest form, bottom-line ethics is likely to foster such destructive business practices as the sale of shoddy products, poor services, broken promises, all sorts of deceptive tactics, and criminal misconduct.

LITTON SYTEMS, INC. v. AMERICAN TELEPHONE AND TELEGRAPH CO.
U.S. COURT OF APPEALS, SECOND CIRCUIT
700 F.2d 785 (1983)

Litton Systems, Inc. (plaintiff) brought a lawsuit against AT&T (defendant), charging that the defendant's violation of federal antitrust law caused the plaintiff to go out of the telephone terminal equipment business. AT&T claimed that the plaintiff's business failed due to mismanagement and employee incompetence and dishonesty.

The court, at the defendant's request, ordered the plaintiff to make available to the defendant's attorneys certain documents that might show that the plaintiff had been mismanaged and that its employees were incompetent and dishonest. Roberts, the plaintiff's full-time attorney (house counsel), falsely informed the court that some of these documents did not exist and falsely stated that he did not have several of them. Roberts removed several pages from some of the documents before delivering them to the defendant's lawyers. He lied when he told the court that the missing pages were not relevant to the defendant's claims of mismanagement, incompetence, and dishonesty.

Prior to trial, the plaintiff retained an outside attorney (general counsel) to try the case. Roberts delivered to general counsel some of the documents that he had told the court did not exist. Although general counsel knew that Robert had falsely stated that there were no such documents, he did not advise the court of their availability. Before the trial began, the defendant learned that Roberts had lied and that general counsel had not let the court know about the documents. When told of the counsels' misconduct, the court delayed the start of the trial so that the defendant could examine the documents.

The jury returned a verdict in favor of the plaintiff that, when tripled as called for by law, amounted to slightly less than $277 million. Under court rules, the trial judge could impose a *just* sanction on the plaintiff, such as setting aside the jury's verdict or dismissing the lawsuit, because the plaintiff's attorneys had acted in bad faith or had willfully failed to comply with the court's order to deliver the specified documents. The trial judge refused to set aside the verdict or to dismiss the lawsuit. However, holding the plaintiff accountable for the misconduct of its house and general counsel, he denied the plaintiff the attorneys' fees that a successful plaintiff would ordinarily be entitled to recover in such a lawsuit. These fees were probably in excess of $10 million.

The plaintiff appealed, claiming that it should not have been denied attorneys' fees. The defendant also appealed, insisting that the trial court should have dismissed the lawsuit because of the misconduct of the plaintiff's attorneys.

OAKES, CIRCUIT JUDGE

The payment of [a plaintiff's] attorneys' fees [by a defendant] is part of the penalty for violating the antitrust laws. At the same time there is no doubt that attorneys as officers of the court must operate on an honor system, and must be appropriately disciplined to provide specific and general deterrence. Given the [trial] court's express findings of bad faith, it could also have imposed sanctions on [the plaintiff]. It is immaterial that [some of the documents called for could not] ultimately [be presented to the jury]. [W]here there is repeated defiance of express court orders dismissal may be an appropriate remedy.

[B]ecause dismissal denies the party access to justice, if the party has a valid claim, dismissal would amount to a windfall to an adversary to be resorted to only when necessary to preserve the integrity of the judicial system, or in similar "extreme circumstances."

We believe that the trial court quite correctly struck a wise balance between conflicting interests in imposing antitrust penalties on the one hand and preserving the integrity [of the process of directing a party to share specified documents with the other party to the lawsuit prior to trial] on the other. Dismissal of the case would be inappropriate in the light of the limited ultimate role that [some of the documents] played. The imposition of the sanction of no award of attorneys' fees and costs is expensive for Litton, to be sure, but the failures and obstructions of house counsel Roberts and the conduct of general counsel led to the sanction. Indeed, where the stakes are as high as they are in this case, the penalties for obstruction of the truth must be impressive if they are to be effective, yet they must not be so drastic or unfair as the penalty of dismissal. We believe that the trial court acted soundly and correctly, as well as wisely, in imposing the sanction. We decline to set it aside on behalf of either party.

Ethical Issues

1. Is it fair to penalize a client for the misconduct of his or her attorney? Why?
2. Would it have been ethical for house counsel to behave as he did if he had acted under the direct instructions of Litton's board of directors? Why?

PROMOTING BUSINESS ACCOUNTABILITY

Companies can engage in a variety of activities to promote business accountability. Table 1–3 illustrates both the general and the particular ways in which this may be done.

CODE OF ETHICS

Code of ethics

a statement of standards of conduct

A statement of the behavior that a profession or a firm recognizes as allowable or impermissible is known as a **code of ethics.** Professional persons have long been obliged to satisfy a code of ethics. In *Picker International, Inc. v. Varian Associates, Inc.*, we saw how under the legal profession's code of ethics lawyers owe clients their undivided loyalty. Lawyers must also competently represent their clients, neither advise their clients to engage in fraudulent or criminal conduct nor assist them in doing so, not bring frivolous lawsuits, and not knowingly make false statements to a court or use false evidence on a client's behalf.

Like professions, many companies have a code of ethics. Commonly, such a code is prepared by the company officers with the assistance of employees who are especially familiar with its operations and with industry practices. Companies subject to extensive governmental regulation are very likely to obtain an attorney's advice as to the conduct that their code should expressly prohibit.

TABLE 1–3   **Enhancing Responsible Firm Behavior**

Action of individual firm	Code of ethics
	Corporate social responsibility
	Social audit
Collective behavior	Public policy management
	Political action committees

A firm may take into account the opinions of ethicists, also referred to as "ethicians," in the preparation of its code of ethics. These are persons respected for their expertise as to the acceptability of different types of conduct. When a firm's code is formulated with the help of ethicists, the codemaking process is usually called the "Delphi method."

The more specifically a firm's code alerts executives and employees not to engage in certain types of illegal behavior and the more forcefully the firm sees to it that the code's mandates are obeyed, the less likely it is that firm officers and staff will violate those mandates and the less likely it is that the firm will be seen as a wrongdoer if one of its executives or employees engages in unlawful behavior that violates a code mandate. As a result the firm may avoid the severe consequences that it might be subjected to if such behavior were regarded as consistent with its policy.

Ordinarily, a code of ethics states in general terms what is expected of the firm's officers and employees. It may simply direct that firm personnel behave ethically, act in good conscience, treat those who deal with the firm fairly, and obey the law. At times a code may call for specific types of behavior. For instance, it may prohibit company personnel from taking or giving a bribe. Concern with the avoidance of even the appearance of impropriety may be reflected in a code provision that bans officers and employees, when they are engaged in firm business, from taking or giving anything worth more than a few dollars. To assure that firm personnel direct all of their efforts to the advancement of the firm's interests, a code may require that the firm be informed if an officer or an employee will benefit personally should the firm be a party to a particular transaction.

A code may include prohibitions intended to end or avoid certain objectionable practices. For example, sexual harassment or invasion of privacy may be expressly banned.

Firms that share common concerns may join together into a **trade association.** Such an association may have a code of ethics that is designed to regulate how member firms behave. Generally, the codes call for such conduct as fair dealing, ethical behavior, and compliance with the law. They may list and prohibit specific types of irresponsible conduct.

Trade association

a group whose members are firms engaged in the same line of business

---

EASTON v. STRASSBURGER

COURT OF APPEALS, FIRST DISTRICT, CALIFORNIA
152 Cal. App. 3d 90, 199 Cal. Rptr. 383 (1984)

The Strassburgers retained Valley of California, Inc. (appellant), a licensed real estate broker, to sell their home after a minor and a major landslide occurred on their property. Valley of California was not informed of the slides or of the action that had been taken to deal with them. Easton, who did not know about the slides, agreed to buy the home for $170,000.

Shortly after the sale there was a massive earth movement on the property. As a result part of the driveway was destroyed, the home's foundation settled, walls cracked, and doorways warped. The value of the home dropped to about $20,000. Estimates of the cost required to repair the damages and prevent a recurrence ranged as high as $213,000. Both of the slides and the earth movement occurred because the builders had not properly engineered and compacted the landfill.

Easton brought a lawsuit against Valley of California, the Strassburgers, and the builders. The judge instructed the jury that a real estate broker has a duty to prospective purchasers to investigate the state of the property offered for sale and to reveal any property defects. A verdict for $197,000 was returned by the jury in favor of Easton, with 5 percent of that amount assessed against Valley of California. It appealed.

KLINE, PRESIDING JUSTICE

Appellant challenges the [trial court's] following instruction to the jury: "A real estate broker is a licensed person or entity who holds himself out to the public as having particular skills and knowledge to disclose facts materially affecting the value or desirability of the property that are known to him or which through reasonable diligence should be known to him."

Admittedly, no appellate decision [in this state] has explicitly declared that a broker is under a duty to disclose material facts which he should have known. We conclude, however, that [there is such a duty].

The primary purpose[s] of [existing state case law] are to protect the buyer from the unethical broker and seller and to insure that the buyer is provided sufficient accurate information to make an informed decision as to whether to purchase [the property]. If a broker were required to disclose only known defects, but not also those that are reasonably discoverable, he would be shielded by his ignorance of that which he holds himself out to know.

Not only do many buyers in fact justifiably believe the seller's broker is also protecting their interest in securing and acting upon accurate information and rely upon him, but the injury occasioned by such reliance, if it be misplaced, may well be substantial. It seems relevant to us that the duty to disclose that which should be known is [such] a formally acknowledged professional obligation that it appears many brokers customarily impose [this obligation] upon themselves as an ethical matter. Thus, the Code of Ethics of the National Association of Realtors includes the provision that a broker must not only "avoid concealment of pertinent facts" but "has an affirmative obligation to discover adverse factors that a reasonably competent and diligent investigation would disclose." This implicit duty of all real estate agents, regardless whether they are members of the aforementioned Association and bound by its Code of Ethics, is reflected in the law. [As noted in a previous appellate court case in this state, a real estate agent] is supposed to possess ordinarily professional knowledge concerning the natural characteristics of the property he is selling; it should [be] apparent that [buyers are ignorant of certain matters that relate to property. [A] broker [is] obliged as a professional person to obtain information about [the condition of real estate] and make a full disclosure of the burdens it imposed on the land.

[We] hold that the duty of a real estate broker, representing the seller, to disclose facts includes the affirmative duty to conduct a reasonably competent and diligent inspection of the residential property listed for sale and to disclose to prospective purchasers all facts materially affecting the value or desirability of the property that such an investigation would reveal.

[Judgment of the trial court is *affirmed*.]

Ethical Issues

1. Is it fair to impose on a broker a legal obligation based on an ethical standard established by the National

Association of Realtors if the broker is not a member of the association? Why? 2. Should the law require a broker to inform a potential buyer of a defect in a seller's property when the broker knows of the defect only because the seller advised the broker of the defect in confidence, the broker agreed not to disclose the defect, and the seller pays the broker's commission? Why?

EXCERPTS FROM PROFESSIONAL AND CORPORATE CODES OF ETHICS

In addition to serving as a measure of the behavior of professionals and businesspersons, codes of ethics signal to the public the types of values that are cherished by a profession or a company.

The following excerpts, one from the code of ethics of an association whose members provide professional services and the others from the codes of ethics of three major corporations, illustrate the visions and concerns that are ordinarily included in a code of ethics.

Excerpts from Code of Ethics of the American Society of Chartered Life Underwriters and Chartered Financial Consultants[1]

First Imperative:
To competently advise and serve the client.

Guide 1.1: A member shall provide advice and service which are in the client's best interest.
   Interpretive Comment.
   A. A member possessing a specific body of knowledge which is not possessed by the general public has an obligation to use that knowledge for the benefit of the client and to avoid taking advantage of that knowledge to the detriment of the client.
   B. In a conflict of interest situation the interest of the client must be paramount.
   C. The member must make a conscientious effort to ascertain and to understand all relevant circumstances surrounding the client.

Guide 1.2: A member shall respect the confidential relationship existing between client and member.
   Interpretive Comment.
   A. Competent advice and service may necessitate the client sharing personal and confidential information with the member. Such information is to be held in confidence by the member unless released from the obligation by the client.

Excerpts from Aetna Life & Casualty Statement of Principles[2]

Vision

Aetna Life & Casualty sees substantial opportunities for growth in insurance and financial services. We are committed to being the best by dedicating ourselves to efficient and effective customer service. We want Aetna to continue to be the kind of organization where people like to work and with whom the public likes to do business.

Mission

Our mission is to enhance the Company's value to its shareholders by providing responsive market-oriented products and services to our customers. We will offer financial security, asset management, health care and administrative services, while always maintaining a position of unquestioned financial strength.

Values and Objectives

Aetna is committed to a set of values and objectives which it believes are essential to achieving its mission and realizing its vision.

The company will maintain the highest ethical standards in conducting its business and will discharge its moral as well as its legal responsibilities.

As a leader within its industry, Aetna will play a significant role in the development of positions on regulatory, legislative, and environmental issues that are important to the achievement of its objectives. The Company will recognize its responsibilities as a corporate citizen by becoming involved in those social issues and concerns where it can make a positive contribution and by providing opportunities for employee voluntarism.

Aetna's employees and agents are the company's greatest assets, and their success is the most critical factor in achieving our mission. We will provide equal employment and personal development opportunities in a results-oriented environment that offers attractive compensation for good performance. Our goal is to emphasize value to the customer and to make it easier to do business with Aetna by challenging each employee and agent to be better tomorrow than he or she is today.

Excerpts from the Code of Ethics of United Technologies Corporation (UTC)[3]

Standards of Conduct

1.1 Conflicts of Interest UTC employees must deal with suppliers, customers and others doing business with the Corporation in a manner that avoids even the appearance of conflict between our personal interests and those of the Corporation. This requirement applies equally to business relationships and personal activities.

1.4 Product Quality and Safety All operating units of the Corporation have the responsibility to design, manufacture and deliver quality products. All required inspection and testing operations must be properly completed.

Likewise, all UTC products must be designed, produced, and delivered with the safety and health of our customers and product users as a primary consideration.

These standards of product quality and safety must be reflected in the operating policies and procedures of UTC entities worldwide.

1.5 Marketing and Selling It is our responsibility to understand our customers' requirements and to satisfy those requirements by offering quality products and services at competitive terms and prices.

We will sell our products and services honestly, based upon their merits, and will not pursue any sale that requires us to act unlawfully or in violation of those standards to win.

2.1 Equal Employment Opportunity It is UTC policy to afford equal employment opportunity to qualified individuals regardless of their race, religion, color, national origin, age, sex, handicap or other factors not related to UTC's legitimate business interests.

This policy applies to all phases of the employment relationship, including hiring new employees, promotions, selection for training programs, compensation administration, and benefit programs.

2.2 Workplace Environment UTC is committed to providing its employees a workplace that is free from recognized safety and health hazards and a work environment free from discrimination, harassment or personal behavior not conducive to a productive work climate.

2.3 Drug and Alcohol Abuse All UTC entities, domestic and outside the U.S., will abide by applicable laws and regulations relative to the possession or use of alcohol and drugs. Corporate policy prohibits the illegal use, sale, purchase, transfer, possession, or presence in one's system of drugs, other than medically prescribed drugs, while on company premises.

2.4 Employee Privacy United Technologies operates on the firm belief of respect for employee privacy and dignity. It is Corporate policy to acquire and retain only that employee personal information that is required for effective operation of the Corporation or that is required by law in the jurisdictions in which we operate. Access to such information will be restricted internally to those with a recognized need to know.

United Technologies will comply with all applicable laws regulating the disclosure of personal information about employees. In any location where applicable law does not regulate the release of such information, the Company will adopt policies designed to protect such information from unreasonable disclosure.

The Corporation's respect for employee privacy normally precludes any concern relative to personal conduct off the job, unless such conduct impairs the employee's work performance or affects the reputation or legitimate business interests of the Corporation.

3.1 Return on Investment It is one of United Technologies Corporation's basic objectives to earn a profit in an ethical manner in order to make investments in the Corporation's future and to provide a superior return on our shareholder's investment.

4.6 Local Laws and Customs UTC international business operations may encounter laws, local customs, and social standards that differ widely from U.S. practice. It is UTC policy to abide by the national and local laws of the countries in which we operate, unless prohibited by U.S. law. When local customs and business or social practices vary from the standards contained in the UTC Code of Ethics, it is permissible to conform to local customs and practices when necessary for the proper conduct of UTC business, and when approved by the cognizant business practices officer.

4.7 Environmental Issues   The Corporation will conduct its worldwide operations in a manner that safeguards the natural environment.

4.8 Community Support   As a good corporate citizen, UTC policy is to support the organizations and activities of the worldwide communities in which we reside. Employees are urged to participate personally in civic affairs. The Corporation will strive to support worthwhile civic and charitable causes.

6.2 Reporting Violations   It is each employee's personal responsibility to bring violations or suspected violations of the UTC Standards of Conduct to the attention of their supervision, the legal department of their operating entity, or to the UTC Ombudsman, as appropriate. Corporate policy prohibits any retribution against employees for making such reports.

Excerpts from General Electric Company [GE]: A Commitment to Integrity[4]

GE is dedicated to the highest standards of integrity. Through our policies and actions, we seek performance and a reputation reflecting the very best we can achieve: a Company that both creates economic value and acts by ethical principle. But when the issue is ethics, it is better that profits be lost than corners cut or rules bent.

The Company must respect and respond to diverse responsibilities and interests. GE—and the individuals who comprise it—are accountable to laws and regulations; to standards of ethics and excellence; to customers and fellow employees; and to the communities and nations in which we work and to whom we sell.

A number of Company policies have been issued which not only address specific standards of ethical conduct but outline the process by which these commitments are to be met. Living by these rules—and the values they express—is the most serious responsibility a GE employee undertakes. Employees must understand that they alone are responsible for their acts and omissions.

All employees are expected to live by the highest standards of ethical conduct in their relationships with each other, the Company, customers, and the public. If they perceive lapses in those standards, they are expected to report them to their superiors. Employees who prefer to report possible violations of laws or Company policies to someone outside their business may contact, on a confidential basis, the Corporate Ombudsman. In every case, if confronted with apparent conflicts between the demands of their jobs and the highest standards of conduct, employees should be guided by their sense of honor until the inconsistency has been reconciled. GE employees are expected to be as vigilantly ethical as they are aggressively entrepreneurial.

It is a managerial responsibility to make ethical behavior and efficient performance complementary. Good managers measure excellence by qualitative values as well as by quantitative results, motivating employees to "do the right thing" while "doing things right." They must encourage all employees to be alert to ethical ambiguity and to ask tough questions, and must respond promptly to employee concerns about possible violations of laws and regulations. We look to management to uphold company policies and standards, and to set the example by instilling a spirit of honor in the work place.

It is a leadership responsibility to sustain an open, accountable environment where such a spirit of honor can thrive. For only in such an environment can a spirit prevail by which every individual member of the GE community shares responsibility for the integrity of the institution as a whole.

These common values and mutual responsibilities provide the framework for specific standards consistent with our commitment to openness, fairness, and respect for customers and communities. Yet prescribing policies is never more than a beginning; fulfilling them must always be a way of life in GE. Integrity is not an occasional requirement but a continuing commitment. It erodes when it is not reinforced; it weakens if it is not applied, as a living standard, to new issues and situations.

GE and each individual GE employee together pledge to comply with these policies to the best of their ability.

CORPORATE SOCIAL RESPONSIBILITY

As stated at the beginning of this chapter, corporate social responsibility is the behavior that society commonly expects of business in matters of public concern. One view of corporate social responsibility is that firms' efforts should be directed exclusively at making profit for investors. In the case of corporations, for example, directors, executives, and employees should seek to make as much profit as possible for the shareholders, who may use it as they wish. If they choose to do so, they may donate some or even all of the dividends they receive to promote matters of public concern, such as improvement of education, medical research, child care, or assisting the poor.

Another view of corporate social responsibility is that a firm's managers should decide what portion of its profits should be used to deal with particular public concerns. A limited form of this view calls for businesses to dependably provide their customers with goods and services. A broader form calls for businesses to devote a portion of their profits for such purposes as improving the ambience in the workplace, making day-care services available to employees, helping employees to advance their own education and that of their children, enhancing the environment, assisting the needy, promoting the arts, and financing colleges, universities, libraries, and museums.

Various reasons have been offered for putting a portion of a firm's profits to public use. These profits depend in part on public acceptance of business activity and public support of the infrastructure in which companies operate. It is in the self-interest of companies to be good corporate citizens. A firm's involvement with matters of public concern is likely to enhance its image. Moreover, such involvement may simply be good business.

A particular industry, as well as business in general, can be harmed by socially irresponsible business behavior. When businesses and businesspeople have a reputation for acting improperly, government restrictions on business are likely to be demanded and imposed. As a result businesses may be denied the flexibility they need and profits may be adversely affected. Socially responsible business behavior is likely to dampen demands for further regulation of business.

Businesses and businesspeople may be parties to good works for reasons entirely unrelated to company self-interest. Like other people, businesspeople usually are interested in particular philanthropic, educational, and humanitarian programs. They can help satisfy their own desires to improve society by persuading their firm to channel a portion of its resources to public interest projects.

Beneficiaries of Corporate Social Responsibility

Internal dependencies
firm's officers and employees

Firms have both internal and external dependencies. A firm's officers and employees are its **internal dependencies.** How they are treated is a measure of the firm's interest in behaving in a socially responsible way. Among the factors that indicate a firm's responsiveness to the needs and desires of its internal dependencies are its policies and procedures on employee advancement, the extent to which it rewards staff performance and other staff contributions to its success, the level of its support for personnel education and training programs, its responses to safety and health problems, its medical and dental insurance programs, and its retirement plan.

External dependencies
the persons with whom a firm deals

A firm's customers, suppliers, lenders, investors, and creditors are among its **external dependencies.** How it treats them—for example, its pricing practices, the quality of its products, and the degree of candor it displays—is also a measure of its social responsibility.

SOCIAL AUDIT

Social audit
a report on a firm's contributions to society

Once a firm adds a particular program to its social responsibility agenda, it may periodically report on that program's success. Such a report is known as a **social audit.** Commonly, the social audit specifies the program's goals, the resources allocated to the program, the steps taken to achieve the program's goals, and the social benefits derived from the program. The social audit may be included in the firm's annual report to apprise shareholders and the public of this aspect of the firm's perception of its social responsibility and to give interested parties an opportunity to evaluate what has been done.

GLOBALIZATION OF CORPORATE SOCIAL RESPONSIBILITY

At one time American companies were free to take a localized attitude toward corporate social responsibility. In most instances their dependencies were persons and businesses located in a particular town or city, a region, several states, or across the nation. The globalization of business makes it necessary for American firms to think of social responsibility in worldwide terms. Consider the issues raised by the following facts.

□□□□

American Twine, Inc. was established in 1902 as a New Jersey corporation. Its home office was originally located in Newark. Although American Twine remained a New Jersey corporation, its home office was moved to other states as it added and dropped product lines. By the end of the 1980s, less than 40 percent of its manufacturing, warehousing, and selling operations took place in the United

States. The remainder were spread across 20 foreign countries, with most of the company's overseas activities carried on in Western Europe, Australia, and Africa. In 1989 American Twine changed its name to GXT International to reflect its global operations. At a board of directors meeting held in early 1990, its chief executive officer, Dole Champion, asked the directors to approve the following policies:

1. Whenever possible, GXT should carry on its manufacturing and warehousing operations in those countries that assure the highest profitability.

2. In the interest of profit enhancement, GXT should devote the money it allocates for educational purposes to those countries in which it is most likely to be able to hire trained personnel at highly favorable wages.

3. GXT planning should be tax sensitive. Every aspect of its business should be conducted so as to assure that its overall tax liability is as low as possible. If it can save taxes by moving operations from the United States to a foreign country, then, other things being equal, that should be done as soon as possible.

Bob Quist, the chairman of the board of directors, objected to the proposals. "After all," he said, "we are an American firm. But tell me more."

Dole continued: "First of all, Bob, next month I am going to ask the board to approve headquartering several of our operations in Western Europe. To get a bigger piece of the pie, we locate top company officers where the action is. Second, our job is to make a profit for our investors. As you know, these include companies and individuals throughout the world. Third, we have a social responsibility to be good citizens in foreign countries. We do more than 60 percent of our business overseas. All that our dependencies in the United States are entitled to is their fair share, nothing more."

Jane August, the chairman of the board, spoke next. She said: "We happen to have been incorporated in the United States, and once we did business only in New Jersey. But that was a long time ago. We are a global enterprise now. We must think of GXT not as an American enterprise, but as a global firm. Certainly, no one here wishes to harm the United States, but as a company that does more of its business abroad than in this country, we cannot be expected to forget our worldwide dependencies. It would be socially irresponsible if we did."

Would you vote to approve the policies recommended by Dole Champion? Why?

□□□□

PUBLIC ISSUE MANAGEMENT

Company policy may call for company involvement in shaping public opinion as to the resolution of certain public problems. This activity is often spoken of as **public issue management.** In this process a company uses staff members or consultants, or both, to prepare a report that (1) identifies issues of present or probable future public interest, (2) anticipates the diverse ways in which those issues may be resolved, (3) states the impact of the possible responses, and (4) proposes the action that should be taken to avoid undesirable results. The kinds of public issues that the company probes and responds to may be limited to

Public issue management
a firm's involvement in promoting or defeating proposed public programs

those that are likely to hurt its profitability or in some way damage its image. After receiving the report, management decides what action, if any, should be taken.

A company that wishes to influence how public issues are resolved may do so by advertising, by employing lobbyists to sway public officials, and by joining forces with leaders and groups that share the company's viewpoint. For example, a corporation may be planning to acquire more land in a particular community in order to expand the output of its most profitable product line. The public issues report reveals that various individuals and a group of local residents want the zoning law to be altered so as to bar the use of any additional land for commercial purposes because of the danger that this would pose to nearby wetlands. To attain their goal, they are forcefully communicating their position to the electorate, lobbying zoning board members, and campaigning on behalf of candidates for public office who share their point of view. Another group, in order to achieve tax benefits and enhance employment opportunities, opposes any change in the zoning law. It is using the same tactics as those used by its opponents.

Advocates of corporate public issue management would say that it is proper for the company to support the group that opposes a change in the zoning law. Although such involvement is in the company's interest, this does not mean that it is acting irresponsibly. Those who oppose corporate action to influence the resolution of public issues would stress the possible abuse of corporate power and the fact that the company's involvement is motivated by its quest for profit.

POLITICAL ACTION COMMITTEES

Political action committee

an association that channels money to elect particular persons to public office

Federal law permits a corporation, labor union, and other groups to establish one or more political action committees. A **political action committee,** commonly referred to as a "PAC," is a distinct entity, separate from the body that organized it. So, although a corporation or a union has organized a PAC, that PAC may not receive corporate or union funds. However, the corporation may solicit its stockholders, executives, and personnel and a union may solicit its members to contribute to the PAC or to other PACs. PAC funds may be used to promote candidacies for federal office in primary and general elections. During a single year an individual may contribute not more than $1,000 to a PAC that supports one candidate and not more than $5,000 to a PAC that supports two or more candidates. An individual's annual PAC contributions may not exceed $5,000.

PACs are limited in their disbursement of funds. For example, in each election a PAC may contribute up to $5,000 to a single candidate.

Obviously, PACs may influence the behavior of public officials who used PAC funds to get elected. The extent to which PAC activities affect the president and members of Congress is difficult to ascertain. Elected officials may receive contributions from PACs that disagree with them as to the handling of a particular problem. Regardless of the extent to which a candidate is beholden to one or more PACs, in the final analysis he or she is answerable to the electorate.

PACs present corporations, labor unions, and other groups with opportunities to abuse the electoral process. Since there is no limit on the number of PACs that a group may organize, an organization bent on maximizing its potential influence on the behavior of elected officials may organize many PACs and then pressure whomever it can to contribute to a number of them. The manner in which businesses, unions, and other groups make use of PACs is a measure of the propriety of their behavior and their sense of social responsibility.

1. Donald Wilson, vice president/purchasing for Albert, Inc., entered into a contract to buy $10 million worth of computer chips from Talmo Corporation. Delivery was to be made in 30 days. One week after the agreement was signed, the price of computer chips fell 50 percent. The chips that Albert agreed to buy from Talmo could now be bought for $5 million. Wilson immediately informed Bart Happ, Albert's chief executive officer, of the price change. Happ convened a meeting of Albert's vice presidents to explore what should be done.

Fred Fair, vice president/corporate affairs, insisted that Albert had to carry out the contract. If it were violated, he insisted, Albert's image would be injured. He pointed out that Albert would not suffer any loss from fulfilling the contract since the $10 million price had been found acceptable before the contract was signed.

Barbara Tims, vice president/finance, stated that the contract should be renegotiated or broken immediately and a new supplier identified. This, she asserted, would significantly improve Albert's quarterly financial report. She called attention to its poor profit picture in the past two quarters.

Janet Morse, vice president/sales, suggested that the contract be broken and recommended that Albert pass one half of the resulting savings on to its customers.

Tom Green, vice president/legal, reported that if the contract were broken and Talmo brought suit, it would probably recover no more than $2 million for its lost profits. Perhaps it would accept $1.5 million to settle its claim and thereby avoid a lawsuit. He remarked that "it makes no sense to just throw away between $3 million and $3.5 million. Let's break the contract and see what happens."

Flavia Mill, who had been a philosophy professor before becoming Albert's vice president/community relations, asserted that it would be wrong to break the contract. She contended that once Albert made a promise, regardless of the legal technicalities it should carry the promise out. Tims challenged Mill. She called attention to the "money game" played by professional athletes. "What do you think renegotiation of contracts by professional athletes is all about?" she asked. "Isn't it nothing more than breaking one contract to get another that assures the athlete more money?" Mill curtly responded: "We are not ballplayers. We are businesspeople. Our firm's code of ethics states that we must act ethically. We have a responsibility to behave lawfully." Tims countered: "We do not pretend to be ballplayers, but as corporate officers it is our job to make a profit for the shareholders. What is unethical about paying Talmo whatever the law requires? It is not a crime to break a contract."

Happ, after thinking for a moment, said: "As the chief executive officer of Albert, I am convinced that Albert must have a reputation for dealing ethically with its suppliers, for doing the right thing. At the same time we must not forget our shareholders. Now let's decide. What should we do?"

What do you recommend be done? Why?

2. Clar Corporation manufactured a variety of household cleansers. Clar's carpet cleanser, Clean As Snow, once enjoyed about a 40 percent market share. During the past three years its market share had shrunk by 30 percent. Clar's four leading competitors charged retailers 25 percent less for their carpet cleansers. A careful analysis of these cleansers revealed that the ingredients used to manufacture them were less expensive than those used to manufacture Clean As Snow. Although beneath-the-surface cleaning significantly extends

the life of a carpet, these products merely cleaned a carpet's surface. In contrast, Clear As Snow was a superb beneath-the-surface cleanser.

Carolyn Lane, vice president/marketing, confronted James Bark, vice president/production, with the proposal that Clean As Snow be reformulated so that it no longer cleaned beneath the surface. Lane showed Bark that this would permit Clar, because of the efficiency of its operation and its ownership of certain patents, to charge 10 percent less than its leading competitors and still be assured of a 15 percent higher profit yield than any of them. She also showed him an eye-catching container in which the newly formulated Clean As Snow would be sold. Across two sides of the container appeared the words "NEW Clean As Snow. You Will See the Difference!"

Bark objected to changing the composition of Clean As Snow. He insisted that it would be wrong to do so, because "our customers out there are entitled to a really clean carpet, through and through. It makes no difference that they see only the surface of their carpets."

Is Carolyn Lane's proposal ethical? Why?

3. Currently, publicly held corporations issue quarterly earnings reports. What effect, if any, does this practice probably have on an executive's attitude toward long-term profit making? How does this practice affect a firm's readiness to partake in socially responsible projects?

4. Park Corp., a large U.S. conglomerate, employed over 20,000 persons in 27 states. Marchant & Co., a French firm, planned to purchase all of Park's outstanding stock for $3.2 billion. A substantial part of the purchase price would come from the sale of so-called junk bonds, bonds offering a high rate of return but at a significant risk that their holders would not be paid. Marchant intended to sell off the least profitable of Park's divisions within months after the purchase and to cut the size of its remaining staff by not less than 25 percent. Ultimately, Marchant would sell all the remaining divisions. The profits Marchant earned would be used to expand its European operations.

Is Marchant's plan ethical? Discuss. Would your answer be the same if Marchant were a U.S. firm that would invest all of the profits in the U.S.? Why?

5. Soon after resigning from the state legislature, in which she chaired the senate consumer affairs committee for more than 10 years, Jill established a consulting firm. Would it be ethical for her to represent local manufacturers who wished to repeal statutes requiring them to compensate consumers for injuries caused by the same sort of products that they sold? Would it be ethical for her to try to persuade members of the state senate to vote in favor of repealing such statutes? Would your answers be the same if the firms that hired Jill had been European and Asian companies? Why?

ENDNOTES

1. The American Society of Chartered Life Underwriters and Chartered Financial Consultants is a national organization of insurance and financial service professionals. The code belongs to the American Society of Chartered Life Underwriters (CLU) and Chartered Financial Consultants (ChFC), and the excerpts are reprinted with the permission of the Society.

2. The document from which the following excerpts have been drawn is regarded by Aetna Life & Casualty as a "statement of principles" rather than a "code of ethics." The excerpts are reprinted with the permission of Aetna Life & Casualty.

3. Reprinted with the permission of United Technologies Corporation.

4. Reprinted with the permission of General Electric Company.

CHAPTER

2

Functions of Law, Justice, and Legal Philosophy

From time to time, courts are called on to decide a party's rights and obligations in the absence of an established rule of law. For example, at one time no established legal principle determined whether a firm's chief executive officer could be convicted of violating a criminal statute if the subordinate to whom he or she had delegated the responsibility of seeing that the firm was in compliance with the law failed to do so; or whether a person who has been tricked into committing a crime by a government official can be found guilty of the crime. In each of these cases, the court's response was yes. The executive who had delegated responsibility and the person who had been tricked into committing a crime could be fined or imprisoned. In all of these cases, the judge's attitude toward the role of law, perception of justice, and ideas about the nature of law played a part in the decision-making process.

This chapter examines the functions of law, the meaning of justice, and differences in ideas about the nature of law. An awareness of these subjects is extremely helpful to business executives. It alerts them to the possibility that despite the absence of law on the subject of a business decision, a legal principle may be in place or may even be created in a lawsuit or criminal proceeding to which they are a party. By thoughtfully considering that possibility, they may avoid undesirable legal consequences.

FUNCTIONS OF LAW

Law is used for the following purposes:

1. *To resolve disputes in an orderly manner.* In the distant past persons often resorted to self-help to settle their differences. However, this means of dispute resolution is unacceptable in a civilized community. Now, when persons disagree about their rights and duties, they ordinarily turn to the legal system for help.

2. *To influence behavior and to establish and allocate the rights and duties of individuals, groups, and governments.* In the absence of law, individual and group rights and duties would probably be determined by brute force. Law determines these rights and duties by peaceful means. For example, a legal principle holds that a person may not intentionally cause others bodily injury or steal their property, and law requires compensation to the injured party for the harm caused by such conduct. Those who engage in it may also be fined or imprisoned. In the absence of law, government officials would be free to treat persons as they please. In nations in which official conduct is rarely, if ever, regulated by law, government officers freely engage in abusive behavior and are responsible for widespread injuries, if not deaths.

3. *To distribute opportunities and resources.* The marketplace may operate in a manner that denies persons opportunities for reasons unrelated to their abilities. Powerful individuals or groups may deny others access to the resources that they must have if they are to succeed. Law can ban such unwarranted denials of opportunities and of access to resources. For example, the 1964 Civil Rights Act prohibits employers from discriminating against potential or current employees because of their sex, race, religion, color, or national origin and the Sherman Antitrust Act outlaws attempts to monopolize markets. Law can also redistribute resources by using revenues gathered from some persons to provide benefits for other persons. Money collected under federal, state, or local tax legislation may be used to provide the needy with food, housing, medical care, and other basic necessities of life.

JUSTICE

Justice has to do with opinions of what is right and what is wrong. There is no universally accepted definition of justice. According to Aristotle, justice is "treating equals equally and unequals unequally, but in proportion to their relevant differences," a very imprecise definition. Another frequently heard definition, by no means more precise, is that justice is fair play. An advocate of Marxism would indeed differ from an advocate of capitalism on the demands of justice with regard to the ownership of property or the distribution of wealth.

At different times and in different places, a particular definition of justice may or may not conflict with law. Over the course of time, American law has approved of slavery, imprisonment of debtors, denial of women's rights, and forced confinement of mentally ill persons who do not pose a danger to themselves or others. In the past, state law did not allow persons to vote unless they owned property that exceeded a designated dollar value, or protect consumers from extremely hazardous products, or shield the environment from senseless devastation, or afford handicapped persons equal access to various activities, or defend endangered wildlife from deliberate destruction. The idea of what justice demands in regard to each of these matters has changed over time, and so too has the law.

How to Decide Whether a Result Is Just

Criteria set by the legal system itself or standards apart from it may be used to determine whether justice has been done in a particular instance.

Internal Procedures and Principles

One way to judge whether justice has been done in a civil proceeding or a criminal case is to decide whether the outcome was arrived at through procedures and principles established by the law itself. Under this concept of justice, so long as such procedures and principles were followed, the result is just, regardless of the desirability of those procedures and principles. Taking justice to mean only the correct application of existing standards invites an "anything goes" view of justice. A legal system that embodies vile procedures and wicked principles could be said to yield just decisions so long as the decisions are arrived at through the use of those procedures and principles.

External Standards of Acceptability

A definition of justice that embodies external criteria of what ought to be done and how people ought to be treated is likely to be more meaningful than a definition that focuses solely on compliance with a system's processes and principles. Such external criteria may be limited to those provided by the value system of an individual or a small group, or they may be far broader in scope, including a national and perhaps even a worldwide view of the proper outcome of a legal controversy.

The use of external standards permits attention to be given not only to whether established legal procedures and rules were properly used but also to the merits of those procedures and rules. If legal procedures and rules are found to be unacceptable in light of such standards, then a party who has lost a lawsuit or a person who has been convicted of a crime was *not* dealt with justly.

When criteria aside from the legal system and the law are used to decide whether justice has been done, all forms of governmental action are open to challenge. For example, the American colonists who subscribed to the Declaration of Independence believed that certain British laws were unjust and need not be obeyed. They relied on external criteria to evaluate and condemn British law.

UNITED STATES v. DURHAM
U.S. DISTRICT COURT, DISTRICT OF DELAWARE
741 F. Supp. 498 (1990)

Durham, who had already been convicted of seven crimes, surrendered to agents of the U.S. Treasury Department's Bureau of Alcohol, Tobacco & Firearms (ATF) after Agent Schenken contacted him and informed him that he had a warrant for his arrest. He was frisked, handcuffed, arrested, subjected to a strip search, dressed, and taken to a processing room where he was placed in a belly chain.

In the processing room Schenken told Durham that he had to read him his *Miranda* rights. This requirement is based on the U.S. Supreme Court decision in *Miranda v. Arizona,* in which the Court ruled that prior to interrogating a person in official custody a law enforcement officer must inform the person that he or she may remain silent, that anything he or she says may and will be used against him or her, and that he or she has a right to the assistance of an attorney. Durham replied that he "knew" his *Miranda* rights. Schenken told Durham that he had to read them anyway, which he did. Durham then said nothing. Schenken asked Durham to read a standard ATF waiver of rights form, which he appeared to do. Durham then signed the section of the form indicating that he had been advised of his rights and that he understood them, but refused to sign the portion of the form that stated he waived his *Miranda* rights. However, Durham told the ATF agents that he "would tell" them "anything that" they wanted to know.

Schenken, another ATF agent, and Durham got into an automobile to drive Durham to court. After the three were in the vehicle for about five minutes, Schenken asked Durham "to tell [him] what had happened." During a 15 to 20 minute conversation, Durham confessed to the crimes for which he had been arrested. He also said that he had escaped from custody three times and that "if he thought the charges were serious, he would have gone to Peru."

Durham asked the court to bar the government's use of his confession on the ground that he did not waive his *Miranda* rights, that his statements had not been given voluntarily, and that "it was apparent to the ATF agents that [he] was unaware of the serious nature of the charges against him." Following a hearing held to determine whether the confession could be used against him, the court delivered the following opinion.

LATCHUM, SENIOR DISTRICT JUDGE

A suspect can, of course, waive his *Miranda* rights; but such a waiver must be made voluntarily, knowingly, and intelligently. The validity of a suspect's waiver of his *Miranda* rights is assessed in light of the "totality of the circumstances surrounding the interrogation." In analyzing the totality of the circumstances, a court "must look at the facts of the particular case, including the background, experience, and conduct of the suspect." Two factors must be considered to determine whether the waiver was voluntary, knowing, and intelligent.

First, the relinquishment of the right must have been voluntary in the sense that it was the product of a free and deliberate choice rather than intimidation, coercion, or deception. Second, the waiver must have been made with a full awareness of both the nature of the right being abandoned and *the consequences of the decision* to abandon it.

The defendant's constitutional right is to "not be *compelled* to give self-incriminating testimony." The Constitution does not, however, require "the police [to] supply a suspect with a flow of information to help him calibrate his self-interest in deciding whether to speak or stand by his rights." Nor is such a result even desirable.

The defendant himself underscored at the time of his arrest that he was already familiar with his *Miranda* rights. He also does not deny that he was read his rights at the time of the arrest in this case. Moreover, he was given a written statement of his rights, which he appeared to read and which he signed in acknowledgement. That the defendant knew he could stand by those rights is clear from his decision to sign only the acknowledgement and not the waiver. That he nonetheless chose to make an oral statement does not undermine the validity of the waiver; it only reflects his judgment. In light of all these circumstances, the Court finds the government has shown that the defendant's *Miranda* waiver was knowing, voluntary, and intelligent.

The Court has reviewed all of the facts in this case. There is simply no basis for concluding that the defendant's statements were coerced or resulted from overly manipulative tactics.

[T]he defendant did not make any complaints about being hungry, thirsty, or in need of a bathroon. He received no threats or promises, and he did not complain about the handcuffs and chains that restrained him while he was seated in the rear passenger seat of the vehicle.

Another important factor is the defendant's familiarity with the criminal system. The defendant was not "'soft, ignorant, or timid.'" He was "'not inexperienced in the ways of crime or its detection, nor dumb as to [his] rights.'" Four of his seven previous convictions were for "violent felonies."

Finally, the ten-minute strip search was certainly not sufficient to transform the defendant's voluntary statements into a coerced confession. Given that the defendant has *seven* prior convictions and, consequently, has been through the "booking" process at least that many times, the Court finds it unlikely that a short and routine strip search would be sufficient to overcome the defendant's will.

The defendant simply confessed because he thought a federal firearms charge was not "serious." The Constitution protects the defendant against government coercion and, at least arguably, deception. But it does not shield him from his own improvidence.

The Court finds that the defendant's waiver of his *Miranda* rights was valid. Further, the statements made by him on the day of his arrest were voluntary. Accordingly, the defendant's [request to bar the use of his statements against him] will be denied.

Legal Issues

1. If a person has a long history of mental illness, suffers from episodes of admitting wrongdoing without having been guilty of it, and is under continuous psychiatric care, must the person be advised that he or she may consult his or her personal psychiatrist before being questioned by a police psychiatrist? Why?

2. Smith sold two pounds of cocaine in violation of state law. After he was charged with a violation of state law, the state prosecutor granted him immunity from state prosecution in return for his testimony against his accomplice, who had also been charged with violating state law. This barred the state from using against Smith any statements that he might make in response to a question by a state prosecutor. Smith did not know that the state grant of immunity also barred the federal government from using those statements against him in a federal criminal proceeding. Two months later Smith was arrested by federal narcotics agents who promptly informed him of his *Miranda* rights. Unaware that the statements he made under the grant of state immunity could not be used in a federal prosecution and believing that the court "might go easy on him" if he cooperated, he repeated to the federal agents the statements that he had made to state prosecutors. Can the statements that Smith made to the federal agents be used against him in his federal trial? Why?

Ethical Issues

1. Margaret Worth, 18 years of age, was arrested for breaking and entering into a department store. After having been advised of her *Miranda* rights, she asked to speak with her attorney, Leland Ross. Ross, who believed that thieves should be punished according to the law, said to her: "You did it; let the police know." A few minutes later, following Ross's advice, and in his presence, Worth delivered a signed confession to the police. The confession was the key evidence that the state used when it prosecuted Worth. She was found guilty. Did Ross behave ethically when he advised Worth to tell the police what she had done? Why?

2. Is it ethical for a judge, who believes that a court should impose the maximum sentence allowed by law on persons found guilty of a crime and who was elected because of his record of being "tough on crime," to try a case in which the accused is in failing health? Why?

LEGAL PHILOSOPHIES

Philosophy and Theory

A person's or a group's point of view on a particular subject is referred to as a **philosophy.** A philosophy is based on a core of accepted values, attitudes, assumptions, and perceptions. When a philosophy is used to predict, judge, or explain facts, behavior, or events, it is referred to as a **theory.** Theories are commonly referred to by a name that concisely states their fundamental premise.

Philosophy
a point of view on a particular subject

For example, everyone is familiar with the term *laissez-faire.* This term refers to the economic theory that businesspersons should be unhindered in the pursuit of their self-interest and that business should be free from government interference.

Theory
the use of a philosophy to predict, judge, or explain

Philosophies of Law

An attitude toward law is referred to as a **legal philosophy.** Just as there are different views about how an economy should be structured, there are different views about the nature of law. These views of law are linked to distinct theories about such factors as the extent to which established legal principles should be honored, how existing or proposed law should be evaluated, or when law should be used to shape behavior.

Legal philosophy
a view of law

A distinct view of law is spoken of as a "school of legal philosophy" or a **school of jurisprudence.** While unique characteristics mark and distinguish the various schools of jurisprudence, some of them share common values.

School of jurisprudence
a particular view of law

Why should one become acquainted with legal philosophies? Why is it not enough for a person interested in law to just become familiar with important legal rules about a particular subject and then to remember those rules? Knowledge of legal philosophies helps one to understand why a court, a legislator, or a government executive behaves in a particular manner. Appreciation of the *attitudes* of judges, legislators, and government executives helps one to correctly anticipate how these officials will respond when confronted with particular questions. Awareness of different legal philosophies gives one reference points for testing the acceptability of legal principles and for judging the desirability of proposed alternatives. Familiarity with the various schools of jurisprudence helps one to probe beyond the explanations that courts, legislatures, and government executives offer to justify their actions.

Table 2-1 presents core views of legal philosophy and identifies legal philosophies that hold those views.

Government Power and Behavior

Hypothetical Case

OFFICIAL DECEPTION AND THE INTEGRITY OF THE LEGAL PROCESS

At the direction of his superiors Jay, an agent of the state Investor Protection Agency (IPA), together with four other agents, initiated an undercover operation to determine whether Key Inc. was violating the state Fraud in the Sale of Securities Act. Pretending they were lawyers, the five agents established what appeared to be a newly organized law firm. Carefully worded public announcements falsely stated that the firm's members had previously been associated with Barton & Oakes, a prominent law firm. Barton & Oakes, which agreed to assist the government, issued a press release in which it falsely stated that the five were graduates of leading law schools and highly talented, and that they were leaving the firm to practice in areas of law that were of no interest to Barton & Oakes. Jay arranged to "accidently" meet Ted White, the president of Key, at a local golf club. White had read the Barton and Oakes announcement and believed that Jay was a highly competent lawyer. White came to regard Jay as a good friend. Jay arranged for IPA to advise Key that in the near future its officers would be asked to discuss several matters with IPA. White contacted Jay and asked him to represent Key. Jay agreed. During three daylong meetings with White, Jay learned exactly how Key had been violating the law. He shared this information with the state attorney general.

Should the government be allowed to use the evidence provided by Jay in criminal proceedings against White and Key? What ethical standard, if any, could an ethicist rely on to refute the claim that Jay behaved unethically? Discuss. Did the law firm of Barton & Oakes behave ethically? Why?

TABLE 2-1	Legal Philosophies		
	Government power and behavior	Natural law	Positivist jurisprudence
	Technique of judicial decision making	Analytical jurisprudence	
	Workability	Pragmatic jurisprudence	
	A people's spirit	Historical jurisprudence	
	Promotion of particular values and goals	Sociological jurisprudence	Social engineering
	Individual centered	Utilitarian jurisprudence Existentialist jurisprudence Jurisprudence of fairness Egalitarian jurisprudence Distributive justice	

Natural Law

Early Greek philosophers were the first to speak of **natural law.** Aristotle was one of the foremost advocates of this philosophy. Natural law philosophy rejects the idea that government is free to establish and enforce whatever legal rules it may choose. It recognizes certain laws as superior to any laws made by government. These laws automatically give persons certain liberties, commonly called "natural rights." The content and range of these liberties stem from what is referred to as "divine law" or simply "higher laws." These laws govern the operation of the universe and the character of humankind. The cornerstone of natural law philosophy is the view that any law made by government that deprives an individual or a group of a natural right is void.

Natural law played a prominent part in the thinking of this nation's founders and continues to significantly influence the content of its law. The Declaration of Independence mentions "Laws of Nature and of Nature's God" as a basis for bringing an end to the political bond between the colonies and Great Britain. Among the "truths" that the Declaration speaks of as "self-evident" are that "all men are created equal, that they are endowed by their Creator with certain unalienable Rights, that among these are Life, Liberty and the Pursuit of Happiness." Since the king's behavior had been "destructive of these ends," the Declaration states that the colonists could rightfully "alter or abolish" their association with Great Britain and form a new government.

Natural law philosophy has been incorporated into the U.S. Constitution. The First Amendment, for example, protects freedom of speech, press, and religion, which can be called natural rights. The Fourth Amendment prohibits government officials from arbitrarily entering one's home in search of evidence of criminal misconduct. The Constitution also bars government from depriving persons of life, liberty, or property without due process of law. The nation's courts have been compelled to determine the limits that this places on governmental action because the term *due process of law* is not defined in the Constitution. One definition is that government must behave in a *fundamentally fair* manner. This definition invites courts to take into account liberties that may be regarded as natural rights in deciding whether due process has been violated. Since there is no master list of natural rights, courts are free to identify a freedom or entitlement never before mentioned as a natural right to justify striking down objectionable governmental behavior.

Positivist Jurisprudence

The legal philosophy that treats law as a lawmaker's commands that courts are to enforce is known as **positivist jurisprudence,** or simply "positivism." The commands may originate from an individual, such as a dictator, or from a group, such as a military junta, or from a legislative body, such as the U.S. Congress or a state legislature. Positivism leaves no room for a court to strike them down on the ground that they conflict with natural law.

Despite the significance of natural law in the U.S. legal system, in various instances American courts follow the positivist view of law. For example, Congress has the constitutional power to impose a tax on the income of individuals. Were a taxpayer to contest the imposition of a 33 percent tax rate on individual income on the ground that this rate denies him the natural right to be free from excessive taxation, a court would not invoke natural law to test the legality of the

Natural law
the view that laws exist that are paramount to any of the laws made by humankind

Positivist jurisprudence
the view that law is a body of commands that courts are to enforce

rate; it would respect the judgment of Congress. A court would apply the same approach to a statute that bars persons from destroying members of a wildlife species that the legislature has classified as endangered.

There is no general rule as to when courts are to invoke natural law, positivism, *or any other legal philsophy.* In each instance the court decides which legal philosophy is appropriate. In doing so, among the factors that it is likely to take into account are the character and purpose of the law in question, the beneficial and injurious effects of enforcing that law, and current individual and societal concerns.

Technique of Judicial Decision Making

Analytical Jurisprudence

Analytical jurisprudence
the view that legal principles are to be painstakingly identified and applied

Like positivism, **analytical jurisprudence** treats an established legal principle as a command, which its proponents commonly refer to as an "imperative." Imperatives must be applied with precision. This makes court decisions predictable. To decide in whose favor to rule, a court is obliged to look inward. Operating in a formal manner, it should find and study pertinent existing legal principles. To arrive at a conclusion, it must logically apply the relevant imperatives to the immediate facts.

Judicial legislation
the creation of legal principles set by courts

A judge may not pay attention either to the merits or the outcomes of relevant legal principles. A court is not free to change these principles even if they are faulty. A court that altered the law would be guilty of **judicial legislation;** that is, it would make law. According to analytical jurisprudence, making law is beyond the province of a court. If a court were free to modify, reject, or establish legal principles, then law could not be precise and the outcomes of lawsuits would be unpredictable. It is for the legislative branch of government to alter, abandon, or replace unsatisfactory legal principles.

FREEDOM NOT TO SUPPORT ANOTHER'S CAUSE OR A FREE LUNCH?

Hypothetical Case

Thomas strongly opposed unionism. Under the terms of the collective bargaining agreement between his employer and the union, an employee who chose not to become a union member need not do so. However, such employees could not be employed for more than 60 days without paying the union's agency fee. The amount of this fee was the same as the amount of the dues paid by union members.

A portion of the dues and the agency fees collected by the union was used to cover the expenses of its officers when they attended meetings which explored such questions as how to increase union membership. The dues and fees also covered the costs of a monthly magazine published by the union and distributed free of charge only to dues-paying members. The magazine contained articles on how unions could strengthen their operations, recruit new members, and promote pro-union legislation. Thomas objected to the use of his agency fee for these purposes.

The union contended that Thomas wanted a free ride, that he wanted to enjoy the job benefits of union members but not pay to obtain them. It also contended that if Thomas, without paying the union's agency fee, could enjoy the benefits of those who paid union dues, then some union members would probably seek to cancel their membership and new employees would be tempted not to join the union.

Aware that he would be discharged if he did not pay the agency fee, Thomas brought a lawsuit in which he asked the court to declare it unlawful to require him to pay an agency fee equal in amount to union dues.

Should Thomas be required to pay the agency fee? Why? Is it ethical to require a person to contribute to an association whose objectives he or she strongly opposes? Discuss.

Pragmatic Jurisprudence

Advocates of **pragmatic jurisprudence** hold that legal rules and court decisions should be evaluated in terms of whether they are operational. To be acceptable under this standard, a principle of law or a court ruling must be capable of achieving the purpose for which it has been designed. The action requested must be such that persons can be reasonably expected to comply with it, that it is highly likely to achieve the objective of the principle or ruling, and that the court can determine whether its decision has been honored.

> **Pragmatic jurisprudence**
> the view that legal rules and court decisions should yield the desired results

□□□□

Bob, an engineer employed by Research, Inc., was the team leader of one of the firm's secret and expensive research projects. When he was offered a position by Cay Company, a competitor of Research, Inc. that was involved in a similar research project, code-named WIN, Bob resigned from Research, Inc. and went to work for Cay Company. Research Inc. brought a lawsuit to bar Bob from working on the WIN project. If the court ruled that Bob could work for Cay Company but could not use any of the information that he had obtained while employed by Research, Inc., an advocate of pragmatic jurisprudence would contend that the ruling was unacceptable because it was impractical. It is unreasonable to expect Bob to erase from his mind the information that he acquired at Research, Inc., and it would be extremely difficult to make sure that he complied with the court's ruling while working on WIN.

□□□□

Unlike analytical jurisprudence, pragmatic jurisprudence rejects the blind application of established legal principles to decide the outcome of a lawsuit. Justice Oliver Wendell Holmes, Jr. (1841–1935), a dynamic spokesperson for the pragmatic school, insisted that in deciding cases, judges must do more than merely apply relevant existing legal principles. They must also consider experience—how people actually behave and how things are actually done. If the application of a traditional legal principle will lead a court to a useless or unworkable result, then it must formulate a new principle, one that will steer it to an acceptable outcome. And it would retain the new principle only if the principle worked. If the principle proved to be unworkable, then it should be replaced by another new principle.

A People's Spirit

Historical Jurisprudence

The legal philosophy that emphasizes the influence on the law of the will or spirit of a nation's people is referred to as **historical jurisprudence.** It speaks of the people's will or spirit as the *volksgeist.* This spirit is found in a people's customs, traditions, and sense of right or wrong. It affects the people's representatives who

> **Historical jurisprudence**
> the view that law embodies the will or spirit of a people

make and apply the law. Despite the emphasis that historical jurisprudence places on the past, those who support it generally insist that law is also influenced by the *zeitgeist*, the spirit of the times. Customs, traditions, and a sense of right or wrong that were once cherished may not satisfy a people's current will or spirit. In response to the *zeitgeist*, legislators or courts may abandon established rules and replace them with currently approved standards. This allows the law to accommodate change. The *zeitgeist* may affect the law only momentarily, or it may result in the permanent replacement of features of the *volksgeist*.

When the *volksgeist* of American society accepted the dominance of the husband, the law barred married women from personally owning land. A married woman who inherited land or purchased land with her own resources could not personally sell it. When the *zeitgeist* would no longer tolerate the idea that married women were subordinate to their husbands, the law responded by giving wives and husbands the same legal rights to own and sell land.

The *volksgeist* of the American people includes the conviction that no person should be imprisoned unless first convicted of wrongdoing. After Japan bombed Pearl Harbor in 1941, the U.S. government deprived tens of thousands of Japanese-Americans of their freedom by confining them to so-called relocation centers although they had not been found guilty of any misconduct. Yielding to the *zeitgeist* triggered by war hysteria, the U.S. Supreme Court, noting that the challenged governmental action took place in time of war, did not come to their assistance. It rejected the contention that the government's action was unconstitutional. Almost 50 years later Congress acknowledged that these persons had been wronged. To somewhat compensate those who were still alive, it enacted legislation that allotted a small lump sum of money to each of them.

Promotion of Particular Values and Goals

Sociological Jurisprudence and Social Engineering

Sociological jurisprudence

the view that legal principles should reflect current behavior and needs

Eugen Ehrlich (1862-1922) is commonly regarded as the originator of the legal philosophy known as **sociological jurisprudence.** Legal principles, according to this philosophy, should be responsive to current human and institutional behavior and needs. The term *living law* is frequently used to describe this jurisprudential school because it emphasizes the requirement that law be flexible enough to take into account actual present-day behavior and the current aspirations of society. The use of law to protect and promote particular societal values and institutions is illustrated in the following paragraphs.

During the 1930s, when the United States was in the midst of the Great Depression, a number of states enacted "mortgage moratorium laws." These statutes barred a bank that held a mortgage on a person's home from enforcing the usual mortgage provision that allows the creditor to compel the sale of the debtor's property that secures the mortgage and to apply the sale proceeds toward the unpaid debt. Banks, relying on the constitutional provision that bars the states from undermining contractual obligations, contended that the statutes were unconstitutional. Noting that the nation was in the midst of a grave economic emergency and that the statutes were to be in effect only during the emergency, the U.S. Supreme Court ruled that they did not violate the Constitution.

More than one legal philosophy may serve as a basis for a particular law or court decision. Thus, the Supreme Court's decision to uphold the mortgage moratorium statutes was consistent not only with sociological jurisprudence but also with historical jurisprudence. The nation's *volksgeist* generally calls for the enforcement of contracts, but its *zeitgeist* during the Great Depression rendered acceptable the suspension of the right to enforce a certain type of agreement.

When firms headquartered in the United States carried on most of the business they transacted within the nation's boundaries and played a key part in the economies of numerous foreign countries, our courts commonly paid prime attention to American firms in deciding whether a domestic firm's conduct illegally injured competition. Now that foreign companies play a significant role in both U.S. and overseas markets, sociological jurisprudence invites U.S. courts to consider how foreign companies behave in the U.S. as well as in overseas markets when the courts are asked to rule that one or more American firms misbehaved in a national or multinational transaction. The failure of courts to consider the behavior of foreign companies now that these companies are important actors in the world economy would be a mark of judicial inflexibility, inconsistent with the idea of living law.

Social Engineering

In 1906 Roscoe Pound (1870-1964) challenged judges and lawyers to abandon what he labeled "mechanical jurisprudence." He objected to courts acting as if law were nothing more than a core of commands, to be sought out and then logically applied, and although a friend of sociological jurisprudence, he did not see law as simply a means of promoting and protecting society's present values and institutions. Instead, he saw law as an *engineering device,* that is, as a tool that should be used to promote selected social objectives. Pound called on those who create and administer law to use the social sciences to determine what new legal concepts are needed and how these concepts should be applied. He emphasized that new legal concepts should be formulated only after competing social interests have been weighed and balanced. More important interests should be protected and promoted at the expense of less important interests. His legal philosophy is commonly referred to as **social engineering.**

Sociological jurisprudence, which stresses the intimate relationship between law and existing societal wants and institutions, is essentially *reactive.* Social engineering, on the other hand, is *proactive.* Advocates of the social engineering school insist that law should be used not simply as a means to satisfy people's present needs and expectations, but also as an instrument to promote particular values, whether or not these values are popular. Employed as Pound wanted it to be, law can be used to cast society into the mold desired by those who make and administer the law.

At one time the U.S. Supreme Court contended that blacks who were denied access to publicly operated schools attended by whites were not denied equal treatment so long as the schools that they attended were equal to those attended by whites. In 1954 the Court unanimously rejected the "separate but equal" doctrine. It asserted that separate was *necessarily unequal* and that the Constitution's requirement of equal protection of the law barred the assignment of public school students on the basis of their race. In this instance the Court used the law proactively, as a tool to establish a new mode of behavior.

The Pregnancy Discrimination Act of 1978 is another example of social engineering. Previously, employers were free to discriminate against pregnant women. The act makes it unlawful for an employer to deny a woman benefits and opportunities for no reason other than that she is pregnant.

Social engineering
the view that law is a means of promoting selected social goals

Individual Centered

Utilitarian Jurisprudence

The school of jurisprudence that evaluates legal principles in terms of the breadth of their beneficial effects is known as **utilitarian jurisprudence.** It is frequently spoken of as a "common sense approach" to law. As tested by utilitarian jurisprudence, a legal principle is just if it contributes to the happiness of most people even if it oppresses some.

Utilitarian jurisprudence may call for the imposition of legal restraints on some sorts of behavior and for the freedom from regulation of other sorts. For example, a few companies may gain, but the lives and well-being of many persons may be put at risk, if there are no legal restrictions on the disposition of life-threatening substances and socially irresponsible companies use the least expensive way to get rid of them. A statute that imposes standards as to the disposition of such substances and penalizes those who fail to comply is in accord with utilitarian jurisprudence. The number of persons who are likely to benefit from the statute is far greater than the number who must bear the cost of complying with it.

Existentialist Jurisprudence

That individuals are ordinarily *helpless* when they deal with powerful persons or organizations is the critical assumption of the legal philosophy called **existentialist jurisprudence.** Proponents of this philosophy advocate legal principles that otherwise defenseless persons may use when they are faced by the crushing demands of mighty forces.

At one time a court would not disturb a contract although one of the parties was devious, shrewd, quick-witted, and in a better bargaining position and therefore fared *far* better than the other party. The party who got the worst of the bargain was supposedly free not to enter into it. Today, if a court finds that an agreement relating to the sale of goods is *unconscionable,* it may, in accordance with the Uniform Commercial Code, come to the victim's rescue by refusing to enforce the contract, or by enforcing only part of it, or by enforcing it on just terms. A court may conclude that an agreement is unconscionable if the party with far greater bargaining power alone decided the contents of the agreement and took outrageous advantage of the other party through provisions itemized in unnecessarily small print; or if the agreement was written in such a way that the party not permitted to take part in drafting it was highly unlikely to anticipate the extent of its adverse impact; or if the benefits that will accrue to the party who wrote the agreement are far unjustly greater than those that the other party will receive.

Jurisprudence of Fairness

In the preceding chapter fairness was discussed as a criterion that is sometimes used to determine whether conduct is ethical. Fairness also has a place in legal philosophy. Under the **jurisprudence of fairness,** a legal rule that promotes fairness is acceptable. Ordinarily, it is far simpler to identify what is unfair than to prescribe what is fair. For example, courts have concluded that a life insurance contract, although it does not say so, imposes an obligation on the insurance company to fairly fulfill its contractual obligations. Thus, if an insurance company refuses to pay a claim submitted by a policyholder when the terms of the policy afford no reason to withhold payment, the company violates its obligation to behave fairly. In such a case, the policyholder is entitled to recover not only "compensatory damages," that is, the amount of money he or she *would have received* if the insurance company had not failed to carry out the contract, but also "punitive damages," that is, an additional amount sufficient to *punish* the company for not treating the policyholder fairly and to *deter* others from engaging in similar conduct.

The legal obligations of persons who *dominate* others or are commonly *trusted* by others are generally determined on the basis of the sort of behavior that can be fairly demanded by a subservient or reliant party. For instance, an invalid who employs an aide to tend to his daily needs because he cannot take care of himself, is likely to come under the domination of the aide. If the aide offers to sell his home to the invalid, there is a likelihood of a "conflict of interest" between them and a risk that the aide will seek to treat the employer unfairly. If the two do enter into a contract and the employer later refuses to carry it out, the aide may bring a lawsuit to enforce it. To win the suit, the aide must establish that he did not use his position to unduly influence his employer and that the contract does not treat the employer unfairly.

Is a debt collection company acting fairly when one of its employees repeatedly telephones a debtor while he or she is at work, or in the early morning hours, or sends the debtor a daily postcard bearing in bold print these words: "YOU ARE A DEADBEAT! IT IS TIME TO PAY, ISN'T IT?" Believing that such tactics are unfair, Congress has restricted them under the Fair Debt Collection Act.

AETNA LIFE INSURANCE CO. v. LAVOIE
SUPREME COURT OF THE UNITED STATES
475 U.S. 813 (1986)

The plaintiffs, husband and wife, obtained a health insurance policy from the defendant insurance company. Following the wife's 23 days of hospitalization, the company's local office received from the hospital a bill in the amount of $3,028.25 for the cost of the hospitalization. The company's local office offered to pay only $1,650.22. Before receiving a copy of all of the wife's hospital records, it sent a letter to the national office indicating that the 23-day hospitalization was unnecessary and that the "[h]ospital records do not indicate anything to the contrary." At one point the national office told the local office to continue denying the request for full payment, but added that "if they act like they are going to file suit," the file should be reviewed.

The plaintiffs brought suit in a state court, asking the court to award them not only compensatory damages in the amount of the balance of the original claim of $3,028.25 but also *punitive damages* for the tort of *bad-faith*-refusal to pay a valid claim. The plaintiffs were awarded the balance of their original claim and $3.5 million in punitive damages. The defendant appealed to the state supreme court.

In a 5-4 decision the state supreme court affirmed the punitive damages award. Two weeks later the defendant asked the court to rehear the case. Before a decision was made on this request, the defendant learned that while the case was pending before the state supreme court, one of the court's five judges, Justice Embry, who voted to affirm the plaintiffs' punitive damages award, had brought two lawsuits against insurance companies in which he asked for *punitive damages* on the ground of *bad-faith* failure to pay a claim. While these two cases were pending, Justice Embry wrote the 5–4 decision in which for the *first time* the state supreme court ruled that an insurance company that acted in *bad faith* could be *liable* for *punitive damages*. The defendant objected to Justice Embry taking part in the decision that the plaintiffs could recover punitive damages. It insisted that he should recuse himself, that is, not take part in the court's deliberations, when it considered the defendant's request for a rehearing. The court rejected the defendant's recusal request and by a 5–4 vote denied the defendant's request for a rehearing. The defendant appealed to the U.S. Supreme Court.

CHIEF JUSTICE BURGER
Delivered the Opinion of the Court

[U]nder the [U.S. Constitution's] Due Process Clause no judge "can be a judge in his own case [or be] permitted to try cases where he has [an] interest in the outcome." [W]hat degree or kind of interest is sufficient to disqualify a judge from sitting "cannot be defined with precision." Nonetheless, a reasonable formulation of the issue is whether the "situation is one 'which would offer a possible temptation to the average judge to lead him not to hold the balance nice, clear, and true.'"

At the time Justice Embry cast the deciding vote and authored the court's opinion, he had at least one very similar *bad-faith-* [italics supplied] refusal-to-pay lawsuit in another [state] court. The decisions of the court on which Justice Embry sat, the [state supreme court], are binding on all [of the state's courts]. We need not blind ourselves to the fact that the law in the area of *bad-faith-* [italics supplied] refusal-to-pay claims in [the state] was unsettled at that time, as the [state supreme] court's close division in deciding this case indicates. When Justice Embry cast the deciding vote, he did not merely apply well-established law and in fact quite possibly made new law; the court's opinion does not suggest that its conclusion was compelled by earlier decisions.

The decision under review firmly established that punitive damages could be obtained in [the state] in a situation where the insured's claim is not fully approved and only partial payment of the underlying claim had been made. Prior to the decision under review, the [state supreme court] had not clearly recognized any claim [for punitive damages] in such circumstances.

[The issues in this case] were present in [at least one of the cases brought by Justice Embry]. Justice Embry's opinion for the [state supreme court] had the clear and immediate effect of enhancing both the legal status and the settlement value of his own case.

We hold simply that when Justice Embry made that judgment, he acted as "a judge in his own case."

We also hold that his interest was "'direct, personal, substantial, [and] pecuniary.'" We hold that the "tidy sum" that Justice Embry received directly [in the settlement of his case, which was reached after he wrote the opinion in which the state supreme court recognized that an insured could recover punitive damages in a *bad-faith*-refusal-to-pay case] is sufficient to establish the substantiality of his interest here.

We conclude that Justice Embry's participation in this case violated the appellant's due process rights. We make clear that we are not required to decide whether Justice Embry was influenced, but only whether sitting on the case then before the [state supreme court] "'would offer a possible temptation to the average judge to lead him not to hold the balance nice, clear, and true.'" The Due Process Clause "may sometimes bar trial judges who have no actual bias and who would do their very best to weigh the scales of justice equally between contending parties. But to perform its high function in the best way, 'justice must satisfy the *appearance* [italics supplied] of justice.'"

Justice Embry's vote was decisive in the 5-4 decision and he was the author of the court's opinion. Because of Justice Embry's leading role in the decision under review, we conclude that the "appearance of justice" will best be served by vacating the decision and remanding for further proceedings.

The judgment of the [state supreme court] is vacated, and the case is remanded for further proceedings not inconsistent with this opinion.

Legal Issues

1. Wilson Pax was the mayor of Cartlon. As mayor, he was responsible for seeing that the city's annual expenditures did not exceed its annual revenues. His duties as mayor included service as a judge of the city's traffic court. As a judge, he could impose fines on persons whom he found guilty of traffic violations. All money paid as fines were treated as part of the city's annual revenues. Are drivers who are tried by Judge Pax on traffic violation charges denied due process of law?

2. After a four-day trial Judge Wells found Ix guilty of theft and sentenced him to imprisonment for the maximum term allowed by law. Ix's conviction was reversed on appeal and a new trial ordered on the ground that Judge Wells repeatedly allowed the prosecution to use inadmissable evidence. May Judge Wells preside at the new trial?

Ethical Issues

1. Generally, state statutes, codes of ethical conduct, or court rules require judges to recuse themselves for "bias or prejudice." Does a judge violate such a statute, code of ethics, or court rule if he or she does not recuse himself or herself in a nonjury case in which one of the parties is represented by the judge's former college roommate?

2. Was it ethical for a judge to try a case in which the attorney for one of the parties was the largest contributor to the judge's election campaign fund in a heatedly contested election that took place *just* six days before the trial began? Why?

Egalitarian Jurisprudence

During the past four decades judges, legislators, and other officials involved with making or administering the law have displayed an unprecedented degree of interest in seeing that persons are treated in the same manner unless there is a justifiable reason not to do so. The idea that similarly situated people should be treated alike is at the heart of **egalitarian jurisprudence.** Although this legal philosophy is related to the jurisprudence of fairness, the latter view of law is keyed to the acceptability of the way in which parties interact with one another, whereas the prime concern of egalitarian jurisprudence is why like people are dealt with differently. For example, a firm may act fairly by paying its employees a decent wage, yet violate egalitarian jurisprudence by refusing to hire women, minorities, or the handicapped. Egalitarian jurisprudence focuses on the acceptability of discriminatory behavior, whether that of government, a corporation, or

Egalitarian jurisprudence

the view that similarly situated people should be treated alike

individuals. In dealing with loan applicants, should a lender treat married women differently from married men? May an employer pay women employees less than it pays men for performing the same kind of work? Advocates of egalitarian jurisprudence would answer "no" to both questions.

The Fourteenth Amendment to the U.S. Constitution bars states from denying persons equal protection of the laws. The U.S. Supreme Court, for example, has ruled that generally, the vote of each person in an election held to select members of a state legislature must be of equal worth; and even though a child's parents are illegally living in the United States, he or she cannot be denied the opportunity to attend a public school that is open to children of U.S. citizens.

Federal and state statutes and city and town ordinances bar various forms of discrimination. Under the Equal Pay Act of 1963, for example, employers must pay equal wages to those who perform like work, regardless of their sex. The Civil Rights Act of 1964 prohibits employers from denying persons equal job opportunities because of their sex, race, religion, color, or national origin. The Age Discrimination in Employment Act of 1967 generally bars employers from discriminating against persons who are 40 or older on the basis of their age. There is legislation that bars various sorts of discrimination against handicapped persons. Some cities have enacted ordinances that prohibit job discrimination because of a person's sexual orientation.

Like egalitarian jurisprudence, court decisions, statutes, and ordinances intended to protect persons from discrimination recognize that there may be legitimate reasons to discriminate against a member of a generally protected class of persons. For instance, an employer that refuses to hire an individual who practices a particular religion because that person lacks qualifications genuinely necessary to perform a particular job—fails to satisfy bona fide occupational qualifications—does not violate the prohibition on religious discrimination of the 1964 Civil Rights Act.

CLEBURNE v. CLEBURNE LIVING CENTERS, INC.
SUPREME COURT OF THE UNITED STATES
473 U.S. 432 (1985)

Cleburne Living Centers, Inc. (CLC) planned to lease a building for use as a group home for 13 mentally retarded men and women. The city of Cleburne, which classified the proposed group home as a "hospital for the feebleminded," informed CLC that it would have to apply for a special use permit under the city's zoning ordinance, which restricted the construction of hospitals for the insane or feebleminded, or alcoholics or drug addicts, or penal or correctional institutions. CLC requested, but was denied a permit by a 3-1 vote of the city council.

CLC filed a lawsuit in federal district court against the city and several of its officials, claiming that the zoning ordinance discriminated against the mentally retarded in violation of the equal rights of CLC and its potential residents. The trial court found (1) that if the potential residents of the home were not mentally retarded, but the home was the same in all other respects, it could be used as a residence under the city's zoning ordinance and (2) that the city council's decision "was motivated primarily by the fact that the residents of the home would be persons who are mentally retarded." In the opinion of the trial court, the zoning ordinance was reasonably related to the city's legitimate interests in "the legal responsibility of CLC and its residents, the safety and fears of residents in the adjoining neighborhood," and the number of people to be housed in the home. It held that the ordinance was constitutional.

The court of appeals reversed, ruling that the ordinance was invalid because it did not substantially further any important governmental interest. The court pointed out that "in light of the history of unfair and often grotesque mistreatment of the retarded, discrimination against them was 'likely to reflect deep-seated prejudice.'" In addition, the mentally retarded, whose condition would not improve, lacked political power. Without group homes the retarded could never hope to integrate themselves into the community. The U.S. Supreme Court agreed to review the appellate court's decision.

JUSTICE WHITE
Delivered the Opinion of the Court

The Equal Protection Clause of the Fourteenth Amendment commands that no state shall "deny to any person within its jurisdiction the equal protection of the laws," which is essentially a direction that all persons similarly situated should be treated alike. The general rule is that legislation is presumed to be valid and will be sustained if the classification drawn by the statute is rationally related to a legitimate state interest. When social or economic legislation is at issue, the Equal Protection Clause allows the states wide latitude, and the Constitution presumes that even improvident decisions will eventually be rectified by the democratic process.

To withstand equal protection review, legislation that distinguishes between the mentally retarded and others must be rationally related to a legitimate governmental purpose.

The constitutional issue is clearly posed. The city does not require a special use permit [in the same area] for apartment houses, multiple dwellings, boarding and lodging houses, fraternity or sorority houses, dormitories, apartment hotels, hospitals, sanitariums, nursing homes for convalescents or the aged (other than for the insane or feebleminded or alcoholics or drug addicts), private clubs or fraternal orders,

and other specified uses. It does, however, insist on a special permit [for] a facility for the mentally retarded.

It is true that the mentally retarded as a group are indeed different from others not sharing their misfortune, and in this respect they may be different from those who would occupy other facilities that would be permitted [in the area] without a special permit. But this difference is largely irrelevant unless [the group] home and those who would occupy it would threaten legitimate interests of the city in a way that other permitted uses such as boardinghouses and hospitals would not. [I]n our view [there is no showing of] any rational basis for believing that the [group] home would pose any special threat to the city's legitimate interests.

[T]he City Council's insistence on the permit rested on several factors. [T]he Council was concerned with the negative attitude of the majority of property owners located within 200 feet of the facility, as well as with the fears of elderly residents of the neighborhood. But mere negative attitudes, or fear, unsubstantiated by factors which are properly cognizable in a zoning proceeding, are not permissible for treating a home for the mentally retarded differently from apartment houses, multiple dwellings, and the like. "Private biases may be outside the reach of the law, but the law cannot, directly or indirectly, give them effect."

[T]he Council has two objections to the location of the facility. It was concerned that the facility was across the street from a junior high school, and it feared that the students might harass the occupants of the home. But the school itself is attended by about 30 mentally retarded students. The other objection was that it was located on "a five hundred year flood plain." This concern with the possibility of a flood, however, can hardly be based on a distinction between the home and, for example, nursing homes, homes for convalescents or the aged or sanitariums or hospitals, any of which could be located on the site without obtaining a special use permit. The same may be said of another concern of the Council—doubts about the legal responsibility for actions which the mentally retarded might take. If there is no concern about legal responsibility with respect to other uses that would be permitted in the area, such as boarding and fraternity houses, it is difficult to believe that the groups of mildly or moderately retarded individuals who would live at [the facility] would present any different special hazard.

[T]he Council was concerned with the size of the home and the number of people that would occupy it. [The trial and appellate courts found] that "[i]f the potential residents of the home were not mentally retarded, but the home was the same in all other respects, its use would be permitted under the city's zoning ordinance." Given this finding, there would be no restrictions on the number of people who could occupy this home as a boarding-house, nursing home, family dwelling, fraternity house, or dormitory. The question is whether it is rational to treat the mentally retarded differently. It is true that they suffer disability not

shared by others; but why this difference warrants a density regulation that others need not observe is not at all apparent. [I]n the words of the [appellate court] "the City never justifies its apparent view that other people can live under such 'crowded' conditions when mentally retarded persons cannot."

[R]equiring the permit in this case appears to us to rest on irrational prejudice against the mentally retarded, including those who would occupy the facility and who would live under the closely supervised and highly regulated conditions expressly provided for by state and federal law.

The judgment of the [court of appeals] is affirmed insofar as it invalidates the zoning ordinance as applied to the home.

Legal Issues

1. Some forms of governmental discrimination deny persons due process of law because they are *invidious,* that it, they are unfair, unreasonable, arbitrary, or irrational. An age discrimination statute passed by Congress barred employers from engaging in age discrimination against most employees over the age of 40. However, the statute limited the protection it afforded to tenured college and university professors to tenured professors between the ages of 40 and 70. Is the discrimination permitted by the statute invidious? Why?

2. The Fourth Amendment to the Constitution secures individuals against *unreasonable* searches and seizures of their belongings in the privacy of their home. What a person knowingly exposes to the public, even in his or her home, is not protected by the Fourth Amendment. To decide whether the Fourth Amendment is applicable, a court takes into account whether the person who claims the protection of the amendment showed an expectation

of privacy and whether that expectation was one that society considers reasonable. When Sanders lived in an apartment he kept the gun with which he had killed a bank guard in a box under his bed. After he became a homeless person, he lived in a cave-like shelter under a highway. He placed the box with the gun in an opening in a concrete highway support located just a few inches from where he slept on a piece of cardboard. Was Sanders then entitled to the same constitutional protection from a police search for the gun as the protection he enjoyed when he kept the gun in his apartment? Why?

Ethical Issues

1. Gray, a long-time farmer, was the founder of Agri Corporation, a large supplier of farm products. To represent the firm in any capacity he would hire only a person who, as he would say, "was raised on a farm. Farmers understand farmers." Kibbs grew up in a large city. When he applied for a position as a computer operator at Agri, his only contact with farming had been a 10-minute visit to a small farm at the age of five. Although he was the best qualified applicant, the firm's personnel director wrote across his job application: "Not a farmer. Do not consider." Was Agri Corporation guilty of unethical behavior? Why?

2. A court rule permitted trial judges to assign a third-year law student to represent persons who were charged with a crime punishable by not more than six months in prison, or a $500 fine, or both, and who lacked money to pay a lawyer to assist them. Jean Royce, who had but a few dollars, was charged with a crime that could result in her imprisonment for up to 30 days, or a $250 fine, or both. When she asked the trial judge to assign an attorney to help her with her defense, she was told that a third-year law student would soon be in touch with her. She insisted that she wanted what she called "a real lawyer." The judge said, "Have no fear. The student who will help you works with 25 other students under the direction of a law professor. I am sure that before long the student will pass the bar examination. All of the students in the program are at least C+ students." Royce replied: "I am not being treated like folks with money. If I had money, I could have a real lawyer, one who has passed the bar examination, has experience, and—who knows—even had a law school grade average of A+." Was it ethical for the court to assign a third-year law student to represent Jean Royce? Why?

Distributive Justice

The legal philosophy spoken of as **distributive justice** calls for government and law to take a variety of factors into account in deciding how economic resources should be distributed. Among those factors are the desirability of equal treatment, the comparative needs of those in quest of government help or the help of the legal system, the contributions to society of those who want help, the public interest, and the availability of resources. When a small entrepreneur's request for a loan from the federal, state, or local government is refused, he or she may have to go out of business, but this personal disaster is likely to have only a slight effect on the general economy. By contrast, the demise of a large enterprise can trigger extensive repercussions. Because resources are necessarily limited, and not all of those in need of public help can be assisted, distributive justice would call for

Distributive justice
the view that law is a means of controlling the distribution of wealth

government to help assure the survival of a large enterprise rather than that of several small firms if helping the small firms would make it impossible to help the large enterprise.

A consumer who has been severely injured because of a defective product may be confronted with personally insurmountable economic problems. Ordinarily, his or her need for financial aid outweighs the damage that the manufacturer will suffer if it is compelled to compensate the consumer for the harm caused by its product. The public interest is served by requiring the manufacturer to bear the cost of the consumer's loss. If the manufacturer were not held accountable, then public funds might have to be used to pay for the injured consumer's needs. In part to assist injured consumers and in part to serve the public interest, product liability law holds the manufacturer accountable for injuries attributable to its product in a variety of circumstances, including circumstances in which the product is not fit for its ordinary use or circumstances in which the product is unreasonably defective. If a product is highly desirable, the manufacturer can pass on to those who benefit from its use some or all of the costs that it incurs to compensate those who are injured by the product.

GREEN v. WALKER
U.S. COURT OF APPEALS, FIFTH CIRCUIT
910 F.2d 291 (1990)

Sidney Green was employed by ARA/GSI International. As a condition of continued employment, ARA/GSI required its employees to undergo an annual physical examination that included chest X-rays. ARA/GSI contracted with Dr. Leslie Walker, the defendant, to conduct those examinations. After examining Green, Dr. Walker submitted to ARA/GSI a report stating that all of the test results were normal. About one year later Green was diagnosed as having lung cancer. Green and his wife, Joni, individually and on behalf of their minor daughter, sued Dr. Walker. They claimed that he had negligently failed to diagnose the beginnings of cancer at the time of the examination and that he had failed to disclose that finding in a timely manner, thus reducing Green's life expectancy and his chances of survival. Shortly thereafter Green died. Dr. Walker asked the district court to dismiss the lawsuit without a trial on the ground that since he had examined Green pursuant to a contract with ASA/GSI, no physician-patient relationship on which to base a malpractice claim existed between him and Green. The district court granted Dr. Walker's request, ruling that Dr. Walker had no duty of care to Green when he examined Green. Joni Green, individually and on behalf of her child, appealed.

POLITZ, CIRCUIT JUDGE

It is a long-established principle of law that liability for malpractice is dependent on the existence of a physician-patient relationship. [T]he existence of the traditional physician-patient relationship on which such liability hinges uniformly has been held to depend upon the existence of a contract, express or implied, that the doctor will undertake to treat the patient or at least engage in diagnosis as a prelude to treatment.

Emphasizing a distinction between treatment and a consultative physical examination conducted at the request and for the benefit of a third party, state courts addressing the issue generally have held that no physician-patient relationship exists between "a prospective or actual employee and the doctor who examines him for the employer."

Like any person, a physician "is responsible for the damage he occasions not merely by his act, but by his negligence, his imprudence, or his want of skill."

The issue presented by the instant case is whether Louisiana jurisprudence supports an extension of the traditional physician-patient relationship to admit of a legal relationship between examining physician and examinee, thus imposing the physician's duty of care in that situation.

> The persons at whose disposal society has placed the potent implements of technology owe a heavy moral obligation to use them carefully and to avoid foreseeable harm to present or future generations. In the field of medicine, as in that of manufacturing, the need for compensation of innocent victims of defective products and negligently delivered services is a powerful factor influencing [the] law. Typically in these areas also the defendants' capacity to bear and distribute the losses is far superior to that of consumers. Additionally these defendants are in a much better position than the victims to analyze the risks involved in the defendants' activities and to either take precautions to avoid them or to insure against them. Consequently, a much stronger and more effective incentive to prevent the occurrence of future harm will be created by placing the burden of foreseeable losses on the defendants than upon the disorganized, uninformed victims.

We live in an age in which the drive for an increasingly productive workforce has led employers increasingly to require that employees subject their bodies (and minds) to inspection in order to obtain or maintain employment. ([C]ommon procedures include blood tests, urinalysis, pulmonary tests, and X-rays.) In placing oneself in the hands of a person held out to the worker as skilled in a medical profession, albeit at the request of one's employer, one justifiably has the reasonable expectation that the expert will warn of "any incidental dangers of which he is cognizant due to his peculiar knowledge of his specialization."

We therefore now hold that when an individual is required, as a condition of future or continued employment, to submit to a medical examination, that examination creates a relationship between the examining physician and the examinee, at least to the extent of the tests conducted. This relationship imposes upon the examining physician a duty to conduct the requested tests and diagnose the results thereof, exercising the level of care consistent with the doctor's professional training and expertise, and to take reasonable steps to make information available timely to the examinee of any findings that pose an imminent danger to the examinee's physical or mental well-being. To impose a duty upon the doctor who performs such tests to do so in accordance with the degree of care expected of his/her profession for the benefit of the employee-examinee, as well as the employer, is fully consistent with the very essence of [the Louisiana] Code.

The decision of the district court is *reversed,* and the matter is *remanded* for further proceedings consistent herewith.

Legal Issues

1. Teet, an employee of Worth Co., was injured while pouring molten steel into a vat. He was immediately examined by Dr. Link, a physician who was employed by Worth. Because Dr. Link

failed to diagnose the full extent of his injuries, Teet lost the use of three fingers on his right hand. He sued Dr. Link for malpractice. Dr. Link's attorney asked the court to dismiss Teet's lawsuit on the ground that since Teet was injured on the job and Dr. Link was employed by Worth, Teet's claim was against Worth, not Dr. Link. What judgment and why?

2. Tests conducted under the direction of Dr. Fred Ferrymate revealed that if Mrs. Diane Moore conceived a child, there was an unreasonable risk that the child would be born with a birth defect. Dr. Ferrymate did not warn Mr. and Mrs. Moore of this possibility. One year after the tests were conducted, Mrs. Moore gave birth to a seriously deformed child. On behalf of the child, Mr. and Mrs. Moore brought a lawsuit against Dr. Ferrymate, asking for a judgment in the amount of $10 million to assure that the child would receive necessary medical care and attention throughout his life. Dr. Ferrymate asked the court to dismiss the suit because he owed no duty to a child who had not been conceived when he conducted the tests. What judgment? Discuss.

Ethical Issues

1. Dr. Suzanne Trish, a physician, was in the full-time employ of LT Corporation. In conducting annual physical examinations of LT employees, she found that those who suffered from even mild asthma were likely to develop serious problems if they worked with the substances that LT used to "wet-dry" its products. When she told her immediate superior, Allan Marr, that she had an ethical obligation to share this information with LT employees who suffered from asthma, he replied: "Suzanne, at LT we are all on the LT team. You know how difficult it is to get good workers. Every time an LT employee leaves, LT incurs a significant cost to train a replacement. That harms not only LT and its stockholders, but also all LT staff members, because there is less to go around for everyone. You work for LT, not the employees who have asthma. Your ethical obligation is to help LT be profitable. LT provides all of its employees with medical coverage. Let their physicians do whatever is called for, even if that means advising them to leave LT." What ethical standard or standards support Marr's point of view? Discuss.

2. Edward Douglas, the chief executive officer of Evans, Inc., told Lee Hawk, the firm's attorney, that "in order to get our budget in line with reality, we must see to it that our older highly paid nonunion employees retire as soon as possible. I will be working with our director of personnel to find out what we must do to persuade them to retire. Your job is to draw up an agreement that they will be asked to sign before receiving the severance check, so that they cannot later sue Evans for age discrimination. I know this plan may violate the spirit of federal and state law that bars age discrimination, but there is no sense in keeping wages high when we can cut them and improve efficiency. Lawmakers just don't know what a business must do to succeed." Hawk replied: "I will gather all of the information available on how employees can surrender their rights to sue for age discrimination and prepare as tight a document as possible to make this program of yours a success." What ethical standard or standards are consistent with Douglas's scheme? Is Hawk's planned course of behavior unethical? Discuss.

1. A law was introduced in the state legislature that barred a firm from doing business with any state agency if less than 5 percent of its employees were 65 or older. A firm could be excused from this requirement only if it showed that despite reasonable efforts it had been unable to meet the 5 percent standard. Opponents of the law insisted that law could not alter human behavior and that it was wrong to saddle employers with the burden of employing persons 65 years of age or older. Advocates of the law insisted that unless something were done to assure that the increasing number of older state residents had access to jobs, the state would have to pay a greater share of the expenses that older persons incurred for food, clothing, shelter, medical care, and social services.

   a. Which legal philosophy or philosophies could the advocates of the law rely on to back their point of view?

   b. Which school or schools of jurisprudence might the opponents of the law use to support their position?

2. "The defendant is accused of murder, a very serious crime. However, our Constitution provides for bail. It would be wrong to deny the defendant bail simply because he is charged with murder. The facts show no reason to believe that he will not obey the orders of this court or to doubt that he will be available when needed, so that the case can promptly proceed to trial. Taking into account the defendant's ties to his community, his past record, and his financial resources, this court sets bail at $500,000." Which jurisprudential school or schools support the judge's conclusion?

3. "This court has carefully examined all of the pertinent cases mentioned in the briefs submitted by the parties' lawyers. It must be recognized, however, that this state's law governing the commercial banking transaction in question has paid attention to the unique nature of the banking business and to the recent changes that have occurred in this sector of American business." Is it likely that the judge who wrote this statement was influenced by the historical school of jurisprudence? Explain your answer.

4. "Law must both change and assure change. If society depended solely on the voluntary action of individuals to do the things that should be done, those things would often not be done. Law must fill the gap; it must see that people behave as they should, even if this means using it to bring about fundamental changes in attitudes and practices." With which legal philosophy or philosophies would you identify the author of the above statement? Why?

5. A state legislator proposed a law to bar motor vehicles from transporting hazardous substances anywhere in the state. Which jurisprudential school would you use as a basis for your support of that law? Why?

6. "What we need are judges who exclusively folllow existing principles to determine the demands of the U.S. Constitution. If judges can freely change the meaning of the Constitution, then we really do not have a constitution. Court decisions that concern the Constitution should be based on what is stated in the Constitution and past court decisions." Which school or schools of jurisprudence are consistent with the above statement? Discuss.

CHAPTER

3

The Judicial and Legislative Process

At present, interest in the views of those under consideration for judicial posts is significantly higher than it has been at other times. Many persons want to know whether such candidates are friendly or hostile to business, support protection of the environment, favor a strict or loose interpretation of the U.S. Constitution, are disposed to harsh or lenient treatment of convicted criminals, or want to restrict or enlarge the extent to which one person's freedom should be permitted to intrude on the rights of another person.

Because of the broad powers of legislators, the views of candidates for legislative office have always been of far greater concern than the views of potential judges. Currently some of the things people want to know about the views of such candidates—for example, their attitude toward the role of government, environmental protection, and the treatment of convicted criminals—are not unlike what they want to know about the views of potential judges. There is also widespread interest in the views of legislative candidates as to subjects about which judges seldom have any say, such as the kinds of taxes levied, tax rates, the powers of governmental agencies, and foreign trade.

This chapter considers the evolution of the judicial and legislative branches of government and examines how judges and legislators go about their tasks. Knowing how judges and legislators perform their duties enables one to appreciate the extent to which the law is affected by their predispositions. A critical link between the judicial and legislative branches is considered in the latter part of the chapter, which focuses attention on the ways in which judges interpret laws enacted by legislators.

COMMON LAW

Our Common Law Heritage

Customarily, English law is referred to as **common law.** Because of the strong influence that English law has had on the basic features of American law, the United States is said to be a "common law country." Other common law jurisdictions include Australia and all the provinces of Canada, except Quebec, whose law originated in French law. France and such other Western European nations as Germany and Italy are said to be "civil law countries." **Civil law** originated in Roman law. Although common law is dominant in the United States, the law of a number of states has been significantly influenced by other legal systems. For instance, some features of the law of such Western states as California and Arizona stem from Spanish law. Various segments of Louisiana law reflect the influence of the body of French law known as the "Napoleonic Code."

English and American judges have traditionally played a key role in lawmaking. At one time the power of the judiciary in common law countries to establish legal principles was a prime difference between common law and civil law. Historically, legal principles in civil law countries originated in some sector of government other than the courts. Either the monarch or a legislative body, or both, made law. For this reason, in civil law countries law was found primarily in written directives called "codes" or "statutes." Today, this once clear distinction between the sources of law in common law and civil law countries no longer exists. Although judge-made law continues to play a very important part in common law countries, a great deal of English and American law now originates in codes or statutes. And in civil law countries judges currently play a far more significant part in the lawmaking process than they did in the past.

Judge-Made Law and Legislated Law

The English Experience

Aside from being used to distinguish the English and American legal systems from some other type of legal system, the term *common law* is used in another context. It is the label given to so-called unwritten or judge-made law. Such law first appears in court decisions.

At one time there were no national courts in England. Courts were then established by local lords, dealt with local matters, and applied local law. In these circumstances, judges understandably took local customs and parochial ideas of right and wrong into account to decide a dispute when they were unaware of any relevant local legal rule. Thus, the principle on which a court based its decision might be nothing more than a statement of customary behavior in legal terms. In this way a custom was transformed into a principle of law that the court used thereafter to decide parties' legal rights and duties. After the Normans conquered England in 1066, England's new kings gradually expanded the role of the national government. Little by little, national courts established by the king displaced the local courts. Judges continued to be the key lawmakers.

Statutory law, unlike judge-made law, is not established in the context of a lawsuit. Statutory law is established in a formal and highly structured way by a body that is usually referred to as a "legislature." This body is composed of

Common law
law of England; unwritten or judge-made law

Civil law
law rooted in Roman law

Statutory law
law made by a body designated to formally make law

legislators, persons whose designated task is to enact laws. The legal principles that a legislature adopts are set forth in statutes, acts, laws, or ordinances.

Parliament
the legislative body that makes England's statutory law

The first meeting of **Parliament,** England's national legislature, has been traced to a gathering of noblemen, knights, and clergy in 1254. In a comparatively short time Parliament became a vigorous lawmaker, but not England's sole lawmaker. Judges continued to be vital participants in the lawmaking process. In some areas of the law, in the absence of a statute enacted by Parliament, judges continued to create law. For example, before Parliament appeared on the scene, judges dealt with disputes that had to do with a "contract," that is, an agreement between parties, and with civil wrongs, referred to as "torts." A tort that puts a person in fear of immediate bodily injury is called an "assault." A "battery" is a tort in which a person is intentionally touched without his or her consent. These are among the oldest recognized torts. It could be expected that unless Parliament enacted a statute relating to contracts or torts, judges would continue to follow court-established legal principles and make new law in these areas.

English Law Comes to the 13 Colonies

By the end of the 13th century, the general structure of the common law that eventually made its way to England's 13 North American colonies was in place in England. The colonial legal systems included courts, a legislative body, and a governor. The link between English law and colonial law was strong. For a time colonists who aspired to become lawyers studied law in England before entering the legal profession back home. Throughout the colonial period a colony's law was essentially the same as English law.

After the Revolutionary War the 13 colonies became 13 states. Each of the states adopted a constitution that for the most part maintained the prewar model of government with its separation of powers among a governor, a legislature, and courts. The U.S. Constitution similarly disperses the powers of the federal government among three branches of government: the president, Congress, and the courts.

Stare Decisis

Precedent
relevant prior court case

Stare decisis
the principle that a court should follow existing law

Courts in the United States, like courts in other common law nations, are expected to decide a lawsuit on the basis of **precedent.** This principle is known as **stare decisis.** "Precedent" consists of prior court cases in which tribunals of equal or higher rank in that jurisdiction decided controversies that involved facts comparable to those in the case now before the court. For instance, Leonard Barker brings suit in a state court against a judge, Spencer, in which he asks for damages because Judge Spencer erroneously refused to admit certain evidence during a trial. In *Arch v. Richter,* a case brought several decades before in which the plaintiff sued a Judge Richter for the very same reason, the state's highest court ruled in favor of Judge Richter on the ground that a judge is immune from liability for erroneously refusing to admit evidence during a trial. In Barker's case *stare decisis* calls for the court to abide by the precedent set in *Arch v. Richter* and to rule in favor of Judge Spencer.

Ad hoc
considering each lawsuit independently of past court decisions

Stare decisis brings a measure of certainty to the law that would be lacking if judges were free to look at each case *de novo,* that is, anew. If judges were free to do that, they would decide cases on an **ad hoc** basis, giving no attention to the results reached in similar prior lawsuits.

Despite the expectation that tribunals will decide cases in accordance with precedent, *stare decisis* does *not* entirely deny courts the freedom to effect change. A court decision may be "overruled," that is, abandoned in favor of a new principle, on the ground that the principle on which the decision was based should not have been adopted in the first place, or fails to take current values into account, or conflicts with current societal interests, or time and again has not been followed by courts although they did not expressly reject it. When a court overrules precedent and announces and uses a new legal principle to decide a case, the new principle becomes precedent for later cases. In time it too may be discarded.

Judges do not always make new law when they are dissatisfied with an existing legal principle. A judge may simply mention the shortcomings of a principle, comply with it, state that a new standard is called for, and invite the legislature to act. This course of action may be due to a variety of reasons. Perhaps the principle in question is firmly entrenched because it has been invoked in a large number of decisions over a long span of time; or perhaps the judge believes that an abrupt departure from the principle would probably cause substantial injury to those who relied on its continued use or that because of the likely far-reaching consequences of changing it, the legislature, rather than a court, should do so.

At times a judge may emphatically condemn an established principle, note that the result of following it would be intolerable, announce a new legal principle, and use that principle to reach a decision. A judge may offer one or more reasons for abandoning an existing principle and replacing it with a new principle. For example, the judge may say that doing so is appropriate because the existing principle, although often referred to in court decisions, has not been literally applied for a long time; or because the new principle, although somewhat different, is merely an extension of the existing principle or merely a logical next step in its evolution; or because the new principle is not entirely new but a previously unstated aspect of the existing principle. Once a new principle has been put in place, it becomes part of the jurisdiction's common law.

Judicial Self-Restraint and Judicial Activisim

The refusal of judges to establish new principles or to immerse themselves in activities in which they have not previously been involved is commonly referred to as **judicial self-restraint.** A **judicial activist,** unlike an advocate of judicial restraint, when convinced that it is appropriate to do so, will break with the past, and invoke a new legal principle or will enter into an activity that has been regarded as beyond the authority of a court.

**Judicial
self-restraint**
the refusal of judges to
initiate changes in the
law

Judicial activist
a judge who is willing to
create new law

□□□□

A prisoner brought a lawsuit in which he challenged the conditions in his prison. In numerous court decisions it had been held that the experts who administer prisons have the authority to decide how prisoners should be treated. A judge who advocates judicial self-restraint would simply abide by precedent and dismiss the suit. A judicial activist would be willing to disregard precedent and rule in the prisoner's favor if convinced that he had been deprived of his constitutional rights.

□□□□

Strict constructionist
a judge who closely fol-
lows the wording of the
Constitution and prior
court decisions

A judge who is a **strict constructionist** would refuse to acknowledge that a particular constitutional right exists unless the Constitution specifically states that there is such a right or unless the right has been recognized in a prior court decision. For example, in 1965 an individual claimed that a state statute deprived her of her right to privacy as guaranteed by the Constitution of the United States. The U.S. Supreme Court agreed. In its decision the Court recognized a constitutional right to privacy although the Constitution does not mention such a right and there were no precedents to support its conclusion. A strict constructionist would not have found that an individual has a constitutional right to privacy and would have rejected the claim that the state statute was unconstitutional.

It should be remembered that despite *stare decisis*, judicial self-restraint, strict constructionism, and the common view that a judge's task is limited to identifying the relevant legal principle or principles and using them to decide a case, a court may, in the vein of judicial activism, conclude that it is appropriate to desert precedent and to introduce and use a new legal principle that it regards as a more suitable rule of law.

Obiter Dictum

Stare decisis allows a court decision in an earlier case to be cited as precedent in a later case only to support the use of the legal principles that the court invoked to decide the earlier case. Principles mentioned by the court that were not invoked to decide the earlier case may not be cited as precedent. For example, if a stockholder brings a lawsuit against a corporate director and the director asks the court to dismiss the suit on the ground that a stockholder may not sue a director, the court's opinion may include a comment as to when one partner may sue another partner. A comment by the court that has nothing to do with the question it is called on to answer—in this instance, whether a stockholder may sue a corporate director—is an **obiter dictum,** commonly spoken of as a *"dictum."* The court's *dictum* on a partner's right to bring suit may not serve as precedent in a later case in which a court is asked to decide a question on that subject.

Obiter dictum
an irrelevant past court
decision

STANFORD v. KENTUCKY
SUPREME COURT OF THE UNITED STATES
492 U.S. 361 (1989)

One of the defendants (petitioners) was 17 years of age when he murdered, robbed, and sexually assaulted a woman. He was sentenced to death under Kentucky law. The other defendant was just over 16 when he murdered a woman during a robbery. He was sentenced to death under Missouri law. Both convictions were affirmed by the respective states' highest courts.

The U.S. Supreme Court agreed to review the two cases and to decide whether the Eighth Amendment to the U.S. Constitution, which bans cruel and unusual punishments, bars a state from imposing the death penalty on a person for a crime committed when the person was below 18 years of age.

JUSTICE SCALIA
Announced the Judgment of the Court.

Neither petitioner asserts that his sentence constitutes one of "those modes or acts of punishment that had been considered cruel and unusual at the time that the [Eighth Amendment] was adopted." At that time the common law theoretically permitted capital punishment to be imposed on anyone over the age of 7. In accordance with the standards of this common-law tradition, at least 281 offenders under the age of 18 have been executed in this country, and at least 126 under the age of 17.

[T]his Court has "not confined the prohibition embodied in the Eighth Amendment to 'barbarous' methods that were generally outlawed in the 18th century," but has interpreted the Amendment "in a flexible and dynamic manner." In determining what standards have "evolved," however, we have looked not to our own conceptions of decency, but to those of modern American society as a whole. As we have said, "Eighth Amendment judgments should not be, or appear to be, merely the subjective views of individual Justices; judgment should be informed by objective factors to the maximum possible extent." This approach is dictated both by the language of the Amendment—which proscribes only those punishments that are both "cruel and unusual"—and by the [respect that we] owe to the decisions of the state legislatures.

"[F]irst" among the "objective indicia that reflect the public attitude toward a given sanction" are statutes passed by society's elected representatives. Of the 37 States whose laws permit capital punishment, 15 decline to impose it upon 16-year-old offenders and 12 decline to impose it on 17-year-old offenders. This does not establish the degree of national consensus this Court has previously thought sufficient to label a particular punishment cruel and unusual.

[P]etitioners seek to demonstrate [a consensus against capital punishment] through [such] indicia as public opinion polls, the views of interest groups, and the positions adopted by various professional associations. We decline the invitation to rest constitutional law upon such uncertain foundations. A revised national consensus so broad, so clear, and so enduring as to justify a permanent prohibition upon all units of democratic government must appear in the operative acts (laws and application of law) that the people have approved.

We also reject petitioners' argument that we should invalidate capital punishment of 16- and 17-year-old offenders on the ground that it fails to serve the legitimate goals of penology. According to petitioners, it fails to deter because juveniles, possessing less developed cognitive skills than adults, are less likely to fear death; and it fails to exact just retributions because juveniles, being less mature and responsible, are also less morally blameworthy.

[I]t is not demonstrable that no 16-year-old is "adequately responsible" or significantly deterred. It is rational, even if mistaken, to think the contrary. The punishment is either "cruel and unusual" (i.e., society has set its face against it) or it is not. The audience for these arguments, in other words, is not this Court but the citizenry of the United States. It is they, not we, who must be persuaded. For as we stated earlier, our job is to *identify* the "evolving standards of decency"; to determine, not what they *should* be, but what they *are*. We have no power under the Eighth Amendment to substitute our belief in scientific evidence for the society's apparent skepticism. In short, we emphatically reject petitioner's suggestion that the issues in this case permit us to apply our "own informed judgment."

We discern neither a historical nor a modern societal consensus forbidding the imposition of capital punishment on any person who murders at 16 or 17 years of age. Accordingly, we conclude that such punishment does not offend the Eighth Amendment's prohibition against cruel and unusual punishment.

The judgments of the Supreme Court of Kentucky and the Supreme Court of Missouri are therefore
Affirmed.

Legal Issues

1. Should the Supreme Court of the United States take into account what it perceives to be a practice followed by many states to decide whether that practice violates a mandate of the Constitution of the United States? Why?

2. What significance, if any, should the Supreme Court assign to professional views on a particular subject to decide the constitutionality of a state statute? Why?

Ethical Issues

1. Justice Brennan wrote a dissenting opinion in the *Stanford* case, and three other members of the Supreme Court joined in the opinion. In addition to offering various other reasons for his opposition to inflicting the death penalty on persons who commit murder before the age of 18, he wrote: "I believe that to take the life of a person as punishment for a crime committed when below the age of 18 is cruel and unusual punishment and hence is prohibited by the Eighth Amendment." Is it ethical for a judge to base his or her decision as to whether a certain action is constitutional on nothing more than his or her personal opinion? Why?

2. Justice O'Connor, who in part agreed with Justice Scalia's reasons, and concurred in the judgment of the Court in *Stanford v. Kentucky,* wrote in a separate opinion that the Court had a "constitutional obligation to judge whether the '[connection] between the punishment imposed and the defendant's blameworthiness' is proportional." Would it be correct to say that this statement of Justice O'Connor is based on the ethics of fairness? Why?

JUDICIAL REASONING

Trial Court

A lawsuit is begun in a "trial court."[1] If after the suit has been brought, the parties are still unable to resolve their dispute, then, after completion of the preliminary steps discussed in the next chapter, they proceed to trial. In a jury case the trial is conducted before a judge and a jury. In a nonjury case it is conducted before a judge.

The rules of law that the parties to a lawsuit must follow so as to enforce their rights and to protect themselves from uncalled for liability are known as principles of *procedural* or *adjective* law. The rules of law that courts use to decide the rights and duties of the parties to a lawsuit are known as principles of *substantive* law.

Nonjury Trial

A trial judge is involved in two distinct types of reasoning in a nonjury trial. One has to do with facts, the other with law.

Fact-Finding

As a **fact-finder,** the judge must decide what did or did not happen. Generally, this requires the judge to determine whether evidence is or is not *credible.* For example, he or she must determine whether a witness is telling the truth. This assessment may be influenced by such factors as the judge's personal experiences, opinions as to what is and what is not likely to happen, beliefs as to how people generally behave under certain conditions, attitudes toward particular sorts of conduct, views about people and events, and practical wisdom. For instance, a judge is unlikely to be easily convinced of the truthfulness of a witness who has been convicted five times of lying during a court proceeding. However, if evidence from a person who the judge believes is credible is consistent with what that witness said, the judge may conclude that his or her testimony is true. A judge may not believe a witness who, while testifying, drinks a great deal of water, perspires profusely, and constantly fidgets, because the judge may take such reactions as indications that the witness is lying. A witness's testimony is likely to be open to serious doubt if she remembers in detail a not particularly memorable conversation that took place more than six years earlier and supports the claim of the party who called her to testify but denies any recollection of a number of very recent startling events that are detrimental to this party.

Fact-finding
the determination of what did or did not occur

Application of the Law

Once the facts have been determined, the judge is ready to consider the legal consequences of what occurred. He or she must identify the relevant legal principles and then apply them to the facts to arrive at a decision as to the parties' rights and duties. This requires answers to a variety of questions. What are the relevant precedents, if any? What decision do they call for? Is this result consistent with the judge's vision of justice? If not, should the precedents still be followed, or should the existing principles be modified or rejected? How much attention should be given to *stare decisis?* If justice does require the introduction of a new principle, what should it be? How should it be worded? In what way should the rejection of precedent be explained?

The Opinion

After the legal principles to be used have been identified and logically applied to the facts, the judge is ready to announce a decision. The decision may merely state which party has been successful, how much money that party is entitled to receive, and how it is to be received. In addition, the judge may write a brief or lengthy **opinion.** Generally, an opinion includes the judge's conclusions as to the facts, a presentation, discussion, and analysis of the selected legal principles, and an explanation of the reasoning by which the judge arrived at the decision. When the decision is based on past court cases, ordinarily those cases are identified together with the principle or principles that they used.

Opinion
a judge's explanation of the outcome of a lawsuit

    If the unsuccessful party, on the basis of past decisions, urged the judge to rule in his or her favor, the opinion may explain why those decisions were not followed. Perhaps they are said to be inapplicable because they dealt with an entirely different set of facts or because the portions of those decisions on which the unsuccessful party relied merely contain *obiter dicta*. The opinion may include what purports to be an objective evaluation of the current worth of the precedents. Perhaps they are condemned on the ground that they are at odds with society's present-day values, needs, or aspirations or that they simply do not work. The opinion is likely to emphasize the virtues of the newly announced principle and to offer rationales for its use. Usually, it will include remarks intended to convince the parties, other judges, and whoever else is involved or interested that the decision is correct.

On occasion there is no precedent concerning the exact issue that is before the court. In such instances the opinion is very likely to mention related issues for which there is precedent and to use such precedent in support of the principle or principles on which the decision has been based.

Jury Trial

Fact-Finding

In a jury trial the fact-finding function is performed by the jury. To perform this function, the jury, like the judge in a nonjury case, considers the credibility of testimony and evaluates the evidence.

As described in the next chapter, the judge is not a passive participant in a jury trial. For example, the judge informs the jurors of the legal rules that they must follow to arrive at their decision, and the judge must reject the jury's conclusion if he or she finds that it is not reasonably related to the evidence.

Appellate Court

The Appeal Process

A party who is dissatisfied with the result arrived at in the trial court ordinarily has a right to "appeal" the decision, that is, to have it reviewed by a higher court.[2] That court is called an "appellate court." An appellate court examines what occurred in one or more lower courts in order to determine whether the *law* is satisfied.

The first appeal is generally heard by either three or five judges. The party that loses in the first appellate court may be entitled to appeal. A second appeal is ordinarily allowed for such reasons as these: it is authorized by statute; the decision of the first appellate court is not unanimous; the subject matter of the lawsuit makes it desirable to have a higher appellate court review the action of the lower courts; or the first appellate court believes that it is in the interest of justice that a higher court reexamine the case and authorizes the losing party to appeal to a higher appellate court. In many instances the higher appellate court itself grants the losing party's request that the decision of the lower appellate court be reviewed. Commonly, the appeal is heard before, and decided by, a five or seven-judge court.

Opinions

In addition to announcing its ruling, an appellate court may publish an opinion. The format of an appellate court's opinion resembles that of a lower court's opinion. The opinion includes a statement of the facts, a presentation and analysis of the pertinent legal rules, the court's reasoning, and such explanation as the judges believe appropriate to justify their decision. If the appellate court agrees with the action of the lower court, its opinion is likely to refer to the same precedents as those used by that court and to support the result with a like explanation. The opinion may offer additional precedents and rationales to reinforce the appellate court's conclusion.

In a case in which all the appellate judges are of the same mind and there is but a single opinion presented, one judge's name appears at the beginning of the opinion even if other judges and judges' clerks took part in writing it. If all the members of an appellate court agree on the result, but one or more differ from the rest as to the reasons for reaching it, there will be an **opinion of the court,** the opinion that contains the thinking shared by most of the judges, and a **concurring opinion,** a separate opinion written by a judge who does not agree with the explanation contained in the opinion of the court. Other judges may join in the concurring opinion. The larger the number of judges assigned to an appellate court, the greater is the likelihood that there will be concurring opinions.

In instances in which the judges differ as to what should be done, there are likely to be at least two opinions—a **majority opinion,** which presents the position taken by most of the judges, and a **minority opinion,** (or "dissenting opinion"), which presents the position of the judge or judges who disagree with most of the court's members. Occasionally, the dissenting judge or judges do not present an opinion and simply state that they dissent.

On occasion an appellate court's opinion does not bear a judge's name. Instead, where a judge's name ordinarily appears in such an opinion, one finds the term **per curiam,** which means "opinion of the court." A *per curiam* opinion is generally used when there is unanimous support for the opinion and the matter in question is relatively uncomplicated. Such an opinion usually refers to other cases that have already set the stage for the outcome.

Judicial Recusal

In Chapter 2 we examined restrictions the U.S. Constitution imposes on a judge trying a particular case. A 1974 act of Congress establishes additional grounds that disqualify a federal judge from partaking in a proceeding. Under this statute a judge must **recuse** himself or herself, that is, decline from taking part in a case in which a *reasonable person* who knows all of the facts would conclude that the judge's impartiality *might* be questioned. Among the specific instances in which the statute requires a judge to recuse himself or herself are: (1) he or she has a personal bias or prejudice concerning a party to the proceeding, or has personal knowledge of disputed evidentiary facts concerning the proceeding aside from what he or she learned as a judge in the proceeding; (2) while in private practice he or she served as a lawyer regarding the matter in controversy; (3) while employed by the government he or she acted as a lawyer, adviser, or material witness concerning the proceeding or expressed an opinion as to how it should be resolved; (4) he or she knows that his or her spouse, or a minor child who resides in his or her household, has a financial interest in the subject matter in controversy, or the spouse or minor child is a party to the proceeding or has some other interest that could be substantially affected by the outcome of the proceeding; or (5) his or her spouse, parent, grandparent, great grandparent, child,

Opinion of the court
the opinion of most of the judges

Concurring opinion
an opinion that contains a judge's own reasons for agreeing with the court's decision

Majority opinion
presents the position taken by most of the court's judges

Minority opinion
presents the position taken by the judge or judges who disagree with most of the court's members

Per curiam
a court's opinion for which no judge is identified as the author

Recuse
a judge's refusal to participate in a lawsuit

grandchild, brother, sister, uncle, aunt, nephew, or niece is a party to, or a lawyer in, the case. State statutes or state court rules impose one or more of the same sort of restrictions on state judges that Congress has imposed on federal judges.

Federal and state judges must have an *open mind* as to the outcome before they become involved in a proceeding. For example, a judge who has publicly announced his or her decision in a case before the trial begins may not judge the case. However, a judge is not disqualified from judging a case even though his or her judicial philosophy differs from that of any of the parties to the proceeding. It is not realistic to believe that judges have no viewpoint at all on any of the legal issues on which they must rule during a trial or an appeal. Considering the age and experience of the persons who generally become judges, it is unlikely, and probably undesirable, that they have no viewpoint about certain aspects of the law, such as the constitutionality of particular types of governmental action, the meaning of particular statutes, or the constraints that particular common law principles impose on individuals. But a judge is obliged to recuse himself or herself if he or she gives the impression that a personal point of view of the law, or prior experiences, or the nature of the controversy prevents him or her from carefully considering the facts and the law applicable to the proceeding. To assure public confidence in the judicial branch of government, it is essential that court decisions be the end products of a fair and impartial process and that they are based on the evidence presented and suitable application of relevant legal principles.

SHACKIL v. LEDERLE LABORATORIES
SUPREME COURT OF NEW JERSEY
561 A.2d 511 (1989)

Two days before her second birthday, the plaintiff was inoculated with DPT, a combined diphtheria pertussis tetanus vaccine. As a result she was stricken with chronic encephalopathy and severe retardation, which required her to be institutionalized. Thirteen years later her parents learned of the linkage between DPT and her injury. The plaintiff brought suit against the pediatrician who administered the DPT injection and Lederle, a manufacturer of the DPT vaccine. Unable to establish that Lederle made the DPT used by the pediatrician, who had purchased DPT from Lederle and five other manufacturers, one of which was no longer in business, the plaintiff added the four remaining manufacturers as defendants. Prior to trial, the court dismissed the lawsuit because the plaintiff failed to identify which manufacturer made the DPT dose administered by the pediatrician.

A divided appellate court reversed. It opted for a "risk modified market share" approach to manufacturer liability. Under this standard, when a plaintiff demonstrates that the specific manufacturer of a defective product proven to have caused an injury cannot be identified, he or she may bring suit against the manufacturers that together have a substantial share of the market, that is, almost all of the manufacturers that could have distributed the product to the plaintiff. Once this has been done, it is up to the defendants to show that they did not distribute the product to the plaintiff, or that they have a reduced market share, or that their product posed a lower risk than the one that injured the plaintiff. The extent of each manufacturer's liability is based on the potential risk of injury caused by its product. The court refused to use the pure market share standard under which a manufacturer's liability is simply based on its market share. The defendants appealed.

CLIFFORD, JUSTICE

Although proof of causation-in-fact is ordinarily an indispensable ingredient of [a plaintiff's proof of defendant liability], exceptions have nevertheless arisen that have allowed plaintiffs to shift to defendant or a group of defendants [the obligation to show that they did not cause the plaintiff's injury]. These exceptions include [risk] modified market share liability, the theory that we are urged to adopt in this case.

The seminal market share case is *Sindell v. Abbott Laboratories* [in which the plaintiffs] brought [suit] against the manufacturers of the drug DES for injuries [that first appeared long after the drug was used. DES was prescribed for pregnant women to prevent miscarriage and was later proved to be linked to cellular abnormalities]. [P]laintiffs were unable to identify the manufacturer who actually produced the injury-causing product. The California Court held that the inability to identify a defendant was not fatal to [a] plaintiff's [lawsuit], provided plaintiff join[s] as defendants a "substantial share" of manufacturers who produced or supplied the [injury-causing] DES. The burden would then shift to the defendant manufacturers to demonstrate that they could not have produced the DES [dose that caused the injury]. Any manufacturer that could not exculpate itself would be held liable "for the proportion of the judgment represented by its share of the [DES] market."

[I]mportant policy considerations supported the court's decision. [A]s between an innocent plaintiff and negligent defendants, the latter should bear the cost of injury. [A] DES manufacturer was in a better position to insure against the risk of injury.

[To decide] whether New Jersey should expand current principles of tort law to adopt risk-modified market share liability in the DPT context [w]e turn to the thrust of this appeal: the public-policy and public-health considerations that would accompany the imposition of market share liability in this context.

This Court has adopted the basic tenet that "[t]he torts process, [that is, the body of legal principles that hold persons accountable for civil wrongdoing], like the law itself, is a human institution designed to accomplish certain social objectives." One of the primary objectives is to ensure "that innocent victims have avenues of legal redress, absent a contrary, overriding public policy." In this case we are presented with a difficult circumstance in which societal goals, in encouraging the use and development of needed drugs, would be thwarted by the imposition of unlimited liability on manufacturers in order to provide compensation to those injured by their products.

We deem it a matter of paramount importance that this case involves a vaccine—a product regarded as essential to the public welfare. Before the vaccine's appearance, the disease pertussis claimed the lives of thousands of children in the United States each year and left many others with severe injuries. In one epidemic alone, pertussis was responsible for as many as 7,518 deaths [and] affecting a total of 265,269 children. As a result of national immunization efforts begun after the development of the vaccine, the country showed a ninety-nine percent reduction in the number of reported cases and an even more dramatic reduction in the number of deaths.

Those efforts notwithstanding, pertussis, not having been entirely eradicated, continues to pose a threat to the health of this country's children. [A] recent study indicates that DPT immunization rates have fallen sharply since 1980, particularly in nonwhite infants.

Recent trends in the production and distribution of DPT have threatened the supply of the vaccine, with a predictable effect on the nation's immunization efforts. There are now only two commercial entities willing to produce DPT vaccine as contrasted with five in 1984. The overwhelming reason for the decrease in the number of manufacturers is the "extreme liability exposure, [the] cost of litigation, and the difficulty of continuing to obtain adequate insurance."

In addition to the policy of ensuring the continued use of this essential drug is the more immediate need to develop a safer alternative vaccine. The creation of an alternative-vaccine design is a slow and complex process that demands the consolidated efforts of scientists, researchers, government agencies, and manufacturers. More importantly, it involves significant expense, shouldered almost entirely by vaccine manufacturers.

It is apparent that DPT manufacturers would have difficulty sustaining the increased cost attendant on the imposition of market share liability while simultaneously covering ascending research costs in order to halt the unfortunate sequence of events that spawned this appeal, as well as continuing to meet current production needs. Of broader concern is the effect of market share liability on the develop-

ment of other experimental drugs, such as a vaccine against the spread of acquired-immune-deficiency syndrome (AIDS).

[W]e have chosen to posit today's ruling on the regressive effect that collective liability would have on the social policy of encouraging vaccine production and research.

[T]he imposition of market share liability in this case would cut against the societal goals of maintaining an adequate supply of lifesaving vaccines and of developing safer alternatives to current methods of vaccinations. Our aim is not to insulate vaccine manufacturers from liability, but to acknowledge a painful reality—the excessive exposure to liability that imposition of this novel theory would produce would inevitably discourage highly useful activity.

Reversed. The judgment for defendant manufacturers is reinstated. No costs.

Legal Issues

1. After repeated increases in the cost of medical malpractice policies and threats by physicians that they would stop practicing certain specialties, the state legislature enacted a law limiting the damages that a victim of medical malpractice could recover from the guilty party for the harm that was done. Under the law, a victim might not be compensated for all of the pain and suffering caused by the defendant. Within a year the number of new malpractice cases brought in the state declined and the cost of malpractice insurance decreased by 15 percent. Is the law just? Why?

2. The federal Age Discrimination in Employment Act (ADEA) generally bars employers, including state governments, from forcing the retirement of employees over the age of 40. The act excludes persons appointed to state "policy-making" positions. A state law

mandated that all appointed state judges retire at the age of 70. An appointed state judge who had been forced to retire at 70 brought a lawsuit in which he asked the court to order his reinstatement on the ground that his forced retirement violated ADEA. In defense of its action, the state insisted that judges had to be capable of exercising the same sort of discretion in decision making that was required of all state-appointed policy-making officials and of engaging in the same sort of thoughtful judgment. The judge's attorney maintained that traditionally judges had not been involved in policy-making since their role was to simply find and apply the law. What judgment? Why?

Ethical Issues

1. Is the court's decision in *Shackil* consistent with pragmatic ethics? Why?

2. Which standard or standards of business ethics could be cited to support the court's decision in *Shackil?* Why?

HOW TO BEST CURB PEEPING

Hypothetical Case

Walker rented an apartment in a 175-tenant building owned by James Corporation. In each of the three preceding years, the corporation's profits had been seriously limited because it had had to pay more than $250,000 a year for damages to the building caused by irresponsible tenant behavior. Unknown to Walker, James Corporation's chief of security, Terry Rigid installed cleverly hidden television cameras and microphones in what he regarded as high-risk apartments and hallways. Everything transmitted by the cameras and microphones was taped for possible later use.

After living in the building for six months, Walker discovered two television transmitters and three microphones in his apartment. Outraged, he consulted Timothy Lane, his attorney. Lane informed him that state law did not prohibit what James Corporation had done. Then Lane said: "But isn't this an excellent chance for us to take the lead in striking a blow for ethical landlord behavior? Let's sue your landlord for intrusion on your privacy." Walker agreed, and Lane promptly brought suit.

Betty Villes, James Corporation's attorney, asked the judge to dismiss the suit on these grounds: state law did not prohibit what her client had done; her client's actions were reasonable in light of what had occurred in the past; and Walker's lease gave her client the right to enter his apartment as needed to protect its property. Villes further stated: "If the law is to be changed, then it is for the legislature to do so. If courts are to make new law and impose damages on my client, then everyone must live in fear of being punished later for doing something that was lawful when it was done."

Lane asked the court not to dismiss the suit. He conceded that neither past state court decisions nor state laws supported his client's right to damages, but, he insisted, judges had a duty to see that the law reacts to change and deals with unethical behavior. If tenants had to await action by the state legislature, they might never be protected from the humiliation that could result from secret landlord surveillance. Lane added: "The clause in the lease that allows James Corporation to enter Walker's apartment to protect its property does not allow it to move in with him."

Should the court rule for James Corporation for the reasons given by Villes, or should it rule for Walker? Why? If the court explores whether James Corporation behaved ethically, what ethical standards should it take into account to arrive at a decision?

THE LEGISLATIVE PROCESS

Legislative Structure

Bicameral

a lawmaking body with two houses

As we have seen, the English Parliament was established by the end of the 13th century. It is a **bicameral** body, that is, a two-house legislature. It is made up of a House of Commons and a House of Lords. Congress, the legislative body established by the U.S. Constitution, is also bicameral. It is composed of a House of Representatives and a Senate. Figure 3-1 shows the structure of the House.

Unicameral

a lawmaking body with one house

Generally, state legislatures are bicameral. Nebraska's legislature is **unicameral,** that is, composed of a single house. Local governments commonly use a unicameral legislative body.

Origin of a Statute

Statute

a law established by a lawmaking body

Ordinance

a law established by a local unit of government

Unlike judges, legislators can establish a new legal principle without having to wait for an immediate need to resolve a controversy between particular disputants. They may create law at any time. They do this by enacting a **statute,** which is also called an "act." (A law adopted by a local legislative body, such as that of a city or a town, is commonly referred to as an **ordinance.**) Like a legal principle

FIGURE 3–1   **House of Representatives**

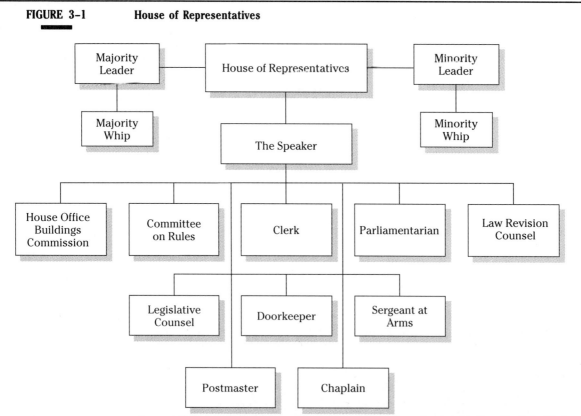

Source: Office of the Federal Register, National Archives and Records Administration, *The United States Government Manual, 1990/91* (Washington, D.C.: U.S. Government Printing Office, July 1, 1990).

established by a court, the behavior specified by a statute is a legal principle that is enforceable through the courts.

A statute originates as a *bill,* a written document containing the provisions of a proposed law. It may be initiated because of a legislator's personal point of view; or it may be a legislator's way of responding to the suggestion of a public official, or a respected constituent, or a group of citizens; or it may simply be a legislator's effort to enact an item in the platform of his or her party. Regardless of its source, a bill is generally seen by its proponents as a means of dealing with an unsatisfactory state of affairs. For example, widespread consumer clamor about defective automobiles prompted numerous states to enact so-called lemon laws. These statutes typically entitle a car buyer to a refund or a new automobile after he or she has made repeated unsuccessful attempts to have the seller correct a significant defect in the one he or she bought.

Passage of a Bill by the House of Representatives

Drafting a Bill

Although there are differences between the steps that the U.S. House of Representatives takes to pass a bill and those taken by the U.S. Senate, or the nation's 50 state legislatures, or local legislative bodies, there are striking similarities in the procedure that all of them use. The following examination of how the House of Representatives passes a **bill** that, if approved by the Senate and the president, will become a statute, illustrates the manner in which almost all of the nation's legislative bodies adopt a law.

Bill
a proposed law

The first step is to **draft** the bill, that is, to write the proposed law. Although a member of the House of Representatives may perform this task, ordinarily one or more members of the legislator's staff participate in it. At times the president, a federal agency, one or more special interest groups, or one or several persons who have a stake in the proposed law may be intimately involved in its preparation. In such instances the interested party or parties may even provide the legislator with a draft of the bill. If the legislator finds the draft acceptable, it may be treated as if he or his staff had prepared it. Otherwise, the draft is reworked so that it is to the legislator's liking. Once the bill is in an acceptable form, it is ready for **introduction,** that is, to be submitted for consideration by the House of Representatives.

Draft
the initial form of a proposed law

Introduction of a bill
the submission of a proposed statute for consideration by a legislative body

Introduction and Deliberation

To submit the bill, the legislator places it in the "hopper," a box located in the chamber in which the House of Representatives conducts its business. The bill is assigned a number so that it can be readily identified. For example, the 291st bill placed in the hopper during the first session of the 102nd Congress (1991) is numbered H.R. 291, 102nd Congress, 1st Session.

House **legislative committees** play a critical part in the legislative process. They are established by the rules of the House. Their task is to study and report on proposed legislation. The House parliamentarian, who acts on behalf of the Speaker, the person selected by the members of the House to preside over it, decides the legislative committee to which a proposed bill should be assigned. The decision is made on the basis of House rules, custom, and the bill's subject matter. Because of the points of view of the members of particular committees, a

Legislative committee
a group of legislators who have been chosen to evaluate proposed laws

bill may be worded in such a way that it is more likely to be assigned to one committee rather than another.

The committee to which a bill has been assigned may refer it for study to a specialized subcommittee. To assist the subcommittee in its deliberations, interested parties are generally invited to present their points of view on the bill. They may appear before the subcommittee to testify for or against the bill and to provide it with information that supports their position. If the subcommittee concludes that a bill should receive a favorable report, the bill proceeds to the **markup** stage. This is the process of wording the bill in the exact way in which it will be forwarded to the full committee. Because an insertion, deletion, or alteration of even one or two words can significantly change a bill's effect, great care must be taken to assure that the marked-up bill embodies the intentions of the legislators. The subcommittee's report to the full committee will include the bill, the subcommittee's recommendation, and, in most instances, an analysis of the proposed act and a statement of its purpose. Ordinarily, the subcommittee does not report on a bill that it does not favor. In most instances such a failure to report is equivalent to a final rejection of the bill.

Markup
process of wording a bill in its final form

After receiving the subcommittee's report, the committee usually takes the same steps as those that have been taken by the subcommittee, including hearings and markup. If the committee favors the bill, it submits its report to the House Rules Committee. If it does not favor the bill, it will not issue a report. As with the subcommittee, such a failure to report normally marks the death of the bill. In some instances, however, the House Rules Committee may present the bill to the House membership for floor debate. Submission to the House indicates that the Rules Committee does not oppose the bill.

Generally, amendments may be added to the bill during House debate. Now the bill is ready for a vote by the House. The House may approve it or set it aside by voting to return it to the committee to which it was initially assigned or dispose of it in some other manner. If the House votes to approve the bill, it goes to the Senate for consideration.

The Senate may reject the bill, modify it, or approve it. Only when the wording of the bills approved by both the House and the Senate are identical can a bill be presented to the president for consideration. When the two chambers substantially agree on proposed legislation, but the bills they have enacted are not identically worded, both bills are sent to a conference committee composed of House and Senate members. The committee eliminates any differences between the two bills. Once this has been done, a single bill, accompanied by the committee's report, is forwarded to both chambers. If a majority of the voting legislators in the House and the Senate favor the bill, it is presented to the president.

When the president approves of a bill, he signs it. The bill, now referred to as a statute or as an act of Congress, then becomes law or becomes law on the date on which the statute states that it will take effect. Should the president reject a bill, that is, **veto** it, the bill and a statement of his or her objections are sent to the chamber in which the bill originated. If two thirds of that chamber's members vote for the bill, then the bill, together with the president's objections, is forwarded to the second chamber. The bill becomes law if two thirds of the members of this chamber also vote for it.

Veto
an executive rejection of a bill passed by the legislature

A bill may also become law without the president's signature if he does not return it within 10 days (excluding Sunday) after it was presented to him. However, a bill does not become law if the president does not sign it but has been unable to return it within the prescribed 10-day period because Congress adjourned before the expiration of that period. This form of presidential veto is commonly referred to as a **pocket veto.**

Pocket veto

the president's failure to sign a bill; equivalent to a veto

Legislator Partiality

Unlike judges, legislators are not expected to be impartial in the performance of their legislative duties. To garner the support of the electorate, persons in quest of a seat in Congress, a state legislature, a town council, or some other legislative body usually speak out on a variety of subjects prior to their election or while they are in office. Voters are likely to choose and reelect candidates whose expressed points of view they approve. They expect legislators who, while campaigning or while holding office, call for the enactment of certain legislation to vote for bills embodying the legislation that they called for. Legislators who vote contrary to their preelection programs are likely to stir the ire of at least some of the electorate and may not be reelected. Not perceived as impartial participants in the lawmaking process, legislators are free to promote a statute and then to vote for it.

UNIFORM STATE LAWS

A concern shared by companies that do business in a number of states is the differences in the state laws that govern commercial transactions. These differences add to the complexity of interstate transactions. The National Conference of Commissioners on Uniform State Laws was established to reduce the extent of such differences by encouraging state legislatures to adopt the same statutes on a variety of subjects.

The Conference, which has its own constitution and bylaws, is made up of at least three commissioners from each state, the District of Columbia, and Puerto Rico. Judges, lawyers, and law school professors are commonly chosen to serve as commissioners. Governors usually select their state's representatives. The Conference meets annually to determine which subjects warrant uniform state laws. If it finds that a uniform law would be desirable, it assigns a committee the task of drafting such a law. A draft that it approves is thereafter referred to as a uniform law.

A uniform law may include alternative recommendations so as to accommodate possible objections to a particular provision by one or more states. State legislatures that adopt a uniform law are free to choose among the alternative recommendations. States often adapt a uniform law to their unique views on a particular subject either by excluding from their statute portions of the uniform law or by including in their statute provisions not found in the uniform law.

A uniform law that has been widely accepted is the Uniform Commercial Code. This law deals with such subjects as the sale of goods, checks, and stock certificates. It has been adopted, at least in part, by all of the states, the District of Columbia, and Puerto Rico. Some uniform laws, such as the Consumer Credit Protection Code, have been adopted by fewer than 10 states. Anticompetitive practices and monopolization, deceptive business practices, landlord and tenant rights, and protection of trade secrets are among the subjects of other uniform laws that have been drafted and adopted by state legislatures.

STATUTORY CONSTRUCTION

Need to Define Statutory Language

A statute may be so clearly and carefully written that the meaning of its provisions is obvious. When the rights and duties of the parties to a lawsuit are governed by such a statute, the court's task is simple. The court has no need to look beyond the statute's words to determine what legal principle it should use to arrive at a decision.

At times, regardless of how much care legislators take to assure that a statute accurately states a newly established legal principle, the statute's wording is not precise enough to allow a court to rely solely on what the statute says. It is often extremely difficult for lawmakers to grasp all the ramifications of a statute. Unable to foresee all the instances in which the statute will be invoked by the parties to future lawsuits, they fail to clearly say just what it calls for in particular cases.

A law enacted only after bitter controversy may include what many lawmakers regard as distasteful but unavoidable compromises. Or a bill rushed into law near the end of a legislative session may contain a muddled provision that was overlooked in the rush that usually marks the end of such sessions. Or a cloudy amendment that has not been carefully studied by any of its numerous supporters may be incorporated into a bill. Sometimes a bill may be made unclear intentionally in order to ensure its passage. Its sponsors may believe that it would not pass if there were not some uncertainty as to its meaning, and that it would be better to enact a poorly worded law on the subject than none at all. Legislators who oppose the bill may fear the consequences of voter dissatisfaction should they vote against it despite its lack of clarity. The dilemma is resolved by passing a bill that is in part incomprehensible.

If a statute does not clearly indicate whether it is applicable to a particular set of facts, or if a statute is clearly relevant to a question before a court but neglects to specify how it affects the litigants' rights and obligations, a court must look beyond the exact words of the statute to arrive at a decision. This judicial process is referred to as **statutory construction** or "statutory interpretation." The purpose of the process is to identify the intention of the legislature.

Statutory construction
a judicial definition of a statutory provision

Rules of Statutory Construction

Courts use various guidelines to identify the intention of the legislature. If a portion of a statute, read alone, is unclear, a court may turn to the statute's **preamble** to identify the intention of the legislature. This general introductory statement about the statute commonly recites the evils that triggered its enactment and what the legislature sought to accomplish by enacting it. The title of a statute, such as Fair Debt Collection Act, or the headings dispersed throughout its text, such as Unfair Practices, may also hint at its purposes.

Preamble
a statute's general introductory statement

A court's interpretation of a statute must be logical and reasonable. It should not distort the statute. Generally, the terms and phrases of the statute should be given their ordinary meaning. However, this is not done if doing so would lead to an unreasonable, impractical, or absurd outcome or to an outcome that appears to conflict with the overall purpose of the statute.

Technical terms are given their technical meaning, unless the legislature expressly indicates that this is not intended. An exemption is not read into the general language of a statute unless not doing so would produce an unjust or irrational result. In determining the meaning of words found in a particular statute, no attention is paid to how the same words are interpreted for the purposes of another statute if the two statutes deal with unrelated subjects.

To ascertain the legislature's intent, a court may examine the **legislative history** of the statute. In other words, the court may take into account the circumstances surrounding its passage. The court may consider the conditions that existed prior to its enactment and the legal principles that were in effect at that time. Comments made by its advocates and opponents during floor debate may reveal its purpose. Perhaps a legislative committee, subcommittee, or conference committee report contains a declaration of that purpose.

Legislative history
the circumstances in which a statute was enacted

Some rules of statutory construction are based on the premise that the legislature intended to enact a statute in harmony with other legal principles. It may be possible to construe a statute in two ways, of which one would render the statute unconstitutional and the other would not. Faced with these alternatives, a court will construe the statute in the way that renders it constitutional. Similarly, a court will not construe an ambiguous statute in a way that contradicts related legal mandates or clashes with **public policy**—conduct that is currently considered in the best interests of society. A court will read individual portions of a statute as parts of the entire statute to assure that the overall intent of the legislature is respected. This means that the court will clear up an ambiguity in one section of a statute by construing the ambiguity in a way that makes the section consistent with the rest of the statute. When one section of a statute includes certain words that are omitted from the section in which they would ordinarily be found, it is presumed that the legislature purposely omitted them. Because it is also presumed that an amendment to a statute already in force is intended to effect a change in that statute, a court takes the original statute and related statutes into account in determining the meaning of the amendment.

Public policy
conduct that is currently considered in the best interest of society

An ambiguous statute may be liberally or strictly construed. **Liberal construction** interprets a statute loosely. This means that the statute will be read loosely enough to cover subjects not expressly mentioned in it but presumably intended to be covered by it. **Strict construction** interprets a statute narrowly, limiting its application to the subjects specifically included in it.

Liberal construction
interprets a statute loosely

Strict construction
interprets a statute narrowly

A **remedial statute** is one that has been enacted to end an undesirable state of affairs. Generally, it does so by creating a new legal right or by limiting or eliminating an existing legal right. Any uncertainty as to the applicability or meaning of a statute is resolved in a way that the court considers consistent with the legislature's intent.

Remedial statute
a law that is intended to replace an unacceptable legal principle

A statute that changes an established common law principle is said to be in **derogation of the common law.** Presumably, before enacting the statute, the legislature determined what change or changes should be made in existing law. A statute in derogation of the common law is strictly construed.

Derogation of the common law
changing a common law principle

A DEMANDING AUTOMOBILE DEALER AND AN UPSET PURCHASER

When Tony Wake purchased an automobile from Newtown Motors Corporation, he paid Newtown Motors an additional $1,250 for a five year warranty contract. The warranty agreement required the vehicle's oil and oil filter to be changed every three months or 5,000 miles, whichever occurred first.

When Wake had driven the vehicle for three years, its electrical system failed. He then went to Newtown Motors to have the system repaired. This repair was one of the many types

Hypothetical Case

of repairs covered by the warranty. After identifying the problem, Newtown Motors' service manager told Wake that the repair would cost him $2,500. Wake informed her that there should be no charge since he had purchased Newtown Motors' extended warranty. She asked him to show her his maintenance record book. After examining the book, she said to him: "You neglected to have the oil and oil filter changed at the intervals required by the warranty. Since you did not properly maintain your car, the work will cost you $2,500." Wake pointed out to the service manager that neither an oil change nor an oil filter change could have protected the electical system. She replied, "I know that, Mr. Wake. I have been in the business for 25 years. But you did not properly service your vehicle. You cannot now expect Newtown Motors to do any repairs under the warranty. To protect our bottom line, we never perform repairs without charge if a purchaser fails to carry out each and every provision of the warranty agreement. What's fair is fair."

Wake resented the stand taken by Newtown Motors and arranged to have his vehicle towed to the service shop of another dealer whom he paid $2,300 to repair the electrical system.

A state statute provided that if a court found a merchant's refusal to honor a customer's contract "frivolous," the court might grant the customer an award against the merchant for three times the amount of the damages that the customer suffered because of the merchant's misconduct. Wake brought suit against Newtown Motors in which he asked the court to award him three times as much as it cost to repair the electrical system.

Should judgment be entered in favor of Wake? Why? Did Newtown Motors behave in an ethical manner? Why?

SPORTSMEN'S BOATING CORPORATION v. HENSLEY
SUPREME COURT OF CONNECTICUT
474 A.2d 780 (1984)

The plaintiff and the defendant each operated a sport fishing boat. From April through November, weather permitting, their boats set sail twice a day, at 6 A.M. and 1 P.M. The boats carried persons who desired to fish in nearby waters. To reach the plaintiff's parking lot or dock, potential customers had to pass the defendant's dock, ticket booth, and parking lot. The defendant's ticket booth did not indicate that it sold tickets only to those who wished to sail on its boat.

The plaintiff sued to recover damages for lost business from the defendant and to obtain a court order directing the defendant to stop his employees from (1) standing in the street before 6 A.M. on days when it was still dark at that hour and waving flashlights motioning approaching vehicles into the defendant's parking lot and (2) falsely informing customers who asked about access to the plaintiff's dock that the plaintiff's boat was full or not sailing or that persons who fished from the plaintiff's boat had been catching fewer fish than were being caught by persons who fished from the defendant's boat. According to the plaintiff, the defendant had also led some persons who wished to embark on the plaintiff's boat to believe that they were boarding that boat rather than the defendant's. The plaintiff charged the defendant with unfair competition by intimidation, obstruction, or molestation in violation of the Connecticut Unfair Trade Practices Act (CUTPA) and of the tort of unlawful interference with the plaintiff's business.

After hearing the evidence, the trial court ruled that the defendant was not guilty of either a CUTPA violation or a tort because it found that the plaintiff's *evidence* did not show (1) that the defendant's employees made false statements about the plaintiff's business or (2) that potential customers were excessively deterred or misled from proceeding to the plaintiff's dock. The plaintiff appealed.

SPEZIALE, CHIEF JUSTICE

[T]he plaintiff claims that the trial court misinterpreted the evidence. [A]n appellate court must be particularly mindful of its role in the adjudication process. The reviewing court must guard against substituting its interpretation of the evidence as reflected by the cold, printed record for an equally tenable interpretation made by the trial court. "A factual finding may not be rejected on appeal merely because the reviewing judges personally disagree with the conclusion or would have found differently had they been sitting as the factfinder." [An appellate court] "may reject a factual finding if it is clearly erroneous, in that as a matter of law it is unsupported by the record, incorrect, or otherwise mistaken."

In reviewing the record as regards the findings we cannot say that either finding was clearly erroneous.

[A] plaintiff may recover for CUTPA violations only if the proven deceptive acts or practices of the defendant "have a potential effect on the general consuming public." If the plaintiff establishes this public interest, it may recover simply upon showing that the defendant engaged in a deceptive or unfair practice and that the plaintiff suffered an ascertainable loss of money or property thereby.

The Connecticut [legislature] deliberately chose not to define the scope of unfair or deceptive acts proscribed by CUTPA so that courts might develop a body of law responsive to the marketplace practices that actually generate such complaints.

In determining whether a practice violates CUTPA, the court should employ these criteria: "(1) [W]hether the practice, without necessarily having been previously considered unlawful, offends public policy as it has been established by statutes, the common law, or otherwise—whether, in other words, it is within at least the penumbra of some common law, statutory, or other established concept of unfairness; (2) whether it is immoral, unethical, oppressive, or unscrupulous; (3) whether it causes substantial injury to consumers [competitors or other businessmen]."

[T]he trial court concluded that the plaintiff had not met its burden of establishing that the defendant engaged in unfair or deceptive acts or competition. [A]lthough the trial court should have considered the tort and CUTPA claims separately, the plaintiff was not harmed by the trial court's failure to do so.

There is no error.

Legal Issues

1. Carefree Appliances informed its customers that because its sales staff comparison-priced the appliances that it sold, its prices were competitive. If within seven days after the purchase of an appliance a customer could show that the appliance could be bought at a lower price elsewhere within a 100-mile radius, Carefree promised to pay the customer twice the amount of the difference between the price that the customer had paid Carefree and the competitor's price. Although Carefree's prices were generally between 10 percent and 15 percent higher than those

of its competitors, over a five-year period very few of its customers took advantage of its "double the difference" refund offer. The rest either did not bother to find out the prices charged by Carefree's competitors because they thought that Carefree would not have made its offer if it did not in fact charge less than they did, or did not want to take the time to visit Carefree's competitors, or did not think going back to Carefree was worth the hassle even if they did learn of a lower price. Is Carefree Appliances guilty of a CUTPA violation? Why?

2. Vought, Inc. had a contract with Withers Company to purchase 5,000 acres of its property. Tigge, Inc., although aware of the Vought/Withers agreement, was determined to buy the 5,000 acres because it had determined the approximate worth of the mineral deposits that lay beneath their surface. Neither Vought nor Withers knew about these deposits. When Tigge offered to pay Withers three times the amount called for by the Vought/Withers contract, Withers sold the 5,000 acres to Tigge. Should Vought be permitted to recover damages from Tigge on the grounds the Tigge wrongfully interfered with Vought's business? Why?

Ethical Issues

1. High Quality Motors recommends that its customers have their vehicles repaired by its service department. The department's posted hourly service charge for repairs is $42 an hour, but instead of calculating the charge for a particular repair on the basis of the amount of time its mechanics *actually* spend on the repair, it uses a manual compiled by a national automobile dealers association that specifies the amount of time a mechanic *ordinarily* takes to complete that repair. According to the manual, it requires two hours to replace a front-wheel rotor. The mechanics of High Quality Motors completed the job in 45 minutes. Instead of charging $31.50 on the basis of the time the mechanics actually spent, High Quality Motors charged $84 on the basis of the time specified in the manual. Is High Quality Motors' conduct ethical? Why?

2. Gill Kind, the chief executive officer of Wayto Go, Inc., submitted the following proposal at a regularly scheduled meeting of its board of directors:

a. Wayto Go would establish a Competitiveness Division.

b. The division's charge would be to gather intelligence about Wayto Go's domestic and foreign competitors that would help Wayto Go to anticipate and plan to effectively deal with the future operations of those competitors.

Lise Cooper, a director whose only affiliation with Wayto Go was to act as one of its directors, asked Kind whether the division would engage in such behavior as keeping tabs on the personal lives of the top executives of Wayto Go's competitors.

Kind promptly replied: "Yes, Lise, you hit it on the head. We must work at being competitive, and the new division will help us do that."

Cooper responded: "Kind, I just do not like it. Such behavior is plainly unethical."

Kind answered: "I am as ethical as the next person. But business is business. We do not plan to break the law. Winning is not a crime, and that is what the division is supposed to help us do."

Would you vote for Kind's proposal? Why?

1. A state legislature's subcommittee on debtors' rights, while considering a bill that barred debt collection agencies from contacting debtors between the hours of 10 P.M. and 7 A.M., was told by the chief lobbyist of the National Association of Debt Collectors that courts were better equipped than a legislature to design legal principles protecting debtors from abusive tactics that debt collectors might practice. Do you agree? Why?

2. Trial and appellate courts, including the Supreme Court of the United States, permit a party who has been unsuccessful before a court to ask the court for permission to "reargue," that is, to appear before the court again and attempt to persuade it that it should change its decision. Is this procedure consistent with *stare decisis?* What reasons for allowing reargument would you expect a lawyer to rely on? Under what circumstances is it likely that a lawyer's reargument will be successful?

3. A state law provided that an employee who desired to observe up to three of his or her religious holidays during any one year was entitled to be paid in full for each day that he or she was absent from work for this purpose. The plaintiff founded his own religion. He insisted that under the law he was entitled to observe any three days he chose as his religious holidays and to be paid in full by his employer for those days. Was he correct? Why?

4. A workers' compensation law provided that employees were entitled to compensation if "injured on the job." As a result of harassment by his employer, Thomas Jenkins suffered a nervous breakdown. Is he entitled to receive payment under the law? What factors should a court consider to decide the case?

5. "When two states have a statute with exactly the same provision, a court in the state with no precedent as to how the statute should be interpreted should, on the basis of *stare decisis,* abide by a decision of the other state's courts as to the meaning of a particular phrase in the statute." Do you agree with this statement? Why?

6. While an assistant state attorney general, Linda testified in favor of a bill that was being considered by a committee of the state legislature. She told the committee that in her opinion the bill did not violate the state constitution. Thereafter she was appointed to the state supreme court. Two months after her appointment, a case came before it in which the trial court had ruled against the appellant on the basis of the statute on which Linda had testified. The appellant's attorney asked the state supreme court to reverse the trial court's decision on the ground that the statute was unconstitutional. Is Linda obliged to recuse herself from taking part in the court's deliberations on the constitutionality of the statute? Why?

1. In Chapter 4 the trial court process is examined in detail.
2. In Chapter 4 the appellate process is examined in detail.

PART

2

LITIGATION, ALTERNATE DISPUTE RESOLUTION, AND THE ADMINISTRATIVE PROCESS

CHAPTER

4

The Court System

In this chapter we will examine the court system under which businesses operate. When a dispute develops between parties, the court system, when requested, provides an orderly means of achieving justice between them. Every day businesses deal with disputes, most of which they resolve amicably. Many business disputes, however, are settled by the decision of a court.

The first part of the chapter covers the state and federal court systems in the United States and the problems of jurisdiction and venue. The remainder of the chapter covers procedures in a lawsuit prior to trial, during trial, and during the appeals process and also includes a brief look at the methods of enforcing judgments.

COURT SYSTEMS

The people of the United States are governed by both state governments and the federal government. Such rule by two types of governments is called **dual sovereignty.** The dual sovereignty that characterizes our governmental system is reflected in our legal system. Since the state and federal governments each have their own body of laws, each of these governments also has its own system of courts: the state courts maintained in each state and the federal courts maintained by the federal government. Although the state and federal court systems have very different functions, both of these systems have courts of limited jurisdiction, general trial courts, and appellate courts.

The State Court System

As noted in Chapter 3, the state court system is of colonial origin. After the Revolutionary War, the colonial courts continued to function and develop as state courts. Each state now provides for its own court system in its constitution and statutes.

The California constitution, for example, provides for the state's court system as follows: "The judicial power of the State is vested in the Supreme Court, courts of appeal, superior courts, municipal courts, and justice courts."[1] This section expressly provides for the structure of California's court system, from the highest court, the supreme court, to the lowest, the justice courts. A **court of record** is a court that is required to keep a record of its proceedings and can fine or imprison those whom it finds guilty. Since the justice courts merely levy fines and do not keep records of their proceedings, they are not courts of record.

Courts of Original Jurisdiction in the State System

Each state court system has **courts of original jurisdiction**—the trial courts in which cases are initially brought and tried. The courts of original jurisdiction are subdivided into minor courts and general trial courts.

Minor Courts

The various **minor courts** are courts of limited jurisdiction. Jurisdiction means the power of a court to hear a case and render a valid decision. Thus minor courts are "limited" to the types of cases they can hear. Courts of inferior jurisdiction hear cases that involve small amounts of money or special matters such as traffic violations. These specialized courts include the lowest-level trial courts, such as municipal or city courts, justice of the peace courts, magistrate courts, police courts, and traffic courts. Courts of these kinds have jurisdiction over lesser crimes such as misdemeanors, for which punishment is usually a fine or a short jail term to be served other than in a penitentiary. They also have jurisdiction over civil cases between individuals in tort actions for damages (such as claims of negligence in auto accidents) or for breach of contract where the amount in controversy is typically $1,000 or less.

Lower courts of limited jurisdiction often include **small claims courts** that can dispose of small money claims in one decision. To keep the proceeding inexpensive, the parties usually represent themselves without a lawyer and the loser has a right of appeal. Small claims courts generally hear cases involving small amounts

Dual sovereignty
rule by two types of governments

Court of record
a court that is required to keep a record of its proceedings

Court of original jurisdiction
the trial court in which cases are initially brought and tried

Minor courts
courts of limited jurisdiction

Small claims court
a court that handles cases involving small amounts of money

of money. In Michigan, for example, the maximum amount that can be claimed is $1,000; in California, $2,500; and in Arkansas, $3,000. Businesses use small claims courts to sue customers for unpaid debts, while customers frequently use them to sue businesses for the settlement of minor disputes. The advantage of a small claims court is that it can hear cases involving small amounts of money at almost no expense. Litigation costs will not prevent a plaintiff with a legitimate complaint over a small claim from bringing suit in such a court. It is important to note, however, that the plaintiff usually has a choice as to whether to bring suit in the small claims court or in the regular division of the lower trial court. With the choice of the latter comes the right to appeal.

Other courts of limited jurisdiction are probate courts and domestic relations courts. **Probate courts** hear disputes over the validity of wills, administer estates, and oversee the distribution of the assets of deceased persons.[2] **Domestic relations courts** hear family matters such as divorce and custody proceedings. While probate courts and domestic relations courts are not restricted to cases involving certain amounts of money, they are restricted to cases concerning a special subject matter.

General Trial Courts

The **general trial courts** are state courts of general jurisdiction. They can hear all cases except those specifically directed by statute to the minor courts of limited jurisdiction. They are usually organized into districts that comprise several counties.[3] The general trial courts hear many kinds of cases and are able to grant every kind of relief offered by the legal system. However, to bring a case in one of them, the plaintiff must have a claim that exceeds a specific amount, usually $2,000 or $3,000. Since states develop their court systems independently, different states give different names to general trial courts. In some states these courts are called "superior courts," "courts of common pleas," and "district courts." In New York the general trial court is called the "supreme court," a name that can be very misleading to those unfamiliar with that state's court system.

Appellate Courts

The state courts of appellate jurisdiction sit only to review the decisions of the lower courts. This means that a state's **appellate courts** hear appeals from the judgments of its trial courts. Unless an appeal from such a judgment is filed within a certain number of days after the trial, the judgment becomes final. The party who makes the appeal is known as the **appellant,** while the party against whom the appeal is made is known as the **appellee.** An appellant is usually given 60 days to file an appeal.[4] If the appeal is not filed within this time, then the right to appeal is lost and the judgment of the trial court stands.

If a state has only one appellate court, it is usually called the "supreme court" of the state. But in most states intermediate courts of appeals exist between the trial court and the supreme court. These intermediate courts, often called **courts of appeals,** are the courts to which appeal must first be made after the judgment of the trial court has been passed.

The judges of appellate courts are often called "justices." To prevent tie decisions, these courts usually have an odd number of members, such as three, five, seven, or nine. Judges in state courts are selected by election or appoint-

Probate court
a court that hears disputes over the validity of wills, administers estates, and oversees the distribution of the assets of deceased persons

Domestic relations court
a court that hears family matters such as divorce and custody proceedings

General trial court
a court of general jurisdiction that has the power to hear most types of cases

Appellate court
a court that hears appeals from the judgments of lower courts

Appellant
the party in a lawsuit who makes the appeal

Appellee
the party in a lawsuit against whom the appeal is made

Courts of appeals
a court that hears appeals from the judgments of lower courts

ment. Some states combine the two systems, which allows for a first-term appointment and reelection to successive terms.

Like the general trial courts, the appellate courts are given different names in different states. In Hawaii, the intermediate appellate court is simply called the Intermediate Court of Appeals. In Maryland, the intermediate appellate court is called the Court of Special Appeals. Among the states that do not have intermediate appellate courts are Maine, Mississippi, Nevada, Utah, West Virginia, and Wyoming.

An appeal to the state supreme court from the intermediate reviewing court is a matter of privilege. This means that the supreme court may, in the exercise of its discretion, decide to hear the appeal (ordinarily for the most important cases only). After a person has gone to trial over an issue, lost the case, appealed, and lost all appeals, the decision is considered *res judicata* or final. In other words, a litigant who has exhausted all the judicial avenues of relief given by trial and appeal is not allowed to bring the case to court again. A typical state court system is shown in Figure 4-1.

FIGURE 4-1   **A Typical State Court System**

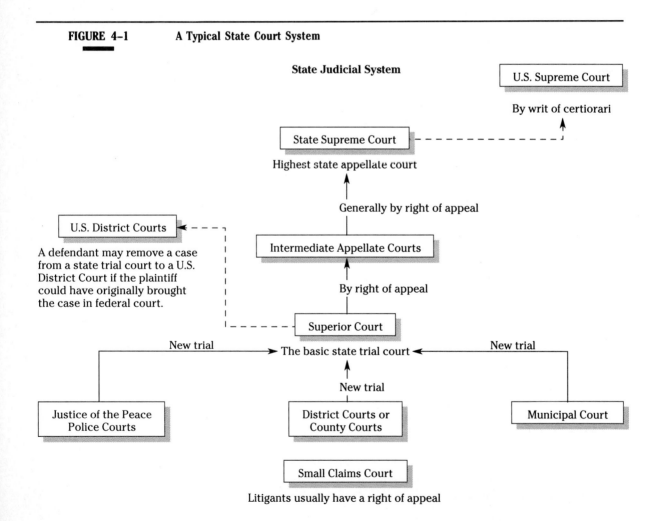

The Federal Court System

The federal courts were established by Article III, Section 1 of the U.S. Constitution, which provides that "the judicial power of the United States shall be vested in one Supreme Court, and in such inferior courts as the Congress may from time to time ordain and establish." The federal court system currently consists of district courts, courts of appeals, the Supreme Court, and several special courts.

District Courts: The Federal Trial Courts

The district courts are the basic trial courts of the federal court system. A plaintiff in the federal courts begins the lawsuit in a district court. One or more district courts are located in each state, thus allowing all citizens access to the federal court system. In states with low populations, such as Wyoming, a federal judicial district covers the whole state; in states with large populations, such as New York, there are several federal judicial districts (see Figure 4-2). Currently, there are 94 federal judicial districts in the 50 states and three U.S. territories: Guam, Puerto Rico, and the Virgin Islands.

District court judges, like all federal judges, are appointed by the president of the United States with the advice and consent of the Senate. Their appointment lasts for the term of their good behavior. The number of judges serving a district, usually from one to six, depends on its population. Although most cases are tried before only one district court judge, some types of cases are tried before a panel of three.

Courts of Appeals: The Intermediate Federal Appellate Courts

Appeals from the judgments of the district courts may be filed with the federal courts of appeals. These intermediate appellate courts hear all appeals from district courts except for a few types of cases for which appeals may be taken directly to the Supreme Court. Another function of the federal courts of appeals is to review the orders of federal administrative agencies, such as the Federal Trade Commission or the Environmental Protection Agency.

Federal law established courts of appeals in various parts of the United States (see Figure 4-3). Eleven courts of appeals each have jurisdiction over all the

---

Federal District Courts   **FIGURE 4–2**

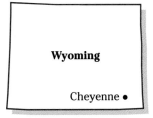

Population: 469,557   Population: 17,558,165

Circuit

a judicial division of a state or of the United States

district courts within several states. These multistate divisions are called **circuits.** For example, the Court of Appeals for the Ninth Circuit hears appeals from the district courts of Montana, Idaho, Washington, Oregon, Nevada, California, and Arizona. It also hears appeals from the rulings of federal administrative agencies for those states.

Like other appellate courts, the courts of appeals hear appeals based on errors of law. The judges for the courts of appeals review the trial proceedings of the district court and the evidence presented in that court to determine whether an error of law was made in the trial.

The courts of appeals were once known as the "circuit courts of appeals," because the judges appointed to them were not stationary, but traveled the circuit. These judges were often called "circuit riders" or "circuit judges." Even though the courts of appeals are no longer called the "circuit courts of appeals," their judges are still called "circuit judges."

Two other courts of appeals have a jurisdiction different from that of the other 11. A separate Court of Appeals for the District of Columbia hears appeals from the federal district court located there. This court of appeals also reviews the rulings issued by federal agencies in the District of Columbia. The other court of appeals is the Court of Appeals for the Federal Circuit, an innovation in the federal court system. The Federal Courts Improvement Act of 1982 created this court. This act eliminated two older courts, the U.S. Court of Claims and the U.S. Court of Customs and Patent Appeals. At the same time it created another court, the U.S. Claims Court. The Court of Appeals for the Federal Circuit hears all patent appeals from the Patent and Trademark Office boards, which are located throughout the

---

FIGURE 4–3   **Federal Judicial System**

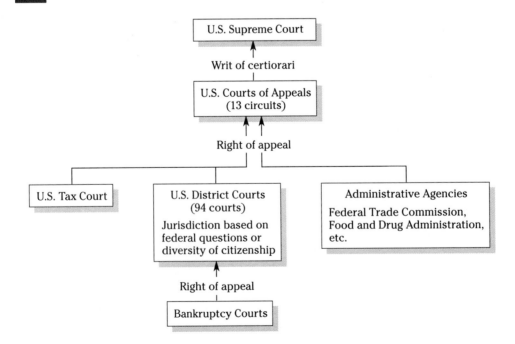

country. It also hears appeals from decisions of the U.S. Claims Court, the trial court in which most monetary claims against the federal government originate.

Appeals from the decisions of the courts of appeals are heard by the U.S. Supreme Court. However, review by the Supreme Court is discretionary—a matter of choice. This means that the Supreme Court has no legal obligation to review the judgment of the courts of appeals, but instead, in almost every instance, must be petitioned for a writ of certiorari. A **writ of certiorari** is an order of a higher court requiring a lower court to forward to it the records and proceedings of a particular case.

The U.S. Supreme Court: The Highest Court of the Land

The Supreme Court of the United States hears appeals primarily from the federal courts of appeals and the state supreme courts. However, it can also hear appeals directly from the federal district courts in special types of cases.

Why is the Supreme Court's decision on whether to hear a case discretionary? Since the litigant, or party to the suit, has already been granted the right to one trial and one appeal, further appeal to the Supreme Court is granted only if the suit poses an issue of substantial federal importance or if an obvious conflict exists between the decisions of two or more courts of appeals.

A practical reason also exists for the Supreme Court's discretionary power to hear cases. The Supreme Court cannot possibly hear the thousands of cases that are appealed to it each year, so it must choose the cases it deems of national importance. In summary, there is no general right of appeal to the Supreme Court. The only possibility of getting a case before the Supreme Court is through the writ of certiorari, and then only if the Supreme Court believes the case is important enough to hear.

The judges of the Supreme Court are called **justices,** and the presiding justice is called the **chief justice.** Like all federal judges, justices of the Supreme Court are appointed by the president with the advice and consent of the Senate. The Constitution makes no provision regarding the size of the Supreme Court, and the number of justices has ranged from 6 to 10. For some years there have been nine justices.

Although there are no special requirements for the position of justice (such as that the person chosen must be a judge or a lawyer), usually those chosen to serve in this capacity have been outstanding men and women of legal experience. The most notable Supreme Court justices in U.S. history include Oliver Wendell Holmes, Jr., John Marshall, Benjamin Cardozo, and Felix Frankfurter.

JURISDICTION: THE POWER OF A COURT TO HEAR A CASE

A decision to bring a lawsuit raises a primary question: In which court do you bring the suit? The word *court* is used in various ways, signifying not only a judge but also the place in which a judge or several judges sit to hear cases. The word **jurisdiction** has a more concrete definition. It refers to the authority of a court to hear a case. Without proper jurisdiction the actions of a court have no legal effect. Selecting a court with such jurisdiction is therefore a very important step after the decision to bring a lawsuit has been made.

Writ of certiorari
an order of a higher court requiring a lower court to forward to it the records and proceedings of a particular case.

Justices
the term that designates judges of the U.S. Supreme Court and of the state supreme courts

Chief justice
the term that designates the presiding judge of the U.S. Supreme Court and of the state supreme courts

Jurisdiction
the authority of a court to hear a case

The authority of a court to hear a case is derived from several sources. The source of a court's jurisdiction depends on whether the court is a state or federal court. State courts are granted jurisdiction by state constitutions and statutes. Federal courts are granted jurisdiction by Article III of the U.S. Constitution and by the Judiciary Act of 1789.[5] Constitutional and statutory grants of power to state and federal courts determine the range and scope of a court's jurisdiction.

For a court to have jurisdiction, it must have both (1) jurisdiction over the subject matter of the lawsuit and (2) jurisdiction over the person or property of the defendant.

Jurisdiction over Subject Matter

The subject matter of the lawsuit is the dispute that has been presented to the court for decision. The dispute, for example, may involve a contract, tort, or crime. What jurisdiction over subject matter means is that the court must have the power to decide the *kind* of case before it. If a court does not have subject matter jurisdiction in a case, then it has no power to hear the case and any decision it renders in the case is without effect.

Jurisdiction over subject matter is usually not a problem with state courts of general jurisdiction. However, it can be a problem in cases before inferior state courts. For example, a typical municipal traffic court would have no jurisdiction over a case involving a contract dispute. Like inferior state courts, federal courts are allowed to hear only certain types of cases and thus are courts of limited jurisdiction.

Subject Matter: State versus Federal Jurisdiction

Federal courts have exclusive jurisdiction over certain kinds of cases, such as federal crimes, copyrights, and bankruptcy. Other kinds of cases commence in state courts, with two exceptions: (1) cases that present a federal question and (2) cases that involve diversity of citizenship. Thus the vast majority of cases are subject to the jurisdiction of state courts.

Federal Question

Federal question cases

cases based on the U.S. Constitution, a federal law, or a treaty of the United States

Cases based on the U.S. Constitution, a federal law, or a treaty of the United States are **federal question cases.** Federal courts have jurisdiction over federal question cases regardless of the amount that the plaintiff claims as money damages.[6] For example, plaintiffs need only allege that an act deprived them of their First Amendment right of freedom of speech to state a cause of action for federal courts.

AN ACCIDENT WHILE ON VACATION

Hypothetical Case

While on vacation, Paula, a citizen of Illinois, was crossing a street in St. Louis, Missouri, when a car driven by David, a citizen of Kentucky, struck her. The car was owned by David's employer, ABC Company, an Indiana corporation whose principal place of business was in Chicago, Illinois. Paula sues both David and ABC Company in the St. Louis federal district court, claiming damages in the amount of $500,000. Does the court have jurisdiction? Why? Assuming that the court has jurisdiction, what law will it apply? Why?

Diversity of Citizenship

Even though no federal question is involved, the federal courts can also hear cases in which the plaintiff and the defendants are citizens of different states if the amount of damages claimed is over $50,000. Such cases are called **diversity of citizenship cases.**[7]

To determine whether diversity of citizenship exists in a case, the citizenship of the litigants must first be ascertained. A person is a citizen of the state in which the current residence at which he or she intends to remain is situated. Assume, for example, that Mr. Lee has a house in Georgia and a winter cottage in Florida. He works in Georgia and lives in his house there with his wife and three children. A citizen of South Carolina sues him in a contract action. For purposes of diversity of citizenship jurisdiction, Mr. Lee is a citizen of Georgia. The plaintiff may sue him in federal court provided that the plaintiff asks in good faith for damages in excess of $50,000.

A corporation may be a citizen of two states. Federal rules provide that for purposes of diversity of citizenship, a corporation is a citizen of its state of incorporation and of the state in which its principal place of business is located, provided that its principal place of business is in a state different from the state of incorporation. A corporation's principal place of business is generally the place in which the corporation makes its policy decisions, usually the home office. Suppose, for example, that Mr. Jones, a citizen of Iowa, brings a suit against Play Toy Corporation for a defect in one of its products. Play Toy Corporation is incorporated in Delaware, but its principal place of business is in Illinois, where it has a factory, distribution center, and home office. Mr. Jones can sue it under diversity of citizenship jurisdiction.

Federal and state courts have concurrent jurisdiction over diversity of citizenship cases and many federal question cases. **Concurrent jurisdiction** means that *both* the federal and state courts can hear the case. This means that plaintiffs in such cases can bring their lawsuits in a federal court or a state court. For example, a plaintiff in a diversity of citizenship action who has a claim for over $50,000 can bring the suit in a federal court or a state court. State and federal courts have concurrent jurisdiction in federal question cases other than those in which federal courts were given exclusive jurisdiction by Congress. However, the parties usually choose to litigate cases involving federal questions in federal courts.

The choice between a state forum and a federal forum is up to the plaintiff.[8] That choice may be based on a lawyer's familiarity with a particular court system or on a lawyer's belief that the lawsuit is likely to receive more favorable treatment in a particular court system.

When a federal district court hears a case solely under diversity of citizenship jurisdiction, no federal question is involved. Since the case does not concern a question of federal law, *the federal court must apply state law.*

Jurisdiction over the Person

For a court to render a valid judgment, it must have not only jurisdiction over the subject matter but also jurisdiction over the parties to the lawsuit or over the property of the defendant. Jurisdiction over the person or property of the defendant may be attained in one of two ways: (1) in personam jurisdiction, or (2) in rem jurisdiction. The jurisdictional power of the court over the person must be

Diversity of citizenship cases
cases in which the plaintiff and the defendant are citizens of different states and the amount of damages claimed is over $50,000

Concurrent jurisdiction
cases that both the federal and state courts are empowered to hear

asserted in a manner consistent with the due process requirements of the Constitution. Due process generally means fair play. Thus the defendant in a lawsuit must receive reasonable notification of the suit and must have a reasonable opportunity to be heard.

A LAWSUIT AGAINST DEFENDANTS FROM ANOTHER STATE

Hypothetical Case

While visiting relatives in Detroit, Sandra purchased a car from the Motor City Dealer Corporation. Three days later, while driving to her home in South Carolina, she was involved in an automobile accident in Virginia. She sustained serious personal injuries when her car was struck from behind, causing the gas tank to explode. Sandra filed a products liability suit in Virginia against the dealer and against the wholesaler who had sold the car to the dealer. She claimed that her personal injuries had been caused by the defective condition of the car when the wholesaler and dealer sold it.

The dealer and the wholesaler were Michigan corporations that did no business in Virginia. They claimed that a Virginia court had no power to require them to defend themselves.

Do you agree with the dealer and wholesaler or with Sandra? Why?

Personal Jurisdiction

Personal jurisdiction
the power of the court over the person of the plaintiff and the defendant

Summons
a notice to the defendant to appear in court and answer the plaintiff's allegations

Service of process
the communication of the summons to the defendant

Personal service
a form of service of process in which the summons is personally handed to the defendant

Substituted service
the form of service of process in which the summons is handed to a member of the defendant's household who is above a specified age

Long-arm statute
a state statute that allows service of process beyond the borders of a state

The power of the court over the person of the plaintiff and the defendant is **personal jurisdiction,** also called "in personam jurisdiction." Personal jurisdiction over the plaintiff is obtained by the plaintiff's filing of the lawsuit. By filing the suit, the plaintiff has voluntarily submitted to the court's jurisdiction. Personal jurisdiction over the defendant is usually obtained by the service of a **summons,** a notice to appear in court and answer the plaintiff's allegations. Fair notice to the defendant that he or she is being sued is accomplished by **service of process**—the communication of the summons (usually with a copy of the complaint) to the defendant. The summons commands the defendant to appear in court or lose by default.

Service of process is usually accomplished by **personal service,** in which the summons is handed to the defendant. Where serving a summons on a particular individual is difficult, **substituted service** is generally valid. The summons is served on any member of the defendant's household who is above a specified age, and an additional copy is mailed to the defendant's home. In some cases service of process is obtained by publishing a notice in a general circulation newspaper and also mailing a summons to the defendant's last known address. Service of process is invalid if it is done improperly, and invalid service of process operates as if it had not been served at all.

Anyone personally served with a summons within a state, even a transient, is subject to the personal jurisdiction of its courts. For example, if Mr. Dennis, a citizen of New York, gets off an airplane in Miami and is served with a summons at the Miami airport, he is subject to the personal jurisdiction of the Florida courts.

Long-Arm Statutes

Currently, each state has a **long-arm statute** that allows the service of process beyond its borders by giving reasonable notification to a defendant outside the state. Before the advent of long-arm statutes, service of process could only be accomplished within the boundaries of a state. Without a long-arm statute, if a person left a state, the state could not serve process on the person and thus could not obtain jurisdiction over him or her.

A U.S. Supreme Court decision in 1945, *International Shoe Co. v. Washington,*[9] expanded state court jurisdiction and opened the way for the passage of long-arm statutes by the states. According to *International Shoe* and other Supreme Court decisions that followed, long-arm statutes that provide a nonresident defendant with due process of law are valid and constitutional. In terms of jurisdiction, due process requires that a defendant who is not present within the forum state must have "minimum contacts" (relationships) with the state so that maintenance of the suit does not offend "traditional notions of fair play and substantial justice." Assume, for example, that Smith and Jones enter into a contract for the sale of goods in the state of Missouri. Jones breaches the contract and then moves to Indiana. Smith sues Jones for breach of contract in Missouri, which has a long-arm statute, and has Jones served with process in Indiana according to the terms of that statute.

Typical long-arm statutes base jurisdiction over out-of-state defendants on various kinds of contacts with the forum state. Jurisdiction is allowed for the following types of contacts:

1. The transaction of business in the state.
2. The commission of a tort[10] in the state.
3. The ownership of property in the state.
4. Entry into a contract in the state.
5. The commission of a particular act outside the state that has consequences in the state.

In the following case, the U.S. Supreme Court considered whether Florida had properly exercised its long-arm statute to obtain jurisdiction over a Michigan resident.

BURGER KING CORP. v. RUDZEWICZ
SUPREME COURT OF THE UNITED STATES
105 S. Ct. 2174 (1985)

Appellee Rudzewicz and MacShara, his business partner, entered into a 20-year franchise contract with Burger King to operate a restaurant in Michigan. Burger King was a Florida corporation whose principal offices were in Miami. Although day-to-day monitoring of the Rudzewicz/MacShara restaurant was conducted by the Burger King district office in Michigan, the Miami office set company policy and worked directly with the restaurant in resolving major problems.

The franchise operated by Rudzewicz and MacShara suffered a decline in business within a year after they signed the contract with Burger King. They then failed to make monthly payments on the franchise. After negotiations with the Michigan district office and the Miami headquarters of Burger King failed, the Miami headquarters terminated the franchise and ordered Rudzewicz and Mac-Shara to vacate the premises. When they refused to do so, Burger King brought suit in a Florida federal district court under Florida's long-arm statute. But Rudzewicz and MacShara argued that since they were Michigan residents and the dispute arose in Michigan, the Florida court lacked personal jurisdiction over them. The court disagreed and entered judgment for Burger King. Rudzewicz and MacShara appealed to the Court of Appeals for the 11th Circuit, which reversed the judgment. Burger King then appealed to the Supreme Court, which granted the petition for certiorari.

JUSTICE BRENNAN
Delivered the Opinion of the Court

The Due Process Clause protects an individual's liberty interest in not being subject to the binding judgments of a forum with which he has established no meaningful "contacts, ties, or relations." *International Shoe Co. v. Washington 326 U.S. at 319.* By requiring that individuals have "fair warning that a particular activity may subject [them] to the jurisdiction of a foreign sovereign," the Due Process Clause "gives a degree of predictability to the legal system that allows potential defendants to structure their primary conduct with some minimum assurance as to where that conduct will and will not render them liable to suit."

Where a forum seeks to assert specific jurisdiction over an out-of-state defendant who has not consented to suit there, this "fair warning" requirement is satisfied if the defendant has "purposefully directed" his activities at residents of the forum and the litigation results from alleged injuries that "arise out of or relate to" those activities. Thus "[t]he forum State does not exceed its powers under the Due Process Clause if it asserts personal jurisdiction over a corporation that delivers its products into the stream of commerce with the expectation that they will be purchased by consumers in the forum State" and those products subsequently injure forum consumers. And with respect to interstate contractual obligations, we have emphasized that parties who "reach out beyond one state and create continuing relationships and obligations with citizens of another state" are subject to regulation and sanctions in the other State for the consequences of their activities. Jurisdiction in these circumstances may not be avoided merely because the defendant did not *physically* enter the forum State. Although territorial presence frequently will enhance a potential defendant's affiliation with a State and reinforce the reasonable foreseeability of suit there, it is an inescapable fact of modern commercial life that a substantial amount of business is transacted solely by mail and wire communications across state lines, thus obviating the need for physical presence within a State in which business is conducted. So long as a commercial actor's efforts are "purposefully directed" toward residents of another State, we have consistently rejected the notion that an absence of physical contacts can defeat personal jurisdiction there.

Once it has been decided that a defendant purposefully established minimum contacts within the forum State, these contacts may be considered in light of other factors to determine whether the assertion of personal jurisdiction would comport with "fair play and substantial justice." Thus courts in "appropriate case[s]" may evaluate "the burden on the defendant," "the forum State's interest in adjudicating the dispute," "the plaintiff's interest in obtaining convenient and effective relief," "the interstate judicial system's interest in obtaining the most efficient resolution of controversies," and the "shared interest of the several States in furthering fundamental substantive social policies." These considerations sometimes serve to establish the reasonableness of jurisdiction upon a lesser showing of minimum contacts than would otherwise be required.

In this case, no physical ties to Florida can be attributed to Rudzewicz other than MacShara's brief training course in Miami. Rudzewicz did not maintain offices in Florida and, for all that appears from the record, has never even visited there. Yet this franchise dispute grew directly out of "a contract which had a *substantial* connection with that State." Eschewing the option of operating an independent local enterprise, Rudzewicz deliberately "reach[ed] out beyond" Michigan and negotiated with a Florida corporation for the purchase of a long-term franchise and the manifold benefits that would derive from affiliation with a nationwide organization. Upon approval, he entered into a carefully structured 20-year relationship that envisioned continuing and wide-reaching contacts with Burger King in Florida. In light of Rudzewicz's voluntary acceptance of the long-term and exacting regulation of his business from Burger King's Miami headquarters, the "quality and nature" of his relationship to the company in Florida can in no sense be viewed as "random," "fortuitous," or "attenuated."

Rudzewicz's refusal to make the contractually required payment in Miami, and his continued use of Burger King's trademarks and confidential business information after his termination, caused foreseeable injuries to the corporation in Florida. For these reasons it was, at the very least, presumptively reasonable for Rudzewicz to be called to account there for such injuries.

Because Rudzewicz established a substantial and continuing relationship with Burger King's Miami headquarters, received fair notice from the contract documents and the course of dealing that he might be subject to suit in Florida, and has failed to demonstrate how jurisdiction in that forum would otherwise be fundamentally unfair, we conclude that the District Court's exercise of jurisdiction did not offend due process. The judgment of the Court of Appeals is accordingly reversed, and the case is remanded for further proceedings consistent with this opinion.

It is so ordered.

Legal Issues

1. How was the fair warning requirement, mentioned in the opinion, met in the *Burger King* case? Explain.
2. According to the opinion, are minimum contacts the only factors to be considered in determining whether the assertion of personal jurisdiction is proper? Why?

Ethical Issues

1. What ethical standard apparently guided Rudzewicz's behavior in his dealings with Burger King? Explain your answer.
2. Assume that before Rudzewicz entered into the 20-year contract with Burger King, his attorney asked that this provision be included in the contract: "Any lawsuit between the parties to resolve a dispute arising under this contract is to be brought in a Michigan state court." Assume further that Burger King used its superior bargaining power to prevent the inclusion of the provision. Under these circumstances and if the only other contacts between Florida and Rudzewicz were those set forth in the case, would it be ethical to permit Burger King to bring suit in a Florida federal district court? Why?

Civil suits
lawsuits over private wrongs committed between individuals

Criminal suits
lawsuits over wrongs committed against the state

In personam jurisdiction
jurisdiction of the defendant that is obtained by arrest in a criminal suit and by service of process in a civil suit

Extradition
the process by which a state or country voluntarily turns the criminal defendant over to the requesting state or country for trial

In rem jurisdiction
jurisdiction of the court over the property that is the subject of the dispute

Jurisdiction for civil suits is different from jurisdiction for criminal suits. **Civil suits** are lawsuits over private wrongs committed between individuals. **Criminal suits** are lawsuits over wrongs committed against the state, because crimes are violations of criminal statutes passed by the state.

In criminal actions, the crime must have been committed within the state for the court to have jurisdiction of the case. **In personam jurisdiction** of the defendant is obtained by arrest in a criminal suit (as opposed to the use of a summons in a civil suit). A defendant in a criminal suit who leaves the state must be extradited to the state in which the crime was committed. **Extradition** is the process by which the governor of the forum state voluntarily turns the defendant over to the governor of the requesting state.[11] If the governor of the state to which the criminal defendant has fled refuses to turn the defendant over to the governor of the state in which the crime was committed, then the defendant remains safe from prosecution.

If the defendant is arrested in a foreign country, the extradition negotiations, based on treaties between the United States and that country, are handled by the federal government. The United States has extradition treaties with most countries.

Jurisdiction Based on Property

There are cases in which property rather than particular parties is involved. In such cases the court can base jurisdiction on the fact that the defendant's property is located within its territorial boundaries. Thus the court can base its authority to render a valid decision on in rem jurisdiction.

In Rem Jurisdiction

A lawsuit concerned with disputes over claims to a particular piece of property involves **in rem jurisdiction.** *In rem* is Latin for "against the thing," the thing being the property. To obtain in rem jurisdiction, the court simply acquires jurisdiction over the property located within its territorial jurisdiction that is the subject of the dispute. Assume, for example, that the Superior Court of Pleasant County has in rem jurisdiction in a dispute regarding a tract of land in Pleasant County, the county in which the court sits. The basis of the in rem jurisdiction is the location of the tract within the territorial jurisdiction of the court.

In rem jurisdiction is generally needed in divorce cases and in cases involving title to real estate because such cases involve "things," that is, marital status or property, instead of personal liability. Again, due process must be met by giving the owners of the property or those who have an interest in it reasonable notice and opportunity to be heard. A defendant cannot be deprived of *property* without due process of law.[12]

Conflict of Laws

Each state has its own statutes, passed by its own legislature. Each state also has a body of judge-made law, or common law, that differs from the judge-made law of other states. For in-state disputes, the litigants must refer to the laws of their state. In such disputes the decisions of other states have no effect but can be used by way of analogy if there have been no previous decisions in the state on the issue being litigated.

Since each state has the power to make its own laws, the laws of the states can and do differ in many ways. For example, more ecology-minded states have stricter laws against pollution, making some acts of pollution criminal that are not considered criminal in states with more lenient laws on pollution. And not only criminal laws but also laws on contracts and torts may be substantially different from state to state. Moreover, the federal government, like the state governments, has its own body of law and procedural rules to govern lawsuits.

The variations of state laws become a problem in disputes over interstate transactions. And rapid developments in communication and transportation have made interstate business transactions more convenient and more common. People often live in one state and work in another, own out-of-state property, or make out-of-state sales or purchases. To resolve conflicts between state laws, each state has developed a set of **conflict-of-laws principles.** These principles, usually considered part of the substantive law of each state, come into play when a dispute involves a conflict between the laws of two states. They allow the courts to decide which state's law is applicable in a given situation.

Conflict-of-laws principles allow a court to decide which state's laws to apply when a dispute involves a conflict between the laws of two states

If a case involving diversity of citizenship is brought in a federal court, that court must apply the law of the state in which it sits. But because the substantive law of the state includes a set of conflict-of-laws principles, the federal court may be required by those principles to apply the law of a state other than the one in which it sits. Since federal question cases concern federal law, state laws are never applied in such cases.

In a typical case in which conflict-of-laws principles come into play, two or more states have the power to hear the case and render a decision. The plaintiff chooses the forum, the court in which the case is tried. Unless the defendant can get a change of venue or remove the case, the plaintiff's choice of court will prevail.

The object of conflict-of-laws principles is to provide the forum court with a means of determining which state law to apply if more than one state is involved. In tort actions, for example, the traditional conflict-of-laws principle is to apply the law of the state in which the injury occurred. Assume that Mr. Harris, while traveling to Canada, drives to New York from his resident state, Maryland. While in New York, he negligently collides with the rear of the auto of Mrs. Williams, a New York resident, at a red light. Since the accident occurred in New York, if a lawsuit is brought in a Maryland court, it will apply the law of New York in determining the rights of the parties.

In contract actions, conflict-of-laws principles vary. The general principle is that states apply the law of the state in which the contract was *made*, though some states apply the law of the state in which the contract was to be *performed*. Assume that Mr. Johnson, a California farmer, meets Mr. Tate, owner of a North Carolina trucking company, at a convention in Illinois, where they draw up a contract for Mr. Tate's distribution of Mr. Johnson's produce in California. Later, when the cost of oil rises sharply, they disagree on the terms of the contract. Mr. Johnson sues Mr. Tate in a California court for breach of contract. The California court could apply the law of Illinois, where the contract was made, or its own law, since the contract was to be performed in California. Alternatively, the court could decide to apply the law of California because that state has the most substantial contacts with the contract action (the plaintiff is a resident and the contract was to be performed there).

Today, many courts simply apply the law of the state that has the most substantial contacts with the matter being litigated. Under the grouping of contacts theory, the court, after grouping the contacts in a given case, has to decide which state has the most substantial contacts with the action being brought. In a contract action, for example, the court would look at who breached the contract, the resident states of the plaintiff and the defendant, the nature of the breach of contract, and so on.

Right of Contracting Parties to Choose the Controlling Law

Generally, the parties to a contract can choose the state law by which they will be bound. In making a contract, for example, the parties might stipulate that a breach of contract action or any other action arising out of their business relationship must be brought in the court system of a particular state. However, if the parties are from the same state and they negotiate, sign, and perform the contract in that state, they cannot stipulate that the law of another state will apply, because they have no contact with another state. Moreover, a court will not uphold a choice-of-law clause if it determines that the clause was inserted fraudulently or mistakenly.

VENUE: THE PLACE OR COURT WHERE A LAWSUIT IS BROUGHT

As noted, to hear a case a court must have subject matter jurisdiction and personal jurisdiction over the defendant (or if the case involves a "thing," such as land, it must have in rem jurisdiction). If jurisdiction is established in several places, where should the trial be held? The best place for the trial is a question of venue. **Venue** is the geographic area in which a case should be tried. Whereas jurisdiction is a question of whether a court *can* hear a case, venue is a question of whether a court *should* hear a particular case over which several courts have jurisdiction. A court may have jurisdiction but not venue. Venue therefore becomes a consideration only when jurisdiction over the case has been established.

Venue
the geographic area in which a case should be tried

Venue is generally provided for in statutes, laws passed by a legislative body. A typical state venue statute provides that for purposes of venue, a suit can be brought in a county where any defendant resides. Assume that Johnson decides to sue Black for breach of contract in a state court of general jurisdiction. Johnson is a resident of County A; Black is a resident of County B. Johnson can sue Black in a state court of general jurisdiction in County B.

Ordinarily, venue statutes also allow suit to be brought in the county in which the cause of action arose. (A **cause of action** is simply a set of facts that entitle a person to judicial relief.) This type of statute allows venue in the county in which the event or transaction that is the subject of dispute actually took place. Assume that Johnson, a resident of County A, runs a stop sign in County C and collides with Black, a resident of County B. Black can sue Johnson in a state court of general jurisdiction in County C.

Cause of action
a set of facts that entitle a person to judicial relief

State venue statutes generally consider corporations to be residents of any county in which they have an office or in which they are "doing business." Statutory provisions establishing venue for corporations are similar to those establishing venue for partnerships. Partnerships are generally considered residents of any county in which a partner resides, in which the partnership has an office, or in which the partnership does business.

Defendants can object to venue, but if they fail to do so at an early time after the case is begun, their later objections to venue are considered "waived" (surrendered). In other words, unless defendants challenge the plaintiff's choice of venue during the initial stages of the lawsuit, they lose their right to do so. On the other hand, objections to jurisdiction cannot be waived because of the failure to object at the appropriate time.

Why do defendants object to venue? One ground is that the requirements of the state venue statute have not been met. More often, though, they object on the ground that the judge, the jury, or even the jury to be chosen is prejudiced. Prejudice is often used as a ground for objection to venue in criminal cases. Criminal defendants will ask for a **change of venue** if they believe that the judge or jury may be prejudiced against them because of, for example, pretrial publicity.

Another important ground for objection to venue is inconvenience, expressed by the Latin phrase **forum non conveniens,** which simply means that the place of trial is not convenient. Inconvenience (which is not just the trouble of coming to court) exists, for example, if an Alaskan plaintiff acquires jurisdiction over a defendant from Florida under a state long-arm statute and demands that the defendant appear in an Alaskan court. The costs of travel and out-of-state litigation might be unfair to the defendant.

A court's decision to invoke the doctrine of *forum non conveniens* involves two considerations: the convenience of the defendant and the interest of the state in which the court is located. Not only should a defendant not be forced to try a case in an extremely inconvenient location, but a state should not be forced to burden its courts with lawsuits not connected to it. When deciding whether to invoke the doctrine of *forum non conveniens,* courts often consider whether the plaintiff is a state resident and taxpayer and where the witnesses and sources of proof are located.

Change of venue
a change of the geographic location of a trial

Forum non conveniens
the inconvenience of the place of trial

BIGGY BURGER'S DISPUTE WITH ITS FORMER FRANCHISEE

Biggy Burger Corporation, a nationwide hamburger chain, terminated an agreement with a local franchisee because the franchisee refused to operate under the policies set forth in the franchise agreement. After the termination the former franchisee continued to operate his restaurant under the name Biggy Burger. Biggy Burger Corporation seeks to stop this unauthorized use of its valuable trade name. What course of action should it take? To which court should it go for the relief it seeks? Explain.

Hypothetical Case

EQUITABLE REMEDIES

Courts of law provide relief for petitioners in the form of money damages. Courts of equity provide "extraordinary," or equitable, remedies in situations in which money damages would be inadequate.

Understanding the difference between courts of law and courts of equity requires looking back into English history. For hundreds of years, there were two separate systems of courts in England: courts of law and courts of equity.

Henry II, king of England from 1154 to 1189, established law courts on a national scale during his reign. These were called "common law courts" because their judges began to reconcile their decisions with those of other law court judges in order to create a body of law "common" to all the people of England.

Although the law courts were established to ensure a consistent judicial system for the English people, their scope was very narrow. This resulted primarily from the fact that they were under the direct control of the king. To obtain a hearing in a law court, an aggrieved party had to buy a writ from the king and present it to the court. A **writ** is a legal document that is either submitted to a court or issued by a court. Writs were designed in advance for specific causes of action; if no existing writ fitted a person's cause of action, or if a writ did not precisely fit the cause of action for which it was purchased, then a court was not allowed to hear the case and the person could not obtain *any* legal relief.

The writ system did not permit flexibility in defining new causes of action. Thus the system of common law was limited primarily to the recognition of a narrow range of property rights at a time when the rapid growth of population and commerce was giving rise to new causes of controversies. In this climate the courts of equity developed.

In the area that became the United States, the colonies generally adopted the English system of law, which was common law supplemented by equity. Today, law and equity have merged in the federal court system and in nearly all of the state court systems. Each court has the power of both law and equity. Therefore, each court is said to be hearing an action at law or a suit in equity depending on the type of relief or damage the plaintiff asks for.

The remedies granted continue to be the primary difference between law and equity. Those most often granted by courts in equity are the injunction and specific performance. An **injunction** is an order of the court commanding a person to do a specific act or to refrain from doing a specific act that threatens irreparable harm to others. Injunctions are often used by courts in settling labor disputes, nuisance cases,[13] and civil rights violations. Courts can enforce injunctions by jailing for contempt of court defendants who refuse to obey them.

Specific performance is another equitable remedy. A court in equity can order a party to perform whatever that party has specifically agreed to perform in a contract. Money damages are often inadequate if the property bargained for in a contract is "unique." Real estate is generally considered unique property, and a purchaser will usually be granted specific performance if the seller tries to back out of a binding contract for the sale of real estate. Suppose, for example, that Susan contracts to sell several acres of land to Barbara but later changes her mind and refuses to sell. A court in equity can compel Susan to specifically perform the contract by making her sell the property to Barbara. The court could not have simply ruled that the land was the property of the plaintiff since an equity court has power only over people and not over property.

However, even though personal services are unique, a court in equity will not order the specific performance of a contract for such services, because being forced to perform personal services is similar to involuntary servitude. Suppose, for example, that Roger, an actor, contracts with a movie studio to play a role in a motion picture. If Roger later refuses to act in the motion picture, a court will not force him to specifically perform his contract. It will instead make him liable to the movie studio for money damages.

If a party refuses to obey a court's decree in equity, the court can order that the party be fined or sent to jail until he or she obeys the order.

An important distinction between law and equity is that a court in an equity suit sits without a jury. A judge in equity decides both the law *and* the facts in the suit.

Writ
a legal document that is issued by a court

Injunction
an order of the court commanding a person to do a specific act or to refrain from doing a specific act that threatens irreparable harm to others

Specific performance
being required to carry out a contract according to its terms

As previously mentioned, in a jury trial a judge decides the law and the jury decides the facts.

In the following case the buyer asked for equitable relief in the form of specific performance from an automobile dealer who breached a contract for the sale of a new automobile.

BECKMAN v. VASSALL-DILLWORTH LINCOLN-MERCURY
SUPERIOR COURT OF PENNSYLVANIA
468 A.2d 784 (1983)

On December 14, 1978, Howard Beckman, the appellant, entered into a written agreement with Vassall-Dillworth Lincoln-Mercury, an automobile dealer, for the purchase of a 1979 Lincoln Continental at a price of $12,286. Four weeks later the appellant learned that the dealer could not find the agreement and had not ordered a car for him from the manufacturer, Ford Motor Company. The dealer was willing to order another 1979 Lincoln Continental, but at a price higher than that in the original agreement. The appellant sued the dealer and the manufacturer for specific performance of the agreement, but the lawsuit was dismissed by the trial court.

MONTGOMERY, JUDGE
Delivered the Opinion of the Court

It is clear that an order for specific performance is inappropriate where the moving party has an adequate remedy at law. Our Court has held that specific performance is a proper remedy when the subject matter of an agreement is an asset that is unique or one such that its equivalent cannot be purchased on the open market. In this case, the record shows that the Appellant was given an opportunity by the dealer to purchase the automobile he wanted, but at a higher price. It may not be ignored that the Appellant could also have sought to purchase the same vehicle from another source. His remedy in such circumstances was to seek damages for any difference between the original order price and the actual purchase price he paid. Because the subject matter of the contract was not unique, and because it is obvious that an adequate remedy at law was available, we agree with the lower court's rejection of the Appellant's demand for specific performance.

Affirmed.

Legal Issues

1. Why didn't the court require the automobile dealer to sell the appellant the Lincoln Continental he wanted at the contract price of $12,286? Explain.

2. If the automobile referred to in the contract had been a one-of-a-kind classic car, would the court have granted the remedy of specific performance? Explain.

Ethical Issues

1. Was it ethical for the automobile dealer to insist that Beckman pay a higher price if he wanted delivery of a Lincoln Continental? Why?

2. Under what standard of ethics, if any, would Beckman have been obliged to purchase a Lincoln Continental from another dealer and then sue Vassall-Dillworth for damages? Explain your answer.

When parties are unable to resolve their disputes, litigation usually results. The following section discusses the steps in a lawsuit, including the pretrial proceedings, the trial proceedings, and appellate proceedings.

PROCEEDINGS PRIOR TO TRIAL

Civil procedure is the process of civil litigation. Civil litigation is the judicial settlement of civil disputes, such as actions in contracts or torts. Both federal and state courts have rules that govern the process of civil litigation. Criminal actions, which differ from civil actions in many respects, are governed by different procedural rules in federal and state courts.

Procedural rules developed to promote judicial efficiency and fairness. In the common law courts of early England, parties shouted their positions before the court. No written record was kept of these pleadings, and the parties and the court had to rely on their memory of what had been said. Now orderly rules of civil procedure reduce confusion and unfairness and written pleadings provide both parties and the court with a record of the issues in controversy.

Pleadings Stage

Pleadings
the initial written statements that each of the parties to a civil suit presents to the trial court

Before a suit reaches trial, the parties and their attorneys must take several steps to bring the litigation before the court. The pleadings are the first of these steps. The **pleadings** are the initial written statements that each of the parties to a civil suit presents to the trial court. Through the pleadings the parties and the court are notified of the basic issues of the litigation. The pleadings serve the important function of limiting the litigation to these issues and thus preventing anything irrelevant to them from being introduced at trial. The pleadings of a case consist of the complaint, the answer, and in some jurisdictions, the reply.

Complaint

Plaintiff
the party who initiates the lawsuit

Defendant
the party who is being sued

The party who initiates the lawsuit is the **plaintiff.** The party who is being sued is the **defendant.** The plaintiff initiates the lawsuit by filing a written complaint with the court. In this communication the plaintiff "complains" about actions of the defendant and asks the court to grant relief. Generally, a complaint contains the name of the court, the names of the parties to the suit, a statement of the court's jurisdiction, and a short, simple statement of the facts that provide the basis of the controversy.

A complaint is not an argument, but an allegation of facts. Plaintiffs do not have to offer proof with a complaint; they simply allege that certain facts are true and that because those facts are true, they are entitled to money damages or other relief from the court. Figure 4-4 provides an example of a complaint.[14]

Service of Process

The defendant is served with a copy of the complaint to give notice that he or she is being sued. Accompanying the complaint is a *summons,* a court order directing the defendant to appear in court within a certain time (usually 30 days) and answer the complaint. The summons brings the defendant under the jurisdiction of the court. Figure 4-5 provides a sample summons.

Example of a Complaint   **FIGURE 4–4**

IN THE SUPERIOR COURT OF
IDEAL COUNTY
STATE OF UTOPIA

CIVIL ACTION NO. 1-77804

James A. Smith
Plaintiff

v.   COMPLAINT ON CONTRACT

Brown Wholesalers, Inc.

Defendant

Comes now, James A. Smith, the plaintiff by and through its counsel Holmes, Hand & Marshall, attorney, and states his complaint as follows:

1. The defendant is Brown Wholesalers, Inc., whose business is located at 15 Bloomdale Street, City of Alpharetta, Ideal County, Utopia, and is subject to the jurisdiction of this court.

2. On or about June 1, 1991, the defendant and the plaintiff entered into a contractual agreement, a copy of which is attached hereto as "Exhibit A" and made a part hereof.

3. The defendant has breached said contractual agreement by failing and refusing to accept delivery of the said tomatoes.

WHEREFORE, the plaintiff demands judgment against the defendant in the sum of $250,000, together with interest and the costs of this action.

Holmes, Hand & Marshall
Attorneys-at-Law

s/s *Frederick R. Holmes*
Frederick R. Holmes
Attorney for Plaintiff
500 High Rent Street
Alpharetta, Utopia

Date: 9/10/91

As noted, serving a copy of the complaint and the summons on the defendant is called "service of process." Serving process on a defendant is usually accomplished by handing these papers to the defendant. Most jurisdictions now allow service of process in other ways such as substituted service, publication, and registered mail.

Generally, the defendant must respond to the plaintiff's complaint within 30 days or lose the case by default. Such a result is called a **default judgment.**

Default judgment
a judgment taken against the defendant if the defendant fails to respond to the plaintiff's complaint

FIGURE 4–5   **Example of a Summons**

IN THE SUPERIOR COURT OF
IDEAL COUNTY
STATE OF UTOPIA

CIVIL ACTION NO. 1-77804

James A. Smith
Plaintiff

v.   SUMMONS

Brown Wholesalers, Inc.
Defendant

To the above-named Defendant:

You are hereby summoned and required to serve upon Frederick R. Holmes, plaintiff's attorney, whose address is 500 High Rent Street, Alpharetta, Utopia, an answer to the complaint which is herewith served upon you, within 30 days after service of this summons upon you, exclusive of the day of service. If you fail to do so, judgment by default will be taken against you for the relief demanded in the complaint.

Date: 9/10/91

s/s John C. Townsend
Clerk of Court

s/s Ann B. Parker
Deputy Clerk

Answer

Answer

a written statement in which the defendant denies or admits each allegation in the plaintiff's complaint

The defendant responds to the plaintiff's complaint with an answer. The **answer** is a written statement in which the defendant denies or admits each allegation of the plaintiff. If the defendant denies the allegations of the plaintiff, the plaintiff must prove them at trial. If the defendant admits every allegation of the plaintiff, then there is no need for a trial because there are no facts at issue. In that event the court would award a judgment in favor of the plaintiff, assuming that the plaintiff's complaint states a cause of action.

The defendant's answer may contain a general denial or one or more specific denials. In an answer containing a general denial, the defendant denies all of the allegations in the complaint. In an answer containing specific denials, the defendant admits that some of the allegations are true and denies the truth of others.

Affirmative defense

the allegation of new matter in the defendant's answer that acts as a bar to the plaintiff's recovery

In some cases the defendant's answer raises affirmative defenses. An **affirmative defense** is the allegation of new matter that, assuming the complaint to be true, acts as a bar to the plaintiff's recovery. Assume, for example, that plaintiff Joe Jackson sues defendant Linda North for negligently running into his car with hers. In his complaint the plaintiff alleges that the defendant committed the tort of negligence and requests money damages for personal injuries to himself and for property damage to his car. In her answer the defendant denies that she was driving negligently and alleges that the defendant was guilty of contributory negligence by speeding and that his negligence contributed to the accident. Contributory negligence is an affirmative defense that, if proven, frees the defendant of liability under the laws of many states—even if the plaintiff proves that the defendant was also negligent. The affirmative defense of the contributory negligence in the above example is an attempt by the defendant to shift some or all of the responsibility for the accident to the plaintiff.[15]

In addition, most states allow the defendant's answer to assert a counterclaim. In a **counterclaim** the defendant asserts his or her own claim against the plaintiff and asks that the plaintiff be required to pay the defendant money damages. The counterclaim does not have to be related to the cause of action (the statement of facts sufficient to support a lawsuit) stated in the complaint. This policy permits *all* of the disputes between the parties to be settled as economically as possible. The plaintiff must respond to the defendant's counterclaim with an answer.

In most jurisdictions the pleading stage ends with the defendant's answer. In those jurisdictions the plaintiff does not have to reply to the defendant's answer. In some jurisdictions, however, the plaintiff must file a **reply** if the defendant's answer alleges new facts. The plaintiff's reply will specifically admit or deny each of these allegations of fact. An answer with an affirmative defense and counterclaim is shown in Figure 4-6.

Counterclaim
the assertion in the defendant's answer of the defendant's own claim against the plaintiff asking that the plaintiff be required to pay the defendant money damages

Reply
a pleading by the plaintiff in response to the defendant's answer

Discovery

Trials shown in movies and on television are often resolved by such surprises as an unexpected witness or the relevation of previously unknown facts. A surprise-laden trial, however, would in fact be very inefficient. In the past lawsuits proceeded directly from the pleading stage to the trial stage. The parties often did not know until the day of the trial what witnesses and evidence the other side would present. Thus, trials were often a battle of wits whose outcome was decided by the skill and cunning of the attorney. Current civil procedure uses the rule of discovery to take as many surprises as possible out of the litigation process. Discovery speeds up the trial process and encourages settlement of the dispute before trial.

How do parties undertake to "discover" what facts the other side possesses or knows about? Depositions and interrogatories are the discovery devices that attorneys use most frequently. The other discovery devices include inspection of documents and property, and physical and mental examinations.

A **deposition** allows the attorneys for the parties to question any person, including a party, regarding the subject matter of the lawsuit. Depositions are taken at a hearing outside the court after due notice has been given to all involved. Usually, they are taken at the office of the attorney for one of the parties. The testimony of witnesses or parties is given under oath, subject to cross-examination, and recorded by a court reporter. The court reporter prepares a transcript that the witnesses must sign. Many jurisdictions allow depositions to be videotaped, which eliminates the need for a written transcript.

Deposition
the sworn testimony of a witness given out of court

Depositions have several advantages. They allow an attorney to observe witnesses while the witnesses are undergoing questioning. They also allow an attorney to seek details from witnesses and to examine witnesses for inconsistencies in their testimony. Thus they offer an attorney valuable opportunities for direct observation that do not exist in procedures in which witnesses respond to

FIGURE 4–6   **Example of an Answer**

IN THE SUPERIOR COURT OF
IDEAL COUNTY
STATE OF UTOPIA

CIVIL ACTION NO. 1-77804

James A. Smith
Plaintiff

v.   ANSWER

Brown Wholesalers, Inc.
Defendant

Now comes defendant, Brown Wholesalers, Inc., through counsel, and in answer to the complaint of plaintiff, James A. Smith, says:

1. Defendant admits the allegations in paragraph one (1) of the complaint.

2. Defendant admits the allegations in paragraph two (2) of the complaint.

3. Defendant denies each and every allegation of paragraph three (3) of the complaint.

AFFIRMATIVE DEFENSE

The defendant alleges that the delivery of tomatoes was refused because said tomatoes were not of the kind and quality specified in the contract.

COUNTERCLAIM

And now comes the defendant in the above-stated case, and for counterclaim says:

1. That on the 30th day of July, 1991, the plaintiff presented for delivery 10,000 cases of tomatoes.

2. That said tomatoes were not good and merchantable Blue Goose tomatoes as called for in the contract, a copy of which is attached hereto as "Exhibit A" and made a part hereof.

3. On the 30th day of July, 1991, the defendant duly demanded that the plaintiff deliver to defendant the goods specified in the contract.

4. On the 21st day of August, 1991, the defendant was forced to purchase in the open market similar goods, of the same quality that the plaintiff agreed to deliver, for which defendant paid the sum of $280,000, which sum was $30,000 in excess of the price for which plaintiff agreed to sell and deliver the goods to defendant.

WHEREFORE, the defendant demands judgment in the sum of $30,000 together with interest and the costs of this action.

Black & Mansfield
Attorneys-at-Law

s/s Lawrence C. Mansfield
Attorney for Defendant
Lawrence C. Mansfield
100 Fees Boulevard
Middleton, Utopia

Date: 9/20/91

questions in writing with the benefit of counsel. Depositons make it possible to obtain the testimony of witnesses who are unavailable for trial.

Depositions are usually requested of the other party and of that party's most important witnesses. The depositions of expert witnesses such as doctors, whose time as expert witnesses is both limited and expensive, are often taken at a hearing before trial and are used at the trial in place of live testimony.

Written **interrogatories** allow one party to send the other party a series of questions that must be answered under oath within a specific time. This exchange of information is accomplished entirely by mail. Unlike depositions, interrogatories are confined to the parties to the case. However, one party may use an interrogatory to demand a list of the witnesses that the other party plans to use at a trial. Interrogatories have the advantage of being relatively inexpensive. A disadvantage of interrogatories is that they do not provide an opportunity to examine witnesses in person.

A party who is answering interrogatories may consult with counsel before doing so. This ensures care in the formulation of answers that may be used in court against the answering party. Figures 4-7 and 4-8 illustrate an interrogatory and an answer to an interrogatory.

Since depositions and interrogatories are given under oath, a falsehood in them will incur the penalty of perjury. Furthermore, if a witness gives one answer in a deposition or interrogatory and another during the trial itself, the deposition or interrogatory may be used to **impeach** (discredit) the witness at trial. To impeach a witness is to call his or her truthfulness into question before the court.

Either party to a case may secure a court order permitting the party or the party's attorney to inspect, copy, or photograph documents or things relevant to the trial that are in the possession or control of others. Typical examples of such things are letters, business records, medical records, and bills. Parties cannot evade inspection by placing such evidence in the hands of others.

If the physical or mental condition of a party is at issue, a court may issue an order requiring the party to submit to a physical or mental examination. For example, in a personal injury action, both parties may request examination of the injured party by physicians.

Summary Judgment

During the discovery stage of litigation, either party may move for **summary judgment.** This is a motion to dismiss a case on the basis of the evidence produced by the discovery process. Such a motion enables the parties to establish that no genuine issue of fact exists. The summary judgment procedure allows the parties to review the facts in a hearing before a judge. At this hearing they may introduce affidavits (sworn statements) of witnesses who would be called if a trial were held. They may also introduce such materials as depositions and documents relevant to the case and admissible under the rules of evidence. If there is no genuine issue of material fact, the judge will rule that no trial is needed and will enter a judgment for the plaintiff or the defendant. This determination on the merits of the case may be appealed to a higher court.

Pretrial Conference

The pretrial conference, a relatively modern development, was unknown at common law. It is a means of coping with congested court calendars by managing trials more efficiently. The **pretrial conference** is a meeting of the judge and the attorneys in the judge's chambers two or three weeks before the trial. At this

Interrogatories

written questions that one party in a lawsuit sends to the other party to obtain sworn written answers to factual questions.

Impeach

demonstrating that a witness at a trial is untruthful.

Summary judgment

a motion to dismiss a case on the basis of evidence produced by the discovery process

Pretrial conference

a meeting of the attorneys and the judge to determine what issues and facts of the case are still in controversy

FIGURE 4–7   **Example of an Interrogatory**

SUPERIOR COURT OF
IDEAL COUNTY
STATE OF UTOPIA

CIVIL ACTION NO. 1-77804

James A. Smith
    Plaintiff

v.

Brown Wholesalers, Inc.
    Defendant

INTERROGATORIES

TO: BROWN WHOLESALERS, INC.

Please take notice that the plaintiff, James A. Smith, demands answers to the following interrogatories under oath within twenty (20) days from the time service is made upon you.

Question No. 1:   Did the plaintiff attempt to deliver 10,000 cases of tomatoes to the defendant?

Question No. 2:   Did the defendant refuse delivery of the said tomatoes?

Question No. 3:   What defenses does the defendant plan to raise?

Question No. 4:   What counterclaims, if any, does the defendant plan to raise?

Question No. 5:   What physical evidence will the defendant present?

Question No. 6:   State the names and addresses of all the witnesses that the defendant will use to testify on behalf of the defendant in the trial of the case.

> *s/s Frederick R. Holmes*
> Frederick R. Holmes
> Attorney for Plaintiff
> 500 High Rent Street
> Alpharetta, Utopia

Date: 11/25/91

---

meeting the attorneys and the judge make decisions and reach agreements on discovery, on exactly what issues and facts are still in controversy, and on the preparation of the trial itself. The pretrial conference encourages out-of-court settlements by the parties before the dispute reaches trial, since during the conference the parties become aware of the strengths and weaknesses of their cases.

The judge issues a pretrial order at the conclusion of the pretrial conference. An illustration of a pretrial order is provided in Figure 4-9.

SUPERIOR COURT OF
IDEAL COUNTY
STATE OF UTOPIA

CIVIL ACTION NO. 1-77804

James A. Smith
Plaintiff

v.

Brown Wholesalers, Inc.
Defendant

ANSWERS OF BROWN WHOLESALERS, INC.
TO INTERROGATORIES

The defendent, Brown Wholesalers, Inc., appeared before the undersigned authority this day, and, being duly sworn, answers said interrogatories:

Question No. 1:   Did the plaintiff attempt to deliver 10,000 cases of tomatoes to the defendant?

Answer: Yes.

Question No. 2:   Did the defendant refuse delivery of the said tomatoes?

Answer: Yes.

Question No. 3:   What defenses does the defendant plan to raise?

Answer: The defendant will claim that the tomatoes presented by the plaintiff were not good and merchantable Blue Goose tomatoes as called for in the contract.

Question No. 4:   What counterclaims, if any, does the defendant plan to raise?

Answer: The defendant will claim that the plaintiff's failure to present tomatoes of the kind and quality specified in the contract caused the defendant to purchase such tomatoes on the open market for a price $30,000 greater than called for in the contract.

Question No. 5:   What physical evidence will the defendant present?

Answer: The contract.

Question No. 6:   State the names and addresses of all the witnesses that the defendant will use to testify on behalf of the defendant in the trial of the case.

Answer: William Swan, Receiving Supervisor, Brown Wholesalers, Inc., 222 Rocky Road, Alpharetta, Utopia.

s/s Robert Q. Brown
Robert Q. Brown
President
Brown Wholesalers, Inc.

Defendant, herein, who being duly sworn states under oath that the above answers to interrogatories are true and correct. Sworn and subscribed before me this the 25th day of November, 1991.

s/s Theodore T. Trueblood
Notary Public

FIGURE 4-9

THE SUPERIOR COURT OF
IDEAL COUNTY
STATE OF UTOPIA

CIVIL ACTION NO. 1-77804

James A. Smith
    Plaintiff

      v.

Brown Wholesalers, Inc.
    Defendant

PRETRIAL ORDER

A pretrial conference was held on January 15, 1992, before me, with Frederick R. Holmes appearing as attorney for the plaintiff and Lawrence C. Mansfield appearing as attorney for the defendant. The following proceedings were had:

1. Plaintiff tendered 10,000 cases of tomatoes and defendant refused delivery of said tomatoes.

2. Defendant purchased 10,000 cases of good and merchantable Blue Goose tomatoes on the open market for a total of $280,000.

3. The issue remaining in the action in whether the tomatoes tendered by plaintiff were good and merchantable Blue Goose tomatoes.

s/s Laura A. Phillips
Laura A. Phillips
Judge, Superior Court
Ideal County

Date: 1/20/92

TRIAL PROCEEDINGS

If a lawsuit is not settled during the pleading or discovery stage, trial proceedings will begin. The parties may be given the option of having the lawsuit decided by either a jury or a judge.

In civil cases the parties usually have a right to a jury trial if the plaintiff is asking for a remedy at law, usually money damages. For nearly all criminal cases, the defendant has the right to a trial by jury. In civil cases a jury trial may be waived (given up) by agreement of the plaintiff and the defendant, while in criminal cases only the defendant has the right to request a **bench trial,** one decided by the judge.[16]

Bench trial
a case in which the judge
makes the decision

Jury Selection

If at the time of trial a jury is desired, the first step in trial proceedings is to impanel a jury. The potential jurors for the case will have been selected at random by the clerk of court from a list of eligible citizens, usually the voter registration list. Approximately 50 persons are called to the courtroom where the *voir dire* will take place. The **voir dire** is the questioning by the attorneys and the judge to determine that the citizens chosen to serve as jurors will be impartial. Where answers to questions indicate that a potential juror may not be impartial, that person can be eliminated by a **challenge for cause.** For example, a person would be excluded from jury service if questioning reveals that he or she has a financial interest in a business involved in the litigation or is a close friend of one of the parties. There is no limit to the number of challenges for cause.

In addition, each attorney has a certain number of peremptory challenges. A **peremptory challenge** allows an attorney to eliminate a prospective juror without giving a cause for doing so. The Supreme Court has ruled, however, that the prosecution cannot use race as a basis for a peremptory challenge in a criminal case, and neither plaintiff nor defendant can use race as a basis for a peremptory challenge in a civil case. The selection process continues until the required number of jurors has been chosen. At common law juries always consisted of 12 persons.[17] The number of jurors has now been reduced, frequently to six persons, in nearly all of the federal courts and most of the state courts.

Voir dire
the questioning by the attorneys and the judge to determine that those chosen to serve as jurors will be impartial

Challenge for cause
the elimination of potential jurors because they may not be impartial

Peremptory challenge
the elimination of prospective jurors without giving a cause

Opening Statements

Once the jury has been selected, each attorney makes an opening statement. The **opening statement** consists of a preview of the case and of the type of evidence that the attorney plans to introduce.

Opening statement
a statement in which an attorney gives a preview of the case and of the type of evidence that the attorney plans to introduce

Presentation of Evidence

The party with the burden of proof proceeds first to present the evidence supporting his or her allegations. **Burden of proof** is the obligation of going forward with the evidence and proving the facts alleged. The plaintiff in a civil case and the prosecution in a criminal case have the burden of proof. In a civil trial the burden of proof for plaintiffs is to prove their case **by a preponderance of the evidence.** This standard requires plaintiffs to convince the jury by the greater weight of their evidence that their allegations are true. One may think of preponderance of the evidence as a one-point victory.

The prosecution in a criminal case needs much more than a one-point victory. To obtain a conviction in a criminal trial, the prosecution is required to prove its case **beyond a reasonable doubt.** This means that its evidence must be so persuasive that the jurors have no reasonable doubt as to the guilt of the accused. Convincing a jury is more difficult in a criminal case than in a civil case. In a civil case the scales of justice must tilt at least slightly in favor of the plaintiff; in a criminal case they must tilt heavily in favor of the prosecution.

The purpose of evidence is to convince the court of the truth or untruth of a matter in dispute. Evidence most frequently consists of the sworn oral testimony

Burden of proof
the obligation of a party to go forward with the evidence and prove the facts alleged

By a preponderance of the evidence
the burden of proof for plaintiffs in a civil trial

Beyond a reasonable doubt
the prosecution's burden of proof in a criminal trial

Direct examination

questioning by the attorney who called the witness

Cross-examination

questioning by the attorney who did not call the witness

Expert witness

a witness who has specialized knowledge in any field

Lay witness

a witness who does not qualify as an expert

Privilege

allows a witness to refuse to testify or allows a person to prevent a witness from testifying

Attorney-client privilege

allows the client to prevent the attorney from testifying concerning matters that the client told the attorney while seeking legal advice

of a witness in response to questions from the attorney and the judge. In addition, opposing counsel usually present physical evidence consisting of business records, letters, weapons used to commit crimes, and other physical items.

The attorney who calls a witness has the first opportunity to examine the witness. This is called **direct examination.** When the direct examination has been completed, the witness is turned over to the opposing attorney for cross-examination. The questions on **cross-examination** are limited to matters that were raised by the direct examination. The cross-examination may be followed by a redirect examination to allow the witness to explain or modify answers given in the direct examination. The scope of redirect examination is limited to matters brought out in the cross-examination. A witness may then be subjected to recross-examination and even beyond. Normally, the examination of a witness does not proceed beyond cross-examination.

The witnesses called are classified as either lay witnesses or expert witnesses. An **expert witness** is one who qualifies as an expert by specialized knowledge in any field. For example, a witness may be called to give expert testimony on accounting, medicine, engineering, sociology, psychology, or economics. The expert witness brings to the court the learning that she or he acquired by training, education, or experience. Any witness who does not qualify as an expert is a **lay witness.**

Based on the rules of evidence, attorneys may object to the introduction of oral testimony and physical exhibits. The purpose of the rules of evidence, which are very technical, is to exclude irrelevant and prejudicial evidence. These rules prevent attorneys from introducing unreliable evidence that would mislead and confuse a jury of laypersons.

A major rule for excluding evidence is called "privilege" or "privileged communication." **Privilege** allows a witness to refuse to testify. It also allows a person to prevent a witness from testifying. Privilege is based on the idea that certain communications should be confidential and that the public interest is served by protecting such communications.

Perhaps the best-known privilege is communication between an attorney and a client. The **attorney-client privilege** allows the client to prevent the attorney from testifying concerning matters that the client told the attorney in confidence while seeking legal advice. The rationale of this privilege is to encourage clients to communicate freely with attorneys without fear that their words can later be used against them. Only the client may waive the privilege.

Other categories of privilege are:

1. *Medical treatment privilege*—protects information that the patient gives the physician.

2. *Spousal privilege*—protects confidential communications between husband and wife.

3. *Priests' (clergy's) penitent privilege*—protects confidential communications between an individual and his or her religious adviser.

4. *Privilege against self-incrimination*—the privilege that the Fifth Amendment grants witnesses in criminal trials who refuse to answer questions that may tend to incriminate them (to show their guilt).[18]

Motion for a Directed Verdict

After the plaintiff's attorney has called all of the witnesses and presented all of the physical evidence for the plaintiff's side, the defendant's attorney frequently makes a motion for a **directed verdict.** By this motion the attorney is contending that the plaintiff has failed to prove his or her case. This means that the evidence presented is so inadequate that a reasonable person could not decide the case for the plaintiff. If the motion for a directed verdict is granted, the judge orders a judgment for the defendant and this concludes the trial. If such a motion is granted, the plaintiff ordinarily appeals. Motions for directed verdicts are usually not granted because the plaintiff's evidence is usually not defective enough to warrant granting them.

At the conclusion of the plaintiff's case, counsel for the defendant presents the defendant's witnesses and physical evidence. When the presentation of the defendant's case has been completed, both parties may make motions for directed verdicts, each party claiming that its evidence is so clear and convincing that a reasonable person could not possibly find for the other side.

Directed verdict
a verdict that the judge tells the jury to render

Closing Arguments

After both parties have finished submitting evidence, the attorneys make closing arguments. Ordinarily, the party with the burden of proof opens the argument and closes it. Typically, attorneys emphasize their evidence and discredit the evidence of the other party and draw a conclusion for the jury.

Jury Instructions

For jury trials, after the closing arguments the judge instructs the jury about the law it is to apply when it retires for deliberation. Typically, the judge tells the jury that its duty is to determine the facts of the case (what actually took place), to apply the rules of law (as given in the **instructions**) to the facts, and to reach a verdict. For example, the judge may tell the jury:

Instructions
the directions that the judge gives the jury about the rules of law it is to apply to the facts of the case

> A corporation under the law is a person, but it can only act through its employees, agents, directors, or officers. The law therefore holds a corporation responsible for the acts of its employees, agents, directors, and officers if, but only if, those acts are authorized. An act is authorized if it is a part of the ordinary course of employment of the person doing it. Whether a particular act was authorized is a question that you must decide on the evidence.
>
> The fact that a plaintiff or a defendant is a corporation should not affect your decision. All persons are equal before the law, and a corporation, whether large or small, is entitled to the same fair and conscientious consideration from you as any other person.

Attorneys usually submit written proposals for instructions to the court. The judge then decides which of the proposed instructions to include in the charge to the jury. A judge's refusal to include a proposed instruction may be the basis for an appeal by the losing party.

Verdict

After receiving the instructions, the jury retires for deliberations and then returns a verdict. The **verdict** is the jury's decision. In civil cases verdicts are ordinarily reached by a unanimous decision, though in some cases they may be reached by three-fourth's of the jurors.[19] For nearly all criminal cases, verdicts must be unanimous.

In civil cases the jury does not determine guilt or innocence. In such cases it assigns fault and fixes the amount of damages. For example, the jury may determine that the defendant breached the contract and was therefore at fault and that the defendant is liable to the plaintiff for $50,000 in damages. In criminal cases juries return a verdict of "guilty" or "not guilty."[20] The steps in a jury trial are shown in Figure 4-10.

FIGURE 4-10   **Example of a Typical Jury Trial**

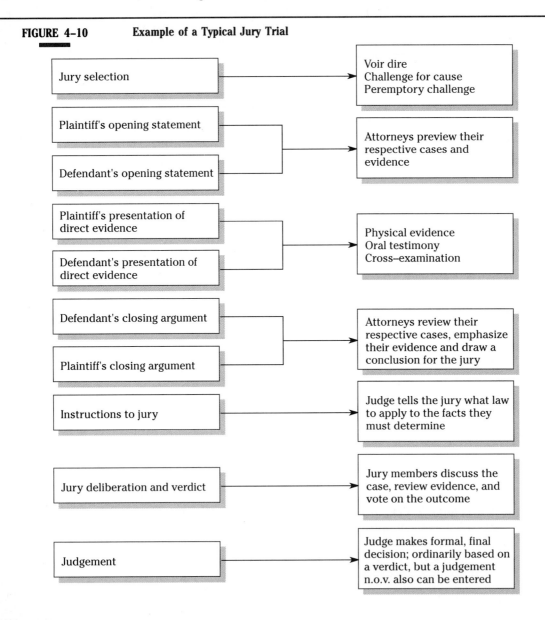

Example of a Judgment   **FIGURE 4–11**

THE SUPERIOR COURT OF
IDEAL COUNTY
STATE OF UTOPIA

CIVIL ACTION NO. 1-77804

James A. Smith
Plaintiff

v.

Brown Wholesalers, Inc.
Defendant

JUDGMENT

This action having been before the court and jury, and the jury having rendered its verdict for the defendant and against the plaintiff on plaintiff's claim and for the defendant and against the plaintiff on defendant's counterclaim:

It is ordered and adjudged that the plaintiff take nothing and the defendant recover of plaintiff on said counterclaim the sum of $30,000, together with interest and the costs of this action.

This 31st day of January, 1992.

s/s *Laura A. Phillips*
Laura A. Phillips
Judge, Superior Court of
Ideal County, Utopia

Postverdict Proceedings

After the jury has returned the verdict, the court may enter a judgment in the records that conforms with the verdict. A **judgment** is the formal, final decision that a trial court gives when a dispute in that court has terminated (see Figure 4–11 for an example). In a jury trial the judgment is ordinarily based on the verdict. The court, however, has control over verdicts and judgments.

It is possible for the court to disregard the verdict and enter a judgment in favor of the losing party. The court may act on its own initiative or on a motion of the losing party, called a motion for **judgment notwithstanding the verdict** or "judgment n.o.v." The standard for granting a motion for judgment n.o.v. is the same as the standard for granting a motion for a directed verdict—the evidence is such that a reasonable person could reach only a verdict in favor of the opposite party. The motion is rarely granted. The party against whom it is granted will almost certainly appeal to a higher court.

The court may also grant a new trial on its own initiative or on a motion of the losing party. Typical grounds for granting a new trial are insufficiency of the evidence, erroneous rulings on instructions, newly discovered evidence, and a

Judgment
the official decision that a trial court gives when a dispute in that court has terminated

Judgment notwithstanding the verdict
a judgment that the court, disregarding the verdict, enters in favor of the losing party

verdict contrary to the instructions. The granting of a new trial occurs only occasionally.

The court also has the power to alter the damages awarded by the jury. At his or her discretion the judge may decide that they are excessive or insufficient and order their reduction to a specified lower amount or their increase to a specified higher amount.

APPELLATE PROCEEDINGS

As previously noted, unlike general trial courts, appellate courts do not "retry" cases. This means that at the appellate level no new evidence may be introduced and there is no right to a trial by jury. The sole duty of appellate courts is to review cases for errors of law in the rulings of the trial court. Typical examples of such erroneous rulings are situations in which the trial judge (1) incorrectly excluded or admitted evidence, (2) improperly stated the instructions to the jury, or (3) incorrectly interpreted state or federal law.

The appellate court bases its decision on its review of the written record of the trial court, along with the written arguments (briefs) and the oral arguments of opposing counsel on mistakes of law. The decision is rendered in the form of a written opinion. If the appellate court concludes that no error of law occurred, it will **affirm** (sustain) the judgment of the trial court. If it concludes that an error of law occurred that was of sufficient magnitude to affect the outcome of the trial, it will **reverse** the judgment of the trial court. In reversing, it will apply the correct rule of law and enter its own judgment. A more common decision of the appellate court that finds an error of law is to **reverse and remand,** which means to send the case back to the trial court for a new trial.

Affirm

the outcome of an appeal in which the higher court sustains the lower court's judgment

Reverse

the outcome of an appeal in which the higher court sets aside the lower court's judgment and enters its own

Reverse and remand

the outcome of an appeal in which the higher court sets aside the lower court's judgment and sends the case back for a new trial

ENFORCEMENT OF JUDGMENTS

A judgment remains a claim against a defendant for the period of time set by state statute, usually 10 to 20 years. In past centuries, a creditor could place a debtor in jail for not paying his or her debts. Imprisonment for debt has been abolished, so that today many debtors are "judgment-proof." If the defendant has no regular job and no property from which the judgment may be satisfied, the judgment may be a barren victory. Thus, before plaintiffs file suit, it is important for them to consider the defendant's financial standing.

After the court has entered a judgment, the losing party (defendant) generally complies with the terms of the judgment. If the defendant refuses to pay, however, since the judgment is not self-enforcing, the plaintiff may enlist the aid of the court to execute (carry out) the judgment. If the judgment is for the payment of a sum of money, the plaintiff's attorney files a request with the clerk of court to issue an instrument.

Writ of execution

a judge's order directing the sheriff to seize enough of the defendant's nonexempt property to satisfy a judgment

Generally, the clerk of court is requested to issue either a writ of execution or a writ of garnishment. A **writ of execution** directs the sheriff to seize enough of the defendant's nonexempt real and personal property to satisfy the judgment and to sell the property at a public auction. (In each state exemption laws provide that certain property is exempt from levy of execution.) The judgment debtor may be questioned under oath in open court to discover assets.

Garnishment is a method by which, under court order, the plaintiff can reach the defendant's wages, bank accounts, or accounts receivable. A federal law limits the amount of wages subject to garnishment to 25 percent of net income, and the limit set by state statutes may be a lesser amount. Garnishment is not a satisfactory method of settling a claim, because the amount collected from wages is small. In addition, after a garnishment has been issued, the debtor often quits his or her job and moves without leaving a forwarding address, thereby making the garnishment unenforceable. Garnishments are discussed in more detail in Chapter 15. The stages of a typical lawsuit are shown in Figure 4-12.

Garnishment
a judge's order that allows the plaintiff to satisfy a judgment by reaching the defendant's wages, bank accounts, or accounts receivable

LAW ABROAD

European Community

Disputes between member states of the European Community (EC) are adjudicated by the Court of Justice of the European Community. The court, seated in Luxembourg, has 13 judges, each of whom is chosen by the member states acting in concert. It was established in 1952 as part of the European Coal and Steel Community, and its functions were enlarged in 1957, when the EC was created.

The court's principal function is to interpret and apply the constitution and the legislative enactments of the EC. Private individuals and businesses may bring some cases before it. National courts may ask it for assistance in interpreting laws of the EC. The court's authority to interpret the laws of the EC and to adjudicate disputes between member states was conferred on it by the member states upon the creation of the EC.

Germany

Although the German legal system includes both federal and state courts, Germany does not have two separate systems of courts. A case begins in a state trial court, and then it may be appealed to an intermediate state appellate court. However, the court of final appeal is a federal court.

Germany's single court system includes special courts whose jurisdiction is confined to particular subjects. Among these subjects are labor relations, taxes, constitutional matters, civil matters, and criminal matters. At the lowest level are the numerous local courts, called *Amtgerichte,* which are located in both small towns and large cities. The Amtgericht are the equivalent of U.S. municipal courts. Their jurisdiction in civil cases is limited to disputes in which the amount at issue does not exceed 5,000 deutschemarks. These courts may consist of one judge or a judge and two laypersons sitting as judges.

The next higher courts, the district courts, called *Landgerichte,* are fewer in number. These courts can act as appeals courts for the local courts. However, the district courts more commonly act as courts of original jurisdiction for civil litigation as, for example, cases in which the amount at issue exceeds 5,000 deutschemarks. Depending upon the type of case, the district courts may consist of three judges or of one judge and two businesspersons acting as assistant judges. However, three professional judges are assigned to cases involving important factual or legal difficulties.

FIGURE 4–12   **Example of a Typical Lawsuit**

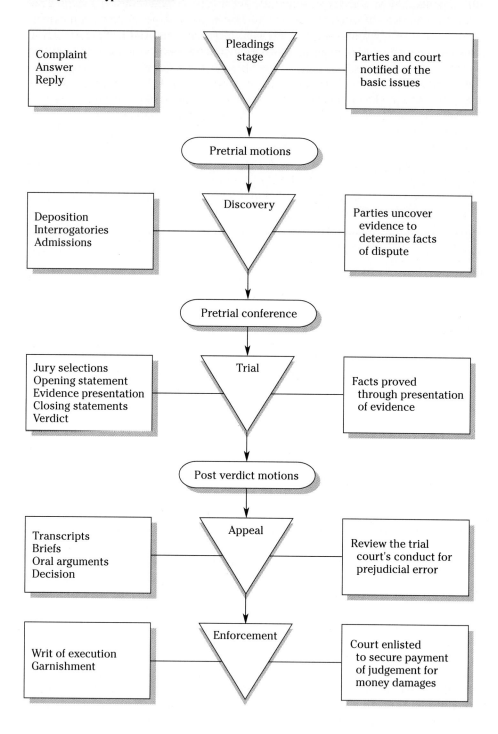

Appeals from the Landgerichte are taken to the *Oberlandesgerichte,* the courts of appeals. These courts, generally located in the largest cities, act as "circuit courts" for the district courts. A court of appeals sits in three- to five-judge panels called "senates"; each senate is headed by a "president." The overall head of the courts of appeals is the "chairman." A crucial difference between American courts of appeals and German courts of appeals is that the German courts of appeals allow new evidence and testimony to be introduced and make new findings of fact. Thus they take appeals on both questions of fact and questions of law.

The highest court is the *Bundesgerichtshot,* the federal supreme court. Like the courts of appeals, it utilizes "senates," including civil senates, criminal senates, an antitrust senate, and senates that handle various other matters. Each senate has five judges. The Bundesgerichtshot, like the Oberlandesgerichte, is empowered to take appeals on both questions of law and questions of fact. As with the U.S. Supreme Court, parties wishing to appear before the Bundesgerichtshot usually have a long wait before their case is heard and decided.

Unlike the U.S. legal system, the German legal system embodies the principle of free admissibility of evidence in both civil and criminal cases. Any evidence is admissible, with the court deciding how much weight to give it. The judge controls the examination of witnesses, asking questions to elicit testimony. The attorneys may then request permission to ask supplementary questions.

Japan

The Japanese judicial system closely resembles the state court systems in the United States. It consists of summary courts, family courts, district courts, high courts and the supreme court. Unlike the United States, Japan has no local or special courts. All of the Japanese courts are called *saibansho,* which means the place where justice is administered.

The summary courts handle civil cases in which the amount in controversy is less than 900,000 yen and criminal cases in which the maximum punishment is less than three years in prison. Appeals from the summary courts concerning civil matters are heard by the district courts; criminal appeals go directly to the high courts.

There are 409 judicial districts, and the usual court of original jurisdiction is the district court. District court cases are generally heard by just one judge. The legal system of Japan does not provide for juries. The district courts have civil and criminal jurisdiction over most civil and criminal cases.

Appeals from district court decisions are made to the high courts, which act as circuit courts of appeals. Cases before these courts are heard by three judges. Commercial cases may be appealed on the basis of error of law or error of fact. For many cases the decision of the high court is final. Appeals from the high courts go to the supreme court (*saiko saibansho*). This court, which sits in Tokyo, has a chief justice and 14 justices. It can sit with all its members in what is called a "grand bench," or it may break off into panels that each consist of five justices.

The appointments to Japan's supreme court differ significantly from the appointments to the U.S. Supreme Court. By law 10 of the justices on Japan's supreme court have to be attorneys, judges, or law professors; the remaining 5 may simply have "broad vision and legal knowledge." The rationale is that these members will broaden the perspective of the court on the important social issues that come before it.

The rules of jurisdiction are contained in the Japanese Code of Civil Procedure. The basic rules are that a lawsuit is brought (1) in the place where the defendant lives, (2) in the place where the property is located for lawsuits involving property, (3) in the place where the tort occurred for tort actions, (4) in the place where business is conducted for lawsuits in which a company is the defendant, or (5) in the place where the defendant has attachable property. The last option may apply to a foreigner with no residence in Japan even if the value of the attachable property is quite small in relation to the amount sued for and is not directly related to the lawsuit.

Creditors can attach a debtor's property in a hearing without giving notice to the debtor.

Pretrial procedure in Japan is quite different from that of the United States. There is no discovery process, which, of course, eliminates interrogatories and depositions.

The scheduling of trials in Japan is strikingly different from the scheduling of trials in the United States. The trial days are not scheduled consecutively. In Japan, after the first day of a trial has been held, the second day is scheduled about a month later; the third day is scheduled about a month after the second day; and so forth. The purpose of this procedure is to encourage the parties to settle their dispute.

In the United States the opposing attorneys control what takes place at a trial. In Japan the judge controls much of what takes place. The judge decides which witnesses will be called and what questions are to be directed to them. Frequently, the judge exercises his or her influence to obtain a compromise between the parties.

There is much less litigation in Japan than in the United States. In 1986 the number of civil cases in Japan was 340,000, only about 30 cases per 10,000 persons. Japan averages about 400,000 traffic accidents per year. However, because of the extensive use of no-fault compensation and the encouragement of alternate dispute resolution, only 5,000 of these accidents go to trial.

REVIEW QUESTIONS & PROBLEMS

1. What important function is served by pleadings?

2. What generally happens if a defendant does not respond to a complaint within 30 days?

3. What discovery device would a party in a lawsuit use in attempting to view the sales receipts in possession of the other party?

4. The plaintiff was a famous singer and actress who lived and worked in California. An article on her private life appeared in the *National Enquirer,* a national weekly newspaper that was sold in grocery stores and other retail outlets. The plaintiff brought suit for libel in California against the author of the article and the editor of the newspaper, both of whom were residents of Florida, in which the corporation that published the newspaper was located. The newspaper had its largest circulation in California. The defendants moved to quash the service of process for lack of personal jurisdiction. The superior court in California granted the motion, and the plaintiff appealed to the U.S. Supreme Court. Should the Supreme Court reverse? Why?

5. Two residents of Indiana collided in an auto accident in Indiana. One of them, the plaintiff, moved to Minnesota and decided to sue the defendant in a Minnesota state court. Since the cause of action arose in Indiana and the defendant resided in Indiana, the plaintiff had to establish that the defendant had "minimum contacts" with Minnesota. The plaintiff persuaded the Minnesota court to grant jurisdiction on the basis that the defendant's insurance company, which was obligated to act for the defendant in the case, did business in Minnesota and had the requisite contacts. The case was appealed and reached the U.S. Supreme Court. How should the Supreme Court rule? Why?

6. Bob paid Sam $10,000 for a car that Sam said was a 1988 Oldsmobile. After driving the car for a few days, Bob visited his friend Charlie, an automobile mechanic. Charlie told Bob that he liked the car but that it was a 1987 Oldsmobile. Bob brought a lawsuit to recover damages from Sam for fraud. The sheriff was unable to locate Sam and thus could not deliver the service of process papers to him. Bob published a notice of the lawsuit in the newspaper of the town in which Sam formerly lived and obtained a judgment against him. Is Bob's judgment valid? Why? Assuming that the judgment is valid and that Sam refuses to pay, what methods could be used to enforce the judgment?

ENDNOTES

1. Cal. Const., Art. 6, fl.
2. In many states, including New York, the probate courts are called "surrogate courts."
3. A large or densely populated county is often designated as one district.
4. Only about 5 percent of judgments are appealed.
5. Article III, Section 1 of the Constitution states: "The judicial Power of the United States, shall be vested in one supreme Court, and in such inferior Courts as the Congress may from time to time ordain and establish." In the Judiciary Act of 1789, the First Congress created a system of federal courts inferior to the U.S. Supreme Court.
6. Federal questions can be raised in a state court and decided by the state court. The federal question can ultimately be appealed from the state court system to the U.S. Supreme Court.
7. Also under the jurisdiction of the federal courts are cases involving ambassadors, ministers, and consuls; admiralty and maritime cases; and cases in which the United States is a party (such as a case in which a citizen sues a federal agency).
8. In a case filed in a state court involving parties of diverse citizenship, a nonresident defendant can remove the case to a federal court provided he or she acts within 30 days from the date of the filing of the complaint in the state court.
9. 326 U.S. 310 (1945).
10. A tort is a private wrong for which the law allows a remedy in an action for damages.
11. The governer of the requesting state submits documents to the governor of the forum state that (1) officially charge the defendant with a crime (the documents include a copy of an indictment or an affidavit in which this charge is made before a magistrate) (2) indicate probable cause that the defendant was in the requesting state when the crime was committed, and (3) indicate that the defendant is in the forum state.
12. The Fifth Amendment provides: "No person shall . . . be deprived of life, liberty or property, without due process of law." The 14th Amendment provides: "nor shall any State deprive any person of life, liberty, or property, without due process of law."

13. Nuisance is the use of property in a way that harms or annoys neighbors.

14. Examples of a summons, answer, interrogatory, answer to an interrogatory, pretrial order, and judgment are provided on the following pages. The examples are based on the contract illustrated in Figure 8-1 in Chapter 8.

15. Other examples of affirmative defenses are a discharge in bankruptcy, fraud, illegality, waiver, the statute of limitations, and the statute of frauds. These defenses are discussed in subsequent chapters.

16. The Seventh Amendment to the Constitution guarantees the right to jury trials in federal civil cases; the Sixth Amendment guarantees the right to jury trials in criminal cases. State constitutions and state laws also guarantee the right to trial by jury.

17. In reviewing the history of the jury trial, the Supreme Court concluded that "the fact that the Jury at Common Law was composed of precisely twelve is a historical accident . . . and wholly without significance except to mystics." *William v. Florida,* 399 U.S. 78 (1970).

18. The Fifth Amendment provides that "no person . . . shall be compelled in any criminal case to be a witness against himself." The Fifth Amendment is more fully discussed in Chapter 10.

19. More than one half of the states have adopted the less than unanimous verdict in civil cases. However, unanimity of the jury is required in federal trials.

20. In approximately 5 percent of all cases, the jury is unable to reach a verdict. This situation is referred to as a "hung jury." The plaintiff or the prosecution must decide whether to retry such cases.

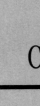

CHAPTER

5

Alternate Dispute Resolution

Lengthy delays in the processing of lawsuits, time-consuming court procedures, the costs of attorney's services, a general lack of knowledge by judges and jurors about complex technology and complicated business arrangements, the growing volume of transnational business transactions, and a widespread insistence on quick resolution of controversies are among the reasons why an ever larger number of disputes are being resolved by means other than a lawsuit. Ordinarily, even after a lawsuit has been initiated, the parties seek to bring it to a close before trial.

The view of many disputants that their controversies should, if possible, be settled "away from courts and trials," has spread to the judiciary and legislative bodies. For years judges have been seeking mechanisms that would allow the parties to lawsuits to bring them to a speedy end. The judicial quest for alternative means of resolving disputes is perhaps best illustrated by the fact that as a result of court decisions many types of controversies that could formerly be resolved only by a court can now be resolved outside the court system. Legislators have also sought to lessen the use of courts. Over a span of many decades, Congress and state legislatures have designed and enacted statutes promoting the use of devices other than a lawsuit to resolve disputes.

This chapter considers negotiation, mediation, and arbitration, the most frequently used alternatives to court proceedings. It also examines less frequently used yet at times highly effective alternatives.

Hypothetical Case

LET'S TALK, LISTEN, AND SETTLE IN

The construction contract between Walt Corp. and Ivid Inc. called for Walt to erect a three-story addition to Ivid's plant for $5.5 million. This amount was to be paid in five equal installments at progress points specified in the contract. Six months after construction began, Ivid received a bill for $1.1 million from Walt. Payment was refused on the ground that Walt had not completed the work as called for by the contract.

Tyne, Walt's president, telephoned Leigh, Ivid's chief financial officer. He asked her whether there was some way to resolve the matter. Leigh replied: "Yes, you do what you promised." Tyne said: "We have. Let's talk."

After a brief discussion, the two agreed on but one thing: that a lawsuit should be avoided at all costs. Leigh suggested that Fair, a builder, who was extremely knowledgeable about all aspects of the construction industry, arbitrate the controversy.

If Walt and Ivid agreed to ask Fair to arbitrate their dispute, would it be ethical for Fair to do so without informing them that within the prior two years, unknown to either Tyne or Leigh, Fair was personally involved in five disputes in which he believed that he had met the contact specifications and in each instance the jury returned a verdict against him? Why? Is Fair legally obliged to recuse himself? Discuss.

The Negotiation Process

Ordinarily, the parties to a dispute settle it themselves. Perhaps they realize on reflection that the source of their dispute is an emotional overreaction to a matter of little or no substance. Even if their dispute does concern something of importance, they may still be able to resolve it by **negotiation,** that is, by personally engaging in a give-and-take process or by having others engage in such a process on their behalf.

Negotiation

a give-and-take process in which the parties themselves settle their dispute

Negotiation is a viable means of dispute resolution so long as both parties stand to benefit from the outcome. To increase the likelihood that the negotiation process will succeed, before initiating negotiations, the parties should gather as much information on their dispute as they can. They should also identify their minimum needs and their nonnegotiable demands. As they haggle, it is likely to become clear to both of them that if their dispute is to be resolved by negotiation, they will probably have to forgo one or more of their initial demands. Unless both of them stand to gain from the proposed resolution of the dispute, they will probably fail to reach a negotiated settlement.

When negotiation leads to a settlement, the parties to a dispute avoid the costs, expenditure of time, and delay that would have confronted them if they had resorted to litigation. Having achieved the settlement themselves, they are likely to be more satisfied with it than they would have been with a court-imposed outcome.

To lock in their agreement, they should put it in writing. This reduces the possibility of a dispute over its terms and may also prove useful if they later resort to litigation. If the parties are again at odds and negotiation proves unsuccessful, the dissatisfied party may bring a lawsuit on the basis of the negotiated agreement if that agreement satisfies the requirements of an enforceable contract.[1] If the agreement lacks the elements of an enforceable contract, then a court will determine the rights and duties of the parties without reference to the negotiated settlement.

Obstacles to Successful Negotiation

Despite the advantages of negotiation as compared to a lawsuit, it is not free of defects. Lack of structure and informality do not assure a just result. One party may be better informed than the other about the issues of the dispute or may be a more clever negotiator. The mental set of the parties to the negotiation may differ. If one party is determined to do whatever must be done to win, even resorting to unethical, deceptive, or intimidating tactics, and the other party is eager to cooperate and willing to surrender significant personal needs so as to speedily resolve the dispute, the compromise reached may be unfair.

Litigation as a Viable Alternative

Judges and juries are likely to shield individuals from their personal incompetence as negotiators and to guard them from undue advantage that may be taken of them by an unethical opponent or by an opponent who is an especially skillful bargainer. However, recourse to litigation does not guarantee an outcome uninfluenced by factors that are unrelated to the merits of the parties' claims. Inequality of wealth, for instance, may affect the outcome of litigation. A richer litigant can more easily afford to pay large amounts of money for the counsel fees and other costs that are ordinarily incurred in a lengthy, hotly contested, and hard-fought lawsuit. If both parties to a case are far from equally able to bear such costs, the result reached by a court may be far different than it would be if both parties were equally able to bear them.

MEDIATION

Another informal way to settle disputes, but one markedly different from negotiation, is **mediation.** Like negotiation, mediation does not use rigid procedures or apply legal principles. Unlike negotiation, it involves the active participation of a third party, a "mediator," selected and paid by the parties themselves. The mediator cannot impose a binding settlement on the disputants, but can assist them in reaching a compromise.

Mediation
use of a third party's help
to resolve a dispute

An effective mediator may persuade the parties to accept a solution that they might not have arrived at on their own. Successful mediation spares the parties the delays, costs, expenditure of time and effort, and annoyances that are part and parcel of a lawsuit.

Essential Mediator Qualifications

An ideal mediator has the talents of a highly skilled manager, is perceived as neutral and fair, is trusted by the parties to the dispute and capable of working effectively with them, is knowledgeable about the subjects of the dispute, and can be depended on to identify the areas of disagreement, to gather and evaluate pertinent information, to inform the disputants of the strengths and weaknesses of their respective claims, and to propose practical solutions. The disputants feel comfortable about sharing with him or her their points of view, aspirations, evidence, and concerns and even the flaws in their positions. As would be expected, they believe that the mediator will not disclose information revealed in confidence.

Mediation Process

To become acquainted with the parties' views of the facts, their actual objectives, and the compromises that they would seriously consider, a mediator must ordinarily speak privately with each of them. There may be information that neither party wants to disclose to the other, but that must be disclosed to the mediator if mediation is to be successful. For example, one party may refuse to tell the other party the rock-bottom amount of money that she would accept but is willing to share this information with the mediator. She tells the mediator that she would settle for $50,000, even though she has repeatedly told the other party that she would reject any amount under $100,000. She has insisted on this amount because of the other party's insistence that he will not pay more than $1,000 for what he characterizes as a "despicable and worthless claim." With the $50,000 amount in mind, the mediator will in private ask the other party what maximum amount he is willing to pay, and he states that $50,000 is as far as he would go. Now the mediator is ready to bring both parties together and suggest a $50,000 settlement. The two may at first insist that the proposed amount is out of the question, but once their initial posturing is over, they are likely to agree with the mediator's recommendation. After all, this is the outcome that both of them actually sought. In this instance negotiation would probably have failed to achieve a solution because the parties were unwilling to share with each other just how far they would go to resolve their dispute.

This scenario is of course a simplification of how mediation usually operates. In most instances it is likely to be far more cumbersome. There may be numerous private exchanges between the mediator and the parties. Perhaps the parties never divulge their actual intentions. There may be sessions at which both parties simply restate their positions. Although the parties agreed to mediation, they may refuse to cooperate with the mediator and each of them may be determined to end the dispute only on his or her own terms. Inequality between the parties in their financial or psychic ability to wage a lawsuit may encourage the more affluent or aggressive party to reject a reasonable solution proposed by the mediator. A mediator's recommendation that seems appropriate in light of what the parties have said during the mediation process may be rejected because it is at odds with their real goals.

Despite the mediator's efforts, it may become clear that the dispute cannot be resolved by mediation unless the parties change their attitudes. At this point the mediator should advise them that he or she believes a solution is beyond reach and should recommend that the mediation process be closed. This may trigger a shift in the parties' positions and open the door to a settlement. If not, some other means must be found to resolve the dispute.

The Mediator's Integrity

A mediator who agrees to assist the parties to a dispute should not relinquish his or her integrity. For instance, if the parties insist on an arrangement that conflicts with the mediator's ethical concerns, or is against public policy, or is a crime, the mediator should resign from any further participation in the mediation process.

The mediator's resignation need not end the parties' attempt to deal with their differences informally. Now that each of them knows where the other stands and they are in apparent agreement on how to settle their dispute, successful negotiation is likely to follow. Of course, if they arrive at an agreement that is unethical, against public policy, or illegal, they may later become defendants in a civil lawsuit or a criminal proceding.

Mediation within the Context of a Lawsuit

Lawyers as Mediators

When mediation fails, a lawsuit may follow. But this need not bring mediation to an end. Once the parties find themselves in the midst of what could be a costly and protracted lawsuit, they may recognize the wisdom of modifying their demands, realistically evaluating proposals for the resolution of their dispute, and carefully considering the likely consequences of their failure to reach a compromise.

The parties' lawyers, who, before the lawsuit began, probably sought to have their clients reach a negotiated settlement, may now assume a role somewhat akin to that of a mediator. Initiation of the lawsuit probably impelled them to further scrutinize the merits of their clients' claims so that they would be able to prepare a complaint or draft an answer and to proceed with the other steps in the litigation process. Thus the lawyers for both parties are probably now in an excellent position to suggest highly attractive ways to resolve the dispute. Moreover, their clients may now be more willing to compromise. The lawyers may therefore be able to convince them of the advisability of considering proposed solutions, to show them the shortcomings of their claims, to explain the strengths of the other party's position, to alert them to the pitfalls they face by allowing the court to rule on their dispute, and to help them to appreciate the benefits of a sensible settlement. On the eve of trial, the litigants and their lawyers must come to grips with the risk of defeat at the hands of the court.

Judges as Mediators

At various times during a lawsuit, judges act as mediators. In many jurisdictions the lawyers for both sides discuss their case before a judge long before the trial is scheduled to begin. At this pretrial hearing the judge explores with the lawyers the possibility of an out-of-court settlement. He or she seeks to determine the extent of the parties' differences, solicits the lawyers' views on how the clients might bring the lawsuit to a close by modifying their positions, offers suggestions on how the case might be settled, and urges the lawyers to prod their clients to come to terms with each other. A diligent and talented judge is sometimes able to hammer out a settlement by working with the clients' lawyers in this way. If not, the parties must await the next step in the lawsuit.

Ordinarily, the judge before whom a case is about to be tried will ask the lawyers whether their clients can reach a settlement. If the lawyers indicate that this could happen, the judge and the lawyers will probably develop possible solutions that the lawyers then present to their clients. Should the lawyer for only one party indicate a readiness to explore the possibility of having his or her client consent to a proposal for avoiding a trial, the judge may suggest to the lawyer for the other party that his or her client be advised of the advantages of not proceed-to trial and of the possible effects of an unfavorable court decision. Some judges, when informed by the laywers for both parties that a compromise is not possible, suggest that they be sure that their clients understand what will confront them if they fail at trial. Even at this late stage, a judge with the skills of a masterly mediator may persuade the parties to reach agreement rather than go to trial. If they do, their agreement may be entered into the **court record,** which reports whatever has occurred during a proceeding, or the trial may be adjourned so that their lawyers can prepare a **stipulation of settlement.** This written statement contains the terms of the agreement. It is signed by the lawyers, at times by the parties themselves, and occasionally, by the judge too. Whether the agreement is entered into the court record or appears in a stipulation of settlement, it is likely to include a provision that a judgment may be entered against the party who fails to abide by its terms. Should such a default occur, the party in compliance with the terms of the agreement is authorized to have a judgment entered in his or her favor against the other party. The judgment is in the same form and has the same effect as a judgment entered after a trial.

Court record
written account of court proceeding

Stipulation of settlement
written statement of a compromise agreement

ARBITRATION

Arbitration
resolution of a dispute by a third party

Like negotiation and mediation, **arbitration** is a consensual arrangement. The fundamental difference between arbitration and the other two alternatives to litigation is that in arbitration the parties have *no* say about the outcome. An "arbitrator" (a single person) or an "arbitration panel" (usually composed of three persons), like a court, hears what the parties and their witnesses have to say and has the final word as to the parties' rights and duties. Because arbitration resembles a lawsuit in some ways, it is often called a "quasi-judicial proceeding."

To resolve one or more disputes by arbitration, the parties must enter into an **arbitration contract** (a binding agreement in which they promise to forgo court action to resolve a particular dispute or any disputes that arise between them) or an **arbitration clause** (a provision in a contract concerning a specific arrangement, perhaps the purchase of equipment or the construction of a building). This clause states that the parties to the contract in which it appears will refrain from bringing a lawsuit against each other should a dispute over that contract arise between them.

Arbitration contract
an agreement to resolve disputes by arbitration

Arbitration clause
a contract provision that calls for arbitration of disputes arising under the contract

Evolution of Arbitration

At one time courts refused to recognize arbitration as a valid means of resolving a dispute. They condemned arbitration as a wrongful intrusion on their exclusive power to resolve controversies. By the beginning of the 20th century, numerous state courts had abandoned the idea that they alone could impose a binding decision on disputants. They treated an arbitration contract or an arbitration clause in the same way as they treated any other contractual obligation. In some states the unenforceability of arbitration agreements was ended through a statute that made such agreements binding so long as they satisfied the provisions of the statute. In 1925 Congress adopted the U.S. Arbitration Act, commonly referred to as the Federal Arbitration Act. Thirty-two states and the District of Colulmbia have adopted the Uniform Arbitration Act, which was drafted in 1955.

Why Choose Arbitration?

For the same reasons that parties prefer to settle their disputes by negotiation or mediation rather than litigation, parties may adopt arbitration as their method for resolving their disputes. This may involve them in the selection of an arbitrator or an arbitration panel. Ordinarily, the person or persons they select to serve as arbitrators are well acquainted with the nature of the transaction in dispute and with related industry and business practices. This makes it highly likely that the decision reached by these persons will be more closely tied to the parties' expectancies and needs than the decisions of a court.

In reaching that decision, an arbitrator or an arbitration panel need not follow the substantive rules of law that a court would be obliged to invoke unless the arbitration agreement requires this to be done. The arbitrator or arbitration panel will probably reach a decision far more quickly and economically than would a court proceeding. In international transactions, uncertainty as to the nation in which a possible lawsuit between the parties will be brought and the consequent inability to anticipate the quirks in that nation's legal system are likely to make arbitration an extremely attractive alternative to litigation.

ENFORCEABILITY OF A SHOTGUN AGREEMENT TO ARBITRATE A DISPUTE

During a collective bargaining session between Tarr Company and the Federation of Clerks Union, Wilton, the union's representative, insisted that the union's contract with Tarr include a provision that a three-person arbitration panel would resolve any disputes that arose between Tarr and the union or a union member and that the union would select the three persons. Wilton told Mark, Tarr's representative, that there would be a strike if Tarr did not consent to the provision that the union select the three persons to serve as panel members. Fearful that a strike would seriously deplete Tarr's already strained financial resources, or even force the firm to go out of business, Tarr yielded.

Two months after Tarr and the union signed their collective bargaining agreement, Walker, one of Tarr's employees, charged that he had been wrongfully denied a promotion. Walker demanded that the dispute be resolved by arbitration. Tarr insisted that arbitration was unacceptable as long as the arbitration panel consisted of three persons named by the union. Tarr brought a lawsuit in which it asked the court to declare the arbitration provision unenforceable because Tarr had not freely agreed to allow the union to name the members of the arbitration panel and since the panel members were selected by the union, they probably would not treat Tarr fairly. The union's attorney insisted that Tarr was bound by the collective bargaining agreement. What judgment? Why? Would it be ethical for the three persons named in the agreement to serve as panel members? Discuss.

Hypothetical Case

Types of Arbitration

Commercial Arbitration

Arbitration of a business-related dispute is known as **commercial arbitration.** An agreement to arbitrate such a dispute may be in the form of an arbitration contract or an arbitration clause. In either case, the agreement to arbitrate is treated like any other contract. Details of the arbitration process, such as the number of arbitrators, the selection of the arbitrator, and the manner in which the arbitrator

Commercial arbitration
arbitration of a business-related dispute

is to perform his or her designated task, may be included in the arbitration agreement. However, the parties may simply say that arbitration is to be carried out according to the rules of a named body, such as the American Arbitration Association, the New York Stock Exchange, the American Stock Exchange, or the National Association of Securities Dealers. When this is done, the parties and the arbitrators are bound by those rules.

Labor Arbitration

Labor arbitration
arbitration of a dispute between an employer and a union or a union member

Arbitration intended to resolve a dispute between an employer and a union or a union member is called **labor arbitration.** A labor arbitration arrangement is entered into between a firm and the union that represents the firm's unionized employees. Generally, the arrangement is part of a collective bargaining agreement that governs many aspects of the employer-unionized employee relationship. Such an arrangement requires that any "grievance," that is, any dispute between a firm and a union member, be resolved by arbitration. Although the union members do not personally sign it, they are generally bound by the arrangement. For example, if such an arrangement is in effect, an employee who claims that the firm wrongfully refused to promote her ordinarily cannot have the matter decided by a court. At times, however, the employee right in question may be of such public importance that the employee is free, regardless of the arrangement, to have a court rule on the dispute. For instance, an employee who claims to have been discriminated against because of race or to have been paid less than the minimum wage established by federal law is not bound by the arbitration clause of a collective bargaining agreement. In such cases the employee may bring a lawsuit to resolve the dispute.

Compulsory Arbitration

Compulsory arbitration
arbitration required by a statute

Unlike commercial arbitration and labor arbitration, **compulsory arbitration,** as its name indicates, is involuntary. It is generally required by a statute establishing arbitration as the alternative to a strike that is likely to cause severe and widespread harm to the public. For example, state law may permit state employees to join a union, but may forbid a strike and require compulsory arbitration when the state and the union are unable to come to terms on particular economic issues.

The Arbitration Process

Commencement

All prearbitration procedures called for by a commercial or labor arbitration agreement must be satisfied before arbitration can begin. For example, an arbitration clause in a contract may provide that at least 10 days before filing a demand for arbitration, the claimant must ask the other party to carry out the terms of the agreement. In that case only if such a request has been made and then not satisfied may the arbitration process begin. The claimant usually initiates it by giving the other party notice that arbitration is demanded in accordance with the terms of the contract. Generally, the notice must state the nature of the dispute, the amount of money involved, and the relief sought.

If the arbitration arrangement names the person who will serve as arbitrator or the persons who will serve on the arbitration panel, that person or those persons must be informed of a party's demand for arbitration. If the arbitration arrangement calls for administering of the arbitration process by a third party, such as the American Arbitration Association, that party must be provided with a copy of both the demand for arbitration and the arbitration agreement and be paid the required fee for its services.

An arbitration agreement need not name the person who will serve as arbitrator, or the persons who will serve on an arbitration panel, or the third party that will administer the arbitration process. Instead, it may merely provide how the arbitrator or arbitration panel will be chosen. When the agreement provides that arbitration is to be conducted in accordance with the rules of a particular organization, then those rules are used to choose the arbitrator or the panel members.

Arbitrational Due Process

In addition to their contractual rights, the parties to an arbitration are entitled to **arbitrational due process.** Although this is not the same standard of fairness that a judicial proceeding assures litigants, it does prevent blatantly unfair treatment. Arbitrational due process requires that each party be given reasonable notice that the arbitration process has begun, be informed of the other party's claims, and be advised of the relief that is being sought. Each party must also be given a reasonable opportunity to offer evidence, to be present throughout the arbitration hearing, to cross-examine witnesses, to examine the other party's evidence, and to be represented by an attorney. In arriving at a decision, an arbitrator, like a judge, may take into account commonly known facts that neither party referred to during the hearing and may use his or her special knowledge on any of the subjects involved in the dispute. Unlike a judge, an arbitrator who needs information on some technical aspect of the proceeding may privately obtain it from experts without the parties' consent. An arbitrator who concludes that the parties have failed to present evidence sufficient for a decision may direct them to submit additional proof.

Generally, if a party who is informed of the time and place of a hearing chooses not to attend, the arbitrator or arbitration panel may still proceed as scheduled. In some states, however, a court order is required to authorize an **ex parte hearing,** that is, a hearing held in the presence of only one of the parties to a dispute. Unlike a mediator, an arbitrator may not communicate with only one of the parties about evidence that relates to the dispute. Each party must have an opportunity to hear, challenge, and rebut the other party's contentions and proof. Only when it is required by the arbitration agreement or a statute is it necessary that witnesses be sworn to tell the truth before they may testify. An arbitrator or arbitration panel is not required to abide by commonly used court procedures or rules of evidence. Except when required by the arbitration agreement, a record of the evidence need not be kept.

Statutes commonly authorize an arbitrator to issue a "subpoena," that is, a directive commanding a person to testify at an arbitration hearing, as well as a "*subpoena duces tecum,*" a directive commanding a person to testify and to bring designated proof, such as certain books and records. Both a subpoena and a *subpoena duces tecum* are enforceable in the same manner that they would have been if they had been issued in connection with a court proceeding.

An arbitrator should in both fact and appearance be impartial and disinterested with regard to the outcome of an arbitration proceeding. Anyone who has a

Arbitrational due process
the procedures that the law requires be used in arbitration

Ex parte hearing
a hearing at which one of the parties to a dispute offers evidence to the decision maker in the absence of the other party

personal stake in that outcome or who has a close blood or economic relationship with one of the parties is ineligible to serve as an arbitrator. As soon as possible, a person who is being considered or has been designated as an arbitrator should inform the parties of any circumstances that might give them cause to doubt his or her impartiality. A person unable to be neutral should recuse himself or herself from serving as an arbitrator. Although a contract may specify that each party is to choose one of three panel members, a party's choice is not supposed to be that party's advocate.

The Decision-Making Process

Arbitrators must personally decide the disputes that they have been authorized to decide. They are not empowered to go beyond their assigned tasks. For instance, an arbitration agreement may call for nothing more than a decision as to whether something did or did not occur. In an arbitration proceeding under that agreement, the arbitrator has no power to decide anything else.

When an agreement does not require an arbitrator to follow established legal principles, he or she is free to use broad principles of justice and equity to determine the parties' rights and duties.

Award

Award
an arbitrator's written
decision

An arbitrator's written decision is known as an **award.** If the arbitration agreement calls for a panel, all of the panelists must be present when the arbitration hearing begins and must take part in the preaward deliberations. Usually, their deliberations are not carried on in the parties' presence. Unless required by the arbitration agreement, neither the facts on which the award is based nor the standards used to determine the parties rights and duties need be disclosed. Unless the arbitration agreement requires unanimous approval, only a majority of a panel's membership need agree on the award. The award should be based on a reasonable interpretation of the evidence.

An award should clearly, precisely, and completely answer all of the questions submitted to the arbitrator. Its terms must be consistent with one another. If not barred from doing so by the arbitration contract, it may call for a remedy or remedies other than those requested by either of the parties.

The arbitrator must inform the parties of the award. If the arbitration agreement or arbitration statute does not require that this be done in a particular way, it may be done in any way that the arbitrator selects. When the parties have been informed of the award, the arbitrator's task is finished.

Judicial Involvement

Selection of Source of Legal Principles

If one of the parties to an arbitration agreement starts a lawsuit to resolve a dispute, the court in which the suit is brought must decide whether the law of the given state, the law of another state, federal law, or even the law of a foreign nation should be used to rule on whether the dispute is to be resolved through arbitration or through litigation.

If the arbitration agreement states the parties' preference as to the jurisdiction whose law should be followed, the court will respect their choice unless it concludes that this would lead to an unjust result. If the agreement makes no mention of jurisdiction, and all of the factors relating to the dispute are connected solely with the state in which the lawsuit has been initiated, the court will use local law to decide the effect of the arbitration agreement. If the arbitration agreement or significant features of the transaction in question have some connection with other states or nations, the court will use local law to decide which state's or nation's law should govern.[2] The court will also consider whether federal law is applicable.

Preaward Judicial Relief

Ordinarily, a court will not allow a party to continue with a lawsuit if there is an agreement calling for the resolution of the dispute through arbitration. In such a situation, a court will ordinarily order that the dispute be resolved through arbitration. Confronted with a party's request that arbitration not be allowed to proceed, a court may order a **temporary stay.** This directs that arbitration not take place for a stated period of time. At some point during this period, the parties can appear before the court to present their positions on what the court should do.

Temporary stay
a court order that bars specified behavior for a stated period of time

There are various reasons why arbitration should not take place. The prearbitration procedure may not have been completed, so that under the arbitration agreement the arbitrator is not yet authorized to proceed; state law requires a written arbitration agreement, but the one before the court is oral; the arbitration agreement is not enforceable because the party who objects to arbitration lacked capacity to enter into a contract; fraud was used to trick the objecting party to accept arbitration, so the arbitration contract is not binding on the parties; or the dispute is "not arbitrable," which means that it involves a matter that only a court can decide upon, such as racial discrimination.

After listening to both parties, the court may conclude that arbitration is appropriate and "vacate," that is, set aside the stay. If the court has been requested to do so, it will "specifically enforce" the arbitration agreement. This means that it orders the parties to arbitrate their dispute in accordance with the terms of their agreement. Should the court conclude that arbitration is inappropriate, it will grant a **permanent injunction**—bar the parties from ever resolving that particular dispute through arbitration.

Permanent injunction
a court directive that certain action never be taken

Postaward Judicial Remedies

Ordinarily, an arbitrator's award is final and binding on the parties. If they honor the award, the dispute is at an end. However, should one of the parties refuse to honor the award, the other party may enforce it through the legal system. This is done by filing a **petition to confirm the award** with the appropriate court. The petition asks the court to convert the award into a judgment. If the request is granted, a judgment is entered that entitles the successful party to the relief specified in the award. The judgment is enforceable in the same way as any other court judgment. A far less complicated process is available in those states that permit an arbitration agreement to provide for the conversion of an award into a judgment simply by filing a copy of the award with the clerk of a designated court.

Petition to confirm the award
request that a court act to make an arbitrator's award enforceable

The party dissatisfied with an award is confronted with the extremely limited power of a court to set it aside. Because the parties have agreed to arbitration, a court has no power to rehear the dispute, or substitute its judgment for that of the arbitrator or arbitration panel, or to act as an appellate body. It may not cancel an award merely because the arbitrator's or panel's determination is based on a standard that it would not have used or that it would have used to arrive at a different conclusion.

Despite the parties' agreement to resolve their dispute by arbitration and the failure of either party to object to arbitration, a court asked to confirm an award may generally consider and rule on such questions as the following: Does the arbitration agreement fulfill the requisites for an enforceable arbitration contract? Does the arbitration agreement violate public policy? Have the prearbitration procedures and the specified process for selecting an arbitrator or a panel been satisfied? Is the dispute arbitrable? Was there arbitrational due process? Did the arbitrator act within the authority conferred by the arbitration agreement? Is the award within the range of the results permitted by the arbitration agreement? Were the law's technical requirements observed?

A court may cancel an award if it finds that any of the answers to these questions unsatisfactory. In addition, a clearly unjust award, an award resulting from arbitrary action, or an award brought about through fraud or corruption will not be allowed to stand.

O.R. SECURITIES, INC. v. PROFESSIONAL PLANNING ASSOCIATES, INC.
U.S. COURT OF APPEALS, 11TH CIRCUIT
857 F.2d 742 (1988)

Under an agreement between WZW Financial Services, Inc. (WZW) and Professional Planning Associates, Inc. (PPA), 20 financial planners resigned from WZW and entered into the employ of a division of PPA. WZW and PPA were members of the National Association of Securities Dealers Inc. (NASD). NASD required its members to resolve disputes between them according to NASD arbitration rules. When a controversy arose between PPA and WZW as to the amount of commission that WZW rather than PPA owed the 20 planners, PPA initiated an NASD arbitration proceeding. Seven months later PPA amended its claim to include O.R. Securities, Inc. (O.R.), also an NASD member, as an additional party to the proceeding. O.R. asked the arbitration panel to dismiss PPA's claim against it. The panel did not expressly rule on this request, but at a hearing did consider the claims of the parties to the dispute. It issued an award in favor of PPA against O.R.

O.R. brought a proceeding in federal district court to vacate the award. It charged that the panel manifestly disregarded the law by making O.R. liable for WZW's obligations to PPA although it had no legal obligation to PPA. The court denied O.R.'s request. It appealed.

GONZALEZ, JUDGE
Delivered the Opinion of the Court

Courts are generally prohibited from vacating an arbitration award on the basis of errors of law or interpretation.

However, several courts have mentioned the proposition that a "manifest disregard of the law" by the arbitrators may warrant vacating the award.

The courts which have recognized the manifest disregard standard define it as necessarily meaning "more than error or misunderstanding with respect to law." [Under this standard,] [m]anifest disregard "may be found 'when arbitrators understand and correctly state the law, but proceed to disregard the same.'"

O.R. contends that the arbitrators exhibited a manifest disregard of the law when they held O.R. jointly and severally liable.

The arbitrators' decision fails to provide any explanation for their conclusion that O.R. is liable to PPA. It is well settled, however, that arbitrators are not required to explain their reasons for an award. O.R. argues that the arbitrators' silence, combined with their failure to rule on [its motion to dismiss], compels a finding that the panel ignored the law.

Contrary to O.R.'s arguments, "the absence of express reasoning by the arbitrators [does not] support the conclusion that they disregarded the law." In fact, when the arbitrators do not give their reasons, it is nearly impossible for the court to determine whether they acted in disregard of the law. "[T]o allow a court to conclude that it may substitute its own judgment for the arbitrator's whenever the arbitrator chooses not to explain the award would improperly subvert the proper functioning of the arbitral process."

If a court is to vacate an arbitration award on the basis of manifest disregard of the law, there must be some showing in the record, other than the result obtained, that the arbitrators knew the law and expressly disregarded it. We recognize that this would be extremely difficult where the arbitrators failed to state the reasons for their decision. However, we repeat that a party seeking to vacate an arbitration award on the ground of manifest disregard of the law may not proceed by merely objecting to the results of the arbitration. To do so would result in relitigation of the claim, in violation of the basic purpose of arbitration: a fast, inexpensive resolution of claims.

The record of the arbitration proceedings in this case shows that the issue of [O.R.'s] liability was clearly presented to the arbitrators and the arbitrators declined to state reasons for their conclusions. This ends the inquiry. O.R. cannot be permitted to relitigate the merits of its claim.

[T]he judgment of the district court is *affirmed.*

Legal Issues

1. Under the stance taken by the court in *O.R. Securities, Inc.,* how could a party establish that an arbitrator acted with manifest disregard of the law?
2. Must an arbitrator keep a record of the proceedings if the arbitration agreement makes no mention of the need to do so?

Ethical Issues

1. Is it ethical for an arbitrator who is well versed in the law of the state in which a dispute is arbitrated to follow the law of another state or a foreign nation because of his or her dissatisfaction with the outcome called for by local law? Why?
2. Is it ethical for an arbitrator not to reveal the standards that he or she used to arrive at an award? Would your answer be the same if an arbitrator did not disclose the standards that he or she used because they had recently been expressly rejected by the state's highest court? Discuss. Is it ethical for an arbitrator to use standards based on nothing more than his or her personal sense of right and wrong? Why?

UNIFORM ARBITRATION ACT

The Uniform Arbitration Act contains many of the already discussed principles of arbitration law. However, a number of its provisions invite attention. To be enforceable, the arbitration agreement must be in writing. A court may not stay arbitration on the ground that the party demanding arbitration has not shown that his or her claim is enforceable in a court or that he or she is entitled to an award. If the arbitration agreement does not state how an arbitrator should be selected or if the person named is unable to serve, at either party's request a court will appoint an arbitrator. An award brought about by what the act calls "undue means"—that is dishonesty—may be set aside. An award may also be set aside if an arbitrator or arbitration panel exceeds its power, unreasonably rejects a request to postpone the arbitration hearing, or improperly refuses to hear evidence material to the dispute and thus substantially prejudices a party's rights, or if there was no arbitration agreement and the party who challenges the award objected to the arbitration but still participated in it.

When a court sets aside an award for some reason other than its finding that there is no binding arbitration agreement, it may order a rehearing. For instance, a rehearing is ordered when an award is canceled because the arbitrator exceeded his or her power or failed to satisfy a necessary step during the hearing. If the court concludes that the same arbitrator should not rehear the dispute, it will appoint a new arbitrator and, when possible, do so as specified in the arbitration agreement. If the arbitration agreement does not state how an alternate should be selected, the court determines how a substitute should be chosen and then chooses one.

A court may modify an award if there is an obvious numerical miscalculation or an obvious mistake in describing a person or a piece of property. It may also eliminate any portion of an award that has to do with a matter beyond the arbitrator's power, so long as that portion is not a critical element of the award and so long as its elimination does not affect the parties' rights or duties.

FEDERAL ARBITRATION ACT

The Federal Arbitration Act is based on the constitutionally granted power of Congress to regulate interstate commerce and commerce on the high seas and navigable waters. The act applies to written contracts that involve *maritime* or *interstate* transactions. Its definition of maritime transactions includes agreements to ship goods or to charter, supply, or repair vessels. The act does not cover contracts that concern seamen, railroad employees, or other employees in the transportation business. Arbitration agreements, the arbitration process, and the role of the courts are treated in essentially the same manner under this act as they are treated under the Uniform Arbitration Act. When an arbitration agreement or process is covered by the Federal Arbitration Act, the act's directives apply to challenges of any aspect of the agreement or process in either a federal court or a state court.

VOLT INFORMATION SCIENCES, INC. v. LELAND STANFORD JUNIOR UNIVERSITY

SUPREME COURT OF THE UNITED STATES
489 U.S. 468 (1989)

The contract between the defendant construction firm (Volt) and the plaintiff university (Stanford) called for the installation of electrical conduits on the plaintiff's California campus. It included a provision that all disputes between the parties "arising out of or relating to [the]contract, or the breach thereof" would be resolved by arbitration. A choice-of-law clause in the contract directed that "[t]he Contract shall be governed by the law of the place where the Project is located." Volt demanded arbitration when a dispute arose over whether it was entitled to be compensated for the extra work it performed. Stanford responded by filing a lawsuit in a California state court against Volt and two other companies that were involved in the construction project. There was no arbitration agreement between Stanford and these companies. Volt petitioned the court to compel arbitration. Stanford asked that arbitration be stayed. Under California law, arbitration could be stayed pending the outcome of related litigation between a party to an arbitration agreement and any parties who were not signatories to the agreement if there was "a possibility of conflicting rulings on a common issue of law or fact" in the arbitration and a court proceeding. Following state law, the court denied Volt's petition and stayed the arbitration proceeding pending the outcome of the litigation.

The state appellate court affirmed. It acknowledged that the parties' contract involved interstate commerce, that the Federal Arbitration Act (FAA) governs contracts in interstate commerce, and that the FAA, unlike California law, contains *no* provision permitting a court to stay arbitration pending resolution of related litigation involving parties not bound by the arbitration agreement. It ruled that by specifying that their arbitration agreement would be governed by "the law of the place where the Project is located," the parties had made California's law a part of the agreement. It rejected Volt's contention that even if the parties had agreed to arbitrate under California law, the state's law was preempted (displaced) by the FAA because the contract involved interstate commerce. It also ruled that to apply the FAA rather than California law to the contract "would force the parties to arbitrate in a manner contrary to their agreement." After the state supreme court denied Volt's request that it review the state appellate court's decision, Volt sought relief in the U.S. Supreme Court.

CHIEF JUSTICE REHNQUIST
Delivered the Opinion of the Court

[The appellant, Volt,] acknowledges that the interpretation of private contracts is ordinarily a question of state law. But [it] nonetheless maintains that we should set aside the [state appellate court's] interpretation of [the contract's arbitration clause].

[FAA] was designed "to overrule the judiciary's long-standing refusal to enforce agreements to arbitrate," and place such agreements "upon the same footing as other contracts."

But FAA does not confer a right to compel arbitration of any dispute at any time; it confers only the right to obtain an order directing that "arbitration proceed *in the manner provided for in [the parties'] agreement.*" [The state appellate court ruled that the parties had incorporated state law into their agreement. It did not find] that appellant had "waived" an FAA-guaranteed right to compel arbitration of this dispute, but [found] that it had no such right in the first place because the parties' agreement did not require arbitration to proceed in this situation.

There is no federal policy favoring arbitration under a certain set of procedural rules; the federal policy is simply to ensure the enforceability, according to their terms, of private agreements to arbitrate. Interpreting a choice-of-law clause to make applicable state rules governing the conduct of arbitration—rules which are manifestly designed to encourage resort to the arbitral process—simply does not offend the rule of liberal construction [of FAA], nor does it offend any other policy embodied in FAA.

The question remains whether, assuming that the choice-of-law clause meant what the [state appellate court] found it to mean, [California law] is nonetheless preempted by [FAA] to the extent [that state law] is used to stay arbitration under this contract involving interstate commerce. It is undisputed that this contract falls within the coverage of the FAA, since it involves interstate commerce, and that FAA contains no provision authorizing a stay of arbitration in this situation.

The FAA contains no express preemptive provision, nor does it reflect a congressional intent to [include one]. The question before us, therefore, is whether application of [state law] under this contract in interstate commerce, in accordance with the terms of the arbitration agreement itself, would undermine the goals and policies of FAA.

[W]e have recognized that the FAA does not require parties to arbitrate when they have not agreed to do so nor does it prevent parties who do agree to arbitrate from excluding certain claims from the scope of their arbitration agreement. *It simply requires courts to enforce privately negotiated agreements to arbitrate, like other contracts, in accordance with their terms.* [Italics supplied.]

In recognition of Congress' principal purpose of ensuring that private arbitration agreements are enforced according to their terms, we have held that FAA preempts state laws which "require a judicial forum for the resolution of claims which the contracting parties agreed to resolve by arbitration." But it does not follow that the FAA prevents the enforcement of agreements to arbitrate under different rules than those set forth in the Act itself. Indeed, such a result would be quite inimical to the FAA's primary purpose of ensuring that private agreements to arbitrate are enforced according to their terms. Arbitration under the Act is a matter of consent, not coercion, and parties are generally free to structure their arbitration agreements as they see fit. Just as they may limit by contract the issues which they will arbitrate, so too may they specify by contract the rules under which that arbitration will be conducted. Where, as here, the parties have agreed to abide by state rules of arbitration, enforcing these rules according to the terms of the agreement is fully consistent with the goals of FAA, even if the result is that arbitration is stayed where the Act would otherwise permit it to go forward. By permitting the courts to "rigorously enforce" such agreements according to their terms, we give effect to the contractual rights and expectations of the parties, without doing violence to the policies behind the FAA.

Affirmed.

Legal Issues

1. Because the state appellate court's construction of the contract could have deprived Volt of a federal statutory right, should Chief Justice Rehnquist in this instance have rejected the rule that construction of a contract is a matter of state rather than federal law and should he have independently reviewed the state appellate court's decision as if the U.S. Supreme Court were sitting as California's highest appellate court dealing with a matter of state law? Why?

2. If the arbitration provision in the parties' agreement in the *Volt Information Sciences, Inc.* case was not specifically discussed or drawn by their attorneys, but simply copied from a standard form construction contract, should the Supreme Court have construed the provision as it did? Discuss.

Ethical Issues

1. Is it ethical for an attorney to advise a client to sign a contract with an arbitration clause without having first discussed the advantages and disadvantages of arbitration with the client? Why?

2. Is it ethical for lawyers who represent parties to a contract to include a standard arbitration clause in the contract rather than an arbitration clause specifically tailored to meet the unique interests of the parties they represent? Why? Should lawyers ascertain their clients' concerns regarding arbitration before allowing them to sign an agreement that contains an arbitration clause? Discuss.

DISPUTE RESOLUTION ACT

In 1980 Congress passed the Dispute Resolution Act. It is intended to assist states and other interested parties in giving all persons convenient access to effective, fair, and inexpensive mechanisms for the expeditious resolution of disputes. In the act Congress notes that for most people means for the resolution of minor disputes are largely unavailable, inaccessible, ineffective, expensive, or unfair and that the available means are generally inadequate or unsatisfactory. It descibes this state of affairs as "contrary to the general welfare of the people" and points out that many parts of the country lack the resources needed to develop essential procedures for the resolution of disputes between consumer and seller, landlord and tenant, and so on.

To foster improvement, the act establishes a process by which state and local governments, state or local governmental agencies, and nonprofit organizations may apply for federal financial assistance to establish or maintain alternative mechanisms for the resolution of disputes. The attorney general of the United States is directed to establish a Dispute Resolution Program in the Department of

Justice. The program must include a Dispute Resolution Resource Center and a Dispute Resolution Advisory Board. The Dispute Resolution Resource Center is to serve as a national clearinghouse for the exchange of information concerning the improvement of existing dispute resolution mechanisms and the establishment of new dispute resolution procedures. Among the tasks entrusted to the center are the provision of technical assistance to state and local governments, and the granting of funds for the improvement of dispute resolution mechanisms.

CONVENTION ON THE RECOGNITION AND ENFORCEMENT OF FOREIGN ARBITRAL AWARDS

The United Nations Convention on the Recognition and Enforcement of Foreign Arbitral Awards has been in force in the United States since 1970. The United States and 75 other nations are signatories to the agreement. Each signatory nation agrees to recognize and enforce arbitral awards made in any other party to the convention in the same way that it would enforce arbitral awards made within its own jurisdiction. The convention is applicable only to written agreements that call for the arbitration of disputes over commercial transactions.

The tribunal that is asked to recognize and enforce an award may refuse to do so if one of the parties to the arbitration agreement lacked capacity to contract, or if the agreement is not valid under the law of the nation in which the award was made or under the law of the nation whose law the parties specified should govern it. An award is unenforceable if the party against whom it was made was not properly notified of the appointment of an arbitrator or of the arbitration proceeding or not permitted to present his or her case before the arbitrator, or if the arbitrator lacked power under the arbitration agreement to make such an award, or if the subject matter of the agreement may not be settled by arbitration under the law of the nation in which recognition and enforcement is sought or is against the nation's public policy.

The convention does not apply if all of the parties to a dispute are U.S. citizens, unless the dispute relates to property located abroad or is based on a contract that calls for performance or enforcement abroad or can be reasonably viewed as having some connection with one or more foreign states. For purposes of the convention, a firm that is incorporated or has its principal place of business in the United States is treated as a U.S. citizen.

Federal district courts have original jurisdiction over any action or proceeding covered by the convention regardless of the amount of money in dispute. The arbitration agreement may stipulate which district court is to hear disputes regarding the agreement. In the absence of such a stipulation, venue is determined by the same rules that control which district court may hear a civil suit. The convention does not bar a party from bringing a lawsuit in a state court, but it governs the rights and duties of the parties to such litigation. In such cases the state court must abide by the legal principles embodied in the convention. At any time prior to trial, the defendant may request that the lawsuit be transferred to the federal district court of the geographic area in which the state suit is pending.

MITSUBISHI MOTORS CORPORATION v. SOLER CHRYSLER-PLYMOUTH, INC.

SUPREME COURT OF THE UNITED STATES
473 U.S. 614 (1985)

Chrysler International, S.A. (CISA), a Swiss corporation, and Mitsubishi Heavy Industries, a Japanese corporation, jointly established Mitsubishi Motors Corporation (Mitsubishi), a Japanese corporation whose principal place of business was in Tokyo. CISA entered into a distributor agreement with Soler Chrysler-Plymouth, Inc. (Soler), a Puerto Rican corporation, that authorized Soler to sell Mitsubishi vehicles in Puerto Rico. On the same day, CISA, Soler, and Mitsubishi entered into a sales agreement which provided for direct sale of Mitsubishi products to Soler and fixed the terms and conditions of such sales.

The "Arbitration of Certain Matters" clause in the sales agreement stated that "all disputes, controversies, or differences which may arise between" the parties "out of or in relation to" designated portions of the sales agreement "or for the breach thereof, shall be finally settled by arbitration in Japan in accordance with the rules and regulations of the Japan Commercial Arbitration Association."

Mitsubishi denied Soler's request for permission to resell some Mitsubishi vehicles in North, Central, and South America. After the parties' attempts to negotiate their differences failed, Mitsubishi brought a lawsuit against Soler in the Puerto Rico federal district court under the Federal Arbitration Act and the Convention on the Recognition and Enforcement of Foreign Arbitral Awards. In its complaint Mitsubishi asked the court for an order to compel arbitration. Soler's answer included a counterclaim alleging that Mitsubishi had violated the sales agreement and conspired to restrain trade in violation of the Sherman Act by refusing to permit Soler to resell some Mitsubishi vehicles outside of Puerto Rico. Mitsubishi filed a request with the Japan Commercial Arbitration Association for arbitration to begin.

After a hearing the district court ordered Mitsubishi and Soler to arbitrate most of the issues that they raised, including the alleged violations of the Sherman Act. Because of the international character of the Mitsubishi-Soler arrangement, it rejected the generally followed rule that a violation of rights conferred by the Sherman Act are "of a character inappropriate for enforcement by arbitration."

The court of appeals reversed the portion of the district court's judgment that ordered arbitration of Soler's Sherman Act claims. Mitsubishi's petition for certiorari was granted.

JUSTICE BLACKMUN
Delivered the Opinion of the Court

Soler argues that a court may not construe an arbitration agreement to encompass claims arising out of statutes [such as the Sherman Act that are] designed to protect a class to which the party resisting arbitration belongs "unless [that party] expressly agreed" to arbitrate those claims.

[W]e find no warrant in the Arbitration Act for implying in every contract within its ken a presumption against arbitration of statutory claims. The Act's centerpiece provision makes a written agreement to arbitrate "in any maritime transaction or a contract evidencing a transaction involving commerce valid, irrevocable, and enforceable, save upon such grounds as exist at law or in equity for the revocation of any contract." The "liberal federal policy of favoring arbitration agreements," manifested by this provision and the Act as a whole, is at bottom a policy guaranteeing the enforcement of private contractual arrangements: the Act simply "creates a body of federal substantive law establishing and regulating the duty to honor an agreement to arbitrate." As this Court recently observed, "[t]he preeminent concern of Congress in passing the Act was to enforce private agreements into which parties had entered," a concern which "requires that we rigorously enforce agreements to arbitrate."

[A]s with any other contract, the parties' intentions control, but those intentions are generously construed as to issues of arbitrability. [T]he Act itself provides no basis for disfavoring agreements to arbitrate statutory claims by skewing the otherwise hospitable inquiry into arbitrability.

That is not to say that all controversies implicating statutory rights are suitable for arbitration. We must assume that if Congress intended the substantive protection afforded by a given statute to include protection against waiver of the right to a judicial forum, that intention will be deducible from text or legislative history. Having made the bargain to arbitrate, the party should be held to it unless Congress itself has evinced an intention to preclude a waiver of judicial remedies for the statutory rights at issue.

[W]e conclude that concerns of international comity [the respect paid by a nation's courts to the decisions of another nation's courts], respect for the capacities of foreign and transnational tribunals, and sensitivity to the need of the international commercial system for predictability in the resolution of disputes require that we enforce the parties' agreement, even assuming that a contrary result would be forthcoming in a domestic context.

[P]otential complexity should not suffice to ward off arbitration. [A]daptability and access to expertise are hallmarks of arbitration.

[W]e also reject the proposition that an arbitration panel will pose too great a danger of innate hostility to the constraints on business conduct that antitrust law imposes. International arbitrators frequently are drawn from the legal as well as the business community; where the dispute has an important legal component, the parties and the arbitral body with whose assistance they have agreed to settle their dispute can be expected to select arbitrators accordingly.

[A]t least where the international cast of a transaction would otherwise add an element of uncertainty to dispute resolution, the prospective litigant may provide in advance for a mutually agreeable procedure whereby he would seek his antitrust recovery as well as settle other controversies.

Where the parties have agreed that the arbitral body is to decide a defined set of claims which includes those arising from the application of American antitrust law, the tribunal should be bound to decide the dispute in accord with the national law giving rise to the claim. [S]o long as the prospective litigant effectively may vindicate its statutory cause of action in the arbitral forum, the [Sherman Act] will continue to serve both its remedial and deterrent function.

Having permitted the arbitration to

go forward, the national courts of the United States will have the opportunity at the award-enforcement stage to ensure that the legitimate interest in enforcement of the antitrust laws has been addressed. The Convention reserves to each signatory country the right to refuse enforcement of an award where the "recognition or enforcement of the award would be contrary to the public policy of that country." While the efficacy of the arbitral process requires that substantive review at the award-enforcement stage remain minimal, it would not require intrusive inquiry to ascertain that the tribunal took cognizance of the antitrust claims and actually decided them.

As international trade has expanded in recent decades, so too has the use of international arbitration to resolve disputes arising in the course of that trade. The controversies that international arbitral institutions are called upon to resolve have increased in diversity as well as complexity. Yet the potential of these tribunals for efficient disposition of legal disagreements arising from commercial relations has not yet been tested. If they are to take a central place in the international legal order, national courts will need to "shake off the old judicial hostility to arbitration," and also their customary and understandable unwillingness to cede jurisdiction of a claim arising under domestic law to a foreign or transnational tribunal. To this extent, at least, it will be necessary for national courts to subordinate domestic notions of arbitrability to the international policy favoring commercial arbitration.

Accordingly, we "require this representative of the American business community to honor its bargain," by holding this agreement to arbitrate "enforce[able] in accord with the explicit provisions of the [Federal] Arbitration Act."

The [case is] *remanded* for further proceedings consistent with this opinion.

Legal Issues

1. Prior to *Mitsubishi Motors Corporation v. Soler Chrysler-Plymouth, Inc.,* a Sherman Act claim was not arbitrable whether it had to do with a domestic or an international business transaction. Was it appropriate for the Supreme Court, without any action by Congress, to effect a change in the enforcement process of a national policy established by a statute almost a century old? Why?

2. In a process that includes arbitration followed by a confirmation proceeding, is a Sherman Act claim likely to receive the same sort of attention that it would receive if it were handled entirely by a court? Discuss.

Ethical Issues

1. A contract between an American firm and a Japanese firm involves a business relationship that for the most part is confined to transactions carried on in the United States. At the insistence of the Japanese firm, the American firm consented to include in the contract an arbitration clause providing that any disputes under the contract should be resolved by the rules of the Japan Arbitration Association, with the hearing to be held in Tokyo. The American firm had never before dealt with a Japanese company, while the Japanese firm had engaged in numerous transactions with American companies. During the arbitration hearing the Japanese firm contends that it acted in accordance with the Japanese view of ethical business conduct. The American firm insists that the panel should take into account the American rather than the Japanese view of ethical business

conduct. Should the American firm's request be respected? Why?

2. An arbitrator discovers that one of the parties in an arbitration proceeding is guilty of a grave business crime. Is the arbitrator ethically obligated to call this to the attention of the appropriate law enforcement authorities? Why? Does it matter whether the arbitrator is or is not an attorney? Why?

OTHER ALTERNATE FORMS OF DISPUTE RESOLUTION

Minitrial

Minitrial

a privately sponsored hearing that resembles a court trial

Persons who are unable to negotiate a resolution of their dispute may wish to test the validity of their positions in a trial type of setting while they still retain the option of hammering out a compromise by themselves. They can do this through a **minitrial.** The particulars of their dispute are set forth in a written agreement that states when the minitrial will take place and what procedure will be used. Both parties are free to terminate the process at any time. So as not to prejudice their rights should they be unable to settle their dispute in this fashion, they agree not to disclose in future litigation anything that occurs during the minitrial.

An impartial adviser, chosen by the parties, officiates at the minitrial. The adviser may be selected because of his or her familiarity with the kind of subject matter involved in the dispute or because of his or her expertise in law. The parties decide on the adviser's role. They may want the adviser to serve as a passive participant—that is, to simply hear the evidence they offer—or to behave as if he or she were deciding the case as an arbitrator or a judge. An active adviser may pose questions that test the worth of each party's case and may offer an opinion as to how a trial would resolve the dispute. Unlike an arbitrator or a judge, an adviser at a minitrial has no authority to make a binding decision.

Before the minitrial is held, the parties may exchange information, such as statements as to what their witnesses would testify and what documents they would offer in evidence in a court trial. The parties may also give the adviser the information that they have gathered through inquiries about each other's case. The parties may use witnesses and experts to support their contentions. The attorneys for the parties are allotted a limited time to present their clients' cases to the adviser. The usual rules of evidence are not followed.

If the minitrial does not lead to a settlement, the parties may proceed to mediation, arbitration, or litigation.

Court-Related Arbitration

Small Claims Arbitration

Many states use a mix of informal and formal dispute resolution processes in small claims courts. A case may or may not be heard by a judge. Just before the trial, the parties may choose to have an arbitrator rather than a judge decide their dispute. If they do, they are required to sign a statement in which they agree that the arbitrator's decision will be final, binding, and unappealable. Small claims arbitrators are attorneys who have volunteered their services. They hear cases that the court assigns to them.

Before hearing a case, a small claims arbitrator, like a judge, often explores the possibility of having the parties adjust their differences between themselves. If they are unable to do so, the arbitrator will hear the case. Small claims proceedings are somewhat informal and do not adhere strictly to the usual court procedures and rules of evidence. After the hearing, or within the next few days, the arbitrator announces his or her decision. It has the effect of a court judgment and is enforceable as such.

Court-Mandated Arbitration

Court-mandated arbitration, commonly called **court-annexed arbitration,** is used in some states to resolve certain types of tort or contract disputes in which the damages sought by the plaintiff are less than a specified amount, perhaps $15,000. Such cases are heard by lawyers who, like small claims arbitrators, have volunteered to assist the court. As in small claims arbitration, the arbitrator is likely to urge the parties to negotiate their dispute and even to offer his or her assistance in their negotiations. If the parties cannot achieve a negotiated solution the arbitrator will hear the case and hand down a decision. Unlike the ruling of an arbitrator in a small claims case, that decision has no effect if either party rejects it. The court then tries the case *de novo,* as if arbitration had never taken place. To discourage bad faith rejection of the arbitrator's decision, if the party who rejects it is unsuccessful in the trial, he or she may be subjected to sanctions, such as being held liable for the successful party's attorney's fees and trial costs for which an unsuccessful litigant is usually not responsible.

Court-annexed arbitration
a form of arbitration required as part of a lawsuit

Hired Judge

A state statute or court rule may allow the parties to a lawsuit to hire a former judge or a lawyer to act as a judge in their case. A person hired for this purpose is commonly spoken of as a **hired judge** or a "private judge." For purposes of the lawsuit, the hired judge is treated as if he or she were a public judge. His or her decision has the same effect and may be appealed in the same way as a decision made by a public judge. An appellate court may affirm, modify, or reverse the decision for the same reasons that it would so treat a like decision of a public judge.

Hired judge
a person knowledgeable in law whom parties pay to rule on their claims

Mock Jury Trial

Before a lawsuit proceeds to trial, some jurisdictions give the parties' lawyers an opportunity to present a summary of their clients' contentions to a simulated jury made up of persons whom the court has summoned for possible service as actual jurors. After hearing the summaries, these persons, known as "mock jurors," are asked to return a verdict. The parties' lawyers may then ask them how they went about their work and why they arrived at their verdict.

Because of the mock jurors' view of the plaintiff's rights and the defendant's responsibilities, as well as their responses to the lawyers' postverdict questions, one or both of the parties may decide that it would be wise to vigorously explore the possibility of reaching a negotiated solution.

The use of mock jurors in the fashion described is known as a **mock jury trial.** Because of the way in which the jurors are apprised of the evidence and the speed with which the "trial" is carried out, this alternate method of dispute resolution is also referred to as a "summary jury trial."

Mock jury trial
a "trial" in which persons behave as if they were jurors

OMBUDSPERSON

An **ombudsperson** acts on behalf of people who wish to dispose of claims without resort to litigation. Sweden was the first nation to use individuals who performed this function. At one time ombudspersons could be found only in government. As a government employee, the ombudsperson's duty is to examine charges that government officials or employees have wrongfully deprived individuals of an entitlement. For example, an individual who has been refused a license, or access to a public health program, or a payment under a government program informs the ombudsperson of what has occurred. Generally, the ombudsperson then contacts the officials or employees who were involved in the refusal in order to become better acquainted with the facts and law in question. If convinced that an error might have been made, the ombudsperson will ask these officials or employees to reconsider their decision. Should they refuse to do so, the ombudsperson may investigate the matter further. If the investigation concludes the claimant has been wronged, he or she will ask the officials or employees to change their decision.

The ombudsperson's power is limited to his or her ability to persuade officials or employees to do the right thing. An ombudsperson lacks the power to order an official or employee to correct an error or to seek relief within the court system. If the ombudsperson's effort to bring about a just result fails, he or she may submit a report on the issue to a designated superior who is either authorized to take the necessary action or is in a better position than the ombudsperson to persuade the errant official or employee to do so.

Today, ombudspersons can be found in businesses, universities, and other types of organizations. Like the ombudspersons who work with government officials, these ombudspersons look into complaints of improper behavior. For instance, instead of seeking a remedy through a federal or state agency or a lawsuit, a company employee who believes that he was improperly denied a promotion because of his religion may inform the ombudsperson of the supposed discriminatory action. The ombudsperson's discussions with company officials and employees may confirm the employee's charge. When this is so the ombudsperson then calls the matter to the attention of the proper company official so that appropriate steps may be taken to correct the wrong. Effective use of ombudspersons enables companies to undo wrongs and to avoid costly litigation.

REVIEW QUESTIONS & PROBLEMS

1. Forel Department Stores entered into a six-month contract to purchase 100 refrigerators from Litok Manufacturing Company on the first day of each month, beginning with January 1991. An arbitration clause provided that any disputes regarding the contract would be resolved by arbitration. The contract was not renewed. Two months after the last delivery, Forel brought a lawsuit against Litok in which it claimed that Litok had delivered 20 defective refrigerators. Litok asked the court to stay the lawsuit and compel Forel to proceed to arbitration. Forel insisted that since the contract with Litok had not been renewed, the arbitration clause was no longer in effect. Should the stay be granted? Why?

2. A contract between Victorian Corporation and Townsend Construction, Inc. called for Victorian to deliver to Townsend 60,000 steel pipes, 12 feet in length

and 6 inches in diameter, in 10 shipments of 6,000 pipes each. An arbitration clause in the contract provided for the settlement by arbitration of disputes regarding the quality or quantity of the pipe delivered. Townsend informed Victorian that the second shipment contained only 5,600 pipes. When Victorian said that it had delivered 6,000 pipes, Townsend informed Victorian in writing that it would demand arbitration to resolve the dispute unless Victorian delivered 400 pipes within five days. Victorian, by letter, advised Townsend that it would not take part in arbitration. Three days later Townsend brought a lawsuit for breach of contract against Victorian. Victorian asked the court to dismiss the lawsuit and direct Townsend to proceed to arbitration. Should the court grant Victorian's request? Why?

3. Whittles was president of Greater Advertising, Inc., a Delaware firm that operated offices in 16 states. To assure that he had sufficient "private time," he resided in Wisconsin, where Greater Advertising did not have an office. His three-year employment contract provided that arbitration would be used to settle any disputes arising under the contract. One year before the contract was to expire, the Greater Advertising board of directors informed Whittles that his work was unsatisfactory, that he had been guilty of insubordination, and that effective immediately he was no longer employed by Greater Advertising. The firm rejected Whittle's request for payment for the year remaining under the contract. When Whittles demanded arbitration, Greater Advertising insisted that since he had broken the contract, he could not now demand that it be enforced. Whittles petitioned a federal district court for an order compelling arbitration. His attorney insisted that the Federal Arbitration Act govern the case. Greater Advertising contended that state law had to be followed. Is Whittle's lawyer correct? Why?

4. Under the contract between Jiffy Building Cleaners and Multi-Oaks Realty Company, Jiffy agreed to complete specified office cleaning services satisfactorily after the close of each business day. An arbitration clause stated that any dispute arising under the contract would be settled by arbitration. Tyrone Griff, president of Jiffy, angry at Multi-Oaks because of a comment made to him by its president, ordered Jiffy's officers and employees to suspend performance of the contract for a two-week period. Afterward Multi-Oaks demanded arbitration of its claims against Jiffy for compensatory and punitive damages and Jiffy took part in the arbitration proceeding. A unanimous arbitration panel, finding that Jiffy's action was intended to injure Multi-Oaks, awarded Multi-Oaks compensatory damages of $50,000 and punitive damages of $500,000. When Multi-Oaks asked that the award be confirmed, Jiffy objected. Jiffy's lawyer insisted that since Multi-Oaks's claims were based on a breach of contract, the portion of the award that granted Multi-Oaks punitive damages was against public policy and should therefore be deleted from the award. Multi-Oaks lawyer insisted that the court could not take public policy into account and should confirm the award in its entirety because an arbitration panel was not required to abide by established legal principles. Was Jiffy's lawyer correct? Why?

5. A contract between Omnioto Corporation and LaFarge Products Company required Omnioto to deliver 7,500 transformers to LaFarge. An arbitration clause stated that arbitration would be used to settle all disputes regarding the contract. LaFarge discovered that the transformers were defective, and soon afterward it was able to convey this information to 98 percent of the persons to

whom it had sold one of them. Omnioto refused to repair or replace the transformers. In its request for arbitration, LaFarge claimed that all of the 7,500 transformers it received were defective. The arbitrator agreed with LaFarge and awarded LaFarge damages.

Six weeks later Barbara sued LaFarge. She had purchased an Omnioto transformer from LaFarge and had been injured because it was defective. LaFarge had been unable to notify her of the defect. To assure that it would be reimbursed for the money that it would have to pay Barbara, LaFarge asked the court to bring Omnioto into the lawsuit as a third-party defendant and to award LaFarge a judgment for the amount that it would have to pay Barbara. Omnioto, which had complied with the terms of the arbitration award, insisted that to recover a judgment against Omnioto, LaFarge's evidence would have to prove that the transformer Barbara bought had been defective when Omnioto delivered it to LaFarge. Was Omnioto correct? Why?

ENDNOTES

1. See Chapter 8 for the essentials of a contract.
2. This subject is discussed in detail in Chapter 4 under the heading "Conflict of Laws."

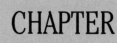

CHAPTER

6

The Administrative Process

Time and again lawmakers conclude that a certain sort of behavior cannot adequately be regulated through private initiative, market forces, or legal principles that are enforced exclusively by courts. They are likely to create a distinct government body to oversee such behavior. Congress, for example, has created government bodies to insulate employees from risk of injury in the workplace and to shield persons from exposure to hazardous substances. Like Congress, state and local legislative bodies create government entities that deal with a broad array of matters. For example, a state legislature may create a government unit to protect wildlife or a city or town council may set up a government unit to assure orderly land development.

This chapter considers the legal principles that affect the creation of government bodies charged with carrying out legislative programs, the organization of these bodies, the limits within which they must operate so that they do not deprive persons of their legal rights, the ways in which they establish and enforce their directives, how these bodies decide whether the law or their mandates have been violated, how they are kept within their constitutional and legislatively prescribed limits, and how courts determine whether to approve or reject their decisions.

APPEARANCE OF THE MODERN ADMINISTRATIVE AGENCY

For centuries, government officials have engaged in such administrative activities as the collection of taxes, the granting or denying of the privilege of engaging in certain sorts of activities, and things as commonplace as the delivery of mail. However, the modern **administrative agency,** also referred to as a "regulatory agency," is a government body that has been created to regulate business and business-related matters and to put into effect and oversee particular legislative policies. Prior to the use of administrative agencies, federal, state, and local legislative policies were ordinarily effected through the enactment of a statute outlawing certain behavior. A violation of the statute could lead to civil or criminal liability. Whoever was authorized to enforce the statute could seek the appropriate relief and sanctions through the court system.

In the 1880s there was widespread clamor urging Congress to do something about such railroad practices as charging unreasonable rates and unjustly discriminating against certain shippers and communities. Congress could have responded in the usual way—that is, it could have passed a law that made those practices illegal, and it could have let those who wished to enforce the law seek judicial relief. There were good reasons for Congress not to use this method.

Although Congress had a general idea of what it wished to accomplish and could specify the sorts of conduct that it wished to make unlawful, it was not in a position to continuously monitor how railroads treated shippers and communities. Moreover, its members were for the most part unqualified to determine what rates were unreasonable or what should be done to eliminate unacceptable railroad practices.

If Congress did deal with the challenged railroad practices in the usual way, the courts would have had to become intimately involved with the implementation and enforcement of its railroad policies. But the judicial process is not especially well suited to monitor such matters as rate setting on an ongoing basis. Courts do not apply or formulate rules of behavior outside the context of a lawsuit. Furthermore, they are not equipped to initiate investigations, seek out wrongdoers, or gather evidence. They leave these tasks to those who seek to enforce the law.

Congress concluded that the three constitutionally established branches of the federal government—the executive, legislative, and judicial branches—should not be directly responsible for implementing the new regulatory policies and wielding authority over the complex railroad industry. So in 1887 Congress established what is commonly regarded as the first modern administrative or regulatory agency, the Interstate Commerce Commission (ICC). Although the act that created the ICC directed that all railroad rates should be "just and reasonable," it did not authorize the ICC to impose such rates on railroads. Not until 1906, when Congress granted the ICC the power to replace unjust and unreasonable rates with just and reasonable ones, did the ICC become a truly regulatory agency.

Since the creation of the ICC, Congress has repeatedly established agencies to administer economic, social, and even political policies. At present there are scores of federal agencies. Although they are not mentioned in the Constitution, these creatures of Congress are commonly referred to as the "fourth branch of government" because of the important role they play.

Today, state, county, and municipal governments also make extensive use of administrative agencies to carry out a variety of legislative programs. For the most

Administrative agency
a body that regulates business and/or administers particular legislative policies

part these entities are created in the same way that Congress creates federal agencies. They perform their functions in essentially the same way as their federal counterparts.

COMBATING THE TRANSMISSION OF AIDS

Hypothetical Case

After drawing blood from an AIDS patient, a hospital resident left the needle in a pile of waste that was on a table. A moment later Dr. Ingel, a surgeon who was then wearing gloves, was pricked with the needle when she pushed aside the waste to make room for a patient's chart. She contracted AIDS. Shortly thereafter she launched a campaign to persuade the state legislature to do something to protect hospital personnel and handlers of waste who were repeatedly exposed to the risk of contracting AIDS from waste contaminated with the AIDS virus. In response to her efforts, a number of state legislators sponsored the AIDS-Free Workplace Act.

The act provided for the creation of an AIDS-Free Workplace Commission that would set standards and regulate workplaces in which persons were likely to be exposed to the AIDS virus. The commission's powers would include the adoption of standards of labeling, handling, and destroying materials that might be contaminated with the AIDS virus; the identification, through mandatory testing, of health care employees infected with the AIDS virus; and the imposition of penalties on employers and health care providers who failed to comply with the commission's standards.

What are the advantages and drawbacks of entrusting a government body with the mentioned powers instead of enacting a statute that establishes required standards of behavior for employers and health care providers and authorizes persons who contract AIDS as a result of the fault of employers or health care providers to institute suit against them?

Would it be ethical to include in the AIDS-Free Workplace Act a provision barring the commission from disclosing the names of persons who tested positive for AIDS? Discuss.

LIMITATIONS ON AGENCY BEHAVIOR

Constitutional and Statutory Constraints

The manner in which federal agencies go about their duties must satisfy the demands of the U.S. Constitution and acts of Congress. State and local agencies must satisfy the demands of the federal Constitution, state constitutions, and applicable acts of Congress and must operate within the limits established by the state legislature.

Administrative Procedure Acts

In order to promote a high degree of uniformity in federal agency practice, eliminate behavior that was regarded as unacceptable, and introduce desired procedural reforms, Congress passed the Administrative Procedure Act (APA) in 1946. The act was repealed in 1966 when its provisions were incorporated in Title 5 of the United States Code under the subhead "Administrative Procedure." Despite the change, the surviving provisions of the 1946 law are still commonly referred to as the Administrative Procedure Act or APA. (See Appendix B.)

State legislatures have adopted state administrative procedure acts. The Uniform Model State Administrative Procedure Act of 1961 has been adopted by 28 states and the District of Columbia, and 3 states have adopted the Uniform Model State Administrative Procedure Act of 1981. Aside from other restraints, state agencies are obliged to operate in accordance with the principles contained in their state's administrative procedure legislation. Since the tasks of state agencies generally bear a striking resemblance to the tasks of federal agencies, it is not surprising that many of the principles embodied in state administrative procedure acts are similar to, or identical with, the principles embodied in the federal APA.

Agency Expertise

Ideally, an agency would be staffed only by persons who possess expert knowledge about the subjects within its jurisdiction. In reality this is often not so. For example, it is not unusual for a person without special knowledge regarding the subjects dealt with by an agency to be appointed as its head. Before long, however, such a person will probably become knowledgeable about those subjects. Moreover, an agency usually has a core of career personnel who can be of tremendous assistance to newcomers. Courts generally assume that an agency is an expert on the activities entrusted to its care and will respect its decisions on a wide range of subjects. A court is not likely to freely set aside an agency's decision on a subject that, in the court's view, requires unique, in-depth knowledge. In such situations, absent special circumstances, the court is likely to *defer,* that is, respect the agency's decision. On the other hand, there are a variety of areas in which courts regard their own knowledge as paramount. For example, a court is likely to freely reject an agency's interpretation as to whether a constitutional provision does or does not allow the agency to behave in a particular manner.

Public Notification of Agency Plans and Action

Statutes enacted by Congress are readily available to the public. The APA requires that certain types of information about agency processes, actions, and decisions be published in the **Federal Register** (FR). This journal is published by the federal government on every working day. Annually, the Office of the Federal Register publishes all of the current agency rules in the **Code of Federal Regulations** (CFR).

Federal Register
daily journal published by the federal government that reports federal agency processes, actions, and decisions

Code of Federal Regulations
annual publication of the federal government that contains current federal agency rules

Independent agency
regulatory and/or administrative body that is separate from any other unit of government

Dependent agency
an administrative agency lodged within some sector of government

TYPES OF ADMINISTRATIVE AGENCIES

An **independent agency** is separate from any other unit of government. The Federal Trade Commission (FTC), which is charged, among other things, with taking action against persons who engage in unfair or deceptive trade practices, is an independent agency. So too are the Securities and Exchange Commission (SEC), which regulates many aspects of the securities business, and the Nuclear Regulatory Agency (NRA) which determines whether to grant applicants permits to build and operate nuclear reactors.

A **dependent agency** is not a distinct entity. It is lodged with another sector of government, usually the executive branch, of which the president is the head. Agencies lodged in the executive branch are commonly referred to as "executive agencies." The Department of Commerce, for instance, is an executive dependent agency.

AGENCY STRUCTURE

An agency may be headed by one person or several. When the agency head is one person, he or she may be called "secretary," such as the secretary of commerce, or "commissioner," such as the commissioner of the Internal Revenue Service, or "director," such as the director of the U.S. Information Agency. In agencies headed by several persons, there are commonly a chairperson and two or four other persons who are called either "board members" or "commissioners." The Federal Trade Commission, for instance, has a chairperson and four commissioners. This agency's table of organization appears in Figure 6-1.

ESTABLISHMENT OF AN ADMINISTRATIVE AGENCY

Once Congress or a state, county, city, or town legislative body has decided that the best way to carry out a desired policy is through the use of an administrative agency, it will pass an "enabling act." Such an act states the policy adopted by the

Federal Trade Commission   **FIGURE 6–1**

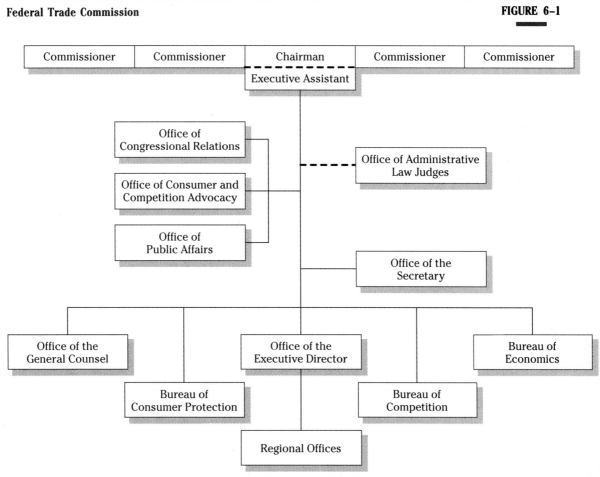

Source: The United States Government Manual, *1990/91* (Washington, D.C.: U.S. Government Printing Office, 1990), p. 592.

legislative body, creates the agency empowered to carry that policy out, specifies how the agency is to perform its tasks, and may specify when, and to what extent, a court may determine whether it has acted lawfully.

HILLS DEVELOPMENT COMPANY v. TOWNSHIP OF BERNARDS
SUPREME COURT OF NEW JERSEY
510 A.2d 621 (1986)

In response to two decisions of the Supreme Court of New Jersey that found a zoning ordinance unconstitutional if it did not provide a municipality with a realistic opportunity to contruct its fair share of the regional need for low- and moderate-income housing, the New Jersey legislature passed the Fair Housing Act. This act created an administrative agency, the Council on Affordable Housing (CAH). The CAH was authorized to define housing regions, to specify regional needs for low- and moderate-income housing, to set criteria and guidelines that would enable municipalities within each region to determine their fair share of the region's needs for such housing, and to decide whether municipal zoning ordinances and related measures satisfied the decisions of the state supreme court.

The act required the transfer to the CAH of most of the pending and future court cases to which the state supreme court's decisions might be applicable. A court might overturn a CAH decision only if there was "clear and convincing evidence" that a contrary result was warranted.

In 12 pending state trial court cases that involved municipal zoning ordinances in some way, there was opposition to transfer to the CAH. The constitutionality of the Fair Housing Act was challenged. In all but one of the cases, the court denied a transfer. Those who objected to the courts' action appealed.

WILENTZ, CHIEF JUSTICE,
Delivered the Opinion of the Court

[The Fair Housing Act] represents a substantial effort by the other branches of government to [fulfill a] constitutional obligation [of municipalities announced by this court]. It deals with one of the most difficult constitutional, legal, and social issues of our day— that of providing suitable and affordable housing for citizens of low and moderate income. [W]e believe that if the Act works in accordance with its expressed intent, it will assure a realistic opportunity for lower income housing in all those parts of the state where sensible planning calls for such housing.

Instead of depending on chance— the chance that a builder will sue—the location and extent of lower income housing [under the Fair Housing Act] will depend on sound, comprehensive statewide planning, developed by the Council and aided by the State Development and Redevelopment Plan (SDRP) to be prepared by the newly formed State Planning Commission. Its statewide scope is an extensive departure from the unplanned and uncoordinated municipal growth of the past.

The Act recognizes that zoning and planning for lower income housing is a long-range task, that goals must be changed periodically, revisions made accordingly, and results evaluated.

When supplemented by SDRP, the Act amounts to an overall plan for the state. It is a plan administered by an administrative agency with a broad grant of general power, providing the flexibility necessary [to carry out the constitutionally required result]; it is a plan that will necessarily reflect competing needs and interests resolved through value judgments whose public acceptability is based on their legislative sources.

This Act represents an unprecedented willingness by the Governor and the Legislature to face the issue [of assuring the availability of low- and moderate-income housing] after the unprecedented [decisions] by this Court. The particularly strong deference owed to the Legislature relative to this extraordinary legislation is suggested in [what this Court said in one of the two decisions that gave rise to the Act now before this Court]. "[W]hile we have always preferred legislative to judicial action in this field, we shall continue until the Legislature acts—to do our best to uphold the constitutional obligation [as to the availability of shelter for persons with low and moderate incomes]. In the absence of adequate legislative and executive help, we must give meaning to the constitutional doctrine in the cases before us through our own devices, even if they are relatively less suitable."

We hold that the Act is constitutional and order that all of the [pending cases] be transferred to the Council. Those transfers, however, shall be subject to such conditions as the trial courts may find necessary to preserve the municipalities' ability to satisfy their [constitutional] obligation.

No one should assume that [this decision] signals a weakening of our resolve to enforce the constitutional rights of New Jersey's lower income citizens. The constitutional obligation has not changed our determination to perform that duty. What has changed is that we are no longer alone in this field. The other branches of government have fashioned a comprehensive statewide response to the [constitutional obligation of municipalities.] This kind of response, one that would permit us to withdraw from this field, is what this Court has always wanted and sought. It is potentially far better for the State and its lower income citizens.

We therefore reverse the judgments below [in all of the cases in which the trial court denied transfer and affirm the case in which transfer was ordered].

Legal Issues

1. If the CAH rules that a particular town should set aside 50 acres for low- and moderate-income housing could that town satisfy the CAH ruling by arranging to have another town set aside 50 acres for such housing and by paying that town an agreed amount of money to help it fund its own program to construct low- and moderate-income housing? Why?

2. What facts would you want to know in order to decide whether the CAH is an independent agency or a dependent agency?

Ethical Issues

1. Is the objective of the CAH as discussed in *Hills Development Company v. Township of Bernards* an example of legislative approval of utilitarian ethics? Why? Is the objective consistent with ethical egoism? Why?

2. What view of ethics, if any, could properly serve as a rationale for requiring private developers to set aside a specified amount of their own resources to meet a town's obligations under the Fair Housing Act?

DELEGATION

The U.S. Constitution vests in Congress the power to enact laws. This, however, does not bar **delegation.** Congress may enact a statute that establishes a policy, sets general standards of permissible and banned behavior, and "delegates," that is, gives an official or a body authority to put the policy and standards of the statute into practice and to manage the statute's requirements day by day. The official or body may establish rules of conduct to perform its duties.

A delegate's function is to formulate the *details* necessary to attain the general objectives mandated by Congress and to oversee the operation of the program enacted by Congress. Because the Constitution gives Congress the power to *enact* law, it prohibits **abdication.** This means that Congress may not surrender to another sector of government its authority to enact the basic law on any particular subject.

The distinction between delegation and abdication makes it necessary that a statute intended to delegate rulemaking power contain intelligible standards that a court may use to determine whether the delegate has acted within the authority granted by Congress. If an act of Congress empowering a delegate to establish rules does not contain comprehensible statutory guidelines within which the delegate must operate, then the grant of power is an abdication of legislative power rather than a delegation, and therefore unconstitutional.

Delegation

the transfer by Congress of a portion of its power to an administrative agency

Abdication

the surrender by Congress of its authority to legislate

AGENCY EXECUTIVE AUTHORITY

An administrative agency generally has **executive power.** This law enforcement power allows an agency to engage in police activities, such as conducting investigations to root out wrongdoers, and to bring charges against those suspected of unlawful behavior, either through a proceeding handled within the agency or through a court. A successful prosecution does not necessarily end an agency's responsibility for law enforcement. If a guilty party fails to comply with the directive of an agency or the judgment of a court, the agency can take whatever steps are necessary to see that the directive or judgment is obeyed. This is generally done by initiating further proceedings before the agency or a court.

Executive power

the authority to enforce the law

RULES AND RULEMAKING

Rules

An administrative agency is generally vested with "quasi-legislative power," that is, with the authority to set standards of behavior. When, through the **promulgation,** that is, the establishment of standards, a federal agency exercises that authority, it behaves in essentially the same way as Congress. A standard promulgated by an agency, is called a "rule" or "regulation." The process by which rules are promulgated is referred to as **rulemaking.**

A **rule** is similar to a statute in that it is not intended to apply to just one or only a few particular individuals. It is directed at the behavior of many unnamed people. For instance, an Internal Revenue Service (IRS) directive stating that a

Promulgation

establishment by an agency of a standard of conduct

Rulemaking

the process by which an agency establishes a standard of behavior

Rule

a standard of conduct set by an agency through the exercise of its power to legislate

certain type of expenditure may never be treated as a business expense is a rule because it applies to all firms, not merely one or a few. But if the IRS announces that Terry Wynn owes $50,000 in federal taxes as a result of his involvement in a particular transaction, that announcement is not a rule, because it is directed solely at Terry Wynn.

Types of Rules

An **interpretative rule** contains an agency's explanation of a term or provision found in the legislation that the agency administers.

A rule that expands on the terms or provisions of a statute and concerns the rights and duties of parties is known as a **substantive rule,** or a "legislative rule." So long as such a rule is constitutional, authorized by legislation, consistent with the relevant legislation, and promulgated in the manner required by the statute, it has the force of law. Its purpose is to effect legislative policy, by expanding on the provisions of a statute or statutes that are under the agency's charge.

Rules relating to agency organization, procedure, or practice are a third category of agency rules. These are called **procedural rules.**

Interpretative rule
an agency's definition of a statutory term or provision

Substantive rule
a rule that expands on the terms or provisions of a statute

Procedural rule
an operational standard set by an agency

VI-CONCRETE COMPANY v. STATE DEPARTMENT OF ENVIRONMENTAL PROTECTION
SUPREME COURT OF NEW JERSEY
556 A.2d 761 (1989)

Under the New Jersey Pollution Control Act, it is unlawful for any person to discharge any pollutant without either a valid New Jersey Pollution Discharge Elimination System (NJPDES) permit issued by the commissioner of the state's Department of Environmental Protection (DEP) or a permit granted by the federal Environmental Protection Agency. Under this act, the commissioner may by regulation *exempt* sanitary landfills and other land means of waste disposal from the permit requirement. The act confers authority on the DEP to compel present owners of closed sanitary landfill sites to bear the cost of installing and maintaining monitoring wells on those sites. The wells are intended to monitor the discharge of pollutants into the state's waters.

In 1976 Vi-Concrete purchased a 9.5-acre tract of land on which an asphalt plant had been built in 1970. Unknown to Vi-Concrete, a prior owner had used the property as a landfill during the 1960s. Vi-Concrete never used any part of the property for that purpose. In August 1985 the Water Resources Division of the DEP issued Vi-Concrete an NJPDES permit—Vi-Concrete had not applied for one—requiring that it install and maintain four ground water-monitoring wells on its property because the property had at one time been used as a landfill. The estimated cost of installation was about $10,000, and the cost of the quarterly tests that all permit holders were required to make would be approximately $12,000 a year. Vi-Concrete filed an appeal with the DEP. The commissioner ruled that the DEP had the authority to issue an NJPDES permit to the owner of a closed landfill even though it had *not* promulgated a rule that required owners of *closed landfills* to incur the expense of installing and maintaining monitored wells. After Vi-Concrete had appealed unsuccessfully to a lower appellate court, the state supreme court granted its request for a review of the action taken by the DEP.

STEIN, JUSTICE
Delivered the Opinion of the Court

[T]he question before the Court is one of statutory interpretation, whether the Commissioner's issuance [of an] unsolicited permit to Vi-Concrete can be reconciled with the language and objectives of the Pollution Control Act.

We consider first the provisions of the Pollution Control Act and its pertinent regulations. The Act prohibits the discharge of pollutant without a federal or NJPDES permit.

The parties acknowledge that the Commissioner has not exercised his power to exempt sanitary landfills from the Act's permit requirements. To the contrary, the regulations under the Act set forth detailed requirements for sanitary-landfill permit applications among which is a specific requirement for the installation of groundwater-monitoring wells. [W]e read these regulations to apply to operating and not closed landfills.

The core of [Vi-Concrete's] resistance to the DEP's action is its contention that it should not have received a permit because it was not "discharging" any "pollutants" into the state's waters. The State responds that the Commissioner has adopted regulations pursuant to which NJPDES permits may be issued without an application based on information possessed by the Department. On the question of whether Vi-Concrete is a discharger under the Act, the State's position is that all landfills, active or closed, are "dischargers" for purposes of the Pollution Control Act.

We are unpersuaded by the State's literal reading of the Pollution Control Act that the Legislature intended all closed landfills to be issued NJPDES permits. The State's argument that all landfills, active or inactive, leach pollutants that may migrate into the state's waters, and hence are "dischargers," reads too much into the terminology used by the Legislature to establish the Act's permit requirements. The Legislature did not mandate that NJPDES permits be issued to all closed sanitary landfills. We construe the Act to authorize the issuance of a NJPDES permit to the owner of a closed landfill, but only if the DEP has a substantial evidential basis for its belief that the landfill actually is discharging pollutants that might flow or drain into the state's waters.

This is plainly a subject on which the agency should proceed by rulemaking in order both to "inform the public and guide the agency in discharging its authorized function." In the course of a rule-making proceeding, DEP should consider and determine the nature and extent of the discharges from closed landfills that would warrant the agency's resort to the permit procedure, the standards for determining the imposition and extent of monitoring procedures, and the criteria for determining the appropriate permittee when the agency can identify both the prior operator of the landfill and its present owner. Because the agency did not proceed by rulemaking, and because no proof was offered to demonstrate the presence of an actual discharge of pollutants from the site, we hold that the NJPDES permit issued to Vi-Concrete was not validly authorized.

[W]e hold that the NJPDES permit issued by DEP is invalid, and reverse the judgment of the [appellate court].

Legal Issues

1. What is the purpose of the court's requirement that the New Jersey Department of Environmental Protection have rules in place before it may issue NJPDES permits to owners of closed sanitary landfills?

2. What type or types of rules does the court's decision require the New Jersey Department of Environmental Protection to promulgate?

Ethical Issues

1. When, if ever, would an advocate of ethical egoism favor the court's decision? Why?

2. Would it be consistent with utilitarian ethics for the New Jersey Department of Environmental Protection to apply a rule authorizing it to issue an NJPDES permit to a person who purchased a closed sanitary landfill prior to the promulgation of the rule and was then unaware that the property had been used as a sanitary landfill? Why?

Rulemaking

Two distinct types of procedures may be used to promulgate rules. One is "informal rulemaking" and the other is "formal rulemaking." The enabling legislation and other federal statutes, in particular the APA, specify which type of procedure an agency must follow in promulgating a rule.

Informal rulemaking, often referred to as "notice and comment," simply requires the agency to notify the public that it is considering the adoption of a proposed rule and to announce that interested persons are free to submit written comments that may state their point of view, present arguments in support of their position, and provide supporting data. To assure that those who may wish to comment are aware of the agency's planned action, the FR must publish the text or substance of the proposed rule together with an announcement of the period during which comments may be filed with the agency. Under this procedure, neither those who support nor those who oppose the action are entitled to appear before any agency official to present their reasons to challenge the positions taken by others.

> **Informal rulemaking**
> a loose method of creating an agency rule

Under informal rulemaking, the agency considers the comments it receives but is not required to adopt or reject a rule on the basis of those comments or evidence in support of its decision. When an agency promulgates a rule in this way, it must also state the basis for its action and the purpose of the rule.

The enabling statute may expressly require **formal rulemaking.** Even when this statute does not do so, formal rulemaking may be required by the APA, which states that such rulemaking is necessary if the statute that confers rulemaking powers on the agency stipulates that a rule promulgated by the agency must be based on a record after there has been an opportunity for a hearing.

> **Formal rulemaking**
> a rigorous method of creating an agency rule

Formal rulemaking requires that the FR give notice of a proposed rule and of the opportunity to participate in the rulemaking process. Interested persons may appear before the agency at the time and place specified in the FR, state their positions and support them by evidence, be apprised of contrary positions and

**Substantial evidence
in the record**

sufficient proof for a reasonable person to reach
a particular conclusion

evidence, test the credibility of the contrary evidence by cross-examination, and offer rebuttal evidence. In formal rulemaking, unlike informal rulemaking, the agency's decision must be based on **substantial evidence in the record.** This means that a reasonable person, after considering the proof offered, could arrive at this conclusion. As with informal rulemaking, the agency must state the basis for its action and the purpose of the rule.

Rulemakers: Neutrals or Advocates?

Agency officials who engage in the rulemaking process are not likely to be neutral decision makers. They will probably be predisposed to favor a suggested rule that is apt to help the agency to fulfill its charge under the enabling act and related legislation. But a positive or negative predisposition toward a proposed rule is different from a final decision as to its acceptability. An agency official may take part in rulemaking even though he or she has a point of view on the rule in question but is barred from taking part if his or her mind is unalterably closed before rulemaking begins.

ADJUDICATION

Adjudication

the method by which an
agency decides an indi-
vidual's rights and duties

An agency exercises its "quasi-judicial power" when it engages in the adversarial process known as **adjudication** or "order-making." This is the method by which an agency decides such questions as whether a particular party should receive or be deprived of a benefit, property, or some other legally protected interest. In the course of an adjudication, an agency determines facts, applies the law, and, to the extent that it is empowered to do so, grants relief.

Order

an agency directive that
is similar to a court
judgment

The APA defines adjudication as the "agency process for the formulation of an order." An **order** is akin to a court judgment. The APA describes it as the "final disposition" in an agency process other than rulemaking.

Everyday examples of adjudication are a proceeding in which an agency decides whether a firm is guilty of an unfair trade practice, or an environmental protection agency seeks to impose a penalty on a firm that the agency's investigators consider guilty of illegally dumping hazardous waste.

Figure 6-2 contains an overview of the adjudication and internal and judicial review process for a typical federal agency.

Evidentiary and Administrative Hearings

Evidentiary hearing

an agency proceeding
that closely resembles a
trial

**Administrative
hearing**

an agency proceeding
that is similar to a trial
but lacks one or more of
its key features

The constitutional mandate that no person may be deprived of property without due process of law requires that an adjudication process provide a party who may suffer the loss of a benefit, property, or a legally protected interest with some form of hearing. An **evidentiary hearing** closely resembles the judicial process. In an **administrative hearing,** however, one or more of the essential elements of a court proceedings are absent. For example, a party may have no opportunity to present oral evidence on his or her behalf, or to confront the government's witnesses, or to cross-examine them, or to rebut the government's evidence by offering the oral testimony of witnesses. In an administrative hearing, the party against whom the agency is about to act may receive a written notice of the basis of the agency's action and may be provided with written statements on the critical facts in

Overview of Federal Agency Adjudication and Internal and Judicial Review Process   **FIGURE 6–2**

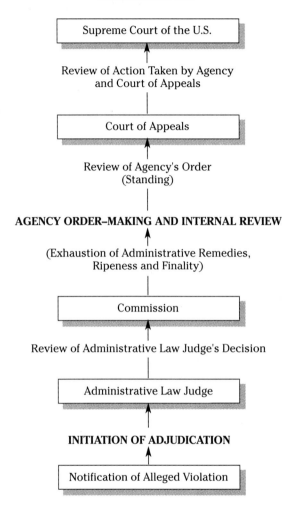

JUDICIAL REVIEW

Supreme Court of the U.S.

Review of Action Taken by Agency
and Court of Appeals

Court of Appeals

Review of Agency's Order
(Standing)

AGENCY ORDER–MAKING AND INTERNAL REVIEW

(Exhaustion of Administrative Remedies,
Ripeness and Finality)

Commission

Review of Administrative Law Judge's Decision

Administrative Law Judge

INITIATION OF ADJUDICATION

Notification of Alleged Violation

question. He or she may be allowed to challenge the agency's charge by submitting a written response together with supportive written statements.

Because due process is not a technical concept with a fixed content, such
factors as time, place, and circumstances determine whether an evidentiary or
merely an administrative hearing is required. The factors taken into account to
decide this question include the following: the importance of the affected private
interest; the risk of error if an evidentiary hearing is not held; the complexity of the
case; whether written evidence rather than oral testimony is acceptable in light of
the important part that credibility and veracity play in arriving at a proper decision;
and the merits of the government's justification for not holding an evidentiary
hearing. If, on balance, consideration of such factors favors an evidentiary hearing, an administrative hearing denies a party due process of law.

In addition to satisfying due process, a hearing must meet the procedural
standards of the enabling legislation, the APA, other relevant statutes, and the
agency's rules.

Elements of an Evidentiary Adjudication

An evidentiary hearing must meet the following standards.

Notification

A party who is likely to be affected by an adjudication must be suitably notified of the initiation and nature of the proceeding. The agency must give such a party notice of the source of the agency's authority to proceed, the portion of the statute and regulation that he or she allegedly violated, the nature of the supposed misconduct, when and where a hearing will be held, and the questions of law and fact that will be ruled on.

Administrative Law Judge

An administrative law judge (ALJ) presides over an adjudication conducted by a federal administrative agency. He or she performs essentially the same duties as a judge in a court. ALJs are appointed by the agency. The APA provides that they may not have any duties incompatible with their judiciary role. For example, an ALJ may not be involved in agency investigations or prosecutions.

As in a court proceeding, the parties to an adjudication are entitled to be heard by a fair and impartial fact finder. An ALJ who has made up his or her mind on the facts or has publicly announced the outcome before hearing the evidence, or has a financial stake in the result, is required to recuse himself or herself. But an ALJ may proceed to hear a case even if his or her judicial philosophy would plainly work to a party's disadvantage.

Hearing and Presentation of Evidence

A party to an adjudication, like a party to a court proceeding, is entitled to the assistance of counsel throughout the proceeding. Both the agency and the party are entitled to offer evidence to support their claims and to refute each other's evidence. The accused must have the opportunity to testify on his or her behalf. Witnesses presented by the agency and the supposed wrongdoer may be cross-examined, and the value and credibility of the evidence they offer may be challenged.

Time of Hearing

Ordinarily, a hearing must be held before an agency takes action that adversely affects an individual or an enterprise. But when the public interest requires it, an agency may act before a hearing takes place. For example, the Federal Drug Administration (FDA) may make a preliminary finding that a widely sold drug has caused numerous deaths and that its continued sale will lead to more loss of lives. In such an instance the FDA may immediately bar any further sale of the product and hold an evidentiary hearing at a later time.

Official Notice

Official notice
an ALJ's authority to treat something not beyond reasonable dispute as true in the absence of evidence

The **official notice** principle allows an ALJ to treat something as true in the absence of evidence even if this conclusion is not "beyond reasonable dispute." This administrative law principle has its origin in the assumption that an ALJ is an expert on subjects over which the agency has jurisdiction. To assure that a party to an order-making proceeding is not a victim of an ALJ's mistaken belief, the APA requires the ALJ to inform the parties that he or she intends to make official notice the basis for his or her decision on a fact or facts not shown by evidence presented during the hearing. The parties must be advised that if they choose to contest such a decision they may do so by showing that the decision is unwarranted.

Failure to Follow Agency Rule

An agency may decline to follow agency rules in particular cases in order to achieve what it perceives as a laudable objective. If this were commonly done, the expected orderliness and predictability of agency action would be lost. Absent extremely extenuating circumstances an agency is required to abide by its properly promulgated rules to determine the rights and duties of the parties.

Stare Decisis

ALJs are ordinarily expected to abide by past adjudications in arriving at a decision. Agency respect for previously announced principles is as beneficial in the adjudication process as *stare decisis* is in court proceedings. It promotes a high degree of stability, provides individuals and firms with guidelines to the conduct of their affairs, and permits those faced with or involved in an adjudication to anticipate, with some certainty, how the ALJ will rule.

Agency decisions, like those of courts, are not eternal. As we have seen, judges abandon precedent and establish new legal principles when it is appropriate to do so. The decision of an ALJ who forsakes precedent is expected to include a reasonable justification for his or her rejection of an established principle. Among the commonly offered rationales are changes within the affected industry and changes in the business environment. To invoke either of these rationales, the ALJ must carefully point out the differences between past and present conditions. A court that is asked to review the propriety of the ALJ's rejection of precedent will scrutinize the justification. If the justification is reasonable, the court will not overturn the challenged decision. Otherwise, it may reverse the decision on the ground that the agency did not explain why it failed to abide by one of its own standards.

Substantial Evidence in the Record

The APA requires that the ALJ's decision be based on substantial evidence in the record. This standard is satisfied if, on the basis of the evidence, a reasonable person could reach the same decision as that reached by the ALJ. To satisfy the APA, the ALJ's decision must include a statement of his or her findings and conclusions, together with the bases that support them.

REVIEW

Internal Review

The enabling legislation or an agency rule may provide that the agency itself is to conduct the first review of an ALJ's decision. In such instances that decision is the agency's **initial decision.** To have the agency review it, the dissatisfied party generally appeals to the person or persons who head the agency.

Initial decision
an ALJ's ruling in an adjudication

Ordinarily, the person or persons who hear an appeal have the same general powers as an ALJ. Unlike an ALJ, however, they do not hear any testimony. The evidence they examine is confined to the record of what took place before the ALJ. The procedure they use to evaluate the ALJ's decision must assure fair treatment of the parties. Whether the reviewing body affirms, modifies, or reverses the ALJ's decision, its action must be supported by substantial evidence in the record.

Eligibility for Judicial Review

Judicial review

a court's evaluation of the legality of agency action

A party who suffers a legal wrong, or is aggrieved, or is adversely affected because of an agency rule or order is generally entitled to have a court evaluate the legality of the agency's action. This process is known as **judicial review.** A court can evaluate an agency's action only if the following four conditions are satisfied.

Standing

Standing

the personal effects that give an individual the right to participate in a legal dispute

To challenge an agency's action, a party must have **standing.** This requirement originates in part in the constitutional mandate that restricts the power of federal courts to rule only on "cases" or "controversies." To meet this demand, a person must be "aggrieved," that is, adversely affected by what the agency has done. The APA permits only a person who is "adversely affected or aggrieved by agency action" to obtain judicial review.

A party has standing if he or she has been injured by the challenged action, if a favorable court decision would undo or reduce the injury caused by the ALJ's decision, and if the interest that he or she is seeking to protect is "arguably within the zone of interests to be protected or regulated by the statute or constitutional guarantee in question." The injury in question need not be economic in nature. It can be an injury to aesthetic, recreational, or environmental interests.

Exhaustion of Administrative Remedies

Exhaustion of administrative remedies

the complete use of all the agency procedures available to correct an agency error

Generally, judicial review of agency action, such as an ALJ's decision, is not available until all possible steps have been taken to secure relief within the agency. This doctrine is known as **exhaustion of administrative remedies.** On occasion exhaustion is unnecessary, such as when such action would be futile, or despite the party's prodding the agency has failed to act, or because of extraordinary circumstances the party faces impending irreparable harm of a protected right and the agency cannot grant adequate or timely relief.

Primary jurisdiction

the doctrine that relief must be sought through an agency before it is sought through a court

Related to, but fundamentally distinct from, the exhaustion doctrine, is the doctrine of **primary jurisdiction.** This doctrine ends a lawsuit on the ground that the plaintiff should not have initiated it. Instead, the plaintiff should have *first* sought relief from the appropriate agency, such as when the complexity of the facts and issues makes it desirable that use be made of agency expertise before a court becomes involved or relevant statutory policy would be better served if an agency deals with the matter initially.

Ripeness

Ripe for review

the doctrine that an agency must rule on a legal issue before a court will consider it to spare a party distress

To prevent what courts regard as premature judicial scrutiny of agency action, a proceeding must be **ripe for review.** This standard is known as the "ripeness doctrine." Under this doctrine, a matter is ready for judicial intervention when a court can come to grips with the legal issues because they have been sufficiently resolved by the agency and a party or parties would be caused substantial hardship if prompt judicial action is not taken.

Finality

The APA authorizes judicial review of agency action only when the agency's involvement has been completed. This requisite is known as **finality.** Courts use a pragmatic test to determine whether an agency proceeding has terminated. Only after an agency has formally announced its decision and communicated the decision to the affected parties is the APA's finality test satisfied.

Parameters of Judicial Review

The scope of a reviewing court's scrutiny of an agency's conduct and of a reviewing court's power to override an agency's decision is governed by constitutional requirements, judicially set standards, and the statute under which the reviewing court is authorized to act. Seldom is a reviewing court empowered to proceed *de novo* when judicial relief is requested by a party who was unsuccessful before the agency. When a reviewing court is thus empowered, it does not need to give any attention to the agency's judgment. Otherwise, its authority to probe and alter agency action is limited. In general, a reviewing court may examine an agency's action to see whether it should be modified or reversed for any of the following reasons.

1. The decision is unconstitutional.
2. The agency's action is **ultra vires,** that is, beyond the powers delegated to the agency by the legislature.

3. In the course of rulemaking or during an adjudication, the agency neglected to observe one or more required procedures.
4. The decision was not based on substantial evidence in the record. When substantial evidence in the record supports the agency's decision, the reviewing court will defer to the agency even through on the same record it would have arrived at a contrary result. This will be done because the agency is the expert and the reviewing court will not substitute its judgment for that of the agency.
5. The statutory authority of the reviewing court requires it to set aside an agency decision that it finds arbitrary, capricious, an abuse of discretion, or otherwise not in accordance with law. A decision is arbitrary or capricious if a reasonable person could not arrive at it. An agency whose statutory power authorizes it to exercise its discretion is not free to do whatever it pleases. It must use its discretion soundly. An agency abuses its discretion when it acts unreasonably.

WHEN SHOULD A PROCEDURAL ERROR INVALIDATE AN AGENCY'S DECISION?

Hypothetical Case

An ALJ of the state Liquor Commission rejected Park's request for a license. During the hearing he excluded evidence that for more than 10 years Park had designed highly successful newspaper advertising campaigns for several of the nation's largest liquor manufacturers. He ruled that he lacked sufficient business experience to satisfy the agency's regulation that to obtain a license an applicant must show suitable experience to probably successfully engage in the wholesale liquor distribution business.

Park appealed to the agency commissioner. She ruled that the ALJ had erred in refusing to hear evidence of Park's advertising experience because there was a link between that experience and his probable success in the wholesale liquor distribution business. However, noting that such evidence would not be enough to entitle Park to a license and that he offered no other evidence of suitable experience, she affirmed the ALJ's decision.

Park asked the appellate court to reverse the agency's decision because of the admitted mistake by the ALJ. What judgment? Why? Under what view or views of ethics would the commissioner's ruling to affirm the ALJ's decision be acceptable? Why?

Prejudicial Error

A party to an agency proceeding is not guaranteed an error-free process. The APA directs the reviewing court to take the rule of prejudicial error into account. An error is prejudicial only if it probably influenced the outcome and thus caused the unsuccessful party substantial harm. In the face of such an error, the reviewing court may set aside the agency's decision. However, a reviewing court will not disturb an agency's decision on account of an error that probably had no effect on the outcome.

BLINDER, ROBINSON & CO. v. SECURITIES & EXCHANGE COMMISSION
U.S. COURT OF APPEALS, DISTRICT OF COLUMBIA
837 F.2d 1099 (1988)

The SEC brought a civil enforcement suit in a federal district court in which it charged that Blinder, Robinson & Co. and its president had violated the antifraud provisions of federal securities laws and SEC rules. The trial court granted the SEC's request for injunctive relief against both the firm and its president. After they had appealed unsuccessfully to the court of appeals, the Supreme Court denied their petitions for certiorari.

During the appellate stage of the litigation in which the SEC sought injunctive relief, the SEC instituted an administrative proceeding against Blinder, Robinson and its president to determine what sanctions, if any, the SEC should impose on them for violations of federal securities laws. The ALJ ordered that they be suspended from engaging in certain types of transactions for a specified period of time. This order was appealed to the full Securities and Exchange Commission by the SEC and by the firm and its president. The Commission affirmed the ALJ's suspension order as to Blinder, Robinson but changed the president's 90-day suspension to a permanent ban on dealing in securities. After that ban had been in place for two years, the president could ask that it be lifted. Both Blinder, Robinson and its president appealed.

STARR, CIRCUIT JUDGE
Delivered the Opinion of the Court

[The firm's president] argues that the procedures employed by the SEC and its staff run afoul of the Fifth Amendment's Due Process Clause. Here is the way [he] summarizes his claim:

Having prevailed on its contested lawsuit, the SEC now is seeking to exercise quasi-judicial discretion to decide how severely [he] should be sanctioned for the conduct that was the subject of the lawsuit. If the Commission's proposed course is permitted, a plaintiff will have become a judge of its own claim. [He] maintains that the Constitution "does not permit a transformation of litigation roles" so as to permit a litigant to become a judge in its own case.

[F]airly viewed, [the petitioner's claim] represents nothing less than an assault on the constitutionality of a principal feature of the Administrative Procedure Act itself. That familiar statute, enacted by Congress over forty years ago, represents a comprehensive charter for the conduct and operation of modern administrative agencies. Among other things, the APA prohibits agency staff from combining prosecutorial and adjudication functions in the same case. *But it expressly exempts agency members from this prohibition of combined functions.*

The permissibility of the APA-sanctioned regime under the Constitution has been strongly suggested (if indeed not settled) by the Supreme Court. [T]he Court [has stated]:

> Congress has addressed the issue in several different ways, providing for varying degrees of separation of functions to virtually none at all. For the generality of agencies, Congress has been content with section 5 of the [APA], *which provides that no employee [may combine functions] but which also expressly exempts from this prohibition "the agency or a member or members of the body comprising the agency."* [For purposes of this portion of] section 5 the term "employee" means a person who was involved in investigating or prosecuting the case, or a factually related case, or an ALJ who presided at the reception of evidence in the case.

[The Supreme Court has not found it unconstitutional for] "members of an administrative agency [to] investigate the facts, institute proceedings, and then make the necessary adjudications." "[It has not questioned] the Administrative Procedure Act."

[The Supreme Court] invoked the administrative agency model in language that bears directly on the question [that the petitioner] brings before us [when it observed]:

> It is also very typical for the members of administrative agencies to receive the results of investigations, to approve the filing of charges or formal complaints instituting enforcement proceedings, and then to participate in the ensuing hearings. *This mode of procedure does not violate the Administrative Procedure Act, and it does not violate due process of law.*

Whether the adversarial proceeding is before an agency-designated ALJ or a federal district court judge, the relationship obviously remains one of adversariness between agency and opponent. [By first proceeding against the petitioner in federal district court, the SEC afforded him] the not insubstantial advantage of the neutral forum with its attendant procedures and protections (including the rules of evidence and procedure) that may not obtain in an agency adjudication.

[A]cceptance of [the petitioner's] broad due process attack would accede precisely to what the Supreme Court has warned against, namely a sweeping due process challenge that "'would bring down too many procedures designed, and working well, for a governmental structure of great and growing complexity.'"

The subsequent administrative proceeding does not, fairly viewed, constitute a second bite at the apple for an agency that had failed to convince [a court] of the merits of a particular remedy. Instead, based upon the district court's judgment, the SEC subsequently initiated procedures expressly ordained by Congress. This, we are satisfied, does not run afoul of any values of fundamental fairness embodied in the Due Process Clause. Indeed, to accept petitioners' broadside would do violence to the core value of flexibility (coupled with appropriate procedural protections) that has been the hallmark of modern administrative process.

Indeed, a moment's reflection suggests that acceptance of [the petitioner's] claim under the Due Process Clause would do considerable violence to Congress' purposes in establishing a specialized agency to regulate in the difficult and challenging world of financial markets and securities regulation. Ironically, the wisdom of Congress' handiwork is suggested by the brief of [the petitioner's] own firm, whose words, we believe, aptly capture the considerations in forming Congress' policy choice in this respect:

> While courts are best equipped to adjudicate whether statutory violations occurred, Congress believed the SEC's particular expertise would best enable it to choose among available administrative disciplinary sanctions and to discern the interests of the investing public.

[Petitioners also challenge the SEC's refusal to consider evidence relating to the sanctions to be imposed upon them.] In brief, we are persuaded that the fundamental principle of administrative law that an agency act in a nonarbitrary, noncapricious fashion is necessarily implicated by the SEC's refusal to permit evidence with respect to a salient factor. That is, in meting out sanctions, the Commission cannot adequately weigh the factors that it concedes should be considered without having before it the full set of facts necessary for reasoned consideration.

Thus, our analysis is inevitably affected by the Commission's error in refusing to consider [relevant] evidence. [W]e remand the case to the Commission for further action consistent with this opinion.

It is so ordered.

Legal Issues

1. To what extent, if any, do you think the court's decision is based on respect for agency expertise? Discuss.

2. Under the reasoning of the court of appeals, could there be circumstances in which a federal agency's pursuit of an individual or an enterprise through repeated resort to court and agency proceedings would constitute a denial of due process of law under the Fifth Amendment? Explain.

Ethical Issues

1. When would it be unethical for an administrative agency to initiate an agency proceeding against a firm who was successful against the agency in a lawsuit having to do with the same firm's conduct? Why?

2. Would it be ethical for the SEC to usually impose harsher penalties on smaller or newer firms than it does on old-line or more established firms? Discuss.

EXECUTIVE ORDERS

Executive order

a presidential directive that has the force of law

The president may issue an **executive order** to execute a particular policy. Such a directive has the effect of law. The president's power to make an order stems from either the U.S. Constitution—which vests the executive power of the federal government in the president, requiring him to "take Care that the Laws be faithfully executed," and also designates him the commander in chief of the army and navy—or an act of Congress.

Just as Congress may delegate lawmaking power to an administrative agency by authorizing it to make rules and regulations to carry out a legislative mandate, Congress may delegate to the president lawmaking power by authorizing him to issue executive orders to effect a congressional policy. For example, Congress, having enacted legislation to promote United States trade with certain under-developed nations, has authorized the president to determine which products from these countries may be imported duty-free.

GOVERNMENTAL MISCONDUCT AND OFFICIAL RESPONSIBILITY

Sovereign Immunity

The doctrine of **sovereign immunity** bars individuals and enterprises from recovering damages for injury caused by governmental misconduct. Governments, however, may waive their immunity under this principle. Time and again, the United States does so on behalf of *particular individuals* through the passage of "private bills" either by the House of Representatives or the Senate. Through the passage of "public laws," Congress permits *untold numbers of persons* to sue the United States.

Sovereign immunity
the freedom of governments from legal liability

A private bill approved by the House or Senate is referred to the U.S. Claims Court. Such a bill might ask this court to report whether it would be equitable to waive the statute of limitations so that a named party could bring a lawsuit against the United States or whether certain facts show that a named party has a legal or equitable claim against the federal government. In its report the court might recommend the sort of relief that Congress should grant. For example, the court might find that a named party does have an equitable claim and might recommend that Congress award the party a specified amount of money.

In 1946 Congress enacted the Federal Tort Claims Act. This statute permits persons to bring suit against the United States in federal district court to recover damages for injury or loss of their property, or personal injury or death caused by the negligent or wrongful act or omission of any employee of the government while acting within the scope of his or her employment, under circumstances where the United States, if a private person, would be liable for damages under the law in effect in the locale where the injury occurred. Among the exceptions to this broad waiver of sovereign immunity are that the United States is not liable for (1) any claim based upon the exercise or the failure to exercise a discretionary function or duty on the part of a federal employee whether or not such discretion is abused, or (2) any claim arising in a foreign country, or (3) a claim for damages caused by the fiscal operations of the U.S. Treasury or by the regulation of the monetary system.

The Federal Employees Liability Reform and Tort Compensation Act of 1988, with but two exceptions, limits the relief available to persons who bring a lawsuit against a U.S. employee for injury or loss of their property, or personal injury or death, caused by a negligent or wrongful act or omission by the employee while he or she was acting within the scope of his or her office or employment, to the relief that the injured party may recover against the United States under the Federal Tort Claims Act. The 1988 act does not grant U.S. employees immunity from personal liability for claims based on a violation of (1) the U.S. Constitution or (2) a U.S. statute which authorizes a lawsuit to be brought against a U.S. employee.

Under the Act the United States is substituted as the party defendant in the lawsuit brought against the employee once the Attorney General certifies that the claimed injury occurred while the employee was acting in the scope of his or her office or employment. The United States may use any defense that the employee could have used if he or she remained the defendant.

At one time the doctrine of sovereign immunity barred persons injured by the action of either state or local governments from suing these political units. Now, either because of state court decisions or state laws, in most states persons injured by government employees while these employees were acting within the scope of their official duties may recover damages from state or local governments if similar behavior by private persons would have entitled the injured persons to relief.

Official Immunity from Civil Liability

Absolute immunity

the exemption of government officials from liability for any wrongful conduct that occurs while they are acting within the scope of their official duties

Qualified immunity

the exemption of government officials under certain circumstances from legal liability for wrongful conduct that occurs while they are acting within the scope of their official duties

Federal officials may enjoy either absolute or qualified immunity. **Absolute immunity** completely excuses an official from civil liability for wrongful conduct that occurs while the official is acting within the scope of his or her official duties. **Qualified immunity** exempts an official from liability for a wrong done within the scope of his or her official duties if (1) there were reasonable grounds for believing that the act was legal and (2) the act was not done with malice or in bad faith. This means that an official who knew or should have known that his or her conduct was unlawful or who acted with a malicious intent cannot rely on qualified immunity to avoid liability.

Federal judges, ALJs, and others who act in a quasi-judicial capacity enjoy absolute immunity with regard to their adjudication duties. Prosecutors enjoy absolute immunity with regard to their participation in the "judicial" phase of a criminal prosecution. This immunity applies to such activities as evaluating and marshaling evidence, filing charges, presenting the government's case in court, engaging in plea bargaining, and negotiating parole. Prosecutors enjoy only qualified immunity with regard to their police activities, such as arresting or interrogating persons or disseminating information learned through these activities to the press.

The president of the United States has absolute immunity from civil liability for his official acts. Other high-ranking federal officials generally have but qualified immunity, if while acting in the scope of their duties, they deprive a person of a constitutional right.

Official Misstatement

Repeatedly, to justify its rejection of a party's claim that he or she is entitled to relief because of a statement by a federal official, the U.S. Supreme Court has declared that "men must turn square corners when they deal with the government." This rule has been used against a party when he or she would have been granted relief if the defendant was a private party. Those who deal with the federal government are expected to know the law and in most instances are *not* expected to rely on the advice of an official that is contrary to law. However, the government may be held accountable if the detriment to the party who relied on the incorrect advice is *extremely severe* and because of the official's error the agency's action is *fundamentally unfair.*

□□□□

An agency official provided Mark with an erroneous interpretation of the relevant portion of the law as to what he must do to receive a $1,200 social security benefit. He believed what he was told, relied on it, and acted accordingly. Because he followed the advice given to him he became ineligible to receive the $1,200. The agency refused to award him the $1,200. Mark would not be successful in a lawsuit to recover the $1,200 even if he showed that he behaved as he did on account of the official's erroneous advice. Mark had ready access to the law, and the loss caused him was not extremely severe, nor was the agency's action basically unfair.

□□□□

A state court may grant relief to a party who has been injured on acount of an official's misstatement when, given the same facts, a federal court would not do so.

ACCESS TO THE RECORDS OF FEDERAL AGENCIES

Restriction on Availability

The Privacy Act, passed by Congress in 1974, recognizes that the collection, maintenance, use, and dissemination of information about individuals by federal agencies may endanger the right of individuals to privacy. To limit intrusion on the privacy of individuals, the act establishes a number of standards and procedures.

A federal agency may gather, keep, use, and share the records of identified persons only for necessary and lawful purposes. The records may contain information about such matters as educational background, financial transactions, and medical, criminal, or employment history. The agency must establish adequate safeguards to assure that such records are current and accurate and that they are not misused.

The Privacy Act allows persons to inquire whether an agency has records that pertain to them. If it does, they may gain access to the records, obtain a copy, have them corrected or amended as necessary, and prevent the agency from using or revealing their contents for other than lawful agency purposes.

Among the records that need not be disclosed under the Privacy Act are those that are kept by the Central Intelligence Agency or relate to various aspects of law enforcement.

A person may bring a civil lawsuit in a federal district court against any agency that violates the act. In addition to providing other relief, such as ordering the agency to correct its records, the court may award a plaintiff who has substantially prevailed in the lawsuit a judgment against the United States for reasonable attorney's fees and other costs that he or she incurred because of the litigation.

Mandatory Disclosure

Administrative Procedure Act

The APA requires agencies to publish in the FR information about their structure, operations and office locations and about how to obtain copies of their decisions. If an agency does not publish its decisions promptly and does not offer copies of the decisions for sale in accordance with its published procedures, the agency must make available for public inspection and reproduction final opinions, including concurring and dissenting opinions, orders in adjudication proceedings, and policies and interpretations that have not been published in the FR, as well as administrative manuals and instructions affecting the public that it gives to staff members. If necessary to prevent a clearly unwarranted invasion of individual privacy, an agency may delete identifying details from the opinions, policies, and interpretations, or staff manuals and instructions that it makes available or publishes.

Freedom of Information Act

In 1966 Congress passed the Freedom of Information Act. Its purpose is to assure public access to government records that federal agencies might otherwise unnecessarily shield from public view. Agencies are required to promptly comply with a party's lawful request for a copy of a record. Among the records exempt from the act are records that the president by executive order correctly classifies as secret in the interest of national defense or foreign policy; records that relate solely to internal personnel rules and practices; records that contain trade secrets; records that contain privileged or confidential commercial or financial information; medical and other personnel files whose disclosure would be clearly unwarranted invasions of personal privacy; and certain types of investigatory records compiled for law enforcement purposes. If a record contains information exempt from the act that can be reasonably segregated from the rest of the information it contains, then the agency must provide the record after having deleted the information exempt from the act. Should an agency choose to do so, it may reveal information that need not be disclosed under the act.

GOVERNMENT IN THE SUNSHINE ACT

The purpose of the Sunshine Act, in effect since 1976, is to allow the public to obtain, to the fullest practicable extent, information regarding the decision-making processes of many federal agencies. The act applies only to agencies headed by a collegial body of two or more members, a majority of whom are appointed by the president with the advice and consent of the Senate.

Generally, at least one week before holding a meeting, an agency must make a public announcement of the time, place, and subject matter of the meeting, indicate whether the meeting is open or closed to the public, and give the name and telephone number of the official who has been designated to deal with requests for information on the meeting. In the case of a closed meeting, the agency must make available to the public a full written explanation of its decision to close the meeting and must identify the persons who are expected to attend it and their affiliations.

REGULATORY FLEXIBILITY ACT

The purpose of the Regulatory Flexibility Act of 1980 is to introduce into the rulemaking and enforcement processes the principle that it is sometimes inappropriate to treat large and small firms alike. To put this principle into effect, the act directs agencies, consistent with the objectives of their rules and applicable statutes, to take into account the size of the businesses under their jurisdiction when they formulate their regulatory and informational requirements. The Regulatory Flexibility Act also requires that in adopting regulations to protect the nation's health, safety, and economic welfare, agencies should seek to avoid the imposition of unnecessary burdens on the public.

ADMINISTRATIVE CONFERENCE OF THE UNITED STATES

The Administrative Conference of the United States consists of between 75 and 91 persons. Among the members of the conference are the chairperson, who is appointed by the president with the advice and consent of the Senate; the chairperson of each federal independent regulatory board or commission or an individual designated by the board or commission; the head of each dependent agency lodged in the executive branch of government or some other administrative agency, who is designated by the president, or an individual designated by the head of the department or agency; and other persons appointed by the president.

Congress established the conference to provide a suitable arrangement through which federal agencies, assisted by outside experts, might cooperatively study mutual problems, exchange information, and develop recommendations for action by the proper authorities so that, while private rights were fully protected, regulatory activities and other federal responsibilities might be carried out expeditiously in the public interest. The conference studies the efficiency, adequacy, and fairness of the administrative procedures used by administrative agencies in carrying out administrative programs and, when appropriate, makes recommendations to administrative agencies; arranges for the interchange among administrative agencies of information that might be useful in improving their procedures; collects information from administrative agencies; and publishes reports that it considers useful for evaluating and improving administrative procedures.

REVIEW QUESTIONS & PROBLEMS

1. An act of Congress directs that a regulation of an agency may be promulgated only after a hearing and must be based on the record. Could the agency satisfy this statutory requirement by using the notice and comment process? Why?

2. You have heard that within the last several weeks a federal agency promulgated a rule that may significantly affect your firm. Where would you ordinarily look to find the complete text of this rule? Why?

3. Basic Health Products Corporation was charged with marketing the drug cytripaspro without satisfying the provisions of an agency rule that prohibits

the sale of any drug dangerous to human health unless a label on its package contains a warning of the potential harm that could result from its use. In the course of the adjudication, the ALJ recalled having read that eminent researchers were convinced that grave harm could result from even the short-term use of cytripaspro. What must the ALJ do if she plans to use this information to support her decision? Discuss.

4. After a hearing the ALJ concludes that the use of principles invoked in prior agency decisions would excuse the defendant firm from statutory liability but that this result is unsatisfactory because the industry of the defendant firm, once extremely fragmented, is now dominated by three huge firms that together control 95 percent of the market. In his decision the only explanation he offers for not following the established principles is that they are "clearly inapplicable." The firm appeals to the three-member agency board which affirms his ruling and notes in its ruling that the agency's prior rulings are "obviously not pertinent." On appeal to the court of appeals, the firm's attorneys ask it to reverse the agency's decision on the grounds that neither the ALJ nor the agency board stated why precedent was not followed. What judgment? Why?

5. Wells, a retired sociologist, was concerned that a large corporation, Ato Exhaust, Inc., would avoid liability in an adjudication hearing. He took careful notes of the evidence submitted by the agency and the firm during the hearing. The ALJ ruled in favor of Ato Exhaust. Wells was convinced that this ruling was not based on substantial evidence in the record. After the director of the agency issued a decision affirming the ruling, Wells filed a notice of appeal to have a court of appeals review the agency's action. The firm asked the court to dismiss the appeal on the ground that Wells lacked standing. What judgment? Why? What ethical standard or standards would support a court ruling that Wells had standing? Discuss.

6. Shortly after an adjudication hearing began, James Forceful, the attorney for Good Products, Inc., challenged a ruling by Elizabeth Ware, the ALJ. Over Forceful's objection she permitted a document unfavorable to Good Products to be placed in evidence. Forceful shouted: "Ware, you are incompetent and an obstacle to justice." Ware immediately ordered him to leave the room, saying that as far as she was concerned, he no longer represented Good Products, Inc. Carr, the president of the firm, then asked Ware to adjourn the case so that the firm could obtain another attorney. Ware told him: "Sir, the facts are really simple. Why waste time and taxpayers' money? We will now proceed." After strongly objecting to "what is being done," Carr handed Ware a note that read: "As president of Good Products, Inc., I want this in the record. I object to not being allowed to retain another attorney. I am not an attorney, and I am not ready to pretend that I am. I demand an adjournment." After reading the note, Ware said, "I have already ruled on your request. You have my answer." Ware remained in the hearing room but refused to allow any of Good Products' witnesses to testify or to offer any documents into evidence on its behalf. The witnesses called to testify by the agency were not cross-examined. Ware ruled against Good Products. On appeal, the five-person agency commission affirmed. Good Products, Inc. appealed to the court of appeals. Forceful, once again representing the firm, insisted that his client had been deprived of due process? What judgment? Why?

7. Timmons, Inc. was charged with a violation of an agency rule limiting the amount of hazardous waste that could lawfully be disposed of in an individual container. Shortly before the charge was to be heard by René Carl, an ALJ, she held a press conference. When asked her opinion about the agency's enforcement policy, she noted that she was to hear a case in which a vigorous agency investigation had led to the filing of charges although the corporate defendant had resorted to various types of misrepresentation to avoid discovery. Facts contained in her statement made it clear that she was talking about Timmons. Before the hearing was to begin, the attorney for Timmons asked Carl to recuse herself. He stated: "You announced your decision yesterday. Without hearing the evidence, you concluded that my client was guilty." Carl replied: "Since my mind is not unalterably closed, I can fairly hear this case. Your request is denied. Let's get to work." A week after the hearing was completed, Carl ruled that Timmons was guilty as charged. The five-person agency commission affirmed her ruling. Timmons, Inc. appealed to the court of appeals. Its counsel insisted that Carl was obliged to recuse herself. What judgment? Why?

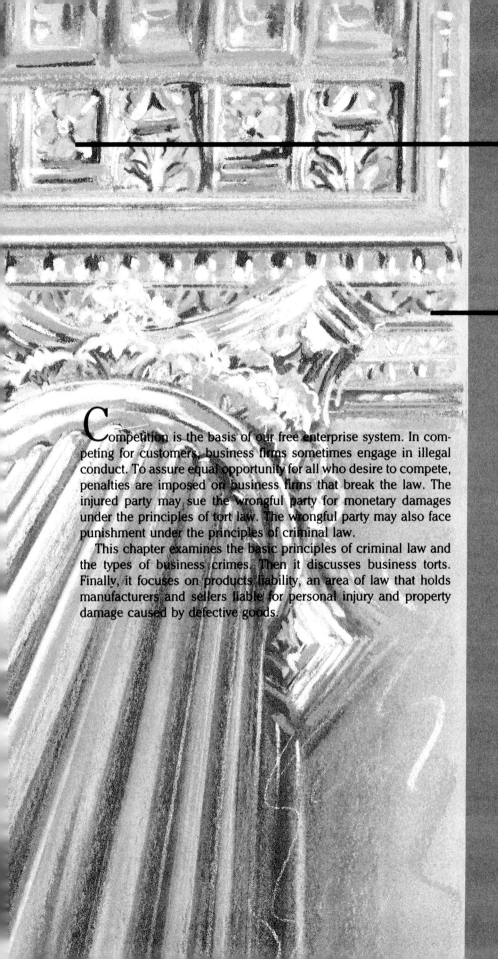

CHAPTER

7

Business Crimes and Business Torts

Competition is the basis of our free enterprise system. In competing for customers, business firms sometimes engage in illegal conduct. To assure equal opportunity for all who desire to compete, penalties are imposed on business firms that break the law. The injured party may sue the wrongful party for monetary damages under the principles of tort law. The wrongful party may also face punishment under the principles of criminal law.

This chapter examines the basic principles of criminal law and the types of business crimes. Then it discusses business torts. Finally, it focuses on products liability, an area of law that holds manufacturers and sellers liable for personal injury and property damage caused by defective goods.

Crime

an offense against society that is prosecuted by the government

Tort

a private or civil wrong that involves the breach of a legal duty

COMPARISON OF CRIMES AND TORTS

A **crime** is a breach of duty owed to society and thus an offense against society as a whole. Since criminal law protects society as a whole, the state or federal government prosecutes those accused of crimes on behalf of the people. A **tort** is a private or civil wrong that involves the breach of a duty owed only to the injured party. Tort law provides compensation for the damage suffered. The party injured by the tort is therefore allowed to sue the tortfeasor, the person who committed the tort, for monetary damages.

A single wrongful act may be classified as both a tort against the individual and a crime against the state. Tort law recognizes that some individuals are guilty of certain harmful acts and that those injured deserve compensation for their injuries. For example, if an employee has stolen property belonging to his employer, the employer can sue the employee for compensation equal to the value of the property stolen. This would be a tort suit—a civil lawsuit between private parties in which one of the parties seeks compensation for a wrong committed by the other party.

In addition to the tort suit, the state may arrest the employee and prosecute him for the crime of larceny—the wrongful taking of the personal property of another. Since the crime is a wrong against society, the state brings a criminal prosecution to protect both the individual victim and the other members of society. Thus the same act may be both a tort and a crime.

NATURE OF BUSINESS CRIMES

Most of the acts recognized as crimes today have been prohibited by law for centuries. However, as society changes, what we view as wrongful acts also changes. Society evaluates the new methods that people devise to earn rewards, and state legislatures and Congress may enact new criminal statutes to outlaw those methods. All of the acts classified as crimes must be specified in statutes passed by either state legislatures or Congress.

The federal and state penal laws do not characterize any criminal act as a business or white-collar crime. Generally, any nonviolent illegal act related to a legitimate occupation and committed by an individual or a firm to obtain business or personal advantage can be called a "business crime" or a "white-collar crime." The bribery of a public official and an improper donation to a political campaign might be such crimes. So too might a false statement in a financial report, the unlawful trading of publicly held stocks, tax evasion, embezzlement, and shoplifting.

Persons of high respectability and social status often commit white-collar crimes in the course of their occupations. Today, the use of the terms *business crime* and *white-collar crime* has been broadened, and no single definition is universally accepted. In fact, the term *white-collar crime* usually refers to the offender's social status.

The financial impact of business crimes on the public is enormous. Business crimes add about 15 percent to the prices of all goods sold in the United States. The cost of business crimes surpasses that of larceny, robbery, burglary, and auto theft combined. Illegal price-fixing agreements by competing companies often artificially inflate consumer prices for goods and services. The business losses caused by employee theft or embezzlement are passed on to consumers in the form of higher retail prices.

Despite the personal interest that consumers should have in preventing or punishing business crimes, these crimes continue to enjoy a great deal of public tolerance, in part perhaps because such crimes, unlike violent crimes, are hardly visible to the public. They appear to be "victimless" because they harm no one physically. The financial losses are usually suffered by large corporations. In addition, the businesses victimized by such crimes often do not prosecute the offenders. Generally, businesses fail to file formal complaints because (1) the losses are covered by insurance, (2) prosecution may be difficult, or (3) they fear a public relations problem if they report the losses.

Criminal Law Principles

To understand business or white-collar crimes, one must first understand basic criminal law principles. The steps in a criminal prosecution differ significantly from the steps in a civil trial, discussed in Chapter 4. The criminal process contains safeguards specifically designed to protect the rights of accused persons.

Classification of Crimes

Crimes are classified as either felonies or misdemeanors, depending on the possible punishment specified by statutes. **Felonies,** which may be punishable by death or by imprisonment in a federal or state penitentiary for more than one year, are more serious than misdemeanors. Examples of felonies are murder, arson, and the theft of property valued at over $250.

Misdemeanors, on the other hand, are punishable by a fine or by confinement in a local jail for a maximum of one year. Trespassing, reckless driving, and disorderly conduct are common misdemeanors.

A **petty offense,** often called an "infraction of the law," is less serious than either a misdemeanor or a felony. Petty offenses include minor traffic violations, parking violations, and violations of the building code. Such offenses are punishable by a few days in jail or a small fine, or a combination of the two.

Historically, criminal law has been primarily the concern of the states. State legislatures pass criminal statutes that the state courts then enforce. However, there is also a federal criminal code. Federal crimes are violations of laws passed by Congress. Typically, these laws relate to functions of the federal government or involve federal personnel or institutions. For example, counterfeiting, illegal immigration, spying, and assaulting a federal officer are federal crimes. The federal government may also use its general regulatory powers to aid state law enforcement groups in curtailing crimes with a national impact. Kidnapping, violations of civil rights, and transportation of stolen vehicles across state lines are examples of such crimes.

Criminal Prosecution

Before a person can be imprisoned or fined for committing a crime, the person must be convicted of the crime. An arrest occurs when a person is taken into custody, usually by police officers, in order to be charged with a crime. Criminal prosecution is brought by the state or federal government in its own name, not that of the victim, so a criminal case might be called *State of Illinois v. Smith* or

Felony
a serious crime whose maximum punishment is death or more than one year in a federal or state prison

Misdemeanor
a crime less serious than a felony whose maximum punishment is a fine or not more than one year in a local jail

Petty offense
a minor violation of the law (such as speeding or illegal parking) whose primary punishment is a fine

United States v. Brown. In such a case, the victim is not a party but will only serve as one of the witnesses.

Arrest

An arrest is the first step in a criminal prosecution. The authority to arrest may be based on (1) the commission of a crime in the arresting officer's presence, or (2) the belief of the arresting officer that the person arrested has committed a crime, or (3) a warrant issued by a court. An arrest warrant can be issued only upon an affidavit that establishes probable cause for believing that the person to be arrested has committed or is about to commit a crime. *Probable cause* can be defined as a substantial likelihood that the person has committed or is about to commit a crime. Thus a substantial likelihood of criminal activity rather than just the possiblity of criminal activity is required.

In the first two situations, in which police officers act without a warrant, the arrest is also subject to the standard of probable cause. This means that it may be subject to after-the-fact review by a judicial officer.

In the landmark case of *Miranda v. State of Arizona,*[1] the Supreme Court held that an arrested person may be questioned by the police only after having been warned of his or her rights. These rights, often called "Miranda rights," include the right to remain silent, to be represented by an attorney (by a state-appointed attorney if the arrested person cannot afford one), and to have an attorney present during questioning. If the arresting officer fails to give the Miranda warnings, statements made by the arrested person, including a full confession, may not be used in evidence against that person in a trial following the arrest.

Indictment

The Fifth Amendment requires an indictment by a grand jury for serious federal crimes.[2] The grand jury, usually numbering 15 to 23 persons, must find that the evidence is sufficient to require the accused to stand trial. Thus the grand jury acts as a buffer between the individual and the powers of the government. The purpose of the grand jury is to reduce the possibility that innocent persons will bear the expense and publicity of being brought to trial for serious crimes.

The Fifth Amendment grand jury requirement does not apply to the states. However, all of the states screen felony cases by either a preliminary hearing before a judge or a grand jury review, or both. Generally, the standard that is used to determine whether there is sufficient evidence to justify bringing a person to trial is the same probable cause standard that a police officer uses when making an arrest.

Trial

The next step after the indictment or preliminary hearing is the actual trial. As noted in Chapter 4, the accused person does not have to prove his or her innocence. The burden of proof in a criminal trial lies with the prosecutor for the state or federal government. The prosecution establishes the guilt of the accused person by convincing the jury that the defendant is guilty beyond a reasonable doubt. If the jury returns a "not guilty" verdict, this does not necessarily mean that the defendant is innocent. It merely means that the jury was not convinced that the evidence was sufficient to establish the guilt of the accused beyond a reasonable doubt.

Criminal Intent

To establish the guilt of the accused, the prosecution must prove beyond a reasonable doubt that his or her criminal act (**actus rea**) was accompanied by criminal intent (**mens rea**). What constitutes criminal intent varies according to the wrongful act. The act of murder, for example, is the taking of a life accompanied by the intent to kill; the act of forgery is the altering of a check accompanied by the intent to defraud the owner of the checking account.

After a trial resulting in a conviction, an accused may appeal the jury's verdict on any legal error committed during the trial. An acquittal, however, ends the case. The Fifth Amendment provides that no person can be put in jeopardy of life or liberty twice for the same offense.[3] This prohibition against double jeopardy prevents the prosecution from appealing the acquittal.

Criminal Punishment

If a conviction for a business or white-collar crime is not appealed or an appeal is unsuccessful, a person convicted of such a crime may be punished by imprisonment or a fine, or a combination of the two. A corporation, as a legal entity separate from its shareholders, directors, and officers, cannot be imprisoned. A convicted corporation is punished by a fine or in extreme cases by a revocation of its charter.[4] These fines are often merely symbolic, only a small portion of the illegal gain. However, there has been a trend toward the imposition of heavier penalties by the courts, and in some cases courts require payment of a fine equal to or greater than the illegal proceeds of specific criminal acts (if those proceeds can be determined).

TYPES OF BUSINESS CRIMES

This section briefly discusses some of the more common types of business crimes. Human inventiveness in the commission of business crimes makes it impossible to treat them all or to examine all of the methods that have been used to carry them out. The types of business crimes that this section discusses are (1) computer crimes, (2) bankruptcy frauds, (3) bribery, (4) larceny and embezzlement, and (5) violation of the Racketeer Influenced and Corrupt Organizations Act (RICO).

Computer Crimes

The present period of world history will probably be known as the "computer age." Computers handle the financial transactions of governments and nearly all large business enterprises. Even small neighborhood businesses have turned to computers for use in keeping records and handling financial transactions. Money circulates largely as digital information in computer memories.

Naturally, criminals have found ways to manipulate computers for personal and business gain. The detection of such manipulation is often difficult since data can be rearranged, accounts altered, confidential information obtained, and all evidence of the tampering erased within seconds by anyone with access to a computer and the knowledge needed to break its security codes.

The annual financial losses due to computer crimes, according to some experts, run into hundreds of millions of dollars. Multimillion-dollar computer

Actus rea
a criminal act

Mens rea
a criminal intent

thefts have been discovered. Federal officials say that in a bank robbery the average loss is $3,200; in a nonelectric embezzlement, $23,500; and in a computer fraud, $500,000.

As few as one percent of computer crimes may be discovered. One reason for this is that computer crimes are extremely difficult to detect. Another is that firms victimized by computer crimes are reluctant to admit publicly that their computer security system has been breached. When perpetrators of computer crimes are prosecuted, their cases rarely reach trial, because the affected businesses usually allow such cases to be plea-bargained—negotiated between the prosecutor and the accused in exchange for an agreed sentence. This keeps the case from being reported and prevents adverse publicity.

Criminal laws are often inadequate to deal with computer crimes. For example, larceny statutes were designed to prohibit the theft of tangible property. However, computer theft often involves the taking of intangible computer software, such as a program on a disc or tape. A program of this kind is not "property" as defined by the traditional criminal law statutes. The federal government and almost one half of the states have therefore modified their larceny statutes to include the theft of electronic impulses from computers.[5] Some state laws now define larceny as the theft of a "thing of value," thereby making the theft of computer time illegal. Unfortunately, even these laws are inadequate. Thus the law of computer crimes is still in its formative stages, with the authorities struggling to keep their criminal laws abreast of the new technology.

Computer crimes can take many forms. In one case employees stole material and then altered inventory records so that the stolen material was not immediately missed. In another case an outsider accessed a company's computerized inventory files and ordered the delivery of inventory to a certain location. Upon delivery of the order, the criminal sold the inventory and programmed the computer not to send a bill for the inventory delivered. In still another case a computer employee who had learned of an impending layoff altered the computer program so that payroll checks continued to be sent to terminated employees.

Congress has not yet passed a comprehensive federal statute on computer crime. The Counterfeit Access-Device and Computer Fraud Act, passed in 1984, makes it a federal crime to access a computer without authorization. However, it is not a general-purpose computer crime statute. The Federal Computer Systems Protection Act, which would make it a federal offense to damage a computer or to use a computer for unauthorized purposes, has been introduced each year since 1978.

The following case discusses whether the use of a computer is property subject to theft.

STATE v. MCGRAW

INDIANA APPELLATE COURT, SECOND DISTRICT
459 N.E.2d 61 (1984)

Michael McGraw was a computer operator for the Indianapolis Department of Planning and Zoning. As a sideline, he operated a business selling Naturslim, a diet product. He used the computer service leased by Marion County to maintain data relating to his business, such as client lists and birth dates. Employees of the

Department of Planning and Zoning were not authorized to use the computer service for personal affairs, and McGraw was reprimanded at least once for doing so. The department eventually discharged him because of his unauthorized use of the computer service. Following his discharge, McGraw asked a co-worker to obtain a printout of the Naturslim data that he had stored in the computer and then to erase the information. The co-worker, however, reported this request to his supervisor, and an investigation followed that revealed the extensive use of the computer by McGraw.

The trial court dismissed the charges against McGraw on the ground that his actions did not constitute an offense against the state of Indiana. On appeal, the appellate court found the "only real question" to be "whether the use of a computer is a property subject to theft."

NEAL, PRESIDING JUDGE

The sole issue on appeal is whether the unauthorized use of another person's computer for private business is theft under the statute as a matter of law.

Theft is defined by IND.CODE 35-43-4-2(a) as follows:

> A person who knowingly and intentionally exerts unauthorized control over property of another person with intent to deprive the other person of any part of its value or use, commits theft, a Class D felony.

IND.CODE 35-41-1-2 defines property:

> "Property" means *anything of value; and includes a gain or advantage or anything that might reasonably be regarded as such by the beneficiary;* real property, personal property, money, labor, *and services;* intangibles; commercial instruments; written instruments concerning labor, services, or property; written instruments otherwise of value to the owner, such as a public record, deed, will, credit card, or letter of credit; a signature to a written instrument; extension of credit; trade secrets; contract rights, choses-in-action, and other interests in or claims to wealth; electricity, gas, oil, and water; captured or domestic animals, birds, and fish; food and drink; and human remains.

The State essentially argues that the theft statute comprehends a broad field of conduct and a wide range of activities, and is sufficiently broad to prohibit McGraw's acts here.

McGraw's initial arguments involve a close examination of the pertinent statutory language. The theft statute, he argues, is divided into a conduct portion "knowingly and intentionally exerting unauthorized control over the property of another person" and the intent portion, "with the intent to deprive the other person of any part of its value or use." The word "use" does not appear in the conduct portion; therefore, the unauthorized control must be over the property itself. Further, he argues, IND.CODE 35-41-1-2, which defines property, does not include the word "use" as such, and IND.CODE 35-43-4-1(a), which defines "exert control over property," does not employ the term "use." Additionally, he contends that "services" as used in IND.CODE 35-41-1-2 is limited to the context of labor.

Inasmuch as the evidence clearly supports the fact that McGraw knowingly and intentionally used the city-leased computer for his own monetary benefit, the only real question is whether "use" of a computer is a property subject to theft. The sufficiency question will not be discussed separately.

No Indiana case under the modern

theft statute exists which addresses this question. We view McGraw's arguments as derived from old common law concepts which do not control the much broader definition of property and theft contained in modern statutes. The case most applicable to the instant one is *Moser v. State,* (1982) Ind.App., 433 N.E.2d 68. In *Moser,* the defendant was charged under IND.CODE 35-43-5-3(a)(6) with the offense of deception by avoiding a lawful charge of cable television. The court, referring to IND.CODE 35-41-1-2 (the property definition) stated that the "receiving of cable television signals was receiving something of value, whether a service, or signal, or a combination thereof, from someone who had a possessory intent in it." However, this case is not wholly on point because IND.CODE 35-43-5-3(a)(6) refers specifically to television services.

A search of the holdings of other jurisdictions regarding computer-related crime has turned up cases which are neither particularly helpful nor on point.

[A]n Indiana decision similar to *Moser* found that electricity, a service, may be stolen.

We deem McGraw's interpretation of the statutes overly restrictive. In short, he is arguing old common law precepts pertaining to larceny. In our view his contentions are inapposite to the plain meaning of the statutory sections involved herein.

Computer services, leased or owned, are a part of our market economy in huge dollar amounts. Like cable television, computer services are "anything of value." Computer time is "services" for which money is paid. Such services may reasonably be regarded as valuable assets to the beneficiary.

Thus, computer services are property within the meaning of the definition of property subject to theft. When a person "obtains" or "takes" those services, he has exerted control. Taking without the other person's consent is unauthorized taking. Depriving the other person of any part of the services' use completes the offense. IND.CODE 35-43-4-2(a). Further, we disagree that it is a defense to exerting unauthorized control that the owner was not using the property at the time.

Judgment *reversed.*

Legal Issues

1. What is the "real question" in this case?
2. Why did the court decide that computer services are property?

Ethical Issues

1. Is the court's view of how Indiana's theft statute should be interpreted comparable to the application of an imperative advocated by a priori ethics, or is it comparable to the establishment of a standard through a close evaluation of the facts advocated by situation ethics?
2. Among the arguments made in support of McGraw's contention that he did not violate Indiana's theft statute were (a) that he merely used his employer's computer and the statutory definition of property did not include the word *use* and (b) that the computer was not in use when he used it. Is the court's interpretation of the statute consistent with the way in which a proponent of pragmatic ethics would evaluate the acceptability of a person's behavior? Why?

Bankruptcy Frauds

A debtor may commence voluntary bankruptcy proceedings by filing a petition for bankruptcy, or a debtor's creditors may petition a court to commence involuntary bankruptcy proceedings. The bankruptcy laws, which are discussed in detail in Chapter 15, require the debtor to disclose all of his or her assets. The trustee in bankruptcy takes title to all of these assets and sells them to pay off the creditors, according to detailed rules. Although bankruptcy actions are heavily regulated, they provide ample opportunity for the commission of white-collar or business crimes.

A common bankruptcy crime is the fraudulent transfer of assets either before or after the bankruptcy petition has been filed. Since the laws of bankruptcy provide that the trustee in bankruptcy will take title to the debtor's assets, debtors are often tempted to illegally place them beyond the trustee's reach. For example, a debtor may "sell" assets to a trusted friend at a very low price and then "repurchase" them after the bankruptcy proceedings have been completed. The ways in which assets may be fraudulently transferred is limited only by the imagination of debtors and their accomplices.

Some debtors plan bankruptcy. A planned bankruptcy is a scam that uses business credit as its vehicle. A business dealing in merchandise that can be sold quickly, such as televisions and stereos, is established. The business purchases the merchandise on credit, then pays for it promptly. This process continues until the creditors are willing to offer the business a substantial line of credit. The owners of the business then order a very large shipment of merchandise on credit, sell it at bargain prices for cash, and close the business. When they fail to pay for the merchandise, the creditors file an involuntary petition in bankruptcy against the business. They often recover little or nothing because the assets of the business have been depleted and the wrongdoers have disappeared.

AN UNSAFE CHRISTMAS PRESENT

Hypothetical Case

Hunters, Inc., a producer of hunting equipment, manufactured 30.06-caliber hunting rifles. Because it failed to distribute the rifles to retail stores in time for the Christmas season, sales of the rifles lagged behind the sales of other Hunters products. To reach his sales quota for the quarter, Irving Underhanded, a Hunters salesman, gave the manager of Bargain Gun Basement Store a cash "incentive payment" of $5,000 to stock additional Hunters rifles.

Mr. Brown bought one of the rifles as a Christmas present for his 18-year-old son. Several days after Christmas, Mr. Brown and his son were on a hunting trip. Although the hammer of the son's rifle was in a safe, nonfiring position, the rifle discharged when the son stumbled and fell. The bullet struck Mr. Brown in the arm.

An investigation determined that the rifle had been defectively designed. It discharged accidentally because of an extraheavy firing pin. The addition of a spring could have prevented the accidental discharge.

Is Hunters, Inc. liable for the damages resulting from the personal injuries suffered by Mr. Brown? Is Bargain Gun Basement Store liable? Or are both liable? Explain. Did Irving Underhanded's payment to the manager of Bargain Gun Basement Store constitute a business crime? Why?

Bribery

State laws generally define **bribery** as illegally offering or promising to offer anything of value to a person for doing something that is in the private interest of the bribe giver or the bribe taker. Thus bribery is an intentional violation of "trust" or "fiduciary" duty in return for a special favor or benefit. The person offering the bribe and the person receiving it are equally guilty. Bribery offenses have a substantial impact on American businesses, with one study indicating that their costs run as high as $20 billion annually. Three types of activity may constitute the crime of bribery: (1) commercial bribery, (2) bribery of public officials, and (3) bribery of foreign officials.

Commercial Bribery

In nearly all states, **commercial bribery** consists of bribing an employee in order to influence the employee's conduct in relation to the affairs of his or her employer.[6] Commercial bribery may take place in such aspects of business as sales, service contracts, advertising, purchasing, and engineering. The purpose of the bribery may be to retain current customers or obtain new customers, to cover up false financial statements, to conceal short deliveries, or to cover up inferior products or services.

Bribes usually take the form of cash. However, employees have been induced to violate their duty of trust by bribes in the form of lavish entertainment or of "loans" that they are not expected to repay. Ostensible tipping may also be a commercial bribe. In 1978 a major brewing company was convicted for having its beer salesmen intentionally overtip by $20 at bars to induce the use of its products.[7] Customary tipping in appreciation of service is never a commercial bribe. Kickbacks and payoffs are often commercial bribes. If John, who works for X Company, pays Molly, who works for Y Company, to give him information about the proposed market for Y Company's new product, both John and Molly are guilty of commercial bribery.

While there is no general federal law prohibiting commercial bribery, numerous federal statutes and regulations outlaw the corrupt extension of anything of value to influence commercial transactions in services or products regulated by federal law. The Clayton Act, the Robinson-Patman Act, and the Sherman Antitrust Act (discussed in detail in Chapters 18 and 19) specify criminal penalties for such activities on the federal level. To prevent "sweetheart" contracts between management and labor, the Labor Management Reporting Act of 1959 (discussed in Chapter 14) makes it illegal for an employer to give or lend anything of value to a labor union, its officers, or its members. It is also illegal for an employer to make payments to a third party on behalf of a union official. In one case a company was convicted of making payments to a union official's girlfriend.

Bribery of Public Officials

Attempting to influence a public official to serve a special interest rather than the public interest is a crime. A person elevated to a public office owes a duty not to use his or her office for private gain. Public officials have been bribed, for example, to obtain zoning permits, to prevent the prosecution of criminal violations, to secure particular votes on legislation, and to protect illegal gambling activities.

Bribes of public officials are usually in the form of money. However, cases have held that such a bribe can be a sexual favor, a diamond ring, price discounts, or anything else that the recipient of the offer considers valuable.

The offer of a gift, favor, or money to a public official is not a crime unless a criminal intent is present. If a criminal intent is present, the crime is committed when the gift, favor, or money is offered, even if the public official does not accept or perform the requested act. However, a criminal intent is usually not present when a donor entertains a public official merely to create a generally friendly business climate, provided the entertainment is not conditioned on the official's performance of a particular act. To discourage bribery and close legal loopholes, the receipt of gifts by federal public officials is governed by a complex set of rules and reporting requirements.

Bribery of Foreign Officials

Bribes, kickbacks, and other forms of illegal payments to foreign officials are specifically prohibited under the Foreign Corrupt Practices Act (FPCA), passed in 1977. This act was passed after the Watergate investigations had revealed that Lockheed Aircraft Corporation gave $25 million in "questionable" payments to Japanese government officials in exchange for the purchase of commercial airliners. Shortly thereafter, it was revealed that between 1975 and 1977 more than 400 U.S. corporations had made more than $800 million in questionable payments to foreign officials to facilitate business contracts and other favors from foreign governments.

The FCPA prohibits U.S. corporations from offering anything of value to foreign government officials. Both the corporation and its representatives are subject to strict civil and criminal penalties. The Foreign Corrupt Practices Act is discussed in detail in Chapter 20.

Larceny and Embezzlement by Employees

A 1984 study by the National Institute of Justice, the research branch of the U.S. Department of Justice, estimated that one third of all office and plant workers steal from their employers. According to the U.S. Chamber of Commerce, between 60 and 75 percent of inventory shortages can be attributed to employee theft. Research studies indicate that inventory shrinkage due to employee theft adds at least 2 percent and possibly as much as 4 percent to the cost of retail goods. Nearly 1,000 businesses are forced into bankruptcy by employee theft each year.

Larceny (theft) is the taking of property belonging to another with the intent to deprive the owner of the property. Larceny by employees can take many forms. The following are everyday examples of employee theft: a retail clerk charges a friend $5 for a shirt priced at $20; an office worker takes home a package of pencils; a highly paid executive pads the business account that he submits to his employer.

Larceny
the taking of another's property with the intent to deprive the owner of it

Embezzlement is the wrongful deprivation of property that belongs to another by a person already in lawful possession of it. A bank accountant, for example, may embezzle by funneling money into a personal bank account and shuffling the books to cover up the crime. Banks and other businesses that must give employees access to large amounts of money face the greatest embezzlement problem.

Embezzlement
the wrongful deprivation of another's property by a person entrusted with authority to handle or manage it

Research has shown that employees embezzle because they are living beyond their financial means. These employees usually do not have a criminal record, and detection of their embezzlement is often difficult. Thus many crimes of embezzlement are never reported. Moreover, criminal prosecution of the embezzlers who are caught seldom deters others. For these reasons the nationwide losses due to embezzlement are greater than the nationwide losses due to robbery and burglary combined.

Racketeer Influenced and Corrupt Organizations Act

Since 1951 Congress has wrestled with the problem of organized crime's infiltration into otherwise legitimate businesses. In 1970 Congress enacted the Organized Crime Control Act, a package of bills designed to stem organized crime. Title IX of the act is labeled the Racketeer Influenced and Corrupt Organizations Act (RICO). The stated purpose of RICO is "the elimination of the infiltration of organized crime and racketeering into legitimate organizations operating in interstate commerce."

Although RICO provides civil penalties, as well as criminal penalties, it resulted in only a trickle of private civil litigation during the 1970s.[8] Attorneys assumed at first that it was directed only against organized crime, but they gradually discovered its applicability in ordinary civil commercial suits. These suits ranged from common law fraud cases to complex securities and antitrust cases. The defendants were not mobsters but respected members of the business community. A trickle of RICO cases against legitimate businesses became a rushing stream. Ordinary business disputes are now being handled as federal "racketeering" cases.

Since a private citizen injured by a RICO violation may recover three times the actual damages, plus the court costs and attorney's fees, attorneys have become quite creative in molding private commercial claims to satisfy the RICO statutory requirements. To better understand the applicability and scope of RICO, let us examine its provisions and their interpretation by federal courts.

Statutory Provisions of RICO

RICO prohibits four basic activities: (1) using income derived from a "pattern of racketeering activity" to acquire a financial interest in an enterprise (for example, Mr. Big cannot use "dirty money" to purchase McDonald's shares); (2) acquiring or maintaining an interest in an enterprise through a "pattern of racketeering activity" (for example, Mr. Big cannot acquire an interest in McDonald's by threatening to kidnap its president); (3) conducting the affairs of an enterprise through a "pattern of racketeering activity" (for example, Mr. Big cannot increase McDonald's sales by threatening physical violence to Burger King patrons); and (4) conspiring to violate provisions (1), (2), or (3).

Once the terms of RICO have been clearly defined, it is relatively easy to apply. The key definitions follow:

1. *Person.* RICO defines a "person" as "any individual or entity capable of holding a legal or beneficial interest in property." Therefore, individuals, corporations, partnerships, and trusts are subject to RICO claims.

2. *Enterprise.* Rico defines "enterprise" as "any individual, partnership, corporation, association, or other legal entity, and any union or group of individuals associated in fact although not a legal entity." Courts have held that this term

comprises legitimate businesses (a vending machine company, a trucking firm, a restaurant, an automobile dealership, a hotel); labor unions; government agencies (a police department); and groups of individuals (a prostitution ring, a loan shark group, a credit card ring).

3. *Racketeering Activity.* The offenses listed by RICO as constituting "racketeering activity" may be divided into four categories: (a) crimes of violence (including murder, kidnapping, and extortion); (b) crimes involving illegal goods and services (including pornography, gambling, and drugs); (c) crimes involving labor organizations; and (d) crimes involving commercial fraud (including commercial bribery, industrial espionage, securities fraud, mail fraud, wire fraud,[9] copyright infringement, and trade secret infringement). Of these four categories, RICO is most often used to deal with claims of commercial fraud, particularly mail fraud and wire fraud.

4. *Pattern of Racketeering Activity.* A "pattern of racketeering activity" is defined by RICO as at least two instances of a crime covered by it within a 10-year period, for example, two or more instances of securities, wire, or mail fraud. However, the instances must be interrelated. Federal courts have found the following to constitute a pattern of racketeering activity: (a) the acceptance over a 2½- year period of four bribes from parents who wanted their children admitted to graduate school and (b) a penitentiary warden's participation in three related acts of bribery.

Court Interpretation of RICO

Defendants have attempted to limit the application of RICO in two ways. They argue (1) that RICO is limited to activities involving organized crime and (2) that the plaintiff must establish a "prior conviction." If successful, the first argument would eliminate most commercial fraud litigation under RICO. The second argument requires the plaintiff to establish that the defendant was previously convicted of a "racketeering activity" in order to allege a "pattern of racketeering activity" under RICO. In *Sedima, S.P.R.L. v. Imrex Co.,*[10] the Supreme Court rejected both arguments.

Since RICO permitted a private civil suit by "any person injured in his business or property," the Court concluded that RICO claims were not limited to "racketeering injuries."[11] And since the statute stipulated that a "racketeering activity" need only be "chargeable," "indictable," or "punishable" under specified criminal laws and the word *conviction* did not even appear in any relevant part of the statute, the Court concluded that racketeering activity consisted not of acts for which the defendant had been convicted but acts for which the defendant could be convicted.

Numerous potential areas for the application of RICO have been opened up by the Court's expansive interpretation of RICO in *Sedima.* Among these areas are commercial bribery, industrial espionage, trade secret misappropriation, copyright infringement, and commodities fraud.

RICO Trends

Almost one half of the state legislatures have passed so-called Little RICO statutes. These statutes are patterned after the federal RICO statute, but many of them provide more extensive remedies, such as private injunctive relief and punitive damages. For example, Georgia's Little RICO statute entitles a successful plaintiff to treble damages, punitive damages (in certain cases), and injunctive relief.

In *Sedima* the U.S. Supreme Court stated that if the statutory language of RICO encompassed too broad a spectrum of defendants, "its correction must lie with Congress." In response, several bills to amend RICO have been introduced in Congress, but no amendments have yet been passed. Plaintiffs' lawyers have argued that Congress intended the civil provisions of RICO to be a powerful tool for weeding out fraud in private business practices. Defendants' lawyers, on the other hand, have expressed concern about the epidemic of RICO-created triple-damage lawsuits in which noncriminals are branded as racketeers.

NATURE OF BUSINESS TORTS

The basis of the free enterprise system of the United States is the right to freely begin a business and compete for customers. The history of this country demonstrates that business competition leads to economic prosperity. However, it may also give rise to unethical or illegal behavior that limits lawful businesses and causes others to suffer financial losses. To ensure fair business practices, laws restricting unfair trade have been imposed. Americans demand that individuals and corporations engaging in business maintain high ethical standards. To achieve this goal, an area of law known as "business torts"[12] has been developed. **Business torts** are defined as wrongful interference with the business rights of others. This broad category includes such torts as "unfair competition" and "wrongful interference with contracts."

Business torts
wrongful interference
with the business rights
of others

For purposes of brevity and simplicity, the discussion of the complex topic of business torts will be divided into the following categories: (1) interference with business relations; (2) infringement of trademarks, patents, and copyrights; and (3) disparagement of reputation.

INTERFERENCE WITH BUSINESS RELATIONS

The tort of interfering with business relations includes interference with contractual relations (1) during the *making* of a contract and (2) during the *performance* of a contract. Interference during the performance of a contract occurs most often in employer-employee relations.

Interference with the Making of a Contract

Contracts express the understandings and intentions of businesspersons when they buy, sell, or undertake other business deals. Contracts are actually nothing more than agreements, oral or written, between parties. The rights of a party to contract for performance of business services are necessary for the orderly conduct of business. These rights are recognized as property rights, and the law opposes interference with them.

If a person or a firm intentionally induces another person or firm to refrain from entering into a contract with a third party, that person or firm has committed the tort of *interference with the making of a contract.* This does not apply to socially acceptable interference that is privileged or justified. It applies to interference that goes beyond fair competition and whose purpose is to deprive another person or firm of business.

False statements that adversely affect the reputation of one of the parties can constitute interference with the making of a contract. Suppose, for example, that Charlie Client strongly dislikes Sam Stockbroker. Upon learning that Ima Investor is about to allow Sam to invest a large amount of money for her, Charlie falsely tells her that Sam has embezzled money. As a result, she does not allow Sam to invest the money. Since Charlie's malicious action causes Ima not to enter into the contract, it constitutes a business tort. Sam could obtain a judgment against Charlie for wrongful interference with the making of a contract through unjustified conduct and, perhaps, for disparagement of his reputation, a tort discussed later in this chapter. Had Charlie Client threatened to kill Ima Investor if she contracted with Sam Stockholder, then Charlie would be guilty of wrongful interference with the making of a contract through illegal means.

A justified or privileged inducement not to engage in business with another does not result in a tort. For example, in an attempt to induce state legislatures to ratify the Equal Rights Amendment, the National Organization for Women (NOW) urged organizations not to hold conventions in states that had failed to ratify it. A federal court of appeals held that this was not an improper interference with prospective contractual relationships, because the boycott was privileged under the First Amendment.[13]

The courts distinguish between competition and predatory actions in recognizing interference with the making of a contract. No tort results if bona fide competition, carried on in a justified and legal manner, causes a potential customer not to contract with a certain business. For example, Jay's Towel Shop may, by offering better service or lower prices, induce regular customers to stop dealing with Tanya's Towels and buy their new merchandise from it. Provided that Jay did not open his shop as a predatory action, he would be privileged to lure customers away from Tanya.

Although a business may properly attempt to attract the general public, it may not attempt to directly divert customers from another business. For example, if Jay stationed employees at the entrance of Tanya's store to encourage Tanya's customers to shop at his store instead, Tanya could recover for his wrongful interference with a business relationship. Jay would have been attempting to divert to his store customers who had been attracted by Tanya's advertising and goodwill.

COMPETING FIRMS SELLING REAL ESTATE

Seventh Heaven Company was developing and promoting Seventh Heaven Acres, a vacation home real estate development. As part of its promotional campaign, Seventh Heaven provided lodging for prospective buyers at a motel that it owned. A former employee of the company approached buyers in their motel rooms, where he persuaded them to rescind their contract with Seventh Heaven and to purchase property at a lower price from his company, Restful Acres Company.

Shangri-La, Inc., another competitor of Seventh Heaven, began an extensive newspaper, radio, and television advertising campaign promoting its real estate development. Because of the campaign, Dave broke his contract with Seventh Heaven and entered into a contract with Shangri-La.

Did the former employee's actions on Seventh Heaven property constitute a business tort. Why? Did Shangri-La, Inc. commit a business tort? Why?

Hypothetical Case

Interference with the Performance of a Contract

The right to expect performance under an *existing contract* enjoys even greater protection than the right to contract. If a contract is breached by one of its parties, the innocent party can bring an action in contract to recover payment for damages caused by the breach. Such a lawsuit differs from an action in tort because it deals with the terms of the contract.

However, if a third party unjustifiably interferes to induce one of the parties to breach the contract, the innocent party to the contract can bring an action in tort against the third party for the damages caused by the *interference with contract performance* (commonly called "inducing breach of contract"). This action in tort can also be brought against any third person who attempts to make performance of the contract more difficult. In the securities example above, if an actual contract had already been signed between Ima Investor and Sam Stockbroker when Charlie Client interfered, Stockbroker could bring an action against Client for interference with the performance of a contract.

Charlie Client would be liable for wrongful interference with the performance of the contract if these four elements were present:

1. Client knew of the existence of the contract and intended to cause Investor to breach it.
2. Client's actions were not legally justified.
3. Investor breached the contract as a result of Client's actions.
4. Stockbroker suffered damages because of the breach.

A contract may include a provision that allows either party to terminate the contract at will, usually after a brief period of notice to the other party. Termination at will simply means that either party may choose to terminate the contract at his or her election without being liable for damages for breach of contract. Despite this freedom, however, a third person is not privileged, without justification, to intentionally induce one of the parties to terminate the contract at his or her election without being liable for damages for breach of contract.

The leading case of interference with contract performance is *Texaco, Inc., v. Pennzoil Co.*[14] In late 1983 Pennzoil Company approached Getty Oil Company about the possibility of purchasing a significant portion of Getty Oil's outstanding stock. On January 3, 1984, Pennzoil and Getty Oil drafted a Memorandum of Agreement under which Pennzoil was to purchase about three sevenths of Getty Oil's outstanding shares of stock for about $110 a share. The remaining four sevenths would be owned by the Sarah C. Getty Trust. Pennzoil and the trust were to operate Getty Oil on the basis of their respective stock ownership.

On the evening of January 6, 1984, representatives of Texaco Oil Company met with Gordon Getty, trustee of the Sarah C. Getty Trust, to discuss the purchase of the trust's shares. Texaco offered Getty $125 a share, Getty accepted the offer, and a merger agreement between Texaco and Getty Oil was signed on the same evening.

In February Pennzoil filed suit against Texaco, alleging that Texaco had tortiously induced Getty Oil to breach a contract to sell its shares to Pennzoil. In 1983 a Texas jury returned a verdict in favor of Pennzoil in an amount exceeding $11 billion. The Texas Court of Appeals later reduced the judgment to about $9 billion.

INFRINGEMENT OF TRADEMARKS, TRADE NAMES, PATENTS, AND COPYRIGHTS

Trademarks

Generally, a **trademark** is any word, symbol, or design that a manufacturer affixes to its products so that consumers may readily identify them. For example, the back pocket stitching design on Levi Strauss blue jeans is a trademark. Trademark laws prohibit manufacturers from copying or closely imitating the trademark of a competitor. These laws serve two basic purposes: (1) to protect consumers from deception concerning the origin of a product and (2) protect the "investment" of the trademark owner. For example, if L & K Cola Company were permitted to copy the red and white can design used by Coca-Cola Bottling Company, consumers would be confused and L & K Cola Company would get a "free ride" on the goodwill and advertising expenditures of Coca-Cola.

While not technically a trademark because it does not identify tangible goods, a **service mark,** which identifies services, receives the same treatment as a trademark. Car rental, laundry, and automobile repair businesses, for example, may use a service mark to identify their services.

Although trademarks are usually registered with state and federal agencies, they are protected regardless of registration. A trademark becomes the exclusive property of the first firm to employ it in marketing a product or service. Since such a firm enjoys a common law property right in its trademark, an unregistered, but protected, trademark is known as a **common law trademark.**[15]

Trademarks registered with the U.S. Patent and Trademark Office (PTO) are protected by federal law—the Lanham Act of 1946. Trademark registrants must submit five drawings of the trademark and a filing fee to the PTO. An approved trademark receives a certificate of registration that is valid for 20 years and renewable for an additional 20 years. However, the registrant must file an affidavit (a written statement of facts confirmed by an oath) at the end of five years stating that the approved trademark is still in use. Failure to file the affidavit results in cancellation of the trademark. The renewal requirement is imposed because companies have hoarded trademarks for possible future use.

A 1989 amendment to the trademark law allows companies to apply for trademarks without first marketing the products that they identify. The purpose of the amendment was to remove the competitive advantage of European companies over U.S. companies. Under the laws of Europe, and now of the United States, companies can lock up a trademark by filing a notice of a bona fide intent to use it. This allows companies to protect a trademark for three years without actually using it.

For several reasons a trademark registrant might be denied a certificate of registration. A trademark cannot be deceptive, immoral, merely descriptive, or so similar to one already in use that the general public is likely to be confused. When the PTO or the courts examine potential trademarks, they typically place them in one of four categories: (1) arbitrary and fanciful; (2) suggestive; (3) descriptive words, personal names, and geographic places; or (4) generic.

Trademarks that are classified in the first two categories, arbitrary-fanciful and suggestive, are always registerable, provided they are not too similar to a prior trademark. Exxon for gasoline, Kodak for cameras, and Rolex for watches are

Trademark
artwork, symbol, or design placed on a product to identify its manufacturer

Service mark
artwork, symbol, or design intended to identify the services provided by a company as well as the company

Common law trademark
an effective unregistered trademark that is acquired by the first firm to employ it

examples of arbitrary and fanciful trademarks. These words have no meaning apart from their distinctive use as trademarks. Teflon when used by a manufacturer of refrigerators, Hawaiian Tropic when used by a manufacturer of suntan oil, and Eveready when used by a manufacturer of batteries and flashlights are examples of suggestive trademarks. But the trademark Teflon is arbitrary and fanciful if a shoe manufacturer uses it.

The third category of trademarks—descriptive words, personal names, and geographic places—is not registrable since the words in this category should be available to everyone. The Phone Company as a name for a telephone and telephone equipment store and The Computer Store as a name for a computer retail company were merely descriptive and could not be registered as trademarks. Raisin-Bran as a name for a breakfast food was denied a trademark because the name merely described the ingredients of the product, and Grandma Jones could not become a registered trademark for cake mixes because every person has the right to use his or her name in connection with a business. However, a personal name accompanied by a unique design might be registrable. Thus the name Grandma Jones accompanied by a distinctive picture of a little old lady on a rocker might be registrable. Similar registrable examples include McDonald's accompanied by a large yellow "M" and Betty Crocker accompanied by the face of a woman.

Secondary meaning

the public's association of a trademark with a particular manufacturer and with the quality of a product

Even a trademark that is merely descriptive, a personal name, or a geographic place will be protected if it has acquired a secondary meaning. A trademark acquires a **secondary meaning** when, through long use in connection with a product, the consumer public associates it with a particular manufacturer and thus draws a conclusion as to the quality of the product. Cream of Wheat, for instance, is a merely descriptive trademark that has acquired a secondary meaning through over 100 years of extensive advertising by Nabisco Brands, Inc. Coca-Cola is a trademark that has acquired a secondary meaning as applied to beverages. In a famous trademark infringcment case, *The Coca-Cola Company v. The Koke Company of America*,[16] the Supreme Court in 1920 enjoined the Koke Company from using the work "Koke" to identify its products. The court held that the word was so similar to Coca-Cola's name that it would confuse purchasers. For most persons the name Coca-Cola signified the product of The Coca-Cola Company rather than a compound of particular substances.

Generic trademarks, the fourth category, are never registrable. Generic terms that designate a class of goods cannot become protected trademarks even if they have acquired a secondary meaning. Examples of such terms are *monopoly, cellophane, cola, aspirin, thermos,* and *lite* or *light.*

Trademark infringement

the accidental or intentional use of a trademark so similar to another as to probably confuse the public

Once a trademark has been created for a product, it is protected against infringement by products of the same kind. A **trademark infringement** occurs when a firm uses a trademark whose similarity to a previously established trademark of another firm is likely to confuse the consumer public. In such cases, the owner of the established trademark may receive court-granted injunctive relief and damages (compensation from the defendant for economic losses that have resulted from the infringement).

The following two cases illustrates this process. The manufacturer of a novelty beer can used the trademark Battlin' Bulldog Beer, and the University of Georgia brought suit claiming that the trademark infringed on its registered service mark, which depicted an English bulldog wearing a sweater on which the letter "G" and the word "BULLDOGS" were emblazoned. In *University of Georgia Athletic Ass'n v.*

Laite,[17] the court granted an injunction against the manufacturer. It concluded that the manufacturer had infringed on the University of Georgia's service mark because its trademark was likely to confuse the consumer public, which would probably think that the University of Georgia had approved the use of the trademark on the beer cans.

In another case, *Lucas Films Ltd. v. High Frontier,*[18] the court found little or no likelihood of confusion. George Lucas, the owner of the Star Wars trademark, sued a public lobby group that referred to President Reagan's Strategic Defense Initiative program as "star wars." The court decided that the consumer public was not likely to infer that Lucas had approved this use of his trademark. It also decided that he had suffered no economic harm from this use.

LAW ABROAD

European Community

A distinguishing feature of European Community law concerning trademarks is the "exhaustion of rights" principle. Under this principle, once a trademarked product has been marketed in one EC member state by the trademark owner (or with the owner's consent), the trademark rights cannot be used to keep that product off the market in other member states. For example, if a Danish chocolate company sells its trademarked candy bar in all of the EC member states except Spain, it cannot prevent the sale of the candy bar in Spain on trademark grounds. This policy, like most of the substantive law of the EC, is designed to promote the free movement of goods among member states.

Another trademark principle of the EC is the "common origin" principle. This principle comes into play when two companies in two countries both have the same trademark for a product or products. Such a situation usually occurs when a company that does business in several EC member states sells its operations and trademark rights in a particular country to a company in that country. In the common market created by the EC, the result is that different companies with the same products and trademark are competing against each other. For example, imagine that 10 years ago a German coffee manufacturer sold its subsidiary operations in France and Belgium, including the rights to its distinctive trademark, to a company in each of these countries. Now three companies have the same fairly acquired trademark. Because of the common origin of the trademark, these companies may not sue one another for trademark infringement.

Germany

Merchants, commercial partnerships, and corporations may apply to the Federal Patent Office for registration of a trademark intended to distinguish their goods. Such a trademark can be words or pictures, or both, but there are certain restrictions. For example, a tea company cannot use a figure of a Chinese person as a trademark, because such figures are widely employed in the tea trade. Also not allowed are trademarks that are simply numbers or a single letter.

Those who oppose the registration of a new trademark can express their opposition to the Federal Patent Office. Protection of a new trademark occurs upon registration. The right to exclusive use of a trademark is granted for 10 years from the date of registration; this right may be renewed as often as desired. Nonregistered trademarks may be protected on the basis of their use and their reputation.

The laws that protect service marks are essentially the same as the laws that protect trademarks.

There is reciprocity of trademark protection between Germany and the United States. Germany grants protection to trademarks registered in the United States, and vice versa.

Japan

Trademarks may be written characters, designs, or signs—or any combination thereof—that are used to distinguish the merchandise or goods of a person or a firm. To be protected, a trademark must be registered with the Patent Office. Generic or insufficiently distinctive trademarks, trademarks that resemble governmental designs, and inappropriate or offensive trademarks cannot be registered. A proposed trademark that conflicts with an existing trademark requires the consent of the holder of the existing trademark. The rights granted by trademark registration last 10 years, and renewals are readily available.

Infringement of a trademark exposes the violator to injunctions, actions for damages, and criminal prosecution. An application for cancellation of a trademark can be filed on the ground that it has been used improperly by its owner or licensee or that it has not been used for three years or more. Foreign trademarks may be registered in Japan.

Patents

Patent
the right to the exclusive manufacture and sale of an invention

Patent law gives a legal monopoly to the owner of an invention. A **patent** grants the owner a nonrenewable right, for 17 years, to exclude others from making, using, or selling the patented invention. Designs for a manufactured article, say a new toy or a fabric, may also be patented. Patents for designs last for a shorter time than patents for inventions.

The patent laws are intended to protect the invention or discovery of a process, machine, manufacture, or composition of matter. They reward inventors for the time and money they invest on risky endeavors. Granting inventors a temporary monopoly provides them with an opportunity to earn a rate of return that makes their investment worthwhile.

An individual who files a patent application with the Patent Office must show in detail how his or her invention or discovery satisfies a three-part test: (1) novelty, (2) utility, and (3) nonobviousness. The novelty element prohibits a patentable invention or discovery from being substantially similar to a previously patented invention or discovery. The utility element requires the patenter to demonstrate that the invention or discovery is useful. An invention that has no known use cannot be patented. The nonobviousness element requires that the invention or discovery not be obvious to a person of ordinary skill in the field of the invention or discovery. Each of these elements involves a question of fact that the Patent Office must determine. If two patent applications are filed for the same invention, the Patent Office holds a proceeding to determine who invented it first. The first inventor will receive the patent.

In employment situations, questions regarding the ownership of patents often arise. If an employee develops a patentable process or machine during working hours or while using the employer's equipment and materials, the patent probably belongs to the employer. For example, the fact that Joe Engineer quit his job with Southern Bell before applying for a patent will not entitle him to the patent if he developed his invention while working for Southern Bell. Frequently, employees sign an employment contract providing that any inventions related to the employer's business that they develop while working for the employer and even for a one- or two-year period after the termination of their employment belong to the employer. Courts generally uphold such provisions.

A patent owner must place notice of his or her patent on a discovery or invention. Notice consists of the word "Patent" or the abbreviation "Pat." followed by the patent number. Using or selling a patented invention without the authority of the patent owner is a business tort known as **patent infringement.** In the case of a patented process, all the steps of the process must be copied for an infringement to exist. Litigation for patent infringement is long and costly. Consequently, patent owners often settle infringement cases by selling the infringer a license to use the patent instead of incurring the costs of a lawsuit.

Patent infringement
the use or sale of a patented invention without authorization from the patent holder

International trade has given rise to the sale of patented inventions in foreign countries. To protect such inventions, it is necessary to obtain patent protection in those countries. While U.S. patent laws provide protection from domestic infringement, they do not apply to violations by foreign manufacturers. However, a patented product cannot be assembled in an unauthorized fashion outside the United States for international sales. An unauthorized U.S. businessperson who supplies component parts of a patented invention to a foreign manufacturer is liable under the Patent Law Amendments Acts of 1984.

An invention or discovery whose patent expires becomes public property. However, creative patent owners can extend the life of their patents by discovering or inventing a novel, useful, and nonobvious improvement.

LAW ABROAD

European Community

The laws covering patent protection vary widely among nations. And while most nations attempt to respect the patent laws of other nations, a patent dispute between the citizens of two nations can become very complicated.

However, the EC, through the Convention for the European Patent of the Common Market, has developed a simple solution: the community patent. This patent requires only one application process and is recognized in all of the EC member states. Thus a Portuguese firm that develops a new type of computer memory storage can obtain such a patent and be assured of patent protection throughout the EC.

Each EC member state retains its own system of issuing patents. The community patent is just a way of extending the protection afforded by that system.

Germany

Patent protection is available in Germany for inventions that have potential industrial use. The inventor must file an application with the patent office, which makes sure that an invention is patentable before granting a patent. The patent entitles the owner alone to take advantage of the patented item. If the patent holder's rights are violated, the patent holder can require that the violation cease and a suit for damages may be available in the case of intentional or negligent violation.

The Federal Patent Court (Bundespatentgericht) decides appeals from decisions of the Patent Office's Examination Department and Patent Division. Such appeals may be taken to the Board of Appeals of the Patent Court, and ultimately to the federal supreme court (Bundesgerichtshof).

Patent protection is effective for 20 years from the date of application. Persons without a residence or business establishment in Germany must be represented by an attorney in their dealings with the Patent Office. Germany recognizes the patent of the European Community. It is also a party to international agreements to respect the patents granted by other nations, such as the International Convention of Paris and the Berne Convention.

Japan

Applications for patents are made at the Patent Office, and patent rights come into existence only by registration with the Patent Office. A foreigner residing or doing business in Japan can apply for a patent on the same footing as a Japanese citizen. A nonresident of Japan who wishes to apply for Japanese patent protection must be represented in Japan by either a lawyer or a patent agent. Inventions of new "high-grade" articles and new industrial processes may be patented in Japan, with two exceptions: (1) material manufactured by means of atomic reaction and (2) items potentially hazardous to public health, morals, or order.

If several applications for a patent on the same invention are filed, the first applicant is the only one entitled to the patent. If those applications are filed on the same day, no applicant is entitled to the patent. Upon request, examiners of the Patent Office will review a patent application. Patent rights last for 15 years from the date of application, and this term can be extended 5 years. Patents can be transferred, inherited, or pledged (placed as security for a loan); however, registration with the Patent Office is usually required.

Copyrights

Copyright
the exclusive right to control the copying and distribution of a literary or artistic work

Generally, a **copyright** is the exclusive right granted by federal law to the copyright holder to print, reprint, publish, copy, and sell the literary or artistic work of an author or creator. Copyright protection extends to books, periodicals, newspapers, dramatic and musical compositions, letters, works of art, photographs, pictorial illustrations, and motion pictures. Under the Copyright Act of 1976, it extends for the author's life plus an additional 50 years after the author's death.

Like trademark protection, copyright protection arises automatically when a work has been created in fixed form. Registration with the U.S. copyright office is not required to protect the work since it *immediately* becomes the property of the person who created it. However, unless the work is registered, a copyright infringement action cannot be instituted. Unlike the patent laws, the copyright laws do not require novelty and inventiveness. In fact, a copyrightable work may be substantially similar to a work previously copyrighted.

Although registration is not required for protection, notice of a copyright is recommended. To protect a work against infringement, the copyright owner must affix to each copy of a published work the word *copyright* or its abbreviation

"Copr" or "©" followed by the year of first publication of the work and the name of the author. An example follows: © 1992 Mary R. Smith.[19]

Several categories of material are ineligible for the protection of the copyright laws. The copyright system, for example, protects the particular expression of an idea, but not the idea itself. In one case an artist who had painted a picture of a cardinal sued a second artist, who painted a similar picture of a cardinal. The court held that although the ideas in the two paintings were similar, they were expressed differently. Consequently, the second painting did not infringe on the copyright of the first. Works that have not been fixed in a tangible form of expression are also ineligible for copyright protection. An unwritten or unrecorded speech, for example, is not protected by the copyright laws.

For years telephone companies maintained that the information contained in the white pages of their telephone directories was protected by copyright. In 1991, in *Feist Publications v. Rural Telephone Service Co.,*[20] the Supreme Court unanimously rejected this view. The Court held that mere listings of facts or data such as the white pages listings of names, addresses, and telephone numbers, could not be copyrighted, that only compilations of facts or data possessing some element of originality could be copyrighted. Thus the yellow pages of telephone books are copyrightable because their arrangement involves creativity and originality. As a result of this ruling, every company that compiles and vends information will have to determine whether its service will have copyright protection.

The first U.S. copyright statute, enacted in 1790, protected only maps, charts, and books. Since the enactment of that statute, the spectrum of copyrightable material has expanded considerably. Most recently, the Semiconductor Chip Protection Act of 1984 added computer programs etched into a computer microchip to the list of copyrightable material. The act, however, limits copyright protection for such programs to 10 years.

No copyright will protect an author's work throughout the world. However, most countries recognize the copyright laws of other countries through copyright treaties. The United States is a member of the Universal Copyright Convention (UCC), which became effective in 1955. Manufacturers in the United States may affix the symbol © and/or the word *copyright* on the goods they export to countries that are UCC members.

A work whose copyright has expired is in the public domain and may be exploited without permission. Mark Twain's *Huckleberry Finn* is an example of a work that is now in the public domain. Many publishers have copied and sold such works.

The Copyright Act of 1976 permits fair use of copyrighted material without permission of the copyright owner. The act defines *fair use* as copying "for purposes such as criticism, comment, news reporting, teaching (including multiple copying for classroom use), scholarship, or research" without infringing on the exclusive rights of copyright owners. The statute enumerates four factors to be considered in determining whether the use of a copyrighted work is fair: (1) the nature of the work, (2) whether the use is commercial or nonprofit, (3) the amount of the work used in relation to the whole, and (4) the effect of the use on the potential market or value of the work. Copying a number of poems in order to save students the cost of purchasing an anthology would not constitute fair use. However, copying one or two of E.E. Cummings's poems for classroom distribution would constitute fair use, since such use of the poems is reasonable and not harmful to the copyright owner.

Infringement of a copyright requires the actual copying of a copyrighted work without permission. The infringer need only copy a substantial part of the work to commit the business tort of copyright infringement. In one case, a newspaper infringed on the copyright of a graphics company's artwork. The newspaper copied a picture entitled "Ronbo," which superimposed a photograph of Ronald Reagan's face on a muscular body that was firing a machine gun. The court decided that this was not fair use and awarded the copyright owner damages for the infringement.

Some of the most hotly contested copyright infringement disputes occur when a copyrighted work is satirized or parodied. Courts, however, generally permit parody and satire as fair use of a copyrighted work. In one case the court decided that the television series "The Greatest American Hero" made fair use of Superman's traits when it parodied American superheroes. In another case the court found fair use despite the copying of the first 6 bars of a 38-bar song. The composers of the song "When Sunny Gets Blue" brought a copyright infringement action against a disc jockey who called his parody of the song "When Sonny Sniffs Glue." The parody ran for 29 minutes as a comedy record album. The decisive factor in determining whether a parody or a satire constitutes fair use is a recognizable economic effect on the parodied or satirized work. If a parody results in a significant economic loss to the owner of the copyright to such a work, the courts usually find that it constitutes *unfair* use.

LAW ABROAD

Germany

The period of copyright protection for literary, musical, and other types of original creative works is 70 years after the author's death. Photographic works and the works of performing artists, film producers, broadcasters, and manufacturers of mechanical devices are protected for 25 years. Except models and designs, no copyright registration is necessary for such works. Germany is also a member of the Berne Convention of 1886, which most countries, though not the United States and the USSR, adhere to. This agreement extends protection to the musical and literary works of member countries. Germany is also a member of the Universal Copyright Convention, whose protection is not quite as sweeping as that granted under the Berne Convention.

A particularly interesting feature of copyright protection in Germany is that manufacturers, distributors, and users of tape recorders (even private, noncommercial users) have had liability for royalty payments extended to them. In addition, Germany has enacted a law modeled after the U.S. Semiconductor Chips Protection Act of 1984, which grants protection to semiconductor chips.

Japan

No application for copyright need be made for literary, scientific, artistic, or musical creations. This means that copyright protection is extended when a work has been created. Transfers or pledges of copyrights must be registered at the Ministry of Education, however, if the new owner seeks to enjoy the privileges of copyright.

Copyright protection extends for the life of the author and for 50 years after the author's death. Motion pictures and photographs also enjoy 50 years of posthumous protection. Infringement of copyrights gives rise to suits for injunctions against unauthorized use and for damages. Japan is a party to the Berne Convention.

DISPARAGEMENT OF REPUTATION

The laws of our society impose a general duty on all members of the society to avoid the tort of **defamation**—making false statements that damage the reputation of another. When a person breaches this duty by communicating such statements orally, the tort of **slander** is committed. When such statements are communicated through writing, the tort of **libel** has been committed. Libel has traditionally been considered more serious than slander, but the distinction between the two has become less meaningful.

The tort of defamation does not occur unless the damaging statement is communicated to a third person (this is called "publication"). For example, a damaging statement about Tom that only Tom hears is not defamatory since the statement has not damaged Tom's reputation.

Libel and slander become business torts when false statements are made about the reputation or quality of a party's business. Suppose, for example, that when Joe's Supermarket switched from Mary's Market Supply to another supplier, an angry Mary falsely stated to many people that the meat sold by Joe's Supermarket weighed less than the amount stated on the package. If the communication of those statements caused Joe's Supermarket to lose sales, Mary committed the business tort of **disparagement of reputation.** If, however, only Joe heard Mary make the statements, the tort of disparagement of reputation did not occur because the reputation of Joe's Supermarket was not harmed by them.

The tort of defamation can occur in the employer-employee relationship. The following scenario is typical: A person applies for a job, and the prospective employer contacts the person's former employer for a letter of reference. The letter of reference states why the person was discharged, the prospective employer does not hire the person, and the person files a defamation suit against the former employer based on the letter of reference.

The former employer is granted a **qualified privilege** in most states. This means that if the former employer provided mistaken information in a good faith belief that the information was accurate, the former employer is protected. To prove defamation, the former employee is required to show that the mistaken information was provided with malice (ill-will or spite).

Approximately one third of all defamation lawsuits are related to employment. The threat and reality of defamation lawsuits have drastically reduced the flow of truthful information between former and prospective employers. Job references are now extremely difficult to check because most attorneys advise employers to refrain from discussing former employees.

In the following case a fired employee sued his former employer for defamation based on the former employer's communications within the company and to a prospective employer.

Defamation

false statements made by one person that damage the reputation of another person

Slander

a defamation that is communicated orally

Libel

a defamation that is communicated in writing

Disparagement of reputation

communication of false statements about the business practices of a person or a company that tends to damage the person or company in the eyes of the public

Qualified privilege

the right of a former employer to give another employer information about an employee's work habits and abilities; even if the information given is incorrect, no suit may be brought unless malice is shown

TURNER v. HALLIBURTON COMPANY, INC.
SUPREME COURT OF KANSAS
722 P.2d 1106 (1986)

Together with others, Hiram Turner, the plaintiff-appellee, an employee of Halliburton Company, Inc., stole company tools from another employee's truck. The theft occurred outside a local café on Turner's day off from work. Turner had been drinking and did not remember the event, but his companions later testified that the tools were taken to play a joke on the employee. After one of the companions was arrested for the theft, Turner returned the tools to Halliburton. William Arend, the Halliburton manager, terminated Turner's employment because of his role in the theft. Although Arend discussed the reason for the termination only with supervisory and managerial personnel, as required, it became common knowledge to the other Halliburton employees.

Shortly thereafter Turner was refused employment by Ark City Packing Company. The refusal was based on an employer reference in which Halliburton stated that Turner had been terminated for "stealing company property." Subsequently, Turner filed suit against Halliburton Company and Arend (the defendants-appellants), for defamation of character based on communications to (1) other managerial employees and (2) the prospective employer. The trial court entered judgment in Turner's favor, and the defendants appealed.

HOLMES, JUSTICE

The first issue raised by appelllants is that they were entitled to prevail, as a matter of law, in the defamation action because they were privileged in their communications and no evidence was presented to support a finding of actual malice.

In any proceeding where the plaintiff complains that he or she has been defamed, a number of affirmative defenses are available, among them privilege and truth. A qualified or limited privilege is granted to those with a special interest or duty in the subject matter of the [alleged defamatory] communication. The availabilty of a limited privilege is generally restricted to those situations where public policy is deemed to favor the free exchange of information over the individual's interest in his or her good reputation. One such qualified privilege exists with respect to business or employment communications made in good faith and between individuals with a corresponding interest or duty in the subject matter of the communication.

Where a defamatory statement is made in a situation where there is a qualified privilege, the injured party has the burden of proving not only that the statements were false, but also that the statements were made with actual malice—*with actual evil-mindedness or specific intent to injure.*

While Turner alluded to the fact that his termination because of theft was widely known, he failed to produce any evidence to prove that this information came from communications from the defendants.

The evidence relied upon by appellee to establish actual malice is detailed in his brief and will be reviewed here in the best possible light from appellee's standpoint. Arend, at the termination meeting, accused Turner of theft of the tools, other thefts, and of fencing property in Gueda Springs; Arend did not undertake his own outside investigation after being advised Turner was involved in the missing tools incident; there were discrepancies between the police officers' testimony and that of Arend as to when the officers first talked to Arend and gave him the information that Turner was involved; Arend made statements to police that Turner may have been involved in other thefts of company property and was being watched; Arend also stated he wanted Turner prosecuted; Ryser valued the tools at $80.00, while Arend valued them at cost less 20%, for a figure of $125.88; Halliburton had a list of 69 different grounds for termination, but Arend chose stealing company property, knowing this would go into Turner's records and possibly be relayed to other prospective employers; and Arend had a bad attitude at the conference wherein Turner was terminated.

Employee conduct, particularly involving theft, is a matter within the bounds of the qualified privilege pertaining to communications within the company. All of the Halliburton personnel who testified to having knowledge of the communications were shown to be managerial-level employees with an interest in the situation. While evidence was offered to indicate the defendant Arend was upset about the taking of Halliburton property, no evidence tended to establish an evil motive on the part of the defendants. Therefore, with respect to the intracompany communications, it does not appear Turner overcame the defendants' privilege by proving actual malice.

A privilege also existed with respect to communications between Halliburton and Ark City Packing. Therefore, it is also necessary for Turner to demonstrate actual malice on the part of the defendants to be entitled to recover on this claim.

At trial the plaintiff presented Carolyn Borror, who was in charge of screening applicants at Ark City Packing Co. Borror testified that she had accepted an application for employment from the appellee. Turner's application indicated that he had formerly worked for Halliburton and the reason for his unemployed status was "layoff." When Borror checked with Turner's former employer, Halliburton, she was informed that Turner was terminated for "stealing company property." This information was provided over the telephone by Wilbur Bright, and subsequently confirmed by written communication. Again there is absolutely no evidence that the appellants acted with evil-mindedness or specific intent to injure Turner. The rule would also appear to preclude recovery on the basis of Turner's consent to or request for the communication to Ark City Packing Co.

The communications with the police department were initiated by the police during a routine investigation of the reported theft of the Halliburton tools. There was a duty on the part of Halliburton's employees to cooperate in that investigation, and the communications were subject to a qualified privilege.

We hold that, based upon this record, when all of the facts and the inferences to be drawn therefrom are resolved in favor of Turner, there is no credible evidence to support a finding of actual malice upon the part of the defendants.

Reversed.

Legal Issues

1. According to the court, under what types of situations is the granting of a qualified privilege appropriate?
2. How does the court define actual malice?

Ethical Issues

1. What view or views of ethics support the recognition of a qualified privilege on behalf of an employer-defendant in a defamation suit brought by a former employee who claims that the employer made a false statement about him or her to a potential new employer? Why?

2. Is it consistent with bottom-line ethics to recognize a qualified privilege on behalf of an employer-defendant in a lawsuit brought by a former employee because the employer made a false statement about the former employee to someone who, but for that statement, would have hired the former employee? Why?

PRODUCTS LIABILITY

Products liability
liability on the part of the manufacturer and seller of a product for injuries caused by a defective product

Manufacturers and sellers are liable for damages caused by defective products that injure consumers, users, or bystanders. This liability is called **products liability.** Products liability law encompasses four legal theories of recovery: (1) the contract theory of warranty, (2) the tort theory of negligence, (3) the tort theory of strict liability, and (4) the tort theory of misrepresentation.

The responsibility for injury in products liability cases usually rests with the manufacturer; however, the wholesaler, retailer, and other sellers in the channel of distribution may also be held responsible. Under modern products liability principles, the lawsuit may be brought by a buyer of the defective product, a user of the product, or a bystander who is injured by the product. Although a claim in products liability can be based on four legal theories, strict liability now predominates as the basis of recovery.

Recent years have witnessed an explosion in products liability litigation. The increased resort to the courts of persons injured by products and the increased acceptance by states of strict liability as a basis of recovery have taken a heavy toll on the business community. Products liability insurance premiums have skyrocketed; in such industries as sporting goods, they have increased thousands of percent. As a result some small companies have stopped carrying such insurance. "Going naked" renders these companies particularly susceptible to business failure not only because they face the possibility of uninsured claims but also because distributors and retailers are reluctant to carry products that lack the protection of insurance coverage. Yet another effect of the increase in products liability litigation has been the hesitancy of companies to develop and market new product lines, especially in high-risk areas such as the pharmaceutical industry.

Liability Based on Warranty

Warranties are a part of products liability law. A warranty is some undertaking of the seller with respect to the goods sold and thus a part of the sales contract. Even a seller who never uses the word *warranty* may be answerable in damages to the buyer for a breach of warranty.

A buyer, user, or injured bystander can recover in contract from any seller for damages based on breach of the seller's express or implied warranties. Thus a person who buys goods from a retailer may hold the retailer or the manufacturer liable if the goods do not meet the warranty's standards of quality. It is not necessary for the buyer to prove that the seller was negligent.

In the past, laws dealing with business transactions were not uniform throughout the United States. To achieve uniformity, 49 states have adopted the Uniform Commercial Code, which is designed to deal with the most common problems that arise in business transactions. Article 2 of the Uniform Commercial Code deals with contracts for the sale of goods. A good is tangible personal property— property that has a physical existence, and it is movable. The sale of an automobile, jewelry, books, and clothing is an example of a *sale of goods.*[21] Under Article 2 of the Uniform Commercial Code, such a sale may involve an express warranty and implied warranties of merchantability and fitness.

Express Warranties

The Uniform Commercial Code defines an **express warranty** as a guarantee created by any affirmation of facts or any promise made by the seller that relates to the goods sold and becomes part of the basis of the bargain. Mere opinions stated about the goods are "sales talk" or "dealer puff," and do not create warranties. If a dealer states that a car has a 350-cubic-inch engine, this is a representation of fact and creates a warranty. On the other hand, if a dealer states that a car has a "good engine," this is merely an opinion and does not create a warranty. Express warranties can be created when the seller does not use the words *warranty* or *guarantee* or when the seller has no intention of making a warranty. Labels on merchandise, such as "100 percent cotton," can result in express warranties. In some cases a seller's conduct can bring about an express warranty. For example, drawing a sample of fabric from the mass to be sold creates an express warranty that the quality of the entire mass will conform to that of the sample drawn.

Implied Warranties

The implied warranties of merchantability and fitness may be imposed by law simply because a sale of goods was completed, even though the seller made no representations or promises relating to the goods. A **warranty of merchantability** is implied in all contracts for the sale of goods if the seller is a merchant. A **merchant** is generally a professional who deals in the class of goods involved in the transaction. *Merchantability* means that the goods are *fit for the ordinary purpose for which such goods are used.* To be merchantable, the goods need not be perfect, but they must meet the standard of average quality.[22] Thus a heater must heat, an air conditioner must cool, and food must be fit for human consumption. On the other hand, no warranty of merchantability is implied if Smith sells his home heater to a friend, since Smith is not a merchant dealing in heaters.

An implied **warranty of fitness** for a particular purpose is created (1) if the seller knows at the time of contracting that the buyer intends to use the goods for a particular purpose and (2) if the seller knows that in purchasing the goods, the buyer is relying on the seller's skill or judgment. For example, suppose that a buyer asks a seller for help in finding a pair of shoes for mountain climbing. If the seller recommends a pair for that purpose, then an implied warranty that the shoes are fit for climbing mountains is created. In all cases of the fitness warranty, the buyer's reliance on the seller's judgment must be proved. A buyer who asks for a particular brand of climbing shoes cannot prove reliance on the seller's skill and judgment.

Express warranty
a guarantee created by a specific factual statement or promise made by a seller that influences the buyer to purchase the goods

Warranty of merchantability
the implied promise that goods are fit for the purpose for which they are sold

Merchant
a professional who deals in the class of goods involved in a transaction

Warranty of fitness
the implied promise that goods are fit for the purpose for which they are sold

Exclusion or Modification of Warranties

The Uniform Commercial Code provides detailed rules for the exclusion of warranties. Express warranties, once made, are difficult to exclude. The Uniform Commercial Code provides that an express warranty can be excluded by clear, specific language. However, a disclaimer of this kind is ineffective if it is inconsistent with the words or the conduct that created the express warranty. An agreement containing an express warranty and a clause disclaiming the express warranty almost always contains inconsistent clauses. In a case in which a seller sold a machine described as a "haybaler," the sales contract also contained a disclaimer of all express and implied warranties. The machine did not bale hay, and the buyer successfully sued for breach of express warranty.

The inconsistency between an express warranty and a disclaimer is resolved in favor of preserving the warranty. A seller who does not wish to be liable for an express warranty should not say or do anything that might create one. Once an express warranty has been made, it is extremely difficult to disclaim.

The seller may disclaim the implied warranty of merchantability either orally or in writing. However, the exclusionary language must mention the word *merchantability,* and if the disclaimer is in writing, it must be conspicuous. The disclaimer may be a general statement such as "There are no warranties that extend beyond this writing." General terms—for example, "as is" and "with all faults"—may also be used to exclude implied warranties. To disclaim or limit a warranty, the seller must comply with the detailed rules of the Uniform Commercial Code.

Liability Based on Negligence

Negligence
the failure to exercise the degree of reasonable care that a person of ordinary prudence would employ

Negligence exists when a duty of reasonable care owed to someone is breached, resulting in injury to the person to whom the duty is owed. A business that manufactures a consumer product must use reasonable care to assure that the product is safe for its intended use. Reasonable care must be used in every phase of the production process: in designing the product; in manufacturing and assembling the parts; in testing, inspecting, and packaging the finished product; in placing adequate instructions for use of the product; and in providing warnings of dangers. For example, a failure to properly tighten the bolts securing the gas tank to the body of an automobile will make an automobile manufacturer subject to a negligence claim by an injured plaintiff.

A claim based on negligence does not require a contractual relationship, called "privity of contract," between the parties since the action is one of tort and not contract. Thus, without regard to a contractual relationship, an injured plaintiff may successfully sue by providing that the manufacturer or the seller was negligent. Section 395 of the *Restatement, Second, of Torts* states the rule of negligence as follows:

> A manufacturer who fails to exercise reasonable care in the manufacture of a chattel (personal property) which, unless carefully made, he should recognize as involving an unreasonable risk of causing physical harm to those who use it for a purpose for which the manufacturer should expect it to be used and to those whom he should expect to be endangered by its probable use, is subject to liability for physical harm caused by its lawful use in a manner and for a purpose for which it is supplied.

To recover on a negligence theory, the plaintiff must prove that the defendant's conduct did not meet the standard of reasonable care. Obtaining such proof is often difficult, however, as the defendant is usually reluctant to voluntarily provide necessary information and an examination of the defendant's manufacturing process, which may be far from the plaintiff's residence, may be required. It may be possible to demand such information through court process, but this can be costly.

Res Ipsa Loquitur

In some cases the plaintiff can rely on the doctrine of **res ipsa loquitur**—"the thing speaks for itself." A presumption of negligence may arise if it is shown that (1) the defendant had exclusive control over the product when the negligent act occurred, (2) the product defect is of a type that ordinarily does not occur unless the defendant was negligent, and (3) the injury was not due to any voluntary action or contribution on the plaintiff's part. In such a case the thing does speak for itself; that is, the accident furnishes proof of negligence.

The *res ipsa loquitur* doctrine often solves evidentiary problems because it shifts the burden of disproving negligence to the defendant, who is often in a better position than the plaintiff to find and present evidence. Once the presumption of negligence has been established, the defendant is forced, by threat of automatically losing, to counter the presumption. In one case the plaintiff, a waitress in a restaurant, was injured when a soft drink bottle exploded while she was placing it in the refrigerator. The plaintiff testified about the handling of the bottle after its delivery to the restaurant, but she offered no direct proof of the defendant's negligence in manufacturing and preparing the bottle. The plaintiff recovered on the basis of *res ipsa loquitur,* which shifted the burden of proof to the bottling company. The company could not disprove the inference.

Res ipsa loquitur
a situation in which it is obvious that an accident could not have occurred unless the defendant was negligent; literally, "the thing speaks for itself"

Negligence per Se

In many states negligence may be established by proving that the manufacturer violated a statute, ordinance, or regulation in producing an article. Governments at all levels—federal, state, and city—have imposed duties on manufacturers of goods. The Food and Drug Administration, for instance, issues regulations related to the marketing of impure, adulterated, and misbranded foods, drinks, cosmetics, and drugs. In most cases involving a claim for damages, proof that the defendant violated a regulation is sufficient to establish **negligence per se;** that is, negligence as a matter of law.

Negligence per se
negligence as a matter of law

Defective Design

Another method of establishing negligence is to prove that the damages resulted from a defective design of the product. The product may have no physical flaw, but the manufacturer failed to exercise reasonable care in its design; that is, the manufacturer's plan, structure, specifications, or choice of materials fell below the standard of safety expected by society. An automobile manufacturer who designs an automobile whose gas tank is positioned in such a way as to explode upon minor rear-end impact may be liable for negligent design if sued by a plaintiff injured in such an explosion. The use of a common design is not an absolute defense. Thus the plaintiff could prevail even though the entire automobile industry placed gas tanks in a similar position.

In the following case the Supreme Court of Alabama considered the issue of whether a motorcycle helmet was defectively designed.

HARLEY-DAVIDSON, INC. v. TOOMEY
SUPREME COURT OF ALABAMA
521 So.2d 971 (1988)

Bobby Dale Toomey sued Harley-Davidson, Inc. for injuries sustained in a motor-cycle accident, claiming defective design of a Harley-Davidson motorcycle helmet. At the time of the accident, Toomey was wearing a "full face" helmet that he had purchased from a friend, who had purchased it from a Harley-Davidson dealer. Toomey's wife had purchased the "flip-up" face shield that he was wearing with the helmet from the same dealer.

Toomey testified that although it was a clear morning, his face shield had suddenly clouded with condensation, completely obscuring his vision. As a result, he lost control of the motorcycle on a sharp curve, entered the left lane, and hit an oncoming automobile. His left elbow was shattered, and his right leg was later surgically amputated below the knee. Toomey claimed that the helmet lacked ventilation to prevent interior fogging and that it was not hinged so as to allow the user to quickly flip it up if visibility became inhibited.

Harley-Davidson contended that the helmet and face shield were not defective or unreasonably dangerous to expected users and that the plaintiff was contrib-utorily negligent. The jury awarded the plaintiff $1 million at trial, and the defen-dant appealed.

PER CURIAM

Bobby Toomey called as a witness George Greene, a consulting engineer, who testified that in his expert opinion the helmet and face shield as designed, manufactured, and sold were defective because they did not provide ventila-tion to prevent fogging and did not have a means of removing the face shield if it became fogged. Greene testified that one of the specific goals of design and safety engineering is to identify hazards and eliminate them by design rather than guard against them with warnings. He also stated that fogging in helmets is a well-known occurrence and that Harley-Davidson was aware of it, be-cause it also manufactured nonfogging face shields during the same time Toomey's full-face shield was made. He further testified that as early as 1975 it was within the state of the art to de-sign a full-face helmet that had an easily flipped up face shield and had ventilation to prevent fogging.

We agree with the trial judge's deter-mination that there was a scintilla of evidence that the helmet and shield were defective as designed. When asked for the basis of his opinion that the helmet was defective, Greene re-plied:

> Because the face shield is extremely dif-ficult to remove, it cannot be removed quickly with one hand, and because fog-ging is a problem that is well known. You know, there are many other ways you could obscure your vision, . . . even besides fogging, but you have to be able to get that shield off there quickly, sir.

Toomey testified that he attempted to raise the face shield but was unable to do so. The only eyewitness to the acci-dent, Judith Coleman, whose auto-mobile Toomey hit, testified that just before the collision, she saw Toomey, in a quick motion, try to get the shield up, but to no avail. She also testified that immediately after the accident when she approached Toomey, as he lay in the middle of the road, he told her that it was not her fault, that his shield had fogged up.

"Defective" is defined as "not meet[ing] the reasonable expectations of an ordinary consumer as to its safety," and a product is in a defective condition when "at the time the product leaves the seller's hands, it is in a condition not contemplated by the ultimate consumer." Reviewing the record, we find it apparent that there was at the very least a scintilla of evidence to support a finding that the helmet was defective.

Harley-Davidson claims that Toomey did not sufficiently acquaint himself with the helmet before he wore it on the day of the collision and that his accident was a result of his own inability to properly use it. The trial judge, in denying Harley-Davidson's motion for a directed verdict and motion for judgment notwithstanding the verdict, held that the evidence did not show that Toomey was contributorily negligent as a matter of law. In his order he stated that "there was clear and convincing evidence that the products sold and distributed by defendants in this case were defective and unreasonably dangerous when put to their intended uses and that these defects proximately caused the plaintiff's injuries and damages."

The testimony at trial reflects that Toomey was wearing the helmet properly with all four snaps fastened; there is no evidence that he failed to exercise reasonable care in wearing the helmet. Upon raising the affirmative defense of contributory negligence, defendant has the burden of proving that (1) plaintiff failed to use due care for his own, or . . . his property's, safety and (2) that such a failure was a proximate cause of the injury. The trial judge's rejection of this ground as a basis for directed verdict or JNOV and his submission of the contributory negligence issue to the jury were correct.

Affirmed.

Legal Issues

1. How is the term *defective* defined in this case?
2. According to this court, what must the defendant prove in order to show the plaintiff's contributory negligence?

Ethical Issues

1. How would a firm whose executives were dedicated to bottom-line ethics view the court's treatment of the defendant's claim that the plaintiff was not entitled to recover damages because of contributory negligence?
2. An attorney has an ethical obligation to behave as the advocate of his or her client. An attorney also has an ethical obligation to be honest with the court. Based on the facts you have read in the above case, did the defendant's attorney behave ethically in asking the court to dismiss the plaintiff's claim because of contributory negligence? Why?

Strict Liability in Tort

In the past, a person injured by a defective product was often without a remedy since he or she could not prove negligence and the seller had not made a warranty. Since the early 1960s, however, courts have been imposing the doctrine of strict liability on manufacturers for injuries caused by their defective products.

As a matter of public policy, courts have concluded that the costs of injuries resulting from defective products should be borne by the manufacturers who put such products on the market rather than by persons who are powerless to protect themselves against such injuries. This doctrine does not make manufacturers absolute insurers against injuries resulting from the use of their products. Strict liability is imposed only on manufacturers who sell defective products that are unusually dangerous to the user or consumer or to his property.

The doctrine of strict liability in tort for defective products was first announced in 1963, in *Greenman v. Yuba Power Products, Inc.*[23] In that case the wife of the plaintiff purchased a Shopsmith (a combination power saw and drill) and gave it to the plaintiff for Christmas. The plaintiff then purchased the attachments needed to use it as a lathe. While the plaintiff was using the Shopsmith, a piece of wood flew out of it and struck him on the forehead. The plaintiff then sued the manufacturer to recover for the injuries he sustained.

The California Supreme Court imposed strict liability on the manufacturer without requiring the plaintiff to prove that the manufacturer had been negligent. The court stated:

> A manufacturer is strictly liable in tort when an article he places on the market, knowing that it is to be used without inspection for defects, proves to have a defect that causes injury to a human being.

Within 10 years after *Greenman,* almost all of the states, by either legislation or court decision, had adopted strict liability in tort. The application of this doctrine varies, but most states apply it as announced by the American Law Institute, in *Restatement of Torts,* Section 402A:

(1) One who sells any product in a defective condition unreasonably dangerous to the user or consumer or to his property is subject to liability for physical harm thereby caused to the ultimate user or consumer or to his property, if
   (a) the seller is engaged in the business of selling such a product, and
   (b) it is expected to and does reach the user or consumer without substantial change in the condition in which it is sold.
(2) The rule as stated in subsection (1) applies although
   (a) the seller has exercised all possible care in the preparation and sale of his product, and
   (b) the user or consumer has not bought the product from or entered into any contractual relation with the seller.

Comment i of Section 402A states that for a product to be unreasonably dangerous, "the article sold must be dangerous to an extent beyond that which would be contemplated by the ordinary consumer who purchases it, with the ordinary knowledge common to the community as to its characteristics."

As can be seen from the *Restatement,* the injured party does not have to be the buyer. It should be noted that such restatements of the law are prepared by the American Law Institute, an organization of prominent lawyers, judges, and law professors. These pronouncements are very influential. However, they are not the law until the courts have adopted them.

Strict liability in tort is not governed by the provisions of the Uniform Commercial Code. It is imposed as a matter of public policy. Judges have given the following reasons for imposing it:

1. The costs of injuries resulting from defective products should be borne by the manufacturers who put such products on the market rather than by persons who are powerless to protect themselves against such injuries. The manufacturers can absorb the losses through insurance and increased prices.

2. Transferring the financial risk from the user to the manufacturer increases the incentive of manufacturers to police their operations and produce safe products.

3. It is difficult to examine complex or packaged products at the time of purchase, and manufacturers often represent through advertising that the products are safe to use. Users of such products are therefore especially susceptible to injury.

Availability of Strict Liability

The drafters of the *Restatement* extended protection to injured users or consumers but took no position on harm to other persons. Since the issuance of the *Restatement,* most courts have allowed strict liability recovery to injured *bystanders.* In one case the plaintiff was driving an automobile whose head-on collision with another automobile was caused by a defect in that automobile. The plaintiff, who was neither a user nor a consumer, recovered from the manufacturer of the other automobile on the basis of strict liability. The court reasoned that bystanders who lack the opportunity of prior inspection are entitled to at least the same protection as that given to buyers and users.

Most courts limit strict liability to cases involving personal injury. Where the plaintiff suffered only *property damage,* the seller is not liable under this doctrine. In such cases suit can be brought for breach of warranty or negligence. If that is done, recovery may be more difficult because it is then necessary to prove that a warranty existed and was breached or that the manufacturer did not exercise reasonable care.

Strict liability applies only if the seller is in the business of selling the product. It cannot be imposed on the casual seller, such as an owner selling his or her personal car. The term *seller,* however, has been extended to include lessors and those who render a service for a fee. The doctrine has therefore been applied in situations in which the defendant *leased* defective goods that caused personal injuries. In such situations, however, it is applied only if the defendant is in the business of leasing such goods. Thus recovery was allowed in strict tort liability from a rental agency that leased a van whose defective brakes caused injury to the plaintiff.

Market Share Liability

A novel theory of products liability was introduced in 1980 in a California strict liability case, *Sindell v. Abbott Laboratories.*[24] Between 1945 and 1971, approximately 2 million pregnant women took the drug DES (the synthetic hormone diethylstilbestrol) to prevent miscarriages. The drug, which had been approved by the Food and Drug Administration, was marketed by approximately 300 pharmaceutical companies, frequently under generic names.

While DES apparently had no adverse effect on the mothers, scientists reported in the 1970s that it had caused vaginal cancer and other abnormalities in some daughters of its users. Lawsuits were dismissed because the plaintiffs were unable to show which of the 300 manufacturers had produced the drug that injured them. In the California case, however, the court shifted the burden of proof to the defendant manufacturers, requiring them to prove that they had not produced the drug that injured the plaintiff. The manufacturers were unable to do this since their information was no better than that of the plaintiff. The court then created a market share test under which the manufacturers' share of the damages was based on their share of the national DES market in 1971, when the drug was banned.

Several states subsequently adopted a similar theory of market share liability in DES cases.[25] This theory may be extended to cases involving other types of goods (e.g., asbestos.) that (1) are the same across an industry and (2) are not identifiable as the products of a particular manufacturer.

Defenses

A seller or manufacturer may raise defenses that will defeat the plaintiff's claim. Most of these defenses center on the plaintiff's conduct as a factor contributing to the injury. Some of the defenses apply only in negligence cases, while others may be used to defeat a cause of action based on strict liability or warranty. The defenses used most often are contributory negligence, comparative negligence, assumption of risk, and misuse. In many states defendants can also find protection in statutes of repose and seller's exemption statutes. A few states permit defendants to raise the defense of sufficient instructions and warnings.

Contributory negligence
the doctrine under which recovery by the plaintiff is barred if both the plaintiff and the defendant were negligent

Under the doctrine of **contributory negligence,** both the plaintiff and the defendant have been negligent and each party's conduct was a contributory cause of the injury. When proved, contributory negligence is a complete bar to recovery by the plaintiff. Suppose that the defendant manufacturer produces a ladder whose load-bearing capacity is reduced by an off-center rivet. Suppose further that the plaintiff sustained an injury when he negligently placed the ladder on uneven, muddy terrain that increased the strain on the already weak ladder and thus caused it to collapse. The plaintiff's contributory negligence would defeat recovery.

Comparative negligence
the doctrine under which the negligence of the defendant and the plaintiff are compared and damages are divided on the basis of their respective percentages of fault

The hardships resulting from the doctrine of contributory negligence have caused over one half of the states to allow recovery based on the doctrine of comparative negligence. **Comparative negligence** permits a jury to divide the damages between the plaintiff and the defendant on the basis of their respective percentages of fault. If, for example, the defendant manufacturer is responsible for 60 percent of the fault, then it is liable for only 60 percent of the plaintiff's damages. Most states do not recognize either contributory negligence or comparative negligence as a defense in strict liability or warranty cases.

Assumption of risk
a defense in which the defendant shows that the plaintiff knew the risks or defects of a product but nevertheless chose to use it

Almost every state allows the defendant to prove that the plaintiff assumed the risk of a defective product. Based on the defense of **assumption of risk,** the plaintiff who voluntarily encounters a known danger is generally not allowed to recover. The defendant who uses this defense must prove that the plaintiff knew of the defect but nevertheless chose to use the product. In one case a worker was struck in the chest and abdomen when a pressurized valve that he was trying to open blew off. Evidence showed that he knew the valve stem was broken before the accident occurred. The jury concluded that he assumed the risk of injury when he tampered with the valve.

After acquiring a product, purchasers sometimes use it in a manner that was neither intended nor reasonably foreseeable by the manufacturer. Under the laws of every state, a manufacturer or seller is not liable for the plaintiff's deliberate **misuse** of a product. For example, a seller is not liable if a plaintiff is injured because he or she knocks a soft drink against a radiator to remove the cap. This product is not expected to be foolproof when it leaves the seller's hands. In some cases in which the misuse was forseeable by the manufacturer, the defendant has been held liable. Warning of the dangers of such use sometimes provides protection for the manufacturer. Both assumption of risk and misuse are defenses in cases based on strict liability, negligence, and warranty.

In response to the evolution of products liability laws, at least 31 states have passed statutes designed to limit the seller's liability for injuries caused by his product. The most popular statutes of this kind have been **statutes of repose.** These statutes limit the time, beginning with a product's manufacture, sale, or delivery, in which the plaintiff can bring suit. Beyond this time the seller cannot be liable.

A number of states have enacted **seller's exemption** statutes, which protect retailers, wholesalers, and other nonmanufacturer distributors from strict liability, though not from negligence and warranty recovery. In most of these states, the nonmanufacturer distributor is liable in strict liability if the manufacturer is insolvent or cannot be sued.

A few state legislatures have enacted statutes permitting the presumption that a product is not unreasonably unsafe if the manufacturer can establish that the product is accompanied by *sufficient instructions and warnings.* These legislatures assume that the plaintiff acts unreasonably if he uses a product in a manner contrary to instructions or warnings.

Reimbursement

Although the elimination of the privity of contract requirement permits the injured plaintiff to sue the manufacturer, the retailer and other distributors are often named as defendants or as a subgroup among a group of defendants that includes the manufacturer. Any seller of a defective product is potentially liable to the injured plaintiff. If a retailer pays the entire claim, what are its rights against the other sellers in the chain of distribution? The general rule is that any seller can recover from the supplier who caused the product to be dangerously defective. The innocent retailer is entitled to reimbursement from the manufacturer or dealer who either breached the warranty or sold an unreasonably dangerous product.

Misrepresentation

The seller of a *nondefective* product may be liable in tort for injuries to a user or consumer. The *Restatement,* Section 402B, states that a seller who *misrepresents* a material fact to the public with regard to the character or quality of the product through advertising or labeling may be liable for physical harm to a consumer or user. The liability may be imposed even though the seller *innocently* misrepresented the product and the plaintiff did not purchase the product from the seller. The rationale of the *Restatement* is that consumers obtain most of their information on products from sellers and producers. Quite naturally, this information

Misuse

a defense in which the defendant shows that the plaintiff deliberately used a product in a manner neither intended nor foreseeable by the manufacturer

Statute of repose

a statute limiting the time in which a plaintiff may bring a products liability lawsuit

Seller's exemption

a statute exempting retailers, wholesalers, and other nonmanufacturer dealers from strict liability on the products they handle

places the products in the most favorable light possible. Thus the sellers should be held responsible for their misrepresentation to the public.

The facts in the widely publicized case of *Crocker v. Winthrop Laboratories, Div. of Sterling Drugs, Inc.*[26] provide a good illustration of misrepresentation. After extensive testing by the federal government and Winthrop Laboratories, the painkiller Talwin was approved as a nonaddictive prescription medicine. Winthrop innocently advertised and marketed the drug among the medical profession as "free and safe from *all* dangers of addiction." Based on this information, a physician used Talwin to treat a patient who developed an addiction to it that caused his death. Despite the manufacturer's good faith and the rarity of the patient's reaction, the manufacturer was found liable. The product was not defective, but the manufacturer was held to be a guarantor of its representation that the product was not addictive.

Figure 7-1 provides a summary of the defenses to the different theories of recovery of product liability claims.

Products Liability and Criminal Liability

As discussed, a corporation whose defective product causes an injury is liable in damages in a products liability lawsuit. As a result of a recent trend in the law, the defective product can also subject the corporation to a criminal indictment.

A corporation is a separate legal entity. This means that it has an existence separate from the existence of its owners and employees.[27] Although a corporation is an artificial person created by law and cannot formulate the necessary criminal intent (*mens rea* or "guilty mind") required for conviction, it may still be criminally responsible for its actions. Thus a corporation can be indicted for a crime committed within the scope of employment of its officers, its top-level managerial employees, and, on occasion, even its lower-level employees. The corporation commits the criminal act through its authorized employee, while the criminal intent is the intent of the authorized employee.

A possible explanation for the trend toward criminal prosecutions of corporations is the broader definition of *mens rea* promulgated by the Model Penal Code. This code, a body of uniform criminal laws adopted by most states, was revised in 1962 to eliminate common law definitions of criminal action. It now includes

---

FIGURE 7-1   **Product Liability Defenses**

Theories of Recovery	Exclusion or Modification of Warranty	Assumption of the Risk	Misuse	Contributory negligence	Comparative fault	Statute of Repose	Seller's exemption
Warranty	X	X	X				
Negligence		X	X	X	X	X	
Strict Liability		X	X			X	X
Misrepresentation*							

* A defendant charged with misrepresentation may defeat a plaintiff's claim by contending that the misrepresentations were not a material fact or that the plaintiff did not rely on the misrepresentations. Chapter 8 contains a more thorough discussion of the essential elements of misrepresentation.

mere recklessness under the definition of *mens rea,* so that specific intent is no longer required for an action to be criminal.

Indiana v. Ford Motor Company[28] is a famous case in which a corporation was charged with a criminal act due to the recklessness of persons in supervisory positions. The faulty design of Ford Motor Company's Pinto automobile resulted in the death of several people when a Pinto was struck in the rear by another car. In a products liability lawsuit against the company, the jury awarded millions of dollars to the family of the deceased. The state of Indiana later brought a criminal prosecution against Ford Motor Company for its role in the design and manufacture of the Pinto. The company was charged with a criminal act due to the recklessness of persons in supervisory positions in failing to warn customers of an alleged defect in the Pinto. Although Ford was acquitted after a jury trial, the Indiana court held that the proper elements for a criminal charge existed.

LAW ABROAD

European Community

The former laws of many EC member states based liability for defective products on negligence. The EC, however, uses a no-fault liability standard for damages caused by defective products. A defective product is one that does not provide the safety a person is entitled to expect. Consumers need prove only that the damages they sustained were caused by a defect in the product, regardless of the fault or negligence of the producer or supplier. A number of defenses are available to the producer.

The statute of limitations is three years from the date that the plaintiff knew or should have known of (1) the damage, (2) the defect, and (3) the producer's identity. There is, however, a 10-year maximum period of liability from the date when a product was put into circulation. This time limitation may be changed by the laws of the member states.

Liability for damages caused by services is not covered. Here the individual law of the member states applies.

American manufacturers and distributors seeking to do business in Europe should be aware of this strict liability standard. However, it is also important to note that products liability litigation is much less frequent in Europe than in the United States, where contingent fees, class action lawsuits, enormous punitive damages, and other factors have spawned a flood of such litigation in recent years.

Germany

Decisions of the federal supreme court have established a high standard of products liability for manufacturers. If injury to a person or damage to property occurs when a product is used as normally intended, the manufacturer must show that the product was neither defective nor inherently defective when it was manufactured or sold. In other words, the burden of proof is on the manufacturer to show that the product was safe when manufactured and that any defects in the product or dangers posed by it were created after it left the manufacturer's hands. Without such proof the manufacturer is liable for damages caused by the product.

REVIEW QUESTIONS & PROBLEMS

1. The case of *Miranda v. State of Arizona* set out certain rights that an individual being held in police custody must be granted. What are these rights? Would a failure to grant these rights be a basis for appealing a conviction? Explain.

2. Using computer programs to defraud companies is a growing category of business crime. What are the main factors that contribute to the criminal abuse of computers? Explain.

3. Buyer purchased a car from Sam's Used Cars. The sales contract specified that the car had been driven "36,509 miles," the reading on the odometer. Buyer subsequently talked to the owner who had sold the car to Sam's. He stated that the odometer reading was over 60,000 miles when Sam's bought the car. Is Sam's Used Cars liable for breach of express warranty? Why?

4. The Reading Railroad computerized its freight car flow to improve its freight operation. Evan, a Reading employee, manipulated the computer program so that missing freight cars would not show up on the railroad's records. Eventually, he made off with hundreds of $60,000 boxcars and the freight inside, which he then sold for his own profit. (*a*) In this situation, did Evan's computer manipulation of the boxcars constitute embezzlement? Explain. (*b*) Assuming that Evan was not a Reading Railroad employee but an outsider who had accessed Reading's computer system on his home computer, would he be held guilty of computer fraud? Explain. (*c*) How would current laws deal with such an outsider? Explain.

5. When Patsy, a Food and Drug Administration inspector, examined a shipment of a nonprescription drug manufactured by Illcore Corporation, she noticed that some of the pill bottles were cracked. Rita, an Illcore employee, offered her $80,000 to overlook this "small" defect and approve the goods for shipment. (*a*) What profit-oriented arguments might Rita make to defend her action? Are any of them justifiable over the long term in light of multimillion-dollar products liability lawsuits? Explain. (*b*) If Illcore discovered and ignored Rita's bribe and a consumer suffered adverse effects from the drug, could Illcore be charged with a crime? Explain.

6. A woman drank about half a fifth of bourbon a day during her pregnancy. Her child was born with fetal alcohol syndrome, mental retardation, physical deformities, and other defects. The woman sued Jim Beam Brands Company for $4 million in damages for negligence in not stating on its whiskey labels that alcohol consumption by pregnant women could cause birth defects. The woman testified that she would have given up drinking had the labels carried such a warning. Her husband, also an alcoholic, testified that he would have stopped her from drinking if he had been aware of the dangers.

   Witnesses for Jim Beam testified that relatives and friends had repeatedly warned the woman about the dangers of drinking alcohol while pregnant. Other witnesses testified that she had drunk beer in bars during her pregnancy. Evidence was also introduced that she drank rubbing alcohol, which had borne warning labels for years.

   Should Jim Beam Brands Company be held liable? Why? (*Note:* The lawsuit was brought prior to the passage of a federal law requiring all containers of alcoholic beverages to carry warnings about birth defects and other health hazards.)

1. 384 U.S. 436 (1966).

2. The Fifth Amendment provides that "no person shall be held to answer for a capital, or otherwise infamous crime, unless on a presentment or indictment of a Grand Jury."

3. The Fifth Amendment states that "no person . . . shall be subject for the same offense to be twice put in jeopardy of life or limb."

4. The grant of power from the state that permits the corporation to exist.

5. The states that have passed computer crime laws are Alaska, Arizona, Colorado, Delaware, Florida, Georgia, Illinois, Iowa, Massachusetts, Michigan, Minnesota, Missouri, Montana, New Mexico, North Carolina, Ohio, Rhode Island, Tennessee, Utah, Virginia, and Wisconsin.

6. In those states that have not prohibited commercial bribery, the only remedy of the victim is to resort to the civil court for an injunction and to ask for recovery of damages.

7. *U.S. v. Joseph Schlitz Brewing Co.,* case no. 78 CR 33 (Wisconsin 1978).

8. Of the district court RICO decisions brought prior to 1985, only 3 percent were decided in the 1970s, 2 percent in 1980, 7 percent in 1981, 13 percent in 1982, 33 percent in 1983, and 43 percent in 1984.

9. The crimes most likely to involve business are securities fraud, mail fraud, and wire fraud. The antifraud provisions of securities law are discussed in Chapter 14. The federal mail fraud and wire fraud statutes make it a crime to use mail or wire communication in furtherance of a scheme to defraud. 18 U.S.C. 1341, 1343.

10. 105 S. Ct. 3275 (1985).

11. Even the statute's authors realized that RICO would extend beyond organized crime. Senator McClellan, chairman of the subcommittee that created the statute, wrote that "it is impossible to draw an effective statute [referring to RICO] which reaches most of the commercial activity of organized crime, yet does not include offenses commonly committed by persons outside of organized crime as well." 46 *Notre Dame Lawyer* 55, 143-44 (1970).

12. As noted in Chapter 4, a tort is a private wrong for which the law allows a remedy in an action for damages.

13. *State of Missouri v. National Organization for Women, Inc.,* 620 F.2d 1301 (1980).

14. 729 S.W.2d 768 (Tex. 1987).

15. Although registration does not create a trademark, the owner of a registered trademark or service mark obtains protection that is not available to common law trademarks or service marks, which are enforced only in the trading areas served by their owners.

16. 254 U.S. 143 (1920).

17. 756 F.2d 1535 (1985).

18. 227 U.S.P.Q. 967 (1985).

19. Under the old copyright statute, publication (communication to third parties) of the work without the required notice resulted in the loss of copyright protection. The Copyright Act of 1976 diminished the harshness of the notice required. If copyrighted works are published without the required notice, the owner will not lose the copyright if (1) only a few items are published, or (2) upon discovering the omission, the owner attempts to give copyright notice to all holders of the published works, or (3) a third party publishes the works despite a written agreement between the third party and the copyright owner that copyright notice would be affixed to the published works.

20. 111 S. Ct. 1282 (1991).

21. The Uniform Commercial Code and sale of goods are discussed more fully in Chapter 8.

22. An analogy is the letter grade "C."

23. 377 P.2d 897 (1963).

24. 607 P.2d 924 (1980).

25. The theory has been accepted by courts in the states of California, New York, Washington, and Wisconsin.

26. 514 S.W.2d 429 (Tex. 1974).

27. A more detailed explanation of corporations is presented in Chapter 11.

28. 24 CRL 2454 (1979).

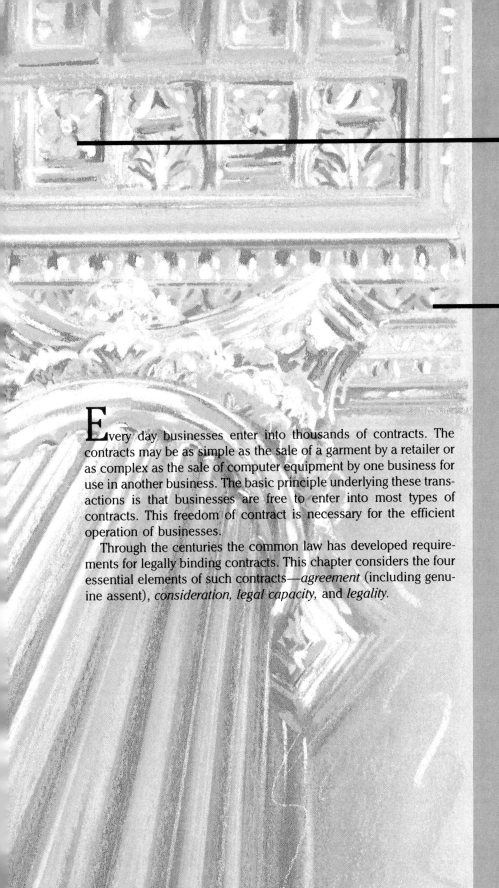

CHAPTER

8

Essentials of a Contract

Every day businesses enter into thousands of contracts. The contracts may be as simple as the sale of a garment by a retailer or as complex as the sale of computer equipment by one business for use in another business. The basic principle underlying these transactions is that businesses are free to enter into most types of contracts. This freedom of contract is necessary for the efficient operation of businesses.

Through the centuries the common law has developed requirements for legally binding contracts. This chapter considers the four essential elements of such contracts—*agreement* (including genuine assent), *consideration, legal capacity,* and *legality.*

Contract
legally enforceable prom-
ise or group of promises

NATURE OF A CONTRACT

A **contract** is a legally enforceable promise or group of promises. However, not every promise constitutes a contract. Suppose that Al asks Barbara to go with him to a dance and that Barbara agrees to do so. Suppose further that when Al arrives at her dormitory to pick her up, he discovers that she has left with someone else. Since courts will not uphold social agreements, such as a "date," Al cannot sue Barbara for breach of contract. On the other hand, a promise to make monthly payments for a new car is legally enforceable. For a contract to be enforceable, these basic requirements must be met:

1. *Agreement*—mutual assent by both parties based on an *offer* by one party and its *acceptance* by the other party.
2. *Consideration*—the price requested by the party making a promise and received in exchange for the promise.
3. *Competent parties*—the legal ability of the parties to contract. A contracting party who is not of legal age, sane, or sober does not have the capacity to contract and in certain circumstances, has the right to disaffirm or cancel a contract.
4. *Legality of purpose*—the objective of the contract is not opposed to public policy and not prohibited by statute or common law.

Figure 8-1 illustrates these requirements.

Knowing the four essential elements of a contract makes it possible to distinguish between enforceable and unenforceable promises. These elements will be discussed in the following sections.

Classification of Contracts

Various kinds of contracts are legally recognized. Familiarity with their features is necessary for an understanding of contract law.

Express contract
an agreement whose in-
tentions and terms are
stated in clear, definite,
and explicit words

Express and Implied Contracts

In an **express contract** the parties state their intentions and terms explicitly, either orally or in writing, when the contract is formed. For example, if Jack tells

---

FIGURE 8-1
▬▬

A Typical Contract

This agreement, made and entered on June 1, 1991, between Robert A. Smith and Brown Wholesalers, Inc., whereby Smith promises to produce and sell, and Brown Wholesalers, Inc. promises to buy, 10,000 cases of good and merchantable Blue Goose tomatoes under labels and specifications designated by Brown Wholesalers, Inc. in this contract, at a price of $25 per case or $250,000 total. Brown Wholesalers, Inc. agrees to pay for said tomatoes, one half to be paid on delivery, and the other half in 30 days from the date of delivery.

/s/ *Brown Wholesalers, Inc.* Buyer
/s/ *Robert A. Smith* Seller

This contract meets the basic requirements: (1) agreement, (2) competent parties, (3) consideration, and (4) legality of purpose.

Chrissy: "I will mow your yard for $10," and Chrissy replies: "That sounds good to me," an express contract is formed.

In many situations, however, contracts are made whose terms are not expressly stated. When the actions of the parties and the surrounding circumstances indicate that an agreement has been reached, an **implied contract** is formed. Implied contracts arise often in everyday life. For example, when Bob drives his car into the neighborhood automobile repair shop, describes his problem, and says "Fix the engine" to the owner, an implied contract is formed. From the conduct of the parties, a court could infer a promise by the owner to use reasonable means to repair the engine and a promise by Bob to pay a reasonable price for the services.

A **quasi contract** is created in those unusual circumstances in which one party has been unjustly enriched at the expense of the other party. Suppose that the Cardinal Ice Cream Company sends Supplier X a check for $5,000 because it mistakenly believes that the money is owed to Supplier X when in fact the money is owed to Supplier Y. Cardinal could recover the money from Supplier X on a quasi-contract basis. Since it would be unfair to allow Supplier X to keep the money, the courts resort to a legal fiction and imply a promise in law. In most cases the obligation is based on the amount of the unjust enrichment.

Bilateral and Unilateral Contracts

Traditional contract law recognized a distinction between bilateral and unilateral contracts. In a **bilateral contract,** *both* parties make promises. If Shirley promises to sell her car to Lenny for $10,000 in exchange for Lenny's promise to buy the car for $10,000, a bilateral contract is formed. A bilateral contract consists of a *promise for a promise.*

In a **unilateral contract,** only *one* party makes a promise. A unilateral contract usually involves a *promise for an act.* When Higgins says to Thomas, "I will pay you $100 if you find my lost wristwatch and return it to me," Higgins has made a promise to pay Thomas for the act of finding the missing watch. Thomas can accept this promise only by finding it. A promise by Thomas that he will find and return the watch would not result in the formation of a contract.

Valid, Void, Voidable, and Unenforceable Contracts

A **valid contract** is one that meets all the requirements for the formation of a contract. Valid contracts are enforceable in court by either party.

Void contracts lack one or more of the requirements of a contract and thus are not really contracts. Such contracts have no legal effect. Since one requirement of a valid contract is that the act agreed upon be legal and robbing a bank is illegal, a contract between Frank and Jesse to rob a bank is void.

Voidable contracts can be rescinded (canceled) at the election of one or both of the parties. A voidable contract is legally enforceable unless the party with the power of avoidance chooses to cancel it. Since minors generally have the legal power to cancel their contracts, if Joanie, a 16-year-old, purchases a motorcycle from Arthur, an adult, a voidable contract is formed. Both parties remain legally bound by its provisions unless Joanie chooses to cancel it. Contracts in which fraud is present are also voidable.

Unenforceable contracts meet the legal requirements for contract formation but are not legally enforceable because of some other rule of law. For example,

Implied contract

an agreement whose intentions and terms are indicated by the actions of the parties and the surrounding circumstances

Quasi contract

an agreement created by courts to offset the unjust enrichment of one party at the expense of the other party

Bilateral contract

an agreement in which both parties make promises

Unilateral contract

an agreement in which one party makes a promise in exchange for an act by the other party

Valid contract

an agreement that meets the requirements of a contract—agreement, consideration, competent parties, and legality of purpose

Void contract

an agreement that is without legal effect because it lacks one or more of the requirements of a contract

Voidable contract

an agreement that can be rescinded by one or both of the parties but is legally enforceable unless one of the parties chooses to rescind it

Unenforceable contract

an agreement that is not legally enforceable because a defense to the agreement exists

certain types of contracts, such as contracts for the sale of land, are not enforceable unless they are in writing. If Howard's agreement to sell Don 50 acres of land for $100,000 meets the requirements of a contract, but the agreement is not in writing, the contract is unenforceable.

The Purpose of Contracts

The social institution of contracts is found in almost every society in which goods and services are exchanged. Without the legal recognition of contract rights, parties would be reluctant to enter into agreements involving future performance. In a society consisting mainly of farmers and hunters, for example, David, a small, weak farmer, might not sell grain to Conan, a large, strong hunter, in exchange for Conan's promise to pay for the grain next week unless David knows that the law will assist him in enforcing the contract.

Contracts are also necessary in a complex industrial society. Long-range planning involving enforceable assurances of performance is vital to the operation of any large business. Annie, a bicycle manufacturer, cannot operate her business profitably unless she can count on the promise of suppliers to provide the various parts she needs to make her bicycles.

Contracts have provided the basis for economic evolution from barter systems to massive industrial complexes. As the business world becomes more complicated, contracts will assume even greater significance.

THE UNIFORM COMMERCIAL CODE

Over the years a wide variety of state laws were enacted to govern commercial transactions. As interstate commerce grew, it became apparent that these laws should be as uniform as possible. In response to this need, in 1941 the American Law Institute and the National Conference of Commissioners on Uniform State Laws joined forces in drafting the Uniform Commercial Code (UCC), a modern, uniform law governing commercial transactions. It took over seven years for 1,200 of the brightest legal minds in the United States to draft the code. In 1954 Pennsylvania, by unanimous vote of its legislature, became the first state to adopt the UCC.

Afterward the UCC was adopted by every other state except Louisiana, which has adopted only certain articles.[1] The UCC was also adopted by the District of Columbia and the Virgin Islands. This widespread adoption has not resulted in complete uniformity, however. Several states enacted alternative versions of some portions of the UCC, and other states have amended their versions of the UCC. In addition, some UCC provisions have been interpreted differently by various state courts. All in all, though, the UCC has done much to eliminate confusion in commercial transactions.

Goods
tangible property that is movable

Personal property
property that can be moved from place to place

The UCC is divided into 11 articles designed to deal with a wide variety of problems that commonly arise in commercial transactions.[2] Perhaps the most important of these articles for businesses is Article 2, Sales, which governs all contracts for the *sale of goods*. Essentially, the term **goods** means *tangible, personal property*.

Personal property is movable. Thus it can be carried from place to place. Land and things firmly attached to land are classified as real property.

To classify property as goods, it must also be **tangible property,** which means that it must have a physical existence. Intangible property, such as stocks, bonds, patents, and accounts receivable, are not classified as goods.

Thus *a contract for the sale of tangible, movable property is governed by the rules of Article 2, Sales, of the UCC.* The sale of jewelry, automobiles, wheat, or the like constitutes a sale of goods. The sale of real estate and the sale of services, such as contracts of employment and contracts of insurance, are covered by contract law. While the rules governing sales of goods are based on statutory law, contract law consists of common law rules.

The UCC imposes a duty of good faith on the buyer and seller in the performance of a sales contract. *Good faith* is defined by the UCC as "honesty in fact" in performing obligations assumed in the contract. For example, if the terms of the contract provide that either the buyer or the seller will set the price at the time of delivery, the party responsible for setting the price must act in good faith; the price set must be reasonable.

AGREEMENT—OFFER AND ACCEPTANCE

As previously noted, an essential element of contracts is an **agreement**—a "meeting of the minds" between the parties. An agreement is formed when one party, called the "offeror," makes an offer to another party, called the "offeree," who accepts the offer. Thus an agreement consists of two parts—an *offer* and an *acceptance.*

Offer

In contract law an **offer** is what the offeror promises to give in return for a specific act or promise by the offeree. An offer gives the offeree the power of accepting and thereby creating a binding contract. Whether a proposal is legally an offer depends on whether (1) the parties actually *intend* to enter a contract, (2) the proposed terms are sufficiently *definite,* and (3) the offeror has *communicated* the offer to the offeree. It should also be remembered that an offer can be terminated by the acts of either party and by the terms of the offer.

Intent

For a contract to be formed, both parties must have the **intent to contract.** This intent is measured, not by the subjective intentions of the parties, but by the manifested intentions of the parties. Courts look to the parties' acts, words, and other circumstances in deciding whether a **reasonable person** would be justified in believing that an offer was made. A contract cannot be formed if an offer is made in the heat of excitement, in anger, or in jest. For example, if Oliver says to Ralph in a serious manner, "I'll sell you my 1991 Mercedes for $5,000," and Ralph replies, "You've got a deal," a contract has been formed and Oliver must sell the car to Ralph even if it is worth much more than $5,000. Oliver may be able to prove that he made the offer in jest, but a court would find the offer serious, since a reasonable person would conclude that a valid offer had been made. Oliver's actual intent would not concern the court.

The following case helps show how courts determine whether an offer was made in jest or with an intent to contract.

BARNES V. TREECE
COURT OF APPEALS OF WASHINGTON, DIVISION 1
549 P.2d 1152 (1976)

Barnes sued Treece and Vend-A-Win, Inc. to recover on a reward offer. Vend-A-Win was engaged in the distribution of punchboards (a gambling device), and Treece, a vice president, testified before the state gambling commission: "I'll pay $100,000 to anyone who finds a crooked board. If they find it, I'll pay it."

Barnes heard Treece's statement on the television news and also read newspaper reports of the statement. A number of years earlier, while employed as a bartender, Barnes had purchased two fraudulent punchboards. Barnes located these punchboards, telephoned Treece, and asked him whether his offer had been made seriously. Treece replied that it had been made seriously and told Barnes to bring the punchboards to his office. Although Barnes presented Treece with a fraudulent punchboard, both Treece and Vend-A-Win refused to pay the $100,000.

The trial court held that a contract existed but that only Treece was obligated. Barnes appealed.

CALLOW, JUDGE

The first issue is whether the statement of Treece was the manifestation of an offer which could be accepted to bind the offeror to performance of the promise. Treece contends that no contract was formed. He maintains that his statement was made in jest and lacks the necessary manifestation of a serious contractual intent.

When expressions are intended as a joke and are understood or would be understood by a reasonable person as being so intended, they cannot be construed as an offer and accepted to form a contract. However, if the jest is not apparent and a reasonable hearer would believe that an offer was being made, then the speaker risks the formation of a contract which was not intended. It is the objective manifestations of the offeror that count and not secret, unexpressed intentions. Corbin, *Contracts* § 34 (1963):

> If a party's words or acts, judged by a reasonable standard, manifest an intention to agree in regard to the matter in question, that agreement is established, and it is immaterial what may be the real but unexpressed state of the party's mind on the subject.

The trial court found that there was an objective manifestation of mutual assent to form a contract. This was a matter to be evaluated by the trier of fact. The record includes substantial evidence of the required mutual assent to support the finding of the trial court. Although the original statement of Treece drew laughter from the audience, the subsequent statements, conduct, and the circumstances show an intent to lead any hearer to believe the statements were made seriously. There was testimony, though contradicted, that Treece specifically restated the offer over the telephone in response to an inquiry concerning whether the offer was serious. Treece, when given the opportunity to state that an offer was not intended, not only reaffirmed the offer but also asserted that $100,000 had been placed in escrow and directed Barnes to bring the punchboard to Seattle for inspection. The parties met, Barnes was given a receipt for the board, and he was told that the board would be taken to Chicago for inspection. In present-day society it is known that gambling generates a great deal of income and that large sums are spent on its advertising and promotion. In that prevailing atmosphere, it was a credible statement that $100,000 would be paid to promote punchboards. The statements of the defendant and the surrounding circumstances reflect an objective manifestation of a contractual intent by Treece and support the finding of the trial court.

The trial court properly categorized Treece's promise of $100,000 as a valid offer for a unilateral contract. The offer made promised that a contract would result upon performance of the act requested. Performance of the act with the intent to accept the offer constituted acceptance. The trial judge entered a specific finding that Barnes performed the requested act of acceptance when he produced a rigged and fraudulent punchboard. We concur with the trial court's holding that a binding unilateral contract was formed between Barnes and Treece and uphold the conclusions of the trial court in that regard.

Affirmed.

Legal Issues

1. If a party makes an offer that she intends as a joke, can a court still construe her words as a valid offer to contract? Why?

2. In the *Barnes* case, what facts did the court consider to determine whether Treece's promise of $100,000 could be construed as a valid offer?

Ethical Issues

1. To support its decision that Treece's statement as to the payment of $100,000 could be taken as an offer, the court noted that large sums are spent on the advertising and promotion of gambling in present-day society. Would a proponent of expectancy ethics approve of taking this factor into account in concluding that the statement could be taken as an offer? Why?

2. Is it fair to use an objective standard to determine whether a party's stated proposal was made in jest? Why? If a court based its decision on pragmatic ethics, would it use a subjective test to determine whether a proposal was made in jest? Explain your answer.

Advertisements

Problems often arise with advertisements offering goods for sale at a stated price. Courts generally hold that such advertisements are not offers but invitations to negotiate. This rule has been extended to catalogs, price lists, and price quotations. The rule reflects the commercial realities of the situation. If such an advertisement were treated as an offer, then everyone who read or heard it could bind the seller to a contract. The seller's limited supply of the advertised goods would soon be exhausted, but the seller would still be contractually bound to the disappointed buyers. Most advertisements do not meet the objective intent to contract standard.

Nearly all of the states have enacted statutes that prohibit the advertising of goods without an intent to sell the goods as advertised. Thus it is illegal to advertise goods for sale merely to attract customers to the advertiser's place of business.

It is possible, however, for an advertisement to be an offer. An advertisement is an offer to sell if the terms of its promise are so definite that they show a genuine intent to contract. Advertisements that solicit performance are likely to be held as offers to sell. Suppose that an advertisement states: "We offer to sell 3 General Electric washing machines, Model 321, price $129, worth $375, to the first three persons who enter our store on Saturday, November 14. Doors open at 9 A.M. sharp." This clear, definite, and explicit advertisement leaves nothing open for negotiation. Thus it is an offer to sell, and the first three persons in the store can make an acceptance that creates a binding contract.

Definiteness

Definite offer
an offer whose terms are clearly stated

A **definite offer** is one whose terms are clearly stated. The terms of the offer must be precise enough for a court to ascertain the intention of the parties and to identify their contractual duties. An offer by Tony to sell all the eggs Julie desired at $0.50 a dozen would be void for indefiniteness unless Julie indicated in her acceptance the quantity she desired.

The UCC broadens the strict common law requirement of definiteness for contracts that involve a sale of goods. Under Article 2, Sales, a contract does not fail for indefiniteness, even if the parties did not expressly agree on all of its terms, if a court finds (1) that the parties intended to form a contract and (2) that the contract is definite enough to allow the court a reasonable basis for granting an appropriate remedy (2-204). Further, the UCC contains several sections that provide a method for courts to fill in missing contract terms, such as price, place of delivery, and time of delivery. For example, a contract for the sale of 100 chain saws that omits the price is still a binding contract. The price will be a reasonable price at the time of delivery.

Communication of Offer

Communication of the offer
the transmission of an offer by the offeror to the offeree

An offer can take effect only if the offeror transmits the offer to the offeree. In such a **communication of the offer,** the offeror indicates an intent to be bound by its terms. By the same token, the failure to communicate an offer may mean that the offeror does not wish to enter into a contractual relationship. Suppose that Herman tells his friend Lily that he intends to sell Darlene his car for $1,200 and that Lily tells this to Darlene, who then calls Herman and says "I accept." No contract was formed since Herman did not communicate his proposal to Darlene and thus never gave her a power of acceptance.

Likewise, the writing and mailing of an offer by the offeror is not effective as an offer until the offeree receives it. If the letter containing the offer is not received, no offer has been made.

Termination of an Offer

Once an offer has been made, the offeree has the power to accept it and thereby create a contract. For practical reasons, however, the power to create a contract cannot exist indefinitely.

Revocation of the offer
cancellation of the legal effect of an offer

Revocation of the offer is within the offeror's power at any time prior to acceptance even if the offeror agreed not to revoke it for a specified period of time. If the offer states "This offer will remain open for 10 days," the offeror can still revoke it at any time before the expiration of the 10 days. However, there are two situations in which an offer may be irrevocable: (1) an option contract and (2) a firm offer.

Option Contract An offer becomes irrevocable if the parties enter into a separate agreement known as an **option contract.** If the offeree gives the offeror something of value to hold the offer open for a stated period of time, the offer cannot be revoked for that period of time since the offeree has purchased the right to accept or reject it during that time.

Firm Offer The UCC sets forth another kind of irrevocable offer that can occur if the offeror is a merchant. A **merchant,** broadly speaking, is a professional businessperson who deals in goods. In Section 2-205, the UCC provides that if a merchant signs a written offer to buy or sell goods in which it is stated that the offer will be held open for a specified period of time, the offer is irrevocable. Such an offer is termed a **firm offer.** The UCC limits the period of irrevocability to three months. A written offer from Albert, an appliance salesman, states: "At any time during the next 45 days, I well sell you a Model 490 washing machine for $350. Signed, Albert." This is a firm offer, and it must be held open for 45 days even though the offeree gave no consideration.

Lapse of Time An offer that does not contain a stated time period will be terminated by the passage of a "reasonable time." How much time is regarded as "reasonable" depends on the circumstances. Offers covering items that fluctuate rapidly in price, such as stocks and bonds, have an extremely short duration. Offers covering the sale of land may last several days.

Acceptance

The second part of an agreement is an acceptance. An **acceptance** is an offeree's indication that he or she is willing to be bound by the terms of the offer. An acceptance usually takes the form of an express statement, but any language or act indicating assent to the offer is sufficient. Only the offeree has the power of acceptance.

Unequivocal

The acceptance must be definite and unequivocal. Courts say that it must be a "mirror image" of the offer. Thus a proposed acceptance that changes any terms of the offer automatically terminates the offer. Such an acceptance is usually treated as a counteroffer. If Sam offers to sell his house to Barbara for $120,000 and Barbara replies, "I accept your offer provided you put a fresh coat of paint on the house," Barbara no longer has the power to accept Sam's offer. Her attempted acceptance operates as a counteroffer since it has changed the terms of the offer.

An acceptance that varies the terms of the offer is to be distinguished from a "grumbling acceptance" that merely expresses dissatisfaction with the contract. If Barbara states, "I accept your offer, but I wish the price were lower," her acceptance is effective.

In Section 2-207 the UCC allows acceptances that vary the terms of an offer in certain circumstances. These circumstances ordinarily occur when merchant sellers and merchant buyers use their own printed forms in making offers and acceptances for sales of goods. The printed terms and conditions of the forms seldom match.

Option contract
an agreement in which one party gives something of value to the other party to hold the offer open for a stated period of time

Merchant
a professional business person who deals in goods

Firm offer
a merchant's written offer to buy or sell goods in which it is stated that the offer will be held open for a specified period of time; becomes irrevocable for the time specified or up to three months

Acceptance
the offeree's assent to the terms of the offer

Hypothetical Case

THE BUYER REMAINS SILENT

Robert, a salesman for Mathews Sewing Machine Company, wrote Paul, the owner of Paul's Sewing Machine Store, a letter that said: "I have a very special deal on our sewing machines for new customers. I will sell you Model Number Z–400 at 50 percent off list price. The Z–400 is widely advertised and our leading seller. The price is $225 per machine, which is 50 percent off list price. I have five machines left, and if I don't hear from you within 10 days, I will ship the machines and bill you $1,225 plus tax." Paul did not reply, and after 10 days passed, Robert shipped the sewing machines. Paul refused to accept or pay for them. Robert sued Paul for breach of contract. Is Paul legally obligated to pay damages for breach of contract? Why?

Silence as Acceptance

**Silence
of the offeree**
not an acceptance of the offer unless there is a duty to speak

Generally, the **silence of the offeree** does not imply an acceptance of the offer. The basis of contract law is the voluntary agreement of the parties. However, the parties' prior course of dealings may create a duty on the offeree to specifically reject an offer. In this situation the offeree's silence constitutes an acceptance. Suppose, for example, that for the past several years the Manufacturing Company sold goods to Wholesaler, Inc. and that during this time Wholesaler returned any unwanted goods and paid for the other goods within one month. Suppose further that Manufacturing Company makes a particular shipment and Wholesaler fails to return any goods within one month. Wholesaler's failure to reject the goods obligates Wholesaler to pay for them. Wholesaler's silence is a manifestation of consent because of the prior business dealings between the parties.

Communication of Acceptance

If the offeror and offeree negotiate face-to-face or by telephone, the acceptance takes effect instantly. However, if they negotiate by mail or telegraph, there is necessarily a lapse between the time the acceptance is sent and the time it is received.

**Deposited
acceptance rule**
the effectiveness of the acceptance of an offer when sent provided the means of communication is reasonable

The general rule is that an acceptance takes effect only when the offeror receives it. The courts have created an exception to this rule: The **deposited acceptance rule** provides that an acceptance takes effect when sent provided the means of communication chosen is reasonable. Suppose that Tom Brown, a Chicago businessperson, mails an offer to Ann Jones in Los Angeles and that Jones accepts by telegram. The acceptance is effective when it is deposited in the telegraph office because this is a reasonable means of communication. Thus a binding contract results even if Brown never receives the telegram. The risk of loss for damages caused by delay or nondelivery is on Brown, the offeror.

The offeror can specify conditions of acceptance in the offer, such as the time, place, or method of communicating the acceptance. Any variance makes the acceptance ineffective. Thus Brown could have protected himself by making this stipulation in his offer to Jones: "A telegram of acceptance must be received in my office by 1 P.M. September 15."[3] This places on Jones, the offeree, the risk of loss for damages caused by a delay or nondelivery of the telegram.

It should not be presumed, however, that an offeree may not use an unreasonable means of communication to accept an offer. This is permissible, but the acceptance is effective only when the offeror receives it.

In the following case the court was faced with the issue of whether the offeree had accepted the offer before the offeror withdrew it.

CUSHING V. THOMSON
SUPREME COURT OF NEW HAMPSHIRE
386 A.2d 805 (1978).

A member of the Clamshell Alliance sued Thomson, the governor of New Hampshire, to enforce a contract renting the National Guard armory in Portsmouth to the alliance, an antinuclear protest group. The Portsmouth Clamshell Alliance sought to rent the armory from the state for a benefit dance. The state mailed a signed contract offering to rent the armory to the alliance for a specified time. The offer could be accepted by returning the signed agreement within five days. Cushing, a member of the alliance, signed and mailed the contract soon after receiving it, and the state received the contract within the five-day limit. After the acceptance was mailed but before it was received, Governor Thomson ordered withdrawal of the rental offer. The trial court ruled that a contract had been formed and ordered specific performance. Both parties appealed from portions of the trial court's decision.

OPINION OF THE COURT

The first issue presented is whether the trial court erred in determining that a binding contract existed. Neither party challenges the applicable law. "To establish a contract of this character . . . there must be . . . an offer and an acceptance thereof in accordance with its terms . . . : [W]hen the parties to such a contract are at a distance from one another and the offer is sent by mail, . . . the reply accepting the offer may be sent through the same medium, and the contract will be complete when the acceptance is mailed . . . properly addressed to the party making the offer and beyond the acceptor's control." Withdrawal of the offer is ineffectual once the offer has been accepted by posting in the mail.

The defendants argue, however, that there is no evidence to sustain a finding that plaintiff Cushing had accepted the adjutant general's offer before it was withdrawn. Such a finding is necessarily implied in the court's ruling that there was a binding contract. The implied finding must stand if there is any evidence to support it.

Plaintiffs introduced the sworn affidavit of Mr. Cushing in which he stated that on April 3 he executed the contract and placed it in the outbox for mailing. Moreover, plaintiffs' counsel represented to the court that it was customary office practice for outgoing letters to be picked up from the outbox daily and put in the U.S. mail. No testimony was submitted in this informal hearing, and the basis for the court's order appears to be in part counsels' representations, a procedure which was not objected to by the parties. Thus the representation that it was customary office procedure for the letters to be sent out the same day that they are placed in the office outbox, together with the affidavit, supported the implied finding that the completed contract was mailed before the attempted revocation.

Because there is evidence to support it, this court cannot say as a matter of law that the trial court's finding that there was a binding contract is clearly erroneous, and therefore it must stand.

In deciding the legal issues of contract law in this case, we, of course, are not passing on the aims or activities of the Clamshell Alliance.

Decision for plaintiff.

Legal Issues

1. Why was the governor's attempted withdrawal of the rental offer ineffectual?

2. What rule makes the action taken by the Clamshell Alliance a proper acceptance? Explain.

Ethical Issues

1. Is there any standard of ethics that would treat as ethical an offeror's revocation of an offer because someone has offered to pay the offeror a price higher than that set forth in the offer? Under which standard or standards of ethics would such a revocation be regarded as unethical?

2. The court accepted the plaintiff's claim that its customary office practice was to mail letters on the same day that they were placed in the outbox. Was the court's willingness to accept this claim fair in light of the fact that there was little or no likelihood that anyone who dealt with the plaintiff would know how often this does not occur? What standard of ethics could the court have used to buttress its conclusion? Explain your answer.

LAW ABROAD

Germany

Offers made through personal negotiations between parties, including offers made by telephone, must be accepted at once. Offers made by mail or telegraph remain open only so long as it takes the offeree to reasonably reply. Acceptance occurs only upon receipt by the offeror. If a specified amount of time is set for acceptance, the acceptance must be received by the offeror before that time elapses.

Japan

Offers that specify a fixed time period for acceptance cannot be withdrawn before the end of that time period. Accepting an offer only partially or conditionally can be seen as both a refusal and a counteroffer. Acceptance is effective as soon as it is sent to the offeror. Acceptance can be indicated by an act that signifies to both parties that a contract has been made.

GENUINENESS OF ASSENT

An agreement may be unenforceable even though it contains the four basic requirements of a contract and appears to be valid otherwise. Occasionally, parties enter into a contract in which their consent does not express their real intent. This lack of voluntary consent, which may occur because of fraud or misrepresentation, makes the contract unenforceable.

Fraud

Generally, **fraud** is a dishonest method by which one party gains an unfair advantage over another party. The essential elements of fraud are as follows:

1. Misrepresentation of a material fact.
2. Justifiable reliance by the injured party.
3. Intention to deceive the injured party.
4. Legal damages to the injured party

To clarify, a *fraud* occurs when an intentional misrepresentation of a material fact causes a party to enter into a transaction and thereby suffer a monetary loss.

The essence of fraud is the misrepresentation of a **material fact.** To constitute fraud, the misrepresentation must concern a past or present fact. A mere expression of opinion or a prediction of what will happen is not a statement of fact and therefore not fraudulent. A misrepresentation is material if it induced a party to enter into a contract. Fraud does not occur only when false statements regarding material facts are made. In some cases silence or nondisclosure may constitute fraud. Similarly, misrepresentations may be made by conduct as well as by false statements.

The injured party must have placed **justifiable reliance** on the misrepresentation. A buyer who knew the facts before entering into the contract cannot prove such reliance. In addition, a buyer's reliance on the seller is not justifiable if the buyer's knowledge or opportunity to learn the facts is equal to that of the seller. The injured party must prove that the misrepresentation was made with an intent to deceive. Finally, the injured party must have sustained legal damages because of the misrepresentation. Suppose that Sam represents the car he sells to Bill as a 1990 Thunderbird when, in fact, it is a 1989 Thunderbird and Sam knows this. Since the 1989 and 1990 Thunderbirds look very similar, Bill would be justified in believing Sam's statement. Thus Sam has committed fraud in the sale of the car because he made the statement with the knowledge that it was false and with an intent to deceive.

By acting promptly, the injured party may either rescind the contract or sue in court for damages, including punitive damages. For example, a buyer who purchased property because of fraud can rescind the contract by returning the property. The seller is then obligated to return the purchase price. Instead of rescinding the contract, a buyer who can show that financial injuries resulted from a fraud can obtain actual and punitive damages. The actual damages are the difference between the actual value and the represented value of the property that the buyer received. The punitive damages are damages to punish the seller for the seller's intentional misrepresentation.

Fraud
the intentional misrepresentation of a material fact that causes a party to enter into a transaction and thereby suffer a monetary loss

Material fact
an act or event that induces a party to enter into a contract

Justifiable reliance
the reasonable belief of an injured party that a misrepresentation is true

Misrepresentation
the innocent misstatement of a material fact that causes a party to enter into a contract and thereby suffer a monetary loss

Misrepresentation

A lawsuit for **misrepresentation** can occur if all the elements of fraud are present except that the person making the misrepresentation honestly believed that the statement was true. The remedy for misrepresentation is limited to rescission.

CONSIDERATION

Courts will not enforce gratuitous promises. Generally, neither party can bind the other to the terms of the agreement unless the promisee has given up something of value in exchange for the promisor's promise. This means that the promise of each party must be supported by consideration.

Consideration
the promisee's giving or promising to give something of value to the promisor in exchange for the promisor's act or promise

The **consideration** element of contracts requires the promisee to "earn" the right to enforce the promisor's promise by agreeing to give up something of value in exchange for the promise. Thus the promisee must incur a legal detriment under the contract. For example, if Skip promises to give Ernie a new car and Ernie has not promised anything in return, Ernie cannot bind Skip to his promise since it was not supported by consideration. Consideration is usually defined as a legal detriment, bargained for and given in exchange for an act or a promise. It is the price for the promise or act that makes the contract enforceable.

Legal Detriment

A legal detriment may be an act or a promise, depending on whether the contract is unilateral or bilateral. In a unilateral contract the performance of the act is the consideration, while in a bilateral contract each promise serves as consideration for the other promise. A legal detriment can be of two types. **Legal detriment** occurs where, in exchange for the promisor's promise, parties perform an act or promise to perform an act that they are not otherwise legally obligated to perform. Legal detriment also occurs where, in exchange for the promisor's promise, parties refrain from doing something or agree to refrain from doing something that they have a legal right to do.

Legal detriment
in exchange for the promisor's promise, doing or promising to do that which one has no legal obligation to do or the refraining from doing or promising to refrain from doing that which one has a legal right to do

Legal detriment does not have to coincide with monetary value. In one case an uncle promised to pay his nephew $5,000 if the nephew gave up drinking, smoking, swearing, and gambling until he was 21 years of age. The nephew lived up to his end of the bargain and legally enforced his uncle's promise. The court found legal detriment in the nephew's refraining from doing something that he had the right to do.

Bargained For and Given in Exchange

The legal detriment must be bargained for and given in exchange for the promisor's promise. The promisee's promise or act must be the consideration requested by the promisor in exchange for his or her promise. In other words, what is relied on as consideration must be given and received in exchange for the promise before it will operate to make the promise binding.

Pre-existing Contractual Duties

Generally, an agreement to perform a **pre-existing duty** is not consideration. A promisee who agrees to do something that he or she is already bound to do does not incur a legal detriment since nothing of legal value has been given up.

Most pre-existing duty problems involve contractual duties. Such problems often arise where the parties to an existing contract attempt to modify it, without furnishing new consideration in support of the modification. For example, assume that ABC Corporation and Superior Construction Company enter into a contract under which Superior is to build a new ABC office building for $675,000. After construction is under way, the owner of Superior requests an additional $50,000 from the president of ABC to complete the project. ABC's president agrees to the price increase, and Superior completes the project. If ABC then refuses to pay Superior the extra $50,000, Superior cannot successfully sue ABC for it since no new consideration was supplied by Superior when ABC promised to pay the additional amount. To be enforceable, modification of an existing contract requires new consideration.

The UCC **modification of sales contracts rule** makes an exception to normal consideration rules. Section 2-209 (1) of the UCC provides that "an agreement modifying a contract [for the sale of goods] needs no consideration to be binding." For example, assume that Cunningham Hardware agrees to sell Arthur's Auto Shoppe 50 gallons of paint, to be delivered on June 6. Cunningham Hardware is unable to make delivery on time, and the buyer and seller then agree to a delivery date of June 15. Arthur's later demands delivery on June 6. Under the UCC, Arthur's is bound by the terms of the modified agreement even though Cunningham Hardware supplied no new consideration. The purpose of the UCC modification rule is to facilitate sales transactions by making it easier for businesspersons to adapt to changing circumstances.

Apart from the UCC, the common law **unforeseeable difficulties** rule upholds modifications unsupported by new consideration if a party's performance is impossible or highly impracticable. Courts apply this rule only in exceptional situations. They do not regard such things as price increases, bad weather, and strikes as unforeseeable difficulties. On the other hand, if a builder discovers that quicksand underlies a roadbed in an area where quicksand is very unusual, the promise to pay the builder for the additional cost of construction is enforceable even though it is unsupported by new consideration. Because of the unforeseeable difficulties, the pre-existing obligation rule does not apply.

Past Consideration

The term **past consideration** is misleading since past consideration is generally viewed as no consideration at all. If the promisee's performance was completed before the promisor's promise was given, then it cannot be consideration supporting the promise. Even if the promisee's performance involves a legal detriment, it was not "bargained for and given in exchange" for the later promise. If Bud says to his neighbor, "I will pay you $125 for the swell bicycle you gave me last year," and subsequently does not pay, his neighbor cannot enforce the promise. Consideration is lacking because Bud did not promise to pay the $125 in exchange for his neighbor's promise to give him the bike.

**Pre-existing
duty rule**
the rule that promising to do that which one already has a legal duty to do is not consideration

**Modification of sales
contracts rule**
UCC rule under which changes in the terms of sales contracts are enforceable without consideration

**Unforeseeable
difficulties rule**
the rule that modification of a contract without consideration because of unforeseeable difficulties is enforceable

Past consideration
the doctrine that the promise of something that has already been given is not consideration

Promissory Estoppel

In certain cases a valid contract can be formed without consideration. Where one party detrimentally relies on the promise of another party, the doctrine of **promissory estoppel** may operate to enforce the contract even if consideration was not given. This doctrine has three elements:

1. A promise has been made on which the promisee is likely to rely.
2. The promisee has reasonably relied on the promise.
3. Injustice can be avoided only by enforcing the promise.

All three elements must be present for promissory estoppel to apply. For example, assume that Shirley was working as a bottle inspector at Shorty Brewery when Richie, president of C&H Publishing Company, offered her a job as a secretary. Relying on Richie's promise of employment, Shirley quit her job at the brewery, but Richie then refused to hire her. The doctrine of promissory estoppel would bind Richie to his promise even thought it was unsupported by consideration on Shirley's part. Since Richie should have foreseen that Shirley would quit her job in reliance on his promise, he is estopped (prevented) from revoking the promise.

LAW ABROAD

Germany

Consideration need not be given for a contract to be valid. This means that gift contracts are valid and enforceable.

Hypothetical Case

A MINOR BUYS A SPORTS CAR

Mike, a 17-year-old who looked at least 21, purchased a sports car from Ace Used Car Sales. He paid $1,200 down and signed a contract agreeing to pay $200 a month for the next 48 months. After he had the car for one week, he decided to see how fast it would go. At 119 mph, one of the tires blew out, causing the car to swerve off the highway and flip over. The car was totaled, and Mike was hospitalized. The day after his release from the hospital, he had the remains of the car towed to Ace Used Car Sales, whose owner he told that he was returning the car. He also told the owner that he wanted Ace to refund his $1,200. Is Ace Used Car Sales legally obligated to refund Mike's down payment? Why?

CAPACITY TO CONTRACT

The law regards certain parties as incompetent to enter into contracts. Lack of **capacity to contract** is usually caused by infancy, insanity, or intoxication. Contracts entered into by individuals who lack the capacity to contract can be rescinded by them.

When a contract is rescinded for lack of capacity, it is usually because one of the contracting parties is an infant, or minor. Over 40 state statutes now define a minor as a person who has not yet reached 18 years of age. When the 26th Amendment to the U.S. Constitution lowered the voting age in national elections from 21 to 18, most state legislatures also lowered the age of capacity to contract. A minor can rescind a contract by indicating to the adult party the intention not to be bound by it. Upon rescission of a contract, the parties go back to their position before they entered into the contract. The minor is entitled to receive from the adult party everything that he or she has given under the contract, and the minor must return to the adult party everything that he or she has received under the contract and still possesses.

The right of the minor to rescind the contract is absolute. The minor can disaffirm the contract even if he or she no longer has the consideration. In one case a minor purchased an engagement ring on credit from a jewelry store. His fiancee broke off the engagement but refused to return the ring. The court ruled that the minor could rescind the contract even though he could not return the ring to the store. Thus the minor was able to recover all of the money that he had paid the store.

The minor may disaffirm the contract at any time before reaching the age of majority and for a reasonable time thereafter. If the minor chooses not to disaffirm, the contract is binding. A minor who fails to disaffirm within a reasonable time after reaching the age of majority has ratified (approved) the contract. In this situation the minor loses the right to disaffirm.

It is important to note that *only* the minor may disaffirm the contract. The adult party is bound to the contract unless the minor decides to rescind it. The purpose of the law is to protect minors from the consequences of their folly as youths.

Contracts for necessaries entered into by minors are treated differently. Necessaries include food, clothing, shelter, medical attention, basic education, and tools of trades. Minors are liable for the reasonable value of those necessaries that adult parties furnish to them. Suppose that John, a minor who receives no support from his parents, charges $350 of clothing that he bought from a store. John can rescind the contract but is liable to pay for the reasonable value of the clothing— which may or may not be the contract price. Suppose, however, that John's parents had been furnishing him with clothing at the time of the contracting. In that case the clothing would not be a necessary and John can rescind the contract without any obligation of payment.

States have enacted statutes that preclude minors from rescinding certain types of contracts. For example, minors cannot rescind contracts for life or health insurance on their own lives. In most states minors cannot rescind contracts for educational loans, bank account agreements, enlistment in the armed forces, and marriage.

Contracts involving insane or intoxicated adults may be voidable. The capacity of such adults to contract is determined by whether they were capable of understanding the nature and purpose of the contract when they entered into it. If not, they can rescind the contract.

A judicial hearing is occasionally held to determine whether an adult party is mentally competent. If the court determines that the adult is mentally incompetent, it appoints a guardian and future contracts of the mentally incompetent adult are void.

In the following case the Supreme Court of Wisconsin had to decide whether a minor was entitled to the return of the purchase price of a car that had been damaged before the minor's disaffirmance of the sales contract.

HALBMAN V. LEMKE
SUPREME COURT OF WISCONSIN
298 N.W.2d 562 (1980)

James Halbman, Jr., a minor, purchased a 1968 Oldsmobile for $1,250 from Michael Lemke. Lemke was an employee at a service station managed by Halbman. Halbman paid him $1,000 and agreed to pay him $25 a week on the balance. About five weeks later a connecting rod on the car's engine broke. Halbman had the car repaired but did not pay the repair bill.

The garage that repaired the car eventually removed its replacement engine to cover the cost of the repairs and then towed it to Halbman's home. During the time that the car was at the garage and at Halbman's home, it was rendered unsalvageable by vandalism.

Halbman attempted to disaffirm the purchase contract by returning the title to Lemke and demanding the return of the $1,100 that he had paid Lemke. Lemke counterclaimed for $150, the amount still owing on the purchase price. The trial court entered judgment for Halbman and Lemke appealed.

CALLOW, JUSTICE

The sole issue before us is whether a minor, having disaffirmed a contract for the purchase of an item which is not a necessity and having tendered the property back to the vendor, must make restitution to the vendor for damage to the property prior to the disaffirmance. Lemke argues that he should be entitled to recover for the damage to the vehicle up to the time of disaffirmance, which he claims equals the amount of the repair bill.

Neither party challenges the absolute right of a minor to disaffirm a contract for the purchase of items which are not necessities. That right, variously known as the doctrine of incapacity or the "infancy doctrine," is one of the oldest and most venerable of our common law traditions. [I]t is generally recognized that its purpose is the protection of minors from foolishly squandering their wealth through improvident contracts with crafty adults who would take advantage of them in the marketplace.

In this case we have a situation where the property cannot be returned to the vendor in its entirety because it has been damaged and therefore diminished in value, and the vendor seeks to recover the depreciation. A minor, as we have stated, is under enforceable duty to return to the vendor, upon disaffirmance, as much of the consideration as remains in his possession. When the contract is disaffirmed, title to that part of the purchased property which is retained by the minor revests in the vendor; it no longer belongs to the minor. The rationale for the rule is plain: a minor who disaffirms a purchase and recovers his purchase price should not also be permitted to profit by retaining the property purchased. The infancy doctrine is designed to protect the minor, sometimes at the expense of an innocent vendor, but it is not to be used to bilk merchants out of property as well as proceeds of the sale. Consequently, it is clear that, when the minor no longer possesses the property which was the subject matter of the contract, the rule requiring the return of property does not apply. The minor will not be required to give up what he does not have.

Where there is misrepresentation by a minor or willful destruction of property, the vendor may be able to recover damages in tort. But absent these factors, as in the present case, we believe that to require a disaffirming minor to make restitution for diminished value is, in effect, to bind the minor to a part of the obligation which by law he is privileged to avoid. [Some courts hold] that a disaffirming minor must do equity in the form of restitution for loss or depreciation of the property returned. Because these cases would at some point force the minor to bear the cost of the very improvidence from which the infancy doctrine is supposed to protect him, we cannot follow them.

[A]bsent misrepresentation or tortious damage to the property, a minor who disaffirms a contract for the purchase of an item which is not a necessity may recover his purchase price without liability for use, depreciation, damage, or other diminution in value.

Affirmed.

Legal Issues

1. According to the court, what is the purpose of allowing a minor to disaffirm a contract for the purchase of an item that is not a necessary?
2. Why did the court refuse to require Halbman to make restitution to Lemke for the diminished value of the car?

Ethical Issues

1. Should the law hold infants to the ethical level of fair behavior that could ordinarily be demanded of a person of the infant's age, general knowledge, education, and experience? Why?
2. Although minors are generally excused from contract liability, minors who are guilty of misrepresentation or willful destruction of property may be required to make restitution for the diminished value of the property that they return to a seller when they cancel a contract? What ethical standards support this view? Discuss.

LAW ABROAD

Germany

A person is considered a minor until the age of 18. A minor can enter into a contract only with the consent of a parent or a guardian (in certain cases the consent of a guardianship court may also be required).

If a parent or a guardian, with the consent of a guardianship court, authorizes a minor to start his or her business, the minor is automatically considered to have attained majority as far as debts and obligations related to the business are concerned. Similarly, if a minor takes a job (with the consent of a parent or a guardian), he or she is considered to have attained majority in regard to transactions connected with the job.

Japan

The minimum age for capacity to contract is 20, but marriage emancipates the individual. A minor can contract only with the approval of parents or a guardian.

Contracts entered by a minor without the consent of parents or a guardian are voidable.

ILLEGALITY

The fourth basic requirement of a valid contract is a legal objective. **Illegal contracts** are void—neither party to such a contract has the option of choosing whether to rescind or enforce the contract. The detriment to society of enforcing contracts to perform illegal acts outweighs the benefits to society of freedom to bargain.

Types of Illegality

An agreement is illegal if either its formation or its performance (1) involves the commission of a crime or tort, (2) is contrary to statute, or (3) is contrary to public policy.

Contracts Involving a Crime or Tort

The rule against enforcement of illegal contracts is most clearly applicable to agreements that call for the commission of a crime or a tort. If Louise pays Bently $50,000 to kill her husband and Bently fails to perform the job, Louise will be unable to enforce the agreement since it clearly involves crime. Similarly, an agreement to commit a tort—for example, a promise to pay a newspaper $10,000 to print a libelous article—is unenforceable.

Contracts Made Illegal by Statute

Certain types of agreements have been rendered illegal by statutes. All of the states have *anti-gambling statutes* that make gambling illegal. Gambling is the creation of a risk for the sole purpose of bearing the risk. For example, bets on the outcome of a sports event and obligations that arise from operating games of chance are gambling since the parties create a risk for the sole purpose of bearing the risk. States have created numerous exceptions to the anti-gambling statutes. For example, more than one half of the states have legalized betting at racetracks, 14 states allow off-track betting, 2 states allow casino gambling, and most states have legalized bingo games.

Many states have also passed **Sunday laws,** which prohibit work and various types of business transactions on Sunday. Thus contracts that call for the sale of certain kinds of goods on Sunday may be illegal. In many states, for example, the sale of alcoholic beverages on Sunday is a prohibited contract.

In addition, most states have passed **usury laws,** which limit the interest that can be charged in contracts to borrow money. These laws are discussed in Chapter 15.

Contracts Made Illegal by Public Policy

Public policy is an important concept, but one that is difficult to define. Basically, public policy is determined by the court's view of what is in the best interest of society as a whole. That view changes with changing societal conditions and with the public's changing views on acceptable forms of behavior. A court may declare a contract illegal because the contract is against public policy, so that enforcement of the contract would be detrimental to society.

Contracts in restraint of trade—contracts that restrict competition—are one type of agreement that many courts have viewed as contrary to public policy. An important principle of the American economic system is free competition. In certain circumstances, however, courts have allowed reasonable restrictions on competition. Courts closely scrutinize agreements that limit competition in order to determine their reasonableness.

Contracts in restraint of trade
contracts that restrict competition

Generally, agreements whose *only* purpose is to restrain competition are illegal. However, restraints on competition that supplement contracts are legal if they are intended to protect contractual interests and are no more restrictive than is reasonably necessary to protect those interests. When a business is sold, for example, the contract usually protects the goodwill of the business that the buyer purchases. Thus a clause in the contract may provide that the seller will not enter a similar business in competition with the buyer. Such a restriction is enforceable if it is limited to a reasonable geographic area and a reasonable period of time. Suppose that Lee, who owns a small mattress factory in Albany, New York, sells the factory to Scott and that a clause in the sales contract provides that Lee will not open a competing mattress factory in the state of New York. This agreement not to compete is unenforceable because the geographic limitation on competition is unreasonably large: Scott's business would not be threatened by the loss of customers in, say, New York City. However, a clause restricting competition in the Albany area would be reasonable and enforceable.

An agreement by Lee not to open a competing business for the next 10 years would probably also be unenforceable, because the time limitation on competition is unreasonably long. Most courts, however, would uphold an agreement restricting competition for up to five years.

In addition to being against public policy, contracts in restraint of trade may be in violation of statutes that declare monopolies unlawful. These antitrust statutes are discussed in Chapters 18 and 19.

Many employment contracts contain provisions that prevent employees from competing with or working for a competitor of their employer if they quit or are fired. Although technically "in restraint of trade," such a provision is not automatically illegal. If the provision is necessary to prevent a former employee from revealing trade secrets or "stealing" customers and is limited to a reasonable time period, it will probably be enforceable.

Courts will generally view noncompetition agreements with skepticism. They will closely examine the length and geographic scope of the ban on competition.

Effect of Illegality

It should be kept in mind that when an agreement is illegal, the parties are usually not entitled to assistance from the courts. Neither party can sue to obtain performance or recover money. The court leaves the parties where it finds them. The rationale for doing so is that this discourages the making of illegal contracts.

Unconscionable contracts are so one-sided that they offend the conscience. Such contracts are discussed in Chapter 15. This chapter examines how federal and state laws, as well as administrative regulations and court decisions, have changed traditional private contract law to protect consumers who enter into contracts with businesses.

Unconscionable contracts
contracts so unfair that the courts will not enforce them

LAW ABROAD

Germany

The Civil Code contains the main provisions of German contract law. However, special provisions are found in the Commercial Code and in the laws on checks and bills of exchange.

Japan

In Japan contracts are controlled by special sections of the Civil and Commercial codes. A typical Japanese contract is quite different from an American contract. In the contract, which is usually only one page in length, the parties state their rights and obligations and their agreement to negotiate any future problems in good faith. Many Japanese believe that in a contract dispute, establishing contractual rights is less important than negotiating in a spirit of harmony to ensure the continuation of a successful business relationship.

In their international contracts the large Japanese companies have changed to a more Western view. These contracts define the contractual duties of the parties more carefully. Still, like the domestic contracts, they emphasize trust and reflect a strong belief that cooperation between the parties should be the goal.

REVIEW QUESTIONS & PROBLEMS

1. Can a contract in restraint of trade be enforceable? Why?

2. The enforceability of contracts is essential to the economic system of the United States. Explain.

3. A minor purchased a computer from Computer Store for $1,000. He paid $100 down and signed a contract promising to pay the rest in monthly installments. When a payment was past due, Computer Store sued the minor. One month after the suit was filed, the minor became 18 years old and disaffirmed the contract by returning the computer and demanding the return of the $400 he had already paid. The minor claimed the defense of lack of capacity. Was this an effective defense? Why?

4. While in Pop's Grocery Store, where she had a charge account, Rachel took a gallon of milk off a refrigerated shelf and held it up so that Pop saw her. Pop nodded his approval, and Rachel walked out of the store with the gallon of milk. Did Pop's Grocery Store and Rachel enter into a contract? Why?

5. Lally owned and operated Lally's Barber Shop, a business in Rockville, Connecticut. He sold the shop "together with all goodwill" to Buyer. The bill of sale contained this clause: "The seller agrees in and for the consideration received that he will not engage in the barbering business for a period of five years from this date in the city of Rockville." Nine months after the sale, Lally set up a one-chair barbershop in his own home, which was about 300 feet from the shop he had sold to Buyer. Buyer brought suit for an injunction to restrain Lally from operating this barbershop. Is Buyer entitled to an injunction? Why?

6. After 30 years of employment, Elbert retired from Pittman Lumber Company, receiving a pension of $700 per month. Pittman, the sole owner and president of the company, happened to meet Elbert two years later and asked him how

he was enjoying his retirement. Elbert responded that even with social security benefits he did not have enough money to live on because of medical bills due to his wife's serious illness. Pittman, who had always appreciated Elbert's loyalty, said "Don't worry. I will see that Pittman Lumber Company pays you an additional $300 per month for the rest of your life. You have been such a good and loyal employee that you certainly deserve to enjoy retirement." Elbert smiled, shook Pittman's hand, and said, "I'm going home now and tell my wife the good news." Is Elbert legally entitled to the $300 per month that Pittman promised him? Why?

1. Louisiana has adopted Articles 1, 3, 4, and 5 of the UCC but not Article 2, which covers sales of goods.

2. The UCC consists of 11 articles (chapters). The eight articles covering substantive areas of law are as follows: Article 2, Sales; Article 3, Commercial Paper; Article 4, Bank Deposits and Collections; Article 5, Letters of Credit; Article 6, Bulk Transfers; Article 7, Warehouse Receipts, Bills of Lading, and Other Documents of Title; Article 8, Investment Securities; Article 9, Secured Transactions, Sales of Accounts, and Chattel Paper.

3. The expression "received by the offeror" ordinarily means that the acceptance must be delivered to the offeror's residence or place of business. If the offeror is absent at the time of delivery, the necessary communication has nevertheless been made.

CHAPTER

9

Enforceability of Contracts

The four essential elements of a valid contract were discussed in Chapter 8. However, the courts may refuse to enforce contracts that contain these elements. This chapter discusses (1) contracts that must be in *writing* to be enforceable, (2) contracts that may be enforced by a *third party*, (3) contracts whose obligations may be legally *discharged* without having been completed, and (4) contracts under which breach of contract usually entitles the innocent party to certain legal *remedies*.

FORM OF CONTRACTS REQUIRED BY LAW

It is commonly believed that oral contracts are not enforceable. In fact, most oral contracts are just as enforceable as written contracts. Certain kinds of contracts, however, must be in writing to be enforceable. All of the states have enacted **statutes of frauds** that set forth those kinds of contracts. The first statute of frauds, enacted in England in 1677, was designed to prevent fraud in contracts that were frequently vulnerable to fraud or contracts in which the results of fraud would be particularly damaging. The state statutes of frauds are very similar to the original statute of frauds.

A typical statute of frauds, including the UCC provisions for sales of goods, requires a writing for the following types of contracts:

1. Contracts to answer for the debts of others.
2. Contracts for the sale of land.
3. Contracts not to be performed within one year.
4. Contracts for the sale of goods for $500 or more.

> **Statute of frauds**
> a statute providing that certain types of contracts will not be enforceable unless they are in writing

Effect of Failure to Comply

A statute of frauds provides that oral contracts falling within its provisions are **unenforceable**, not void or voidable. Should a party who is being sued for breach of contract assert the statute of frauds as a defense, the court will not enforce an otherwise valid contract falling within the statute of frauds if it cannot be proved by a proper writing. Assume that Marty told Harris: "I'll pay you $5,000 for your land" and that Harris replied: "You've got a deal." If Harris subsequently refused to sell the land to Marty and Marty sued to enforce the contract, it would be up to Harris to raise the statute of frauds as a defense. Otherwise the court would enforce the contract provided Marty could establish its terms in court.

Where both parties have fully performed their obligations under a contract, the statute of frauds cannot be used as a defense even though its provisions cover the contract. Full performance of the contract assures the court that a contract did in fact exist. If Marty paid Harris the $5,000, moved onto the land, and made improvements to the land, the contract falls outside the statute of frauds because sufficient evidence of its existence has been established.

Courts may also use the doctrine of **estoppel** as a basis for allowing recovery on oral contracts covered by the statute of frauds. If the party seeking to enforce such a contract has relied on an oral promise to his or her detriment and will suffer an unconscionable hardship and loss if the promise is not enforced, courts may hold that the defendant is estopped (prevented) from asserting the statute of frauds as a defense. Likewise, if a party to an unenforceable oral contract has rendered part performance under the contract, thus benefiting the other party, the doctrine of **quasi contract** would allow the recovery of the reasonable value of such performance. Thus the statute of frauds does not completely bar the enforcement of oral contracts that are required to be in writing; it makes such contracts unenforceable only in certain contexts.

> **Unenforceable contract**
> a legal contract for which the courts will deny the plaintiff any remedy because a defense to the contract exists

> **Estoppel**
> a legal bar to alleging or denying a fact because of one's previous statements or actions to the contrary

> **Quasi contract**
> an obligation created by law as a remedy for unjust enrichment

Promise to Pay for the Debt of Another

Guaranty contract

a third party's promise to fulfill the obligation of an original party to the contract if the original party fails to perform

A promise by one person to be responsible for the debts or default of another person falls within the statute of frauds. Such promises are generally referred to as "guaranty contracts." A **guaranty contract** provides that a third party, the guarantor, will perform the duties that another party, the debtor, owes under a separate contract, if the debtor fails to perform. Assume that Donald, owner of Don's TV Sales, borrows $10,000 from ABC Bank to finance the acquisition of additional inventory, agreeing to repay the bank over a 5-year period. Assume further that in order to improve its position ABC Bank obtains the promise of Donald's sister, Susan, to pay back the loan if Donald fails to do so. Susan's promise is a guaranty because she is liable *only* if Donald fails to perform. Thus Susan's promise is enforceable only if it is in writing.

Primary liability

the liability of the party to the contract who is absolutely required to perform

An important distinction that must be made in this area is the difference between guaranty contracts and original contracts of the third party. Original contracts need not be in writing in order to be enforceable. A party to an original contract is subject to **primary liability** under the contract, whereas a guarantor is only secondarily liable. A **primary promise** occurs if the third party agrees to be liable whether or not the debtor defaults.

Primary promise

a third party's promise to fulfill the obligation of an original party to the contract whether or not that party performs

For example, assume that ABC Bank lent the $10,000 to both Donald and Susan, both of whom agreed to repay the loan. Donald and Susan are therefore co-obligors on the loan and are both primarily liable to repay it. ABC Bank can collect the loan payments from either of them. The promises made by Donald and Susan are *original* promises and thus need not be in writing to be enforceable. Here Susan's debt is her own from the beginning. She is not promising to answer for Donald's debt if he does not pay. Figure 9-1 illustrates a guaranty contract.

FIGURE 9-1

A Guaranty Contract

In this figure businessperson B seeks to borrow $10,000 from bank S, but B's credit history is not strong enough for S to lend B the money without a guaranty. C promises S that she will pay back the $10,000 if B fails to do so. Under the statute of frauds, C's promise must be in writing.

Contracts for the Sale of Land

Since the time when land was the primary indicator of wealth, land has been recognized as a special form of property. Thus the statute of frauds requires written contracts for the sale of land or the transfer of an interest in land. The expression "interest in land" is interpreted to include any contract whose performance will affect rights in land ownership. Such contracts include transfers of mineral rights, contracts to mortgage, and contracts granting easements to land.

Partial performance under a land sales contract may remove the writing requirement.

Contracts Not to Be Performed within One Year

Important provisions of long-term oral contracts are highly likely to be forgotten or distorted. Thus long-term contracts must be evidenced by a writing. The statute of frauds requires, perhaps arbitrarily, that contracts whose terms preclude their performance within one year must be in writing to be enforceable.

The courts have interpreted this requirement to mean that if the terms of the contract make it *at all possible* to perform the contract within one year, the contract does not have to be in writing. Assume that Alice, a famous movie star, makes an oral commitment to a small studio to act in a series of four motion pictures. Although the studio is usually capable of producing only two movies a year, the contract need not be in writing, since it is *possible* that the studio will complete the entire series within one year.

It is important to note that the one-year period begins when the parties enter into the contract. Suppose that Life Insurance Company agrees on March 15, 1991, to employ Smith for one year and that Smith is to begin work on April 1, 1991. The contract must be in writing as it cannot be performed within one year of the contract date.

The Required Writing

The statute of frauds does not require a formal written document signed by both parties. All that it requires is a **memorandum** of the contract signed or initialed by the party denying its existence. This memorandum may be a telegram, a letter, a receipt, or any other writing indicating the existence of the contract. It may be a single writing or a series of documents that clearly relate to the same agreement.

Memorandum
an informal record or account

The memorandum, whatever its form, must contain the essential elements of the contract. It must name both parties; it must describe the subject matter of the contract; and it must specify the consideration.

Contracts for the Sale of Goods for $500 or More

The UCC (2-202) provides that a contract for the sale of goods for $500 or more must be in writing to be enforceable. If Stella Perkins orally offers to sell 1,000 pounds of crabmeat at $5 per pound to Paul Drake, who orally accepts the offer, the agreement is unenforceable because it is not in writing.

The entire contract need not be in writing to satisfy the statute of frauds provisions of the UCC. The UCC requires only an informal writing. The writing must (1) indicate the existence of the contract, (2) contain the signature of the party to be charged on the contract, and (3) indicate the quantity of the goods sold.

The following writing would comply with the UCC writing requirement:

I agree to sell 1,000 pounds of crabmeat to Paul Drake. Signed, Stella Perkins

This writing binds Stella (the party to be charged) under the UCC. It does not bind Paul since it does not bear his signature. However, if both Paul and Stella are merchants and Paul does not object within 10 days after receiving the writing, the statute of frauds defense is unavailable to him. The fact that he did not object to the writing is viewed as evidence that the contract existed, making the protection of the statute of frauds unnecessary.

Written confirmation
a writing sufficient to satisfy the statute of frauds if it is not objected to within 10 days after receipt by a merchant buyer or seller

Thus, the UCC writing requirement can be satisfied by a **written confirmation** of the oral agreement between merchants. The merchant who receives the written confirmation and does not object in writing within 10 days after receiving it cannot use the statute of frauds as a defense.

The UCC contains several exceptions to the writing requirement. A writing is not required for sale of goods contracts in the following situations:

1. The goods (1) are to be *specially manufactured* for the buyer, and (2) are not suitable for sale in the seller's ordinary course of business, and (3) the seller has made a substantial beginning of their manufacture or procurement. Suppose that the Brown for President Campaign Committee orally contracts with ABC Company for $100,000 of campaign buttons imprinted with Brown's picture and name and that the committee rejects the contract after ABC has made a substantial beginning. The oral contract is enforceable since the buttons cannot be sold in the ordinary course of ABC's business.

2. A *part payment* or a *part delivery* has been made and accepted. The oral contract is enforceable to the extent that the seller accepted payment or to the extent that the buyer accepted the goods. Suppose that Buyer orally agrees to purchase six computers at a price of $800 each from Seller. Seller makes an initial delivery of three computers, which Buyer accepts, but Buyer then rejects the contract. Seller can sue for breach of contract for the partial performance of the three computers that Buyer accepted.

3. The party who is being sued *admits the existence of the contract* in court or in pleadings. In the previous example, if Buyer admits in court having entered into an oral contract for five computers, the oral contract is enforceable as to the quantity of goods admitted.

The next case presents an interesting situation in which the contract consisted of two or more writings, only one of which was signed by the party to be charged.

D.P. SERVICE, INC. v. AM INTERNATIONAL
U.S. DISTRICT COURT N.D. ILLINOIS, E.D.
508 F. Supp. 162 (1981)

D.P. Service, Inc. sued AM International, Inc. for breach of an alleged distribution agreement. D.P. Service (DP) alleged that a written agreement with AM International (AM), dated July 1, 1978, established DP as a non-exclusive distributor of AM's products in Illinois. AM argued that any alleged contract was unenforceable because neither AM nor any of its agents had ever signed a written agreement and because any claimed oral agreement would run afoul of the statute of frauds. AM made a motion to dismiss, alleging that the complaint failed to state a claim upon which relief could be granted. (The contract was formed in California, so the federal court in this diversity of citizenship case applied California law).

SHADUR, JUDGE

California's Statute of Frauds, Cal. Civ. Code, Section 1624, provides:

> The following contracts are invalid, unless the same, or some note or memorandum thereof, is in writing and subscribed by the party to be charged or by his agent:
>
>> 1. An agreement that by its terms is not to be performed within a year of the making thereof . . .

Because the Distributorship Agreement specifies a 24-month term, renewable for two additional periods of 12 months each, it was not valid unless there was a writing sufficient to take it out of the Statute of Frauds.

As a general rule the "in writing" requirement may be satisfied by a contract comprising two or more writings, only one of which need be signed by the party to be charged. Corbin, *Contracts*, Section 512. California follows that general rule.

DP acknowledges that the original Distributorship Agreement is unsigned by AM but argues that later documents, signed by AM, constitute a sufficient writing in conjunction with the original. Complaint Exhibit E [document submitted to the court by the plaintiff] is a letter from AM to plaintiff, signed by AM's Vice President–Sales Donald Novak, referring to "your current Distributor Contract" (quite plainly a reference to AM's printed form of Distributorship Agreement, Exhibit A, which DP had signed). Exhibit F, a letter from AM's President Edgar Bolton to DP, states that AM "fully intends to honor the agreement we have with your organization."

The Court cannot rule as a matter of law that the Exhibits attached to DP's complaint do not constitute writings sufficient to avoid the Statute of Frauds.

Legal Issues

1. What kinds of agreements are invalidated by the writing requirement of the statute of frauds?
2. How did DP avoid the statute of frauds? Explain.

Ethical Issues

1. On September 1, 1990, Rob, the purchasing agent of Wayco, Inc. entered into an oral agreement with Trigger Corporation to buy 10 heavy-duty electrical heating units at Trigger's usual price of $1,000. Delivery was to be made on October 15, 1990. Ten days later, because of the unexpected bankruptcy of Quick-Ease Company, one of Trigger's competitors, comparable heating units could be bought from Quick-Ease's stock at $750 each. When Thomas, Wayco's president, learned that the arrangement with Trigger was oral, he instructed Rob to tell Trigger not to deliver the units and to purchase units from Quick-Ease. Rob protested. "Boss," he said, "we have an ethical obligation here. It was no one's fault that we forgot to put the agreement in writing. We have done business with Trigger for a decade, and time and again we have done business without a written contract. It is unethical to back off on a legal technicality." Thomas replied: "There is nothing unethical

about acting lawfully. We have a duty to our shareholders. That is what I am thinking of." Would it be ethical for Rob to follow Thomas's instructions? Why?

2. Chris Lamb asked Linda Care, his attorney, to accompany him to the office of Tam Park. Chris told Linda: "Please remember, I want a deal that I can easily avoid. If you think I am making an error, just speak up." After two hours of negotiations, Lamb agreed to purchase $18,000 worth of merchandise from Park. Lamb then said: "Tam, let's shake on this." Park replied: "Delighted." After Chris and Linda left Tam's office, Linda told Chris: "You know, the arrangement is not enforceable because it is not in writing." Chris thought for a moment and then said: "Linda, that's great. I now have the flexibility I need."

Was it ethical for Linda Care not to inform Tam Park that the oral arrangement was unenforceable? Would your answer be the same if during the negotiations Park mentioned that if she made an arrangement with Lamb, she would not try to sell the merchandise to anyone else and that the goods were seasonal and would have to be sold at a significantly lower price within a day or two? Why?

LAW ABROAD

Germany

Oral contracts are not prohibited and may be proved by a variety of means. Although there is no concept comparable to a statute of frauds, certain contracts must be in writing. A written agreement is required, for example, for a contract to sell land and for one party's guaranty of another party's obligations.

Japan

Japan does not have a specific statute of frauds. However, certain contracts, such as wills and corporate instruments, are required to be in writing.

Hypothetical Case

ORAL PROMISES AND THE SEASIDE HOTEL

The Seaside Hotel needed five new vacuum cleaners. A sales representative from Murphy Appliance Store said to Sally Morris, the hotel's purchasing agent, "The vacuum cleaners that we sell have a 24-month guarantee, and if any of them breaks down during this warranty period, we will lend you one without charge while it's being repaired."

Sally purchased five vacuum cleaners from Murphy Appliance Store, but the contract she signed did not mention the sales representative's promise of free use of a vacuum cleaner. A year later Sally arranged to have one of the vacuum cleaners returned to Murphy Appliance Store for repair. At that time she was informed that any use of a borrowed vacuum cleaner would be subject to a daily rental fee. Did Murphy Appliance Store breach its contract with Seaside Hotel? Why?

The Parol Evidence Rule

Whenever an agreement is reduced to writing, the **parol evidence rule** excludes evidence of prior or concurrent oral agreements that would vary the written contract.

The parol evidence rule is based on the premise that the best evidence of a written contract is the writing itself. While defective memories, wishful thinking, or bad intent may color the oral statements of the parties to the contract after a dispute has arisen, the written contract is relatively clear and incontestable.

The parol evidence rule bars proof of oral terms even if the parties actually agreed to them. Thus, when a contract is reduced to writing, it is important to include all of its material terms.

Exceptions to the Parol Evidence Rule

Exceptions to the parol evidence rule are recognized where the writing is not in fact the best evidence of the contract. Thus a party can introduce oral evidence in situations in which the oral evidence:

1. Tends to prove that an oral agreement was entered into *after* the formation of the written contract.
2. Shows that one or both of the parties lacked voluntary consent when they entered into the contract.
3. Assists the court in interpreting unclear or ambiguous contracts.
4. Fills in the missing terms of incomplete contracts.

Parol evidence rule

the rule that a written contract cannot be changed by evidence of prior or concurrent oral agreements

RIGHTS OF THIRD PARTIES

Thus far the discussion has centered on the rights and duties of the original parties to the contract. Ordinarily, after having entered into a contract, only these parties have rights and duties under it. In two situations, however, a third party can enforce a right or assume a duty created in a contract. These situations are assignments of contracts and third-party beneficiary contracts.

Assignments of Contracts

A party to a contract may transfer his or her contractual rights to a third party. Such a transfer of contractual rights is referred to as an **assignment.** The party who makes the assignment is called the **assignor,** and the party who receives the assignment is called the **assignee.** The assignee is entitled to any performance that the assignor was to receive under the original contract. This means that the other party to the original contract, who is called the **obligor,** must render performance to the assignee. Suppose, for example, that a number of customers of Smith Manufacturing Company owe Smith $50,000 that is to be paid over a six-month period. However, Smith is in need of immediate cash and therefore assigns its rights under its contracts with these customers to Ace Factoring Corporation for $40,000. The customers (obligors) who owed the $50,000 to Smith (the assignor) must now pay it to Ace (the assignee). Although this assignment involves

Assignment

the transfer of a legal right from one party to another party

Assignor

the party who transfers a legal right to another party

Assignee

the party to whom a legal right is transferred in an assignment proceeding

Obligor

a party to a contract who owes a duty to another party to the contract

consideration, assignments usually do not have to be supported by consideration to be enforceable. Figure 9-2 provides an illustration.

Contracts that Are Assignable

Generally, the assignor can assign rights under the contract without the consent of the obligor. Some contracts, however, cannot be assigned over the obligor's objections.

Contracts involving personal rights and duties cannot be assigned without the obligor's consent. Elements of personal skill, judgment, or knowledge are an essential part of such contracts. Thus the substitution of one party for another would materially affect the performance required of the obligor.

Employment contracts and contracts of lawyers and other professionals with their clients are unassignable without the obligor's consent. An assignment of such contracts over the obligor's objection violates the obligor's freedom of contract. Of course, if the obligor consents, such assignments are enforceable.

Any assignment that would place an additional burden or risk on the obligor without the obligor's consent is unenforceable. Assume that Jones Family Farm, Inc. entered into a contract with Tiny Feed Company, a small animal feed manufacturer, to supply all of the corn that Tiny required in its operation. Tiny could not assign its contractual rights to Ralston-Purina Company, a very large feed manufacturer, since Ralston-Purina would require a great deal more corn than would Tiny. If Jones consented, however, the assignment would be enforceable.

Another type of contract that cannot be assigned without consent is one that

---

FIGURE 9–2   **Assignment of Contract Rights**

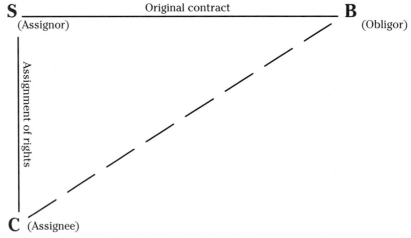

In this figure B owes $425 to S and S assigns his rights to receive the money to C. S is the *assignor,* the party who transfers rights under the contract. C is the *assignee,* the party to whom the rights are transferred. C can now enforce the contract against B through court proceedings if B fails to pay the money owed.

contains a clause expressly prohibiting assignment. Courts will generally embrace a non-assignability clause, such as "any assignment of this contract is void."

In addition, most states have statutes that prohibit the assignment of future wages by wage earners. The purpose of these statutes is to prevent unscrupulous parties from taking advantage of wage earners. Some states allow such assignments but regulate the amount of wages that may be assigned.

When an assignment is made, the assignee receives no greater rights than the assignor had under the original contract. This means that the obligor can assert the same defenses against the assignee, such as illegality, fraud, or lack of consideration, that he or she could have asserted against the assignor.

Notice of Assignment

When an assignment is made, the assignee should immediately notify the obligor. If notice is not given and the obligor renders performance to the assignor, the obligor has discharged his or her obligations under the contract and owes no additional duties to the assignee.

Delegation of Duties

In some circumstances an obligor may *delegate* his or her duties under the contract to a third person. While an assignment of contractual rights extinguishes all of the assignor's rights under the contract, a delegation of duties does not usually extinguish the obligor's responsibilities. An obligor is still liable to the promisee if the delegatee, the person to whom the duties are delegated, fails to perform them properly. An exception occurs if the parties enter into a **novation,** a separate agreement in which the promisee to the original contract releases the promisor from liability.

Novation
the substitution of a new contract for an old one by mutual agreement

Duties may generally be delegated without the obligor's consent unless they are of a nature personal to the obligor. For example, if Johnny Jones, the owner of the Kit-Kat Nite Club, hired Susan Smith to sing at his club for two weeks, Susan would be unable to delegate her duties under the contract. This is so because Johnny contracted for Susan's personal artistic skill. Duties involving such skills are not delegable since there is no objective standard for determining whether performance by a delegatee would be the equivalent of performance by the delegator.

LAW ABROAD

Germany

Debts may be assigned by an agreement between the assignor and the assignee. Formal notice to the debtor is not required, but is advisable, so as to prevent confusion for the debtor.

Japan

Rights in either real or personal property can be assigned by means of a valid declaration of intent. To be effective against third parties, the assignment of real property must be recorded and the assignment of personal property must be accompanied by delivery. Obligations that are by their nature assignable may be assigned unless the parties have expressed intentions to the contrary. An assignee who is specifically named must give notice to the obligor.

Third-Party Beneficiaries

As previously noted, persons who are not actual parties to a contract generally have no rights to enforce the contract. However, if a contract has been made for the express purpose of benefiting a third party, the third party can enforce the contract. A third party who benefits from a contract set up and performed by others is called a **third-party beneficiary.** Three types of third-party beneficiaries are recognized: creditor beneficiaries, donee beneficiaries, and incidental beneficiaries. Only creditor and donee beneficiaries can enforce contracts made by others.

If a contract is made for the express benefit of a third person who is a creditor of the promisee, the third person is a **creditor beneficiary.** Suppose that May Brown, owner of May's Limousine Service, purchases a van on time from Mid-Town Motors and subsequently sells the van to Dave Philbin, owner of Dave's Custom Delivery, with the understanding that Dave will make her remaining payments to Mid-Town. Mid-Town is a creditor beneficiary of May and Dave's contract. Once May delivers the van to Dave, Mid-Town is entitled to recover the payments from Dave, but it still retains its original right to recover the payments from May.

Where the promisee's purpose in entering the contract was to make a gift to a third person, the third person is a **donee beneficiary.** A life insurance policy is a primary example of a donee beneficiary contract. The owner of the policy (the promisee) pays premiums to the insurance company (the promisor), which promises to pay benefits to a beneficiary on the death of the insured. If the insurance company fails to pay on the death of the insured, the donee beneficiary may sue to enforce the contract. Unlike a creditor beneficiary, who can sue either of the parties to the contract, the donee beneficiary can recover only from the party who promised to perform for the benefit of the donee.

In some circumstances the performance of a contract intended to benefit only the promisee may also incidentally benefit a third party. Such a third party is referred to as an **incidental beneficiary.** Incidental beneficiaries do not receive any rights under the contract and cannot sue for nonperformance. Suppose that a landowner enters into a contract for the construction of a shopping mall. The surrounding landowners whose property will increase in value are incidental beneficiaries since the contract was not made primarily for their benefit. Thus an abandonment of the project would not give them the right to sue either of the contracting parties for breach of the contract. Figure 9–3 illustrates a contract with a third-party beneficiary.

In the next case some members of the public were injured by a union's strike in breach of its collective bargaining agreement. The Supreme Court of Washington considered whether the injured members of the public could sue as third-party beneficiaries of the collective bargaining agreement.

Third-party beneficiary

a person who benefits from a contract set up and performed by others

Creditor beneficiary

a person who, because of the promisee's specific obligation to that person, benefits from a contract set up and performed by others

Donee beneficiary

a person who, because the promisee intends to provide a gift to that person, benefits from a contract set up and performed by others

Incidental beneficiary

a person who benefits indirectly or accidentally from a contract set up and performed by others

BURKE AND THOMAS v. INTERNATIONAL ORGANIZATION OF MASTERS
SUPREME COURT OF WASHINGTON
600 P.2d 1282 (1979)

On the eve of Labor Day weekend in 1976, the International Organization of Masters, Mates, and Pilots, the licensed bargaining agent for officers of the Washington State Ferry System, called a strike of its members. These public employees either did not report to work or refused to perform their tasks, causing a complete cessation of normal ferry services during the holiday weekend. The strike was in breach of the existing collective bargaining agreement between the union and the toll bridge authority.

In November 1976 the plaintiffs in the case filed a class action suit against the union. The named plaintiffs were Washington corporations doing business in the area and individual residents who were dependent on the ferry system for transportation and allegedly derived a substantial portion of their income from tourism. The plaintiffs alleged that the unauthorized strike caused them to suffer economic disruption and harm as well as inconvenience, disruption, and interference in their daily lives. It also alleged that the strike was especially harmful to businesses and residents in the area because of their reasonable expectation of increased business and income from the heavy tourist traffic normally experienced over the Labor Day weekend. The plaintiffs contended that the strike was in violation of the

---

Third-Party Beneficiary Contract

FIGURE 9–3

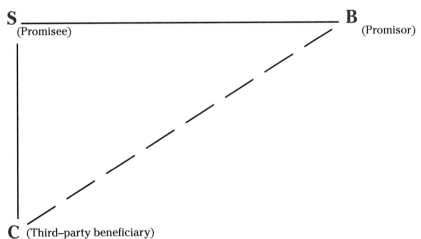

In this figure S delivers her stereo to B in exchange for B's promise to pay $425 to C. S is the promisee, B is the promisor, and C is the *third-party beneficiary* since she is named in the contract as the beneficiary of B's promise. C is a creditor beneficiary if S's main purpose in making the contract is to discharge an obligation to C; C is a donee beneficiary if S's main purpose in making the contract is to confer a gift to C.

collective bargaining agreement and asked for damages in excess of $1 million as third-party beneficiaries.

HOROWITZ, JUSTICE

This case raises the question whether members of the public who are incidentally injured in their personal or business relationships by an unauthorized strike of public employees have a private claim for relief or cause of action against the employees' union to recover damages.

Petitioners first claim that as members of the public they are third-party beneficiaries of the collective bargaining agreement between the union and the public employer, and may therefore maintain an action against the union for breach of its contractual promise not to strike. The creation of a third-party beneficiary contract requires that the parties intend that the promisor assume a direct obligation to the intended beneficiary at the time they enter into the contract. No such intent may be inferred from the facts alleged here.

Collective bargaining between a union representing public employees and the public employer is a tool for improving the relationship between employer and employee. The intent of the contract is thus, presumptively, to agree to the terms and conditions of employment as between the parties. Petitioners contend, however, that the intent of the parties here was that the public employees would assume a direct obligation to members of the public which could be privately enforced by that public. The effect of such an agreement, of course, would be to put the union members in the place of the state agency which is obligated to provide the service to the public. Petitioners point to no language in the contract which indicates such an intent. Nor do they put forward any other evidence tending to show that the parties here intended any consequence other than the normal agreement to the terms and conditions of employment. There is therefore no evidence that the requisite intent to create a third-party beneficiary relationship is present. In the absence of such an intent, no third-party beneficiary contract exists.

Affirmed.

Legal Issues

1. What does the creation of a third-party beneficiary contract require?
2. What was the intent of the contract according to the court?

Ethical Issues

1. At the beginning of June, Patricia Tyne, president of a union, informed the members of the union executive committee that management was more likely to meet the union's demands if a planned strike against a pharmaceutical firm did not begin until October 1, when the firm usually converted to a double shift to replenish its supply of various prescription drugs that it alone produced. She said: "Based on my 30 years of union experience, I think that if we handle the strike in this way, our members will benefit overall by between 2 and 3 percent." Claudia Fair, a new member of the executive committee, strongly objected. "We all know," she said, "that the firm makes medical products to treat gravely ill people. To purposefully put these people in fear that they may not obtain the drugs they need is just wrong. We can actually kill people. It is unethical." Tyne replied: "There will be no problem if management meets our demands. Although they are high, it is

management's responsibility, not ours." Is Tyne's proposed course of action unethical? Why?

2. Suppose that a court ruled that a party could not recover damages because she was only an incidental third-party beneficiary. Would this ruling satisfy your view of what is ethical if the third party acted in reliance on the contract and would suffer extensive monetary losses as a result of the court's decision? Why?

TERMINATION OF CONTRACTS AND REMEDIES

The duties assumed by the parties to a contract do not last forever. There are various methods for discharging contractual obligations. However, if one party fails to properly discharge his or her obligations under the contract, the injured party is given certain remedies for breach of the contract. A remedy is the method of enforcing a legal right.

Discharge

The **discharge** of a contract occurs when all of the obligations under the contract have been extinguished. In most situations a contract is discharged when both of the contracting parties have performed their contractual obligations fully and completely. For example, the debtor pays the creditor the full amount due under the loan and the creditor surrenders the collateral to the debtor. The duties of the contracting parties can be discharged in a variety of ways. The most common are discussed below.

Discharge
the completion of all the obligations of the parties under a contract

Agreement

The parties to a contract are always free to make a new **agreement** that alters or terminates the original agreement. Since contracts are created by mutual agreement, they may also be terminated by mutual agreement, provided the new contract is supported by consideration.

Agreement
the language in which parties commit themselves to the discharge of their obligations under a contract

Conditions

The duty to perform a promise is usually established when the parties enter into a contract, while the time for performance is usually set for a future date. However, the contract may contain a **condition,** a clause that makes a party's duty to perform contingent on the happening of an uncertain event. Contractual obligations may be terminated through the failure of a condition precedent or the occurrence of a condition subsequent.

Condition
a clause in a contract that makes a party's duty to perform contingent on the happening of an uncertain event

Condition Precedent If a future event is to take place before a party is obligated to perform, the contract contains a **condition precedent.** A contract to purchase land, for example, may state: "This contract is conditional upon buyer obtaining financing in the amount of $75,000 from a lending institution within 30 days of this date." Here obtaining a loan is a condition precedent. If the buyer is unable to obtain a loan within the stated time, the obligations of both parties are discharged.

Condition precedent
a future event that must take place before a party is obligated to perform contractual obligations

Condition subsequent

a future event whose occurrence discharges a duty to perform contractual obligations

Condition Subsequent A contract with a **condition subsequent** discharges a duty to perform if a future event takes place. Suppose that the following is stated in an agreement to purchase a restaurant near a factory, with monthly payments to be made for 10 years: "In the event that the factory closes permanently, this agreement shall be void." Here the buyer has incurred a duty to perform, but that duty is discharged if the factory closes. The primary distinction between a condition precedent and a condition subsequent is that the occurrence of a condition precedent gives rise to a contractual duty, whereas the occurrence of a condition subsequent extinguishes a contractual duty.

Concurrent conditions

the requirement that both parties to a contract perform their duties at the same time

Concurrent Conditions A contract with **concurrent conditions** provides that both parties are to perform their duties at the same time. A contract for the sale of land usually provides that the seller is to deliver the deed at the same time that the buyer pays the purchase price.

Performance

As previously noted, most contractual duties are discharged by performance. When both parties completely perform their promises under the contract, no legal problems arise. However, parties to contracts do not always perform their duties in the manner that they have promised to perform them. Courts generally recognize three degrees of contract performance: complete performance, substantial performance, and material breach of contract.

Complete performance

the duties that both parties to a contract must perform in full and as agreed in order to discharge their obligations under the contract

Complete Performance Some contractual duties can be discharged only by **complete performance.** In regard to such duties, even minor breaches of performance will result in a failure to discharge the promisor's obligations. Suppose that Tina Carson, an accountant, contracts to prepare a client's tax return for $250. If the client gives Tina a check for $230 in payment for her services, the client's contractual duty has not been discharged. Tina has fulfilled her obligations and is entitled to receive the total contract price in return. Other types of contractual duties that require complete performance are the delivery of a deed in connection with a land sale contract and, in some instances, the delivery of goods.

Substantial performance

less than perfect contract performance that conforms to the contract in all major aspects

Substantial Performance It is not humanly possible to perform many types of contractual duties perfectly. This holds true for the duties involved in construction contracts and many other kinds of personal service contracts. Slight deviations from contractual terms and specifications are expected in such instances. However, the duties are usually capable of being substantially performed. **Substantial performance,** though less perfect than complete performance, conforms to the contract in all major respects. The promisor must make a good faith effort to comply with the terms of the contract but is excused for minor deviations in performance. For example, assume that Toni Garrett, a building contractor, agreed to build a house for $75,000. The contract called for the use of "beige" paint on the exterior of the house. However, Toni mistakenly painted the house with "off-white" paint, a shade virtually identical with "beige." Since the deviation from the specifications was minor and done in good faith, Toni will be held to have substantially performed her duties under the contract. The promisor who substantially performs is entitled to recover the contract price less any damage suffered by the other party due to the defective performance. Table 9-1 summarizes the methods by which a contract can be discharged.

In the following case the issue was whether the building contractor substantially performed its contract.

GEORGE BUTKOVICH & SONS, INC. v. STATE BANK OF ST. CHARLES
APPELLATE COURT OF ILLINOIS, SECOND DISTRICT
379 N.E.2d 837 (1976)

On May 16, 1969, the plaintiff, George Butkovich & Sons, Inc., a building contractor, entered into an agreement with Herbert Grane, Jr., the defendant, under which the plaintiff would make numerous improvements to the defendant's house. The defendant was to pay $19,290 in agreed-upon installments. The defendant paid the first $10,000 due on the contract. Subsequently, however, disputes arose concerning the plaintiff's performance. The defendant alleged instances of poor quality in the plaintiff's workmanship and also alleged that the plaintiff did not make some of the improvements agreed upon. The plaintiff sued the defendant for the balance due under the contract plus payments for extra expenses. The trial court found for the plaintiff, holding that the plaintiff had substantially performed. The defendant appealed.

WOODWARD, JUSTICE

The ordinary rule applied in cases involving building contracts is that a builder is not required to perform perfectly, but rather, he is held only to a duty of substantial performance in a workmanlike manner. The purchaser who receives substantial performance of the building contract must pay the contract price less a credit as compensation for any deficiencies existing in what he received as to what strict performance would have given him.

On the other hand, a contractor whose work amounts to less than substantial performance has no right to the contract price; in that situation, the builder's right is, under a theory of quantum meruit, a right to recover only reasonable compensation for value received by the purchaser over and above

---

Methods by Which a Contract Can Be Discharged   **TABLE 9–1**

Reason	Action
Agreement	Parties agree to alter or terminate original contract
Failure of condition precedent	Event upon which contract is conditioned does not occur
Occurrence of condition subsequent	Event whose occurrence terminates the contract
Concurrent conditions	Parties perform their duties simultaneously
Complete performance	Parties perform their duties with no deviations from the contractual terms and specifications
Substantial performance	Parties perform their duties with slight deviations from the contractual terms and specifications

the injury suffered by the builder's breach. What will be considerd substantial performance of a building contract is difficult to define and whether substantial performance has been given will depend on the relevant facts of each case. We shall therefore proceed to examine those facts in connection with the case.

[I]t is undisputed that plaintiff failed to install water stops. According to plaintiff, a water stop could be caulking or a solid material poured up against a wall with fresh concrete; according to defendant, a water stop is a piece of usually vinyl material, nonporous in nature that is placed in between the cement floor and the foundation wall. The parties in general did agree that the purpose of water stops is to prevent water from coming in.

While admitting that the water stops were not installed, plaintiff argues that the contract makes no reference to water stops, that water stops are mentioned only in the specifications for the house. Further, that there was no testimony that the absence of water stops contributed to the water in defendant's premises.

While the trial court found nothing in the evidence to show that defendant's water problem was proximately caused by the lack of water stops, the real question here is whether plaintiff did comply with the terms of the contract. The contract itself does not enumerate that water stops were to be installed; however, the contract here, which is set out above, is in quite general terms and would be difficult, if not impossible, to carry out without the use of the specifications, which, according to plaintiff, did require the installation of water stops. Further, the Supplemental Conditions [in the contract] provide in part:

> The contract shall consist of the specifications, the drawings, the proposal form, and the Owner-Contractor Agreement.

Finally, there was testimony that prior to entering into the contract, the parties held lengthy discussions on the potential water problem in connection with the plans and specifications for defendant's residence.

Defendant contends that while the plans called for the installation of wire mesh and reinforcing wire under all floors, plaintiff failed to install reinforcing wire mesh in the basement floor. Plaintiff argues that the reinforcing mesh, like the water stops, was not mentioned in the contract, and that defendant offered no testimony that any damage was suffered as a result of such an omission. However, John Butkovich, supervisor for plaintiff, testified that page three of the specifications calls for reinforcing wire; it was placed in the garage floor, but he did not know about the basement floor; as a rule they do not put it in the basement floor.

Donald Smith, a licensed surveyor who surveyed the property for defendant, testified that he found the defendant's residence to be 8⅞″ below the level required in the plans and only 3″ higher than the adjoining residence.

Thus, considering the omissions from the contract, coupled with the evidence of the poor quality of the workmanship as outlined above, this court is of the opinion that the finding by the trial court that plaintiff substantially performed its contract with defendant is against the manifest weight of the evidence.

Reversed and *remanded.*

Legal Issues

1. Based on the material in the text and the comments of the court in this decision, if a builder fails to substan-

tially perform, what can the builder recover?

2. In general terms, how did the court determine whether substantial performance occurred?

Ethical Issues

1. Which ethical standard or standards would support the principle that a party to an agreement who fails to substan-

tially perform a contract may recover damages only on the basis of quantum meruit? Which standard of ethics, if any, would support the proposition that a person who intentionally does not substantially perform a contract is not entitled to any relief? Explain your answers.

2. Which standard or standards of ethics would be consistent with the plaintiff's behavior? Why?

Material Breach

A performance that falls below substantial performance is a material breach. A **material breach** occurs where the performance of the promisor fails to meet the level of perfection that the other party reasonably expects under the contract. In the example above, assume that instead of making a minor mistake with the paint, Toni intentionally used substandard lumber, rendering the house dangerously unsafe. In this instance Toni will be held to have materially breached the contract. A promisor who materially breaches a contract cannot sue the other party under the contract and is liable for damages arising from the breach. The promisor may be entitled to recover from the other party the reasonable value of benefits conferred.

Material breach
a substantial breach by one party to a contract that permits the other party to suspend the performance of its obligations under the contract and sue for damages

Anticipatory Breach

One party's indication of nonperformance to the other party, before the time for performance arises, is an **anticipatory breach.** An anticipatory breach usually has the same legal effect as material breach since the innocent party can immediately sue for damages. Assume that on May 5, Ace Asphalt, Inc. contracts to pave the roads in a subdivision beginning on June 15. On June 1 Ace informs the developer of the subdivision that it will not perform. Under the doctrine of anticipatory repudiation, the developer may treat the contract as breached and hire another company to pave the roads. The developer may also institute suit against Ace, if the breach causes damages to the developer. This example involves an express repudiation, but repudiation may also be implied from the promisor's actions.

Anticipatory breach
one party's indication of nonperformance to the other party before the time for performance has arrived

Legal Impossibility

In some circumstances it becomes impossible for a promisor to perform his or her duties under the contract. The doctrine of **legal impossibility** recognizes this and will discharge the promisor's contractual duties in such circumstances. However, courts have developed a very narrow definition of impossibility. Additional hardship does not discharge the contract. A manufacturer would ordinarily not be relieved from performance if a strike prevented the manufacturer from delivering goods ordered under a contract. A legal impossibility occurs when *no one* can perform the contractual duty. An obligation that can be fulfilled by persons other than the promisor is not a legal impossibility. Suppose that Sam, the owner of a

Legal impossibility
the doctrine under which a promisor's contractual duties are discharged because circumstances have made it impossible for the promisor or anyone to fulfill them

clothing store, cannot pay his creditors because his bank has closed and he has lost a substantial portion of his funds. Sam will not be discharged from his contracts because he is saying, in effect, "I cannot do it," not "It cannot be done."

The courts have recognized only four basic situations in which the promisor is excused from performance because of impossibility: (1) the death or incapacitating illness of the promisor, (2) intervening illegality, (3) destruction of the subject matter, and (4) commercial impracticability.

Hypothetical Case

A DEBTOR BECOMES DISABLED

Marty, an elderly bachelor who lived alone, signed a one-year contract to take dancing lessons at Darlene's Dance Studio. His very friendly female dancing instructor told him that he was "an especially good learner" and encouraged him to sign up for additional lessons. Marty entered into a contract for five years of dancing lessons at a total cost of $38,000. Shortly afterward, he was involved in an automobile accident that prevented him from returning to work or walking. His only source of income was a small disability pension. Marty refused to pay Darlene's Dance Studio under the contract and also stopped making payments on a loan from Friendly Fred Finance Company that he had made in order to purchase a new car. Can Darlene's Dance Studio legally collect the $38,000 from Marty? Why? Can Friendly Fred Finance Company take legal action against Marty? Why?

Death or Illness of Promisor   In a personal service contract, such as an employment contract, the death of the promisor terminates the contract. Since such contracts are based on the unique services of the individual promisor, the promisor's death renders performance impossible. In a nonpersonal service contract, on the other hand, the death of the promisor does not discharge the contract. The promisee may enforce such contracts against the promisor's estate.

Illness will excuse performance, if the circumstances make it impossible for the promisor to substantially perform.

Intervening Illegality   If a contract becomes illegal as a result of a change in laws, the parties are excused from performing. Performance may also become illegal because of government regulations, such as some of the restrictions that the government imposed during World War II. Relief is not provided, however, for laws or government regulations that merely make performance more difficult.

Destruction of the Subject Matter   If prior to performance, the subject matter of the contract is destroyed through no fault of the promisor, a legal impossibility is created. The "subject matter" of a contract generally includes all of the items essential to its performance. If substitutes are available, performance is not excused even if it becomes more difficult or expensive.

Commercial impracticability
the doctrine under which nonperformance is excused if unforeseeable events make performance highly impracticable or unreasonably expensive

Commercial Impracticability   Nonperformance may be excused in situations that fall short of impossibility. If unforeseeable events make performance highly impracticable or unreasonably expensive, the doctrine of **commercial impracticability** or commercial frustration operates to free the promisor from his or her contractual duties. Only exceptional circumstances can excuse a business from its promises. Changing market conditions do not provide an excuse for breaking contracts. Increases in the cost of labor and raw materials are other risks that businesses assume when they enter into contracts. The events that trigger the doctrine of commercial impracticability are events that were unforeseeable at the time of contracting. Such events include severe shortages of supplies or raw materials caused by wars, embargoes, or crop failures, that result in substantial cost increases or total unavailability to the promisor. Suppose that ABC Company contracts to sell certain machinery to a buyer in a foreign country. Suppose further that the U.S. government bans the importation of a raw material needed to produce the machinery. ABC Company is unable to fulfill its promise, but it is not liable for breach of contract. It is excused from performance of the contract because the unforeseeable contingency resulted in commercial impracticability. The doctrine of commercial impracticability was first adopted in the UCC, and thus it applied initially only to sales contracts. However, it has recently been extended to all other types of contracts.

Statute of Limitations

Once a party to a contract has breached the contract, the other party has a certain amount of time in which to initiate a suit. Such amounts of time are specified in various **statutes of limitations.** In most states the statute of limitations varies from 2 to 8 years on oral contracts and from 4 to 15 years on written contracts. The statute of limitations for sales of goods is four years, whether the contract is written or oral (2-725). The time limit begins running when the contract is breached. A failure to bring suit within the specified time results in a discharge of liability for breach. The purpose of the statute of limitations is to prevent ineffective lawsuits. If a plaintiff, for example, waits 20 years to file suit, it is likely that evidence will have been lost, witnesses will have moved away or died, and memories will have faded.

**Statute
of limitations**
a law limiting the time in which a suit may be brought

LAW ABROAD

Germany

The German statute of limitations can prevent a party from enforcing a claim to a debt or obligation, but it does not extinguish the debt or obligation. Therefore, a party prevented from collecting a debt through the courts may satisfy it by keeping any security (collateral) given by the debtor, even though the statute of limitations has expired.

The usual limitation period is 30 years, but there are many exceptions. A two-year period applies to many everyday transactions, a four-year period to certain business claims. On tort claims for damages, the limitation period is three years.

Japan

Statutes establish limitations on the time in which a suit may be brought. These limitations operate automatically; even the consent of both parties cannot waive them.

Japanese courts distinguish extinctive prescription from the broader concept of limitations of actions. Extinctive prescription occurs when the obligation of one party to another party is lost by the other party's failure to demand enforcement. It occurs after 10 years for obligations in general, after 5 years for obligations arising out of commercial transactions, and after 20 years for all other obligations, excluding ownership. Extinctive prescription might, for example, prevent a doctor from collecting on a bill for services rendered 13 years earlier. In all likelihood the bill would be uncollectable because the obligation would be said to have been extinguished by the passage of time.

Remedies

The court's objective in remedying a breach of contract is to put the injured party in the same position that he or she would have occupied had the contract been performed. This is usually done by awarding monetary damages, although other types of remedies may be called for in special situations.

Damages

A variety of damages may be awarded in contracts, depending on the particular circumstances.

Actual damages
the actual financial loss resulting from a breach of contract

Actual Damages A party suing for breach of contract is entitled to recover an amount equal to the actual financial loss resulting from the breach. Such damages are called **actual damages** or "compensatory damages." The purpose of these damages is to make the injured party whole, that is, to compensate the injured party for his or her injuries. Assume, for example, that Farmer Jones breaches his contract to supply corn to Splitz Brewing Company. Thus Splitz had to procure its corn from another source and paid $2,500 more than was called for under its contract with Jones. In a suit for breach, Splitz would be entitled to recover at least $2,500 as actual damages.

Consequential damages
losses that are not a foreseeable result of a contract breach

Consequential Damages Sometimes the plaintiff suffers damages that are not a foreseeable result of the breach. Such **consequential damages** (also called "reliance damages") are not recoverable unless the breaching party had reason to foresee them when the contract was formed. Assume that Splitz Brewing Company contracts to have Wildcat Truckers, Inc. deliver a shipment of corn without advising Wildcat that it is shutting down production awaiting delivery of the corn. If Wildcat delivers the corn three days late, in a suit for breach of contract Splitz would be limited to the award of actual damages only and could not recover the profits it lost as a result of the shutdown.

Nominal damages
a very small award of damages, such as $1, where a technical breach of a contract has occurred but no actual loss has been suffered

Nominal Damages Where there has been a technical breach of a contract but no actual loss, the court may award a small amount, such as $1, as **nominal damages.** While such awards are of no financial significance, they do recognize the wrongful conduct of the breaching party and they are usually accompanied with an order requiring the breaching party to pay court costs.

Liquidated damages
a specified amount of damages that are available in the event of a breach of contract

Liquidated Damages In some cases the contract may specify the amount of the damages that are recoverable in the event of a breach. Such damages, called **liquidated damages,** are given effect as long as the amount agreed upon is a reasonable forecast of the actual damages. However, if the amount is unreasonably excessive, the court may deem it a "penalty" and will not uphold it. The plaintiff must then prove actual damages.

Punitive Damages   Punitive damages are usually not recoverable for breach of contract. **Punitive damages** are awarded only if the situation warrants penalizing the defendant for his or her conduct, as would be the case, for example, if the defendant committed the tort of fraud. Thus an unscrupulous car dealer who intentionally makes false statements to sell a defective car may be liable for punitive damages as well as actual damages. In addition, punitive damages may be specifically authorized by statute.

Punitive damages

compensation in excess of actual damages that serves as a punishment in tort law; not usually available in contracts cases

Duty to Mitigate Damages

In the event of a breach, the nonbreaching party has a duty to *mitigate* or minimize the damages. Without incurring unreasonable risk or expense, the nonbreaching party must take reasonable steps to reduce the actual loss. In the Splitz Brewing example, even if Wildcat Truckers knew that the brewery would be shut down until it delivered the corn, Splitz would have been under a duty to mitigate damages by seeking still another supply of corn if reasonably possible. Splitz could not just sit back and allow damages to mount up while waiting for Wildcat to deliver the corn.

A wrongfully discharged employee is entitled to damages for the unpaid wages for the remainder of his or her employment contract. To minimize damages, however, the employee is required to seek work of a similar nature in the same community. The employee is not required to accept inferior employment or to accept a similar job in a different locale.

Equitable Remedies

Where the legal remedies of damages are not sufficient to fully compensate the injured party, the court may grant an **equitable remedy.**[1] Courts grant equitable remedies only when they feel that justice is served by doing so. Two commonly used equitable remedies are specific performance and injunction.

Equitable remedy

a legal action in which a court of equity uses its power to serve justice because the legal remedies of damages are not sufficient to fully compensate the injured party

Specific Performance   An order for **specific performance** requires the party who breached the contract to do precisely what he or she promised to do under the contract. A court may order specific performance where the unique subject matter of a contract makes money damages an inadequate remedy for the party injured by a breach of the contract. Contracts for the sale of real property are traditionally treated as unique for purposes of specific performance. Contracts involving antiques, heirlooms, and stocks of closely held corporations may warrant specific performance. Works of art may also warrant specific performance. On the other hand, contracts involving most types of personal property, such as a car, cannot be enforced by specific performance.

Specific performance

a court order requiring the party who breached a contract to do precisely what he or she promised to do under the contract

Injunctions   Some exceptional circumstances warrant the grant of an injunction. An **injunction** is a court order that forbids the defendant to do certain acts specified by the court. It is available only where a breach of contract is likely to harm the plaintiff irreparably. For example, many contracts for the sale of a business include enforceable clauses prohibiting the seller from competing with the buyer for a specified period of time in a specific geographical area. Where the

Injunction

a court order forbidding a defendant from doing acts specified by the court seller breaches such a clause, the buyer may be entitled to an injunction prohibiting the seller from doing so.

LAW ABROAD

Germany

Contracts for the benefit of third parties are valid. In general, third parties acquire a direct right to enforcement of such contracts. Specific performance, not damages, is the typical remedy sought. To collect damages, the obligor must be given notice that establishes a time for performance. If performance does not take place by that time, damages will be sought.

German law recognizes impossibility as an excuse for nonperformance. The interpretation of contracts is based on the true intention of the parties.

Japan

Either party in a bilateral contract may refuse to perform until the other tenders performance, unless the situation is one in which the obligation to perform has not yet accrued. A third party's right under a contract, created by the original parties to the contract, cannot be extinguished.

REVIEW QUESTIONS & PROBLEMS

1. Distinguish commercial impracticability from impossibility as a means of discharging a contractual obligation.

2. When are consequential damages recoverable?

3. Joan agreed to sell her sailboat for $15,000 and Ron agreed to purchase it. When Ron later refused to purchase the boat, Joan advertised it and managed to sell it for $16,500. Joan now sues Ron for breach of contract. What damages, if any, should she be allowed to recover? Why?

4. Charles White died owing Ellen Brown $10,000. Charles's will named Bob White, his brother, as executor to handle his estate. Bob orally promised Ellen that she would be paid the $10,000, even if he had to pay it to her personally. The funeral expenses and the expenses of the last illness were paid first, as required by state law. These payments depleted the assets of the estate, and Ellen sued Bob on his promise to personally pay her the $10,000. Should Ellen recover? Why?

5. On October 28, 1990, Farmer entered into an oral contract to sell 20,000 bushels of wheat to Grain Elevator at a price of $1.80 per bushel. Farmer delivered 20,000 bushels of wheat but refused to deliver the remaining 12,000 bushels. Farmer sold 12,000 bushels of wheat to a grain elevator in another state at a price of $5.35 per bushel. Grain Elevator was forced to purchase 12,000 bushels of wheat at $6.50 per bushel. Grain Elevator sued Farmer for damages. Farmer pleaded the statute of frauds as a defense. At the trial the attorney for Grain Elevator questioned Farmer as to the existence of the contract:

Q. So your testimony is that there was an agreement for you to sell 20,000 bushels of wheat?

A. Yes.

Q. And that agreement was made in October, October 28 of 1990, is that correct?

A. Yes.

Is Farmer liable for actual damages to Grain Elevator?

6. Greg, a general contractor, entered into a written contract with the school board to construct a new high school. Greg then entered into a subcontract with Ready Roofing Company under which Ready Roofing was to erect the roof of the new high school for $100,000. Through the fault of neither party, a labor dispute at the construction site delayed work on the school for a year. During that time Ready Roofing reported to Greg that the costs on which it had based its estimate for the roofing job had risen by $15,000. Ready Roofing sought an increase in the contract amount or release from the contract, but Greg did not give it either. When work on the school began, Ready Roofing refused to perform and Greg was forced to engage another roofer at a higher price. Greg sued Ready Roofing for the price difference. Could Ready Roofing defend itself on the ground of legal impossibility? Why?

7. Veronica, a famous movie star, entered into a contract with Big Studios to play the female lead in the musical *Bloomer Girl*, in which she would be able to use her talents as a dancer and actress. Veronica's compensation for playing this role was to be $750,000. Subsequently, Big Studios decided not to produce *Bloomer Girl* and offered Veronica the same compensation to play the female lead in *Big Country, Big Man*, a western. Unlike *Bloomer Girl*, which was to have been filmed in California, the western was to be filmed in Australia. Other terms of the offer varied from Veronica's contract. In the western Veronica would not have the approval rights for the screenplay or the director accorded her in the contract for the musical. Veronica sued Big Studios for money due under her contract and for damages resulting from the breach of contract. Big Studios contended that no money was due Veronica, because she failed to mitigate damages by unreasonably refusing to accept the role in the western. How do you think the court ruled? Why?

---

1. Equity was discussed in Chapter 4.

ENDNOTES

PART

4

CONSTITUTIONAL LAW

10. The Constitution and Government Regulation of Business

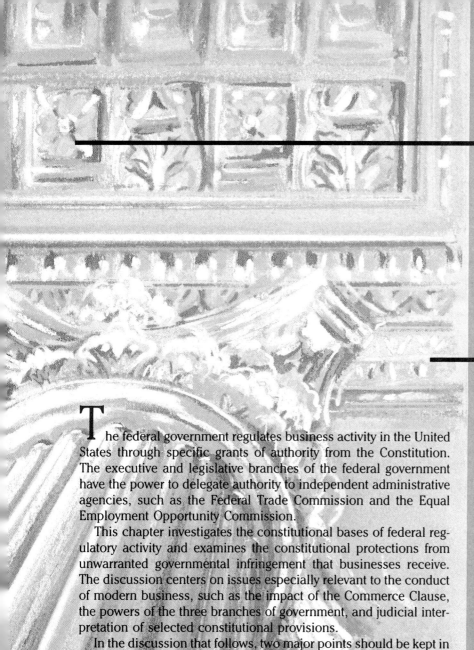

CHAPTER

10

The Constitution and Government Regulation of Business

The federal government regulates business activity in the United States through specific grants of authority from the Constitution. The executive and legislative branches of the federal government have the power to delegate authority to independent administrative agencies, such as the Federal Trade Commission and the Equal Employment Opportunity Commission.

This chapter investigates the constitutional bases of federal regulatory activity and examines the constitutional protections from unwarranted governmental infringement that businesses receive. The discussion centers on issues especially relevant to the conduct of modern business, such as the impact of the Commerce Clause, the powers of the three branches of government, and judicial interpretation of selected constitutional provisions.

In the discussion that follows, two major points should be kept in mind:

- □ The U.S. Constitution is the foundation of our legal system.
- □ The Supreme Court makes the final determination regarding the constitutionality of actions taken by the legislative and executive branches of the federal government.

THE COEQUAL BRANCHES OF GOVERNMENT: LEGISLATIVE, EXECUTIVE, AND JUDICIAL

The federal government comprises three branches: executive, legislative, and judicial. The U.S. Constitution provides for a division of authority among these branches.

Separation of Powers

The framers of the Constitution firmly believed that concentrating too much power in one branch of government posed great dangers to individual liberties. Thus, they created three separate branches of government—judicial, legislative, and executive. Each of these branches is free from the control of the others, and each has a particular function to perform. Generally, the judicial branch interprets the laws, the legislative branch makes the laws, and the executive branch enforces the laws.

The Constitution disperses the power of government in two directions. One of the directions is vertical, with authority divided between the federal government above and the state and local governments below. The 10th Amendment provides that "the powers not delegated to the United States by the Constitution, nor prohibited by it to the States, are reserved to the States respectively, or to the people." Hence, the state governments may exercise those powers not delegated to the federal government or prohibited to the states. Consequently, neither the national government nor local governments completely control the affairs of individuals. A majority rule in one government is balanced by a majority rule in another government.

The other direction is horizontal, involving a dispersal of authority within the federal government itself. Not only is each branch of the federal government free from the control of the other branches, but each branch also has the power to restrict in some way the exercise of the authority vested in the other branches. This system of **checks and balances** ensures that no branch of our federal government is devoid of restraint. The president appoints high cabinet officers, but Congress checks the president by ratifying the appointments. Congress passes laws, but the president checks Congress through the veto power, and Congress in turn checks the president through the power to override the veto by a two thirds vote. The courts check the legislative and executive branches through the power to determine whether the actions of those branches are constitutional. Congress checks the courts through the power to approve federal judges appointed by the president. Figure 10-1 illustrates the system of checks and balances.

Checks and balances constitutional restraints that prevent any of the three branches of the federal government from becoming too powerful by having each branch check and balance the powers of the other two branches

The Role of Congress

Article I of the U.S. Constitution endows Congress only with the "legislative Powers herein granted." Congress, therefore, has only *limited* powers—the powers specifically granted to it by the Constitution. Those powers include the enactment of legislation pertaining to tax collection, commerce, patents, bankruptcies, money coinage, counterfeiting, and support of the army and navy. Article I, however, also empowers Congress to "make all Laws which shall be necessary and proper" to carry out the purposes of the specific powers. The Necessary and Proper Clause, often referred to as the "elastic clause," has greatly expanded the power of Congress to legislate. The courts must determine which exercises of congressional power are in fact necessary to carry out the powers "implied" by the Constitution.

The best-known and earliest interpretation of the Necessary and Proper Clause was made in 1819, in the famous case of *McCulloch v. Maryland.*[1] This case involved the Baltimore branch of the Second Bank of the United States, a bank created by Congress. When the bank had been in existence for a year, Maryland passed a law requiring all nonstate banks to either pay the state $15,000 annually or pay a tax on each bank note issued. Chief Justice Marshall[2] found that the Constitution implicitly forbade a state tax on a federal institution. In reaching this conclusion, he determined that the Necessary and Proper Clause expanded, rather than restricted, congressional authority. In his classic statement of the doctrine of implied powers, he said:

> We admit, as all must admit, that the powers of government are limited, and that its limits are not to be transcended. But we think the sound construction of the Constitution must allow to the national legislature that discretion, with respect to the means by which the power it confers are to be carried into execution, which will enable that body to perform the high duties assigned to it, in the manner most beneficial to the people. Let the end be legitimate, let it be within the scope of the Constitution, and all means which are appropriate, which are plainly adapted to that end, which are not prohibited, but consist with the letter and spirit of the Constitution, are constitutional.[3]

The System of Checks and Balances   **FIGURE 10–1**

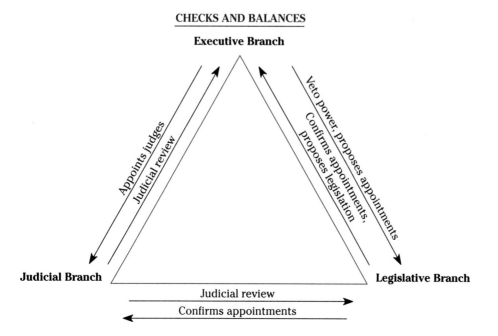

CHECKS AND BALANCES

Thus, Marshall construed the word *necessary* to signify all laws that were "appropriate" to achieve an end authorized by the Constitution.

The great expansion of the federal legislative power over the years has been based on the Necessary and Proper Clause. The drafters of the Constitution could not anticipate the necessity of regulating railroads, airlines, television stations, and space exploration. Congress, however, passed laws regulating them on the ground that those laws were necessary and proper to the Commerce Clause. (The Commerce Clause is explained later in this chapter.)

The elasticity of the Necessary and Proper Clause has given the federal government "implied power." Implied power is not, however, unlimited power. Every expansion of the federal government's power must be firmly affixed to a power specifically enumerated in the Constitution.

The Role of the Executive

The executive powers provided by the Constitution are vested in the president of the United States, whose duty is to enforce all laws, even by calling out the Armed Forces if necessary. The Constitution gives the president the specific power to intervene in domestic and foreign affairs. Even with the system of checks and balances, the extensive rights and duties that the Constitution extends to the president make the office one of the most powerful in the world, if not the most powerful.

The president's domestic powers include the authority to appoint ambassadors, federal judges, and other officers of the United States. Equally important are the president's implied domestic powers, which derive primarily from the express constitutional obligation to enforce the laws. Presidents can influence the judiciary by submitting to it, through the Department of Justice, their views on constitutional and statutory interpretation. Presidents can also influence the outcome of legislation by enforcing some legislation stringently and other legislation laxly.

As the commander in chief of the army and navy, the president has considerable power to conduct foreign affairs. This power, of course, significantly affects international relations. In addition, the Constitution specifically authorizes the president to make treaties with foreign countries, subject to Senate approval. For example, treaties between the United States and certain foreign countries protect aliens from those countries in the area of employment opportunities while they are in the United States.

Executive authority in international affairs is checked by congressional authority. Treaties negotiated by the president require the consent of two thirds of the Senate. As commander in chief, the president depends on the approval of the army and navy budget by Congress. And as previously noted, Congress has the power to regulate foreign commerce.

The Role of the Judiciary

Judicial review
the power of the judiciary to declare acts of the legislative and executive branches unconstitutional

The judiciary has the power to determine whether the acts of the legislative and executive branches of the federal government are constitutional. This power of **judicial review** was not expressly stated in the Constitution. Chief Justice Marshall[4] asserted it in 1803, in the landmark *Marbury v. Madison*[4] decision, the first decision in which the Supreme Court declared an act of Congress unconstitutional. Thus the Supreme Court assumed the authority of judicially reviewing the acts of the legislative and executive branches of government. Our constitutional system relies to a great extent on the doctrine of judicial review because that doctrine places a limit on the various departments of government. The Supreme Court has the final word on interpreting the Constitution. Judicial review was discussed in Chapter 6.

GENERALIZATION OF CONSTITUTIONAL INTERPRETATION

In the *Marbury* case Chief Justice Marshall clearly established the Supreme Court's role as the final interpreter of the Constitution. Some provisions of the Constitution are so unambiguous that they require little or no interpretation. This clause in Article I is an example: "The Senate of the United States shall be composed of two Senators from each State, chosen by the Legislature thereof, for six Years; and each Senator shall have one Vote." This language is so precise that only one interpretation is possible.

By contrast, many other provisions were drafted in general terms. The Founding Fathers realized that they could not anticipate the complex needs of a developing nation, so they left certain provisions vague in order to give the Constitution flexibility. Article I gives Congress the power to "lay and collect Taxes." These four words, which are the basis of our federal taxation system, do not indicate what kinds of taxes Congress can impose, and what the tax rates should be, or how the taxes should be collected.

The general terms of the Constitution are the main reasons why it has survived for more than 200 years. They permit flexibility of interpretation that allows courts to apply the words of the Constitution to new problems as they arise. This is why the document is often referred to as "the living Constitution."

In the following sections, we will see how the Supreme Court has interpreted parts of the Constitution that affect businesses. But first we must examine how the federal courts respond when they are confronted with an issue of constitutional interpretation.

Case or Controversy Limitation

Article III provides that the federal courts can decide constitutional issues only when actual cases or controversies are presented to them. They will not issue advisory opinions. They must be presented with genuine disputes involving the rights and liabilities of opposing parties. The Supreme Court cannot, on its own initiative, declare a law unconstitutional. An aggrieved party must first challenge the law in court.

Standing to Raise Constitutional Questions

A litigant has standing to raise constitutional issues if the litigant's personal rights are directly affected by legislation or other governmental action. The litigant must show not only unconstitutionality, but also that he or she has been personally injured by enforcement of the legislation or the governmental action. A party cannot litigate a hypothetical injury. For example, federal taxpayers generally have no standing to challenge the constitutionality of federal expenditures since the individual interests of these taxpayers are too minute, indeterminable, and uncertain. Any injury that they sustain is not a personal injury but an injury common to the population in general.

Political Question Doctrine

The Supreme Court will not review constitutional issues that are "political questions." The **political question doctrine** is based on the principle of separation of powers. Political matters are not suitable for judicial review. To illustrate: Questions pertaining to foreign affairs are primarily reserved to the legislative and executive branches of government, which have the expertise and authority to decide such questions. Thus, the Supreme Court will not review questions of this kind. For example, the Supreme Court steadfastly refused to hear cases intended to establish whether U.S. participation in the Vietnam conflict violated the constitutional power of Congress to declare war. In 1979 the Supreme Court would not decide whether President Carter could terminate a treaty with Taiwan without the approval of Congress. The Court regarded the treaty issue as a nonreviewable political question.

INTERPRETATION OF SELECTED PROVISIONS OF THE CONSTITUTION AFFECTING BUSINESS

As noted, the Founding Fathers drafted the Constitution in broad terms that require judicial interpretation. This section considers such interpretation of important constitutional provisions that affect businesses. The first four are contained in the Constitution itself: The others are contained in the Bill of Rights—the first 10 amendments to the Constitution.

The Commerce Clause: Basis of Federal Regulation of Business

An important constitutional power that pertains to businesses is the ability of Congress to regulate foreign commerce and commerce between the states. Article I, Section 8 of the Constitution contains the Commerce Clause, which states: "Congress shall have Power" to "regulate Commerce with foreign Nations, and among the several States." This clause provides the constitutional basis for the regulatory power of Congress over domestic and international business. It also imposes, by implication, certain limitations on the authority of state governments to regulate business. Before the Constitution was adopted, local governments established regulatory barriers against interstate commerce to obtain commercial advantages for themselves. Through the Commerce Clause the framers of the Constitution reduced the obstacles to the free flow of interstate and foreign commerce.

Foreign Commerce

Under the Commerce Clause, Congress has the *exclusive* power to regulate all aspects of **foreign commerce.** This means that state governments have no constitutional authority to regulate foreign trade. Although the Commerce Clause itself gives no indication that state power in this area is wholly excluded, numerous

Supreme Court cases have held that the simple existence of the clause operates as an inherent constitutional limitation on the authority of the states. The reason is that the states have no legitimate interest in the federal government's dealings in foreign trade.

Federal power over foreign commerce includes not only the regulation of imports and exports, but also the sale of imported goods within the states. For example, if the legislature of State A enacted a statute prohibiting the sale of shoes imported from Taiwan, this statute would be held unconstitutional as a violation of the Commerce Clause.

Interstate Commerce

Early Supreme Court cases determined that the Commerce Clause could be used to invalidate state legislation that obstructed the flow of **interstate commerce.** For example, in 1824, in the landmark case of *Gibbons v. Ogden,*[5] the Supreme Court held that a state regulation affecting commerce is invalid if it conflicts with a federal law. The state of New York had granted Ogden a monopoly to operate coastal steamboats between New York and New Jersey, and the federal government had issued a steamboat license for the same purpose to Gibbons. Chief Justice Marshall resolved the controversy by holding that a federal law regulating interstate commerce overrules state regulation of the same activity. Marshall's opinion clearly established the power of the federal government to deal with national economic problems.

Interstate commerce business activity that takes place in more than one state

Marshall's opinion in *Gibbons* defined the commerce power of the federal government very broadly to include "every species of commercial intercourse." This broad interpretation referred to interstate commerce and not to commerce completely internal to a state. Later Supreme Court cases interpreted the Commerce Clause to permit congressional regulation of any business activity that *affects* the flow of interstate commerce.

In 1941, in another landmark case, the Supreme Court held that the Commerce Clause applies to **intrastate commerce** that affects interstate commerce. In *United States v. Darby,*[6] a lumber manufacturer was charged with violating the Fair Labor Standards Act, which established minimum wages and maximum hours for employees engaged in producing goods for shipment in interstate commerce. The Court held that manufacturing that took place entirely within one state was subject to this act. The *Darby* Court found that Congress could regulate intrastate commercial activities that *affected* interstate commerce.

Intrastate commerce business activity that is confined to a single state

The Affectation Doctrine, the modern view of the Commerce Clause, holds that any business activity that *appreciably affects* interstate commerce, directly or indirectly, is subject to federal regulation. The doctrine has been applied to such diverse areas of business activity as farm production, manufacturing, and public accommodations. In *Heart of Atlanta Motel, Inc. v. United States,*[7] the Supreme Court upheld the constitutionality of Title II of the 1964 Civil Rights Act, which forbids racial discrimination in places of public accommodation, such as restaurants, hotels, and theaters. In this case the court held that the act could be used to prohibit racial discrimination in a motel that refused to rent rooms to blacks. Although the motel's operations were apparently local, they affected the free movement of interstate travelers and were therefore subject to federal regulation. Almost any legislative exercise of the commerce power will be upheld as long as its effect on interstate commerce is not inconceivably remote.

State and Federal Regulation of Business

The Commerce Clause does not prevent the states from regulating commerce that crosses state lines. The states may regulate areas of commerce that Congress has not preempted.

Individual states often enact legislation to protect the health, safety, morals, or general welfare of their citizens, as noted in Chapter 16. In enacting such legislation, they are exercising their **police power,** which is reserved to the states under the 10th Amendment. As discussed, the 10th Amendment reserves to the states those powers not specifically delegated to the federal government. Police power measures include state highway regulations, state milk regulations, state hunting and fishing regulations, and state environmental protection laws.

The police power of the states is subject to restrictions by the U.S. Constitution. In protecting its citizens, the state legislature must not pass laws that conflict with congressional legislation. Thus a state statute is invalid if it attempts to regulate an area that (1) has been reserved for exclusive federal control, (2) imposes an undue burden on interstate commerce, or (3) discriminates against interstate commerce.

Police power

the power of the state government to enact laws that protect the health, safety, morals, or general welfare of its citizens

Preemption

The Supremacy Clause, in Article VI, provides that the U.S. Constitution and the federal laws of the United States shall be the "supreme Law of the Land." This clause, which establishes the supremacy of the federal government, is the basis of the **preemption doctrine.** Under that doctrine, when Congress preempts (takes for itself) an area of lawmaking, its legislation is exclusive and any conflicting state legislation is invalid in that area. The Supremacy Clause, therefore, empowers Congress to preempt state regulation in particular areas of lawmaking.

Congress may enact legislation *expressly* preempting state legislation in a particular area. It may do this by including language stating that federal law will control the entire area. More commonly, Congress does not state an intent to preempt state legislation, so that when a conflict between federal and state law develops, courts must determine whether *implied* preemption has occurred. Factors that may be relevant to a finding of implicit federal preemption include the following:

Preemption doctrine

the doctrine that the states may not pass laws conflicting with the laws passed by Congress in a subject area

1. The federal legislation is highly comprehensive, leaving little doubt that Congress intended the area in question to be subject to federal rather than state control.
2. The area has traditionally been identified as federal.
3. The state and federal regulatory schemes are nearly identical.
4. Congress has previously exhibited an extensive interest in the area.
5. The need exists for a high degree of national uniformity of regulation.

If some or all of these factors are present, the federal law may be held to be exclusive and to override state regulation in the same area.

A compelling need for *national uniformity* of regulation is the most important factor in determining whether the preemption doctrine applies. For purposes of expediency and administrative convenience, certain aspects of commerce require uniform regulation. An Illinois statute, for example, required that all trucks using state highways be fitted with curved mud flaps unlike those in use in other states, forcing interstate truckers to equip their trucks with special mudguards. The Supreme Court declared the Illinois requirement invalid on the grounds that national uniformity was clearly necessary in this area of commerce and that the requirement unjustifiably impeded the flow of interstate trucking.

SELLING APPLE JUICE ACROSS STATE LINES

Adam, who owns an apple juice processing plant in State A, sells a good deal of apple juice in Pleasantville, a city in State B. Pleasantville passes an ordinance requiring that all apple juice sold in Pleasantville be processed and bottled within 10 miles of the city. Can Adam successfully challenge the ordinance? Why?

Hypothetical Case

Undue Burden and Discrimination   Most subject areas are not affected by the need for exclusive control. States are free to regulate these areas, but may not enact legislation that imposes an undue burden on interstate commerce or that discriminates against interstate commerce.

The question for the courts to decide is whether state laws place an **undue** (unreasonable) **burden on interstate commerce.** In making such decisions, the courts balance the competing state and federal interests. A few states unduly burdened interstate commerce by enacting statutes requiring railroads to stop at small towns along their main route. Similarly, the courts found state laws that subject goods crossing state lines to unreasonable delays to be unconstitutional. State laws that make the shipping of goods across state lines more expensive are also violations of the Commerce Clause. A Madison, Wisconsin, ordinance made it unlawful to sell milk as "pasteurized" unless the milk had been processed and bottled within 5 miles of the center of Madison. Enforcing this ordinance would have compelled out-of-state dairies to locate a facility within the borders of Wisconsin. The Supreme Court concluded that the ordinance was not essential for the health of Madison's citizens and that it made the conduct of interstate commerce more expensive.

Similarly, local regulations that discriminate against interstate commerce in favor of local business are unconstitutional. An ordinance passed by a city in Vermont required nonresident photographers to file performance bonds and pay license fees. In annulling the ordinance as a **discrimination against interstate commerce,** the Supreme Court stated: "While interstate commerce may be required to pay its way, it must be placed on a plane of equality with local trade and commerce."

The Constitution does not define specific areas of the state and federal control over interstate commerce. The Supreme Court, therefore, sits as the referee to determine what the competing interests of state and federal governments may or may not do with respect to interstate commerce. With the importance of the Commerce Clause today, the Supreme Court in effect involves itself in the formulation of business policies.

In the following case the issue is whether a federal law preempts a Florida statute.

Undue burden on interstate commerce the doctrine that state laws impeding interstate business activity are invalid

Discrimination against interstate commerce the doctrine that state laws unreasonably favoring intrastate business activity over interstate business activity are invalid

BONITO BOATS, INC. v. THUNDER CRAFT BOATS, INC.
SUPREME COURT OF THE UNITED STATES
489 U.S. 141 (1989)

Bonito Boats, Inc. developed a hull design for a fiberglass recreational boat marketed under the name of Bonito Boat Model 5VBR. The company never filed a patent application to protect the design of the hull or the "direct molding process" that it used to produce the hull. After the 5VBR had been on the market for six years, the Florida legislature enacted a statute prohibiting the use of a direct molding process to duplicate unpatented boat hulls and forbidding the knowing sale of such hulls.

Bonito Boats subsequently filed an action in a Florida trial court alleging that Thunder Craft Boats, Inc. had violated the statute by using a direct molding process to duplicate the 5VBR hull and by selling the duplicated hulls. The trial court, later affirmed by the Florida Court of Appeals and the Florida Supreme Court, dismissed the complaint on the ground that it conflicted with the federal patent law and thus violated the Supremacy Clause of the U.S. Constitution. The U.S. Supreme Court granted certiorari.

JUSTICE O'CONNOR
Delivered the Opinion for a Unanimous Court

Article I, Section 8, clause 8, of the Constitution gives Congress the power "[t]o promote the Progress of Science and the useful Arts, by securing for limited Times to Authors and Inventors the exclusive Right to their respective Writings and Discoveries." The Patent Clause itself reflects a balance between the need to encourage innovation and the avoidance of monopolies which stifle competition without any concomitant advance in the "Progress of Science and the useful Arts." As we have noted in the past, the clause contains both a grant of power and certain limitations upon the exercise of that power. Congress may not create patent monopolies of unlimited duration, nor may it "authorize the issuance of patents whose effects are to remove existent knowledge from the public domain, or to restrict free access to materials already available." Protection is offered to "[w]hoever invents or discovers any new and useful process, machine, manufacture, or composition of matter, or any new and useful improvement thereof." 35 U.S.C. Section 101. Since 1842, Congress has also made protection available for "any new, original, and ornamental design for an article of manufacture." 35 U.S.C. Section 171. To qualify for protection, a design must present an aesthetically pleasing appearance that is not dictated by function alone, and must satisfy the other criteria of patentability. From the Patent Act of 1790 to the present day, the public sale of an unpatented article has acted as a complete bar to federal protection of the idea embodied in the article thus placed in public commerce.

In this case, the Bonito 5VBR fiberglass hull has been freely exposed to the public for a period in excess of six years. For purposes of federal law, it stands in the same stead as an item for which a patent has expired or been denied: it is unpatented and unpatentable.

Our decisions have made it clear

that the Patent and Copyright Clauses do not, by their own force or by negative implication, deprive the States of the power to adopt rules for the promotion of intellectual creation within their own jurisdictions. Thus, where "Congress determines that neither federal protection nor freedom from restraint is required by the national interest," the States remain free to promote originality and creativity in their own domains.

Nor does the fact that a particular item lies within the subject matter of the federal patent laws necessarily preclude the States from offering limited protection which does not impermissibly interfere with the federal patent scheme. States may place limited regulations on the use of unpatented designs in order to prevent consumer confusion as to source.

The Florida statute is aimed directly at the promotion of intellectual creation by substantially restricting the public's ability to exploit ideas which the patent system mandates shall be free for all to use. The Florida law substantially restricts the public's ability to exploit an unpatented design in general circulation, raising the specter of state-created monopolies in a host of useful shapes and processes for which patent protection has been denied or is otherwise unobtainable. It thus enters a field of regulation which the patent laws have reserved to Congress. The patent statute's careful balance between pub-

lic right and private monopoly to promote certain creative activity is a "scheme of federal regulation . . . so pervasive as to make reasonable the inference that Congress left no room for the States to supplement it."

We therefore agree with the majority of the Florida Supreme Court that the Florida statute is preempted by the Supremacy Clause and the judgment of that court is hereby affirmed.

It is so ordered.

Legal Issues

1. When are the states allowed to adopt rules for the promotion of intellectual property? Explain.

2. What did the Court mean when it stated that the "Patent Clause itself reflects a balance between the need to encourage innovation and the avoidance of monopolies which stifle competition"? Explain.

Ethical Issues

1. What view of ethics is consistent with the idea that originality and creativity should be protected through either federal or state legislation? Discuss.

2. What view of ethics is embodied in the Court's contention that "States may place limited regulations on the use of unpatented designs in order to prevent consumer confusion as to source"? Why?

The Contract Clause

The **contract clause** of the Constitution, in Article I, Section 10, forbids state legislation that impairs "the Obligation of Contracts." This clause was originally adopted to prevent the states from enacting laws that would interfere with contractual arrangements between private citizens. Its primary purpose was to prevent state laws that granted relief to debtors.

In subsequent years, however, the Supreme Court relied on the Contract Clause to strike down a wide variety of state laws that retroactively affected the contractual

Contract clause
the clause in the Constitution that prohibits states from passing statutes that unduly interfere with existing contracts

obligations and property rights of private parties. For example, a Minnesota statute imposed greater obligations on the pension plans of private employers than had been assumed by the private employers. The statute provided that employees who had worked for certain Minnesota employers for more than 10 years became vested in the company pension plan. The pension plan of Allied Structural Steel Company, which had been established before the enactment of the statute, did not grant vesting within that period of time. When Allied closed its plant, the statute required it to pay pension benefits to employees who would not have received them otherwise. In *Allied Structural Steel Co. v. Spannaus,*[8] the U.S. Supreme Court held that the Minnesota statute was an unconstitutional impairment of a contractual relationship.

The prohibitions of the Contract Clause have been extended to state statutes that alter contracts to which the state is a party. Thus state statutes that alter the contractual pension rights of state employees are unconstitutional.

The Full Faith and Credit Clause

Full faith and credit clause

the clause in the Constitution that requires the courts in one state to recognize and enforce the final judgments of the courts in other states

Article IV, Section 1 provides a mechanism for the enforcement of judgments in different states: "Full Faith and Credit shall be given in each State to the . . . judicial Proceedings of every other State." The **full faith and credit clause** guarantees that a final judgment in one state will be recognized and enforced in all the other states. Suppose that XYZ Foods Company obtains a judgment for $25,000 against Perch Supplies, Inc. in California. XYZ Foods could enforce this judgment against property that Perch owns in Oregon. The Oregon courts are required to give the California judgment the same effect (the same "faith and credit") that the California courts would give it. Perch's Oregon property could therefore be seized to satisfy the judgment.

The Full Faith and Credit Clause is a useful means of ending litigation. It puts to rest matters that have been decided between adverse parties in any state. This means that the Oregon courts will not reconsider the details of the first suit. The only issue open to them is whether the California court had proper jurisdiction.

LAW ABROAD

European Community

The courts of European Community member states must adhere to special rules regarding reciprocity with the courts of other member states.

Germany

The judgments of courts of a foreign nation are enforced in Germany if the courts of that nation offer reciprocal treatment to the judgments of German courts. However, the judgment of a foreign court is held to be unenforceable if, according to German law, the foreign court lacked appropriate jurisdiction or if the defendant was a German citizen who was not served with jurisdiction or through German authorities. The judgment of a foreign court can also be refused enforcement on grounds of public policy. Reciprocity exists between German courts and

U.S. federal courts though it may or may not exist between German courts and U.S. state courts.

Japan

A final judgment of a foreign court will be recognized as binding in Japan only if four conditions have been met. First, the jurisdiction of the foreign court has not been denied by Japanese law or treaties. Second, if the losing party is a Japanese citizen, publication has not been the only method of service employed. Third, the judgment has been in accordance with Japanese standards of public orders and good morals. Finally, the foreign court has reciprocated judgment by recognizing the judgment of Japanese courts.

If these conditions have been met, the final judgment will be executed only after a competent Japanese court has affirmed the validity of the judgment in a special action.

Complete reciprocity between Japanese and U.S. courts has not yet been established by treaty, but reciprocity with a particular jurisdiction will generally be granted upon proof that Japanese judgments are recognized in that jurisdiction.

The Privileges and Immunities Clause

Article IV, Section 2 provides: "The Citizens of each State shall be entitled to all Privileges and Immunities of Citizens in the several States." The **privileges and immunities clause** prevents a state from discriminating against nonresidents. The Founding Fathers intended this clause to have a unifying effect on the loose confederation of states that preceded the adoption of the Constitution. "Privileges and immunities" are "rights." As citizens pass from state to state, they acquire the rights of citizens in the states through which they pass.

The Privileges and Immunities Clause guarantees a citizen of Michigan who visits Ohio the same basic rights in Ohio as those possessed by the citizens of Ohio. Thus a noncitizen of the host state has the same access to police protection and the court system as citizens of the host state. To further illustrate: Any state law that bars nonresidents from acquiring property in the state or imposes higher taxes on nonresidents violates the Privileges and Immunities Clause.

States may restrict the rights of nonresidents in matters that pertain to local government. For example, a state may pass reasonable laws concerning residency requirements for voting or require that nonresident students make higher tuition payments to a state university. Further, since corporations are not "citizens," a state may tax nonresident corporations more heavily than domestic corporations, provided the tax is reasonable.

Under the privileges and immunities standard, laws that discriminate on the basis of residency will be sustained only if they reasonably relate to a legitimate state objective. Two Supreme Court cases involving this standard are instructive.

In *Toomer v. Witsell*,[9] a Georgia fisherman challenged the enforcement of a South Carolina statute regulating commercial shrimp fishing. The statute required a $2,500 per year license fee from nonresidents for each shrimp boat they operated and only $25 per day for resident shrimpers. The Supreme Court held that the statute violated the Privileges and Immunities Clause since it created a commercial monopoly for South Carolina residents. The simple fact of nonresidency,

Privileges and immunities clause
the clause in the Constitution that prevents a state from denying the citizens of other states the basic rights that it extends to its own citizens

said the Court, cannot serve as the basis of discriminatory treatment unless there are valid independent reasons for the discrimination.

In *Baldwin v. Montana Fish & Game Commission,*[10] the Supreme Court applied privileges and immunities analysis to Montana's recreational hunting license system. Nonresidents of Montana were required to pay $225 for the privilege of hunting elk, while residents could purchase a license for only $9. The Court upheld the statute despite its challenge to the Privileges and Immunities Clause: "Elk hunting by nonresidents in Montana is a recreation and a sport. It is not a basic right or an essential activity, interference with which would frustrate the purposes of the formation of the Union." Thus the right of citizens to exploit the limited resources of a state in which they are nonresidents may be restricted despite the protection of the Privileges and Immunities Clause.

THE BILL OF RIGHTS

Bill of Rights
the first 10 amendments to the Constitution, which protect the liberties of citizens from actions of the federal government

The first 10 amendments to the Constitution are referred to as the **Bill of Rights**. Many citizens resisted ratification of the constitution because it did not contain provisions that protected the individual from actions of the federal government. (These citizens remembered, all too well, the power of the king of England.) In 1789 the First Congress proposed to the state legislatures 12 amendments that afforded such protection. The 10 amendments that were ratified became effective in 1791.[11]

The first 10 amendments were drafted to protect the liberties of citizens from actions of the federal government. However, the Supreme Court has determined that nearly all of the liberties guaranteed by the Bill of Rights are "fundamental" and are, therefore, protected by the due process clause of the 14th Amendment. Thus, the first 10 amendments protect our liberties from actions of both the federal government and state governments.

The provisions of the Bill of Rights that significantly affect businesses are contained in the First Amendment, the Fourth Amendment, and the Fifth Amendment.

The First Amendment

The First Amendment guarantees to each individual (1) freedom of religion, (2) freedom of speech, (3) freedom of press, (4) freedom of association, and (5) freedom to petition the government for the redress of grievances. Freedom of religion and freedom of speech issues have the greatest impact on businesses.

Freedom of religion clause
a clause in the First Amendment that limits the power of Congress to advance or inhibit any religion

Freedom of Religion   The First Amendment protects religious activities: "Congress shall make no law respecting an establishment of religion, or prohibiting the free exercise thereof." The purpose of the **freedom of religion clause** is to separate church and state. Hence, it guarantees every person the freedom to follow any religion as long as the practice of that religion does not endanger society.

The first part of the First Amendment is known as the Establishment Clause, since it prohibits the establishment of a state-supported church or an official state religion. In some of the colonies a particular church was supported by taxation. The Establishment Clause prevents such involuntary support of a state-approved church.

The second part of the First Amendment is known as the Free Exercise Clause. It prohibits government interference with the practices of any religion except for practices that are injurious to the welfare of its members or others. For example, the government can prohibit the handling of poisonous snakes as part of a religious group's worship. Similarly, the use of illegal drugs in religious ceremonies is not protected by the First Amendment's Free Exercise Clause.

Many states have enacted Sunday closing laws, commonly called "blue laws," that require local businesses to close on Sunday. These laws were originally enacted to ensure that all would observe the Sabbath of the dominant Christian group. Although they have been challenged as being in violation of the First Amendment, the Supreme Court has upheld them despite their religious origin on the basis that providing for a uniform day of rest is a legitimate governmental objective. The Court concluded that the purpose of the Sunday closing laws had become nonreligious.

Freedom of Speech   The portion of the First Amendment that is most significant for business reads: "Congress shall make no law . . . abridging the freedom of speech." The **freedom of speech clause** essentially guarantees the rights of citizens to advocate and exchange ideas—even unconventional ideas—free of governmental interference.

Like other constitutional guarantees, the right to speak freely is not absolute. The Supreme Court has found it necessary to balance First Amendment liberties against societal interests. Speech that threatens to induce violence or unlawful activity does not promote the free exchange of ideas and is not protected. Justice Holmes employed a famous example in 1919 by observing that the First Amendment does not protect a person who falsely shouts "fire" in a crowded theater.

In addition, the First Amendment does not protect speech that defames the character or reputation of an individual or a business. Defamation by published words or pictures is called **libel;** defamation by spoken words or gestures is called **slander.** If Amy Brown fails to fulfill her obligations under a contract to John Jones and Jones falsely tells third persons that she is a liar or a crook, Brown may recover damages from Jones for slander. If Jones writes that Brown is a liar and crook in a letter that a third party reads, Brown may recover damages from Jones for libel.

Suppose that Smith, a newspaper publisher, prints an article that falsely refers to the governor as a liar and a crook. Can the governor recover damages for libel from the newspaper and Smith? In determining libel and slander, courts apply a standard for "public officials" and "public figures" that is different from the usual standard. Public officials are persons in high places of government. Public figures are persons whose appearances before the public have made them celebrities. Examples of people whom courts have held to be public figures include an actor, a professional baseball player, an athletic director for a university, and a retired army general.

To prove libel or slander, a public official or a public figure must show actual *malice*. "Malice" is a technical term signifying that the false statement was made intentionally and either with knowledge that it was false, or with a reckless disregard for whether it was true or false. "Reckless disregard" means that the defendant entertained serious doubts as to the truth of the statement. By contrast, a private person who sues a media defendant for defamation need only show that the defendant *negligently* published a false statement.

Freedom of speech clause

a clause in the First Amendment that limits the power of Congress to prohibit the free expression of ideas

Libel

published words or pictures that injure a person's reputation or character

Slander

spoken words or gestures that injure a person's reputation or character

A trend in the law is for plaintiffs in libel cases to also allege the intentional infliction of emotional distress. In the following case the Supreme Court considered whether a defendant sued by a public figure was entitled to the same level of free speech protection for the intentional infliction of emotional distress as the level required for allegations of libel.

HUSTLER MAGAZINE v. FALWELL
SUPREME COURT OF THE UNITED STATES
485 U.S. 46 (1988)

The Reverend Jerry Falwell, a nationally known minister and commentator on public issues, filed a complaint to recover damages for libel and intentional infliction of emotional distress arising from *Hustler* magazine's publication of an advertising satire or parody that depicted Falwell as having engaged in a drunken, incestuous relationship with his mother in an outhouse. The tort of emotional distress occurs where a party's conduct is so outrageous that it causes a strong emotional response in another party. Generally, the conduct has "to be regarded as atrocious, and utterly intolerable in a civilized community" (*Restatement of Torts, Second*, section 46, comment).

A jury found against Falwell on the libel claim but awarded him $200,000 in damages for emotional distress. The court of appeals affirmed the trial court's verdict. Both parties appealed to the Supreme Court, which upheld the ruling against Falwell in the libel complaint and rendered the following decision on the emotional distress complaint.

CHIEF JUSTICE REHNQUIST
Delivered the Opinion of the Court

This case presents us with a novel question involving First Amendment limitations upon a State's authority to protect its citizens from the intentional infliction of emotional distress. We must decide whether a public figure may recover damages for emotional harm caused by the publication of an ad parody offensive to him, and doubtless gross and repugnant in the eyes of most. Respondent [Falwell] would have us find that a State's interest in protecting public figures from emotional distress is sufficient to deny First Amendment protection to speech that is patently offensive and is intended to inflict emotional injury, even when that speech could not reasonably have been interpreted as stating actual facts about the public figure involved. This we decline to do.

At the heart of the First Amendment is the recognition of the fundamental importance of the free flow of ideas and opinions on matters of public interest and concern. "[T]he freedom to speak one's mind is not only an aspect of individual liberty—and thus a good unto itself—but also is essential to the common quest for truth and the vitality of society as a whole." We have therefore been particularly vigilant to ensure that individual expressions of ideas remain free from governmentally imposed sanctions. The First Amendment recognizes no such thing as a "false" idea. As Justice Holmes wrote, "The ultimate good desired is better reached by free trade in ideas— . . . the best test of truth is the power of the thought to get itself accepted in the competition of the market."

The sort of robust political debate encouraged by the First Amendment is bound to produce speech that is critical of those who hold public office or those public figures who are intimately involved in the resolution of important public questions or, by reason of their fame, shape events in areas of concern to society at large.

Of course, this does not mean that *any* speech about a public figure is immune from sanction in the form of damages. Since *New York Times Co. v. Sullivan,* we have consistently ruled that a public figure may hold a speaker liable for the damage to reputation caused by publication of a defamatory falsehood, but only if the statement was made "with knowledge that it was false or with reckless disregard of whether it was false or not." False statements of fact are particularly valueless; they interfere with the truth-seeking function of the marketplace of ideas, and they cause damage to an individual's reputation that cannot easily be repaired by counterspeech, however persuasive or effective. But even though falsehoods have little value in and of themselves, they are nevertheless inevitable in free debate, and a rule that would impose strict liability on a publisher for false factual assertions would have an undoubted "chilling" effect on speech relating to public figures that does have constitutional value. Freedoms of expression require "breathing space." This breathing space is provided by a constitutional rule that allows public figures to recover for libel or defamation only when they can prove *both* that the statement was false and that the statement was made with the requisite level of culpability.

Respondent argues, however, that a different standard should apply in this case because here the State seeks to prevent not reputational damage, but the severe emotional distress suffered by the person who is the subject of an offensive publication. In respondent's view, and in the view of the Court of Appeals, so long as the utterance was intended to inflict emotional distress, was outrageous, and did in fact inflict serious emotional distress, it is of no constitutional import whether the statement was a fact or an opinion, or whether it was true or false.

Generally speaking, the law does not regard the intent to inflict emotional distress as one which should receive much solicitude, and it is quite understandable that most if not all jurisdictions have chosen to make it civilly culpable where the conduct in question is sufficiently "outrageous." But in the world of debate about public affairs, many things done with motives that are less than admirable are protected by the First Amendment. Thus while such a bad motive may be deemed controlling for purposes of tort liability in other areas of the law, we think the First Amendment prohibits such a result in the area of public debate about public figures.

Were we to hold otherwise, there can be little doubt that political cartoonists and satirists would be subjected to damages awards without any showing that their work falsely defamed its subject.

Respondent contends, however, that the caricature in question here was so "outrageous" as to distinguish it from more traditional political cartoons. There is no doubt that the caricature of respondent and his mother published in *Hustler* is at best a distant cousin of the political cartoons described above, and a rather poor relation at that. If it were possible by laying down a principled standard to separate the one from the other, public discourse would probably suffer little or no harm. But we doubt that there is any such standard, and we are quite sure that the pejorative description "outrageous" does not supply one. "Outrageousness" in the area of political and social discourse has an inherent subjectiveness about it which would allow a jury to impose liability on the basis of the jurors' tastes or views, or perhaps on the basis of their dislike of a particular expression. An "outrageousness" standard thus runs afoul of our long-standing refusal to allow damages to be awarded because the speech in question may have an adverse emotional impact on the audience. Speech does not lose its protected character . . . simply because it may embarrass others or coerce them into action.

Admittedly, these oft-repeated First Amendment principles, like other principles, are subject to limitations. We recognized that speech that is "'vulgar,' 'offensive,' and 'shocking'" is "not entitled to absolute constitutional protection under all circumstances." We held that a State could lawfully punish an individual for the use of insulting "'fighting' words—those which by their very utterance inflict injury or tend to incite an immediate breach of the peace." These limitations are but recognition of the observation that this Court has "long recognized that not all speech is of equal First Amendment importance." But the sort of expression involved in this case does not seem to us to be governed by any exception to the general First Amendment principles stated above.

We conclude that public figures and public officials may not recover for the tort of intentional infliction of emotional distress by reason of publications such as the one here at issue without showing in addition that the publication contains a false statement of fact which was made with "actual malice," *i.e.,* with knowledge that the statement was false or with reckless disregard as to whether or not it was true. This is not merely a "blind application" of the *New York Times* standard; it reflects our considered judgment that such a standard is necessary to give adequate "breathing space" to the freedoms protected by the First Amendment.

For reasons heretofore stated this claim cannot, consistently with the First Amendment, form a basis for the award of damages when the conduct in question is the publication of a caricature such as the ad parody involved here. The judgment of the Court of Appeals is accordingly
Reversed.

Legal Issues

1. According to this decision, what is at the heart of the First Amendment? Explain.

2. What must a public figure show to recover for the tort of intentional infliction of emotional distress? Why?

Ethical Issues

1. The Court notes that a public figure may hold a speaker liable for the damage to his or her reputation caused by publication of a defamatory falsehood only if the statement was made "with knowledge that it was false or with reckless disregard of whether it was false or not." Is this standard consistent with the attitude toward ethics held by a person who contends that a person who behaves fairly behaves ethically and that unfair behavior is unethical? Explain your answer.

2. Is Chief Justice Rehnquist's observation that "even though falsehoods have little value in and of themselves, they are 'nevertheless inevitable in free debate'" consistent with pragmatic ethics? Why?

Prior restraint
of speech

the prohibition of speech
by the government be-
fore it has been seen or
heard

Prior Restraint   Courts have consistently ruled that **prior restraint of speech** presents a far greater danger to freedom of speech than does punishing people who have made injurious statements. Such restraint is ordinarily held unconstitutional because it suppresses the free exchange of ideas and prevents some opinions from receiving public scrutiny. Under a system in which speech is suppressed, a government censor privately decides what ideas can and cannot be expressed. The general public is never aware of what kinds of things it is forbidden to see or hear.

The First Amendment prohibits the government from using prior restraint to censor publications. A famous 1971 case, *New York Times Co. v. United States*,[12] commonly called "The Pentagon Papers Case," illlustrates this point. The *New York Times* and the *Washington Post* were printing classified documents, entitled "History of U.S. Decision-Making Process on Vietnam Policy," that had been leaked to them. Publication of the documents was a highly charged political issue since it occurred during the Vietnam conflict. The U.S. government petitioned the Supreme Court for an injunction to prevent the publication of further installments. The Court stated that any system of prior restraint bore a heavy presumption of unconstitutionality that the government seeking to restrain had the burden of justifying. The government did not meet its burden in this case. The Court suggested that the two newspapers deserved commendation for serving a purpose of the First Amendment—prohibiting the government's suppression of embarrassing information.

The question that courts must determine in prior restraint cases is whether a greater danger to freedom of speech is posed by suppressing the alleged illegal speech before it occurs or by subjecting the speaker to punishment subsequent to the illegal speech. Generally, prior restraint is the greater danger because when the speaker is punished, the public has at least been given the opportunity to find out what he said. Only a compelling state interest can justify prior restraint.

Symbolic speech
conduct designed to con-
vey a message

Symbolic Speech   Certain forms of **symbolic** (nonverbal) **speech** are protected by the First Amendment. When conduct is designed to convey a message, it is equated to speech and thus entitled to constitutional protection. The Supreme Court has acknowledged the communicative nature of such conduct as displaying flags or wearing armbands.

Only certain kinds of communicative acts are protected. In *United States v. O'Brian*,[13] the Court upheld the federal statute that prohibited the burning of draft cards. In an antiwar protest in 1966, O'Brian burned his draft card on the steps of a Boston courthouse. He was convicted and appealed to the Supreme Court, but the Court rejected his view that the statute restricted his freedom of expression. Since the purposes of selective service registration constituted a sufficient government interest with only incidental restrictions on free speech, the First Amendment did not protect the symbolic act of burning draft cards.

However, the Supreme Court has held that the burning of the U.S. flag can be considered expressive conduct and is thus protected as speech under the First Amendment. In the 1989 case of *Texas v. Johnson*,[14] a defendant who burned a U.S. flag during a protest against the Republican National Convention in Dallas, Texas, had been convicted of desecrating a venerated object, a violation of a Texas criminal statute. The Supreme Court held that prosecution of the defendant could not be justified on the basis of attempting to keep peace in a community or to preserve the flag's symbolic value. Congress responded to this decision by passing the Flag Protection Act of 1989, but the Supreme Court quickly held this act to be unconstitutional in another case.[15]

Picketing, a form of symbolic speech, is protected by the First Amendment when it is for a lawful purpose. However, it must be conducted in an orderly manner. This condition gives courts authority to regulate the number and sites of pickets, to ban violent picketing, and to punish pickets who disregard court orders.

A CORPORATION BECOMES POLITICALLY ACTIVE

A proposed statute that outlaws the transportation of hazardous nuclear waste is coming before the state legislature. The chairman of the board of XYZ Company, a small corporation engaged in this activity, plans to use corporate funds to publicize arguments against the proposed statute. However, a state law forbids the use of corporate funds for such purposes. Can the chairman of the board carry out her plan? Why?

Hypothetical Case

Corporations   The First Amendment protects the speech of corporations as well as individuals. In *First National Bank v. Bellotti*,[16] the Supreme Court considered a Massachusetts criminal statute that prohibited a corporation from spending money "for the purpose of influencing or affecting any of the property, business, or assets of the corporation." The First National Bank and other corporations challenged the statute as being in violation of the First and Fourteenth Amendments. They wanted to advertise their opposition to a proposed amendment to the Massachusetts constitution that authorized the state legislature to enact a graduated personal income tax. The state contended that the First Amendment did not protect advertising. The Court held, however, that corporations, like natural persons, are entitled to free speech rights. In striking down the statute, it said:

> We find no support in the First or Fourteenth Amendments, or in the decisions of this court, for the proposition that speech that otherwise would be within the protection of the First Amendment loses that protection simply because its source is a corporation that cannot prove, to the satisfaction of a court, a material effect on its business or property.

Thus the First Amendment protects the right of corporations to spend money to promote *political issues* submitted to voters in ballot referendum. However, corporations and trade associations are restricted from using corporate treasuries on behalf of *candidates for political office.*

In *Austin v. Michigan Chamber of Commerce*,[17] in 1990 the Supreme Court upheld a Michigan law that prohibited corporations from using general treasury funds for expenditures in connection with the elections of state candidates. The Chamber of Commerce wanted to use the funds to buy a newspaper advertisement supporting a particular candidate. The Court said that the Michigan law served a compelling state interest by reducing the threat that huge corporate treasuries would be used to unfairly influence elections for political office. Laws similar to the Michigan law have been enacted by 20 other states and the federal government. Under these laws, a corporation may make campaign contributions only by establishing special funds or political action committees. These funds or political action committees are to be funded solely by contributions from individuals, either employees or members of the political action committee. Everyone who contributes to these funds must understand that their money will be used for political purposes.

Thus, although corporations are entitled to First Amendment free speech rights, they do not enjoy the same free speech rights as individuals.

Commercial Speech The First Amendment protections apply to **commercial speech**—speech that advertises a product or service for business purposes. In the past, advertising statements by businesses lacked freedom of speech guarantees. Today, however, commercial speech is given almost the same degree of protection as other forms of speech. To qualify for First Amendment protection, the commercial speech must be truthful and not misleading. Thus, it enjoys only a qualified protection since the government can regulate commercial speech, such as advertising, that is untruthful or misleading.

The commercial speech doctrine originated in 1924 in *Valentine v. Chrestensen.*[18] Chrestensen distributed a handbill advertising a former navy submarine that he operated as an amusement attraction in New York City. He was convicted of violating the city's sanitary code forbidding the distribution of advertising matter in the streets.

In upholding the conviction, the Supreme Court set forth the original commercial speech doctrine, which held that speech whose primary purpose is commercial is not subject to First Amendment protection. In 1975 the Supreme Court reviewed this doctrine in the case of *Virginia Pharmacy Board v. Virginia Citizens Commerce Council.*[19] A Virginia statute declared it to be "unprofessional conduct" for a licensed pharmacist to advertise the prices of prescription drugs. The Commerce Council, a consumer group, challenged the statute, claiming that consumers would benefit from the advertising of prescription drugs. The Supreme Court declared the statute unconstitutional.

A primary justification for the Court's ruling was the importance of a free flow of commercial information to the consuming public. The Court noted:

> Advertising, however tasteless and excessive it sometimes may seem, is nonetheless dissemination of information as to who is producing and selling what product, for what reason, and at what price. So long as we preserve a predominantly free enterprise economy, the allocation of our resources in large measure will be made through numerous private economic decisions. It is a matter of public interest that those decisions, in the aggregate, be intelligent and well informed. To this end, the free flow of commercial information is indispensable.

Commercial speech does not enjoy the same degree of protection as other speech. The Court was careful to point out that the state or federal government has the power to prohibit untruthful or misleading commercial speech. In particular, the government can issue regulations restricting commercial speech to a reasonable time, place, and manner. In *Ward v. Rock Against Racism,*[20] a New York City regulation restricting the noise level of rock concerts in Central Park was upheld as a reasonable regulation of the time, place, and manner of expression of commercial speech.

Recently, courts have upheld legislation that restricts commercial speech if the legislation significantly promotes social interests such as health and safety. In *Posadas de Puerto Rico Association v. Tourism Co. of Puerto Rico,*[21] for example, the Supreme Court upheld a regulation that prohibited advertising for legal casino gambling aimed at citizens of Puerto Rico. In *Board of Trustees v. Fox,*[22] it upheld a regulation that banned private companies from staging parties promoting house-

---

Commercial speech
speech that advertises a product or service for business purposes

wares in student dormitories. According to the Court, the correct standard of review for commercial speech requires that the means of restriction be narrowly drawn and that they be no more extensive than is reasonably necessary to further substantial state interests.

The following case provides an example of the regulation of commercial speech. An organization of practicing accountants challenged a state law that restricted the professional tasks they were allowed to perform.

ACCOUNTANT'S SOCIETY OF VIRGINIA v. BORMAN
U.S. COURT OF APPEALS
860 F.2d 602 (4th Cir. 1988)

Accountant's Society of Virginia, Inc., an organization of practicing accountants, most of whom were not licensed certified public accountants (CPAs), challenged a Virginia statute that restricted the professional tasks the non-CPA accountants might perform by prohibiting them from using certain terms in the documents they prepared for clients. The non-CPAs were not allowed to give an "assurance" regarding a financial statement or to use the following expressions: "generally accepted accounting standards," "public accountancy principles," "generally accepted auditing principles," and "generally accepted auditing standards." They were also barred from using these terms in a report: *audit, audit report, independent audit, attest, attestation, examine, examination, opinion,* and *review.*

The district court found the statute a valid regulation. The Accountant's Society appealed.

BUTZNER, SENIOR CIRCUIT JUDGE

The accountants first claim that [the statute is] unconstitutional because, by forbidding non-CPAs from describing the "principles" and "standards" they use in compiling financial statements and by preventing non-CPAs from identifying their reports by certain technical labels, the statute impermissibly regulates their commercial speech.

To be sure, the First Amendment protects commercial speech. The Supreme Court, however, has long recognized that governmental regulation of the professions is constitutional if the regulations "have a rational connection with the applicant's fitness or capacity to practice the profession."

Professional regulation is not invalid, nor is it subject to First Amendment strict scrutiny, merely because it restricts some kinds of speech. A statute that governs the practice of an occupation is not unconstitutional as an abridgment of the right to free speech, so long as "any inhibition of that right is merely the incidental effect of observing an otherwise legitimate regulation."

The task, then, is locating the point at which "a measure is no longer a regulation of a profession but a regulation of speech or of the press."

One who takes the affairs of a client personally in hand and purports to exercise judgment on behalf of the client in the light of the client's individual needs and circumstances is properly viewed as engaging in the practice of a profession. In such a situation, the professional's speech is incidental to the conduct of the profession, and government regulation limiting the class of persons who may practice the profession cannot be said to have enacted a limitation on freedom of speech or the press subject to First Amendment scrutiny. The key to distinguishing between occupational regulation and abridgment of First Amendment liberties is in finding a personal nexus between professional and client.

Here the accountants attempt to portray the preparation of financial reports by non-CPAs as analogous to speech or publications addressing the general public. They minimize the existence of any client relationship between non-CPAs and the businesses for which they perform services and prepare reports, asserting instead that no personalized advice is given, either to any third party or to the client.

But non-CPAs undoubtedly perform personal services for their clients. They exercise their professional judgment in making individualized assessments of each client's financial situation, for which they are compensated by the client. While the information compiled by accountants and bookkeepers may be directed at third parties, it is not aimed at the general public. Rather, such information typically is used by lenders and insurers and has been prepared and circulated for the pecuniary benefit of the client, who has paid the accountant to prepare it. Clearly, the relationship between accountant and client gives rise to "a personal nexus between professional and client." The statute in question restricts only accountants' communications with and on behalf of their clients, as a means of regulating the professional activities of non-CPAs.

Accordingly, we hold that the restrictions imposed by Va.Code Ann. Sections 54-102.31(C) & (D), on the use of certain terms in the work product of non-CPAs, amount to the permissible regulation of a profession, not an abridgment of speech protected by the First Amendment. The district court

correctly concluded that Sections 54-102.31(C) & (D) are constitutional.

The Code also restricts the words unlicensed accountants may use in holding themselves out to the public. A non-CPA may not "describe himself as or assume" any of several "titles or designations," including "certified public accountant, CPA, public accountant, PA, certified accountant, CA, chartered accountant, licensed accountant, LA, registered accountant, RA, independent auditor, or auditor." Section 54-102.31(B).

The accountants challenge the district court's determination that Virginia constitutionally may prohibit non-CPAs from assuming the title "public accountant" and its abbreviation "PA." They argue that the district court erred in holding without evidentiary support that those terms may be restricted because their use by non-CPAs might be misleading.

We agree with the district court that the words "public accountant" and "PA" are business or trade labels, analogous to advertising. Unlike the restricted vocabulary discussed in Part II, these words are not communications between a professional and his client, and may not be restricted as an incidental part of the regulation of a profession. Rather, these words are commercial speech.

Notwithstanding the initial classification of a communication as commercial speech, it falls outside the protection of the First Amendment, if the communication is false, deceptive, or misleading. Thus, appellants' assertion that a search for the least restrictive means of regulation is required here, cannot withstand analysis. If the use of the title "public accountant" by non-CPAs is misleading, it may be prohibited by the state, because the First Amendment does not protect misleading commercial speech. In a prior case this court held that the First Amendment "poses no barrier to any remedy . . . reasonably necessary to the prevention of future deception" by the use of commercial speech.

The state has an interest in assuring the public that only persons who have demonstrated their qualifications as certified public accountants and received a license can hold themselves out as certified public accountants. The Supreme Court has held that "advertising for professional services" may be prohibited "when the particular content or method of the advertising suggests that it is inherently misleading or when experience has proved that in fact such advertising is subject to abuse." We believe that use of the title "public accountant" by a non-CPA fairly could be characterized as inherently misleading, given the possibility, accurately stated by the district court, that "some members of the public would believe the title . . . has the state's imprimatur."

The similarity of the title "public accountant" to "certified public accountant" is self-evident. In defining "misleading" for the purpose of the regulation of commercial speech, the Supreme Court has explained that when the possibility of deception is self-evident, the state need not survey the public. Accordingly, the Board was not required to make an elaborate evidentiary showing at trial in order to establish the misleading nature of the regulated speech. The ban on the use of "public

accountant" or "PA" by unlicensed accountants, in Section 54–102.31(B), is a constitutionally permissible regulation of misleading commercial speech, as the district court correctly held.

Affirmed.

Legal Issues

1. Why did the court uphold the restriction on the use of the title "public accountant" by a non-CPA?

2. Did the court find unconstitutional the sections of the statute that forbade non-CPAs from describing the "principles" and "standards" they used in compiling financial statements? Why?

Ethical Issues

1. The court noted that the Supreme Court had long recognized the constitutionality of governmental regulation of the professions if the regulations "have a rational connection with the applicant's fitness or capacity to 'practice' the profession." Which view of ethics would you most closely associate with this standard of permissible regulation of professional behavior? Why?

2. Is it ethical to permit the Virginia statute to be applied to a person who, although not a CPA, used the title "public accountant" in his business dealings for more than a decade when it was lawful to do so? Why?

The Fourth Amendment

The Fourth Amendment protects against unreasonable searches and seizures. It states: "The right of the people to be secure in their persons, houses, papers, and effects, against unreasonable searches and seizures, shall not be violated, and no Warrants shall issue, but upon probable cause." The **unreasonable searches and seizures clause** of the Fourth Amendment requires that criminal search warrants be issued only upon a showing of probable cause. "Probable cause" means that a reasonable ground must exist for suspicion regarding criminal activity associated with the premises to be searched. The suspicion must be based on circumstances that support a prudent belief in their validity. Evidence obtained from an unreasonable search and seizure is inadmissible in court.

Unreasonable searches and seizures clause
a clause in the Fourth Amendment that prohibits government searches and seizures of persons or property without a search warrant issued by a court upon a showing of probable cause

In the past the courts interpreted the Fourth Amendment protections to apply only in criminal situations, such as arrests or the search and seizure of articles from a suspected individual's home or car. In criminal cases, with a few notable exceptions, the police are required to have a valid search warrant.[23]

The standards for obtaining a criminal search warrant are stringent because of the importance of the individual's right to privacy. An affidavit setting forth circumstances that show probable cause is submitted to a neutral and detached magistrate (a judge of an inferior court) for consideration. The search warrant that the magistrate issues must be precise as to the place to be searched and the items to be seized.

Today, the Fourth Amendment also protects businesses from unwarranted and unreasonable *administrative* searches and seizures. In civil matters involving a business, if the owner of the business or the owner's representative demands a search warrant, administrative inspectors are required to have one before conducting a search. The standards for obtaining an administrative search warrant are much less stringent than those for obtaining a criminal search warrant. Obtaining an administrative search warrant requires the showing of a neutral enforcement plan that assures that selective enforcement through administrative searches will not occur. For example, under the Occupational Safety and Health Act, which provides for the inspection of possible safety violations, the standard of probable cause for a search warrant is met by showing a pattern of accidents in the industry of the particular business for which the search warrant is requested.

In civil cases, as in criminal cases, there are exceptions to the rule requiring search warrants. A search warrant is not required in the following administrative situations:

1. Seizures of contaminated food. Here the need for government intrusion outweighs the interests of the property owner.

2. Searches of businesses in intensely regulated industries, such as the liquor, strip mining, and firearms industries. These businesses may be inspected without a warrant on the theory that highly regulated industries pose a more urgent public interest than other industries. Warrantless searches of these businesses are regarded as necessary to ensure that government regulations are being upheld, and the owners have, in effect, consented to such searches by entering this kind of business.

In sum, the owners of most businesses can demand a search warrant prior to an administrative inspection. Attorneys generally advise businesses to consent to a warrantless search unless the search involves harassment or unfair treatment. The owner of a business in food or a highly regulated industry should be aware that the business is subject to warrantless searches.

The Fifth Amendment

The Fifth Amendment provides every person with (1) the right to indictment by a grand jury in federal criminal cases, (2) protection against being tried twice for the same crime (double jeopardy), (3) protection against compulsory self-incrimination ("pleading the Fifth"), (4) due process of the law, and (5) just compensation if private property is taken for public use. Of most concern to businesses are due process and just compensation.

Due Process Both the Fifth and Fourteenth amendments provide that no person shall be deprived of "life, liberty, or property, without due process of law." The Fifth Amendment applies to actions of the federal government, while the Fourteenth Amendment applies to actions of the states. "Due process of law" means that the law must "play fair." This principle protects the rights of the individual from the arbitrary exercise of the powers of government. Questions of due process are fundamentally questions of fairness. Thus, the federal and state governments cannot act unfairly with regard to the various interests constituting "life, liberty, and property."

The law specifies both "substantive due process" and "procedural due process." **Substantive due process** requires that the provisions of laws be fair and not arbitrary. Courts apply a "substantive review" test only to laws that affect the fundamental rights of individuals under the Constitution. When a statute restricts a civil liberty, such as freedom of speech, the right to vote, or the right of privacy, courts will examine the underlying purpose of the statute. That purpose must promote a compelling interest of government. Such a statute is unconstitutional unless the government interest that it promotes is more important than the restriction of a civil liberty that it imposes.

Procedural due process requires that the proceedings under which the government takes some action affecting life, liberty, or property be fair. In procedural due process, unlike substantive due process, the court does not examine the fairness of the law that is being enforced.

A state statute that imposes a penalty of life imprisonment on any person found guilty of murder promotes a legitimate government objective and, therefore, complies with the requirements of substantive due process. If the process through which the statute moves, however, does not include such steps as indictment, trial by jury, and appellate review, the requirements of procedural due process have not been met. The same statute can, of course, be challenged on the basis that it denies both substantive due process and procedural due process.

In both civil and criminal proceedings, the guarantee of procedural due process extends certain rights to individuals threatened with the loss of "life, liberty, or property." The term *life* has relevance only in connection with the death penalty. *Liberty* issues, on the other hand, commonly arise when government action restrains or threatens to restrain an individual's physical freedom or freedom of choice. For example, law enforcement officials must comply with various procedural requirements in making arrests. Similarly, proper procedures must accompany restrictions on a person's ability to engage in an activity or a profession. For example, a CPA's license to practice can be revoked for improper conduct, but the CPA is entitled to a hearing and must be given reasonable notice of the charges and an opportunity to present objections to them. Finally, procedural due process affecting *property* interests arises in several contexts. For example, the Supreme Court has recognized certain "entitlements" as falling within the definition of "property." The right to continued government employment is a property entitlement. Statutes often specify the continued employment of a government worker except when certain conditions have not been fulfilled. Before a government worker whose employment is protected by such a statute can be terminated, due process requires a hearing to determine whether the worker has in fact not met the statutory conditions.

Just Compensation for Private Property   In the United States, ownership of private property is a basic right of individuals. The federal government and state governments, however, have the inherent power of **eminent domain,** the power to take private property for public use. This power is limited by the Fifth Amendment, which provides that private property shall not be "taken for public use, without

Substantive due process

the requirement that the provisions of the law be fair and not arbitrary

Procedural due process

the requirement that governmental proceedings affecting life, liberty, or property be fair and not arbitrary

Eminent domain

the government's power to take private property for public use by paying the property owner a fair price just compensation." Thus the exercise of eminent domain is limited to situations in which private property is taken for a public use and the property owner is justly compensated. Although the clause "taking" applies specifically to the federal government, courts have held, in decisions based on the due process clause of the Fourteenth Amendment, that it also applies to the states. If a city government, for example, wishes to lengthen an airport runway, the owners of the land needed for this purpose cannot refuse to let the city have it, since this is a public use. However, these landowners are entitled to "just compensation."

In a discussion of eminent domain, it is necessary to examine closely the meaning of "taking," "public use," and "just compensation."

What constitutes a "taking"? The answer is clear when property is physically appropriated. For example, the construction of a government dam that floods nearby land has destroyed the use of the land and entitles its owner to just compensation. The question can arise, however, even when property is not appropriated. A taking can occur from the impairment of an owner's use and enjoyment of land because of public improvements being made on adjacent land. In one case the court held that the construction of an interstate highway whose entrances and exits were not reasonably close to land on which a restaurant stood had damaged the land's value as a site for a restaurant. The owner of the land was entitled to consequential damages because the nearby taking had detrimentally affected the property.

Through the exercise of their police power, governmental bodies can regulate property without paying compensation. Excessive governmental regulation that deprives an owner of land of its entire use and value can amount to a taking that requires the payment of just compensation to the injured landowner. Environmental protection laws and zoning regulations often result in takings.

Under the Fifth Amendment, the right to take private property through the exercise of eminent domain is limited to taking for a public use. The courts ultimately determine what is meant by "public use."

The traditional view of "public use" is that the government can take private property only when the property is to be used for public purposes, such as the construction of public highways, schools, and hospitals. Today, a broader view allows private property to be taken for public purposes even though it will not actually be used by the public. Most states have enacted legislation providing for the exercise of eminent domain in urban renewal efforts. Housing authorities have been given the power to acquire private property by condemnation and to sell it to private real estate developers. The redevelopment of blighted areas in large cities is of concern to the government since it affects the health and safety of the public. In addition, the power of eminent domain can be delegated to highly regulated public utility and railroads. A railroad, for example, can appropriate land to construct railroad tracks over the optimum route. Although the public does not actually own the appropriated land, the public benefits from improved service and reduced transportation costs.

Another eminent domain issue is how to set "just compensation." Generally, the state must pay the owner the fair market value of the property taken. This is the price that would be agreed upon between a willing buyer who does not have to buy and a willing seller who does not have to sell. Property owners who are dissatisfied with the government's valuation of their property have the right to challenge it in court. "Just compensation" does not, however, cover all of the losses suffered by property owners. The owner who has been forced to relocate a business is usually not compensated for loss of profits, loss of goodwill, or moving expenses. Courts reason that only the real property was condemned, not the business.

The Fourteenth Amendment

The Fourteenth Amendment, adopted at the close of the Civil War, contains two important clauses: the due process clause and the equal protection clause. Section 3 of the amendment prohibits states from depriving any person of "life, liberty, or property, without due process of law." The interpretation of the Fourteenth Amendment's due process clause is practically the same as that of the due process clause of the 5th Amendment.

The Fourteenth Amendment also introduced a new constitutional guarantee, the equal protection clause: "No State shall make or enforce any law which shall . . . deny to any person within its jurisdiction the equal protection of the laws." This clause was originally intended to protect the newly freed slaves from actions by state governments. It is now understood to guarantee that the government will treat similar individuals in a similar manner.

Equal protection clause

the clause in the Fourteenth Amendment that prevents federal and state laws from establishing unreasonable classifications of persons

Rational basis review

the test used by courts to determine whether the classifications in state and federal laws are reasonably related to a legitimate governmental objective

Strict scrutiny review

the test used by courts to determine whether classifications in state and federal laws based on a fundamental constitutional right or a suspect class are necessary to promote some compelling governmental purpose

Fundamental right

any right guaranteed by the constitution

Suspect class

a statutory classification based on race, religion, national origin, alienage, or sex

Equal Protection of the Law   The **equal protection clause** has no counterpart in the Constitution applicable to *federal* legislation. However, since the Supreme Court has held that due process under the Fifth Amendment is violated by federal laws that unfairly treat one class of persons differently from another class, the equal protection clause applies to federal laws as well as state laws.

In determining whether a statute creates unreasonable classifications and violates the equal protection clause, the courts apply two tests: rational basis review and strict scrutiny review.

Rational Basis Review   Equal protection does not require that the law treat all persons or all things equally at all times. What it requires is that the classifications of persons made in a statute be reasonable. The traditional test that courts use to determine whether such classifications are reasonable is the **rational basis review.** Under this test, a statute is constitutional if its classifications of persons are *reasonably related* to a legitimate governmental objective.

Many statutes classify persons for special treatment. In 1938, for example, the Fair Labor Standards Act established the standard workweek as 40 hours, with ovetime pay at the rate of 1½ times the employee's regular rate of pay. Clearly, this statute does not treat all employees equally, as it does not apply to executives and administrators. Still, its classification is constitutional because the classification promotes a legitimate governmental objective—the protection of workers subject to possible abuse by management. The statute does not deny equal protection to executives and administrators, because their situation is different from that of the employees who receive the benefits of the statute.

Strict Scrutiny Review   The second test employed by the courts is **strict scrutiny review.** This standard applies to legal classifications based on a fundamental constitutional right or a suspect class. A **fundamental right** is any right guaranteed by the Constitution, such as the right to vote or freedom of association. A **suspect class** is a statutory classification based on race, religion, national origin, alienage (citizenship status), or sex.[24] A statute containing classifications based on any of these criteria is constitutionally "suspect." To be upheld as constitutional, such a statute must be necessary to promote some *compelling state purpose*.

The strict scrutiny review has been employed to strike down a number of laws discriminating against racial minorities. *Brown v. Board of Education*,[25] decided in 1954, is among the most famous race discrimination cases. In *Brown*, parents of minority children challenged state laws that provided for the segregation of children in public schools solely on the basis of race. The Supreme Court, in a unanimous opinion, held that classifications based on race in the field of public education constitute a denial of equal protection. Clearly, such classifications did not promote a compelling state purpose. The *Brown* decision applied only to public schools, but in subsequent decisions the principle it embodied was applied to other public facilities, such as public beaches, city golf courses, stadiums, theaters, office buildings, and public transportation.

Where questions of reverse discrimination favoring minorities have arisen, the Supreme Court has tended to uphold minority preferences. In *Regents of the University of California v. Bakke*,[26] the Supreme Court invalidated a state medical school admissions quota that favored minorities. However, the *Bakke* decision, while striking down a strict quota system, did not deny schools the right to use race as a consideration in the admission process. In *Fulliolove v. Klutznick*,[27] the Court upheld a federal provision requiring that 10 percent of each public works grant go to minority contractors.

LAW ABROAD

Germany

The foundation of Germany's government is the Basic Law (*Grundgesetz*), which went into effect on May 23, 1949, four years after Germany's surrender in World War II. The Basic Law, like the U.S. Constitution, is a democratic constitution containing a formal declaration of human rights. Like England, Germany has a parliamentary government. The government consists of a *Bundestag,* an elected assembly; a federal council; a president; and a chancellor. (The president is the formal chief of state; the chancellor is the head of the federal government.)

Like the U.S. courts, the German courts are strongly independent and have the right to declare laws unconstitutional and void. German judges are bound solely by the codified law and the constitution; in contrast, U.S. judges are generally bound by the principle of *stare decisis*.

Germany's highest court is the Federal Constitutional Court. In 1951, in the *Southwest State Case*, that court first set aside a law as unconstitutional. Thus *Southwest* is known as Germany's *Marbury v. Madison*. In *Marbury*, the U.S. Supreme Court presented elaborate reasoning for the principle of judicial review. In Germany, the law explicitly confers this power on the Federal Constitutional Court.

Japan

The current Japanese constitution was implemented during the occupation of the Allied Powers after World War II. The constitution retained the institution of the monarchy, but the emperor's role is purely ceremonial. A two-house Diet serves as the sole law-making body. The Diet selects a prime minister from among its members. The prime minister selects and heads a cabinet. A majority of the cabinet must be Diet members. The House of Representatives can force the cabinet to resign upon a vote of no confidence.

Japan has an independent judiciary that has the power of judicial review over legislative and executive acts. The Supreme Court of Japan heads the judiciary. The cabinet appoints its members; unlike U.S. Supreme Court justices, they are subject to recall at the next general election and at 10-year intervals.

Japan's constitution has an elaborate, U.S.-inspired bill of rights. Among the rights not found in the U.S. Constitution are the following:

Academic freedom

The right to maintain minimum standards of wholesome and cultured living.

The right to work.

Japan's constitution is unique in that it renounces war.

REVIEW QUESTIONS & PROBLEMS

1. Describe the constitutional allocation of powers among the branches of the federal government. How does this separation of powers protect the citizens of the United States?

2. Business operations often extend across state borders, subjecting businesses to both federal laws and the laws of different states. Would it be advantageous to businesses to deal with a single national jurisdiction instead of a variety of jurisdictions? Explain. Are any constitutional problems inherent in a single national jurisdiction? Explain.

3. A statute enacted by the state of Connecticut provided, for tuition purposes, that the nonresident status of a state university student at the time of application would continue for the student's entire period of attendance at a state university. Does this statute violate the due process clause of the Fourteenth Amendment? Explain.

4. An Oklahoma statute prohibiting the sale of 3.2 percent beer to males under the age of 21 and females under the age of 18 was challenged under the equal protection clause of the Fourteenth Amendment as discriminatory, because males between the ages of 17 and 20 were more likely to be arrested for drunk driving and killed or injured in traffic accidents than were females of the same age group. Do you think the U.S. Supreme Court agreed with this argument? Explain.

5. The state of Illinois adopted a statute that allowed judges to order that defendants in criminal cases be imprisoned if they did not pay a court-ordered fine. Such defendants were to remain in jail until the fine was paid or was satisfied at the rate of $5 per day of imprisonment. This statute was challenged by a defendant convicted of petty theft and sentenced to one year of imprisonment and a $500 fine. The defendant was an indigent (needy and poor) and unable to pay the fine. Therefore he would have been forced to spend an additional 100 days in jail to work off the fine. Does the statute violate the equal protection clause? Explain.

6. Consolidated Edison Company of New York, an electric utility, was prohibited by the New York Public Service Commission from inserting material concern-

ing "the benefits of nuclear power" in its billing envelopes. The commission did not bar the utility from sending bill inserts discussing topics that were not "controversial issues of public policy." The utility challenged the commission's action in court. Eventually, the case reached the U.S. Supreme Court. Based on the text material dealing with the speech of corporations, what ruling do you think the Supreme Court made? Why?

END NOTES

1. 17 U.S. (4 Wheat) 316 (1819).

2. John Marshall served as the fourth chief justice ot the Supreme Court of the United States from 1801 to 1835. Marshall was born in Virginia in 1755. Although he had little formal training in law, he attained great stature while practicing law in his native state. During his tenure as chief justice, he expanded the power of the federal government by expanding the power that the Constitution had granted it and by limiting the power of the states. As a strong advocate of national government, Marshall wrote in one opinion that a narrow construction of the Constitution "would cripple the government." His opinions, noted for their clarity, force, and persuasiveness, strengthened the judicial branch of the federal government.

3. *McCulloch v. Mayland,* 17 U.S. (4 Wheat) 316, 421 (1819).

4. 5 U.S. 137 (1 Cranch) 1803.

5. 22 U.S. 137 (9 Wheat) 1 (1824).

6. 312 U.S. 100 (1941).

7. 379 U.S. 241 (1964).

8. 438 U.S. 234 (1978).

9. 334 U.S. 385 (1948).

10. 436 U.S. 371 (1978).

11. The two amendments that were not ratified specified compensation for members of Congress and provided for the reapportionment of congressional representation.

12. 403 U.S. 713 (1971).

13. 391 U.S. 367 (1968).

14. 109 S. Ct. 2533 (1989).

15. *United States v. Eichman,* 110 S. Ct. 2404 (1990).

16. 435 U.S. 765 (1978).

17. 110 S. Ct. 1391 (1990).

18. 316 U.S. 52 (1924).

19. 425 U.S. 748 (1976).

20. 110 S. Ct. 23 (1989).

21. 478 U.S. 328 (1986).

22. 109 S. Ct. 3028 (1989).

23. In criminal cases no search warrant is necessary for (1) search incident to a lawful arrest, (2) search of an automobile if the automobile will not be available at the time that a search warrant can be obtained, (3) search of things held in plain view when the police are legitimately on the premises, (4) search if consent by the person searched or by the owner of the property searched is voluntarily given, (5) search of a person stopped by a police officer under a reasonable suspicion of a crime, and (6) search in emergency situations in which the person or items searched could be disposed of before a search warrant can be obtained.

24. For sex-based classifications the Supreme Court uses an intermediate scrutiny test—higher than rational basis, lower than strict scrutiny. This is the standard for the intermediate scrutiny test: "Classifications by gender must serve important governmental objectives and must be substantially related to achievement of those objectives." *Craig v. Boren* 429 U.S. 190 (1976).

25. 347 U.S. 483 (1954).

26. 438 U.S. 265 (1978).

27. 448 U.S. 448 (1980).

PART

5

CORPORATE LAW

11. Corporate Law

CHAPTER

11

Corporate Law

Both the complexity of business ventures and the capital necessary to finance them have grown. As a result, managing the inherent risks of new businesses has become increasingly difficult for individuals and small groups. Over the years the corporate form of business organization has greatly increased in importance as a means of dealing with management and finance problems. Still, other forms of business organizations are available. An entrepreneur may choose from a variety of forms. Which one is best depends on the nature of the business and on the characteristics of the individuals who organize it.

This chapter explains the advantages and disadvantages of several forms of business organizations. It then presents some of the most pertinent aspects of corporate law, including the duties and rights of shareholders, directors, and officers. Finally, it examines the termination of corporate existence.

FORMS OF BUSINESS ORGANIZATIONS

Selecting a form of legal organization is one of the first decisions that the founders of a business must make. Businesses range from individual proprietorships and partnerships to giant corporations. Less frequently used forms of business organizations include cooperative associations, joint ventures, and syndicates. This section will discuss the basic structure of each form and will indicate the factors that should be considered in selecting a form.

Factors Used in Selecting a Form of Business Organization

Each form of business organization has advantages and disadvantages. Which form is chosen can well determine whether a business succeeds or fails. Factors that should be considered in selecting a form of business organization are:

1. *Taxes.* The amount of taxes paid can vary greatly for different forms of business organizations. Thus taxes are probably the most crucial factor that should be considered.
2. *Control.* The owners must decide whether complete control over the business is essential. In some forms of business organizations decisions can be made only after consulting with other interested parties, such as partners or a board of directors.
3. *Liability.* In some forms of business organizations, the owner's personal assets are exposed to liability for the obligations of the business. In such forms, these assets can be seized by the creditors of the business.
4. *Capital.* An essential consideration is the amount of capital required to start the business. Some forms of business organizations have a greater ability to attract capital than do other forms.
5. *Ease of Formation.* The difficulty and cost of setting up a business vary with the form of organization. Some forms require compliance with detailed procedures specified by state law. Other forms do not require governmental approval.
6. *Continuity.* If the owner dies, suffers a severe personal injury, or becomes bankrupt, some forms of businesses continue, while others terminate. The problems of the heirs in selling a discontinued business depend on its form of business organization.

With these factors in mind, we can explore and compare forms of business organizations. Table 11-1 compares the sole proprietorship, partnership, and corporation and summarizes the essential factors that should be considered in selecting a form of business organization.

The Sole Proprietorship

Sole proprietorship
a business owned and operated by one person

The least complex form of business organization is the sole proprietorship. A **sole proprietorship** is a business owned and operated by one person. A sole proprietor is considered self-employed because the owner is an active operator of the business. More than three fourths of all the businesses in the United States are sole proprietorships. The vast majority of these firms are small businesses, employing fewer than five workers. Mom-and-pop grocery stores, small restaurants, and bakeries are examples of such businesses that can be found in every city and town.

Partnerships

The most basic form of business involving two or more owners is the partnership. A **partnership** is an association of two or more persons to carry on as co-owners of a business for profit. A partnership is similar to a sole proprietorship but has more than one owner. The owners of an ordinary partnership are called "general partners." The general partners conduct the business, share in its profits, and have an unlimited personal liability to its creditors. Suppose that Adams, Brown, and Clay form an ordinary partnership, with each serving as a general partner. Suppose further that the partnership is unable to pay all of its debts. The partnership creditors, after first proceeding against the partnership assets, could have the court seize the personal assets of Adams, Brown, and Clay and sell them at public auction to pay the creditors.

Partnership
an association of two or more persons to carry on as co-owners of a business for profit

---

Comparison of Forms of Business Organizations   **TABLE 11–1**

	Sole Proprietorship	Partnership	Corporation
Taxation	Owner taxed as individual on net profits	Each partner taxed as individual on pro rata share of net profits, whether or not they are distributed	Double taxation: corporation taxed on the net profits; shareholders taxed on dividend income*
Control	Direct control by owner	Control shared with partners	Shareholders control through election of directors and majority vote on important matters
Capital	Low ability to attract outside capital; limited to contribution of proprietor and borrowed funds	Low ability to attract outside capital; limited to contributions of partners and borrowed funds	High ability to attract outside capital through investment by large numbers of shareholders
Liability	Unlimited liability for the debts of the business	Unlimited liability for the debts of the partnership	Liability limited to amount of investment; no personal liability for corporate debt†
Ease of formation	High ease of formation; need only comply with routine business licensing procedures	High ease of formation; no formal state organizational regulations; created by agreement among partners‡	Low ease of formation; must comply with strict state regulations
Continuity	Terminates upon death or retirement of owner or upon bankruptcy	Terminates upon agreement, death or withdrawal of a partner, or bankruptcy	Can be perpetual; death of shareholder has no effect on existence of corporation

* Corporations that qualify can avoid double taxation by selecting the option provided by Subchapter S of the Internal Revenue Code. If a corporation has 35 or fewer stockholders, it can be treated as a partnership for income tax purposes. The income of Subchapter S corporations is taxed only as personal income to the shareholders.

  The Subchapter S option has become extremely popular since the passage of the Tax Reform Act of 1986. For the first time since 1913, when the income tax was first imposed, the maximum individual tax rates are lower than the corporate tax rates for taxable income over $25,000. A Subchapter S corporation funnels its earnings to the owners. The corporation retains the advantages of limited liability.

† The advantage of limited liability for small corporations is somewhat exaggerated. Ordinarily, the credit strength of a small corporation is somewhat questionable. If a corporation has limited assets and capital, lenders are reluctant to extend credit to it only on the basis of its ability to pay. Thus lenders will usually require its owners, the principal stockholders, to cosign or guarantee loans personally. However, these stockholders are protected from obligations of the corporation imposed by law, such as taxes.

‡ Partnerships are easy to form, but a well-drafted partnership agreement may be 20 pages long and involve a substantial attorney's fee.

Partnerships are less common than sole proprietorships or corporations, but they may be found in many fields. Many partnerships may be found in such professions as law, medicine, and accounting and in such businesses as retailing, wholesaling, and agriculture. To understand this form of business organization, close examination of the definition of partnership is necessary.

Association   A partnership is an **association,** which implies a voluntary coming together. Since a partnership is a voluntary arrangement, if a partner in a law firm has a son who was recently licensed to practice law, he cannot force the other partner or partners to accept his son into the partnership.

Association
a collection of persons who voluntarily joined together to achieve a common objective

Two or More Persons   At least *two persons* are necessary to form a partnership. Ordinarily, one thinks of a person as a human being. However, a partnership can consist of a combination of individuals, a corporation, another partnership, and other associations.

Carrying On a Business   A partnership must be *carrying on a business.* The word *business* includes every trade, occupation, or profession. Partnerships can be formed, for example, by plumbers, businesspersons, certified public accountants, and doctors.

Whether or not a business is being carried on depends on the extent of the undertaking. Suppose that several independent retail clothing stores agreed to purchase a carload of shirts at a discount price with the understanding that the shirts would be divided among them. The stores did not form a partnership, because this single purchase was not "carrying on a business." For a partnership to exist, a series of transactions must be conducted over a period of time.

Co-owners
joint owners of a business

Co-Owners   The members of a partnership must be **co-owners.** This means that they must be joint owners of the *business,* and as such have a voice in its management and a share in its profits. They need not co-own the property used in the business. Conversely, individuals can be co-owners of property and not be partners.

Profit   The purpose of a partnership must be to make a profit, and unless the co-owners of a business share its profits, it will not qualify as a partnership. Suppose that a group of church members holds a bazaar once every month for a year to raise money for the church. The group does not constitute a partnership because its members do not intend to make profits for themselves. Activities conducted by a nonprofit group do not form a partnership.

Partnerships are easy to start. The only requirement is that at least two persons agree to begin a business in the form of a partnership. The partnership agreement may be oral, written, or implied from the conduct of the parties. The conduct of the parties must indicate that they formed a business and intended a relationship that included the essential elements of a partnership—the sharing of profits, losses, and a voice in management.

A partnership agreement need not comply with any particular formalities. However, a well-drafted agreement will contain the following provisions:

1. The name of the partnership. If the partners choose to operate the business under a name other than their own, they must file a certificate in the county records, which ordinarily are located in the county courthouse, and pub-

lish a notice in the local newspaper. For example, if Sam and Joe decide to call their business the Happy Times Pizza Parlor, they are required to file a certificate in the county records. The certificate and a newspaper ad give notice to all persons that they are doing business as the Happy Times Pizza Parlor.

2. The amount of capital that each partner will contribute. When the business is dissolved, if there is any money left after the creditors have been paid, the capital that each partner has contributed is returned.

3. How profits and losses will be shared. If the parties do not agree on this provision, then profits or losses are shared equally, regardless of whether one partner contributes more capital or spends more time running the business than the other.

4. The salaries of the partners, if any. The partners are not entitled to salaries unless the partnership agreement so provides. For example, if Sam spends 60 hours a week operating the pizza parlor but Joe spends only 5 hours a week checking the books, Sam is not entitled to a salary unless the partnership agreement so provides. The law regards the return of profits as compensation for the time and efforts of the partners unless the partnership agreement specifies otherwise.

5. A "buy-and-sell" provision. This provision becomes important if a partner dies or withdraws from the partnership. It determines whether the remaining partner or partners have an option to purchase the interest of that partner, the means for determining the price, and the time and method of payment.

6. The location and nature of the business.

7. The authority of the partners to bind the partnership to contracts.

8. How the business will be managed. This provision covers, for example, who will purchase supplies, keep books, and be in charge of selling.

9. Whether the partnership will pay interest on capital contributed.

10. How the books of the partnership will be kept.

11. The duration of the partnership.

Limited Partnership

In general, a **limited partnership** consists of at least one general partner and one or more limited partners. The duties and liability of the general partners are the same as those of partners in an ordinary partnership. Management of the business is conducted by the general partner or partners. Limited partners are mere investors in the limited partnership.

The distinguishing feature of a limited partnership is that the maximum liability of a limited partner is restricted to the amount of capital that the limited partner contributed to the firm. Suppose Adams, Brown, and Clay form a limited partnership, with Clay participating as a limited partner. If the partnership cannot pay its debts, the personal assets of Adams and Brown stand liable for the entire amount owed. By contrast, Clay's liability is limited to the amount of capital that he invested in the partnership.

However, the exemption of a limited partner from personal liability is conditional. A limited partner who participates in the control of the business may be

Limited partnership
a partnership in which the liability of some partners is limited to the amount of capital they contributed

personally liable to partnership creditors. A majority of the states have adopted the Revised Uniform Limited Partnership Act. The act states that a limited partner is liable as a general partner *only* to those creditors who had actual knowledge of the limited partner's participation in control of the partnership.

Unlike a partner in an ordinary partnership, the limited partner is a creature of state statute. Therefore, the formal requirements of the state statute must be *closely* followed. For example, a "certificate of limited partnership" describing the nature of the partnership and the names of the general partners and limited partners must be filed in the records of the county in which the business is situated. In addition, a notice of the limited partnership must be published in a local newspaper. Some states require that the word *limited* be a part of the partnership name. It is important that such requirements be met. Otherwise, the limited partnership will be treated as a general partnership, with the limited partner having an unlimited personal liability.

The primary advantage of a limited partnership is that it can raise capital by attracting investors who are not interested in managing the business. These investors will share in the partnership's profits and can only lose the money they contributed. Limited partnerships are often used as tax shelters, particularly in real estate operations.

One disadvantage of a limited partnership is that the limited partner cannot participate in the management of the business, which can be a problem in attracting investors. Sometimes the limited partner can, however, do such things as inspect the books and provide advice on the operation of the business, as long as the advice does not amount to control of the business. Control of the business is generally a participation in the decision-making process, with the same degree of control as that of a general partner.

Another disadvantage is that a sale of limited partnership interests is a sale of securities. Thus the sale is subject to regulation by the Securities and Exchange Commission, as discussed in Chapter 17.

LAW ABROAD

Germany

Partnerships and Limited Partnerships   In German law, partnership is reserved for commercial enterprises. While not a legal entity, a partnership is entitled to carry on business and acquire rights in the name of the firm and it may sue or be sued under the name of the partnership. Upon the foundation of a partnership, its name must contain the names of all of the partners or there must be words indicating partnership.

Every partner is entitled and obligated to participate in the management of the business. Some partners may have more or less control in the business, and their remuneration may vary accordingly. The partners are jointly and severally liable for all of the firm's debts and liabilities. Any new partner joining the firm becomes liable for all of its debts. Creditors in a bankruptcy action against the partnership may follow it up by bringing bankruptcy proceedings against each partner.

In a limited partnership, there is at least one partner whose liability is unlimited, along with one or more partners whose liability is limited to the amount of capital that they brought into the business. A limited partner cannot participate in management and unless granted a special power of attorney, cannot represent the partnership in dealings with third parties. A limited partner's name cannot be part of the firm's name.

Japan

Partnerships and Limited Partnerships   Partnership as it is understood in the United States does not exist in Japan. However, two categories of business associations, informal associations and partnership corporations, have features similar to those of U.S. partnerships. An informal association is created when several parties formally agree to contribute to a common undertaking. The association acts through majority votes by its members, but every member is empowered to transact ordinary affairs on its behalf unless specific objections are raised. Profits and losses are shared in proportion to the respective contributions of members unless the association contract provides otherwise. If the duration of the association is not fixed, any member may withdraw at any time, provided the withdrawal does not prejudice the interests of the association at that time.

A partnership corporation is formed through articles of incorporation that state the value of the contribution made by each of its members. A new and independent legal personality results from this type of business association. Managers may be appointed, but every member has the right and duty to administer the affairs of the partnership corporation. In the event of insufficient assets, all members are jointly and severally liable for the firm's obligations. If a specific term for the existence of the partnership corporation has not been set, a member may withdraw with six months' notice.

The limited partnership corporation differs from the partnership corporation in that members may have either unlimited or limited liability for corporate obligations. The liability status of each member must be stated in the articles of incorporation. Members with unlimited liability have rights and duties similar to those of the members of a partnership corporation, while members with limited liability cannot act on behalf of the limited partnership corporation. They are merely entitled to inspect and supervise.

Corporations

Most of the business *sales* in the United States are made by corporations. Nearly all large business firms are corporations. This is so because a sole proprietor or several partners cannot provide sufficient capital to finance a national or multinational business such as General Motors or Exxon. By incorporating, a firm can sell stock and attract investors, who become shareholders.

Not all corporations are large. Many small businesses choose this form of ownership because it provides limited liability for the owners. Statistics indicate that 95 percent of all corporations have fewer than 100 shareholders. Indeed, the greatest concentration of corporations is found in the wholesale and retail fields, and most of the corporations in these fields are small.

A corporation comes into existence by an act of the state. In 1819 the Supreme Court defined a **corporation** as "an artificial being, individual, intangible, and existing only in the contemplation of law." Thus a corporation is a legal entity, which means that it has a legal existence separate and apart from the existence of its owners. For most purposes, sole proprietorships and partnerships are not legal entities.

Corporation
an artificial being that is created through a charter granted by a state and has the right to do business in accordance with the terms of its charter

A corporation consists of the shareholders, who own the business, and the board of directors, whose members the shareholders elect to manage the business. The board elects officers, such as a president and several vice presidents, who run the daily operations of the business.

Since a corporation is a legal entity, it possesses nearly the same rights as a person. It can enter into contracts, buy or sell property, sue or be sued in its own name, and perform other acts that are necessary to carry on a business. Suppose that a corporation needs a certain piece of land. The president, an officer, or some other representative of the corporation negotiates with the seller and signs the contract. However, these acts are done on behalf of the corporation. The corporation owns the land, and title is listed in its name.

LAW ABROAD

Germany

Corporations   There are two principal types of corporations in Germany. These can be formed for a wide variety of purposes, although they are usually formed for a business purpose. The first type is the *Aktiengesellschaft,* a corporation limited by shares, which is equivalent to an American stock corporation. The second type is the *Gesellschaft mit beschränkter Haftung,* a company with limited liability whose equivalent does not exist in American law.

Japan

Corporations   Japan's Commercial Code provides for three types of business corporations or companies: (1) *Gomei Kaisha,* partnership corporations; (2) *Goshi Kaisha,* limited partnership corporations; (3) *Kabushiki Kaisha,* joint stock corporations. All three types may be organized without any special act of government approval by compliance with the appropriate legal regulations concerning formation and subsequent registration. All business corporations have to establish a principal office and register its location; branch offices must also be registered. Of the three types of corporations, the *Kabushiki Kaisha* are the most common type and the one that most closely resembles the Anglo-American stock company. The *Gomei Kaisha* differ fundamentally from Anglo-American partnerships in that a new and independent legal personality is created when one of them is born.

Other Forms of Business Organizations

Although sole proprietorships, partnerships, and corporatons are the dominant forms of business organizations, a few other types are widely used in certain fields. These types include cooperative associations, joint ventures, and syndicates.

Cooperative Associations

Cooperative association
an association owned by its members and operated for their benefit

In general, the **cooperative association,** or "co-op," as it is commonly known, is an association owned by its members and operated for their benefit. Cooperatives are usually organized as corporations. State statutes specify the particular requirements of incorporated co-ops. Like corporations, cooperatives must obtain a charter from the state, but a cooperative differs from a corporation in these respects:

1. The cooperative is owned by the user-members, and each member has only one vote regardless of the number of shares owned.

2. All of the cooperative's capital is owned by the members, but there is a limit to the amount that any member may own.

3. The cooperative pays its members interest on their investments.

4. The members of the cooperative share in its profits in the form of patronage dividends. These are paid according to the amount of business that each member transacts with the cooperative, such as buying and selling through it.

Cooperatives may take the form of partnerships. If so, the members are subject to personal liability.

The largest cooperatives are agricultural cooperatives that market the products grown by their members, for example, Sunkist oranges. Credit unions, which are actually nonprofit savings and loan associations, are one of the most common types of cooperatives. Credit unions hold over $179 billion in assets. One out of every six Americans belongs to a credit union. Typically, these associations limit participation to the employees of a particular employer. To become a member, an employee purchases shares in the credit union, earns interest on the money deposited, and is eligible to borrow money from the credit union.

A type of cooperative that has developed recently is the consumer cooperative. The consumer cooperative buys goods and sells them to its members. It obtains items at discount prices and passes the savings on to its members.

Joint Venture

For all practical purposes a **joint venture** is a form of partnership. The relationship of the parties in a joint venture and the organization of a joint venture are so similar to those of a partnership that the rights, duties, and liabilities of the associates in a joint venture are generally tested by the rules that govern partnerships. The two forms of organization differ in the extent of the business that they undertake. A joint venture is created for a limited purpose or a single transaction. If 30 investors join together to buy 100 acres of farmland near a city, this creates a joint venture. The joint venture ends when the land is divided and the lots are sold.

Joint ventures are becoming the predominant method of large-scale manufacturing investment around the world. A typical example occurs when an American company joins with a foreign company to produce and sell a particular product. For both sides, the joint venture is a means of sharing capital and risk and of utilizing each other's technical strength. General Motors Corporation and Toyota Corporation formed a joint venture to build a new model car in California. At the same time, they both carried on their separate enterprises, which is characteristic of the participants in joint ventures.

Joint venture
a business association created for a limited purpose or a single transaction

Syndicates

A **syndicate,** also called an "investment group," is an association of individuals or companies to finance a particular project. A typical project of syndicates is the construction of an apartment complex. The parties of a syndicate can be partners,

Syndicate
an association of individuals or companies to finance a particular project

limited partners, or shareholders in a corporation. The parties of real estate syndicates are often simply joint owners of property, with no legally recognized business arrangement. Unlike joint ventures, syndicates are financial enterprises and they need not terminate after their purpose has been achieved. A common example of the syndicate form is the underwriting syndicate, a group of investment banking companies that join together to sell a large issue of corporation stocks or bonds.

Franchises

Franchising

granting an individual or a group the right to market the products or services of a parent firm in a particular territory

A common way of doing business in the United States is **franchising.** The franchising relationship is a contractual agreement in which the "franchisor" owns a trade name, trademark, or copyright and distributes goods and services through a "franchisee." The franchisor gives the franchisee the franchise. The franchisee is a local business outlet owned by an independent entrepreneur. The franchisor supplies national advertising and permits the franchisee to use its trade name, trademark, or copyright and its marketing techniques. In return, the franchisee ordinarily pays a percentage of its gross sales to the franchisor. Major franchisors include McDonald's, H&R Block Tax Services, and Holiday Inn.

FORMATION OF THE CORPORATION

Promoter

the individual or legal entity that does the legal groundwork for incorporation

If after weighing the advantages and disadvantages of the forms of business organizations, a person selects the corporate form, it is important to contract with a **promoter,** the individual or legal entity that does the groundwork for the establishment of a corporation. The formation and operation of corporations are largely controlled by state law, which can vary greatly from one state to another. Thus an important decision of promoters is selecting the state of incorporation.

Role of Promoters

Promoters bring corporations into existence. In performing their functions, they enter into contracts on behalf of proposed corporations.

Functions of Promoters

A promoter discovers a business opportunity and investigates its feasibility. Recognizing its profit potential, the promoter brings together the resources and personnel needed to operate the new enterprise. The promoter finds a suitable location for the enterprise and either purchases the property or negotiates a lease. Contracts are entered into for the equipment and materials necessary to the future corporation. Personnel to operate the corporation are hired. Most important, the promoter finds individuals who are willing to finance the corporation—to buy shares in it and to lend it money. The promoter plans advertising and completes the paperwork necessary to begin business operations. Essentially, the promoter is the motivating force behind the formation of a corporation.

Quite often, two or more promoters are involved in the creation of a corporation. Such promoters are engaged in a *joint venture* on behalf of the proposed corporation. A promoter is not always an individual; a partnership or a corporation can also be a promoter.

Two important legal questions arise in creating the new corporation: Is the promoter liable on the contracts entered into before incorporation? Is the corporation liable on those contracts? These questions will be answered in the next section.

Liability on Contracts

To secure necessary facilities and financial backing, the promoter enters into contracts with third parties on behalf of the new corporation. That corporation is not automatically liable on such preincorporation contracts. It becomes liable if the board of directors chooses to adopt the contracts. Thus the board of directors is free to reject contracts made by the promoter.

The corporation may impliedly adopt a preincorporation contract by knowingly accepting its benefits. Assume that the promoter enters into a preincorporation contract for the purchase of raw materials. After incorporation the board does not formally adopt the contract, but the manager accepts a partial delivery of the raw materials and begins using them in the manufacturing process. The manager's actions constitute an acceptance of the contract, and the corporation is therefore bound to accept and pay for the remaining raw materials.

To obtain the agreement of third parties, the promoter generally must accept personal liability on preincorporation contracts. In this situation the promoter remains liable if the corporation is never formed or if the new corporation refuses to act on the contracts.

Promoters can, however, protect themselves. The contract can expressly provide that the promoter is not liable if the corporation is never formed or if it does not adopt the contract. Obviously, many third parties are reluctant to enter into such contracts.

Choosing a State of Incorporation

A corporation is a legal entity created under state law. Since the individual states have the right to charter corporations, they also have the right to impose reasonable regulations on them. State corporation laws offer varying degrees of flexibility and operating freedom. This makes choosing the state in which to form a new corporation an important decision.

Ordinarily, a corporation incorporates in the state where it will conduct most of its business. If a corporation plans to do business in several states, the laws governing corporations in these states should be compared. A corporation should not incorporate in a state where it does not plan to do any business, since this might lead to increased organizational expense or double taxation. Which state should be chosen depends on several factors:

1. State corporate taxes. State share transfer taxes, franchise taxes, and income taxes differ among the states.
2. The general powers of corporations in the state.
3. The organizational fees and the amount of capital required to start a corporation.
4. The shareholder approval necessary for certain business transactions, such as mergers and consolidations with other corporations.

5. The records that the state requires of a corporation. The laws of many states give management greater flexibility to attract corporate business.

6. The flexibility that the state corporate statutes grant to management in running the corporation. Whether or not these statutes have been interpreted by court decisions is also important. A well-tested body of case law eliminates uncertainty as to their meaning.[1]

LAW ABROAD

Germany

Foreign Corporations   Foreign corporations can do business in Germany by means of a branch office, a subsidiary, or a joint venture with a German company. Most foreign corportions find a joint venture with a German company to be preferable, because establishing a branch office or a subsidiary exposes them to much higher taxes. Branch offices are seldom used—generally for special reasons. A bank may use a branch office with access to the entire resources of the parent bank for prestige reasons. A corporation may establish a branch office from which it expects losses for several years because the losses can be set off against the profits of the parent corporation.

All forms of commercial activity, within certain rules, are open to foreign corporations. There are no requirements as to the nationality of the employees or managers of a foreign corporation doing business in Germany.

Foreign companies—companies incorporated or established under foreign law and doing business in Germany—are not subject to the codetermination laws. Subsidiaries incorporated in Germany are usually subject to codetermination. (Codetermination is discussed in a later section.)

Requirements for Incorporation

After the state in which to incorporate has been chosen, the articles of incorporation, referred to as the "charter," are prepared. The charter is a legal document written by an attorney and signed by the incorporators. The incorporators are the individuals who apply to the state for incorporation. A majority of the states now require a minimum of only one incorporator. Thus one person can form a corporation. In general, the articles of incorporation contain the following information:

1. *Name and address of the proposed corporation.* The name must include the word *corporation, company,* or *incorporated* or the abbreviation for one of these words. For example, creditors who deal with Smith & Sons, Inc. will know that the business is a corporation and that Smith, his sons, and other investors therefore have limited liability. To avoid confusion, the name cannot be deceptively similar to the name of another corporation doing business within the state.

2. *The purposes for which the corporation has been organized.* A business corporation may be formed for any lawful purpose. Banks, insurance companies, public utilities, and railroads, however, cannot incorporate under the general corporation statutes. These businesses are required to incorporate under specialized statutes.

3. *Financial information about the corporation.* The number of shares that the corporation has authority to issue and the number that it has actually sold must be given. The characteristics of each share class must also be given.

4. *The duration of the corporation.* The charter for most corporations states that its existence "shall be perpetual." Thus the life of the corporation is not affected by the death, retirement, or bankruptcy of a stockholder. This assures creditors, employees, and owners a degree of security. As long as a corporation is successful, it may continue indefinitely.

5. *Names and addresses of the incorporators.* When the articles of incorporation are filed with the secretary of state, a filing fee must be paid. This fee is usually calculated as a percentage of the number of shares that the articles of incorporation authorize the corporation to issue. Some states also require that the articles of incorporation be published in a newspaper of general circulation in the county where the corporate office is situated.

Certificate of Incorporation

The corporation comes into existence upon the issuance of a certificate of incorporation, which is also called a charter. The date of the certificate's issuance is important for record-keeping and other business purposes. A corporation is a creature of the state and exists only by the state's permission. The certificate of incorporation is a state's grant of power to conduct business in the form of a corporation. Figure 11-1 presents an example.

Organizational Meetings

After the certificate of incorporation has been issued, the incorporators hold an organizational meeting at which they elect a board of directors. The first board of directors conducts another organizational meeting to issue stock, adopt the promoter's contracts, elect officers, adopt a corporate seal, and—probably the most important item of business—adopt bylaws.

Bylaws are rules governing the internal affairs of the corporation. They contain provisions specifying the time and place of the annual shareholders' meeting, the required notice for meetings, the necessary quorum for conducting a meeting, the number and qualifications of directors, and other provisions regulating the internal management of the corporation. The bylaws must be consistent with the articles of incorporation and state laws. Unlike the articles of incorporation, the bylaws are not filed with a state official.

Bylaws
the rules governing the internal affairs of a corporation

Most state corporation statutes provide that the board of directors can amend the bylaws. However, the shareholders are empowered to repeal or change amendments adopted by the board of directors.

MANAGEMENT OF THE CORPORATION

Role of Shareholders

A share of stock represents ownership in the corporation. As owners of the corporation, shareholders share its profits and at dissolution they share its assets. Shareholders also perform various functions by voting at properly called meetings.

The most important shareholder functions are (1) election and removal of directors, (2) amendment of articles and bylaws, and (3) approval of extraordinary corporate transactions. Shareholders can sue the corporation to enforce their legal rights and assure the proper performance of their functions.

Shareholders' Meetings

Shareholders cannot act individually. Their power is exercised collectively at *shareholders' meetings.* However, the corporation laws of most states now permit shareholders to act without a meeting by unanimous written agreement among themselves. Still, the shareholders' meeting is the most common method for the exercise of shareholder functions.

FIGURE 11–1   **An Example of a Certificate of Incorporation**

CERTIFICATION OF INCORPORATION

OF

SPECIALTY MANUFACTURING, INC.

We, the undersigned, desiring to form a corporation for profit under the general corporation laws of the state of New York, do hereby make, subscribe, acknowledge, and file this certificate for that purpose, as follows:

Article I.   The name of the proposed corporation is Specialty Manufacturing, Inc.

Article II.   The principal office of the corporation is to be located in the city of Newton, county of Lexington.

Article III.   Richard Lewis, with offices located at 1920 Broadway, Newton, New York, is the registered agent on whom process may be served.

Article IV.   The purposes of the corporation are to design and manufacture custom industrial machine parts and to engage in any other lawful activity for which corporations may be formed under the laws of the state of New York.

Article V.   The term of existence of the corporation shall be perpetual.

Article VI.   The amount of capital stock of the corporation shall be $500,000 divided into 1,000 shares of preferred stock, par value $100 per share, and 40,000 shares of common stock, par value $10 per share.

Article VII.   (a) Each share of common stock shall be entitled to one (1) vote on all matters. (b) Cumulative voting shall not be permitted on any matter.

Article VIII.   The names and the post office addresses of the three directors of the corporation, who are also subscribers to this Certificate of Incorporation, and the number of shares of common stock that each agrees to subscribe for, are:

David Jackson, 133 Davis Road, Newton, 3,000 shares
Ralph Roberts, 121 Broad Street, Newton, 3,000 shares
Arthur Stone, 63 Laurel Avenue, Newton, 3,000 shares

Article IX.   All of the subscribers to this certificate are of full age; a majority of them are citizens of the United States; and at least one of them is a resident of the state of New York. In witness whereof, we have made, signed, and acknowledged this certificate this first day of August, 1991.

(Signed) _David Jackson_____

(Signed) _Ralph Roberts_____

(Signed) _Arthur Stone_____

Annual and Special Meetings

There are two types of shareholders' meetings, annual and special. Most of the state corporation statutes require *annual meetings* of shareholders. The most important purpose of these meetings is to elect the board of directors. Shareholders' meetings may also act on the directors' proposals for stock option plans and amendments to the articles of incorporation. *Special meetings* are called to transact business that cannot wait until the next annual meeting. A typical example is a special meeting called to obtain approval of the director's resolution for a merger with another corporation. A special meeting of shareholders can be called by the directors or by shareholders with 10 percent or more of the voting shares.

Notice of Meeting

State laws require that *written notification* of a shareholders' meeting be sent to each shareholder a reasonable time before the meeting is to be held. The notice must state the place, date, and time of the meeting. For a special meeting, the notice must state the purposes of the meeting. The business transacted at a special meeting must be limited to the purposes stated in the notice.

Any actions taken at a shareholders' meeting for which proper notice has not been given is legally ineffective. For example, the election of directors or the approval of corporate action at such a meeting will be void and will have to be done again at a meeting for which proper notice has been given. Attendance at a shareholders' meeting is an automatic waiver of notice, unless the shareholder attends only to object to the holding of the meeting and the lack of proper notice. A shareholder can also waive the notice requirement by signing a written waiver of notice before or after the meeting.

Quorum at Meetings

Official shareholder action cannot be taken at a meeting, unless a **quorum** of shareholders is present. The quorum requirements for a shareholders' meeting are set out in the bylaws or the articles of incorporation. A quorum is usually at least one third of a corporation's outstanding shares.

Quorum
the number of share-holders' votes required to transact business at a shareholders' meeting

Voting Rights of Shareholders

The voting rights of a shareholder depend on the type of stock that the shareholder owns. Corporations can issue two types of stock, preferred and common, but if they issue only one type, it will be common stock. Owners of common stock share in the profits and assets of the corporation in proportion to the number of shares they own. These shareholders enjoy no special rights or privileges over other classes of stock. Ordinarily, only owners of common stock have voting rights.

Preferred stock may be issued if it is authorized by the articles of incorporation. Even though owners of preferred stock usually have no voting rights, this class of stock has rights superior to the rights of common stock. Holders of preferred shares receive preference in the distribution of dividends and in the distribution of assets if the business is dissolved.

Cumulative voting

a system of voting in which each share of common stock is entitled to one vote for each director that is to be elected

Voting pool

an agreement among shareholders to vote their combined stock in accordance with a plan

Proxy

a written authorization directing the person holding it to vote the shares of the named shareholder; also the person with the authority to vote the shares

Owners of common stock are usually entitled to one vote per share. If Mary Brennan owns 5,000 shares of common stock, she can cast 5,000 votes. Some states require **cumulative voting** in the election of officers. Under this plan, each share of common stock is entitled to one vote for each director that is to be elected. If 10 directors are to be elected, Mary Brennan has 50,000 votes, which she may cast for one candidate or divide among a number of candidates. The purpose of cumulative voting is to give minority shareholders an opportunity to be represented on the board of directors.

Cumulative voting becomes especially important if voting pools are used. In a **voting pool,** smaller shareholders come together and vote their combined stock in accordance with a plan, such as electing two or three members to the board of directors.

Shareholders can cast their votes without attending shareholders' meetings. A written authorization, called a **proxy,** directs the person holding it—the appointee—to vote the shares of the named shareholder. Both the appointee and the written authorization are referred to as a "proxy." Because most shareholders do not attend the shareholders' meeting in person, proxies are an essential means of attaining a quorum.

Proxy voting is often also the means that management uses to control a corporation. Management may solicit proxies prior to the shareholders' meeting by sending information to the shareholders and asking those who will not attend the next meeting to appoint as their proxy a director of the corporation or another individual friendly to management. Most shareholders will sign and return the proxy statement, enhancing management's control. Figure 11-2 presents an example of a corporate proxy.

Both the federal government and state governments have extensive laws regulating the offering and sale of stock and other securities by corporations. These laws are discussed in detail in Chapter 17. Chapter 17 also contains an extensive discussion of the regulation of proxy solicitation.

FIGURE 11–2

Example of a Corporate Proxy

KNOW ALL MEN BY THESE PRESENTS that I, the undersigned, being the owner of <u>500</u> shares of the capital stocks of the XYZ Corporation, state of Utopia, do hereby constitute and appoint <u>Holly Rand</u> and <u>Matt Smith</u>, my true and lawful attorneys, for me and in my name, place, and stead, with power of substitution, to vote as my proxy all shares of the undersigned for the election of directors and upon any and all matters that may be considered at the regular, annual meeting of stockholders of the XYZ Corporation, to be held at the offices of the said company at <u>113 Cedar Street</u> in the city of <u>Pleasantown</u>, Utopia on the <u>24th</u> day of <u>November</u>, <u>1991</u>, or at any meeting or meetings held in lieu of, or in substitution for, said annual meeting, or at any adjourned meeting thereof, and threat to vote the number of votes or shares of stocks the undersigned would be entitled to vote if personally present, as fully and with the same effect as the undersigned might or could do if personally present.

In witness thereof, I, <u>Paige Adams</u>, have hereunto set my hand this <u>19th</u> day of <u>September</u>, <u>1991</u>.

Witness: <u>Stacy Donaldson</u>   /s/ <u>Paige Adams</u>
                                                                         Stockholder

Election and Removal of Directors

The most important power of shareholders is control over the corporate directors' positions. The corporation's shareholders elect the board of directors at the regular, annual shareholders' meeting. Most of the state corporation laws require three directors, but provide that the number of directors need not exceed the number of shareholders. Thus a corporation with only one shareholder needs only one director in order to satisfy these laws.

An elected director generally holds office until the next annual meeting. However, shareholders have the right to remove directors with or without cause. Under the common law, shareholders have always had the power to remove directors for cause, such as failing to attend a specified number of directors' meetings, acting adversely to the corporation's interests, or committing fraud on the corporation. Today, states permit shareholders to remove a director without cause at any time. Such action requires a hearing and a majority vote by stockholders, and is subject to review by courts.[2]

LAW ABROAD

Germany

Codetermination of Corporations   Many types of German corporations are required by law to have supervisory boards, half of whose members are elected by employees and half by shareholders. The purpose of this requirement is to give employees and labor unions a larger voice in determining their economic future. Enterprises in the mining and steel-making industries have their own distinct codetermination scheme, while enterprises in other industries are covered by more general legislative schemes.

The Codetermination Law of May 4, 1976, illustrates how codetermination works. Under this law, a supervisory board of 12 members (six shareholders' representatives, four employee representatives, and two union representatives) is required in certain types of corporations with over 2,000 employees but not more than 10,000. The supervisory board elects one of its members as chairman and another as vice chairman. The supervisory board appoints the members of the corporation's board of management. Codetermination is found in many types of German business enterprises, but its features vary according to the size of the corporation, the type of corporation, and the nature of the corporation's activities.

Amendment of Articles of Incorporation

Any amendment to the articles of incorporation must be approved by the shareholders. Since the shareholders own the corporation, their ownership rights will be affected if its structure is modified by amendment. To amend the articles of incorporation, the board of directors ordinarily adopts a resolution stating the proposed amendment. The shareholders entitled to vote are then given proper notice of the proposed amendment and the meeting at which action will be taken on it. The amendment is adopted if it is approved by a majority of the shares voted at that meeting. Since the original articles of incorporation are filed with the secretary of state's office, amendments must also be filed.

Extraordinary Corporate Transactions

Extraordinary corporate transactions also require shareholder approval. The board of directors conducts most corporate affairs, but the shareholders have managerial control over extraordinary transactions. A special meeting of shareholders is usually called for the approval of such transactions. Shareholder approval is mandatory because of the potential effects of extraordinary transactions on the ownership of the corporation. Since the shareholders own the corporation and their interests will be affected by such transactions, these should be submitted to them for their approval. Extraordinary corporate transactions include mergers, consolidations, and the sale of substantially all corporate assets. In mergers and consolidations two corporations are usually combined. Obviously, the shareholders of the two corporations should be given the opportunity to decide whether they approve such a transaction.

Shareholders' Rights of Action

Shareholders, as the owners of a corporation, can take legal action to protect their interests. Basically, there are three types of shareholder lawsuits: (1) *individual lawsuits,* in which an individual shareholder sues the corporation to enforce his or her rights under the share contract; (2) *class action suits,* in which a number of shareholders sue the corporation collectively when their claims arise out of the same facts; and (3) *shareholder derivative lawsuits,* in which a shareholder or a group of shareholders sue third parties on the corporation's behalf when harm has been done to the corporation. Shareholder derivative lawsuits are the most important type.

Shareholder Derivative Lawsuit

When a corporation suffers a wrong, its directors usually file suit in the corporation's name. If the directors fail to act, for whatever reason, a shareholder or a group of shareholders may file a derivative lawsuit. In this type of action, the suit is on behalf of the corporation to assert the corporation's claims against managerial officers or third parties. The shareholder or shareholders initiate the suit, but the corporation is named as the plaintiff. Any recovery belongs to the corporation.

A derivative suit can be brought to redress harm done to the corporation or to recover benefits that directors or officers have diverted from the corporation. Excessive employee salaries, secret profits by employees, waste of corporate assets, or payment of unauthorized dividends are situations in which shareholder derivative lawsuits have been brought. Such lawsuits are allowed because the shareholders, as owners of the corporation, are affected by any harm done to it.

In past years the shareholder derivative suit was frequently used to harass directors and officers. Some shareholders threatened such suits to force the corporation to purchase their stock at an exorbitant price or to make a lucrative, out-of-court settlement. To control these abuses, states imposed strict requirements that a shareholder must meet before bringing a derivative suit. The two most important requirements are: (1) the shareholder must have owned the stock when the alleged wrong occurred, and (2) the shareholder must make a prior demand on the directors to bring suit on behalf of the corporation. This gives the directors a reasonable amount of time to correct the alleged wrong to the corporation.

The following case illustrates the importance of making a prior demand on the directors in a shareholder derivative suit.

LEWIS v. GRAVES
U.S. COURT OF APPEALS, SECOND CIRCUIT
701 F.2d 245 (1985)

Harry Lewis, a shareholder of J. Ray McDermott & Co., Inc. (McDermott), instituted a shareholder derivative suit on behalf of McDermott on March 28, 1978. His complaint challenged the propriety of a merger of McDermott with another corporation and a distribution of stock to officers and directors under a stock plan. The trial court dismissed his complaint because he had not made a demand on the directors of McDermott to institute a suit or take over his derivative action. On appeal, Lewis asserted that such a demand was excused because of the doctrine of futility.

CARDAMONE, CIRCUIT JUDGE

We review on this appeal the single issue of whether the district court erred in dismissing plaintiff's shareholder derivative suit for failure to make a demand upon the directors of defendant J. Ray McDermott & Co., Inc. (McDermott).

Requirements for demand upon directors by a plaintiff who pursues the extraordinary remedy of a derivative suit have been recognized for over a century in this country. Thus the Supreme Court's statement that a derivative plaintiff must show to the satisfaction of the court that he has exhausted all the means within his reach to obtain, within the corporation itself, the redress of his grievances, and this [effort] must be made apparent to the court, is still a useful guide.

We [now] focus on the primary purposes of the demand rule. The rule is intended to give the derivative corporation itself the opportunity to take over a suit which was brought on its behalf in the first place, and thus to allow the directors the chance to occupy their normal status as conductors of the corporation's affairs. Permitting corporations to assume control over shareholder derivative suits also has numerous practical advantages. Corporate management may be in a better position to pursue alternative remedies, resolving grievances without burdensome and expensive litigation. Deference to directors' judgments may also result in the termination of meritless actions brought solely for their settlement or harassment value. Moreover, where litigation is appropriate, the derivative corporation will often be in a better position to bring or assume the suit because of superior financial resources and knowledge of the challenged transactions.

Despite the strong policy and practical advantages favoring exhaustion of intracorporate remedies, the demand requirement is not without exception. Under the law of this circuit, demand need not be made where "futile." As correctly recognized by the district court, the decision as to whether a plaintiff's allegations of futility are sufficient to excuse demand depends on the particular facts of each case and lies within the discretion of the district court. Thus the district court's holding—that plaintiff's allegations of futility were insufficient—cannot be reversed unless it constituted an abuse of discretion. We find none.

Demand is presumptively futile where the directors are antagonistic, adversely interested, or involved in the transactions attacked. Pointing to the fact that all of the McDermott directors at the time of the complaint had previously approved the Babcock acquisition and the Stock Plans distributions, plaintiff argues that their acquiescence in the dealings complained of was sufficient "involvement" to excuse demand. We agree with the district court, however, that absent specific allegations of self-dealing or bias on the part of a majority of the board, mere approval and acquiescence are insufficient to render demand futile.

Excusing demand on the mere basis of prior board acquiescence would obviate the need for demand in practically every case. The single fact that the plaintiff named as defendants more than a majority—in this case all—of McDermott's then serving directors in our view falls short of excusing demand. To construe it as sufficient would mean that plaintiffs could readily circumvent the demand requirement merely by naming as defendants all members of the derivative corporation's board. Permitting plaintiffs to employ this tactic would eviscerate a rule that this Court observes.

Affirmed.

Legal Issues

1. What is the essential purpose of the demand rule? Explain.
2. In what type of situation does an exception to the demand rule arise? Discuss.

Ethical Issues

1. Should a shareholder be permitted to bring a lawsuit to compel a corporation to adopt a code of ethics? Why? Should a shareholder be permitted to bring a derivative suit to enforce a corporation's code of ethics? Why?
2. Is there an ethical basis for the requirement that before bringing a derivative suit, a shareholder must demand that the corporation's board of directors act? Discuss. Is there an ethical basis for judical recognition of exceptions to the requirement that before bringing a derivative suit, a shareholder must comply with the demand requirement discussed in *Lewis v. Graves*? Explain.

ROLE OF THE BOARD OF DIRECTORS

State corporation laws provide that a board of directors is to manage the business and affairs of a corporation. The board of directors, therefore, is the governing body of a corporation. As such, it elects and appoints corporate officers, approves corporate dividends, and makes policy decisions affecting the corporation. It delegates much of the daily business of the corporation to the corporate officers. Thus its role is a supervisory one. In managing the corporation, it must be concerned with objectives other than the profit motive.

Purposes of Corporation from Directors' Viewpoint

The profit motive is the reason a business exists. Thus, as shapers of corporate policy, directors are driven by the need to assure the financial success of the corporation. However, they must be concerned with more than the blind pursuit of profit. Corporations, like other business entities, must act as responsible members of the business community. The restatement of a nonbinding but judicially persuasive collection of "model" corporation law offers guidance in this area:

The Objective and Conduct of the Business Corporation

Corporate law should provide that the objective of the business corporation is to conduct business activities with a view to corporate profit and shareholder gain, except that, even if corporate profit and shareholder gain are not thereby enhanced, the corporation, in the conduct of its business:

(a) is obliged, to the same extent as a natural person, to act within the boundaries set by law,

(b) may properly take into account ethical principles that are generally recognized as relevant to the conduct of business, and

(c) may devote resources, within reasonable limits, to public welfare, humanitarian, educational, and philanthropic purposes.

Meetings of the Board of Directors

A director acting in his or her individual capacity has no authority in the management of the corporation. The directors carry out their duties as the governing body of the corporation through meetings. Directors' meetings are either regular or special. The time and date of regular meetings are established in the bylaws. In small corporations, regular meetings may be scheduled only once a year since the directors are usually active in the business and familiar with its daily operations. In large corporations, the directors typically hold regular meetings once a month. Unless required by the bylaws, notice of regular meetings does not have to be given to directors. When special meetings are necessary, reasonable notice must be given to each director.

At meetings, action is taken through formal resolutions adopted by a majority of the directors present. Each director has only one vote regardless of his or her financial interest in the company. A quorum (consisting of a majority of the directors) must be present for any action taken at a directors' meeting to be valid. Unlike shareholders, directors are not allowed to vote by proxy. To take part in a decision, they must be present at the meeting. This requirement reflects the value that state legislatures place on consultation and collective judgment.

A majority of the states now permit directors to act without calling a meeting. For such action to be effective, all of the directors must give their written consent to it.

The board quite often establishes "executive committees" of its members. These committees can make ordinary management decisions between regular meetings of the entire board. They also make recommendations on special topics or projects to the board. This committee system takes advantage of the particular experience and knowledge of the individual directors.

Officers

The officers of a corporation manage its daily business activities. State statutes generally specify that a corporation must have at least a president, a secretary, and a treasurer. The board may also appoint one or more vice presidents who are responsible for certain functions of the corporation, for example, a vice president of marketing and a vice president of finance. An individual can usually hold more than one corporate office. However, most states do not allow one person to be both president and secretary. The corporation's bylaws establish the number of officers and the general duties and authority of each officer.

Elected and supervised by the board of directors, the officers of a corporation have varied responsibilities. The president nearly always serves on the board of directors. One of the president's important duties is to preside over both share-holders' and directors' meetings. The vice president presides over such meetings if the president is unable to attend. The treasurer controls the corporation funds. He or she binds the corporation on all receipts, checks, and business transacted by the treasurer's office. The secretary, who is usually an attorney, keeps the minutes of all meetings and the written records of the corporation. Besides the president, other officers may serve as members of the board of directors.

Unlike directors, the officers are agents of the corporation. Under agency law, a principal is liable for the contracts entered into on its behalf if the agent had authority to act for the principal. Thus the corporation is bound by the actions of its officers acting within the scope of their authority. (Agency relationships are discussed in Chapter 12.)

The officers serve at the discretion of the board of directors. A majority vote of the directors, with or without cause, can remove an officer.

Both the officers and the directors of a corporation have special duties because of their positions. Their knowledge and skill should be used only to further the best interest of the corporation.

DUTIES OF OFFICERS AND DIRECTORS

Directors and officers owe the corporation a duty of due care and diligence and a duty of loyalty. They are prohibited from taking personal advantage of business opportunities that belong to the corporation. As previously indicated, the corporation or shareholders can bring suit against directors and officers who breach their duties to the corporation.

Duty of Due Care and Diligence

In making business decisions, directors and officers have a duty to exercise due care and diligence. In most states the standard set for directors and officers is that they must act in good faith with such care as an ordinarily prudent person in a like position would use under similar circumstances. Thus a director or officer who failed to inspect important corporate financial records has violated the duty of due care and diligence, since an ordinarily prudent director or officer would have inspected these records.

However, courts have recognized that business management can be risky and uncertain. A doctrine known as the **business judgment rule** holds that directors and officers are not liable for good faith errors in judgment. This doctrine protects directors and officers as long as they act in good faith with the corporation's interests in mind. Although directors and officers are held to a standard of due care and diligence, courts recognize that they can make honest mistakes.

Business judgment rule
the doctrine holding that the directors and officers of a corporation are not liable for good faith errors in judgment

Suppose that the board decides to spend several million dollars for new machinery. Projections indicate that the new machinery will decrease the production cost of a product from 85 cents per unit to 70 cents per unit. Instead, it increases the production cost to 95 cents per unit. Since the directors made an honest mistake of judgment, no breach of duty occurred.

Directors and officers are liable for negligence, either in their actions or in their failures to take action. Suppose that the board failed to take out casualty insurance on the corporation's assets when it was obvious that the corporation should carry such insurance. If a loss occurred, the directors have violated their duty of due care and diligence. They obviously failed to exercise good business judgment.

In the following case the New Jersey Supreme Court faced the issue of whether a director was negligent in not noticing and trying to prevent misappropriation of corporate funds.

FRANCIS v. UNITED JERSEY BANK
SUPREME COURT OF NEW JERSEY
432 A.2d 814 (1981)

The directors and sole shareholders of Pritchard & Baird Intermediaries Corporation (Pritchard & Baird) were Lillian Pritchard; her husband, Charles Pritchard, Sr.; and their sons, Charles, Jr., and William. Charles, Sr., who was also the chief executive officer, maintained close control over the corporation from 1964 to 1968. During this period he began the practice of withdrawing excess corporate funds and identifying them on the corporate books as "shareholder loans." He repaid these "loans" at the end of each year.

In 1968 Charles, Jr., became president and William became executive vice president, thus taking over control of Pritchard & Baird. Charles, Sr., became ill in 1971, and from that time until his death in 1973 he was not involved in the affairs of the corporation. Beginning in 1970, Charles, Jr., and William siphoned funds from the corporation in the guise of "loans." Unlike their father, however, they never paid back the amounts they took. By October 1975, these "shareholder loans" totaled over $12 million. Soon afterward Pritchard & Baird went bankrupt. Lillian Pritchard, while ostensibly a director of the corporation, took no active part in it and paid no attention to its affairs. Even though her husband had warned her that Charles, Jr., would "take the shirt off her back," she did not perform her duties as a director. After her husband's death, her health deteriorated. She died in 1978.

This action was brought on behalf of creditors of Pritchard & Baird to recover over $10 million from Lillian Pritchard's estate. The plaintiffs asserted that she had been negligent in her duties as director, thus making her personally liable for the losses caused by the wrongdoing of her sons. The trial court ruled in favor of the plaintiff.

POLLACK, J., JUSTICE

The primary issue on this appeal is whether a corporate director is personally liable in negligence for the failure to prevent the misappropriation of funds by other directors who were also officers and shareholders of the corporation.

Individual liability of a corporate director for acts of the corporation is a prickly problem. Generally, directors are accorded broad immunity and are not insurers of corporate activities. The problem is particularly nettlesome when a third party asserts that a director, because of nonfeasance, is liable for losses caused by acts of insiders, who in this case were officers, directors, and shareholders. Determination of the liability of Mrs. Pritchard requires findings that she had a duty to the clients of Pritchard & Baird, that she breached that duty, and that her breach was a proximate cause of their losses.

The New Jersey Business Corporation Act makes it incumbent upon directors to

> discharge their duties in good faith and with that degree of diligence, care, and skill which ordinarily prudent men would exercise under similar circumstances in like positions.

[D]irectors must discharge their duties in good faith and act as ordinarily prudent persons would under similar circumstances in like positions.

As a general rule, a director should acquire at least a rudimentary understanding of the business of the corporation. Accordingly, a director should become familiar with the fundamentals of the business in which the corporation is engaged.

Directors are under a continuing obligation to keep informed about the activities of the corporation. Otherwise, they may not be able to participate in the overall management of corporate affairs. Directors may not shut their eyes to corporate misconduct and then claim that because they did not see the misconduct, they did not have a duty to look.

Directorial management does not require a detailed inspection of day-to-day activities, but rather a general monitoring of corporate affairs and policies. Accordingly, a director is well advised to attend board meetings regularly.

Regular attendance does not mean that directors must attend every meeting, but that directors should attend meetings as a matter of practice.

While directors are not required to audit corporate books, they should maintain familiarity with the financial status of the corporation by a regular review of financial statements. In some circumstances, directors may be charged with assuring that bookkeeping methods conform to industry custom and usage.

Of some relevance in this case is the circumstance that the financial records disclose the "shareholders' loans."

In certain circumstances, the fulfillment of the duty of a director may call for more than mere objection and resignation. Sometimes a director may be required to seek the advice of counsel. The duty to seek the assistance of counsel can extend to areas other than the interpretation of corporation instruments. Modern corporate practice recognizes that on occasion a director should seek outside advice. A director may require legal advice concerning the propriety of his or her own conduct, the conduct of other officers and directors, or the conduct of the corporation. In appropriate circumstances, a director would be well advised to consult with regular corporate counsel (or his own legal adviser) at any time in which he is doubtful regarding proposed action. Sometimes the duty of a director may require more than consulting with outside counsel. A director may have a duty to take reasonable means to prevent illegal conduct by codirectors; in any appropriate case, this may include threat of suit.

A director is not an ornament, but an essential component of corporate governance. Consequently, a director cannot protect himself behind a paper shield bearing the motto "dummy director." The New Jersey Business Corporation Act, in imposing a standard of ordinary care on all directors, confirms that dummy, figurehead, and accommodation directors are anachronisms with no place in New Jersey law.

In general, the relationship of a corporate director to the corporation and its stockholders is that of a fiduciary. Shareholders have a right to expect that directors will exercise reasonable supervision and control over the policies and practices of a corporation. The institutional integrity of a corporation depends upon the proper discharge by directors of those duties.

Mrs. Pritchard should have obtained and read the annual statements of financial condition of Pritchard & Baird. Although she had a right to rely upon financial statements prepared in accordance with [New Jersey statute], such reliance would not excuse her conduct. The reason is that those statements disclosed on their face the misappropriation of funds.

From those statements, she should have realized that, as of January 31, 1970, her sons were withdrawing substantial funds under the guise of "Shareholders' Loans." The financial statements for each fiscal year commencing with that of January 31, 1970, disclosed that the working capital deficits and the "loans" were escalating in tandem. Detecting a misappropriation of funds would not have required special expertise or extraordinary diligence; a cursory reading of the financial statements would have revealed the pillage. Thus, if Mrs. Pritchard had read the financial statements, she would have known that her sons were converting funds. When financial statements demonstrate that insiders are bleeding a corporation to death, a director should notice and try to stanch the flow of blood.

In summary, Mrs. Pritchard was charged with the obligation of basic knowledge and supervision of the business of Pritchard & Baird. Under the circumstances, this obligation included reading and understanding financial statements, and making reasonable attempts at detection and prevention of the illegal conduct of other officers and directors. She had a duty to protect the clients of Pritchard & Baird against policies and practices that would result in the misappropriation of money they had entrusted to the corporation. She breached that duty.

Affirmed.

Legal Issues

1. As a general rule, what are a corporate director's basic responsibilities? Explain.

2. Under New Jersey law, is it possible for a director to avoid these responsibilities? Why?

Ethical Issues

1. As noted in Chapter 1, Aristotle contended that to be ethical one must do what is "right" and "good." Does the court's statement of a director's obligations agree with Aristotle's view of ethical behavior? Discuss

2. How might a firm best introduce a newly elected director to its ethical concerns? Why?

Hypothetical Case

EMPLOYEES FORM A COMPETING COMPANY

ABC Company, a retailer of custom-made draperies, had 36 employees. At lunch Tom Underwood, its treasurer, told John Cox, vice president of marketing and a director of the company, that he was dissatisfied with ABC. He suggested they meet after work with Jim Bland, a local entrepreneur, to discuss forming their own company. That evening Underwood, Cox, and Bland decided to go into the custom drapery business in direct competition with ABC Company. Underwood disclosed confidential profit and expense statistics of ABC Company. He also disclosed his participation in a confidential stock bonus plan of the company.

The three selected a location for their new business, selected fabric suppliers, and secured a yellow pages listing. They contracted with a local attorney to incorporate the business as XYZ Company. They opened a bank account and purchased goods and machines in the name of XYZ Company. Cox copied virtually every form and chart used by ABC Company. Approximately a month after their meeting with Bland, Underwood and Cox resigned from ABC Company without prior notice. Three days later Underwood, Cox, and Bland opened XYZ Company. Did Underwood and Cox violate a duty owed to ABC Company? Why?

Duty of Loyalty

Fiduciary duty of loyalty

the obligation that arises from being entrusted to act for the benefit of another

Directors and officers owe a **fiduciary duty of loyalty** to the corporation. A fiduciary is one who is trusted to act for the benefit of another. As fiduciaries, directors must act to further the corporation's interests. They must subordinate personal interests that conflict with the corporation's best interests to their duty of undivided loyalty to the corporation. Suppose that while on the payroll of Acme Company, Ann Brown, its vice president of marketing, establishes a competing business, solicits Acme's customers, and discloses Acme's trade secrets for personal gain. By competing with Acme Company while still an officer of the company, Brown has breached her fiduciary duty of undivided loyalty.

The directors and officers of a corporation are not prohibited from entering into contracts with the corporation. However, such a contract will be upheld as valid only if the director or officer makes a *full disclosure* of all material information and deals fairly with the corporation. A contract of this kind is closely examined, and the director or officer has the burden of proving that it is fair. If a corporation is considering the purchase of land owned by Charles Smith, a director, Smith must make a full disclosure of his financial interests and the terms of the contract must meet a standard of fairness. This standard requires that the land be appraised and that the sales price be reasonably related to its appraised value.

Many state laws specify that a contract between a corporation and a director or officer is valid if *one* of the three following conditions is satisfied:

1. The interest of the director or officer in the contract is disclosed to the board and approved by the disinterested directors.
2. The shareholders approve the contract with knowledge of that interest.
3. The contract is both fair and reasonable to the corporation.

Although directors and officers can contract with the corporation, they cannot compete with it. As fiduciaries, they are held to undivided loyalty to the corporation.

A CORPORATE OFFICER AND AN INVESTMENT OPPORTUNITY

You are the vice president of XYZ, Inc., a small manufacturing corporation. You are aware that the directors of XYZ have been seeking to acquire a controlling interest in a transistor manufacturing corporation in order to diversify XYZ's operations and to assure a constant supply of the parts necessary to manufacture XYZ's products. While negotiating a sales contract for XYZ, you become aware of a suitable candidate for takeover. In fact, the takeover candidate is so appealing that, as an astute and experienced investor, you wish to invest in it yourself. What should you do?

Hypothetical Case

Corporate Opportunity

The doctrine of **corporate opportunity** prohibits a corporate officer or director from taking advantage of a business opportunity that belongs to the corporation. A business opportunity belongs to the corporation if (1) the director or officer becomes aware of it because of his or her corporate position, or (2) the corporation usually deals in such business opportunities, or (3) the opportunity was created or developed with the corporation's money, facilities, or personnel.

An officer or director can violate the corporate opportunity doctrine in various ways. Suppose that Janet Lane, director of a land development company, through her corporate position learns that certain valuable land is being offered for sale and desires to purchase the land herself without disclosing the offer to anyone else in the corporation. Lane cannot take personal advantage of this opportunity since the land falls within the corporation's normal scope of business, and also Lane learned of the opportunity because of her corporate position. As a director, Lane would be free to purchase the land only if the corporation is first offered the opportunity to do so and rejects the offer or if the corporation is unable to finance the purchase.

Officers and directors who violate their duties may be liable under criminal or civil law.

> **Corporate opportunity**
> the doctrine that prohibits a corporate officer or director from taking advantage of a business opportunity that belongs to the corporation

LIABILITY FOR TORTS AND CRIMES

State and federal statutes, as well as the common law, impose civil and criminal liabilities on corporations and their employees. Thus a corporation, as well as its employees, may commit torts and crimes.

Torts

A corporation can act only through its employees. As an employer, it is liable for any torts committed by its employees while acting within the scope of their employment. The participating employees are also liable for harm suffered by third parties. The corporation is liable even if it instructed the employees not to commit the torts, and the employees are liable even if their motive was to benefit the corporation and not to profit personally.

The corporation is liable for torts of *negligence* (unintentional torts) committed within the scope of employment. If an employee making deliveries is speeding and crashes into a parked car, the employee has committed the tort of negligence and both the corporation and the employee are liable to the owner of the car for property damages. Similarly, if an employee commits an *intentional* tort, such as fraud or trespass, while acting within the scope of his or her employment, both the corporation and the employee are liable for damages. The wrongful intent of the employee is transferred to the corporation.

Directors or officers can commit torts against the corporation that employs them. They are liable to the corporation for the harm they caused it by their negligence. In such a case, money damages are awarded to the corporation itself for the harm done to it. Courts usually require proof of more than just mismanagement to find a director or officer guilty of a tort. Corporate managers are liable if their neglect of their job responsibilities—for example, their failure to attend meetings or to review corporate financial records—results in financial injury to the corporation. In addition, the corporation laws of some states impose civil liability on corporate management abuses, such as issuing overpriced or underpriced shares, declaring corporate dividends without proper authorization, or lending corporate funds improperly.

Crimes

Certain acts of individual corporate managers can lead to criminal liability. False entries in corporate records, intentional dishonesty in corporate elections, and misuse of corporate funds can provoke criminal lawsuits. In many states corporate managers are criminally liable for failing to file required reports or filing false reports wtih the secretary of state or any other regulatory agency. If a corporation does not pay its taxes, the director or officer who is responsible for seeing that this is done may be individually liable to the government. Directors and officers have also been held liable for violation of such statutes as antitrust laws and laws prohibiting discrimination in employment. In at least one case, business managers were convicted of homicide for workplace negligence.

Under common law, a corporation could not be held liable for a crime. Courts reasoned that since a corporation was merely a legal entity, it lacked the capacity to form a criminal intent or to be imprisoned. However, modern state criminal codes often make corporations legally accountable for the crimes of high-level managers acting within the scope of their employment. The trend toward applying criminal statutes to corporations is also reflected in such federal legislation as the Sherman Antitrust Act, the Securities Act of 1933, and various laws relating to employment.

The following case concerns a situation in which the prosecution alleged that a corporate manager was criminally liable for violations of federal laws. The prosecution did not allege that the manager was negligent, but that the manager was liable because he held a position of authority over the conditions on which the charges were based.

UNITED STATES v. PARK
SUPREME COURT OF THE UNITED STATES
421 U.S. 658 (1975)

John Park was the president of Acme Markets, Inc., a national food chain with 874 retail outlets, 12 general warehouses, and special warehouses. Park and Acme were charged with violations of the Federal Food, Drug, and Cosmetic Act (FDA). Each count of the complaint alleged that in violation of the FDA they had stored food held for sale in warehouses exposed to rodents and that the food was subsequently adulterated. Acme pleaded guilty to each count, while Park pleaded not guilty.

At trial the evidence demonstrated that government inspectors had advised Park on several occasions that unsanitary conditions existed in the warehouses and that the steps Park took to alleviate the problem had not been satisfactory. The evidence also showed that Park as the chief executive officer of Acme was responsible for providing sanitary conditions for the food Acme held for sale, and that he usually delegated such matters to "dependable subordinates." Park claimed that he should not be convicted, since he was not personally responsible for the FDA violations.

The jury found Park guilty on all counts. The court of appeals reversed the trial court. The Supreme Court granted certiorari.

BURGER, CHIEF JUSTICE

The question presented by the Government's petition for certiorari in *United States v. Dotterweich* and the focus of this Court's opinion was whether "the manager of a corporation, as well as the corporation itself, may be prosecuted under the Federal Food, Drug, and Cosmetic Act of 1938 for the introduction of misbranded and adulterated articles into interstate commerce." [T]his Court looked to the purposes of the Act and noted that they "touch phases of the lives and health of the people which, in the circumstances of modern industrialism, are largely beyond self-protection." It observed that the Act is of "a now familiar type" which "dispenses with the conventional requirement for criminal conduct—awareness of some wrongdoing. In the interest of the larger good it puts the burden of acting at hazard upon a person otherwise innocent but standing in responsible relation to a public danger."

Central to the Court's conclusion

that individuals other than proprietors are subject to the criminal provisions of the Act was the reality that "the only way in which a corporation can act is through the individuals who act on its behalf."

[T]he Court concluded those doctrines dictated that the offense was committed "by all who . . . have . . . a responsible share in the furtherance of the transaction which the statute outlaws."

The rationale of the interpretation given the Act in *Dotterweich,* as holding criminally accountable the persons whose failure to exercise the authority and supervisory responsibility reposed in them by the business organization resulted in the violation complained of, has been confirmed in our subsequent cases. Thus, the Court has reaffirmed the proposition that "the public interest in the purity of its food is so great as to warrant the imposition of the highest standard of care on distributors." In order to make "distributors of food the strictest censors of their merchandise," the Act punishes "neglect where the law requires care, or inaction where it imposes a duty." "The accused, if he does not will the violation, usually is in a position to prevent it with no more care than society might reasonably expect and no more exertion than it might reasonably exact from one who assumed his responsibilities." Similarly, in cases decided after *Dotterweich,* the Courts of Appeals have recognized that those corporate agents vested with the responsibility, and power commensurate with that responsibility, to devise whatever measures are necessary to ensure compliance with the Act bear a "responsible relationship" to, or have a "responsible share" in, violations.

The Act does not, as we observed in *Dotterweich,* make criminal liability turn on "awareness of some wrongdoing" or "conscious fraud." The duty imposed by Congress on responsible

corporate agents is, we emphasize, one that requires the highest standard of foresight and vigilance, but the Act, in its criminal aspect, does not require that which is objectively impossible. The theory upon which responsible corporate agents are held criminally accountable for "causing" violations of the Act permits a claim that a defendant was "powerless" to prevent or correct the violation to "be raised defensively at a trial on the merits." If such a claim is made, the defendant has the burden of coming forward with evidence, but this does not alter the Government's ultimate burden of proving beyond a reasonable doubt the defendant's guilt, including his power, in light of the duty imposed by the Act, to prevent or correct the prohibited condition. Congress has seen fit to enforce the accountability of responsible corporate agents dealing with products which may affect the health of consumers by penal sanctions cast in rigorous terms, and the obligation of the courts is to give them effect so long as they do not violate the Constitution.

Reversed.

Legal Issues

1. Why could Park and not a low-level Acme custodian be held criminally liable for the unsanitary conditions in the Acme warehouses? Explain.

2. What burden of proof does the government have in a case of this kind? Discuss.

Ethical Issues

1. Under the standard of holding corporate agents criminally accountable for causing a violation of law, the Supreme Court decided that if a corporate official contends that he or she was powerless to prevent the violation, the government has the burden of proving beyond a reasonable doubt that the of-

ficial had the power, in light of the duty imposed by law, to prevent or correct the violation. Is this standard more stringent than the standard that pragmatic ethics would demand? Why? When, if ever, would the use of this standard be unfair?

2. Is the Supreme Court's standard for holding corporate officers accountable for criminal violations consistent with the ethical views espoused by advocates of "pragmatic ethics"? Why?

Indemnification

A director or officer who is held liable in a civil or criminal suit may suffer less than a private individual would in similar circumstances. Many corporations pay the costs of any criminal or civil suit against corporate management. Such payment of the costs of directors and officers is known as **indemnification** (reimbursement). It is a means of encouraging participation in corporate management.

Indemnification
reimbursement for legal costs, expenses, or losses inccurred

In most states, to obtain indemnification the director or officer must have been acting in good faith and in the best interests of the corporation. Directors or officers who knowingly violate a state or federal statute are generally not entitled to protection.

The potential liability of corporate executives may prevent the use of unethical and unreasonable means in the corporate sphere. On the other hand, the chance of incurring liability may discourage some people from becoming corporate executives. Indemnification is a compromise between the two possibilities. As an alternative, some corporations carry liability insurance that reimburses their managers.

DISSOLUTION

A corporation automatically ceases to exist at the end of the time period stated in its charter. If the charter of a corporation states that the corporation will exist for five years, the corporation automatically ceases to exist at the end of five years. Usually, as has been noted, the charter of a corporation states that its existence is to be "perpetual." Certain action must take place to terminate perpetual corporations. They are terminated in legal proceedings that involve either a voluntary dissolution or an involuntary dissolution.

Voluntary Dissolution

In a voluntary dissolution, there are two methods by which the corporation can terminate itself. One method is to obtain the written consent of all its shareholders. The more common method is for the board of directors to initiate dissolution and then to obtain approval from two thirds of the shareholders' votes. After shareholder approval has been granted, the officers of the corporation file a certificate of intent to dissolve with the secretary of state.

Once the certificate has been filed, the corporation goes into the "winding up" stage. **Winding up** means that the corporation stops taking on new business and

Winding up
a state just prior to dissolution in which a corporation stops taking on new business and gradually closes out its accounts

performs only those acts necessary to close out its present accounts. While winding up, the corporation gives its creditors notice of dissolution. The assets of the corporation are liquidated and the money received is first used to pay off the creditors. If any money remains, it is distributed to the stockholders. All of the preferred shareholders are paid in full before the common shareholders are allowed to participate in the distribution. When the distribution has been accomplished, the corporation prepares a certificate of dissolution and forwards it to the secretary of state. On the date that the secretary of state signs the certificate, the corporation is officially dissolved.

Involuntary Dissolution

Action to dissolve a corporation *involuntarily* can be commenced by any one of three groups: the state, the shareholders, or the creditors. Since the corporation has been created by the state, the *state* has the right to begin court proceedings to cancel its charter. The grounds for dissolution by the state, such as failure to file an annual report or failure to pay taxes owed to the state, are specified in state statutes.

The *shareholders* can bring suit to involuntarily dissolve a corporation. They must be able to establish either that the directors are deadlocked, so that they can no longer manage the corporation, or that the shareholders are deadlocked, so that it is impossible to elect a board of directors. To prove that the corporation is deadlocked in either of these ways, shareholders are required to show that it is unable to function. This is a very difficult burden of proof to carry.

Courts will also dissolve a corporation if oppression of the minority shareholders by the majority shareholders can be shown. Oppression occurs when those in control take advantage of the minority shareholders. In one case a corporation earned a large profit over a period of years but refused to declare dividends. The court granted relief to the minority shareholders when it was shown that the majority shareholders used the profit to pay salaries and bonuses to themselves.

Finally, the *creditors* of the corporation may institute proceedings to dissolve it. If the corporation does not pay its debts, the creditors can bring suit and ask the court to grant a judgment declaring that the corporation owes a certain amount to them. The creditors may then execute or enforce the judgment by having the sheriff seize and sell the corporation's assets. After the assets have been sold, if the corporation lacks sufficient funds to set the judgment aside and if it is insolvent, the court may order dissolution.

For an involuntary dissolution, the court appoints a receiver who brings in all of the corporation's assets. The assets are sold, and the proceeds of the sale are used to pay off the creditors. If any money happens to be left over, it will go to the shareholders.

Involuntary dissolution, an extreme remedy, is not easily obtained, whether by the state, the shareholders, or the creditors. Courts are reluctant to cancel the charter of a corporation and will refuse to do so if there is some alternative.

**REVIEW QUESTION
& PROBLEMS**

1. One of the main advantages of a corporation is that the owners have limited liability. For a small corporation, however, this advantage is greatly exaggerated. Explain.

2. Explain how the concept of the corporation as a legal entity affects the limited liability of stockholders.

3. John Smith and Charles Brown intend to manufacture and sell railroad cars. Which form of business organization would be most advantageous to them in each of the following situations? Give reasons for your answer.

   a. John and Charles each have only $5,000 to invest, and their ability to borrow is limited. They require at least $500,000 in capital to begin operations.

   b. John and Charles have recently learned that railroad car manufacturers have suffered products liability lawsuits totaling $800,000 within the past year.

   c. John and Charles expect to sustain a loss during the first years of their business.

   d. John and Charles do not have enough capital, but Michael Rogers, who can meet their needs for capital, is willing to invest in the business. All three parties agree that it is important for them to maintain close supervision and control over the operation of the business.

   e. The facts are the same as in *d,* and in addition Michael Rogers wants to avoid the risk of losing his personal assets.

4. A, B, and C formed a limited partnership, with A acting as a general partner and B and C acting as limited partners. However, B and C became involved in the management and operation of the partnership. Subsequently, the partnership went bankrupt and the trustee sought to hold B and C personally liable for its debts. Should they be held personally liable? Explain.

5. Sarah Barnes is the president of XYZ Corporation, an oil refining and marketing corporation. She also owns a large tract of land with underlying known deposits of oil. She wishes to enter into a lease with the corporation, giving it the right to extract the oil. What should she do? Why?

ENDNOTES

1. Delaware is a popular state of incorporation. More than one half of the Fortune 500 companies and about 45 percent of the companies listed on the New York Stock Exchange are incorporated in Delaware. One reason why corporation attorneys favor Delaware is that its corporation laws have been well-tested and therefore provide an element of predictability. Incorporation fees account for about 15 percent of Delaware's revenue.

2. Removing directors without cause may violate their employment contract. Contracts of employment are discussed further in Chapter 12.

PART

6

EMPLOYMENT LAW

The employer-employee relationship cuts across the entire range of business activity. Most business organizations would be unable to operate without the assistance of employees. For example, corporations, which are legal entities, are incapable of doing any kind of business without employees. Partnerships and sole proprietors ordinarily hire employees, since the owners cannot perform all of the necessary tasks.

This chapter discusses the foundation of the employer-employee relationship: the law of agency. In addition to the common law principles of agency, it discusses state and federal legislation that protects the worker: (1) state workers' compensation statutes, (2) the Occupational Safety and Health Act, (3) the Fair Labor Standards Act, (4) state unemployment compensation statutes, (5) the Employee Retirement Income Security Act, (6) the Immigration and Reform Control Act, (7) plant closing laws, and (8) drug testing laws.

AGENCY

Agency
the relationship in which one person is authorized to act for the benefit of and under the control of another person

Agent
a person who is authorized to act for the benefit of and under the control of another person

Principal
a person who hires another person to act for him or her

The law of **agency** deals with the relationship between one person, called the **agent,** who agrees to act for the benefit of and under the control of another person, called the **principal.** The concept of agency is indispensable in the business world. Since a corporation is merely a legal entity, it can function only through employees who act as its agents. Partnerships are dependent on the agency relationship since each partner acts as the agent of the other partner or partners in conducting partnership business. And individuals make frequent use of such agents as real estate brokers and stockbrokers in transacting business.

The most common legal problems involving agency occur when the agent has purportedly entered into a contract with a third party on behalf of the principal. Legal problems also arise concerning the liability of the principal for the torts of the agent. Other important aspects of the law of agency involve the duties that the principal and agent owe to each other and the methods by which the agency relationship may be terminated.

Creation of Agency

Generally, there are no formal requirements for creating an agency relationship. Mutual consent between the parties, expressly stated or implied by conduct, is all that is necessary. However, the appointment of an agent must be in writing when the agent is authorized to effect an interest in real property, in such ways as signing a deed or mortgaging property.

Liability and Rights of the Principal of the Contract

The law of agency is primarily concerned with contracts and the liability of three parties: the principal, the agent, and the third party. A principal is liable on contracts entered into by the agent with the third party, provided the agent had authority to enter into such a contract. If the agent lacked authority, the principal will not be bound on the contract. The one exception to this rule occurs when the principal with full knowledge of the facts subsequently ratifies or affirms the contract. Figure 12-1 provides an illustration.

Hypothetical Case

A DISCHARGED EMPLOYEE CONTRACTS ON BEHALF OF HIS FORMER EMPLOYER

Paul Morton, the purchasing manager for ABM Construction Company, resigned under pressure from ABM. As a long-term employee, he was allowed to use his office for the next two weeks while seeking other employment. During this period, Sam Smith, a salesman for XYZ Construction Supply who had sold construction materials to Morton on behalf of ABM for a number of years, called on Morton and Morton placed an order for ABM supplies with him. When the supplies arrived, ABM refused to accept or pay for them. Is ABM legally obligated to accept the order that Morton placed? Why?

Types of Authority

The authority of the agent necessarily comes from the principal and may be either actual or apparent.

Actual Authority   The authority that the principal intentionally delegates to the agent, expressly or impliedly, is **actual authority.** Express authority is specifically granted to the agent, either orally or in writing. In addition, an agent is impliedly authorized to do those things that are reasonably necessary to carry out the expressly granted authority. Suppose that the owner of a store hires a manager to operate the store and expressly grants the manager the authority to perform such acts as hiring salesclerks, purchasing inventory, and making sales. The manager would also have the implied authority to perform acts reasonably necessary to operate the store, such as contracting for the delivery of heating fuel.

Apparent Authority   **Apparent authority** is the authority that the principal, by words or acts, has led a third party to reasonably believe the agent possesses, even though the agent has no express or implied authority. In the previous example, if the store owner specifically prohibited the manager from extending credit to customers and the manager sold goods on credit to a customer, the owner would be bound on the transaction if credit was extended by managers of the same type of store. In these circumstances, placing the manager in charge of the store clothed the manager with apparent authority to extend credit. Actual authority and apparent authority are illustrated in Figure 12-2.

Ratification

Ordinarily, unauthorized acts of the agent do not bind the principal to the third party. However, the principal may become responsible by making a **ratification** or

Actual authority
the authority that the principal intentionally grants or delegates to the agent

Apparent authority
the authority that the principal, by words or acts, has led a third party to reasonably believe the agent possesses

Ratification
subsequent approval of the agent's unauthorized act

Illustration of an Agent's Authority to Enter into a Contract on Behalf of a Disclosed Principal

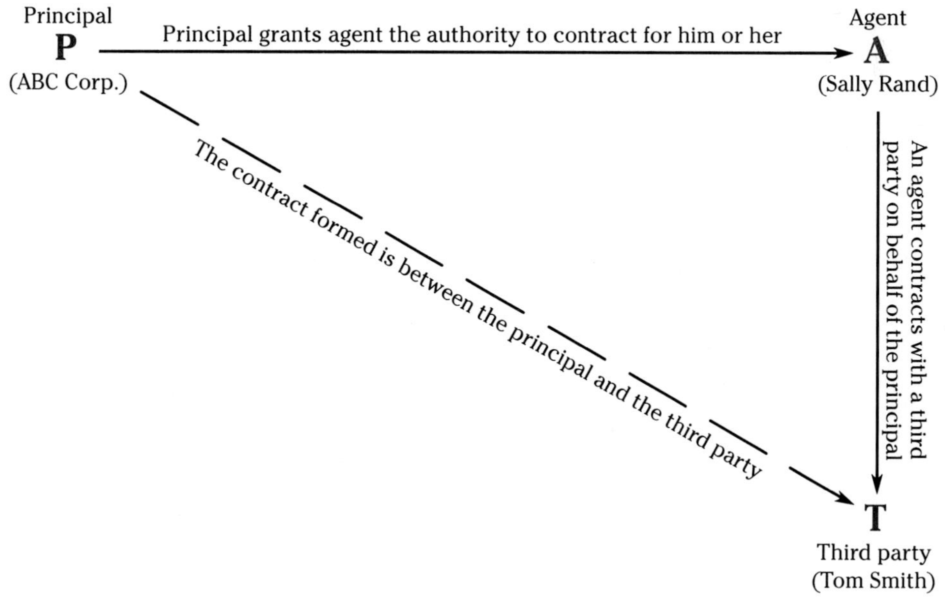

FIGURE 12–1

Example: P appoints A to obtain facilities to house the headquarters of ABC Corporation. After evaluating possible locations and discussing terms with several parties, A signs a lease agreement with T on behalf of P. Since P authorized A to perform this act, P is bound by the agreement.

subsequent approval of the agent's unauthorized acts. For a ratification to be effective, it must be shown (1) that the agent contracted on behalf of the principal and (2) that at the time of ratification the principal had full knowledge of all material facts. If an unauthorized agent orders goods on behalf of the principal and the principal, with full knowledge of the material facts, accepts and pays for the goods, an effective ratification has occurred. Ratification places all three parties in the position in which they would have been if the agent had been authorized to contract at the time of contracting.

Disclosed and Undisclosed Principals

Disclosed principal
contracting between the agent and a third party in which the third party knows of the agency relationship and the identity of the principal

Undisclosed principal
contracting between the agent and a third party in which the third party does not know of the agency relationship or of the identity of the principal

Generally, the agent contracts on behalf of a **disclosed principal,** which means that at the time of contracting the third party is aware of (1) the agency relationship and (2) the identity of the principal. If Sam works for ABC Company as a salesman and identifies himself as a salesman representing ABC when he makes calls on customers, Sam is an agent for a disclosed principal.

On occasion, an agent may be authorized to contract in his or her own name on behalf of an undisclosed principal. An **undisclosed principal** exists where the third party is unaware that the agent is acting on behalf of someone else and therefore, of course, unaware of the principal's identity. If various landowners

---

FIGURE 12–2   **Illustration of Types of Authority Granted by the Principal to the Agent**

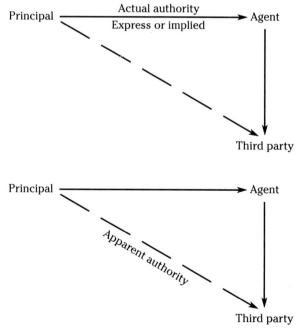

Actual authority is the authority that the principal intentionally delegates to the agent, expressly or impliedly. Express authority is the authority that the principal specifically grants to the agent, either orally or in writing. Agents are impliedly authorized to do the things necessary to carry out the authority that they have been expressly granted.

Apparent authority is the authority that, because of the principal's words or acts, leads third parties to reasonably believe the agent possesses.

know that ABC Company has decided to acquire land for expansion, they are likely to increase the price they charge for the land. To avoid this possibility, ABC Company will contract with an agent to represent himself as the buyer. In this situation ABC Company is an undisclosed principal.

Liability of the Agent to Third Persons

An agent who enters into a contract on behalf of a disclosed principal is not a party to the contract, since both the agent and the third party are aware that the agent intends the contract to be between the principal and the third party. If the principal breaches the contract, the agent cannot be held liable. To avoid liability, an agent acting for a disclosed principal should carefully sign all documents. It is important for the agent to disclose (1) the identity of the principal and (2) the representative capacity of the agent. Here is an example:

The ABC Corporation agrees with Tom Smith . . .
ABC Corporation
by Sally Rand, President

In this example the third party, Tom Smith, knows the identity of the principal, ABC Corporation, for which the agent, Sally Rand, is acting. The third party also knows the representative capacity in which the agent signs, in this example, "President." Thus only the principal is a party to the contract.

In some situations, however, the agent for a disclosed principal can become liable. For example, an agent who enters into a contract on behalf of a principal impliedly warrants that he or she possesses the authority to bind the principal on the contract. If the agent has no authority or exceeds his or her authority, the third party can hold the agent liable for damages for breach of the implied warranty of authority. In the above example, if the principal had refused to accept the goods that the unauthorized agent ordered on principal's behalf, the third party could hold the agent liable for any damages. Further, if it can be proved that the agent intentionally misrepresented his or her authority, the agent may be liable for punitive damages for the tort of deceit.

An agent for an undisclosed principal acts in his or her own name and is therefore a party to the contract and personally liable should the principal subsequently breach it. Courts reason that because the third party must rely solely on the reputation and trustworthiness of the agent, the agent should be required to stand behind the contract. This does not mean, however, that the principal necessarily escapes liability. If the third party learns the principal's identity before the judgment against the agent is enforced, the third party may elect to hold the principal liable rather than the agent.

Tort Liability of Principal and Agent

The law of agency is also concerned with torts that an agent commits while working for the principal. As previously discussed, a tort is a private wrong in which one person causes injury to another person or his property. A third person may hold both principal and agent liable for torts committed by the agent within the scope of the agent's employment.

The agent who commits a tort is always liable to the injured third party. The principal is liable for the torts that the agent committed within the scope of his or her employment. This vicarious liability is based on the doctrine of **respondeat superior,** which means "let the superior respond" or "let the boss answer." The liability of the principal under respondeat superior also applies to the employer-employee relationship. If while making deliveries for the employer, an employee is speeding and negligently crashes into a car driven by a third party, the principal is liable without fault for the agent's tort. The liability is actually *joint and several,* which means that the third party can hold the principal and agent jointly liable or can hold either of them individually liable for the entire amount of damages. The third party, of course, can collect these damages only once. Ordinarily, the third party chooses to proceed against the principal alone, primarily because the principal is in a better financial condition than the agent and is more likely to pay any damages awarded.

The principal has a right of reimbursement from the agent for the amount paid to the third party. This right is seldom exercised because (1) asking employees for reimbursement fosters bad employee relations and (2) employers ordinarily carry enough liability insurance to cover such eventualities.

When an agent has injured a third party, the principal is liable only if two primary conditions have been met. First, an *employer-employee* relationship must be established. An employer is ordinarily not liable for torts committed by independent contractors while performing their job.[1] An **independent contractor** is a person who contracts to do a piece of work for a fixed fee in accordance with his or her own judgment and methods.

The primary distinguishing feature of an independent contractor is that the employer has no *right of control* over how the work is to be performed. The independent contractor is accountable only for a specified result.[2] Suppose that Richard, a carpenter who is in business for himself, contracts with ABC Company to construct an addition to a building. They agree that Richard will work from blueprints and sketches and that he will be paid a fixed amount upon completing the job. ABC Company has no right to control the manner in which he will perform the work. If Richard should be involved in a wreck while on the way to purchase supplies, ABC Company would not be liable, since an employer is not liable for torts inflicted on third parties by an independent contractor while performing his or her job.

The second condition is that the tort must have been committed within the employee's **scope of employment,** that is, while the employee was carrying out the employer's business. If the employee had temporarily *abandoned* the employment when the tort was committed, the employer is not liable. Scope of employment is a question of fact that is often difficult to resolve. Suppose, for example, that a deliveryman departs from his route to visit his girlfriend and has a wreck while on the way to her house. Most courts would hold that the departure was a mere deviation, so that the employer is still liable.

Suppose, however, that after visiting his girlfriend, the deliveryman decides to visit his mother and the wreck occurs while he is on the way to her house. Most courts would hold that at the time of the wreck the deliveryman had abandoned his employment, so that the employer is not liable.

Duties of Principal and Agent

The principal and the agent owe duties to each other. These duties may arise from the contract between them. In addition, the agency relationship implies certain duties in law. The party violating these duties is liable to the other party for damages sustained.

Duties Owed by Agent to Principal

The usual duties imposed on the agent by operation of law are (1) to be loyal to the principal, (2) to obey lawful instructions of the principal, (3) to give notice of material facts, and (4) to account for money and property belonging to the principal. The most important of these duties are loyalty and obedience.

1. *Duty of loyalty.* Because of the agent's fiduciary relationship with the principal, the agent owes the principal the highest degree of *loyalty and good faith.* This means that the agent must not make a secret profit while transacting the principal's business, or accept a personal benefit, such as a gift, without the principal's consent. The duty of loyalty also demands that the agent not disclose confidential information, such as trade secrets, and that the agent act for only one principal in a particular transaction.

2. *Duty of obedience.* The agent also has the duty to *obey* all of the principal's lawful instructions. Courts interpret this duty very strictly. The agent has no discretion to deviate from the instructions given. If an agent instructed to sell for cash only sold on credit, the agent is liable to the principal for damages for nonpayment.

Duties Owed by Principal to Agent

The primary duties of the principal to the agent are (1) to compensate the agent for services rendered and (2) to reimburse and indemnify the agent for money expended by the agent while acting on the principal's behalf.

1. *Duty to compensate.* The principal has a duty to *compensate* the agent for the value of his or her services as agreed in the contract. If the contract does not specify the amount of compensation, the agent is entitled to be paid the reasonable value of his or her services, which is measured by the custom of the community. Courts generally hold that, unless the contract provides otherwise, a salesperson is entitled to compensation for all orders accepted by the principal even if the customer subsequently refuses to accept or pay for the goods.

2. *Duty to reimburse and indemnify.* The principal owes the agent a duty of *reimbursement,* which is repayment of money that the agent expends for the principal's benefit, such as expenses. Unless the contract provides otherwise, if the principal requests the agent to transact business that requires travel but does not provide any funds for travel expenses, the principal is under a duty to reimburse the agent for reasonable travel expenses. The principal must also *indemnify* the agent for any loss that the agent sustains in following the principal's instructions where the agent is not at fault. Situations in which the agent is held liable for trespass while performing his or her duties are a common example of such a loss.

Termination of the Agency Relationship

When the agency relationship is terminated, the agent is freed from fiduciary duties and the principal is no longer obligated to compensate the agent. In most cases, the principal must give notice of the termination to third parties so that the apparent authority of the agent to bind the principal will cease.

The agency relationship may expire by virtue of provisions in the contract. If an agency relationship was created to accomplish a specified result, it terminates when that result has been accomplished. Employment of an agent to sell land terminates when the land has been sold. If a provision in an agency contract specifies that the contract will remain in effect for a definite period of time, say two years, the agency relationship automatically ceases at the end of that period.

If the contract specifies that the agency relationship is to continue for a definite period or until a specified result has been accomplished, either party has the *power* to revoke the relationship at any time. The relationship was entered voluntarily, so either the principal or the agent has the power of renunciation. This is quite different, however, from having the *right* to terminate the relationship. If the revocation is wrongful, the party breaching the contract is liable in damages to the other party. Suppose that an agent hired under a three-year contract was discharged without cause after six months. Although the principal had the *power* to fire the agent, she did not have the *right* to do so. The renunciation of the relationship is effective, but the principal is liable in damages to the agent. Most agency contracts, however, do not specify a definite duration. The relationship is considered to be "at will," and in general either party is free to renounce it at any time.

Certain events may terminate the agency relationship. The death or insanity of either the principal or the agent terminates the agency relationship, though the other party may be unaware of the event. Bankruptcy terminates the relationship only if it affects the subject matter of the agency.

The principal is responsible for notifying third parties that the agency relationship has been terminated. If notice is not given, the agent still possesses apparent authority to bind the principal. The type of notice required depends on the third party. Third parties who have had dealings with the agent are entitled to actual notice, either oral or written. Notice by publication in a newspaper in the place where the agency was carried on is sufficient for third parties who were merely aware of the agency. If an agency is terminated by death, insanity, or bankruptcy, notice to third parties is not required.

In most respects, the law governing the relationship of principal and agent is the same as the law governing the relationship of employer and employee. The main difference is that an employer controls or has the right to control how an employee does the work. As compared with an agent, an employee has little power to exercise initiative or judgment. In addition, an employee ordinarily does not have the authority to enter into a binding contract on the employer's behalf.

LAW ABROAD

European Community

The European Community provisions on agency generally come into play when an agency relationship arises between nationals of different countries—for example, a relationship in which an English manufacturer uses a Spanish agent to sell its goods to Spanish wholesalers.

Principals are bound to act dutifully and in good faith in their dealings with agents. If there is no contractual agreement, the principal is to compensate the agent in accordance with the customary practice of the place where the agent carries on his or her activities. If there is no customary practice, the agent is to be paid a reasonable amount. In particular, the principal is expected to provide the agent with all the documentation necessary for the performance of the contract. The principal is also expected to keep the agent informed of any conditions that would reduce the level of the transactions that the agent anticipated and to inform the agent of any nonacceptance of contracts entered into by the agent. The principal is obligated to reimburse the agent for damages sustained in carrying out the contract.

Agents are expected to attend to the principal's interests, performing all of their duties responsibly and in good faith. Most important, agents should take proper action to negotiate and conclude the transactions that have been entrusted to them, communicating to the principal all the information available. They must also comply with all reasonable instructions.

If the agency agreement is for an indefinite term, either party can terminate it at any time by giving the required notice. The required notice is one month in the first year of the contract, two months in the second year, and three months in the third year and later years. The principal and agent may not agree to accept shorter notice.

Germany

Agency is common in Germany, and permitted with only rare exceptions. German law does not, however, recognize the concept of undisclosed principals. Thus an agent who does not disclose that he or she is acting as an agent acquires no rights or liabilities on behalf of the principal. The agent is personally liable to the third person for damages.

To prove that an agent is the bona fide representative of the principal, the principal may issue a written power of attorney to the agent. The principal may also declare to a third party that the agent has the authority to act for him. The agency relationship may be terminated in much the same way that it was created: by written revocation or oral declaration. The manner of termination of agency is often controlled by contractual arrangement.

German law recognizes several levels of agency, one of which, *Prokura,* confers sweeping authority on the agent. The agent, called the *Prokurist,* has authority to act for the principal in all business matters except the sale of the business itself and the disposal of real estate. A grant of *Prokura* must be recorded in the commercial register, and the principal can revoke it at any time.

Japan

Agency is common in Japan. In commercial transactions the agent must disclose the involvement of the principal or risk having a third party demand that the agent perform the contract.

Third parties can demand proof that the agent has acted within his or her authority. An agent who lacks such proof may be held liable for performance of the contract or for the damages that have been incurred.

Powers of agency are generally assumed to be fairly limited unless specifically stated otherwise. A principal who lets a third party know that an agency relationship exists is bound for any acts that the agent does within the reasonable range of his or her authority.

COURTS AND THE EMPLOYER-EMPLOYEE RELATIONSHIP

The common law principles of agency are broad enough to cover the employer-employee relationship. In the past, if the employment relationship was not for a definite duration, the employer could discharge the employee at any time for any reason. The common law principles have been changing to provide protection to unjustly discharged employees. Protection has also been extended to employees who were fired because they reported unsafe working conditions or their employer's illegal activities.

Termination of Employer-Employee Relations

Employment at will doctrine

the doctrine under which either the employer or the employee can terminate the employment at any time for any reason or for no reason

Most employees are hired for an indefinite amount of time—an employment at will. Under the common law **employment at will doctrine,** either party can terminate the employment at any time for any reason or even for no reason. However, the right of employers to discharge workers has begun to erode as fired workers have been increasingly claiming in court that they were wrongfully discharged. Court decisions in 45 states have restricted the right of the employer to discharge employees.[3] The lawsuits were brought primarily by white male managers who were not covered by civil service and who lacked the protection of a union agreement or of federal statutes, which prohibited the arbitrary dismissal of special segments of the population, such as the handicapped and members of minority groups.

Two principal exceptions to the employment at will doctrine have emerged: (1) firings that conflict with "public policy" and (2) firings that breach an "implied contract." *Public policy* cases emphasize the employer's illegal or wrongful motives. A firing violates public policy if it harms the interests of society. Examples of such firings include dismissal due to refusal to participate in an illegal price-fixing scheme, to commit perjury, or to ignore an obligation to serve on a jury.

Contract theory cases are often based on promises made in an employee handbook that imply a contract under which the employee will be discharged only for just cause. In one case of this kind, the handbook referred to the employee's "permanent status" following a probation period. The company unjustly discharged the employee, because this reference implied a degree of job security. Another wrongful dismissal case arose from a handbook statement that termination for cause could take place only after notification of unsatisfactory performance. The employer-employee "contract" was breached when the employee was fired without warning. In addition to handbook promises, promises of "security" or a "career" in company advertisements can imply contracts.

Many employee handbooks now explicitly state that they are not an employment contract and that the employee can be terminated at any time for any reason. In some companies new employees are being required to sign a statement indicating their understanding that their employment is on an at will basis. Unlike plaintiffs in employment discrimination cases, who can generally collect back pay only, victims of unjust discharges can collect sizable compensatory and punitive damages from their former employer.

California was a pioneer state in establishing the right of fired workers to sue former employers for large damages. In 1988, however, in *Foley v. Interactive Data*

Corporation,[4] the California Supreme Court limited the availability of punitive damages in most wrongful discharge cases. Recovery for a breach of the implied covenant of good faith and fair dealing was limited to lost pay and related economic damages. Tort remedies, including damages for emotional stress and punitive damages, were eliminated. Since the possibility of large punitive damages had been the driving force behind many wrongful discharge cases, this case has reduced wrongful discharge litigation in California.

If the employment contract is for a definite duration, say two years, the employee can be dismissed only for "just cause"—a flagrant violation of company policy. Just cause for dismissal includes theft of company property, fighting, drunkenness, excessive absenteeism and other gross misconduct.

In the following case the employer directed the employee to commit an illegal act.

SABINE PILOT SERVICE, INC. v. HAUCK
SUPREME COURT OF TEXAS
687 S.W.2d 733 (1985)

Michael Andrew Hauck, the plaintiff, was a deckhand on a boat owned by the defendant, Sabine Pilot Service, Inc. A Sabine supervisor instructed Hauck to pump the bilges of the boat into the open water each day. Hauck noted that a sign on the boat specifically stated that it was illegal to pump bilges into the open water. As a result he called the U.S. Coast Guard, which confirmed that it was illegal to do this. He therefore refused to continue pumping bilges into the open water, and Sabine fired him.

Hauck brought suit in a Texas trial court, charging that Sabine had terminated his employment because he refused to engage in an illegal act. Sabine responded that Hauck had been fired for refusing to swab the deck, stand a radio watch, and carry out other assigned duties. The trial court rendered a summary judgment for Sabine. The Texas Court of Appeals reversed and remanded the case for trial, and Sabine appealed to the Supreme Court of Texas.

WALLACE, JUSTICE

The sole issue for our determination is whether an allegation by an employee that he was discharged for refusing to perform an illegal act states a cause of action. This court in *East Line & R.R.R. Co. v. Scott* held that employment for an indefinite term may be terminated at will and without cause. The courts of Texas have steadfastly refused to vary from that holding. However, in the last 30 years the courts of 22 states have made exceptions to the employment at will doctrine and numerous commentators have advocated exceptions to the doctrine. The exceptions advocated by the commentators and adopted by various courts range from very liberal and broad exceptions to very narrow and closely defined ones.

Sabine contends that any exception to the employment at will doctrine should be statutorily created. The Legislature has created exceptions to this doctrine [as noted below]: (discharge for filing a workers' compensation claim); (discharge based on union membership or nonmembership); (discharge because of active duty in the

State Military Forces); (discharge because of jury service); (discharge based on race, color, handicap, religion, national origin, age, or sex). Although the Legislature has created those exceptions to the doctrine, this court is free to judicially amend a judicially created doctrine.

Upon careful consideration of the changes in American society and in the employer-employee relationship during the intervening 97 years since the *East Line & R.R.R. Co. v. Scott* decision, we hold that the situation which led to that decision has changed in certain respects. We now hold that public policy, as expressed in the laws of this state and the United States which carry criminal penalties, requires a very narrow exception to the employment at will doctrine announced in *East Line & R.R.R. Co. v. Scott.* That narrow exception covers only the discharge of an employee for the sole reason that the employee refused to perform an illegal act. We further hold that in the trial of such a case it is the plaintiff's burden to prove by a preponderance of the evidence that his discharge was for no reason other than his refusal to perform an illegal act.

The judgment of the court of appeals is affirmed.

Kilgarlin, J., files a concurring opinion in which Ray, J., joins.

KILGARLIN, JUSTICE, CONCURRING

I concur with this judgment, which gives Michael Hauck an opportunity to prove to a trier of fact that he was discharged for refusing to violate a law. Moreover, I heartily applaud the court's acknowledgement of the vital need for a public policy exception to the employment at will doctrine. Absolute employment at will is a relic of early industrial times, conjuring up visions of the sweatshops described by Charles Dickens and his contemporaries. The doctrine belongs in a museum, not in our law. As it was a judicially promulgated doctrine, this court has the burden and the duty of amending it to reflect social and economic changes.

The court admittedly carves out but one exception to employment at will, but I do not fault the court for the singleness of its exception. The issue before the court was whether a cause of action existed under this particular fact situation: termination of an employee for his refusal to violate a law with a criminal penalty. There was no need for the court to create any other exception to employment at will in order to grant Hauck his requested relief. But our decision today in no way precludes us from broadening the exception when warranted in a proper case.

The court opinion today does not extend an employee's protection as far as any of the other states. Yet the examples of other states will be valuable in examining exactly how broadly the exception in Texas can evolve. In the meantime, an employee in Texas finally has a cause of action when he can show that his employer fired him for his refusal to commit an illegal act.

Although I might have defined the employment at will exception differently, I concur in the court's result and am pleased that an antiquated doctrine has been overcome by the realization that modern times require modern law. I, too, would affirm the judgment of the court of appeals.

Legal Issues

1. What was Sabine's argument for enforcing the employment at will doctrine as it had been enforced in the past? Explain.

2. How did the Supreme Court of Texas change the Texas employment at will doctrine? Explain.

Ethical Issues

1. A principle of law calls for the protection of employees at will from discharge if the discharge is the employer's retaliation against the employee for informing a government agency that the employer had violated the law. In ethical terms, is this principle different from a statute that bars the discharge of an employee because he or she testified against the employer in a workers' compensation hearing? Discuss.

2. Should the legal consequences of discharging an employee for refusing to engage in an unethical act be different from the legal consequences of discharging an employee for notifying the proper government officials that the employer was guilty of an illegal act? Discuss.

Whistle-Blowing Employees

Employers have often discharged employees in retaliation for disclosing dangerous, illegal, or unethical job activities. The employees who make such disclosures are called "whistle-blowers," and making the disclosures is called "whistle-blowing."

A trend toward the protection of whistle-blowing employees has developed. The Civil Rights Act of 1964 makes it illegal for an employer to retaliate against employees who disclose sex or race discrimination in their employment. The Occupational Safety and Health Act of 1970 protects employees who report safety or health hazards. The federal whistle-blower statute[5] passed in 1988 protects employees of defense contractors (companies that contract with the Department of Defense to supply goods or services) who report contract violations. A number of other federal laws also grant protection to whistle-blowers. More than 30 states have passed whistle-blower protection statutes that make it unlawful for either the state or a private employer to fire or discipline an employee for reporting alleged violations of federal, state, or local law to public authorities or for refusing to carry out orders that violate a public policy.[6] Many of these statutes require the employee to first report the violation to the employer and then to allow the employer a reasonable amount of time to remedy the violation. If a reasonable amount of time has passed and the employer has taken no action to remedy the violation, the employee has the right to report the violation to a public body. In addition to injunctive relief, the remedies provided by the whistle-blower statutes are usually reinstatement, back pay, attorney's fees, and court costs.

In about 20 states, courts have based decisions in *retaliatory discharge* cases on whether the violation concerns public policy matters, such as safety and health. If a public policy violation has occurred, the discharged whistle-blower can collect at least money damages. In a Connecticut case an employee was allegedly discharged for calling his employer's attention to deficiencies in the labeling and licensing of products. The Connecticut Supreme Court found that the worker had a legal claim in tort, since the employer's actions, if proven, violated state public policy.

The protection of whistle-blowing employees has been extended to company ethics. The ethical codes of many companies now contain a "squeal clause" that protects and rewards employees who blow the whistle on violations of the ethical code by co-workers.

LAW ABROAD

The court decisions and legislation that protect workers in the United States have been moving toward positions that Japan and most of the European Community countries adopted long ago. Those countries forbid unfair dismissals of workers who have completed a probationary period. The remedy for wrongful discharge is generally compensation, not reinstatement.

In Japan, every employer of 10 or more workers must have clear rules of employment. The employer is required to give the rules to employee representatives and to the Prefectural Labor Standards Supervising Office. The rules cover wages, working hours, holidays and vacations, benefits, termination procedures, and employee issues peculiar to the employer's particular type of business.

Hypothetical Case

A WIDOWER AND WORKERS' COMPENSATION BENEFITS

For the last 15 years of her life, Alice Walker, who died at age 45, worked as a machinist for Acme Machine Works, Inc. Her widower filed for death benefits under the state workers' compensation act, claiming that her job contributed to her death. The workers' compensation insurance company denied him benefits, stating that the death was not job related. He appealed to the workers' compensation board, which also denied him benefits. He then filed suit. Expert testimony at the trial revealed that Alice's death was caused by an irregular heart rhythm that resulted from a combination of a preexisting heart condition and job-related mental stress. The primary sources of the stress were Alice's failure to receive a promotion, her disagreement with the company's management philosophy, and her supervisor's rejection of the suggestions she made. Should Alice's widower be entitled to workers' compensation death benefits? Why?

STATE WORKERS' COMPENSATION STATUTES

Workers' compensation statutes protect workers and their families from the financial consequences of death, injury, or disease resulting from the workers' employment. This section discusses the coverage of workers' compensation statutes and the benefits that they provide.

In 1896 the British parliament passed the first workers' compensation statute. American states began enacting such statutes five years later, and today all 50 states have them. In addition, Congress has enacted three federal workers' compensation programs: (1) the Federal Employers' Liability Act, which covers employees of federal government agencies; (2) the Longshoremen's and Harbor Workers' Compensation Act, which covers shipyard employees; and (3) the Black Lung Program, which covers coal miners. Today, more than 85 percent of the work force is covered by workers' compensation statutes.

Before the enactment of workers' compensation statutes, employees had difficulty in recovering for work-related injuries. This difficulty was due to the common law treatment of workers, which will be discussed next.

Deficiencies of Common Law

Under the common law, workers injured on the job could recover only if they proved that the employer's negligence caused their injuries. Many workers found going to trial and proving the employer's fault extremely difficult. Moreover, even if a worker proved fault the employer would escape liability by proving any one of several defenses.

The burden of proving the employer's fault and disproving the employer's defense prevented many workers from recovering for work-related injuries or death. Even if the court held that the employer was liable for damages, the injured worker faced these problems: (1) expenses of the lawsuit, including attorney's fees; (2) delay from the time of injury to the jury's award of damages; (3) medical expenses owed before the trial was completed; and (4) inadequate jury awards. More efficient and certain protection for employees injured at work was obviously needed.

Coverage

The workers' compensation laws in most states are mandatory. In these states an employer is *required* to provide workers' compensation coverage for its employees. In South Carolina, New Jersey, and Texas, employers may *elect* to be under either workers' compensation coverage or common law negligence. The employers who opt for common law liability are subject to lawsuits for damages by employees and their survivors. The employers do not have the benefit of the common law defenses.

The statutes of all the states exclude certain workers, such as farm workers and domestic help, from workers' compensation coverage. Federal workers are covered by federal compensation laws.

The purpose of workers' compensation statutes is to provide protection for employees and their dependents for work-related injuries, diseases, and death. Whether the employer or the employee is negligent is immaterial, since fault is not an issue. Under workers' compensation laws, the employer is an insurer of job-related harm, provided the following requirements are met: (1) an employer-employee relationship exists; (2) the injury is work related; and (3) the injury resulted from an accident.

To obtain coverage, the *employer-employee* relationship must be established. The employer is not liable for injuries suffered by an independent contractor while performing his or her job. If ABC Company hires Tom Smith, an independent contractor, to install plumbing at the ABC factory and Smith is injured in an accident while performing his job, he is not eligible for workers' compensation benefits.

"Casual workers"—temporary, irregular, and incidental workers—are not covered under workers' compensation laws. However, courts deem it inadvisable to give a general definition of the term *casual.* They decide each case largely on its special facts.

Employees may recover benefits under workers' compensation laws only if the death, injury, or disease is *work related.* A printer who accidentally catches his hand in a press would definitely be entitled to benefits. But if while driving home from work, the same printer stops at a grocery store and slips on the sidewalk, his injury would not be covered since it was not due to a risk or condition peculiar to his job.

In reviewing claims, courts construe the work-related requirement liberally. Thus injuries sustained at company picnics or while participating on a company-sponsored softball team are usually compensable. Although the injuries occurred after working hours and off the job premises, they occurred in the course of an activity that the employer initiated and from which the employer expected to derive benefits. In one case a worker became intoxicated at an office Christmas party and fell out of a third-floor window. A Rhode Island court held that the accident was job related because the worker was expected to attend company social functions.

Courts in all but nine states now recognize job stress as a compensable injury. In Massachusetts, for example, an employee with 22 years of seniority suffered a nervous breakdown when informed that she would be transferred to another department. The state supreme court upheld her claim for workers' compensation benefits despite the company's argument that an emotional disability must result from an unusually stressful event.

For an injury to be compensable, it must result from an *accident.* However, the standard for determining "accident" has broadened over the years. For example, the Supreme Court of Missouri approved an award of benefits to the dependents of a truck driver who suffered a fatal heart attack while making his usual run from Kansas City, Missouri, to Indianapolis. The court noted that the right to compensation is not lost merely because the strains preceding the attack are usual. Although workers' compensation laws do not permit coverage for self-inflicted on-the-job injuries, when a worker in another state permanently damaged his right arm by punching a coffee machine in anger, the court found the injury to be an accident and awarded compensation.

The following case indicates the issues involved in deciding whether an injury is work related.

McCAMMON v. NEUBERT
SUPREME COURT OF TENNESSEE
651 S.W.2d 702 (1983)

David McCammon (plaintiff) was employed by Joe Neubert (defendant) on an hourly basis as a painter's helper and errand boy in Neubert's Paint and Body Shop. On February 15, 1980, McCammon brought his lunch to work, but at the request of his fellow employees he drove approximately a mile to obtain their lunches at a drive-in. After placing the lunch orders, he drove approximately another mile to a bank, where he cashed his paycheck in order to buy enough gasoline to make the return trip to the drive-in and then back to work. Upon leaving the bank, he was involved in an automobile accident in which he injured his hip and left knee, resulting in his total and permanent disability.

McCammon brought suit against his employer and its workers' compensation carrier. He was awarded benefits based on a finding of 100 percent permanent disability. The defendants appealed, contending that his injuries were not work related.

PER CURIAM

[R]ecovery of workers' compensation benefits for injuries suffered by an employee who is not on the premises of his employer but who is on his way to and from his workstation has generally been restricted to those instances in which the employee is proceeding by a means furnished by the employer, or in a manner or over a route required by the employer, and this subjects the employee to a definite risk or hazard.

Our review of the record reveals that no specific time or duration of the lunch hour was ever established by defendant Neubert, but that it was to be taken whenever work permitted; that the time taken by the employees at the lunch hour did not affect their compensation; that the usual lunchtime practice was for one of the employees to take orders from the others and go out and obtain their lunches while his comrades remained at their workstation; and that the lunches obtained often included a lunch for defendant Neubert himself.

There was conflicting testimony, however, as to whether Neubert, on the day plaintiff was injured, actually directed plaintiff to obtain the others' lunches or even was aware that plaintiff had made a trip for that purpose. Plaintiff testified that on February 15, 1980, after his co-workers had yelled to him that they were hungry, Neubert told him specifically to go out and get their lunches; that Neubert told him that when he returned he might have to go out again to get Neubert's lunch; that he told Neubert that he did not have enough gasoline in his car to make the trip for lunch and that in order to do so, it would require the cashing of his paycheck he had received that morning and the purchasing of more gasoline; and that Neubert indeed consented both to his going to the bank and to his purchasing of more gasoline while on his trip for the lunches, but that he was to "hurry back."

From a review of the entire record in the instant case, we hold that there is material evidence to support the chancellor's finding that plaintiff sustained a compensable injury both arising out of and in the course of his employment. We are persuaded by the fact that it was undisputed that the usual lunchtime procedures, which were known and participated in by the employer, regularly involved one of the employees leaving the premises and obtaining lunch for the others who remained at their workstations; that on the date of the accident, plaintiff had indeed brought his lunch to work with him that morning and therefore had no reason to leave work at lunchtime but to obtain lunch for his co-workers; and that plaintiff's journey, although arguably unknown to his employer on February 15, 1980, not only benefited his employer by allowing the other employees to keep on working while plaintiff was obtaining their lunch, but also subjected plaintiff to a definite risk or hazard on the road.

Affirmed.

Legal Issues

1. How important in the court's view was the evidence that "routine practice" occurred? Why?
2. Change the facts of this case so that McCammon could not have recovered.

Ethical Issues

1. Are the court's reasons for permitting McCammon to recover benefits under the state's workers' compensation statute consistent with bottom-line ethics? Why?

2. Does fairness call for courts to loosely or narrowly interpret the requirement of a workers' compensation statute that an employee must have been injured while about the employer's business in order to recover an award? Why?

Occupational Diseases

Occupational disease
a job-related disease

Early workers' compensation statutes did not cover **occupational disease.** However, all of the states now include such coverage. Compensation is provided for any job-related disease. A job-related disease results from exposure to harmful conditions that are present to a greater extent on a particular job than on jobs in general. Among such diseases are lung, skin, and hearing disorders.

Exclusive Remedy

An injured worker is entitled only to the benefits established under the workers' compensation schedule by the state legislature. This means that employees covered by workers' compensation statutes cannot sue their employers for damages. Thus the workers' compensation statute is the *exclusive remedy* for the employee who has sustained a work-related injury. This holds true even if the employee's loss is greater than the benefits provided by the workers' compensation statute. Thus injured workers are entitled to an almost certain recovery, but the benefits are limited. The courts of California and New Jersey allow an exception to the exclusive remedy rule. In those states injured workers can sue the employer for work-related injuries if they can prove that the employer deliberately concealed medical information. In California and New Jersey cases, medical records concealed by the employer indicated that workers had been harmed by asbestos.

The exclusivity of remedies does not prevent workers from suing *third parties* responsible for their injury. Thus a negligent co-worker or the manufacturer of a defective machine that caused a work-related injury is subject to a lawsuit for damages.

Benefits

The benefits provided under workers' compensation statutes vary from state to state. However, all of the state statutes include medical benefits, rehabilitation benefits, and cash benefits. *Medical benefits* pay doctors and hospitals expenses due to the workplace injury. These benefits are sizable since they are ordinarily provided without time or dollar limits. *Rehabilitation benefits* are available for severe injuries that require medical and vocational rehabilitation.

Cash benefits cover physical impairments and wage losses caused by the injury. These benefits are divided into four classifications based on the extent of disablity.

Temporary, Total Disability Benefits   *Temporary, total disability benefits* are made to workers who are totally disabled (unable to work) but whose disability is temporary, so that they are expected to recover and return to work. Such benefits, which typically amount to one half to two thirds of an employee's average weekly wage, up to a specified maximum, are paid until the employee returns to work. Table 12-1 lists the 10 states with the highest maximum benefits and the 10 states with the lowest maximum benefits.

Permanent, Partial Disability Benefits *Permanent, partial disability benefits* are provided when an employee suffers a permanent loss or impairment of any part of the body that results in less than total disability. The disability suffered by an employee who loses an index finger while operating a machine is considered partial because it does not prevent the employee from returning to work. It is permanent, however, and the laws of many states provide a **fixed schedule** for such losses. In such a state the loss of an index finger might be worth $3,150; the loss of a hand, $10,500; and the loss of a foot, $8,750. For unscheduled losses, a percentage of disability is determined based on the employee's loss of earning power due to the injury.

Fixed schedule

a schedule listing the amount of compensation to be paid to workers for particular losses or disabilities

---

Maximum Weekly Benefits for Injured Workers*

TABLE 12-1

Highest state levels	
1. Connecticut	$719
2. Iowa	703
3. Alaska	700
4. Illinois	631
5. New Hampshire	620
6. District of Columbia	584
7. Vermont	559
8. Maine	493
9. Massachusetts	491
10. Maryland	452
Lowest state levels	
1. Mississippi	$218
2. Georgia	225
3. Arkansas	231
4. Oklahoma	246
5. Nebraska	255
6. Tennessee	273
7. Arizona	276
8. Kansas	278
9. Louisiana	282
10. Indiana	294

* Maximum weekly benefits for temporary, total disability for workers' compensation as of January 1991. Most states provide the same amount of maximum weekly payments for temporary, total disability benefits and permanent, total disability benefits.

Source: U.S. Chamber of Commerce.

Permanent, Total Disability Benefits A worker who receives *permanent, total disability benefits* is totally incapacitated and permanently unable to perform gainful employment. The states in which organized labor is strong provide such workers with the highest benefits, sometimes over three times the amount provided in a nonindustrial state.

Death Benefits *Death benefits* are paid to the dependents (spouse and minor children) of an employee who is killed in a work-related accident. The amount of these benefits is based on the number of dependents and is calculated as a percentage of the deceased worker's wages, within a certain minimum and maximum. The benefits also include burial expenses. In California the death benefits amount to $70,000–$95,000 based on the number of surviving dependents.

Funding

Most states require employers either to obtain insurance from a private insurance firm or to qualify for self-insurance by proving that they possess the financial ability to carry their own risk. For large employers that qualify, such as Chrysler Corporation, it is usually cheaper to pay workers' compensation claims themselves.

The premium charged for workers' compensation insurance depends largely on (1) the risk involved in the work, (2) the employer's safety record, and (3) the benefits that the state requires. Thus it is financially advantageous for employers to promote workplace safety.

Administration

In most states an administrative agency, usually referred to as the "workers' compensation commission," administers the workers' compensation laws. A worker whose claim is denied can appeal to this agency. Figure 12-3 provides an illustration. The agency's decision may be appealed to the state courts. However, 95 percent of workers' compensation claims are uncontested, 3 percent are resolved by the state workers' compensation commission, and only 2 percent end up in court. The laws of six states provide for court administration of workers' compensation statutes. In these states claims are filed directly in the state courts.

Workers' compensation statutes vary from state to state, but they all have these goals: prompt and efficient recovery for injured workers, including rehabilitation and the restoration of income, and the promotion of safety and health in the American workplace.

OCCUPATIONAL SAFETY AND HEALTH ACT: PROTECTION OF WORKERS FROM SAFETY HAZARDS

The Occupational Safety and Health Act (OSHA) was passed in 1970. Concerned about the large number of work-related accidents and deaths across the nation, Congress passed the act "to assure so far as possible every working man and woman in the nation safe and healthful working conditions and to preserve our human resources." To encourage employers and employees to reduce workplace hazards, the act established safety and health standards for workplaces.

The act applies to any employer (whether profit or nonprofit) with at least one employee if the employer's business affects interstate commerce. Specifically excluded from the act's requirements are church and religious organizations, the federal government, and state and city governments.

Congress created a new agency, the Occupational Safety and Health Administration (which, confusingly, is also referred to as "OSHA"), to administer and enforce the act. The agency, a part of the Department of Labor, conducts workplace inspections to assure compliance with the government's occupational safety and health standards.

Employees have a right to demand safety and health on the job. As noted, the act forbids employers from punishing workers for complaining to the employer, the union, or OSHA or any other government agency about job safety and health hazards.

Enforcement

Employers are required to comply with health and safety standards issued by the secretary of labor. They are responsible for becoming familiar with the specific standards that apply to their own workplaces. For example, employers must furnish earplugs for employees who work in a workplace that is defined as "noisy." To further illustrate: OSHA regulations now provide right-to-know standards for all employers that produce or import chemicals. These employers are required to provide workers and their customers with detailed sheets that identify the chemicals and describe the appropriate health and safety standards. The purpose of this hazard communication program is to provide employers and employees with an incentive to better protect the workplace from harmful chemical substances.

Illustration of Workers' Compensation Benefits   **FIGURE 12-3**

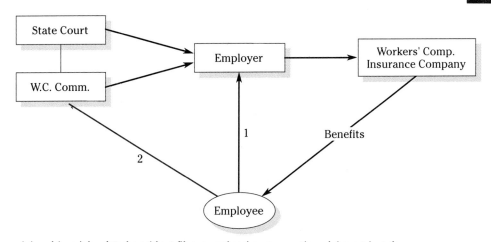

An employee injured in a job-related accident files a workers' compensation claim against the employer (1). The employer forwards the claim to its workers' compensation insurance company, which provides benefits to the employee or denies the claim. If the claim is denied, the employee may appeal to the workers' compensation commission and then to the state courts if the commission denies the claim (2).

Congress recognized that omissions are necessarily inherent in the health and safety standards established under the Occupational Safety and Health Act. Thus the act provides that even where no specific standards apply, employers have an obligation to employees. Its *general duty clause* states that each employer shall furnish "a place of employment that is free from recognized hazards that are causing or are likely to cause death or serious physical harm to employees." This clause obligates employers to eliminate safety hazards that are not covered by any standard.

The act also places duties on employees. Workers are required to observe its health and safety standards. Employees who operate certain machinery, for example, must wear the required personal protective equipment, such as goggles, safety shoes, and earplugs. Although the act does not propose specific penalties, the employer may discipline employees who fail to comply with its standards.

To police the millions of workplaces under its jurisdiction, the Occupational Safety and Health Administration relies primarily on random, unannounced inspections of workplaces by compliance officers. With or without notice to the employer, these compliance officers can enter a business covered by the act at any reasonable time. The employer and a representative of the employees can accompany them during an inspection.

Under language of the Occupational Safety and Health Act, the employer was legally bound to grant the compliance officers immediate entry. However, as noted in Chapter 10, the Supreme Court held that if the owner objected, they could not enter a workplace unless they first obtained a search warrant. The impact of this decision on OSHA has been minimal. Over 96 percent of employers have readily consented to OSHA inspections.

If a violation of the Occupational Safety and Health Act is found to exist, a citation is issued to the employer. The citation informs the employer and employees of the regulations and standards alleged to have been violated and of the date that has been prescribed for correction of the hazard cited. The employer must post a copy of each citation near the place where the violation occurred and must correct the cited hazard by the date prescribed. Failure to do so without good cause results in a penalty for the employer.

An employer may request an informal meeting with OSHA's area director to discuss the citation. Such a meeting often results in a settlement agreement that reduces the citations and penalties. Upon a failure to agree, the employer may contest a citation by filing a notice with the Occupational Safety and Health Review Commission, an independent administrative agency created to hear appeals from citations.

The OSHA area director is authorized to assess penalties for violations of the Occupational Safety and Health Act. These penalties may result in fines of up to $1,000. For repeated violations a fine of up to $10,000 may be assessed for *each occurrence*. A repeated violation is one that may occur if upon reinspection a violation of the previously cited standard or regulation is found, even if the violation involves another piece of equipment or location in the work site. In addition, a fine of up to $10,000 is possible for a violation that the employer intentionally and knowingly commits. This includes gross negligence, in which the employer is aware of the violation but takes no action to correct it. Criminal penalties of up to six months' imprisonment and a $10,000 fine are possible if a willful violation results in an employee's death. These penalties are seldom imposed at the maximum level. Table 12-2 provides examples of penalties that have been proposed by OSHA.

State Plans

The Occupational Safety and Health Act encourages individual states to develop and operate job safety and health plans. Once OSHA has determined that a state program for providing safe places of employment is at least as effective as its own program, federal authority ceases over workplaces in the state. Still, OSHA monitors the state program and will withdraw approval if the state fails to adequately enforce the standards of that program. Approximately one half of the states police workplaces within their borders, with OSHA funding up to 50 percent of the operating costs.

Changes in OSHA

In OSHA's early years, its highest priority was compliance. Compliance officers were sent on inspections without regard to the safety record of the particular workplaces inspected or their industry. Now OSHA targets its inspections to industries and workplaces in which injuries are most likely to occur. It ranks industries by days of work lost per worker and selects workplaces for inspection on the basis of these rankings. Under this system, construction and manufacturing are given the most inspections since they produce the highest percentages of lost-workday cases. Nonhazardous industries, such as retail sales, are usually not inspected unless an employee complains to OSHA that a hazard exists.

Under OSHA's present system, a workplace visit may result in a review of records rather than a full inspection. The compliance officer looks at the safety records and compiles a lost-workday rate. If the rate is lower than the average national rate in manufacturing, the inspection ceases at that point. If it is higher than the national average rate, a complete inspection takes place. Thus frequent and flagrant violators of OSHA's rules receive greater attention. OSHA inspectors

Examples of Penalties Proposed by OSHA (in $ millions)* TABLE 12-2

Company	Amount of Penalty
1. U.S. Steel	$7.2†
2. IBP, Inc.	5.7
3. L'Ambiance	5.1
4. John Morrell & Co.	4.3
5. Bath Iron Worker	4.2
6. Budd Company	3.1
7. Doe Run Company	2.8
8. Friction Division	2.8
9. Ford Electronic and Refrigerator	1.9
10. Zinc Corporation of America	1.9

* The size of the proposed fine is related to the number of violations, with multiple violations increasing the penalty. OSHA is willing to negotiate the amount of the proposed fine if the company gives assurance that it will remedy the safety violations. From 1986 to 1989, OSHA reduced $29.3 million in fines to $9.5 million, a 67.5 percent drop.

† The highest penalty ever proposed because the two steel plants in question had been charged with previous violations.

Source: Occupational Safety and Health Administration, Office of Management Data Systems, 1990.

now focus on the approximately one fourth of manufacturers whose employee lost-workday rate due to occupational injuries exceeds the national average for manufacturing. An employee complaint can, of course, trigger an inspection of an alleged safety hazard that threatens physical harm or an imminent danger.

Since its enactment in 1970, the Occupational Safety and Health Act has been one of the federal government's most controversial laws. In the early years of the Occupational Safety and Health Administration, businesspersons criticized it for harassing businesses with inane but costly rules that were unrelated to safety and health problems—for example, issuing citations for such technical violations as failing to mark factory aisles with white paint and not yellow paint, to mount smaller fire extinguishers 5 feet from the floor, and to use toilets with open-front seats. Labor unions, on the other hand, contended that OSHA failed to curb worker exposure to serious health hazards, such as cancer-causing substances.

Responding to its critics, OSHA changed its direction in the late 1970s. It withdrew or revised thousands of nit-picking regulations and reduced inspections of generally nonhazardous businesses. At the same time, it increased its emphasis on severe health hazards. It issued additional rules regarding worker exposure to such cancer-causing substances as asbestos, benzene, and lead. To protect workers in noisy areas, it required the employer to test the hearing of certain workers annually.

At present, OSHA is focusing on repetitive ergonomic trauma (RET)—injuries to the nerves and muscles resulting from repetitive motions. Such injuries occur in both blue-collar and white-collar jobs. In the poultry industry, for example, one company was assessed a $242,000 fine for willfully keeping workers on jobs that resulted in serious hand and wrist disorders. In this company a worker would cut up as many as 5,000 chickens a day, moving hands and wrist in the same way approximately every four to six seconds. White-collar jobs subject to RET include those that require extensive use of computer keyboards, which has resulted in neck, back, arm, and wrist problems.

Has the Occupational Safety and Health Act accomplished its objective of assuring "safe and healthful working conditions" for "every working man and woman"? The accident and illness figures are inconclusive. However, both labor and business representatives agree that management has become more aware of safety and health issues and that such issues have assumed a more important role in union negotiations.

FAIR LABOR STANDARDS ACT: PROTECTION OF WORKERS FROM UNFAIR AND EXCESSIVE HOURS

The Fair Labor Standards Act (FLSA), passsed by Congress in 1938, sets minimum wage, overtime pay, and child labor standards. The act was passed during the Great Depression, when the unemployment rate was 30 percent, wages were at substandard levels, and many workers were dependent on public relief. Its purposes were (1) to *stimulate the economy* by increasing the purchasing power of low-paid workers; (2) to *reduce unemployment* by making it expensive to pay overtime, thereby giving employers an incentive to hire new workers; and (3) to *reduce the causes of labor disputes* by decreasing long hours and increasing pay in the low-paying jobs.

Coverage

The FLSA coverage extends to all employees of a business that is engaged in interstate commerce or in the production of goods for interstate commerce. In addition, the act specifically applies to employees working for certain businesses, such as laundries, dry cleaners, construction firms, and hospitals. Surveys have indicated that most of the employees who earn the minimum wage are secondary earners. This means that they are not the main breadwinners of their families. About one third of them are teenagers.

Exemptions   Some workers are exempt from the minimum wage and overtime requirements of FLSA. Among these workers are outside sales personnel and administrative, executive, and professional employees. Congress specifically excluded such workers because they are normally in a position to protect themselves. In addition, some workers are included within the minimum wage provisions of the act but exempt from the overtime provisions. Among these workers are highly paid commission employees of retail or service establishments, taxi drivers, employees of railroads and airlines, news editors, and farmers. Application of the overtime provisions to such workers would be impractical.

In 1985 the Supreme Court ruled that state and city governments were subject to the FLSA's minimum wage and overtime provisions. Congress promptly amended the act to permit state and local governments to substitute compensation time for the payment of overtime wages.

Minimum Wage and Overtime Computation

Originally, FLSA specified a minimum wage of 25 cents an hour, a standard workweek of 44 hours, and an overtime rate of 1½ times the employee's regular hourly rate. Amendments to the act have increased the minimum wage and reduced the number of hours in the standard workweek. The amendment that went into effect on April 1, 1991, increased the minimum wage to $4.25 an hour. Employees covered[7] by FLSA are entitled to an hourly wage of not less than this amount. However, the amendment also provides that employers can pay a training wage of $3.61 per hour for workers under 20 years old during the first 90 days of employment. This was the first time that the act contained a provision of this kind. In calculating wages paid, the act allows the employer to include the reasonable costs of meals, lodging and any other facilities provided by the employer as part of the job.[8]

Covered workers have a legal right to overtime pay at not less than 1½ times their regular pay after 40 hours of work in a workweek. FLSA uses a single workweek as the standard and does not permit averaging hours over two or more weeks. For example, an employee who works 35 hours one week and 45 hours the next week—and thus a weekly average of 40 hours for the two weeks—must receive overtime pay for the hours worked beyond 40 during the second week.

Provision for subminimum wages is allowed if special certificates are obtained from the Department of Labor. Learners, apprentices, and handicapped workers can be paid less than the minimum wage. Less than the minimum wage can also be paid to "tipped" employees, such as waitresses, and to full-time students who work in retail or service establishments, in agriculture, or for institutions of higher learning.

Child Labor Provisions

In addition to regulating the minimum wage and overtime pay, FLSA regulates the private employment of child labor. The secretary of labor publishes lists of hazardous jobs that employees under 18 may not do. Such jobs include the operation of a motor vehicle, the operation of machinery, excavation, mining, and jobs that require exposure to radioactive materials. The following regulations govern the kinds and hours of work for youth employed in *nonfarm* jobs:

1. Age 18 or older: any job, whether hazardous or not, for unlimited hours.
2. Ages 16 and 17: any nonhazardous job, for unlimited hours.
3. Ages 14 and 15: outside of school hours, various nonmanufacturing, non-mining, nonhazardous jobs (for example, office work and sales).
4. Age 13 or under: certain approved jobs, such as delivering newspapers or working for parents in a nonhazardous job.

The regulations for *farm work* are less restrictive. Children of any age may be employed by their parents at any time in any occupation on a farm owned or operated by their parents.

Employment of a child below the minimum age specified is considered oppressive and in violation of FLSA.

Enforcement

The Wage and Hour Division of the Department of Labor enforces FLSA. Compliance officers can investigate employers and gather information from them on wages, hours, and other employment conditions. If compliance officers find violations, they can order an employer to revise his or her operations as necessary. An employer who willfully violates the act may be prosecuted criminally and fined up to $10,000. A second criminal conviction may result in imprisonment.

Civil sanctions are also available. An employee can bring suit and recover from the employer for unpaid wages and overtime compensation. In addition, the employee can collect liquidated damages (an equal amount of back pay) plus attorney's fees and court costs. The secretary of labor may sue on behalf of an employee who is reluctant to bring a private suit against the employer. The secretary of labor may also obtain an injunction to restrain an employer from future violations of FLSA.

Most states have enacted laws governing minimum wages, maximum hours, and the employment of child labor. Generally, these laws apply if they provide greater protection to employees than does the federal law.

UNEMPLOYMENT COMPENSATION: FINANCIAL PROTECTION OF WORKERS FROM LAYOFFS

The Social Security Act of 1935 was the origin of the present federal-state unemployment insurance program. The enormous unemployment problem during the Great Depression spurred Congress to aid workers who were unemployed due to economic conditions beyond their control. The Social Security Act imposed a 3 percent federal payroll tax on employers to finance the payment of unemployment compensation. However, employers who paid taxes into a state unemployment compensation plan were excused from paying 90 percent of the tax. Today, the state unemployment compensation laws provide for weekly payments for temporary periods to employees who are no longer working through no fault of their own.

Coverage

To be protected by unemployment insurance, an employee must work for an employer who is required to pay unemployment compensation taxes. As a minimum standard, federal law requires that unemployment compensation taxes be paid by any employer (1) who has at least one or more employees for 20 or more weeks in a calendar year or (2) who pays at least $1,500 in wages in any calendar quarter. Individual states may extend coverage to other employers. A few states, for example, require employers of domestic workers to pay unemployment compensation taxes. However, the following types of employers are usually granted exemptions from paying unemployment compensation taxes: employers of labor for religious, educational, or charitable institutions; employers of labor for small farming operations; employers of federal government labor; and employers of family members. A worker is not entitled to unemployment benefits if the employer is exempt from unemployment taxes.

Benefits

The benefits provided by the unemployment insurance system vary from state to state. In January 1991 the maximum weekly benefits ranged from $140 in the state with the lowest benefits to $423 in the state with the highest benefits (see Table 12-3). Generally, the amount of the benefits is equal to one half of the worker's previous gross full-time weekly pay, up to a specified maximum. Most states pay the benefits for 26 weeks. In times of high unemployment, however, the financing of an additional 13 weeks of benefits by the federal government may be approved by Congress.

Workers who qualify draw unemployment insurance benefits as a matter of right. Need is not a factor. Most states require a waiting period of one week before any payment is made. The purpose of this requirement is to provide the worker with an incentive to actively seek employment.

No contribution is made by employees for unemployment compensation. The benefits are financed by employers through payroll taxes. In all states the covered employer pays a tax rate up to 6.2 percent of the first $7,000 of each worker's annual wages. Of this total, 0.8 percent goes to the federal government to pay for administration of the unemployment insurance program, with the balance going to the state trust fund. In times of high unemployment, if a state's trust fund runs low, the state can borrow from the federal Treasury. Figure 12-4 provides an illustration.

The amount of the unemployment compensation taxes is based on a number of factors, including (1) the state's unemployment rate, (2) the level of benefits mandated by state law, and (3) the employer's layoff and separation record. Employers whose workers have experienced less than average unemployment are required to pay less than employers whose workers have experienced more than average unemployment. The **experience rating** of employers provides them with an incentive to retain employees during recessions.

Experience rating
the employer's record of layoffs, a factor in determining the amount of the employer's unemployment compensation taxes

Qualifications

Even if the employer pays unemployment compensation taxes, a worker must qualify to draw unemployment insurance benefits. For a worker to qualify, the laws of most states require:

1. That the worker be available for work and willing to accept suitable work. The worker must report to the state unemployment office each week and must accept offers of any job for which he or she is *suited by prior training and experience.* Thus a secretary who declines an offer for employment on a factory assembly line is still eligible for unemployment benefits.

2. That the worker be unemployed through no fault of his or her own. A worker who has been laid off due to lack of work is eligible, but a worker who has been discharged for good cause or has left employment voluntarily is not eligible. In all states but New York and Rhode Island, a worker who is unemployed because the worker's union is on strike is not eligible for benefits.

3. That the worker be physically able to work full-time. A worker who for medical reasons can no longer perform a particular job is eligible if he or she can still perform other kinds of work. Thus a carpenter who loses a leg can draw unemployment benefits since he or she can still work at other jobs.

TABLE 12–3 **Maximum Unemployment Compensation Weekly Benefits for Unemployed Workers***

Highest state levels	
1. Massachusetts	$423
2. Rhode Island	334
3. Connecticut	320
4. Pennsylvania	299
5. District of Columbia	293
6. New Jersey	291
7. Ohio	291
8. Alaska	284
9. Maine	282
10. Hawaii	275
Lowest state levels	
1. South Dakota	$140
2. Nebraska	144
3. Mississippi	145
4. Alabama	150
5. Indiana	161
6. Tennessee	165
7. Arizona	165
8. Missouri	170
9. South Carolina	175
10. New Mexico	177

* As of January 1991.
Source: U.S. Department of Labor.

EMPLOYEE RETIREMENT INCOME SECURITY ACT: FINANCIAL PROTECTION OF WORKERS' RETIREMENT PLANS

Millions of Americans are covered under private retirement plans. At the turn of the century, relatively few employers offered such plans. Since then, however, workers' demands for payments after retirement have caused more and more employers to offer private security. Today, private retirement plans cover one half of the workers in the private sector.

The increased popularity of retirement plans is partly due to the tax status of contributions to such plans. Both employer and employee contributions to plans that qualify under Internal Revenue Service regulations are tax-exempt. In addition, earnings on a retirement fund are nontaxable while they are being held in the fund. Retirement benefits are subsequently taxed as personal income only when they are distributed to the retired worker, who is ordinarily in a lower tax bracket at that time.

There are two basic types of retirement plans: contributory and noncontributory. The vast majority are **contributory pension plans,** which are financed by contributions of the employer and employees. In **noncontributory pension plans,** all of the funds are provided by the employer.

In past years retirement plans were largely unregulated and operated solely at the employer's discretion. Unfortunately, many employees never received the benefits stipulated by the plans. This was caused by mismanagement of the plan, workers' voluntary departures from a job in quest of another job, or firings of

Contributory pension plan

a retirement plan that is financed by contributions from both the employer and the employee

Noncontributory pension plan

a retirement plan that is financed solely by contributions from the employer

---

Illustration of the Payment of Unemployment Compensation Benefits

FIGURE 12–4

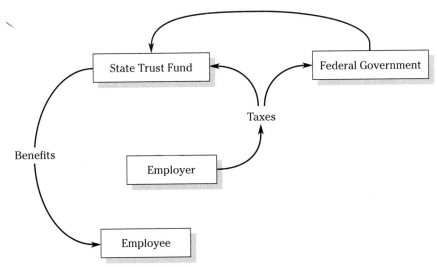

Employees make no contributions for unemployment compensation. Unemployment insurance benefits are funded by payroll taxes paid by employers. Of the taxes collected for this purpose, most goes to the state trust fund, and the remainder goes to the federal government to pay for adminstration of the unemployment insurance program. In times of high unemployment, a state can borrow from the federal Treasury if its trust fund is running low.

workers before the age of retirement. The rate of retirement benefit forfeitures was over 50 percent. As a result, in 1974 Congress enacted the Employee Retirement Income Security Act (ERISA), which established federal regulation of private retirement funds. The act is designed to ensure the benefits of participants in retirement plans against the financial collapse of the plans and to guarantee the payment of promised retirement benefits. The act does not, however, require an employer to establish a retirement plan.

Vesting

Vesting

the legal right that an employee acquires in a retirement plan after completing a required length of service

Before the enactment of ERISA, employees did not vest until shortly before retirement. **Vesting** is the legal right that an employee acquires in a retirement plan after completing a required length of service. Upon vesting, an employee becomes eligible for benefits that it is illegal to take away, though the employee may not be able to collect them until retirement. Before the enactment of ERISA, 30 years of employment were required to qualify for the benefits of a typical retirement plan. An employee who switched jobs or was discharged after 25 years of employment lost all the benefits of the plan.

ERISA requires employers to select one of two minimum vesting schedules. One of the schedules provides 100 percent vesting at the end of five years. The other is a step plan that provides partial vesting based on the following table:

Years of Service	Nonforfeitable Percentage
3	20
4	40
5	60
6	80
7 or more	100

Most employers have chosen the step plan. Under this plan, an employee who quits or is discharged after three years of service is still assured of receiving benefits at retirement. The certainty of benefits after a minimum period of service is a primary objective of ERISA.

To make sure that employees get vested retirement benefits, ERISA established the Pension Benefit Guaranty Corporation (PBGC), a federal agency that insures more than $800 billion in private retirement assets for over 40 million workers. All retirement plans are required to pay the agency annual insurance premiums. If a plan fails, PBGC pays the retirement benefits, up to certain maximums, owed to the contributing employees. The employer is liable to reimburse PBGC for the benefits paid, up to an amount equal to 30 percent of the employer's net worth.

Although the reforms enacted by ERISA were undoubtedly needed, it has had some undesirable effects. It has slowed the growth of private retirement plans and caused some employers to actually abandon their plans. Since the enactment of ERISA, small companies in particular have been reluctant to establish retirement plans. Their reluctance can be attributed in part to (1) the burdensome paperwork requirements of ERISA, (2) the cost of expert advice on retirement plans, and (3) the fact that Congress changes the rules so often. Thus one may question whether

ERISA has been living up to the words of its title—*employee retirement income security.*

IMMIGRATION AND REFORM CONTROL ACT OF 1986

Responding to concerns about rising illegal immigration, Congress passed the Immigration and Reform Control Act of 1986. The act requires employers (even those with as few as four employees) to make sure that their employees are legally eligible to work in the United States. Job applicants, including part-time workers, must produce proof of citizenship or proof of legal residency in the form of a social security card, a U.S. birth certificate, a U.S. passport, a certificate of naturalization, a resident alien card, or various other papers. The act requires *all* newly hired employees—even lifelong residents of the United States—to produce such proof.

Employers who hire illegal immigrants or fail to keep adequate records of employees can be fined $100 to $1,000 for each violation. Employers who knowingly employ illegal aliens can be fined from $250 to $2,000 per illegal employee for a first offense, and repeat offenders can be fined up to $10,000 per illegal employee. The Immigration and Naturalization Service has been vigorous in its enforcement of the act.

An unfortunate side effect of the Immigration and Reform Control Act has been discrimination against legal foreigners, particularly Hispanic- Americans. Employers fearful of hiring illegal aliens have discriminated against job applicants with foreign names or accents. Discrimination on the basis of national origin is prohibited by the act itself, as well as by Title VII of the Civil Rights Act of 1964. Complaints are handled by the Office of Special Counsel for Immigration Related Unfair Employment Practices and the Equal Employment Opportunity Commission.

PLANT CLOSING LAWS

Proposed in Congress as early as 1973, the Worker Adjustment and Retraining Notification Act (WARN) became law in 1988, perhaps in part as a response to the numerous takeovers and corporate restructurings of the 80s. WARN requires that workers be given at least 60 days' written notice of plant closings or mass layoffs so that they can make an earlier start on seeking new employment or on training for different employment. Notice must also be given to labor unions and local governments.

WARN affects only companies with 100 or more employees.[9] Notice must be given 60 days in advance of "plant closing," which is defined as the closing of an employment site that results in the loss of employment for 50 or more workers (excluding part-time workers). In addition, WARN requires notice of a "mass layoff," which is defined as loss of employment by either (1) at least 50 employees (excluding part-time workers) who make up at least 33 percent of the employer's work force or (2) 500 or more employees (excluding part-time workers), whatever their percentage of the work force.

WARN is enforced through private civil lawsuits for lost wages and benefits for each day up to 60 days that notice was not given. Both full and part-time employees, including managers and supervisors, can bring suit for lack of required notice. Courts cannot issue an injunction to stop a plant closing or a mass layoff that violates the act.

Relatively few WARN cases have gone to court. WARN simply does not apply to many smaller businesses, and it provides liberal exemptions that suspend the 60 days' notice requirement. The most imporant exemption applies to employers with a "faltering business" who are actively seeking capital or new business to stay open and reasonably believe that giving notice of a mass firing or layoff would jeopardize their chances of obtaining the capital or business.[10]

DRUG TESTING LAWS

In recent years employers have become increasingly aware of how expensive drug-using employees can be, in terms not only of decreases in productivity but also of increases in workplace accidents and health care costs. Surveys indicate that 19 percent of current employees and 25 percent of applicants are being tested for drugs. Because of privacy concerns, however, employers who use drug testing must proceed with caution. Federal law on this issue is still evolving, and state laws, which generally control the issue, vary widely.

A few general observations may be made. Citing the concerns of public safety, courts have upheld the drug testing of people who work with dangerous machinery. Drug testing of employees who show signs of drug abuse and drug testing as a precondition of employment are not considered unreasonable. Any employer who utilizes drug testing should take great pains to ensure that it is performed accurately and that employee confidentiality is preserved. It is also good policy to explain to employees why drug testing is being used and how it will be carried out.

Congress expressed its concerns about drug use in the workplace by passing the Drug-Free Workplace Act of 1988. Under this act, employers contracting to supply goods or services to the federal government must certify that they maintain a drug-free workplace. This entails having a written policy in which they inform their employees of the dangers of drug use in the workplace and of their intent to keep the workplace drug-free. Employees must also be informed of any penalties that they may suffer if they are discovered to be drug users and of available treatment or rehabilitation services. Employers are not required to test their employees for drugs or to provide drug counseling. A contractor who violates the Drug-Free Workplace Act can be barred from receiving federal contracts for up to five years.

A Guide for Corporate Drug Testing

Because of the wide variations in state laws and a lack of federal decisions on drug testing, many corporations have been reluctant to utilize it. However, a 1989 decision in California (traditionally a state that emphasizes the rights of individuals) illustrates what can be considered reasonable corporate drug testing.

In *Wilkinson v. Times Mirror Corp.,*[11] the California Court of Appeals upheld a drug testing program for employment applicants. In this program the Times Mirror Company gave every person who was selected for employment a "conditional" offer of employment—that is, the offer was conditioned on passing the pre-employment physical, which included a drug test. The drug testing maintained strict concern for privacy—applicants were not observed while they provided the urine sample, and the results of the testing were kept completely confidential.

However, the California Supreme Court has rejected employers' attempts to require random drug testing for current workers in non-safety-related jobs.

LAW ABROAD

European Community

Workday, Overtime, Vacations, Pregnancy Leave, Parental Leave   Most of the countries in the European Community adhere to an eight-hour day. Portugal's standard seven-hour day for white-collar workers and Ireland's standard nine-hour day for industrial workers are two examples of numerous slight variations in the number of hours that may be worked in a day according to law or collective bargaining agreements.

All of the EC member states recognize the principle of overtime, but each handles overtime differently. Denmark and Great Britain allow overtime issues to be decided entirely through collective bargaining, while the other EC nations have legislators decide these issues. Overtime work is voluntary in some of the EC nations, obligatory in others. In Denmark, for example, overtime agreed to by collective bargaining is obligatory. Rates of overtime pay vary widely, with workers in the poorer EC nations earning 25 percent extra pay for overtime, while workers in the more prosperous nations earn 50 percent or 75 percent extra pay.

Workers in the European Community enjoy longer annual vacations than do U.S. workers. According to the 1970 Holidays with Pay Convention, all workers in the EC are supposed to receive at least three weeks of annual leave after one year's service. But 99 percent of British workers get four weeks, while most French workers and 94 percent of German workers get five weeks. In addition, workers are encouraged (sometimes required) to take this leave in blocks of at least 10 to 14 days.

In all of the EC countries, pregnant women and mothers are entitled to time off from work. In Belgium, Germany, and the Netherlands a pregnant woman is entitled to six weeks of unpaid leave before delivery and up to eight weeks of unpaid leave following the birth of her child. These provisions are typical. Many countries also require that mothers who are nursing their babies be given certain periods of time in which to do so.

Most of the EC countries provide some form of parental leave to take care of children. For example, a Danish father is entitled to a two-week unpaid leave following the birth of his child. In Germany and France the parent who takes care of the child is entitled to unpaid leave or a reduction in the number of hours worked until the child's first birthday. In Spain workers are permitted up to three years of unpaid parental leave; however, the right to reinstatement is limited. Great Britain refuses to recognize by law a right of workers to parental leave.

Germany

German statutes specify exactly how much time is required for notice of termination. The length of notice depends on an employee's age, seniority, and special circumstances, such as disability or pregnancy. The notice period, for example, is three months for wage earners with 5 years of employment, five months for wage earners with 10 years of employment. The notice period may be changed by collective bargaining agreements.

Moreover, in firms that employ more than five persons, there must be "socially justified" reasons for dismissing an employee with six months of service. Such reasons include gross employee misconduct or the dire economic circumstances of the employer. If an economic reason is given, the employer must justify "socially" why that employee was chosen for dismissal. Before an employee is dismissed even for urgent economic reasons, the employer must first try to transfer the employee to another job in the company. Generally, the remedy for wrongful discharge is compensation, not reinstatement.

German law contains provisions similar to those of the U.S. plant closing laws. Mass dismissals require prior written notice to the local labor office. No dismissals are permitted for at least one month after notice has been given. The state labor office can shorten or lengthen this period.

Employee councils grant employees extensive rights of codetermination with management on certain matters that affect the employees' social or economic welfare and security. These councils codetermine with management, for example, working hours and the length of vacations.

Most German employers have established pension plans for their employees. Workers become vested after they reach the age of 35 and have 10 years of service. A national pension insurance plan protects pension plans against the employer's insolvency. Employers must review their pension plan every three years to determine whether adjustments for cost-of-living increases are necessary.

Japan

Unproductive workers are often discharged by U.S. companies, which may result in suits for wrongful discharge. There is very little employment litigation in Japan. The Ministry of Labor usually resolves disputes over such issues as wrongful discharge. Large Japanese employers customarily grant permanent employment, which, of course, eliminates wrongful discharge lawsuits for those employers.

The Japan Labor Standards Act of 1947 and other laws provide workers' compensation protection. A job-related injury entitles an employee with 10 months of service to 60 percent of his or her salary in nontaxable benefits.

REVIEW QUESTIONS & PROBLEMS

1. Why did the state legislatures adopt workers' compensation laws?

2. The common law doctrine of employment at will has been eroding. Why have courts been curtailing the employer's freedom to fire?

3. A football player on full scholarship to Indiana State University was severely injured while taking part in the annual spring practice session. The player's financial aid agreement with the university provided that in exchange for

playing football, he would receive free tuition, room, and board; a book allowance; and exemption from laboratory fees. The agreement also provided that this aid would continue if an injury prevented him from playing, though he would be required to serve the university in some other capacity. The student brought suit against the university, claiming that the financial aid agreement constituted an employment contract and thus he was entitled to compensation under the state's workers' compensation laws. Is the student correct? Why?

4. Bond was employed by Uptown Computer Supplies, Inc. While making a delivery in the company van, Bond was speeding and negligently caused a collision with a car driven by Thomas. Thomas was severely injured and brought suit against both Uptown Computer and Bond. Is Uptown Computer Supplies liable? Is Bond liable? Why?

5. The owner of Mucho Gusto Taco Hut and Delicatessen paid the waiters and waitresses less than the minimum wage. A waiter filed a complaint with the Labor Department. The owner responded that the subminimum wage was justified because the waiters and waitresses received tips from the customers. Is the owner correct? Why?

6. The plaintiff and the defendant were business competitors. The plaintiff wanted to buy goods from the defendant but feared that the defendant would refuse to deal with a competitor. The plaintiff engaged Booth as a middleman, and in his own name Booth ordered the goods that the plaintiff needed from the defendant. The goods were delivered to Booth and paid for by him with money that he received from the plaintiff. The goods were defective. Can the plaintiff sue successfully for breach of contract? Why?

ENDNOTES

1. There are exceptions in which the employer is liable for the torts of the independent contractor. These are the two most common exceptions:
   a. The work to be performed by the independent contractor is inherently dangerous. An example is the independent contractor's use of dynamite for blasting in a city.
   b. The work to be performed by the independent contractor is illegal. Thus an employer who hires an independent contractor to collect illegal gambling debts is liable for torts committed by the independent contractor while performing his or her duties.

2. The General Accounting Office reports that billions of dollars in taxes are lost each year because employers misclassify employees as independent contractors to avoid paying social security and unemployment payroll taxes. In addition, the employees who are classified as independent contractors are not included in the company's benefit plans.

3. Montana is the only state that has enacted an employment at will statute. This law prohibits firing without just cause workers who have completed a probationary period. It limits damages to four years of back wages, however, and it requires employers to submit disputes to arbitration.

4. 765 P.2d 373 (Cal. 1988).

5. 10 U.S.C. Section 2409.

6. The states that do not have a whistle-blower protection statute include Alabama, Alaska, Arkansas, Georgia, Idaho, Massachusetts, Mississippi, Nebraska, Nevada, New Mexico, North Carolina, North Dakota, Oklahoma, South Dakota, Tennessee, Vermont, Virginia, and Wyoming.

7. For purposes of minimum wage requirements, a test of annual dollar volume applies to most firms. The revision that went into effect in 1991 exempts companies with annual revenues of $500,000 or less from paying the minimum wage.

8. Many commentators feel that inflation and labor shortages have made the minimum wage almost unimportant. In 1981, 15 percent of hourly workers earned the minimum wage; in 1989 only 6.5 percent of hourly workers earned the minimum wage. This trend is likely to continue.

9. Nine states—Connecticut, Hawaii, Maine, Maryland, Massachusetts, Michigan, South Carolina, Tennessee, and Wisconsin—had enacted plant closing laws prior to the passage of WARN. The federal law supplements state laws that provide for voluntary notice or have a threshold of more than 50 employees for coverage.

10. The Worker Adjustment and Retraining Notification Act also stipulates the following exemptions: (*a*) sudden business changes that were not reasonably foreseeable; (*b*) natural disasters such as flood, earthquake, drought, or storm that cause a plant closing or a mass layoff; and (*c*) a plant closing or a mass layoff that results from a strike or lockout. In addition, the act does not supersede provisions of a collective bargaining agreement that mandate additional notice or additional rights and remedies. Chapter 14 discusses strikes, lockouts, and collective bargaining agreements.

11. 215 Cal. App.3d 1034 (1st Dist. 1989).

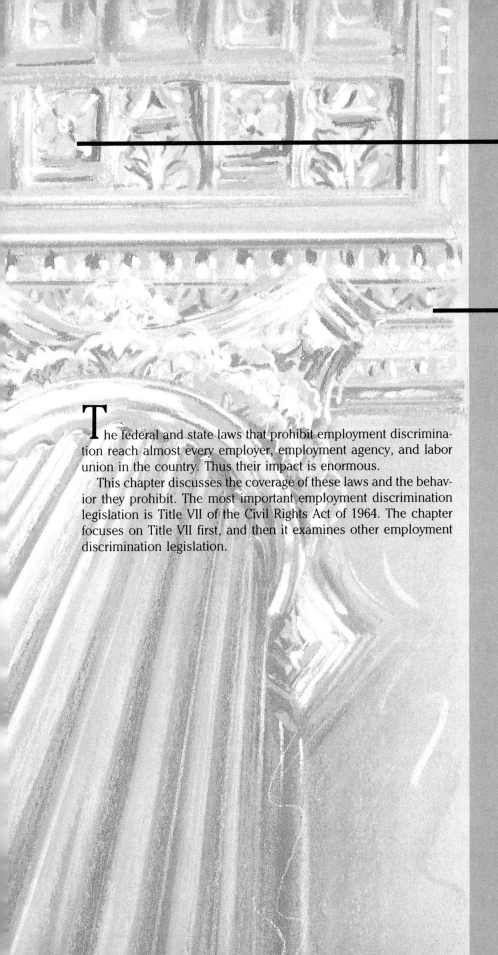

The federal and state laws that prohibit employment discrimination reach almost every employer, employment agency, and labor union in the country. Thus their impact is enormous.

This chapter discusses the coverage of these laws and the behavior they prohibit. The most important employment discrimination legislation is Title VII of the Civil Rights Act of 1964. The chapter focuses on Title VII first, and then it examines other employment discrimination legislation.

BACKGROUND

Employment policy today accords the highest priority to the principle of non-discrimination. In the past management had the right to make employment decisions without external intervention. The common law viewed the relation between the employer and the employee as a private contractual arrangement with which the courts should not interfere. Thus discrimination was common and white males dominated the labor market.

Intrusion on the right to make employment decisions inevitably occurred as the United States industrialized. Prior to the turn of the century, for example, the states passed laws protecting the health and safety of women and children from hazardous working conditions. In the 1950s the civil rights movement gained momentum. The nation became conscious that the American dream was not available for everyone, that equality of opportunity did not exist for blacks and other minorities. American schoolchildren read in a McGuffey's reader: "The road to wealth, to honor, to usefulness, and happiness, is open to all, and all who will, may enter upon it with the almost certain prospect of success."[1] The reality, however, was that minorities, women, and the disabled could not obtain employment that opened up such possibilities. The employment discrimination laws addressed this problem.

In 1964 Congress mandated the elimination by private employers of restrictions on the right to earn a livelihood that were based on race, color, religion, sex, or national origin. In subsequent years other employment discrimination laws were passed. The purpose of these laws is to guarantee equal treatment for all persons in hiring, promotion, discharge, or other employment decisions.

This chapter deals with the following laws:

1. *Title VII of the Civil Rights Act of 1964,* which prohibits discrimination based on race, color, religion, national origin, and sex. Title VII is enforced by the Equal Employment Opportunity Commission, with individual lawsuits permitted if the administrative remedy fails.

2. The *Civil Rights Act of 1866,* which applies to racial discrimination in private employment. This act is enforced through individual lawsuits.

3. The *Age Discrimination in Employment Act of 1967,* which forbids employment discrimination against persons 40 years old and above on the basis of age. This act is enforced by the EEOC, with individual lawsuits permitted if the administrative remedy fails.

4. The *Rehabilitation Act of 1973,* which forbids contractors who do business with the federal government from discriminating against handicapped persons. These contractors are also required to take affirmative action to hire and promote handicapped persons. The act is enforced by the Department of Labor.

5. The *Americans with Disabilities Act of 1990,* which forbids employers of 15 or more employees from discriminating against disabled persons. This act is enforced by the EEOC, with individual lawsuits permitted if the administrative remedy fails.

6. The *Equal Pay Act,* which prohibits wage discrimination on the basis of sex. This act is enforced by the EEOC.

7. *State and city fair employment practice statutes,* which forbid discrimination on the basis of sex, age, handicap, or marital status and have been enacted by some cities and nearly all of the states. The protection of these statutes usually extends beyond that of the federal employment discrimination laws.

The provisions of the federal employment discrimination laws are presented in Table 13-1.

Federal Laws Prohibiting Employment Discrimination

TABLE 13-1

Law	Enforcement	Protected Class	Remedies	Employers Covered	Defenses
Title VII, 1964 Civil Rights Act	EEOC; individual suit permitted if the EEOC remedy fails	Race, color, religion, national origin, sex; employees affected by pregnancy, childbirth, or related medical conditions	Hiring, reinstatement, transfer, promotion, back pay (limited to two years), retroactive seniority, affirmative action programs, attorneys' fees	Businesses engaged in interstate commerce that employ at least 15 persons, labor unions, private and public employment agencies, federal government, state and local governments, government agencies, political subdivisions	Bona fide occupational qualifications, certain testing and educational requirements, height and weight requirements, appearance requirements, seniority systems
Civil Rights Act of 1866	Individual suit	Race (including whites)	Hiring, reinstatement, punitive damages, back pay (unlimited), attorneys' fees	Private employers, state and local governments, unions	
Age Discrimination in Employment Act of 1967	EEOC; individual suit permitted if the EEOC remedy fails	Persons whose age is 40 and above	Hiring, reinstatement, transfer, promotion, back pay (limited to two-three years)	Private employers of 20 or more workers, federal government, state and local governments, employment agencies serving covered employees, labor unions with 25 or more members	Bona fide occupational qualifications, seniority systems, reasonable factors other than age, voluntary early retirement
Rehabilitation Act of 1973	EEOC (no private remedy)	Handicapped persons	Hiring, reinstatement, transfer, promotion, back pay, retroactive seniority, affirmative action programs, imposition of duty to make reasonable accommodations, termination of federal funds	Federal contractors, federal agencies, programs receiving federal assistance	Reasonable factors other than handicap; undue hardship

TABLE 13–1   **Continued**

Law	Enforcement	Protected Class	Remedies	Employers Covered	Defenses
Americans with Disabilities Act of 1990	EEOC; individual suit permitted if the EEOC remedy fails	Disabled persons	Hiring, reinstatement, transfer, promotion, back pay (limited to two years), retroactive seniority, affirmative action programs, attorneys' fees	Persons engaged in commerce who employ 15 or more workers	Reasonable factors other than disability; undue hardship
Equal Pay Act	EEOC or individual suit	Sex	Back pay plus an amount equal to back pay (limited to two-three years)	All employers	Seniority systems, merit systems, pay based on production, pay based on factors other than sex

Hypothetical Case

EMPLOYMENT DECISIONS BY ABC CORPORATION

As personnel manager of ABC Corporation, a widget manufacturer, Harry Smith was responsible for hiring new employees. A sign on the wall behind his desk stated: "All maintenance workers must be at least 5 feet 10 inches tall and weigh at least 190 pounds." ABC Corporation also required that applicants for all jobs, including assembly line and janitorial jobs, have a diploma from a U.S. high school. Under this requirement, applicants who became U.S. citizens after immigrating to this country at age 18 or older did not fare as well as applicants who grew up in the United States.

ABC Corporation hired men, but not women, with pre-school-age children. It hired "women only" for jobs in its quality control department. These jobs consisted of examining widgets for defects.

Harry posted a notice on the plant bulletin board listing the ABC employees who were to be laid off because of a decline in orders. The employees were scheduled to be laid off according to their length of service—the first to be laid off would be the most recently hired employees. In the past few years ABC Corporation had begun hiring women and minorities. Since they had less seniority than most of the other employees, the layoff would affect them more than it affected the other employees.

After posting the notice, Harry called his secretary into his office and promised her a pay raise and promotion if she were sexually "cooperative." She turned down his offer.

In the above fact situation, what violations of employment discrimination laws may have been committed by ABC Corporation? Explain.

TITLE VII OF THE CIVIL RIGHTS ACT OF 1964

The most significant achievement of the civil rights movement was the passage of the Civil Rights Act of 1964. This comprehensive federal law covers a wide variety of discriminatory practices, such as unequal voting rights and segregation in public schools. Title VII, which deals specifically with employment discrimination, is the most comprehensive federal legislation on employment.

Title VII is designed to regulate the employment practices of employers, labor unions, and employment agencies in both the private and public sectors of the economy. Its purpose is to assure equal employment opportunity to all persons, regardless of race, color, religion, national origin, or sex. It applies to discrimination in all aspects of the employment process—from job advertisements through retirement. Its provisions apply to all businesses engaged in interstate commerce that employ at least 15 persons. The small businesses affected by the exemption often employ persons who lack the mobility needed to take a job with a large firm and thus are unable to obtain Title VII's protection.

In 1972 the Civil Rights Act was amended to extend the coverage of Title VII to all state and local governments, government agencies, political subdivisions, and educational institutions. In addition, the Supreme Court ruled in 1984 that the Title VII protections apply to partnerships. Thus partners must follow the federal antidiscrimination laws when they vote on new partners.

Title VII makes it unlawful for an employer to:

1. Fail or refuse to hire, or terminate, any person or otherwise discriminate against any person with respect to the compensation, terms, conditions, or privileges of employment because of race, color, religion, sex, or national origin. This provision covers both employees and applicants for employment.

2. Limit, segregate, or classify employees in ways that tend to deprive any individual of employment opportunities or otherwise adversely affect his or her status as an employee because of the individual's race, color, religion, sex, or national origin.

It should be kept in mind that the purpose of Title VII is to guarantee equal treatment for all employees, applicants for employment, and union members. Title VII does not require an employer to hire or promote any individual. It merely prohibits employment discrimination based on race, color, religion, sex, or national origin. However, there are important exceptions to the basic obligations that Title VII imposes on employers. These will be discussed in a later section.

Disparate Treatment

An employer who discriminates against an employee or a potential employee based on race, color, religion, sex, or national origin is subject to liability for disparate or unequal treatment. **Disparate treatment** is thus intentional discrimination. It might occur, for example, in connection with a discriminatory refusal to hire. After a potential employee has shown that he or she is a member of a protected class (racial minority, nationality, sex, religion) and qualified for a job but was rejected, the potential employee must prove that the hiring practice of the employer served no useful business purpose. An employer who does not have a legitimate, nondiscriminatory explanation for the disparate treatment will be held to have violated Title VII.

In one case a major insurance company agreed to pay damages and back pay to women who had been refused jobs as insurance sales agents in California over a 13-year period. These women said that the company told them that a college degree was a requirement for sales agents. However, men without degrees were

Disparate treatment intentional discrimination by an employer against an employee or a potential employee based on race, sex, religion, or national origin

hired for the jobs. The women also said that the company had told them that sales agents might be required to work at night and that it would not guarantee the safety of female agents. The disparate treatment resulted in a multimillion-dollar settlement for the women.

Mixed Motive

Occasionally, a situation arises in which an employer uses a legitimate, nondiscriminatory reason and an illegitimate discriminatory reason in making an employment decision. Such a situation is called **mixed motive case.** To escape liability for discrimination, the employer must prove that the legitimate, nondiscriminatory reason was so significant that the same decision would have been made if this reason alone had been considered.

In *Price Waterhouse v. Hopkins,*[2] an accounting firm refused to grant a female employee partnership status for both legitimate and illegitimate reasons. The employee's unpleasant personality and her inability to get along with other employees constituted legitimate reasons for not offering her a partnership. However, denying her a partnership because she did not act in a "ladylike" manner (sexual stereotyping) was not a legitimate reason. The Supreme Court held that the employer had the burden of proving that the employee would have been denied the partnership because of the legitimate reasons alone.

Thus a mixed motive case occurs when a protected category (sex, race, religion, national origin, age, handicap or disability) plays a part in an employment decision. The defendant employer then has the burden of proving by a preponderance of the evidence that the same decision would have been made even if the employee's protected category had not been taken into account.

Disparate Impact

Employers may be engaging in discriminatory employment practices without realizing it. However, good intent or a lack of discriminatory motivation is not a mitigating factor if the impact of an employment practice is to discriminate against a protected group. Discrimination based on **disparate impact** occurs when seemingly neutral and objective employment criteria impair the employment opportunities of persons in a protected group, unless those criteria can be justified as a job-related necessity. The concern here is the consequences, not the motive, of employment practices. A city's requirement that fire fighters be at least 5 feet 10 inches tall may at first glance seem nondiscriminatory. However, that requirement may have a disparate impact on groups whose average height is less than 5 feet 10 inches, such as women.

Once disparate impact has been established, the employee must show that the criterion is not a business necessity, that it does not measure job capability. In the above example, the employee would have to prove that a person less than 5 feet 10 inches tall can be an effective fire fighter.

Discrimination by Race or Color

A primary objective of Title VII is the prevention of employment discrimination based on race or color. The emphasis placed on employment and income in the United States makes equal access to jobs essential to the integration of minorities into the mainstream of American society. Under Title VII, applicants for employment must be evaluated on their individual qualifications, not their race or color.

Although the civil rights movement, spearheaded by blacks, spurred Congress to enact the 1964 Civil Rights Act, Title VII's protection against discriminatory employment practices based on race or color is extended not only to blacks but also to such other groups as American Indians and Hispanics. Moreover, although Title VII's prohibition against racial discrimination in employment was intended to protect members of racial minorities, courts have ruled that the protections of Title VII apply equally to members of the majority race. This subject is discussed later in this chapter in the section "Affirmative Action and Reverse Discrimination."

In addition to prohibiting racial discrimination in employment, Title VII prohibits employment discrimination based on skin color. Such discrimination might occur, for example, if a minority applicant with a lighter skin were hired and a more qualified minority applicant with a darker skin were rejected.

For purposes of reporting the numbers of minority employees, the EEOC allows racial classification by minority group. The classification can be accomplished by visual survey and, if necessary, direct personal inquiry.

Discrimination by Sex

Title VII prohibits discrimination based on sex.[3] While the primary purpose of this provision is to protect females, the provision extends to any type of discrimination based on gender. In *Diaz v. Pan American World Airways*,[4] a federal court of appeals held that Pan American World Airways violated the provision by refusing to hire males as flight cabin attendants. Thus Title VII protects males as well as females.

It should be noted that Title VII's sex discrimination protection applies only to gender discrimination, not to discrimination based on sexual preferences or sexual practices. Thus Title VII does not cover homosexuals, bisexuals, or transsexuals (persons whose sex has been changed by surgical or other means). In rejecting a transsexual's claim of sex discrimination, the court noted that although several bills to change the word *sex* to *sexual preference* had been introduced into Congress, none of those bills were enacted. Clearly, Congress did not mean to extend coverage to sexual preference.

Sex discrimination often occurs because of stereotyped assumptions as to what constitutes "male work" and "female work"—for example, the assumption that men are less capable of assembling intricate equipment than women or that women are less capable of aggressive salesmanship than men. Favoring one sex over another because of such assumptions is a violation of Title VII. This means that an employer cannot limit, segregate, or classify male or female employees in a way that would limit their employment opportunities. The principle of non-discrimination requires that males and females be considered on the basis of their individual capacities and not on the basis of characteristics attributed to them.

Fetal Protection Policy

Pregnant workers exposed to radiation or toxic chemicals, while suffering no immediate harm themselves, may be increasing the chances of miscarriage, stillbirth, or birth defects. Some employers, concerned about the well-being of their employees and the possibility of lawsuits, have sought to prevent fetal injuries by restricting jobs involving exposure to toxic substances to males and infertile females. Because the hazards of such jobs meant higher pay, many women have resented their exclusion from these jobs.

Female workers at Johnson Controls, a battery manufacturer, brought suit under Title VII, alleging sex discrimination because they were excluded from jobs that involved exposure to lead, which can disturb neurological development in fetuses. In 1991, in *International Union v. Johnson Controls,*[5] the Supreme Court held that a fetal protection policy aimed solely at women constituted sex discrimination. The Court rejected the use of the bona fide occupational qualification defense (discussed below in the section "Exceptions to Title VII Prohibitions") on the basis of an employer's concerns about the increased cost of fertile women in the workplace or about tort liability for the women's potential offspring. It noted that Johnson Controls had paid little or no attention to medical studies indicating that the exposure of males to lead could cause the same sort of fetal damage.

While labor unions and women's groups were pleased with the Court's decision, employers continued to worry about liability for fetal injuries. The Court tried to reassure them by noting that if the employer "fully informs the women of the risk and the employer has not acted negligently, the basis for holding the employer liable seems remote." However, the dissenting opinion contended that the majority opinion was too optimistic and speculative, stating that the possibility of lawsuits filed by injured offspring (who cannot "assume the risk" that the mother does) would haunt employers for years to come.

Sex-Plus Discrimination

Sex-plus discrimination
the unequal treatment of employees on the basis of sex plus a supposedly neutral requirement

Disparate treatment based on sex takes many forms. **Sex-plus discrimination** involves the unequal treatment of employees on the basis of sex plus a supposedly neutral requirement. An employer who hires both men and women but requires women to have a college degree while hiring men regardless of their educational level is practicing sex-plus discrimination, because there is a plus requirement for women—the college degree. Sex-plus discrimination is often based on marital status or the presence of preschool children in the home.

Sexual Harassment

Sexual harassment
unwelcome sexual advances, requests for sexual favors, and other verbal and physical conduct of a sexual nature

Title VII makes sexual harassment a form of unlawful sex discrimination. The EEOC defines **sexual harassment** as "unwelcome sexual advances, requests for sexual favors, and other verbal or physical conduct of a sexual nature." The courts have recognized two types of sexual harassment: sexual harassment that conditions employment benefits on sexual favors and sexual harassment that creates a hostile or offensive working environment. In *Meritor Savings Bank v. Vinson,*[6] a woman who worked as a bank teller testified that for four years her supervisor had forced her to submit to sexual advances, usually at the bank office, by threatening her job. She failed to alert management or the police because her supervisor had threatened to fire or kill her if she did. Eventually, she quit and sued the bank. The Supreme Court held sexual harassment to be a violation of Title VII. This case makes it clear that the courts may hold an *employer* liable for the sexual harassment activities of an employee even if the victim did not notify the employer of those activities.

The courts have recognized sexual harassment that does not affect economic benefits. An employee who quits because sexual harassment created a hostile or offensive atmosphere in the workplace may sue the employer for damages.

In the following case the plaintiff sued for damages for sexual harassment even though she had not been involved in office sexual relations.

BRODERICK v. RUDDER

U.S. DISTRICT COURT, DISTRICT OF COLUMBIA

685 F. Supp. 1269 (1988)

Catherine Broderick, a 35-year-old white female, was employed as a staff attorney at the Washington Regional Field Office (WRO) of the Securities and Exchange Commission (SEC). During her eight years of employment at the WRO, she encountered or became aware of a number of sexually related incidents involving persons in supervisory positions. These incidents, which were a matter of common knowledge at the WRO, included the following:

• The regional administrator (chief executive) of Broderick's regional field office became drunk at an office party, untied her sweater, and kissed her. At the same party he also kissed another female employee. Broderick claimed that the regional administrator and another supervisor also made sexually suggestive remarks about her dress and figure.

• One of Broderick's former supervisors repeatedly offered her a ride home, and when she finally accepted his offer, he barged into her apartment and toured the premises, including her bedroom. This supervisor, who was foulmouthed and had a penchant for crude and dirty jokes, had an ongoing sexual relationship with a WRO secretary. During a five-year period, the secretary received three promotions, a commendation, and two cash rewards. Although the secretary was not a subordinate of the supervisor, he admitted to having had a direct input into her performance evaluations.

• An assistant regional administrator was noticeably attracted to a staff attorney and socialized with her extensively during business hours. The assistant regional administrator promoted the staff attorney's career by advancing her from a grade GS–11 to a grade GS–14 in a little more than two years.

• Another assistant regional administrator was sexually involved with a clerical worker. The two frequently had long lunches together, occasionally dined and drank together, and regularly jogged together. Once the clerical worker accompanied the assistant regional administrator, her supervisor, on an overnight trip, during which they spent the night in the same hotel room. The assistant regional administrator, however, denied having had sexual relations with the clerical worker on that trip. While under the assistant regional administrator, the clerical worker received two grade promotions, a $300 cash award, and a perfect score in each element of her performance appraisal during one 12-month period.

Because of these sexually related incidents, Broderick sued the SEC for sexual harassment under Title VII of the Civil Rights Act of 1964. She claimed that the combined effect of these incidents was to create a hostile or offensive working environment. David Rudder, chairman of the SEC, was named as defendant in his official capacity.

PRATT, JUDGE

The parties stipulated that the definition of sexual harassment contained in the Equal Employment Opportunity Commission's Guidelines on Discrimination because of Sex, 29 C.F.R. section 1604.11 (1986), is the definition that should be applied in this case. Section 1604.11(a) defines sexual harassment as follows: "Unwelcome sexual advances, requests for sexual favors, and other verbal or physical conduct of a sexual nature constitute sexual harassment when (1) submission to such conduct is made either explicitly or implicitly a term or condition of an individual's employment, (2) submission to or rejection of such conduct by an individual is used as the basis for employment decisions affecting such individual, or (3) such conduct has the purpose or the effect of unreasonably interfering with an individual's work performance or creating an intimidating, hostile, or offensive working environment." Additionally, section 1604.11(g) provides that "(w)here employment opportunities or benefits are granted because of an individual's submission to the employer's sexual advances or requests for sexual favors, the employer may be held liable for unlawful sex discrimination against other persons who were qualified for but denied that employment opportunity or benefit."

The United States Supreme Court recently held that a violation of Title VII may be predicated on either of two types of sexual harassment: (a) harassment that involves the conditioning of concrete employment benefits in return for sexual favors and (b) harassment that, while not directly affecting economic benefits, creates a hostile or offensive working environment. *Meritor Savings Bank, F.S.B. v. Vinson.*

A "hostile work environment" claim is actionable under Title VII if unwelcome sexual advances, requests for sexual favors, and other verbal or physical conduct of a sexual nature are so pervasive that it can reasonably be said that they create a hostile or offensive work environment. Whether the sexual conduct is sufficiently pervasive to amount to harassment and create a hostile or offensive work environment must be determined from the totality of the circumstances. Additionally, Title VII is also violated when an employer affords preferential treatment to female employees who submit to sexual advances or other conduct of a sexual nature and such conduct is a matter of common knowledge.

Evidence of the general work atmosphere, involving employees other than the plaintiff, is relevant to the issue of whether there existed an atmosphere of hostile work environment which violated Title VII.

Ms. Broderick established a prima facie case of sexual harassment because of having to work in a hostile work environment. The evidence at trial established that such conduct of a sexual nature was so pervasive at the WRO that it can reasonably be said that such conduct created a hostile or offensive work environment which affected the motivation and work performance of those who found such conduct repugnant and offensive. Ms. Broderick was herself sexually harassed by Leonard, Hunter, Kennedy, and possibly others. But we need not emphasize these isolated incidents. More importantly, plaintiff, without any doubt, was forced to work in an environment in which the WRO managers by their conduct harassed her and other WRO female employees, by bestowing preferential treatment upon those who submitted to their sexual advances. Further, this preferential treatment undermined plaintiff's motivation and work performance and deprived plaintiff, and other WRO female employees, of promotions and job opportunities. The record is clear that plaintiff and other women working at the WRO found the sexual conduct and its accompanying manifestations which WRO managers engaged in over a protracted period of time to be offensive. The record also establishes that plaintiff and other women were for obvious reasons reluctant to voice their displeasure and, when they did, they were treated with a hostile response by WRO's management team.

In a sexual harassment case involving the claim of hostile work environment, once a plaintiff has established a prima facie case of sexual harassment or retaliation for opposing sexual harassment, the burden shifts to the employer to rebut the plaintiff's harassment claims and to show by clear and convincing evidence that the plaintiff would not have been treated differently if she had not opposed the harassment. This is a higher standard than that required of an employer in a simple gender discrimination case. The reason for this different rule in sexual harassment cases is that "once a plaintiff establishes that she was harassed, . . . it is hard to see how an employer can justify [the] harassment."

In this case, the commission failed to rebut Ms. Broderick's hostile atmosphere, sexual harassment, and retaliation claims by clear and convincing evidence, or even by a preponderance of the evidence. The Commission attempted to meet Ms. Broderick's harassment claims by arguing that Ms. Broderick "was paranoid." Admittedly, plaintiff had problems of personal adjustment before being employed by the Commission in 1979. Whether diagnosed either as "paranoia" or as a "posttraumatic stress disorder," we are satisfied that plaintiff's mental condition was caused and exacerbated by the hostile atmosphere in which she worked.

With respect to plaintiff's opposition and retaliation claims, the Commission's argument that Ms. Broderick's tardiness and her diminished work performance accounted for her performance evaluations and were legitimate reasons for reprimands and threats to terminate her are not persuasive in the overall context of this case. The Commission's allegations of excessive tardiness when tardiness by others was overlooked is sheer "makeweight" and pretext. Ms. Broderick amply demonstrated, through both lay and expert witnesses, that any alleged deficiencies in her work performance, which rested largely on her failure to interact with her supervisors, were directly attributable to the atmosphere in which she worked.

Defendant in effect argues that this is a "quid pro quo" sex harassment case and, except for isolated instances, plaintiff was not sexually harassed. This contention is in error and misses the mark. The Commission's attempt to justify the sexual misconduct on the part of supervisory personnel as "social/sexual interactions between and among employees" which Title VII never intended to regulate is unacceptable on the facts of this case. However relaxed one's views of sexual morality may be in a different context, such views do not cover the pattern of conduct disclosed by the record in this case. We hold, and plaintiff has proved, that consensual sexual relations, in exchange for tangible employment benefits, while possibly not creating a cause of action for the recipient of such sexual advances who does not find them unwelcome, do, and in this case did, create and contribute to a sexually hostile working environment.

The SEC was the employer of, and had authority over, the personnel who persisted in this activity of which it had actual, as well as constructive, knowledge. It took no action. It is therefore liable under agency principles for the acts of these high-ranking subordinates.

[Judgment for plaintiff.]

Legal Issues

1. Why was the evidence concerning the sexual harassment of other

employees relevant to Broderick's case? Explain.

2. Define a "hostile work environment." Explain.

Ethical Issues

1. To determine whether Broderick's work environment was hostile, the court used a "totality of circumstances test" and offered various examples of the factors to be taken into account in determining whether the environment in an employer's workplace is hostile. You have been asked to prepare the section of your firm's code of ethics that deals with matters concerning sexual harassment. What should you include in that section in order to establish the same ethical standards that a court would use to determine whether an employee was a victim of sexual harassment? Discuss.

2. What procedural safeguards would you include in your firm's code of ethics to assure vigorous enforcement of its policy opposing any form of sexual harassment in the workplace? Discuss.

Pregnancy Discrimination Act

The Pregnancy Discrimination Act (PDA) of 1978, which amends Title VII, makes discrimination against women workers based on pregnancy, childbirth, or related medical conditions unlawful sex discrimination under Title VII. The goal of PDA is to assure that women affected by pregnancy and related conditions are treated in the same way as other applicants and employees. For example, PDA protects a woman who is refused a job solely because she has had an abortion. It also prevents an employer from forcing a pregnant woman who is still doing her job properly to stop working until her baby is born.

PDA assures equal treatment in such matters as disability, sick leave, and health insurance. Thus employers' insurance and medical plans must cover pregnancy in the same way that they cover other conditions. This means that an employee who is unable to work because of pregnancy is entitled to sick leave on the same basis as employees disabled by other medical conditions.

The Supreme Court has held that PDA applies to both male and female employees. The Court held illegal an employer's health plan that provided equal benefits for male and female employees but did not provide pregnancy benefits for the dependents of male employees. Thus the Pregnancy Discrimination Act applies not only to female employees but also to the dependent spouses of male employees.

Discrimination by Religion

Members of the mainstream U.S. religions—Protestants, Catholics, and Jews—obviously qualify for protection under Title VII. In addition, exponents of a wide variety of religious beliefs qualify for protection if they sincerely and genuinely hold these beliefs and did not adopt the beliefs for ulterior reasons. The Supreme Court has defined a protected religious belief as one "which occupies in the life of its possessor a place parallel to that filled by God for those admittedly qualifying."[7]

Title VII forbids most employment discrimination on the basis of religion. For example, Title VII is violated if a person is not hired as a secretary with a corporation solely because he or she is a Moslem. In certain situations, however, job selection can be based on religion. Religious organizations may discriminate on the basis of religion in their hiring practices. The *Christian Science Monitor* hired writers and editors who are mainly Christian Scientists. A federal court ruled that as a religious activity of the Christian Science church, this newspaper is exempt from the federal antidiscrimination laws. Similarly, a Baptist minister who seeks a job as a priest in an Episcopal church may be turned down based on religion and the Episcopal church may legitimately require that other employees, such as secretaries and janitors, also be Episcopalian. Title VII's other provisions do apply to religious organizations. Thus religious organizations may not discriminate on the basis of sex, race, color, or national origin. The Episcopal church, for example, may not refuse to hire an applicant as a secretary just because the applicant is male.

In addition to forbidding employment discrimination on the basis of religion, Title VII requires employers to reasonably accommodate religious observances or practices of employees that do not place an undue hardship on the conduct of the employer's business. In one case a bakery in Kentucky fired a worker for failing to work on Sundays. The worker had joined a church that believed its members should not work on Sunday. The court ordered reinstatement with back pay because the bakery had made no attempt to accommodate the worker's religious beliefs. As with this case, most cases of religious discrimination do not arise from prejudice against an employee's religion but from a conflict between an employer's work rule and an employee's religious belief.

In the landmark case of *TWA v. Hardison*,[8] the Supreme Court addressed the issue of what constitutes a reasonable accommodation to an employee's religious beliefs. In that case employees received shift assignments and days off according to seniority, with the most senior employees receiving first choice. Hardison's religion forbade Saturday work, but he did not have enough seniority to avoid being asked to work on Saturdays. When he refused to do so, he was fired. Hardison claimed that his discharge constituted religious discrimination by the employer and the union. The Supreme Court held that alternatives to requiring him to work on Saturdays, such as using a supervisor to fill in, paying overtime to another employee, or breaching the seniority system, would operate as an undue hardship on the employer, that the employer was not required to incur more than a minor cost to accommodate the employee's religious beliefs. In the opinion of the Court, the seniority system itself constituted a reasonable accommodation to the religious and secular needs of all the employees. Thus the employer had taken steps to accommodate Hardison's religious beliefs.

Discrimination by National Origin

Title VII prohibits employment discrimination based on national origin. Basically, national origin is equated with the country from which a person came or the country from which a person's forebears came. Thus refusals to interview, hire, promote, or train a person solely because that person is of French, Italian, or Polish national origin violate Title VII.

The national origin protection of Title VII does not prevent employers from making U.S. citizenship a condition of employment. Under Title VII, however, legal aliens receive the same protection as citizens from discrimination on the basis of race, sex, or religion.

The national origin protection of Title VII extends to discrimination based on factors related to national origin, such as an individual's physical, cultural, or linguistic characteristics. Thus an employer who refuses to hire an applicant who speaks with a foreign accent may be held to have discriminated on the basis of national origin even if the employer does not know what the applicant's national origin is. An exception occurs if an employer refuses to hire an applicant with a pronounced foreign accent because oral communication skills are reasonably related to job performance.

Exceptions to Title VII Prohibitions

A number of exceptions to the prohibitions of Title VII have been recognized. These exceptions include bona fide occupational qualifications, certain testing and educational requirements, height and weight requirements, appearance requirements, and seniority systems.

Bona Fide Occupational Qualifications

Bona fide occupational qualification

a job-related qualification that is reasonably necessary to the normal operation of a particular business

Title VII specifically states that sex, religion, and national origin discrimination is lawful if a bona fide occupational qualification (BFOQ) can be shown. Discrimination on the basis of race or color is never permitted. A **bona fide occupational qualification** is a job-related qualification that is reasonably necessary to the normal operation of a particular business. To discriminate on the basis of a BFOQ, an employer must show that a given sex, religion, or national origin is an actual qualification for performing the given job.

As previously discussed, religion-based BFOQs are sometimes recognized in the employment policies of religious organizations. Sex may be a BFOQ where the moral standards of a community are involved. Thus a BFOQ may be established in restricting employment as a ladies' room attendant to women. In addition, the BFOQ exception has been recognized for jobs requiring physical contact with persons of the opposite sex. For example, a male nurse was legally refused employment in the delivery room of an Oklahoma City hospital and women have been legally prohibited from working as prison guards in contact positions in a maximum security male prison. Sex is an obvious BFOQ for an actor or actress. BFOQs based on national origin are also recognized under Title VII. For example, a Mexican restaurant may refuse to hire non-Mexican waiters in order to preserve a Mexican atmosphere.

Since Congress intended the BFOQ exception to be applied very infrequently, courts and the EEOC have construed it very narrowly. As a result the employer carries a heavy burden of proof. An airline refused to hire male flight attendants because it felt that customer preference for female flight attendants made sex an essential BFOQ for flight attendants. In holding the airline liable for sex discrimination, the court stated that "discrimination based on sex is valid only when the essence of the business operation would be undermined by not hiring members of one sex exclusively." Even when hiring members of a particular sex is convenient, the practice is illegal unless it is a business necessity.

Testing and Educational Requirements

Employers frequently use tests to determine whom they will hire. Title VII allows professionally developed ability tests to be used in the employment process, provided such tests do not discriminate. The Supreme Court decided the first landmark case of judicial requirement for employee selection, *Griggs v. Duke Power Company,*[9] in 1971. The case dealt with the issue of whether administering intelligence tests and requiring high school diplomas were discriminatory acts violative of Title VII.

Duke Power Company instituted the requirement that all job applicants have a high school education. It was found, however, that many employees hired before this requirement was instituted had performed satisfactorily and won promotions. Duke also instituted the requirement that job applicants make a satisfactory score on two professionally prepared standardized aptitude tests. Both of these requirements were instituted after July 2, 1965, when Title VII went into effect. The Supreme Court ruled that under Title VII the requirements that employees have a high school education and pass a standardized intelligence test were unlawful if (1) both requirements acted to disqualify black applicants at a significantly higher rate than white applicants and (2) neither requirement was significantly indicative of successful job performance.

Both requirements did have a discriminatory adverse impact on blacks, and Duke could not carry the burden of proving that the requirements had a substantial relationship to the job skills needed. It could not show that employees with a high school education who passed the tests were necessarily better workers.

In *Griggs* the Supreme Court unanimously held that employment practices, procedures, or tests that are neutral on their face, and even neutral in intent, cannot be maintained if they have a discriminatory impact and are unrelated to the measurement of job capability.

Thus hiring or promotional tests must be valid. A valid test is one that accurately predicts an applicant's ability to perform the job in question. For example, an English grammar test may discriminate among job applicants, yet have little relevance to the performance of an assembly line worker.

The employer's lack of intent to discriminate does not matter. In *Griggs* the Court stated that "good intent or absence of discriminatory intent does not redeem employment procedures or testing mechanisms that operate as 'built-in head winds' for minority groups and are unrelated to measuring job capability."

In its 1989 *Wards Cove Packing v. Atonio*[10] decision, the Supreme Court eased the employer's burden in justifying hiring practices. As a result of that decision, employees or job applicants must establish that a specific hiring practice has a demonstrated adverse impact on the hiring or promotion of the members of a particular minority group. Once this has been established, the employer has the burden of showing that the challenged practice serves legitimate business purposes. If the employer can show this, the employees can win only if they prove that less discriminatory methods of achieving the employer's objective were available.

Some civil rights authorities feel that placing the burden of persuasion on employees and job applicants may make Title VII suits too difficult and expensive for minority groups to bring to trial. Despite this change, however, Title VII suits can still be an effective means of challenging obviously discriminatory employment hiring practices.

The Four-Fifths Rule and Validation of Tests   The Supreme Court in *Albermarle Paper Co. V. Moody*[11] ruled that any employment test that has an adverse impact on minority groups must be validated. The EEOC guidelines consider a test to have an adverse impact if its selection rate for one race, sex, religion, or national

Four-fifths rule

the rule that an employment test has an adverse impact if its selection rate for one group is less than four fifths of its selection rate for the majority group

Criterion validity

the existence of a statistical correlation between test performance and job performance

Content validity

proof that a test samples a real job function

Construct validity

proof that a test measures a psychological trait necessary to a job

Seniority system

a set of rules that bases many personnel decisions on the length of time that employees have worked for an employer

origin is less than four-fifths (80 percent) of its selection rate for the majority group. In other words, no further inquiry will be made if an employer's selection rate for a given protected group is at least 80 percent of the selection rate for the majority group. This formula is called the **four-fifths rule.** When the four-fifths rule is violated, courts often find adverse impact based on the EEOC guidelines. An employer using an employment test that violates the four-fifths rule may be faced with a lawsuit and will be required to provide evidence that the test is related to successful job performance in defending such a suit.

Validation may be achieved by one of three methods. **Criterion validity** is recognized if it is shown that there is a statistical correlation between performance on a test and job performance. This may be done by administering the test to current employees and comparing their test scores with their job performance. **Content validity** establishes that a test samples a job function. A shorthand test for a stenographer would be considered content valid. **Construct validity** denotes the ability of a test to measure a psychological trait necessary to the job. For example, a test measuring calmness under stress may be construct valid for a police officer.

Height and Weight Requirements

Minimum height and weight requirements may violate Title VII if they effectively eliminate certain applicants on the basis of race, national origin, or sex. For example, height or weight requirements in steel, mining, and other industries have denied women high-paid heavy-labor jobs, and the requirement that police officers be at least 6 feet tall may discriminate against women and Americans of Asian or Spanish descent. Height or weight requirements that result in such a discriminatory impact are in violation of Title VII unless the employer can show that the requirements are substantially related to job performance.

Seniority Systems

Employers commonly use seniority systems to differentiate between employees. A **seniority system** is based on the length of service of employees. Seniority systems are specified in nearly all collective bargaining agreements. In addition, many employers who have not entered into collective bargaining agreements make seniority a basis for vacations, retirement benefits, shift selection, promotions, transfers, and layoffs. When the work force is reduced, more senior employees are usually the last to be laid off and the first to be rehired. Thus recently hired members of minority groups are usually the first to be laid off.

Before the passage of Title VII, the hiring practices of many employers discriminated against minority groups. Since its passage, employers have hired on the basis of neutral criteria. A legal question that has arisen is whether Title VII can weaken the seniority rights of white workers if maintaining those rights perpetuates the effects of discriminatory hiring practices.

In *Wygant v. Jackson Board of Education,*[12] the Supreme Court struck down an affirmative action program that laid off nonminorities to preserve the jobs of minorities with less seniority. The Board of Education and the Teachers' Union of Jackson, Michigan, decided to implement an affirmative action program for the hiring of black schoolteachers. The program required laying off white teachers with more seniority to preserve the existing percentage of black teachers if the number of teaching jobs had to be reduced. The Supreme Court held that such discriminatory layoffs placed too great a burden on nonminority teachers and could not be justified by the board's goal of providing minority role models for minority students in order to alleviate the effects of societal discrimination.[13]

Thus a bona fide seniority system (one formulated with no intent to discriminate) does not violate the laws requiring equal employment opportunity even if it has an adverse effect on minority groups. This means that seniority rights take precedence over affirmative action programs even if they perpetuate the effects of past discrimination.

In explaining why it rejected affirmative action programs that took precedence over seniority, but accepted affirmative action programs that granted preferences in hirings or promotions to minorities, the Supreme Court stated:

> While hiring goals impose a diffuse burden, often foreclosing only one of several opportunities, layoffs impose the entire burden of achieving racial equality on particular individuals, often resulting in serious disruption of their lives. That burden is too intrusive.[14]

Affirmative Action and Reverse Discrimination

An **affirmative action program** imposes a duty on employers to correct past discrimination by giving preference to minorities and women in the employment process. There are two situations in which an employer may institute such a program: (1) an employer may *voluntarily* institute an affirmative action program in order to qualify for government contracts; or (2) courts may *order* an employer that has intentionally discriminated against minorities to institute an affirmative action program. Affirmative action programs have been held legal in both situations.

Affirmative action programs
a program that imposes a duty on employers to correct past discrimination by giving preference to minorities and women in the employment process

The executive branch of the federal government has undertaken direct responsibility in the area of affirmative action programs since the genesis of these programs in Executive Order 11264,[15] signed by President Johnson in 1965. An employer with a federal contract is required to analyze its work force in order to determine whether minorities and women are underrepresented in relation to their availability in the local work force. If the analysis reveals significant underutilization of women and minority groups, the employer is required to develop an affirmative action plan for including a representative number of minorities or women in its work force.

Federal contractors must file periodic compliance reports with the Office of Federal Contracts Compliance Programs (OFCCP), the affirmative action enforcement office. The OFCCP can terminate contracts and withhold payments to employers that do not meet the goals of the affirmative action plan. In addition, the employer would be ineligible for future government contracts until the goals have been met. For example, the OFCCP barred a major tire company from doing business with the federal government because it failed to develop an acceptable affirmative action plan in one of its plants. The OFCCP said that in several job categories female and minority workers were "underrepresented in relation to their availability in the work force." Even though this affirmative action dispute involved a small Texas plant and the tire company was a nationwide operation, the OFCCP terminated all of the tire company's contracts with the federal government and barred it from future contracts. The company had previously received at least $40 million annually in federal contracts. No actual discrimination by the company had been proved or even alleged.

Courts have occasionally imposed an affirmative action plan on an employer that has intentionally engaged in discrimination. To correct past discrimination, they have ordered quotas for hiring and promotion. On the other hand, some employers have voluntarily instituted affirmative action plans designed to rectify past or present discrimination. This has prompted some white males to assert that Title VII protects them from sex or race discrimination, just as it protects other groups.

In *Sheet Metal Workers v. EEOC,*[16] the Supreme Court ruled that both mandatory and voluntary affirmative action programs were legal under Title VII. The federal district court found that a New York City union of sheet metal workers had discriminated against nonwhite workers in its recruitment, training, and admission practices. The federal district court ordered the union to stop its discriminatory practices and to establish a 29 percent nonwhite membership quota based on the percent of nonwhites in the relevant labor pool in New York City. The union appealed, and the Supreme Court held that quotas were acceptable as remedies to discrimination even if they benefited persons who had not been discriminated against by a particular employer. The Court noted, however, that the existence of such a quota did not require an employer to accept unqualified individuals.

Several recent Supreme Court decisions have changed the way in which affirmative action programs are implemented. In *Richmond v. Croson,*[17] the Court ruled that the Constitution limits the ability of state and local governments to set aside a certain percentage of their contracts for minority businesses. The Court carefully distinguished this decision from *Fullilove v. Klutznick,*[18] an earlier decision that allowed minority set-asides for *federal* contractors. The decision in *Martin v. Wilks*[19] permits court-approved affirmative action settlements to be reopened if nonminority (white male) employees allege reverse discrimination. And in *Wards Cove Packing v. Atonio,*[20] the Court held that a racial imbalance in the makeup of an employer's work force is not in itself proof of racial discrimination in hiring.

These Supreme Court decisions created concern that the age of affirmative action was over. However, the decisions can best be understood as restraining affirmative action, not rolling it back. Affirmative action is firmly established in the American workplace, and as the proportion of women and minorities in the American work force continues to increase, employers who refuse to hire such workers may not only face lawsuits but also be unable to find the employees they need.

Administration and Enforcement of Title VII

The Equal Employment Opportunity Commission (EEOC) is the federal agency with the primary responsibility for administering Title VII. Its five members, no more than three of whom may be from the same political party, are appointed by the president. The EEOC is empowered to issue legally binding regulations on details of Title VII compliance, as well as nonbinding, advisory guidelines on employment practices. The EEOC has broad investigatory powers under which it can examine and copy evidence, require the production of documents, hold hearings, and subpoena witnesses.

When a discrimination complaint has been filed with the EEOC, or when it has reason to believe that a violation has occurred, it first conducts an investigation to determine whether sufficient evidence of discrimination exists. A private party has

180 days from the time of an alleged Title VII violation to file a complaint, but the EEOC is not bound by the 180-day statute of limitations. If the EEOC discovers sufficient evidence of probable violation of Title VII, it must attempt conciliation. This is a confidential proceeding in which the EEOC attempts to get the employer to eliminate employment discrimination.

As part of the compromise that made it possible to pass the 1964 Civil Rights Act, the EEOC was given almost no enforcement powers. It was limited to investigating charges of unlawful discrimination and attempting to conciliate the dispute between the complaining party and the employer. If these efforts failed, the complaining party could then file a private lawsuit against the employer. A 1972 amendment to the Civil Rights Act provides that if the commission fails to conciliate a meritorious claim, it may file a lawsuit and represent the plaintiff in federal district court. The individual is allowed to file suit personally in federal court, but only after the EEOC and the state employment discrimination agency have elected not to take action.

Among the remedies that federal courts may grant under Title VII are hiring, reinstatement, transfer, promotion, back pay (limited to two years), and retroactive seniority. For example, AT&T agreed to settle out of court by paying $15 million in back wages to 15,000 women and minority men against whom it had allegedly discriminated in job assignment and promotions.

Title VII also permits successful litigants to recover reasonable attorneys' fees, and it specifically prohibits retaliatory discrimination against an employee or an employment applicant for having opposed an unlawful employment practice. Title VII violators may be ordered to institute affirmative action programs.

CIVIL RIGHTS ACT OF 1866

The 13th Amendment, enacted soon after the Civil War, abolished slavery. Congress passed the Civil Rights Act of 1866 to implement the 13th Amendment and assure the civil rights of the freed slaves. Section 1981 of the act provides that all persons in the United States "shall have the same right to make and enforce contracts, . . . and to the full and equal benefit of all laws, . . . as is enjoyed by white persons." This provision of the act has resulted in what are called "1981 suits."

The Civil Rights Act of 1866 lay dormant until after the passage of Title VII. In 1967 the courts, reflecting the social climate of the times, found that the employment relationship was a contract and that Section 1981 was effective as a federal remedy against racial employment discrimination. Because of the phrase "as is enjoyed by white persons," it was widely assumed that Section 1981 applied only to members of minority races. However, the Supreme Court ruled that it applies to "all persons," and therefore protects white persons as well as black persons. Thus white persons are protected by its ban on racial discrimination.

Section 1981 prohibits only intentional discrimination. Therefore, racial discrimination claims based on adverse impact cannot be brought under Section 1981.

In 1989, in *Patterson v. McLean Credit Union*,[21] the Supreme Court further limited the use of Section 1981 in discrimination lawsuits. Patterson, a black woman, had been laid off after having been employed by the defendant credit union as a teller for 10 years. She brought a Section 1981 lawsuit against the credit union, claiming racial harassment and alleging that because of her race the credit union had failed to promote her to accounting clerk and had then discharged her. The Supreme Court ruled that Section 1981 applies only to claims of discrimination in the making or enforcement of contracts and not to claims of other discrimination after a worker has been hired. Since the making of a contract does not include postformation conduct, lawsuits alleging racial harassment or racial discrimination on the job cannot be brought under Section 1981.

The Civil Rights Act of 1866 is often used in racial discrimination lawsuits. Such lawsuits have the following advantages over Title VII lawsuits: (1) they allow more time to file suit (they are not subject to Title VII's 180-day statute of limitations); (2) they do not allow employers to assert a BFOQ defense; (3) since the EEOC does not administer them, they do not require plaintiffs to file a charge of unlawful discrimination with the EEOC before filing a suit; (4) they do not limit back-pay awards to two years of unpaid wages; and (5) they may be filed against employers with fewer than 15 employees.

Hypothetical Case

A CUTBACK IN THE WORK FORCE

Harry Smith, personnel manager of ABC Corporation, called several salesmen into his office and told them that ABC would have to let them go because of a major cutback in orders. The salesmen were all 55 to 60 years old. At a subsequent executive committee meeting, Harry said, "We finally got rid of those old guys who were dragging their feet."

In addition, David McCall, the sales manager, was forced to retire. David was 65 years old and company policy mandated the retirement of managerial personnel upon reaching that age. Although David knew that he would draw an annual pension of $48,000, he wanted to continue working.

In the above fact situation, what violations of employment discrimination law may have been committed by ABC Corporation? Explain.

AGE DISCRIMINATION IN EMPLOYMENT ACT

In 1967 Congress enacted the Age Discrimination in Employment Act (ADEA), which protects persons age 40 and above from employment discrimination based on age.[22] ADEA applies to private employers of 20 or more workers, the federal government, state and local governments, employment agencies serving covered employers, and labor unions with 25 or more members.

ADEA prohibits discrimination against persons age 40 and above in hiring, discharge, pay, promotions, fringe benefits, and other aspects of employment. The treatment of discrimination under ADEA is similar to its treatment under Title VII.

Bona fide occupational qualifications may be established as an exception to ADEA's prohibitions against age discrimination. As with Title VII, the BFOQ exception is interpreted narrowly by the EEOC and the courts. A major airline required flight engineers to retire at age 60, reasoning that age 60 was a BFOQ for flight engineers because there was no reliable test to assure that flight engineers over 60 were fit and would not jeopardize safety. The Supreme Court refused to recognize the BFOQ defense, stating that the BFOQ exception to ADEA had to be construed narrowly: "Even in cases involving public safety, the law requires a stringent test before a company may substitute a blanket age rule for individual testing."[23]

In another case two 62-year-old fire chiefs won an age discrimination lawsuit against a city that required firefighters to retire at the age of 62. The city failed to show the relevance of age 62 retirement, and the court accused it of stereotyping older workers as being unable to handle the job. In yet another case a court failed to find age as a BFOQ for the position of teller at a savings and loan association. The court rejected the savings and loan's argument that older people could not stand on their feet for a long time.

In the past employers established a mandatory retirement age at their discretion. Under ADEA, employees cannot be forced to retire at a mandatory age. An exception to the prohibition of mandatory retirement is that the law does not forbid the involuntary retirement of a bona fide executive at age 65 or older, if the executive will receive a pension of at least $44,000 per year. Like Title VII, ADEA does not prohibit discrimination that results from a bona fide seniority system. In addition, ADEA allows different treatment of older workers based on reasonable factors other than age. For example, inability to perform a particular job satisfactorily could justify a discharge or transfer.

ADEA may be enforced by the EEOC or an individual. Under ADEA, as under Title VII, prior to filing suit on his or her own behalf, an individual must file a charge of unlawful discrimination with the EEOC and any appropriate state agency. The EEOC will first attempt to resolve age discrimination complaints administratively, and if this attempt is unsuccessful, it may initiate court action. Should it fail to take legal action, the individual may file a private lawsuit.

While the ADEA remedies are similar to the Title VII remedies, some courts have awarded additional damages, such as damages for the psychological trauma associated with being fired. Willful violation of ADEA entitles plaintiffs to recover double damages. Employers are prohibited from retaliating against any employee who files an age discrimination complaint or participates in an EEOC investigation.

In the following case the plaintiff was fired for slapping a co-worker. The plaintiff then filed a lawsuit for age discrimination under ADEA.

BLAKE v. J. C. PENNEY
U.S. COURT OF APPEALS, EIGHTH CIRCUIT
894 F.2d 274 (1990)

J. C. Penney fired Euna Fay Blake from her position as a sales associate in the shoe department because she slapped a co-worker. Blake, 56 years of age, was the oldest and best salesperson in her department. During her 17 years with J. C. Penney she had an excellent work record, and in the two years preceding her termination she received the highest possible ratings in the company's annual performance review.

Despite her exemplary performance, Blake's supervisor constantly subjected her to threats of termination for trivial reasons. Her supervisor also constantly reminded her that more was expected of her, in part because of her age.

But Blake's problems began in earnest in 1984, with the hiring of Daniel Hubbard, then 25 years old, as a shoe salesperson. From the beginning Hubbard went out of his way to harass and insult Blake, referring to her as a "senile old woman" and a "crazy old woman." Complaints by Blake to her supervisor, the personnel manager, and the general merchandise manager brought no relief. The personnel manager told her that she "only had three years to go" until early retirement and that she "could stand anything for three years."

These problems came to a head one morning. Blake and Hubbard were working together, and Blake confronted Hubbard in the storeroom for having violated two department policies—waiting on two customers at once and waiting on a customer whom Blake had already approached. When Hubbard responded by saying, "Get out of the way, you senile old thing," Blake slapped him across the face. She was fired several days later.

Blake then filed a suit for age discrimination under ADEA. A jury awarded her $35,000 in lost wages and benefits, but the judge granted a judgment n.o.v. (judgment notwithstanding the verdict), which overturned the jury's decision. Blake appealed to the Eighth Circuit Court of Appeals.

BRIGHT, SENIOR CIRCUIT JUDGE

We cannot agree with the district court's grant of judgment n.o.v. Under the ADEA, a plaintiff may show discrimination by either direct or indirect methods of proof. Blake produced evidence under both methods which reasonably supports her age discrimination claim.

As direct proof of discrimination, Blake submitted evidence that JCPenney subjected her to more onerous working conditions and higher expectations because of her age.

Blake also submitted substantial evidence that JCPenney either tolerated or condoned Hubbard's age-directed insults, which targeted Blake alone. Although JCPenney maintained that it disciplined Hubbard for his age-directed comments, Company personnel records fail to support that claim. In addition, when Blake brought the situation to Personnel Manager Moore's attention just two weeks before her dismissal, Moore, in essence, told Blake that she would have to put up with Hubbard until retirement. An em-

ployer's knowing and informed toleration of age harassment constitutes evidence of age discrimination.

JCPenney contends that the slapping incident comprised an objective, nondiscriminatory reason for summarily dismissing Blake under JCPenney's personnel manual. The evidence before the jury, however, supported a reasonable inference that this proffered reason was pretextual.

In the first place, the Personnel Procedures Manual does not require termination for every instance of physical contact between employees. Rather, the Manual calls for summary dismissal only where the physical contact creates a problem.

Furthermore, the evidence suggests that Hubbard created the problem, not Blake. At trial, JCPenney Store Manager Wayne Hancock conceded that the treatment Blake suffered from Hubbard could constitute provocation for anger. In addition, assuming the jury believed Blake's testimony, JCPenney decided to dismiss her without even contacting her for a statement. This action contravened the procedures recommended by the Company's own personnel manual. Hence, we think that the jury could properly question JCPenney's reasonableness in dismissing Blake under the employee assault provision.

Additionally, the record contained evidence that JCPenney previously had exercised discretion to retain a younger employee after an incident of physical contact.

Moreover, between July 1984 and March 1986, JCPenney also exercised discretion to retain Hubbard even though his conduct may have warranted summary dismissal. Indeed, JCPenney gave Hubbard four separate corrective interviews for numerous infractions, including rudeness to customers, leaving customers to go home, leaving $333.70 in cash receipts unattended overnight, and attempting to take a commission on a return sale. Under the personnel manual, each of these violations could merit summary dismissal. While JCPenney exhibited tolerance for the rule infractions of these younger employees, the Company management team gave Blake no such leeway. The ADEA protects older employees from being treated more harshly than if they were young.

Further, prior to the Hubbard incident, Blake's record contained only one disciplinary notation—over a miscommunication about a Company policy change in 1972. Hence, the jury could reasonably have considered Blake's performance, on the whole, superior to that of Hubbard and Hile and, thus, inferred that the slapping incident constituted a pretext for Blake's dismissal.

Finally, the jury had reason to discount JCPenney's proffered rationales for dismissing Blake (i.e., employee safety/morale). Following the slapping incident, JCPenney allowed Blake to work the rest of the weekend without once checking on her stability. In addition, the jury heard testimony that Blake had never previously struck a coworker and typically walked away from Hubbard's insults without comment. Moreover, the substantial evidence that shoe department personnel liked and respected Blake far more than Hubbard undercut JCPenney's contention that Blake's dismissal was required to sustain morale. Such proof, which discredited the legitimate explanations for Blake's dismissal, comprised evidence of discrimination.

Accordingly, we reverse the judgment n.o.v. and reinstate the jury verdict in Blake's age discrimination claim.

Legal Issues

1. Under ADEA, how may a plaintiff show evidence of discrimination? Explain.

2. Why was Hubbard's work record relevant to this suit?

Ethical Issues

1. What provision should a company's code of ethics make to assure that its officers and employees do not engage in behavior that may serve as indirect evidence of age discrimination? Discuss.

2. Which ethical standard or standards are consistent with the court's statement that "the ADEA protects older employees from being treated more harshly than if they were young"? Discuss.

REHABILITATION ACT OF 1973

The Rehabilitation Act of 1973 forbids discrimination in employment against handicapped persons by federal contractors, federal agencies, and programs receiving federal assistance. In addition, the act requires federal contractors[24] and federal agencies to take affirmative action in hiring and promoting handicapped persons.

The act defines a handicapped person as any person who has a physical or mental impairment that "substantially limits one or more of such person's major life activities." Major life activities include walking, seeing, hearing, speaking, breathing, learning, and working. Thus the definition includes employees with such conditions as mental retardation, emotional disorders, cancer, heart disease, and diabetes, as well as blindness, deafness, amputation, and paraplegia. Drug addition and alcoholism are classified as mental impairments. However, the act was amended in 1978 to specifically exclude alcoholics or drug abusers whose current use of alcohol or drugs prevents them from performing the duties of the job in question.

A 1987 amendment to the act includes "contagious diseases or infections" among handicaps, but the amendment provides that it is not discrimination to deny work to a person who would constitute a direct threat to the health or safety of others. Recent court decisions have held that a person suffering from AIDS can be considered handicapped. Perhaps even a person who has merely tested positive for the HIV virus can be considered handicapped. A worker with AIDS may be fired only if the disease prevents the worker from performing the given job tasks or poses a threat to the health of others. The employer bears the burden of proving that this threat exists. The employer is also responsible for maintaining the privacy of AIDS-infected employees to prevent discrimination against them by other employees.

Under the Rehabilitation Act, employers are required to hire only qualified handicapped persons, after making reasonable accommodation to their handicaps. In determining whether reasonable accommodation has been made, financial cost and business necessity are taken into consideration. Thus an employer would not be required to alter entranceways or workstations to accommodate a qualified paraplegic confined to a wheelchair if doing so would create an undue hardship for the employer.

Courts have ruled that a person hypersensitive to tobacco smoke is a handicapped person under the Rehabilitation Act. Reasonable accommodation to such a person does not require the employer to provide an environment wholly free of tobacco smoke. Separating desks and obtaining the voluntary agreement of other employees to refrain from smoking have been regarded as reasonable accommodations.

The EEOC is responsible for administering the Rehabilitation Act against federal agencies. The act does not create a right to bring a private lawsuit against a federal contractor for discrimination against handicapped persons. In enacting it, Congress did not provide a private remedy for the handicapped, but rather an administrative scheme to remedy violations. The Office of Federal Contract Compliance Programs enforces the act against federal contractors, while the Department of Education administers the act in connection with federally assisted education programs.

Many states have passed statutes prohibiting discrimination against handicapped persons in all employment decisions. Employers in these states are required to comply with both state and federal laws concerning the employment of the handicapped.

AMERICANS WITH DISABILITIES ACT OF 1990

The Americans with Disabilities Act of 1990 (ADA) vastly extended protection against employment discrimination to the handicapped. Studies prior to its passage indicated that almost 45 million Americans (one in six) had physical or mental disabilities and that two thirds of the working-age disabled were unemployed. Unlike the Rehabilitation Act of 1973, which applied only to federal agencies, federal contractors, and recipients of federal grants the ADA applies to all companies with 15 or more employees.

In language similar to that of the Rehabilitation Act, the ADA defines a "disabled individual" as someone who suffers from "a physical or mental impairment that substantially limits one or more of the major life functions" (for example, walking or talking), or has a "record of such impairment" (for example, recovery from cancer), or is "regarded as having such an impairment" (for example, a disfiguring injury or AIDS).

Like the Rehabilitation Act, the ADA requires employers to make reasonable accommodation for disabled workers except when this would place undue hardship ("significant difficulty or expense") on the employer. Following the act's effective date of August 1992, this requirement will be phased in over two to four years, depending on the size of the company. In addition, places of public accommodations, such as hotels, restaurants, motels, gas stations, zoos, and sports arenas, must be made accessible to the disabled. Accessibility includes wheelchair ramps and widened doors.

The fact that the ADA affects many more businesses than does the Rehabilitation Act has caused businesspeople to worry about the vagueness of some of its wording. For example, what precisely constitutes an "undue hardship"—being required to spend $100 or $1,000 or $10,000? Even the ADA's definition of a "disabled person" is so broadly written as to create controversy. However, concerns about the act will undoubtedly wane as the responsibilities it imposes on employers (and the benefits it will offer society) become clearer.

The EEOC enforces the ADA's employment provisions. The remedies provided by the ADA are the same as those provided by Title VII, which include hiring, reinstatement, back pay, and attorneys' fees.

FOREIGN-OWNED COMPANIES OPERATING IN THE UNITED STATES

The antidiscrimination laws of the United States differ from those of other countries. Nevertheless, the Supreme Court ruled, in a 1982 case, that a subsidiary of a foreign company operating in the United States "is a company of the United States" and subject to the provisions of the U.S. antidiscrimination laws.

In that case, several female secretarial employees of a U.S. subsidiary of a Japanese company alleged that the subsidiary hired only Japanese males to fill sales managerial and executive positions. The subsidiary claimed that a 1953 treaty between the United States and Japan exempted it from the Title VII provisions that prohibited employment discrimination based on sex, race, religion, or national origin. The Supreme Court ruled that the treaty exempted only Japanese companies and that the American subsidiaries of such companies were subject to Title VII. The Court noted that Japanese citizenship might be a bona fide occupational qualification for certain positions in Japanese-owned businesses operating in the United States, positions requiring familiarity with the language, culture, and business customs of Japan.[25]

U.S. COMPANIES EMPLOYING AMERICAN CITIZENS IN FOREIGN COUNTRIES

While Title VII of the 1964 Civil Rights Act prohibits discrimination by foreign companies operating in the United States, it does not prohibit discrimination by U.S. companies against American citizens who work abroad for such companies. In a 1991 case involving alleged discrimination against a U.S. citizen working in Saudi Arabia for a U.S. oil company,[26] the Supreme Court held that the 1964 Civil Rights Act did not specifically state that it applied to U.S. citizens working abroad. According to the Court, laws passed by Congress are presumed to have effect only in the United States. Congress, if it chooses, can nullify this decision by amending the 1964 Civil Rights Act.

EQUAL PAY ACT

The Equal Pay Act, passed by Congress in 1963 as an amendment to the Fair Labor Standards Act, makes it illegal for an employer to discriminate on the basis of sex in the payment of wages for equal work. The purpose of the act is to remedy a serious problem of employment discrimination in private industry—paying women less than men for equal work. In mandating equal pay for equal work, Congress did not require that the jobs entitled to equal pay be identical, but only that they be "substantially equal." Thus a violation of the act may be proven if equal pay is not given for jobs requiring substantially equal "skill, effort, and responsibility."

The Equal Pay Act prohibits only wage differences based on sex. Wage differences between the sexes are valid if they are based on any factor other than sex that can be used to differentiate wages among employees—a seniority system, a merit system, a system measuring wages by quantity or quality of production, and so on. Violations of the act may not be corrected by reducing the wages of any employee to eliminate the differential.

The employer may not pay men and women different wages for performing substantially the same work by assigning different titles to that work. For example, if males designated as "environment technicians" and females designated as "janitors" are performing substantially the same work, they must by paid equal wages. The employer can pay different wage rates only for truly different work.

In private employment the Equal Pay Act applies to most of the employees subject to the Fair Labor Standards Act (discussed in Chapter 12), including executive, administrative, professional, and outside sales personnel. In addition, the act covers labor unions and employees of the federal government and state and local governments. The EEOC is responsible for enforcing the Equal Pay Act.

An aggrieved employee can bring suit in a state or federal court for wages withheld in violation of the Equal Pay Act. The employee may also be awarded an amount equal to back pay if the employer acted in bad faith, as well as attorneys' fees and court costs. As an alternative, the employee can file a complaint with the EEOC, which may sue on the employee's behalf.

In the following case the EEOC sued on behalf of six female employees, charging that the employer had violated the Equal Pay Act.

EEOC v. WHITE AND SON ENTERPRISES
U.S. COURT OF APPEALS, 11th CIRCUIT
881 F.2d 1006 (1989)

White and Son Enterprises, an Alabama company, owned and operated by Orvis White and his son Ricky, was engaged in light manufacturing. Female and male employees of the company performed jobs that required similar levels of skill and responsibility, yet the female employees were paid only $4 an hour to start, while the male employees started at $4.50 or $5 an hour. On June 3, 1985, six of the female employees complained to their foreman and Ricky White about the unequal pay and requested a raise. The next day they repeated their complaint to Orvis White, who promptly fired them.

On June 27, 1985, the six women (plaintiff) filed charges with the EEOC, which investigated their claim and filed suit in U.S. district court on June 2, 1987, alleging violations of the Equal Pay Act (EPA). White and Son (defendent) attempted to raise affirmative defenses provided by the Equal Pay Act and Title VII, asserting that its system of pay raises and rates was based on seniority, merit, quantity or quality of production, and factors other than sex, namely prior work experience. The district court denied this motion, and after a trial it entered judgment for the plaintiff. The defendant appealed.

TUTTLE, SENIOR CIRCUIT JUDGE

In order to establish a prima facie case under the EPA, the plaintiff must show "that an employer pays different wages to employees of opposite sexes 'for equal work on jobs the performance of which requires equal skill, effort, and responsibility, and which are performed under similar working conditions.'" Plaintiff need only show discrimination in pay against an employee vis-à-vis one employee of the opposite sex. If, however, other appropriate "comparators," *i.e.,* employees doing substantially equal work, were wrongly excluded from the comparison by plaintiff, defendant must call them to the attention of the court.

The EEOC alleged that the two women who operated the truss saw were paid less than men performing the identical job. In addition, plaintiff claimed that the charging parties working in the Craftwood operation were paid at a lower rate than men working full-time in Craftwood, performing similar jobs. The evidence supports the district court's finding that defendant paid the female employees less than full-time male employees for substantially similar work. The district court did not clearly err when it found that the two women who operated the truss saw, Melissa Aderhold and Florene Bartlett, were paid less than their male counterparts; even their replacements, who were men, were paid higher wages for the same work after these two charging parties left the company. Moreover, the court's finding that the job of large table saw operator is at least equal to a job on the truss table in terms of skill, effort, and responsibility, making them substantially similar, is not clearly erroneous. The court viewed the videotape in evidence of the truss operations, heard the rebuttal testimony to such video, and considered the testimony of employees. As to Ms. Aderholt and Ms. Bartlett, therefore, plaintiff proved that their pay was less in a job which is substantially similar to the job held by the male employees, sufficiently making out an EPA claim.

The district court also found that male employees who were regularly assigned to work at Craftwood were paid more than female employees performing identical work. It is undisputed that all Craftwood jobs but one required equal skill and responsibility. Appellant insists that some male employees in Craftwood were paid less than the charging parties, $3.35 an hour, which defeats plaintiff's discrimination claim. Appellant declares, however, that students were generally the only employees hired at that level. Even though White and Son pays only students the minimum wage, it argues that no distinction should be made between full-time and part-time or student employees for the purposes of appellee's suit. We disagree.

Once plaintiff has established a prima facie case, defendant has the burden to justify the pay difference, based upon one of the four exceptions in the EPA. With such proof lacking here, however, due to defendant's waiver of its affirmative defenses, the prima facie case prevails.

Even if appellant were permitted to assert the defenses that (1) salary was based on prior experience and (2) the pay raise was to reward superior production on the truss table, its arguments must fail. The district court did not clearly err in finding that White and Son had no written or objective system of setting wages. The evidence showed that, in general, appellant did not know what prior experience its employees possessed when they began working at White and Son. Moreover, Shirley Bryan trained male employees for various Craftwood jobs, yet received a lower salary than they did; she had also been with the company longer than at least one man who received a raise before she did. As to the production defense, even assuming appellant rewarded the truss table employees with a pay increase for producing at a certain level, the pay inequities in the areas already mentioned could not be justified by claiming production quantity differed. Because we conclude that plaintiff proved discrimination under the EPA, a violation of Title VII is established a fortiori.

Affirmed.

Legal Issues

1. What was required of the plaintiff to establish a prima facie case? Explain.
2. Why did the defense that salaries were based on prior experience fail?

Ethical Issues

1. Was it unfair for the court not to accept White and Son's contention that paying male student employees

less than full-time women employ-ees showed that it did not violate the Equal Pay Act? Why?

2. Do the provisions of the Equal Pay Act conflict with bottom-line ethics? Why?

COMPARABLE WORTH

In the 1980s the concept of equal pay for equal work was taken one step further, to the view that work of **comparable worth** to the employer ought to be paid equally. This view was embraced by groups of women who worked at low wages in jobs that had traditionally been done by women. Numerous lawsuits were brought under the comparable worth doctrine. An example of such a suit might be one against a manufacturing company that employs only male truck drivers and only female secretaries and pays the truck drivers 50 percent more than it pays the secretaries. The secretaries might sue the company because of the differences in its wage rates for traditionally male and female job classes.

However, courts have received such lawsuits coolly. At a minimum they have required a clear showing that an employer acted *intentionally* in establishing job classifications that resulted in gender-based discrimination. Faced with this burden of proof, the idea of comparable worth appears dead in the water in the U.S. private sector, though it has met with some success in other countries.

Comparable worth
the doctrine that requires employers to provide equal pay for work of comparable value

STATE AND CITY DISCRIMINATION LAWS

Federal employment discrimination laws permit states and cities to enact laws that impose additional requirements on employers. Employers in the states or cities that have enacted such laws are bound by both those laws and the federal laws.

Thus far 45 states have passed their own versions of employment discrimination laws, usually called "fair employment practices laws."[27] The provisions of these laws vary widely, but they usually forbid discrimination on the basis of color, race, national origin, religion, or ancestry in all phases of the employment process. They usually also grant protection beyond that granted by the federal laws. For example, some states prohibit employment discrimination based on marital status or parenthood or limit employment discrimination based on the use of lie detector tests or police or military records.

Many cities have employment discrimination ordinances. For example, the District of Columbia prohibits employment discrimination on the basis of physical appearance, matriculation, sexual preference, political affiliations, or family responsibilities. A Philadelphia ordinance prohibits employment discrimination based on sexual orientation.

State or city employment discrimination laws typically apply to all employers, regardless of the number of employees. In addition, these laws usually cover employment agencies and labor organizations as well as employers. Typically, administrative bodies are empowered to issue rules and regulations and conduct hearings on alleged violations. They are also empowered to take a variety of remedial steps to eliminate employment discrimination if conciliation fails.

EUROPEAN COMMUNITY

Employment Discrimination

A principal concern of the EC is the prevention of employment discrimination based on nationality. Among the EC's efforts to foster openness and equality is the right of workers to move relatively freely between countries. Both public authorities and private individuals are forbidden to discriminate against workers because of their nationality. For example, a British architect who possesses the qualifications required of a French architect cannot be kept from applying for the license necessary to work as an architect in France.

Sex Discrimination

The EC requires each of its member states to give men and women equal pay for equal work. This requirement is intended to improve the living condition of all the people in the EC and to prevent any member state from gaining a competitive advantage by underpaying part of its work force. No other EC legislation is yet in place concerning sexual discrimination or other terms or conditions of employment.

GERMANY

German law requires equal treatment of men and women at the workplace. This means that men and women receive equal pay for equal work and that job distinctions are not based on the worker's sex, though an exception may be made for a bona fide occupational qualification, such as the sex of actors or models. The remedy for employment discrimination is damages but not reinstatement to the job.

JAPAN

Japanese law requires workers to retire at a specified age, usually age 55. These workers frequently find jobs with firms other than the one from which they retired.

REVIEW QUESTIONS & PROBLEMS

1. What does Title VII of the Civil Rights Act of 1964 identify as the principal kinds of discrimination that cause unequal employment opportunities?
2. What factors determine whether an employer is subject to the job discrimination provisions of Title VII?
3. The City of Memphis Fire Department agreed to implement an affirmative action plan to remedy past discrimination against blacks. Subsequently, when

budget deficits required a reduction of fire fighters, the seniority system mandated the layoffs of many of the blacks hired under the affirmative action plan. These black fire fighters sought to enjoin the layoffs. It was argued that remedying past discrimination against blacks was more important than protecting the jobs of whites who had more seniority. Did the layoffs under the seniority system violate Title VII? Explain.

4. Continental Airlines required flight hostesses to comply with strict weight requirements as a condition of their employment. The weight requirements were not imposed because they improved the ability of flight hostesses to perform their duties but because Continental believed that featuring thin and attractive flight hostesses would enhance its ability to compete with other airlines. From 1961 to 1971, Carole Gerdom was a flight hostess for Continental. She was terminated because her weight exceeded the maximum permitted by Continental. She sued Continental, alleging sex discrimination that violated Title VII. Did Continental Airlines violate Title VII? Explain.

5. After Linda Morris, a health club employee, had worked in several positions for the health club over the course of several years, the health club hired a male, David Tashiro, as its athletic director despite the fact that Morris was better qualified for the position. She had more experience than Tashiro, and she had earned a bachelor of science degree in recreation administration, whereas Tashiro had no college degree. Morris sued the health club, claiming that it had violated Title VII by practicing sex discrimination. She alleged that the health club would not hire a woman as athletic director because it wanted to maintain a macho image. Did the health club violate Title VII? Explain.

6. Clark, age 54, was Amtrak's director of budgets and administration. A new supervisor who wanted his own people took over. He told Clark, "We are reorganizing, and there is no place for you." Clark was replaced by a 28-year-old man. Clark's personnel file contained only commendations and praise. Should Clark have an effective lawsuit under the Age Discrimination in Employment Act? Why?

ENDNOTES

1. William Holmes McGuffey, *McGuffey's New Revised Third Reader* (Cincinnati, 1843).

2. 109 S. Ct. 1775 (1989).

3. Ironically, the word *sex* was added to Title VII after the bill had passed the committee and was being debated on the floor of the House of Representatives. In an attempt to defeat the bill, a congressman from Virignia stated that the bill was already so unreasonable that sex might as well be included.

4. 442 F.2d 385 (5th Cir. 1971).

5. 111 S. Ct. 1196 (1991).

6. 106 S. Ct. 2399 (1986). This case was mentioned in Chapter 6.

7. *United States v. Greger*, 580 U.S. 163 (1965).

8. 432 U.S. 63 (1977).

9. 401 U.S. 424 (1971).

10. 109 S. Ct. 2115 (1989).

11. 422 U.S. 405 (1975).

12. 106 S. Ct. 1842 (1986).

13. Private employers are not directly affected by the *Wygant* decision because the decision was based on the 14th Amendment which applies to actions of state and local governments. However, the Court's view of the constitutionality of affirmative action in the public sector usually becomes the law for decisions on what federal civil rights laws allow for the private sector.

14. 106 S. Ct. at 1851–52.

15. The basic concept of this executive order is that doing business with the federal government is a privilege, and thus the federal government can impose conditions on those who enter into contracts to do business with it. Under Executive Order 11264, each federal contractor with 50 or more employees in a contract of $50,000 or more is required to develop an acceptable affirmative action plan with realistic goals and timetables. The order covers approximately 200,000 federal contractors who employ approximately 20 million workers.

16. 478 U.S. 421 (1986).

17. 109 S. Ct. 706 (1989).

18. 448 U.S. 448 (1980). In addition, the minority set-asides by the city of Richmond were a broad race-conscious remedy rather than a plan to correct past discrimination.

19. 109 S. Ct. 2180 (1989).

20. 109 S. Ct. 2155 (1989).

21. 109 S. Ct. 2363 (1989).

22. The 1967 act protected workers aged 40–67. A 1978 amendment extended the act's protection to workers aged 40–70. A 1986 amendment removed the mandatory retirement age for most workers, thereby protecting all workers aged 40 and above, with a few exceptions.

23. *Western Airlines v. Criswell*, 472 U.S. 400 (1985).

24. Employers with a federal contract of $2,500 or more are required to take affirmative action to employ handicapped workers. Employers with government contracts of at least $50,000 must develop a written affirmative action program.

25. *Sumitomo Shoji America, Inc. v. Avagliano*, 457 U.S. 176 (1982).

26. *EEOC v. Arabian American Oil Co.*, 111 S. Ct. 1227 (1991).

27. The five states that have not yet enacted a fair employment practices law are Alabama, Arkansas, Louisiana, Mississippi, and North Dakota.

CHAPTER

14

Union-Management Relations

Although management and labor share in the economic success of a business, their goals are often in conflict. Management seeks to minimize costs, while labor seeks to maximize wages and benefits. Because of the employer's relatively strong bargaining power as compared with that of the individual employee, the individual employee is generally at a disadvantage in dealing with the employer. Consequently, employees have tended to unite in labor organizations to improve their bargaining power. Traditionally, management has fought the formation of such organizations to prevent inroads into its powers.

Disputes between management and labor have historically caused problems not only for the companies involved but for the general public as well, since such disputes often interrupt the flow of commerce. Legislation has been enacted, primarily at the federal level, to balance the power between labor and management and to minimize the harmful effects of their disputes.

This chapter discusses the most important federal laws governing union-management relations and the procedures for implementing those laws. The laws discussed are the Norris-LaGuardia Act, the Wagner Act, the Taft-Hartley Act, and the Landrum-Griffin Act.

UNION MOVEMENT

During the late 1800s the U.S. economy became increasingly industrialized. This triggered an influx of workers into industrialized urban centers. As manufacturing became mechanized, work suitable for unskilled labor developed rapidly.

Worker Concerns

In the early stages of industrialization, employers commanded enormous power over employees. Due to fierce competition companies could stay in business only by keeping production costs as low as possible. One method they used was to pay workers as little as possible. While the average *daily* wage during this period was as low as $1.25, women, children, immigrants, and convicts could be hired for much less, often for as little as 35–50 cents a day. Since a large pool of unskilled workers was available, wages could be drastically reduced when cuts in labor costs were deemed necessary. Despite the low daily wage, workdays were often extremely long. Men, women, and children worked up to 14 hours a day. Breaks were usually limited to mealtimes.

At the same time working conditions were often poor. Many factories had little or no ventilation and high noise levels. The term *sweatshop* was used to describe the small, crowded, unclean workplaces that were all too common. As a result of the poor working conditions, the health of many workers deteriorated. Various illnesses peculiar to certain jobs, such as phosphoric poisoning in the match industry, were labeled "occupational diseases."

The combination of low pay, long hours, and poor working conditions impelled employees to unite in order to increase their bargaining power.

Weapons of Employers to Prevent Unionization

Blacklist
a list of employees involved in union activities

Yellow-dog contract
an employment contract in which as a condition of employment the employee agrees not to join a union

Employers did not sit idly by while their employees attempted to unionize. Two methods that employers used to prevent concerted worker activities were blacklists and yellow-dog contracts. A **blacklist** identifies workers involved in union activities. The circulation of such lists among employers made it difficult for these workers to find new employment in the same trade. A **yellow-dog contract** is an employment contract in which the employee agrees not to join a union as a condition of employment. Violation of the contract subjects the employee to firing.

Common law doctrines were favorable to employers in early industrial America. Employers often charged employees who formed unions with criminal conspiracy in restraint of trade. Courts accepted the argument that worker organizations injured nonmember workers and caused price increases that injured consumers. Workers who raised wages by organizing strikes were held to have illegally benefited themselves at the expense of others.

The first criminal conspiracy case, in 1806, involved a small club of Philadelphia shoemakers. When the shoemakers struck for higher wages, the employers charged criminal conspiracy. The court held that the combination of workers in this case was illegal since the workers' only reasons for striking were to benefit themselves and to injure others. Their illegal reasons made the club itself illegal.

By 1842, however, courts accepted unions as legal organizations. Employers then used the civil courts to stifle unionism. They convinced courts that picketing by striking workers inevitably led to violence, and thus often obtained injunctions against strikes. Union members violating injunctions were subject to fines and imprisonment.

In 1890, with the passage of the Sherman Antitrust Act, Congress inadvertently handed another antiunion doctrine to employers. The Sherman Act was intended to stop the anticompetitive practices of firms. Employers, however, successfully argued that a strike that shut down a plant was a combination in restraint of interstate trade.

Economic pressure was another method that employers used to prevent unionization. If union activity became strong, employers would "lock out" their workers by closing their businesses for a short time. These "lockouts" often destroyed young unions that lacked adequate relief funds. More importantly, the lockouts reminded workers of how much they needed their jobs and how quickly they could lose them. When union members went on strike, employers often hired replacements. The replacements, called "scabs" by the strikers, were usually easy to find, as many immigrants were willing to accept low wages and poor working conditions.

A more subtle method, used by some employers, was to establish company unions in which worker representatives acted as mere puppets of management, allowing it to render the final decision on any labor disputes. To encourage membership in such unions, employers offered bonuses and profit sharing plans to those who joined.

Armed with these and other weapons, employers in early industrial America were able to control workers and curb their ability to organize.

FEDERAL STATUTES

Due in part to the advantages of management, unions gained congressional support. Thus in 1914, when Congress passed the Clayton Antitrust Act, which, like the Sherman Act, was aimed at the anticompetitive practices of businesses, it specifically exempted from the antitrust laws unions that are lawfully carrying out their legitimate objectives.[1]

The Norris-LaGuardia Act

Still, the judiciary remained a major obstacle to the achievement of union goals. The abuse of the injunction as an antilabor tool continued until the passage of the Norris-LaGuardia Act, in 1932. The act barred federal courts from issuing injunctions to prevent peaceful strikes and picketing. It also prohibited yellow-dog contracts. However, it did not require employers to recognize and bargain with unions.

Today, labor-management relations are primarily governed by three pieces of legislation: the Wagner Act, the Taft-Hartley Act, and the Landrum-Griffin Act. The Wagner Act is properly called the National Labor Relations Act, while Taft-Hartley and Landrum-Griffin are actually amendments to the National Labor Relations Act.

The Wagner Act

During the Great Depression of the 1930s, political power shifted toward farm and labor groups. As part of President Roosevelt's New Deal, the National Labor Relations Act of 1935 (Wagner Act), the first comprehensive labor relations legislation, was passed. This act created an affirmative obligation of employers to bargain in good faith with unions.

Previously, Congress had assumed a laissez-faire attitude toward labor-management relations, so that confrontations between labor and management were essentially unregulated. Under the Wagner Act, for the first time, the employer was required to bargain with the labor union selected by a particular group of employees.

The act, which was openly prounion, prohibited certain employer conduct, which it designated as "unfair labor practices," but it did not list prohibitive union practices. It also created the National Labor Relations Board, an administrative agency, to interpret and administer the act.

Taft-Hartley Act

The Wagner Act stimulated the growth of unions. Between 1935 and 1945, the number of union members in the United States increased from 3 million to more than 15 million.

During World War II such consumer products as automobiles and appliances were scarce. After the war consumers expected and demanded these products. Labor leaders, recognizing their strong bargaining position, called crippling strikes to force employer concessions. These strikes exasperated the general public, while the power of individual union leaders (called "labor bosses") caused it to distrust unions. In 1947 Congress reacted by passing the Labor-Management Relations Act (Taft-Hartley Act). The purpose of Taft-Hartley was to balance the power between labor and management, and, in effect, to recognize a third party in collective bargaining, the general public.

The Taft-Hartley Act attempted to restore the balance of power between labor and management by:

1. Forbidding unfair union practices.
2. Prohibiting closed shops.
3. Creating the Federal Mediation and Conciliation Service. This independent agency sends representatives to mediate labor disputes affecting interstate commerce by proposing settlements.
4. Allowing employers or unions to file lawsuits to enforce collective bargaining agreements.
5. Providing an 80-day cooling-off period to postpone lockouts or strikes that threaten the national health or safety. The president appoints a board of inquiry to make recommendations. On the basis of those recommendations, the president may then ask a federal court to issue an injunction prohibiting a lockout or strike for 80 days. After this eighty-day cooling-off period a lockout or strike would be permissible.

Landrum-Griffin Act

During the 1950s Senate investigations uncovered embezzlement of union funds, union corruption, and undemocratic union procedures. To protect individual employees from union abuses, Congress passed the Labor-Management Reporting and Disclosure Act in 1959. This act, commonly known as the Landrum-Griffin Act, established a "bill of rights" for union members. Landrum-Griffin attempted to regulate internal union affairs by guaranteeing the rights of members to attend union meetings, to have a voice in running their union, and to vote by secret ballot. It also established procedures to protect union funds by requiring public financial disclosure from unions and union leaders. Reports on the funds in union treasuries must be filed with the secretary of labor. The main provisions of the Wagner Act, the Taft-Hartley Act, and the Landrum-Griffin Act are outlined in Table 14-1.

PREEMPTION AND STATE LEGISLATION

As noted in Chapters 6 and 10, both the federal government and state governments regulate business activities. In the area of labor-management relations, however, the Supreme Court has ruled that uniformity in administering and interpreting federal labor laws is necessary. Thus, for labor matters that are arguably included

TABLE 14-1   **Summary of the Main Provisions of the Most Significant Federal Labor Laws**

	Unions	Employers
Wagner Act (1935)	Granted the right to organize	Must bargain in good faith
		Must bargain with unions selected by employees
		Designates certain employer conduct as "unfair labor practices"
Taft-Hartley Act (1947)	Forbidden to engage in "unfair labor practices"	Created Federal Mediation and Conciliation Service
	Created Federal Mediation and Conciliation Service	Prohibits closed shops; permits union shops except where states have enacted right-to-work laws
	Permits lawsuits to enforce collective bargaining agreements	Permits lawsuits to enforce collective bargaining agreements
	Provides 80-day cooling-off periods to postpone strikes threatening national health or safety	Provides 80-day cooling-off periods to postpone strikes threatening national health or safety
Landrum-Griffin Act (1959)	Guarantees the rights of members to attend union meetings, have a voice in running their union, and vote by secret ballot	
	Requires public financial disclosure from unions and union leaders	

within the exclusive jurisdiction of the National Labor Relations Act, it is within the power of the National Labor Relations Board, so that, for example, a state court cannot hear an unfair labor practice case or a representation election case. Under the Constitution's Supremacy Clause, a "federal preemption" has removed the states' power to regulate labor relations.

There are exceptions to federal preemption in labor matters. States may exercise authority over labor matters not covered by the NLRA. Disputes over labor activities that involve violence or the threat of violence can be heard by state courts. State courts can also enforce state trespass laws and award damages for harm caused by unlawful strikes or boycotts.

The above summary of federal labor laws reflects our present national labor policy. Through the years Congress has sought to equalize the power of management and labor so that they can reach agreements that are fair to both sides. The final chapter on national labor policy has not, of course, been written.

NATIONAL LABOR RELATIONS BOARD

The National Labor Relations Board (NLRB), an administrative agency created in 1935 by the National Labor Relations Act (NLRA), is charged with the administration and enforcement of the NLRA. The NLRB consists of two divisions: the board itself and the general counsel. The board consists of five members who are appointed by the president, with the advice and consent of the Senate, for a term of five years. The general counsel is appointed by the president for a four-year term, with the advice and consent of the Senate. The actual work of the general counsel is entrusted to 31 regional offices in major cities across the country. Each of these offices is supervised by a regional director.

The board and general counsel are charged with two major responsibilities under the NLRA: (1) supervising elections to determine whether a majority of the workers in an appropriate work unit, known as a "bargaining unit," wish to choose a particular union as their collective bargaining representative and (2) deciding whether employers or unions have engaged in unfair labor practices.

Supervision of representation elections is conducted at the regional level. If a majority of the employees in a bargaining unit vote by secret ballot for a union as their collective bargaining representative, the board certifies that union as the exclusive collective bargaining representative of all the employees in the bargaining unit.

An employer, employee, or union may file charges of unfair labor practices with an appropriate regional office of the NLRB. The charges are then investigated by field examiners in the regional office. If the charges are supported by sufficient evidence, the regional director files a formal complaint against an employer or a union. If the case is not settled by the parties, a public hearing, similar to a trial, is held before an administrative law judge, with an attorney from the regional office acting as prosecutor. The order issued by the administrative law judge is final unless either party, within 20 days, appeals to the board. The board then reviews the case and issues a decision. If it determines that an unfair labor practice has been committed, it is empowered to issue a cease and desist order and to command the offender to take affirmative action to correct the situation.

The NLRB can also order an employer or a union to bargain collectively with the other party in a labor dispute. It cannot, however, force the parties to agree to particular terms of a collective bargaining agreement. The parties to the agreement must set its terms and provisions themselves. In addition, the NLRB can order employers to reinstate illegally discharged employees and pay them lost wages. In cases of unfair labor practices that influence a representation election, the board will set aside the election and require the employees to vote again. Decisions of the board are subject to review by the U.S. court of appeals. Either the aggrieved party or the board may petition the Supreme Court to review decisions of the court of appeals.

Courts have held that the NLRB's powers are broad and discretionary and are subject to limited judicial review. They will not overturn an NLRB order unless it can be shown that the order is an obvious effort to accomplish purposes other than those authorized by the NLRA.

Jurisdiction of the NLRB

Although the NLRA, as amended, covers many millions of employees, its jurisdiction does not extend to all of the employers and employees in the United States.[2] Exercising its broad administrative discretion, the NLRB sets monetary limits to exclude for its jurisdiction employers whose businesses do not significantly affect commerce. For example, retail businesses with an annual gross volume of less than $500,000 are excluded.

Certain groups of employers are specifically excluded from the coverage of the NLRA. Among these groups are the federal government, state and local governments,[3] and railway and airline employers covered by other federal legislation.

The act also specifically excludes such employees as agricultural laborers, domestic workers, and employees of independent contractors. Supervisory and managerial employees are probably the most important employee exclusions of the act. Supervisory employees are employees who have the authority to hire, transfer, suspend, or lay off other employees. Managerial employees are employees who formulate and effectuate management policies. The exclusion of these two classes of employees prevents a conflict of interest between the employer and its own representatives.

As a result of these various exclusions, only slightly more than one half of the total work force in the United States is covered by the NLRA.

EMPLOYER UNFAIR LABOR PRACTICES

The NLRA, as passed in 1935, declared collective bargaining to be a matter of public policy. The act stated that employees have a right both to form unions and to engage in collective bargaining and other activities for their mutual aid and protection. To make this right effective, it defined certain employer acts as unfair labor practices. Congress felt that merely stating the right of employees to organize was not sufficient, that it was also necessary to prohibit employer acts interfering with the right to organize and to bargain collectively.

Section 8(a) makes it an unfair labor practice for an employer to do any of the following:

1. Interfere with employees in the exercise of their rights to form or assist labor organizations.
2. Dominate a union or contribute financial or other support to it.
3. Encourage or discourage union membership by discrimination in regard to hiring, tenure of employment, or conditions of employment.
4. Discriminate against employees for filing charges or giving testimony under the NLRA.
5. Refuse to bargain collectively with the designated representative of a majority of the employees.

Interference with Efforts of Employees to Form or Join Unions

Section 8(a)(1) deems it an unfair labor practice for an employer to interfere with employee efforts to form, join, or assist labor organizations. This catchall provision guarantees the basic rights of employees to organize into labor organizations and forbids all employer activities designed to interfere with the organizational activities of employees.

It prohibits such obvious tactics as blacklisting, espionage (for example, the use of detectives or electonic eavesdropping devices), and threats to fire employees who engage in union organizing. It also prohibits more subtle tactics. In fact, anything that an employer does, says, or puts in writing may constitute an unfair labor practice under Section 8(a)(1) if the action or statement contains threats of reprisals or promises of benefits. For example, an employer may have committed an unfair labor practice by predicting that unionization would result in severe economic consequences if it is within the employer's power to make that prediction come true. In one case an employer's announcement of additional holidays and better vacation benefits was held to constitute an unfair labor practice. Since the announcement was made shortly before the union certification election, the NLRB held that it was intended to cause workers to vote against the union.

On the other hand, an employer is permitted to state his opinion of the consequences of unionization in a nonthreatening manner. The employer's right of free speech protects statements like this one: "It is our considered opinion that if the union is formed, you employees would not benefit in the long run." Employer predictions based on facts over which the employer has no control are also protected, provided the predictions contain no threat of reprisal or promise of benefits.

An employer's work rules may be evidence of an unfair labor practice. An employer is permitted to impose nondiscriminatory rules against the distribution of union literature or the solicitation of union membership during an employee's work time or in work areas. However, management may not restrict the right of employees to conduct such activities in nonwork areas during nonwork time, because doing so would obstruct the employees' right of self-organization.

If an employer questions an employee about union sympathy, is this an unfair labor practice? In the following case, decided in 1984, the NLRB returned to a balancing test established 30 years previously in ruling on an employer's interrogation of a worker about union sympathies.

ROSSMORE HOUSE v. HOTEL AND RESTAURANT EMPLOYEES UNION, LOCAL 11

269 NLRB No. 198 (1984)

Shyr-Jim Tsay, the respondent, operated the Rossmore House, a Los Angeles retirement hotel. In July 1982, Warren Harvey, the hotel cook, contacted representatives of the Hotel and Restaurant Employees Union and arranged to have an employees' meeting held at his house. After the meeting Tsay was sent a mailgram stating that Harvey and another employee were forming a union organizing committee and that the activities of the union organizers were protected under the NLRA.

On August 1, after receiving the mailgram, Ronald Tvenstrup, manager of the Rossmore House, walked into the kitchen and asked Harvey whether what it said was true. Harvey answered yes, and Tvenstrup walked away. Almost a week later, as Harvey was leaving work, Tsay asked him why he was bringing a union into the Rossmore House, and Harvey replied that he was seeking to unionize because of the low pay and the lack of benefits and job security. Tsay then asked Harvey whether the union charged a fee to join and said that he would talk to Tvenstrup about the union.

The union later brought suit against Tsay for unlawful interrogation of employees under Section 8(a)(1) of the NLRA. An administrative law judge heard the case in Los Angeles in October and November 1982 and ruled that the interrogations of Harvey by Tvenstrup and Tsay were violations of the NLRA. Tsay appealed the case to the NLRB.

The judge found the Respondent's statements in both instances to be unlawful interrogations under Section 8(a)(1) of the [National Labor Relations] Act.

[I]n *PPG Industries*, the Board held that questions concerning union sympathies, even when addressed to open and active union supporters in the absence of threats or promises, are inherently coercive.

We will no longer apply the *PPG* standard. We conclude the *PPG* improperly established a per se rule that completely disregarded the circumstances surrounding an alleged interrogation and ignored the reality of the workplace. Such a per se approach had been rejected by the Board 30 years ago when it set forth the basic test for evaluating whether interrogations violate the Act: whether under all of the circumstances the interrogation reasonably tends to restrain, coerce, or interfere with rights guaranteed by the Act.

The Third Circuit recently adopted the same approach, as follows:

> Because production supervisors and employees often work closely together, one can expect that during the course of the workday they will discuss a range of subjects of mutual interest, including ongoing unionization efforts. To hold that any instance of casual questioning concerning union sympathies violates the Act ignores the realities of the workplace.

After careful consideration, we conclude that *PPG* improperly establishes a per se rule that completely disregards the circumstances surrounding an alleged interrogation and ignores the reality of the workplace. Accordingly, we overrule *PPG* and similar cases to the extent they find that an employer's questioning open and active union supporters about their union sentiments, in the absence of threats or promises, necessarily interferes with, restrains, or coerces employees in violation of Section 8(a)(1) of the Act.

In this case, Harvey, an active union supporter, openly declared his union ties by means of a mailgram to the Respondent. We find no violation of Section 8(a)(1) of the Act under either version of the conversation between Tvenstrup and Harvey concerning the contents of the telegram and Tvenstrup's intention to oppose the Union. Nor do we find any violation regarding the second incident when the Respondent's owner asked Harvey why he wanted a union and whether the Union charged a fee. Under the totality of the circumstances, we find the Respondent's questioning of Harvey to be noncoercive, and therefore we shall dismiss the complaint in its entirety.

Order: The complaint is dismissed.

Legal Issues

1. Why were Tsay's questions not unlawful?

2. What questions would have made Tsay's conversation with Harvey unlawful? Explain.

Ethical Issues

1. Which ethical standard most closely resembles the test that the NLRB established to determine whether an employer's interrogation is unlawful under the NLRA? Discuss.

2. The *PPG* standard made it per se unlawful under the NLRA for an employer to interrogate an employee concerning union sympathies. Was this standard more likely than the standard that replaced it to assure employees a fair opportunity to be free from employer pressure in deciding whether to form a labor union, become union members, or have a particular union represent them in collective bargaining? Why?

Domination of a Union

As noted, before the passage of the NLRA, employers often attempted to ward off labor unions by forming company unions. Section 8(a)(2) makes it an unfair labor practice for an employer to interfere with the formation or administration of a union or to contribute financial or other support to a union.

Employers are prohibited from supervising a union's internal management, participating in the formulation of a union's bylaws, or helping to decide the procedure or agenda of union meetings. They are also prohibited from supporting unions by providing meeting places, refreshments, or other logistical support, such as secretaries, telephones, or copying machines.

Sweetheart contract
a collective bargaining agreement in which the union meets the employer's wishes rather than representing the best interests of its members

If a single employer is committing several of these interferences within a single union, the employer is dominating the union. The test is whether the employer's activity has reached a point at which it is reasonable to infer that the union does not truly represent the employees in employer-employee disputes. Domination of the union by the employer could result in a **sweetheart contract,** a collective bargaining agreement in which the union meets the employer's wishes rather than representing the free choice and best interests of its members.

Discrimination in Employment Based on Union Activity

Section 8(a)(3) makes it an unfair labor practice for an employer to encourage or discourage membership in a union by discrimination in any phase of the employment process. This includes discrimination based on union affiliation in hiring, firing, and promotion as well as wages, hours, work assignments, and vacations.

Section 8(a)(3) does not, however, restrict the employer's freedom to select or discharge employees for reasons other than discouraging or encouraging unionization. In one case an employer fired a union member for an offense for which nonunion workers had suffered only minor consequences. The NLRB ruled that the employer committed an unfair labor practice, holding that the employee had been fired because of union activity rather than for legitimate business reasons.

Discrimination for Participation in NLRB Proceedings

Section 8(a)(4) declares it an unfair labor practice to discriminate against workers who file unfair labor practice charges or give testimony under the NLRA. This provision protects employees who exercise their guaranteed rights from employer retaliation, such as discharge, layoff, transfer, or demotion. Congress recognized that employees were in a key position to detect and report employer unfair practices.

Section 8(a)(4) prohibits the same types of actions that Section 8(a)(3) prohibits. The same antiunion motive must be shown, and the employer has the same opportunity to demonstrate that an action was taken for legitimate business reasons.

Discrimination under Section 8(a)(4) may also occur where an employer's action makes the work situation so unpleasant that an employee quits. In one case, a union leader quit because the employer had transferred him to a position in which he was isolated from the other workers and had little chance for advancement. The employer could not show a legitimate business reason for the transfer and was held to have committed an unfair labor practice.

To prove employer discrimination, an intent to affect union activity must be shown. As a defense the employer may claim that a discharge or other allegedly unlawful act was motivated, not by antiunion bias, but by sound business reasons. To determine the actual motivation, the NLRB considers such factors as the employer's record with regard to union activity, the timing of the employer's actions, the work record of the affected employee, and the effects of the act on unionization.

Refusal to Bargain Collectively in Good Faith

Section 8(a)(5) makes it an unfair labor practice for an employer to refuse to bargain collectively with the employees' representatives. This provision is triggered if the employer refuses to confer with the union's representatives after the union has made a proper demand on the employer, for example, by registered letter.

Collective bargaining is the process in which the employer and the union meet at reasonable times and discuss in good faith wages, hours, and other terms and conditions of employment. Once a contract has been signed by both parties, the

Collective bargaining
the process in which the employer and the union meet at reasonable times and discuss in good faith wages, hours, and other terms and conditions of employment

operation and interpretation of the contract are part of the duty to bargain collectively.

The employer is required only to bargain in good faith with the union. The NLRB cannot force an employer or a union to accept any specific provision of a collective bargaining agreement. In one case, for example, it could not force the employer to agree to deduct (check off) union dues from workers' paychecks.

Bargaining in good faith requires the employer to approach negotiations with an open mind in an honest attempt to reach agreement. An employer is under a duty to send to the bargaining table representatives who have the authority to act on its behalf.

An employer's lack of good faith may be shown by its presentation of proposals on a "take-it-or-leave-it" basis or by its failure to make counterproposals to the union's demands. However, the employer is not required to continue bargaining collectively if an impasse in negotiations has been reached.

Is the employer required to get the union's consent before deciding to move a plant for economic reasons? The NLRB addressed that issue in the following case.

MILWAUKEE SPRING DIVISION OF ILLINOIS COIL SPRING CO. v. INTERNATIONAL UNION, UNITED AUTOMOBILE, AEROSPACE, & AGRICULTURAL IMPLEMENT WORKERS OF AMERICA

268 NLRB No. 87 (1984)

Illinois Coil Spring Company consisted of three divisions: Holly Spring, McHenry Spring, and Milwaukee Spring, the respondent in this case. Although the company and its three divisions were a single employer, each of its divisions was a separate bargaining unit.

Milwaukee Spring employed around 99 workers in eight departments, including assembly and molding departments. The union, which had represented its employees for many years, was by contract the sole and exclusive collective bargaining agent for the production and maintenance employees.

In January 1982 Milwaukee Spring asked the union to forego a scheduled wage increase and to grant other contract concessions. When it lost a major customer in March, it proposed to the union that its assembly operations be relocated at the nonunionized McHenry plant to save on labor costs. It also notified the union that it needed wage and benefit concessions in order to continue its molding operations in Milwaukee. In April 1982 the union rejected Milwaukee Spring's proposed alternatives to relocation and refused to bargain further over relocation of the assembly operations. The division then announced its decision to relocate the Milwaukee assembly operations at the McHenry facility.

Although both parties agreed that the relocation decision was economically motivated and that Milwaukee Spring had satisfied its obligation to bargain with the union, the union brought suit against Milwaukee Spring, claiming that it had violated the National Labor Relations Act by moving the assembly operations without the union's consent. In October 1982 the NLRB found that Milwaukee Spring had violated the National Labor Relations Act by failing to get union consent before deciding to move the assembly operations for economic reasons. Milwaukee Spring filed an appeal with the federal court of appeals, and the Board, in an unusual move, asked the court to return the case to the Board for additional consideration. (The 1982 decision is referred to as *Milwaukee Spring I.*) Milwaukee Spring then appealed the decision to the NLRB.

Sections 8(a)(5) and 8(d) [of the National Labor Relations Act] establish an employer's obligation to bargain in good faith with respect to "wages, hours, and other terms and conditions of employment." Generally, an employer may not unilaterally institute changes regarding these mandatory subjects before reaching a good faith impasse in bargaining. Section 8(d) imposes an additional requirement when a collective bargaining agreement is in effect and an employer seeks to "modif[y] . . . the terms and conditions contained in" the contract: the employer must obtain the union's consent before implementing the change. If the employment conditions the employer seeks to change are not "contained in" the contract, however, the employer's obligation remains the general one of bargaining in good faith to impasse over the subject before instituting the proposed change.

Applying these principles to the instant case, before the Board may hold that Respondent violated Section 8(d), the Board first must identify a specific term "contained in" the contract that the Company's decision to relocate modified. In *Milwaukee Spring I* the Board never specified the contract term that was modified by Respondent's decision to relocate the assembly operations. The Board's failure to do so is not surprising, for we have searched the contract in vain for a provision requiring bargaining unit work to remain in Milwaukee.

Milwaukee Spring I suggests, however, that the Board may have concluded that Respondent's relocation decision, because it was motivated by a desire to obtain relief from the Milwaukee contract's labor costs, modi-

fied that contract's wage and benefits provisions. We believe this reasoning is flawed. While it is true that the Company proposed modifying the wage and benefits provisions of the contract, the Union rejected the proposals. Following its failure to obtain the Union's consent, Respondent, in accord with Section 8(d), abandoned the proposals to modify the contract's wage and benefits provisions. Instead, Respondent decided to transfer the assembly operations to a different plant where different workers (who were not subject to the contract) would perform the work. In short, Respondents did not disturb the wages and benefits at its Milwaukee facility, and consequently did not violate Section 8(d) by modifying, without the Union's consent, the wage and benefits provisions contained in the contract.

Language recognizing the Union as the bargaining agent "for all production and maintenance employees in the Company's plant at Milwaukee, Wisconsin," does not state that the functions that the unit performs must remain in Milwaukee. No doubt parties could draft such a clause; indeed, work preservation clauses are commonplace. It is not for the Board, however, to create an implied work preservation clause in every American labor agreement based on wage and benefits or recognition provisions, and we expressly decline to do so.

In sum, we find in the instant case that [the] wage and benefits provisions contained in the collective bargaining agreement [do not] preserve bargaining unit work at the Milwaukee facility for the duration of the contract, and that Respondent did not modify these contract terms when it decided to relocate its assembly operations. Further, we find that no other term contained in the contract restricts Respondent's decision making regarding relocation.

We believe our holding today . . . will encourage the realistic and meaningful collective bargaining that the Act contemplates. Under our decision, an employer does not risk giving a union veto power over its decision regarding relocation and should therefore be willing to disclose all factors affecting its decision. Consequently, the union will be in a better position to evaluate whether to make concessions. Because both parties will no longer have an incentive to refrain from frank bargaining, the likelihood that they will be able to resolve their differences is greatly enhanced.

Accordingly, for all the foregoing reasons, we reverse our original Decision and Order and dismiss the complaint.

Legal Issues

1. Do union contracts ever contain work preservation clauses? Why?
2. Was there any term in the contract that could prevent Milwaukee Spring from moving work from the Milwaukee facility? Explain.

Ethical Issues

1. The NLRB rejected the union's charge that the employer's transfer of work violated the contract. The board explained its rejection in part by observing that its decision would make emloyers more willing to disclose all of the factors that affect their decisions and thus place unions in a better position to evaluate whether to make concessions. Does this rationale indicate that the thinking of the board's members was probably influenced by pragmatic or utilitarian ethics, by both, or by neither? Why?

2. The NLRB asserted that its decision would eliminate an incentive for employers and employees to refrain from frank bargaining and would enhance their ability to resolve their differences. Which value or values did the board members apparently regard as an influence on the conduct of management and labor negotiators during the collective bargaining process? Do you agree with this assessment? Discuss.

UNION UNFAIR LABOR PRACTICES

As noted, the National Labor Relations Act passed in 1935 did not contain any provisions relating to unfair labor practices by unions. In 1947 Congress passed the Taft-Hartley Act. Taft-Hartley changed the direction of labor-management relations by placing restrictions on unions. The most important restrictions are contained in Section 8(b), which prohibits unfair labor practices of unions.

A union becomes subject to an unfair labor practice charge if it:

1. Restrains or coerces employees to join the union or an employer in the selection of his representatives to bargain with the union.
2. Coerces an employer to discriminate against an employee who is not a union member (subject to a legal union shop exception).
3. Refuses to bargain in good faith with the employer.

4. Coerces or induces employees to engage in secondary boycotts for illegal purposes.

5. Levies excessive or discriminatory dues and initiation fees for new members under a union shop contract.

6. Forces an employer to pay for work not performed.

7. Pickets to coerce unionization without seeking an election by workers.

Restraint or Coercion of Employees or Employers

Section 8(b)(1) declares it an unfair labor practice for a union to restrain or coerce employees in the exercise of their right to bargain collectively. Most charges of union unfair labor practices are brought under this provision. Employees have a right to *refrain* from union activities if they choose. Acts of violence, threats, or economic reprisals by unions during strikes or organizing drives are illegal. Thus a union agent's threat that employees will lose their jobs unless they join a union is an unfair labor practice.

Peaceful picketing of the employer's premises is not coercion of employees. However, picketing accompanied by violence or threatened violence is coercion of employees. Thus attacking or threatening nonstriking workers who cross a picket line and blocking a plant entrance or exit are unfair labor practices.

Can a union rely on the threat of fines to keep members in line during strikes? The following case addresses this issue.

PATTERN MAKERS' LEAGUE OF NORTH AMERICA v. NLRB
SUPREME COURT OF THE UNITED STATES
473 U.S. 95 (1985)

In May 1976 the Pattern Makers' League, a national union composed of local associations, amended its constitution to provide the following: "No resignation or withdrawal from an Association, or from the League, shall be accepted during a strike or lockout, or at a time when a strike or lockout appears imminent." This amendment, known as League Law 13, became effective in October 1976 after having been ratified by the league's locals.

In May 1977, when a collective bargaining agreement expired, two local associations of the Pattern Makers' League began an economic strike against several manufacturing companies in Rockford, Illinois, and Beloit, Wisconsin. In September a striking member resigned from the Beloit association after the local association had formally rejected a contract offer. The former member returned to work the next day. During the next three months 10 more members resigned from the Rockford and Beloit associations and returned to work.

The strike ended in December 1977, when the parties signed a new collective bargaining agreement. The local associations then notified the 11 employees who had resigned that their resignations had been rejected as violative of League Law 13. The locals also notified them that as union members they were subject to sanctions for returning to work. Each was fined approximately the equivalent of his earnings during the strike.

The manufacturers, represented by the Rockford-Beloit Pattern Jobbers' Association, filed charges with the NLRB against the Pattern Makers' League and its two locals. The Pattern Jobbers' Association claimed that levying fines against the employees who had resigned was an unfair labor practice in violation of Section 8(b)(1) (A) of the NLRA. The NLRB agreed that Section 8(b)(1)(A) prohibited the union from imposing sanctions on those 11 employees. The U.S. Court of Appeals for the Seventh Circuit enforced the board's order in 1983. The Pattern Makers' League then petitioned the Supreme Court for certiorari, which was granted.

JUSTICE POWELL
Delivered the Opinion of the Court

Section 7 of the Act grants employees the right to "refrain from any or all [concerted] . . . activities." This general right is implemented by Section 8(b)(1)(A). The latter section provides that a union commits an unfair labor practice if it "restrain[s] or coerce[s] employees in the exercise" of their Section 7 rights. When employee members of a union refuse to support a strike (whether or not a rule prohibits returning to work during a strike), they are refraining from "concerted activity." Therefore, imposing fines on these employees for returning to work "restrain[s]" the exercise of their Section 7 rights. Indeed, if the terms "refrain" and "restrain or coerce" are interpreted literally, fining employees to enforce compliance with any union rule or policy would violate the Act.

Section 8(b)(1)(A) allows unions to enforce only those rules that impair no policy Congress has imbedded in the labor laws. The Board has found union restrictions on the right to resign to be inconsistent with the policy of voluntary unionism implicit in Section 8(a)(3). We believe that the inconsistency between union restrictions on the right to resign and the policy of voluntary unionism supports the Board's conclusion that League Law 13 is invalid.

Closed shop agreements, legalized by the Wagner Act in 1935, became quite common in the early 1940s. Under these agreements, employers could hire and retain in their employ only union members in good standing. Full union membership was thus compulsory in a closed shop; in order to keep their jobs, employees were required to attend union meetings, support union leaders, and otherwise adhere to union rules. Because of mounting objections to the closed shop, in 1947—after hearings and full consideration—Congress enacted the Taft-Hartley Act. Section 8(a)(3) of that Act effectively eliminated compulsory union membership by outlawing the closed shop. The union security agreements permitted by Section 8(a)(3) require employees to pay dues, but an employee cannot be discharged for failing to abide by union rules or policies with which he disagrees.

Full union membership thus no longer can be a requirement of employment. If a new employee refuses formally to join a union and subject himself to its discipline, he cannot be fired. Moreover, no employee can be discharged if he initially joins a union and subsequently resigns. We think it noteworthy that Section 8(a)(3) protects the employment rights of the dissatisfied members, as well as those of the worker who never assumed full union membership. By allowing employees to resign from a union at any time, Section 8(a)(3) protects the employee whose views come to diverge from those of his union.

League Law 13 curtails this freedom

to resign from full union membership. Nevertheless, petitioners contend that League Law 13 does not contravene the policy of voluntary unionism imbedded in the Act. They assert that this provision does not interfere with workers' employment rights because offending members are not discharged, but only fined. We find this argument unpersuasive, for a union has not left a worker's employment rights inviolate when it exacts [his entire] paycheck in satisfaction of a fine imposed for working. Congress in 1947 sought to eliminate completely any requirement that the employee maintain full union membership. Therefore, the Board was justified in concluding that by restricting the right of employees to resign, League Law 13 impairs the policy of voluntary unionism.

The Board found that by fining employees who had tendered resignations, the petitioners violated Section 8(b)(1)(A) of the Act, even though League Law 13 purported to render the resignations ineffective. We defer to the Board's interpretation of the Act and so affirm the judgment of the Court of Appeals enforcing the Board's order.

It is so ordered.

Legal Issues

1. Can union members be discharged from employment if they (a) do not pay dues, (b) attend union meetings, or (c) obey union rules? Explain.

2. What is a closed shop agreement? Is it legal?

Ethical Issues

1. Would an advocate of utilitarian ethics view the Court's decision in *Pattern Makers' League* as ethical? Why?

2. From the point of view of a union leader, is the Court's interpretation of the National Labor Relations Act at odds with pragmatic ethics? Why?

Coercing Employers to Discriminate against Nonunion Members

Section 8(b)(2) makes it an unfair labor practice for a union to cause an employer to encourage or discourage membership in a union by discriminating against employees in hiring or firing. This provision does not prevent a union from imposing reasonable rules on membership requirements, dues, and initiation fees and from imposing reasonable penalties on members who do not comply with those rules. Under a union shop agreement, a union may ask an employer to fire employees who fail to pay the union dues or initiation fees. Under such an agreement, however, it is an unfair labor practice for a union to cause an employer to fire employees for any other reasons. In one case a union was held guilty of an unfair labor practice because it brought about the discharge of a worker who offered to pay union dues but would not take the union oath or go to union meetings.

The purpose of unions is presumably to accomplish the objectives of their members by concerted action. Some unions, however, are primarily concerned with strengthening the union itself, and only indirectly benefit their members. Such unions frequently negotiate a "union security clause" in the collective bargaining agreement. This may consist of a checkoff of union dues, in which the employer deducts these dues from the members' paychecks and forwards them directly to the union.

Unions have also tried to negotiate a union security clause that makes union membership a condition of employment. This may be done by means of a closed shop, a union shop, or an agency shop. A **closed shop** requires the employer to hire only individuals who are members of the contracting union. The closed shop grants the union almost complete control over the hiring of employees. It is an unfair labor practice because it allows the union and the employer to discriminate on the basis of union membership. As mentioned, Taft-Hartley specifically prohibits closed shop agreements.

A **union shop** requires employees to join the union after a probationary period of 30 calendar days.[4] In a union shop the employer is required to discharge any employee who fails to become a union member after the probationary period. Approximately two thirds of all the major labor contracts are union shop agreements. Union shop agreements are legal under the NLRA, which also permits agency shop agreements.

In an **agency shop** employees are not required to join the union, but nonmembers begin paying an amount equivalent to union dues within 30 days after being hired. Unions regard the agency shop as a less desirable form of union security than the union shop and negotiate an agency shop only when they cannot obtain a union shop. The rationale for union shops and agency shops is that all workers receive the benefits of a union's representation and collective bargaining negotiations and should therefore share the costs of these services.

State laws in the area of union security are effective. Section 14(b) of the NLRA permits states to enact so-called **right-to-work laws,** which prohibit union shop and agency shop agreements. Such laws have been enacted in 21 states, located primarily in the South and Southwest.[5] Employers in these states cannot require nonunion workers to pay representation fees to a union. This means that union shop and agency shop agreements are effective only in states that have not passed right-to-work laws.

Closed shop
an arrangement that requires the employer to hire individuals who are members of the contracting union

Union shop
an arrangement that requires employees to join the union after a probationary period

Agency shop
an arrangement under which employees who do not join the union are required to pay an amount equivalent to union dues

Right-to-work laws
state laws that prohibit union shop and agency shop agreements

Refusal of Union to Bargain

Section 8(b)(3) makes it an unfair labor practice for a union that is a bargaining representative of the employees to refuse to bargain collectively with the employer. Like the employer, the union must bargain in good faith but is under no legal obligation to reach an agreement.

Hypothetical Case

STRIKING EMPLOYEES PICKET TWO EMPLOYERS

Acme Electronics had a contract to manufacture and deliver 500 computers to Futurama Computer Distributors. However, just as work on the order began, the collective bargaining agreement between Acme and the union expired. Acme's employees, dissatisfied with its pay offer, called a strike and picketed Acme. When Acme arranged to have Budget Electronics manufacture the computers, using Acme managers and supervisors to oversee the work, Acme's employees picketed Budget. Could Acme's employees legally picket Budget? Why?

A **secondary boycott** is a union's use of a strike, picketing, or other pressure against a secondary employer. A *secondary employer* is an employer that deals with the primary employer.

The *primary employer* is the employer with which the union has a dispute. Section 8(b)(4) makes it an unlawful labor practice for a union to engage in a secondary boycott. In other words, it is unlawful for a union to use pressure to compel a secondary employer to stop doing business with the primary employer.[6]

Suppose that Ajax Co. refused to grant a large wage increase to the union and that Employers X, Y, and Z are suppliers of Ajax. Suppose further that the union representing the employees of Ajax Co., by use of pickets at the place of business of X, Y, and Z or other kinds of pressure, influences the employees of X, Y, and Z either (1) to go on strike or (2) to refuse to handle goods sold to Ajax and to require X, Y, and Z to stop delivering goods to Ajax. In both situations the union has engaged in a secondary boycott, because the economic injury is directed against neutral (secondary) employers that are not directly involved in the union's dispute with Ajax.

A **primary boycott** is a union's use of a strike, picketing, or other pressure against a primary employer. A primary boycott directed against Ajax Co., the employer involved in the labor dispute, is legal. Thus a refusal by the union to buy Ajax's products or an attempt by the union with the use of pickets at Ajax's place of business to persuade other *consumers* not to buy Ajax's products is legal. It is also a legal boycott if the pickets persuade employees of other companies not to make deliveries to Ajax. Similarly, a refusal by the union to supply labor (go on strike) to Ajax Co. is legal.

Unions may peacefully distribute handbills at the place of business of neutral employers, without any accompanying picketing, urging consumers to boycott neutral employers. The Supreme Court has ruled that such activity does not have a coercive effect on customers of the neutral employers.

Agreeing with a Union to a Hot Cargo Contract Section 8(e), enacted by Congress in 1959, prohibits a type of secondary boycott action called the **hot cargo contract.** This is an agreement between an employer and a union in which the employer promises not to do business with certain persons or businesses.[7] The mere signing of such an agreement is an unfair labor practice for both the union and the employer.

In a typical hot cargo contract an employer agrees not to handle, use, sell, or transport goods made by an employer with which the union has a dispute or against which it is striking. Prior to 1959 unions often negotiated such contracts as a means of self-protection. Congress outlawed hot cargo contracts because they were seldom voluntary on the employer's part.

Pickets

Peaceful picketing to persuade consumers not to purchase the primary employer's products is permitted. A union can truthfully advise the public, including the customers of a neutral employer, that goods are produced by an employer with which the union has a dispute and ask them not to buy those goods. Thus a union that is engaged in a labor dispute with Super Bread Company can peacefully

Secondary boycott
a union's use of a strike, picketing, or other pressure against an employer that deals with the employer with which the union has a dispute

Primary boycott
a union's use of a strike, picketing, or other pressure against an employer with which the union has a dispute

Hot cargo contract
an illegal agreement between an employer and a union in which the employer promises not to do business with certain persons or businesses

picket the supermarkets that sell Super Bread with signs requesting customers to refrain from buying it because Super Bread Company is unfair to union labor. However, such picketing cannot require the customers of those supermarkets to refrain from shopping at them because they deal with the target employer and cannot be designed to persuade employees of the supermarkets not to transport the target employer's goods or perform services for the target employer.

The Ally Doctrine

Ally doctrine
the doctrine that permits a striking union to picket a secondary employer

The rationale for prohibiting secondary boycotts is that secondary employers should not suffer in a labor dispute between a primary employer and a union. An exception occurs, however, if there is an alliance between the primary employer and the secondary employer. In such instances the **ally doctrine** permits the union to lawfully picket the secondary employer. This doctrine applies where employees of the secondary employer perform work that in the absence of a strike would have been performed by the strikers and where the primary employer and the secondary employer are commonly owned and one controls the other.

Excessive or Discriminatory Initiation Fees Required by Unions

Section 8(5) provides that a union commits an unfair labor practice if it charges an excessive or discriminatory initiation fee under a union shop agreement. The rationale is to protect employees who, because of a union shop agreement, are required to join a union as a condition of employment. Since such an agreement gives employees no alternative to joining the union, the union fees charged must be reasonable and not discriminatory. Union dues are typically $300 per year and up.

Section 8(5) does not set a ceiling on union initiation fees. In determining whether these fees are excessive, the NLRB considers the normal practices of unions in the same industry and the wages currently paid to the affected employees. In one case a $500 initiation fee was held not to be excessive because the fee was in line with the initiation fees of other unions in the same industry and because the affected employees were making $182 a week. In another case an increase in the initiation fee from $50 to $500 was held to be excessive where the starting salaries began at $90–$95 per week. In addition, this increase in the fee was found to be discriminatory against part-time workers and temporary non-union workers.

Featherbedding: Causing an Employer to Pay for Work Not Performed

Featherbedding
the hiring of more workers than are actually needed to perform a task

Under Section 8(e)(6), a union cannot force an employer to pay for services that are not performed or are not to be performed. The term **featherbedding** refers to a union's demand that an employer hire workers despite the fact that the employer has no work for them. This practice began during the Great Depression to create jobs for union members.

However, Section 8(e)(6) only prohibits payment for services that are not performed or are not to be performed. It does not prohibit payment for services that are rendered but useless to the employer. Thus a union can lawfully demand that an employer set up unneeded jobs for employees who are unable to do needed work. In one case two men were assigned to perform one job, one to work and one to watch. The court held that a union could legally coerce employers to hire such a watcher, even if the watcher was not necessary for the safety of the working employee. The courts have approved "make-work" rules if services of some kind are performed, even though the services are unwanted or unnecessary.

Picketing by an Uncertified Union

Under Section 8(b)(7), a union acts illegally if it pickets an employer in order to force the employer to recognize or bargain with an uncertified union. Such picketing is illegal in the following instances:

1. The employer is already bargaining with a certified union.
2. A ballot election has been conducted within the last 12 months.
3. An election petition has not been filed with the NLRB within a reasonable time (not exceeding 30 days) after the picketing began.

Section 8(b)(7) was enacted to assure the effectiveness of the NLRB election procedures. It prohibits certain union tactics that are favored by only a minority of employees. For example, picketing for union recognition at an employer's new stores is prohibited since an election must be held to determine whether the new stores are part of the existing bargaining unit.

However, Section 8(b)(7) permits informational picketing. Such picketing truthfully advises the public that a business does not hire union members or does not have a contract with a union. Informational picketing is allowed as long as it does not disrupt or interfere with the employer's business activities, and it can be done by either a certified union or an uncertified union.

ESTABLISHING THE COLLECTIVE BARGAINING RELATIONSHIP

Under the common law, the employer had no obligation to bargain collectively with employees. Employers could bargain individually or collectively or just arbitrarily set wages, hours, and working conditions. The NLRA guaranteed employees the right to organize and bargain collectively and imposed a duty on employers to bargain collectively with the chosen representative of the employees in an appropriate bargaining unit.

Selecting a Bargaining Representative

The right of employees to bargain collectively does not mean that any group of employees can select a representative that the employer must recognize. Rather, the NLRA provides that a representative chosen by a majority of the employees "in a unit appropriate for such purposes" is to be the exclusive representative of all the employees in that unit. As mentioned, the NLRB is responsible for determining whether a majority of the employees in a bargaining unit desire to be represented by a union and which union a majority of these employees choose as their bargaining representative.

An employer can voluntarily recognize a union as the bargaining representative of its employees, but this usually does not happen. In such cases a petition is filed with the NLRB requesting that the union be certified as the collective bargaining representative. The petition must be substantiated by the support of at least *30 percent* of the employees that the union plans to represent. The union demonstrates the necessary support by having individual employees sign authorization cards that simply state that they want it to represent them.

If the NLRB determines that there is a sufficient showing of employees to conduct an election, it then decides the appropriate bargaining unit. The NLRA imposes express restrictions on the board's authority to determine bargaining units. The board looks to a "community of interests" test since bargaining units generally consist of certain jobs or job classifications. A bargaining unit cannot, for example, include both professional and nonprofessional employees unless a majority of the professionals vote to be included in the same unit as that of the nonprofessionals. Professional employees, such as engineers, share few interests with other employees, and they are usually a minority of a company's employees. The NLRA also provides that employees in skilled crafts must be allowed to vote for a separate unit, even if they are formally in a larger unit. For example, the electricians in a plant may decide to be represented by the International Brotherhood of Electrical Workers, the national union that represents their craft.

Conducting a Representation Election

Once the appropriate collective bargaining unit has been selected, the NLRB schedules an election. Under the board's standard election procedure, the regional directors conduct elections in their regions. The employees eligible to vote in an election are the members of the appropriate bargaining unit. A voting list is prepared, voting hours are set, and polling places on company property are established. Secret ballots are cast with the voters either choosing a union or voting "no union."

To win certification, the union must receive a majority of the votes cast in the election. The union need not poll a majority of all the employees in the bargaining unit who are eligible to vote. For the union to be certified, however, a representative number of the eligible voters must cast ballots. A representative vote is usually the casting of ballots by at least 30 percent of those eligible to vote.

Any party involved in a representation election can file with the NLRB regional director objections to the election procedures or the conduct of the parties. Such objections are usually based on the alleged interference of either the union or the employer with the employees' free choice in voting for a bargaining representative.

Threats or promises of benefits by either an employer or a union may cause the board to set aside a representation election. Employer conduct that has been grounds for setting aside elections includes threatening economic retaliation against employees if the union wins, announcing an additional holiday on the birthday of workers shortly before an election, and granting a large increase in wages on the day of an election. Acts of unions that may cause a representation election to be set aside include threats of picket line violence after the election and a preelection offer to waive initiation fees only for workers who sign union authorization cards before an election.

Prior to the representation election, both the employer and the union distribute campaign literature. The NLRB's policy has been to leave the elections intact even if this literature is not completely accurate. In other words, the NLRB does not analyze the truth or falsity of campaign statements, relying instead on the parties to issue rebuttals. However, the NLRB will set an election aside if campaign literature that is misleading on an important matter cannot be effectively rebutted before the election. In addition, the NLRB prohibits the employer and the union from making election speeches to massed assemblies of employees on company time less than 24 hours before an election. This "24-hour-rule" protects the employees' free choice.

If no objections to an election are filed, or the objections to an election are dismissed, the NLRB certifies either that the election has resulted in a "no union" victory or a union victory.[8] Such **certification** of a union means that the union is the exclusive bargaining representative of the employees in the bargaining unit. Thus the employer must deal with the union on matters concerning its employees.

A union may be decertified, that is, lose its standing as the exclusive bargaining representative of employees in a bargaining unit. A petition for the decertification of a union may be filed by a union, an employee, or a group of employees, but not by the employer. If the petition is supported by at least 30 percent of the employees in the bargaining unit, the board calls a decertification election, and if the union receives less than a majority of the votes cast, the board issues a decertification statement. **Decertification** is a declaration by the NLRB that a formerly certified union is no longer the bargaining representative of the employees in the bargaining unit. The employer then has no legal obligation to bargain with the union. A decertification election cannot occur within a year after a certification election.

Certification
an NLRB declaration that a union is the exclusive bargaining representative of a group of employees

Decertification
an NLRB declaration that a union is no longer the bargaining representative of a group of employees

NEGOTIATING THE COLLECTIVE BARGAINING AGREEMENT

Collective bargaining is the bedrock of our national labor policy. The employer must bargain collectively in good faith with the union that represents a majority of the employees in a designated bargaining unit. The union is also obligated to bargain in good faith. The object of collective bargaining is for the employer and the union to reach a contract, called a "collective bargaining agreement." Provisions of the NLRA govern the various subjects of collective bargaining.

Duration and Scope of Union's Authority

After the results of a representation election for a bargaining unit have been certified, another election cannot be held for that bargaining unit for one year.

Once elected, a union is the *exclusive* bargaining representative for all of the employees in the bargaining unit, whether or not they voted for it. Since the union has the sole authority to represent these employees in matters related to collective bargaining, the employer may not negotiate individual contracts with them. Allowing the employer to do so would undermine the union's efforts. By giving rise to conflicting demands from the union and individual workers, it would probably result in unequal working conditions. Employers have violated the exclusivity principle by soliciting grievance lists from employees and by signing separate contracts with individual employees.

Even the employees are required to deal with their bargaining representative. In a recent case, employees who were members of the minority race demanded to meet with the employer's top officials. When the demand was refused, they picketed and charged the employer with racism. Two of these employees were subsequently discharged. The Supreme Court held that the NLRA did not protect the activities of the discharged employees. Reaffirming the essential role of exclusivity in collective bargaining, the court stated that the right to be free of discrimination "cannot be pursued at the expense of the orderly collective bargaining process under the NLRA."

Duty to Bargain in Good Faith

The NLRA places a duty to bargain in good faith on both the employer and the union. The Act requires both parties to "meet at reasonable times and in good faith with respect to wages, hours, and other conditions of employment."

The duty to bargain in good faith requires both parties to approach negotiations with open minds and a sincere desire to reach an agreement. However, it does not compel either party to agree to a proposal of the other party. In determining whether the duty to bargain in good faith has been violated, the NLRB examines the entire conduct of both parties and decides whether either party has actively sought to frustrate the negotiations at the bargaining table and prevent an agreement.

The board has found some acts to automatically violate the duty to bargain in good faith. These acts include a refusal to bargain, a refusal to execute a written contract whose terms have been accepted orally, constant shifts in position on a contract term, and a blanket rejection of proposals without ever offering counterproposals.

To meet the duty to bargain in good faith, the employer is required to furnish on request information that the union needs for bargaining purposes. This includes information on employee wages, financial benefits, merit pay increases, pension plans, wage classifications, and employee health and safety.

Collective Bargaining Subjects

As noted, the NLRA requires the employer and the union to bargain in good faith "with respect to wages, hours, and other terms and conditions of employment." Thus wages, hours, and conditions of employment are mandatory subjects for collective bargaining. The NLRB has recognized two other categories of collective bargaining subjects: permissive proposals and prohibitive proposals.

A subject's classification affects its treatment at the bargaining table. Neither party can refuse to bargain on mandatory subjects. Either party can refuse to bargain on permissive subjects. Bargaining on prohibitive subjects is forbidden. Even if the parties reach agreement on a prohibitive subject, the outcome of that agreement may not be placed in their contract.

In a number of decisions, the NLRB and courts have defined the *mandatory subjects* of wages, hours, and conditions of employment. These subjects include wage rates, hours of employment, safety rules, sick leave policy, seniority policy, promotions and transfers, layoffs, and stock purchase plans. Such contract provisions as no strike and no-lockout clauses are considered mandatory subjects. Employers must bargain before increasing the prices of in-plant food services (for example, vending machines) even if an independent caterer manages these services. Employers must also bargain concerning some economically motivated management decisions. The Supreme Court has ruled that an employer may legally close its entire business for any reason, even an antiunion reason. However, if an employer with several plants closes only one of them for an antiunion reason, the plant closing is a mandatory subject. Another mandatory subject is subcontracting of bargaining unit work that replaces bargaining unit employees with employees of the subcontractor.

Permissive subjects include working conditions for employees outside the bargaining unit, the terms and conditions of employment for workers hired to replace strikers, the size and composition of the supervisory force, the products to be manufactured, and production schedules. *Prohibitive subjects* include hot cargo clauses, closed shop clauses, pay for work not to be performed, and other practices forbidden by the NLRA.

Although the employer and the union must bargain on mandatory subjects, they do not have to reach an agreement. If they reach a genuine impasse on such a subject, they are both relieved of the duty to bargain further on that subject.

THE CASE OF THE "DISHONEST" BAKERS

Five bakers at a Dee-Licious Doughnut Shop were accused of theft by management. A minimal investigation would have revealed that they were not guilty, but the union did not investigate the case before it went to arbitration and the bakers were fired. The bakers filed suit against the union for part of the wages and benefits they lost. Which side will win the suit? Why?

Hypothetical Case

ADMINISTRATION OF THE CONTRACT

After having entered into the collective bargaining agreement, the employer and the union are obligated to bargain in good faith on disputes alleging violations of contractual provisions. Such disputes are resolved through the grievance procedure contained in the collective bargaining agreement.

The Grievance Procedure

Collective bargaining agreements usually include a formal procedure for handling grievances. The **grievance procedure** comprises the formal steps that must be taken before arbitration is invoked. A grievance (complaint) is initiated by an employee who is represented by the union that is the exclusive bargaining representative for the employee's bargaining unit.

In the first step the employee is represented by a local bargaining unit official, called the "shop steward," who presents the grievance to a lower managerial official, usually the departmental supervisor. If the grievance cannot be resolved satisfactorily at that level, it is sent to higher levels of representatives from the employer and the union. If they cannot resolve the grievance, it goes to arbitration.

Grievances must be stated in writing and signed by the initiator. Most grievances charge that the collective bargaining agreement has been violated. Typical grievances concern wages, job security, and work requirements.

Grievance procedure
an orderly way of handling complaints by union workers

The vast majority of grievances are resolved during the first step of the grievance procedure. Both sides ordinarily make compromises, but when a grievance involves substantial conflicts of policy, it is resolved by arbitration, the last step of the grievance procedure.

As noted in Chapter 5, arbitration is a decision-making process involving a third party. Of the collective bargaining agreements in the United States, 95 percent require the employer and the union to use binding arbitration. The arbitration clause of a collective bargaining agreement sets out a detailed method of choosing the third party, with arbitrators usually being chosen after a dispute has arisen. Many collective bargaining agreements specifying arbitration hearings will follow the rules of conduct established by a professional association, such as the American Arbitration Association. These hearings are less formal than courtroom proceedings. A court will not overturn an arbitrator's decision unless the arbitrator acted outside the authority provided under the collective bargaining agreement, acted in bad faith by not considering the evidence, or otherwise violated the law.

Union's Duty of Fair Representation

The union has a duty to fairly and impartially represent in good faith all of the employees in the bargaining unit. The NLRA specifies that it must represent even those employees who are not union members.

The union's duty of fair representation is breached whenever it acts in bad faith or in an arbitrary or discriminatory manner. A union's refusal to assert the collective bargaining rights of an employee without any reasonable explanation is a breach of its duty of fair representation. In one case the Supreme Court ruled that a union had breached its duty of fair representation by preparing a case for arbitration so carelessly that material evidence favorable to a discharged employee was not discovered. The union was held primarily liable for part of the wages and benefits lost by the employee.

Violation of the union's duty of fair representation is an unfair labor practice that an employee can bring before the NLRB. In addition, the employee can sue the union in state or federal court for breach of that duty.

STRIKES AND RIGHTS OF EMPLOYEES

The strike, a withholding of services by union members, is an extremely important economic weapon for pressuring an employer to meet the demands of employees. The NLRA extends protection to employees involved in certain types of strikes. The degree of protection depends on the type of strike that is being conducted. There are three possibilities: (1) an unfair labor practice strike; (2) an economic strike; and (3) an illegal strike. Employees engaged in an unfair labor practice strike or in an economic strike are entitled to protection under the NLRA.

Unfair labor practice strike

a work stoppage to protest an employer's unfair labor practice

Employees engaged in an unfair labor practice strike are entitled to the highest degree of protection. An **unfair labor practice strike** is conducted to protest an employer's unfair labor practice. A strike that occurs shortly after an employer has committed such a practice is presumed to be an unfair labor practice strike. The employer can hire replacements for the strikers, but the strikers are entitled to full reinstatement when the strike ends even if the employer has to discharge the replacements in order to reinstate them.

Employees engaged in an economic strike have less protection. An **economic strike** is conducted to obtain financial benefits. Such strikes are usually called at the expiration of the collective bargaining agreement to enforce employee demands for concessions concerning wages and working conditions. Economic strikers are entitled to reinstatement only if the employer hired temporary replacements for the duration of the strike. If the employer hired permanent replacements, economic strikers are not entitled to reinstatement. However, replaced economic strikers remain employees. If their replacements leave, they are entitled to reinstatement in their prestrike jobs or substantially equivalent jobs unless they have gotten equivalent jobs elsewhere or the employer can prove legitimate business reasons for not offering reinstatement. In economic strikes the union ordinarily makes reinstatement of strikers a condition to ending the strike.

Employees engaged in an illegal strike can be fired without any right to reinstatement. An **illegal strike** is conducted for unlawful purposes or uses unlawful means to accomplish a lawful purpose. Such strikes include "wildcat" strikes, in which employees act without the parent union's sanction (e.g., a few employees walk out of the plant); strikes in violation of a no-strike clause in a collective bargaining agreement; and strikes that have as their object an unlawful bargaining demand such as a hot cargo contract.

Table 14-2 summarizes the rights of different types of striking employees to reinstatement.

Economic strike
a work stoppage to obtain financial concessions from an employer

Illegal strike
a work stoppage that is conducted for an unlawful purpose or that uses unlawful means to accomplish a lawful purpose

THE DECLINE OF UNIONISM IN THE UNITED STATES

Today, less than 16 percent of the employees in the private sector of the U.S. economy belong to unions. The percentage of unionized employees in the private sector has steadily declined since 1956, when it reached a peak of more than 39 percent. Many leading economists predict that by the year 2000 unionized employees will constitute a single-digit percentage of the employees in the private sector.

Summary of the Rights of Striking Employees to Reinstatement		**TABLE 14-2**
Unfair labor practice strike	Strikers are entitled to full reinstatement when the strike ends even if this means that the employer has to discharge replacement help hired during the strike.	
Economic strike	Strikers are entitled to reinstatement only if the employer hired temporary replacements for the duration of the strike. If the employer hired permanent replacements, strikers are not automatically entitled to reinstatement.	
Illegal strike	Strikers can be fired with no right to reinstatement.	

Why has this decline occurred? Commentators cite the following reasons:

1. The loss of jobs in the traditional manufacturing ("smokestack") industries, such as steel and automobile manufacturing. Employment has shifted to white-collar jobs and the service sector, which have traditionally resisted union organization attempts.

2. The shift of employment from the Northeast and Midwest (which are generally prounion) to the South and Southwest, where workers have historically distrusted unions.

3. Increased management opposition to union organizing. Nonunion employers have been increasingly willing to match union employers with regard to wages, benefits, job security, and work conditions, such as layoffs by seniority, grievance systems, and job posting. Management has vigorously mounted antiunion campaigns. Unions now win less than one half of representation elections, down from 75 percent in 1950. In addition, the number of representation elections has been decreasing since 1960.

4. Work rules that restrict job flexibility. For example, in many situations union workers cannot move from one job to another but are limited to narrow, repetitive tasks. A national poll indicated that 54 percent of Americans believe that unions stifle initiative.

LAW ABROAD

Union-Management Relations in Germany and Japan

Labor-management relations in the United States are adversarial. Federal labor laws pit labor organizations against employers to achieve an optimum balance of interest between the two groups. While the adversarial model of labor-management relations works well in the United States, other models have been adopted elsewhere. In Germany and Japan, for example, cooperation is the basis of labor-management relations.

Germany In Germany, which is typical of most of the countries in Western Europe, workers are involved in the formulation of corporate policy at high levels. They sit on the boards of directors and work councils of many German corporations. The work councils, which are independent of the trade unions, derive their power from German law.[9] The law requires local management to discuss with the work council matters affecting the welfare of employees, such as plant rules and discipline, plant wages, and job classifications. The joint participation of labor and management in decision making is designed to promote cooperative relations between the two groups.

In Germany workers have a constitutional right to belong to a union. The German unions are strong at the national level but weak at the local level. Collective bargaining usually occurs at the state level between the union and the employers' association of an industry. The union and the employers' association can enter into a new contract without discussing the terms with any employees or employers. Generally, the contracts cover a particular region by trades. German law does not recognize closed shops, union shops, or featherbedding agreements. A collective bargaining agreement in one state is usually the basis for settlement in the other states. The collective bargaining agreements usually cover only wages and work time, with general labor laws protecting employees in other areas. Strikes are quite rare in Germany.

Germany has a large body of labor law and special labor courts, *Arbeitsgerichte,* with their own rules of procedure. Labor laws apply to almost every employee, and it is almost impossible to waive them. Unfair labor claims are adjudicated by the *Arbeitsgerichte,* which can also assess damages. These courts, however, cannot prevent strikes by issuing injunctions. Basic labor regulations are found in the Civil Code and the Commercial Code, but special statutes contain most of the provisions of labor laws.

Strict labor relations give employees (particularly pregnant women and nursing mothers) protection against arbitrary dismissal, determine work hours, and govern working conditions for juveniles.

Japan   Since World War II Japan has become the world's number two industrial power. A significant reason for its economic progress has been the purposeful cooperation between the Japanese government and Japanese industry. Another reason has been the cooperation between labor and management in Japan—a cooperation even greater than the cooperation between German labor and management. To spur export growth, unions and management adopted a cooperative system based on the constant sharing of information.

Lifetime employment has been the traditional system in Japan for large companies. Under this system, an employee begins work with a company after finishing his or her education and remains with that company until retirement. Wages and salaries are based almost entirely on seniority. This system gives workers a sense of loyalty to their firms and a sense of security in their jobs. Since managers are trained in the factories, it also encourages better relations between labor and management by reducing the distance between them.

Employees are involved in management decisions at a low level. This is exemplified by the use of quality control (QC) circles.[10] Companies frequently implement improvements suggested by QC circles.

Japanese workers have a constitutional "right to organize and to bargain and act collectively." A Japanese firm will typically have one union that comprises both factory and clerical workers, and this union will belong to a national federation for a particular industry. Strikes are rare, and those that do occur are usually merely symbolic and last no longer than a day. Due to the lifetime employment system, Japanese workers do not fear that new processes will put them out of work or reduce their wages. Rather, they see the company's growth as their own success.

When at least three fourths of a company's regular employees are covered by a contract between the union and the company, the remainder of the employees are also covered. Labor agreements do not require government approval. When these agreements are breached, injunctions and suits for damages are available. Agreements may be made for three years or less.

Labor contracts almost always provide for retirement pensions and large bonuses. They often include many other benefits, such as housing facilities and medical care. Discharges must be preceded by a 30-day notice.

Union membership in Japan now stands at 26 percent of the private work force. This represents a considerable decline from the 1949 peak of 59 percent. Commentators predict that by the year 2000 the unionized percentage of the Japanese labor force will fall below 20 percent.

REVIEW QUESTIONS & PROBLEMS

1. What are the reinstatement rights of strikers? Are these rights different for economic strikers than for unfair labor practice strikers? Explain.

2. Does an employee have to be a union member to be represented by the union bargaining representative for his or her unit? Explain.

3. When ABC Company learns that a union is trying to organize its employees, a company representative announces that employees supporting the union will be the first to be laid off and the last to be rehired in case of a necessary layoff. Is ABC Company guilty of an unfair labor practice? Explain.

4. Ajax Company learns that Union X has been certified as the exclusive bargaining representative of its employees. It allows the union to run a concession stand on its premises. It also pays the rent on the space in which the union's meetings are held. Can Ajax Company do these things legally? Has it committed an unfair labor practice? Explain.

5. Union X, the bargaining agent for the employees of Acme Food Distributing Company, has demanded that Acme agree to refrain from doing business with J & J Groceries, Inc. because J & J is trying to stop its workers from unionizing. What is this type of agreement called? If Union X and Acme enter into the agreement, has each of them committed an unfair labor practice? Why?

6. While negotiating with Union S, Transportation Company, without consulting the union, improves sick pay plans and increases wages of its employees, who are members of Union S. Has Transportation Company bargained in good faith? Why?

7. The employees of Coal Company go on strike for economic reasons. During the strike two employees vandalize the company's property and attempt to injure several replacements. Coal Company discharges the employees. Has Coal Company committed an unfair labor practice? Discuss.

ENDNOTES

1. Unions are subject to the antitrust laws when they take action that does not directly concern a labor dispute. For example, a refusal by union members to handle material furnished by an employer of nonunion workers would illegally restrain the interstate flow of goods.

2. Congress amended the NLRA in 1970 to extend the board's jurisdiction to the U.S. Postal Service and in 1974 to extend the board's jurisdiction to private hospitals and nursing homes. The board itself asserted its jurisdiction over, for example, private colleges and universities, law firms, country clubs, and charitable institutions, depending on their gross yearly revenue.

3. In 1962, however, President Kennedy issued an executive order granting limited collective bargaining rights to federal employees. Statutes in some states grant collective bargaining rights, usually without the right to strike, to state employees.

4. In the construction industry a seven-day union shop agreement is permitted.

5. The 21 states that have enacted right-to-work laws are Alabama, Arizona, Arkansas, Florida, Georgia, Idaho, Iowa, Kansas, Louisiana, Mississippi, Nebraska, Nevada, North

Carolina, North Dakota, South Carolina, South Dakota, Tennessee, Texas, Utah, Virginia, and Wyoming.

6. The Railway Labor Act permits secondary boycotts by railroad unions. Thus a striking railroad union can picket not only the offending railroad but also railroads not involved in the dispute. In this way it can close down the entire railroad industry.

7. Exceptions to the Section 8(e) ban were made for agreements between unions and employers in the construction and garment industries.

8. The Supreme Court has ruled that a union can be certified as the bargaining unit representative without a certification election. A union can ask employees to sign dual-purpose cards that clearly state that the signer authorizes the union to represent him or her for collective bargaining purposes. Such cards count as ballots. *NLRB v. Gissel Packing Co., Inc.* 395 U.S. 575 (1969).

9. In Germany unions are strong at the national level but weak at the local level. Work councils rather than national unions, represent workers locally. They are made up of employees only.

10. Quality control circles have been introduced by some U.S. companies during the past 10 years. Thus far their success has been limited.

PART

7

CONSUMERISM AND ENVIRONMENT REGULATION

CHAPTER

15

Consumer
Protection

Consumerism has become an institution. Today's consumer enjoys rights and protections that have been created by Congress, state legislatures, administrative agencies, and courts. The protection of consumers, however, is not a new development. The unquestioned validity of *caveat emptor* (let the buyer beware) began to erode in ancient times. Before the birth of Christ, usury laws protected consumers who borrowed money. Later the English common law incorporated the concepts of fraud, misrepresentation, and deceit into the principles of contract and tort, thus providing consumers with remedies in commercial transactions.

The first phase of American legislation that protected the consumer came between 1890 and 1920, when such laws as the Sherman and Clayton Antitrust acts, the Pure Food and Drugs Act, and the Federal Trade Act were passed. The most active era in American consumerism began during the 1960s and continued through the mid-70s. During this period consumers gained new legislative protection and remedies in the fields of advertising, credit regulation, contract formation, and debtor-creditor relations. Among the factors that caused this explosion of consumerist legislation were (1) the widespread use of credit; (2) the remoteness of consumer transactions, caused by purchases from nonresident manufacturers; and (3) technological advances, which resulted in products so complicated that buyers became virtually helpless in the marketplace.

This chapter begins by discussing the sources of consumer protection. Next it discusses state statutes that protect consumers. A discussion of federal laws that protect consumers seeking credit follows. The chapter then considers federal laws that protect the consumer as a debtor. Finally, it focuses on the consumer and misleading information in advertising and selling.

SOURCES OF CONSUMER PROTECTION

Consumer protection arises from three sources: (1) private litigation in courts, (2) the rulemaking and enforcement powers of administrative agencies, and (3) legislation enacted by state governments and the federal government.

A primary mechanism for redressing grievances is private litigation, but consumers have been reluctant to sue because of the publicity, expense, and loss of time. However, new developments have been minimizing these obstacles. Some of the most recent consumer statutes allow the recovery of reasonable attorneys' fees, but only if the consumer wins the lawsuit. As noted in Chapter 4, some consumers, to avoid legal expenses, represent themselves in small claims courts, which do not follow strict legal procedures. Many state statutes allow consumers to combine their claims into a class action. In a class action suit, as discussed in Chapter 4, one plaintiff can sue on behalf of all the persons with similar claims. The combined interest of these persons makes the claims for damages large enough to justify retaining an attorney.

Administrative Agencies

Partly becuase of the barriers to private litigation, administrative agencies have become important mechanisms for enforcing consumer rights. For example, the Federal Trade Commission has shifted its emphasis from enforcement of the antitrust laws to consumer protection. The Food and Drug Administration (FDA) enforces the Federal Food, Drug, and Cosmetic Act, which requires periodic inspection of factories, warehouses, and canneries. It also issues regulations related to the certification and advertising of prescription drugs. The consumer protection activities of the Federal Trade Commission (FTC) are discussed in detail later in this chapter.

Legislation

The laws governing consumer transactions are primarily statutory. A number of laws enacted by Congress and the state legislatures limit the actions of sellers and lenders. For example, 49 states have adopted the Uniform Commercial Code. In addition, most of the states have a statute limiting the interest that creditors may charge in lending money. Such statutes are discussed in the following section. State legislatures were the first to protect consumers. Since 1906, however, federal action has produced a series of laws that now outweigh the importance of state consumer protection. Table 15-1 lists some of the major federal consumer protection laws.

THE CONSUMER AND STATE STATUTES

Uniform Commercial Code

Uniform Commercial Code
a comprehensive body of commercial law; adopted by 49 states

Some consumer protection laws are contained in the **Uniform Commercial Code** (UCC). As previously discussed, the code is a comprehensive body of commercial law dealing with sales, commercial paper, investment securities, banking, and secured transactions. The UCC cannot be characterized as consumer legislation,

Major Federal Consumer Protection Legislation

TABLE 15–1

Date	Popular Name	Purpose
1906	Pure Food and Drugs Act	Forbids the marketing of impure, adulterated, and misbranded food, drinks, and drugs; extended in 1938 to cover cosmetic and therapeutic devices and in 1962 to require the pretesting of new drugs for safety and efficiency
1914	Federal Trade Commission Act	Created the FTC; outlaws unfair or deceptive methods of competition; amended in 1938 by the Wheeler-Lea Act to give the FTC jurisdiction over deceptive advertising or sales practices
1939	Wool Products Labeling Act	Demands the accurate labeling of the content of wool products
1951	Fur Products Labeling Act	Outlaws the misbranding of fur products; requires disclosure of the animals actually used
1953	Flammable Fabrics Act	Bars highly flammable fabrics from interstate commerce
1958	Automobile Information Disclosure Act	Requires the posting of suggested retail prices on new passenger automobiles
1959	Textile Fiber Products Identification Act	Requires the identification of most of the textile products not covered by prior federal law
1960	Hazardous Substances Act	Requires prominent warning labels on hazardous household substances
1965	Truth in Packaging Act	Governs the packaging and labeling of consumer goods; requires industry to establish voluntary uniform standards
1966	National Traffic and Motor Vehicle Safety Act	Provides for national traffic and auto safety standards
1966	Child Safety Act	Prevents marketing of harmful toys and inherently dangerous products intended for children; strengthened in 1969
1966	Cigarette Labeling and Ad Act	Requires health warnings to smokers
1967	Wholesome Meat Act	Upgrades meat processing by requiring state standards to meet federal standards
1968	Wholesome Poultry Products Act	Requires states to enact poultry products standards meeting the federal standards
1968	Consumer Credit Protection Act (Truth in Lending)	Demands full disclosure of annual interest rates and finance charges in consumer loans and credit buying; revised and clarified in 1969.
1968	Hazardous Radiation Act	Established standards to limit radiation leakage in electronic products such as television and microwave ovens
1968	Fair Credit Collection Practices Act	Outlaws abuses by debt collectors
1970	Fair Credit Reporting Act	Protects the consumer's reputation by establishing standards for the maintenance and release of consumer credit records
1970	Poison Prevention Packaging Act	Requires the establishment of standards for the childproof packaging of dangerous substances
1972	Consumer Product Safety Act	Created the Consumer Product Safety Commission to establish and police product safety standards
1974	Fair Credit Billing Act	Amends Truth in Lending to govern credit billing and error and dispute resolution

TABLE 15–1   **Continued**

Date	Popular Name	Purpose
1974	Real Estate Settlement Procedures Act	Requires the disclosure of home-buying costs prior to the sale
1975	Magnuson-Moss Warranty Act	Creates federal standards for consumer warranties and allows FTC regulation and enforcement
1975	Consumer Goods Pricing Act	Outlawed "fair trade" by repealing antitrust exemptions
1977	Consumer Leasing Act (Truth in Leasing)	Requires that companies disclose the total costs and terms of leases
1978	Equal Credit Opportunity Act	Forbids discrimination in the extension of credit
1978	Electronic Funds Transfer Act	Governs the allocation of risk and procedures for resolving disputes and errors in the area of electronic banking
1984	Comprehensive Smoking Education Act	Requires a health warning to smokers on all cigarette advertisements

but some of its general principles do protect the consumer. One of the most important of these principles is the doctrine of unconscionability.

Unconscionable contract

a contract so unfair that the courts will not enforce it

Promises that produce unconscionable results will not be enforced. An **unconscionable contract** is a contract so one-sided that it offends the conscience. A gross inequality of bargaining power between the contracting parties has been present in most of the cases that have applied the unconscionability doctrine. In determining bargaining power, courts have been influenced by such factors as lack of education and limited language ability. Where both parties to a contract are businesspersons, courts are less likely to apply unconscionability. As stated in the UCC, unconscionability applies only to contracts for the sale of goods, but by analogy it has been applied to cases involving other kinds of contracts, such as real estate brokerage agreements.

The following fact situations illustrate unconscionable contracts:

Store sells a refrigerator to Hans on credit. Because Hans speaks little English, he does not understand the contract terms, which are written in English. The contract price of the refrigerator was $1,100; the cash price of the refrigerator was $900; the wholesale price of the refrigerator was $348. Store tells Hans that the refrigerator will cost him nothing because he can earn bonuses for every refrigerator that Store sells to one of his friends.

The court would hold this contract unconscionable not only because Hans was unable to understand its terms but because the price was excessive, since the wholesale price was $348. The doctrine of unconscionability applies when the stronger party pressures the weaker party into an agreement, knowing that the weaker party suffers some infirmity, such as ignorance or illiteracy.

Merchant sells Wilma a $514 stereo on credit. Merchant knows that Wilma is on welfare and receives only $218 a month for herself and five children. Wilma already owes Merchant $200 for items purchased previously. A clause in the stereo contract allows Merchant to repossess all of the items Wilma has purchased if she defaults on a single payment of any contract at any time before she has paid her entire debt to Merchant.

The court would hold this contract unconscionable because its terms were so one-sidedly in favor of Merchant, the party with superior bargaining power, and because the court would recognize Wilma's limited education.

The UCC's effectiveness is limited by its reliance on a case-by-case approach. Compared with specific consumer legislation, the code plays a minimum role in consumer protection. The use of repeated lawsuits against a wrongdoer is a frustrating course.

Usury Laws

The law protects consumers by limiting the amount of interest that they can be charged in contracts to borrow money. This protection stems from religious traditions and from the economic hardships created by high interest rates. Most states have usury statutes that impose legal limits on interest rates. **Usury** is lending money at a higher rate of interest than the law allows.

Usury
the lending of money at an illegal rate of interest

State usury statutes used to allow maximum interest rates of 6 or 8 percent. But as rates for corporate borrowers rose, statutory rates for consumers rose along with them. Consumer interest rate ceilings of 18 percent or higher are common today. A loan above the statutory limit is "usurious," and most states prohibit the lender from collecting any interest on usurious loans. Some states, however, allow recovery of the interest at the legal rate, while other states provide for a forfeiture of principal and interest.

Usury laws provide only modest protection for the consumer. Most of the state usury statutes specify the maximum amount of interest that can generally be charged, but numerous exceptions created by special statutes allow higher rates of interest for certain loans. For example, small loan companies and pawnshops often deal with the least creditworthy members of society and therefore can lend money at a rate of interest that may be as high as 36 percent per annum. Annual interest rates charged by a bank credit card are ordinarily 18 percent and above. Moreover, many of the charges to borrowers are not considered interest. In addition to charging the maximum interest rates, in most states the lender can add a fee for closing expenses, such as recording fees, credit reports, and appraisal fees. Some loans are not covered by state usury laws. Most states place no limit on the interest that can be charged businesses.

In the past the maximum rate of interest could be determined merely by examining the state law. But today the federal law may preempt the state usury law. To illustrate, national banks can charge interest at a rate above the maximum usually permitted by state law. The state usury ceiling for mortgage loans is also preempted unless the state acts to reimpose it.

THE CONSUMER AND CREDIT

Credit buying has become the American Way. Consumer credit so pervades our society that paying cash for even small purchases, such as household appliances, is the exception, not the rule. Consumers have clung to the buy-now, pay-later lifestyle despite periods in which interest rates were high and state credit laws were designed to protect lenders. In response to the national trend toward credit buying, Congress enacted laws to protect consumers who utilize installment loans and installment purchases. This section examines laws that Congress enacted to

(1) require the complete disclosure of credit terms, (2) protect the credit reputation of consumers, (3) protect consumers from credit billing errors, (4) forbid discrimination in the extension of credit, and (5) require the disclosure of home-buying costs.

Consumer Credit Protection Act

The increased use of credit by consumers, combined with questionable practices by lenders, caused Congress to pass the *Consumer Credit Protection Act* (CCPA) in 1968. This act, commonly called *Truth in Lending,* is probably the best-known consumer protection legislation. Its purpose is to provide consumers with information on credit costs by requiring lenders to disclose to their customers the true annual percentage rate (APR) and the dollar amount of finance charges. The APR is based on the total finance charges and not just on the amount of interest that will be paid. In theory, the informed consumer will shop around and negotiate for the best credit terms. The CCPA was the first law to require disclosure of credit costs.

Before the CCPA was enacted, lenders stated finance interest charges in various and often misleading ways, which made comparisons of borrowing costs difficult. The APR provides a reliable yardstick for comparing borrowing costs, because Truth in Lending requires that disclosures of the APR be stated in uniform terms. The act does not set a ceiling on interest rates or credit charges.

Truth in Lending also requires that credit terms be disclosed in advertising. If an advertisement contains any credit term, it must include all of the credit terms. Thus if an advertisement says "$100 down, $20 a month" or "only $15 a month," it must also disclose the other credit terms, including the APR, down payment, number of payments, and cash price.

Before Truth in Lending was passed, few consumers realized that when lenders advertised a 6 percent interest rate, the APR spread over three years was actually 11 percent. With installment payments the borrower has the use of the entire balance for only one month, since the money owed is a declining balance. To illusrate, assume that a $12,000 loan is to be repaid in 12 equal monthly installments. The amount borrowed for the first month is $12,000, but for the second month the borrower has the use of only $11,000. The true interest rate reflects the interest paid on the balance throughout the period of the loan. The Truth in Lending disclosures may be printed as a part of the contract to lend money or as a separate document. Most creditors choose to place the disclosures on the face of the loan agreement.

Table 15-2 illustrates a consumer's use of his residence as security for a 10-year loan of $20,000. The Truth in Lending disclosures here are part of the loan agreement. Note that the interest rate based on the payment of interest alone is 12.75 percent but that the APR, 13.25 percent, is one half of 1 percent higher because it is based on all of the finance charges. Many first-time borrowers may be surprised to learn that the total interest on a 10-year, $20,000 loan is over $16,000.

Home as Collateral

Truth in Lending recognizes that consumers often risk losing their homes by using their equity in their homes as security for loans. Borrowers who use their homes

Truth in Lending Disclosure and Loan Agreement

TABLE 15–2

Simple Interest—Real Estate Consumer Note and Security Agreement

Note number <u>741</u> Date <u>March 7, 1992</u>

In this note, the words, *I, me, mine,* and *my* mean each and all of those who signed it. The words *you, your,* and *yours* mean Pleasant Town Savings and Loan Association of Pleasant Town, Any State.

Terms of Repayment: I promise to pay to you or to your order the Amount Financed (see below), together with interest from today's date until paid in full at <u>X</u>, a fixed rate of <u>12.75</u>% per annum, or ___, a variable rate with an initial rate of ___%

per annum, and a Prepaid
Finance Charge of <u>$407.56</u>, [2 points] in the matter described below.

Federal Truth in Lending Disclosures:

Annual Percentage Rate	Finance Charge	Amount Financed	Total of Payments
The cost of my credit as a yearly rate	The dollar amount the credit will cost me	The amount of credit provided to me or on my behalf	The amount I will have paid after I have made all payments as scheduled
13.25%	$16,496.80	$20,378.00	$36,874.80

I have the right to receive at this time an itemization of the Amount Financed.

    <u>X</u> I want an itemization. ___ I do not want an itemization.

My payment schedule will be: <u>X</u> Monthly ___ Quarterly ___ Single payment

This obligation is payable on demand. All disclosures are based on an assumed maturity of one year.

Number of Payments	Amount of Payments	When Payments Are Due
120	$307.29	Monthly

Security: I am giving you a security interest in:

    ___ The goods or property being purchased.

    <u>X</u> Real property located at <u>270 Cedar Street, Pleasant Town, Any State 31502.</u>

    ___ All balances, deposits, and accounts I have or may have with you.

    ___ Collateral, other than my principal dwelling (unless specified above) securing other loans with you.

    ___ Other: _____

Recording Fees and Taxes: <u>$78.00</u>.

Itemization of Amount Financed:

Amount given to me directly	$20,500.00
Amount paid on my account(s)	0

TABLE 15–2   **Continued**

Amount paid as Prepaid Finance Charge	407.56
Amount paid to others on my behalf	0
To public officials—intangible tax	63.00
To public officials—recording fee	15.00
To attorneys for records examination	125.00
To credit life insurer	0
To credit disability insurer	0
To credit bureau	25.00
To appraiser	150.00
To _____	0
To _____	0
Less Prepaid Finance Charge	(407.56)
Amount Financed	$20,878.00
Prepaid Finance Charge:	
Loan fee	$ 0
Discount points	407.56
Other: _____	0
Interest	16,089.24
Total Finance Charge	$16,496.80

I acknowledge receipt of a completely filled-in copy of this note and Federal Truth in Lending Disclosures.
Witness my hand and seal below.

John W. Farmer _____	(Seal)	Mary R. Farmer _____	(Seal)
Borrower		Borrower	
270 Cedar Street		270 Cedar Street	
Address		Address	
Pleasant Town, Any State 31502		Pleasant Town, Any State 31502	
City State Zip		City State Zip	

as collateral for loans have three business days from the date of the transaction to rescind or cancel, without penalty. The three-day cooling-off period applies to the traditional second mortgage loan, in which the borrower uses his or her home as collateral for a fixed loan repayable over a fixed period of time, and to the equity line of credit, in which the borrower uses his or her home as collateral for a form of revolving credit. It does not apply to a first mortgage loan to finance the purchase of a home.

In the following case the borrowers asked a federal district court to rescind a loan agreement secured by their home, based on the lender's failure to disclose to them their right to rescind the agreement.

MAYFIELD V. VANGUARD SAVINGS AND LOAN ASSOCIATION
U.S. DISTRICT COURT, EASTERN DISTRICT PENNSYLVANIA, CIVIL DIVISION
710 F. Supp. 143 (1989)

On August 4, 1986, Anna Mayfield and her husband, the plaintiffs, borrowed money from Vanguard Savings and Loan Association, the defendant, in order to pay some utility bills. The defendant took a mortgage on the plaintiffs' home as security for the loan. Subsequently, the plaintiffs informed the defendant that they were finding it difficult to make the loan payments because of their limited income. The defendant refinanced the plaintiffs' first loan with a new loan written on January 19, 1987, and took another mortgage on the plaintiffs' home to secure the second loan.

On October 28, 1987, counsel for the plaintiffs wrote a letter to the defendant and its attorney rescinding the loan under the Truth in Lending Act. The defendant received the letter on October 30, 1987, but took no action to remove the mortgages. On January 19, 1988, the plaintiffs filed this action to enforce rescission of the loan obligation and removal of the mortgages.

LOWELL A. REED, JR., DISTRICT JUDGE

Whenever a consumer credit transaction results in a creditor acquiring a security interest in an obligor's home, as is the case here, [Truth in Lending] gives the obligor "the right to rescind the transaction until midnight of the third business day following the consummation of the transaction or the delivery of the disclosures required under this section and all other material disclosures required under this part, whichever is later." 15 U.S.C., Section 1635(a). Section 1635(a) requires the creditor to disclose this right to rescind in accordance with regulations promulgated by the Federal Reserve Board. Failure to properly complete the right to rescission form or to provide the consumer with the material disclosures required to be made under TILA extends the rescission period until three days after the disclosures are properly made. If the disclosures are never properly made, the rescission period runs for three years from the consummation of the transaction. 15 U.S.C., Section 1635(f).

In this case, it is uncontested that defendant failed to properly complete the rescission notices and to provide plaintiff with accurate disclosures with respect to both the August 1986 and January 1987 loans. With respect to the rescission notices, the Board's regulations require creditors to provide customers with a notice of their right to rescind that specifies the precise date upon which the three-day rescission period expires. The rescission notices given to plaintiff with respect to both the August 1986 and the January 1987 loans failed to specify the date upon which the three-day rescission period expired. Failure to specify such dates automatically violates the TILA and entitled plaintiff to rescind the loan within the three-year rescission period.

The failure of defendant to correctly make all material disclosures required to be made under 15 U.S.C., Section

1638 also entitled plaintiff to rescind the loan. Section 1638 requires a creditor to disclose the extent of the collateral being taken for the loan. The disclosure statements for the August 1986 and January 1987 loans indicated that the loans were secured by "the property being purchased," which was clearly an incorrect disclosure as these were not purchase-money loans. Plaintiff and her husband purchased their home years before the present security interests in it were taken. The failure to accurately disclose a security interest taken is a material nondisclosure which also entitles a consumer to rescind a loan within the three-year rescission period.

The TILA provides that when an obligor exercises his right to rescission, he or she is not liable for any finance or other charge and any security interest given by the obligor becomes void upon the rescission. Upon receipt of the rescission notice, the creditor must return any down payment or other monies it received from the obligor and take the steps necessary to reflect the termination of the security interest.

Summary judgment for plaintiffs.

Legal Issues

1. Why did the Mayfields have three years to rescind the loan?

2. Suppose that the Mayfields borrowed money from the savings and loan association to *purchase* their home and that the savings and loan association placed a mortgage on the home as security for the loan. Would this have changed the decision of the court? Why?

Ethical Issues

1. The Truth in Lending Act automatically gives a borrower the right to rescind a loan within three years if the lender fails to specify the date on which the three-day rescission period expires. Is this provision consistent with the sort of behavior that an advocate of ethical relativism would expect in lenders? Why?

2. The court concluded that the lender's failure to correctly disclose why the borrowers' home was used as collateral was a material nondisclosure under the Truth in Lending Act. Is this conclusion fair to the lender given the fact that the borrowers were fully aware of the purpose of the loan? Why?

Table 15-3 illustrates a typical form used for giving notice to the homeowner of the right to cancel a traditional second mortgage loan.

Fair Credit Reporting Act

In 1971 Congress enacted the *Fair Credit Reporting Act* (FCRA), a law aimed at credit reporting agencies, such as credit bureaus. Credit bureaus collect information about individual consumers and supply credit reports on these consumers to potential creditors, insurers, and employers. The credit reports include the following types of information:

1. Places of employment and lengths of time worked.

2. Loans outstanding (including the size of the loans, the monthly payments, the collateral given on the loans, and the payment history).

3. Accounts placed for collection.

4. Recorded tax liens.

Table 15-4 illustrates the types of information contained in a credit report.

Inevitably, errors in credit reporting were made and injustices occurred because of irresponsible credit reporting. Typical errors were the reporting of the

---

Example of Notice of Right of Rescission   **TABLE 15-3**

Notice of Right to Cancel

Your Right to Cancel

You are entering into a transaction that will result in a second mortgage or security interest in your home. You have a legal right under federal law to cancel this transaction, without cost, within three business days from whichever of the following events occurs last:

(1) the date of the transaction, which is _____; or
(2) the date you receive your Truth in Lending disclosures; or
(3) the date you receive this notice of your right to cancel.

If you cancel the transaction, the mortgage or security interest is also canceled. Within 20 calendar days after we receive your notice, we must take the steps necessary to reflect the fact that the mortgage or security interest in your home has been canceled and we must return to you any money or property you have given to us or to anyone else in connection with this transaction.

You may keep any money or property we have given you until we have done the things mentioned above, but you must then offer to return the money or property. If it is impractical or unfair for you to return the property, you must offer its reasonable value. You may offer to return the property at your home or at the location of the property. Money must be returned to the address below. If we do not take possession of the money or property within 20 calendar days of your offer, you may keep it without further obligation.

How to Cancel

If you decide to cancel the transaction, you may do so by notifying us in writing at

Pleasant Town Federal Savings and Loan Association
220 East Main Street
Pleasant Town, Any State 06251

You may use any written statement that is signed and dated by you and states your intention to cancel, or you may use this notice by dating and signing below. Keep one copy of this notice because it contains important information about your rights.

If you cancel by mail or telegram, you must send the notice no later than midnight of _____ (or midnight of the third business day following the latest of the three events listed above). If you send or deliver your written notice to cancel some other way, it must be delivered to the above address no later than that time.

I wish to cancel.

_____   _____
Consumer's Signature   Date

I acknowledge that I received two copies of the above notice on the transaction date stated above.

_____
Consumer's Signature

unpaid debts of persons with similar names, and of credit disputes that had already been resolved. However, the individuals whose credit standing was damaged by such errors had no right to check the files of the credit reporting agencies for inaccuracies or to demand that the files be corrected.

Under the FCRA, a consumer who is denied credit, insurance, or employment because of an adverse report must be informed of the reason for the rejection and must be given the name and address of the credit reporting agency that issued the report. The consumer can, within certain time limits, determine the nature of the information in his or her file and the names of the persons who received the report. If the consumer contends that the information in the file is inaccurate, the credit reporting agency must reinvestigate the facts within a reasonable time, which the industry accepts as 30 days. If the agency made an error, it must either correct the error or remove the erroneous information from the file. Should a dispute arise between the consumer and the agency concerning the accuracy of the information in the file, the consumer can submit a 100-word written statement of his or her version of the facts. This statement is inserted in the consumer's file and must be included in all of the agency's future reports on the consumer.

An important provision of FCRA requires the removal of obsolete data from the files of credit reporting agencies. Most adverse information, such as records of arrest, convictions, lawsuits and judgments, cannot be reported after seven years. After 10 years bankruptcy adjudication cannot be reported.[1]

TABLE 15–4   **Types of Information Compiled by Credit Bureaus**

A typical individual credit report contains the following sections:

Personal Identification (supplied by applicant): Subject's name and current address, former addresses, marital status, number of dependents, age, social security number; spouse's name.

Employment History (supplied by applicant): Subject's current employer, position, monthly salary; subject's past employers and dates left.

Other Information (from public records of the county and the court): Accounts of the subject assigned to collection agencies; legal judgments rendered against the subject; amounts owed by the subject; marital status, divorce notices, deaths, marriages, bankruptcies, court judgments, disposition of lawsuits, and liens.

Inquiries: Identity of merchants, banks, etc. seeking information on the subject in the last 90 days.

Credit History (supplied by past creditors and by merchants with which the subject has done business): Names and types of organizations, banks, credit card companies, merchants, etc. to which the subject has owed money in the past and the subject's payment history. This section generally includes the following items on each account:

Date the account was opened.
Terms of the account agreement (basically how soon the subject must pay after receiving a bill).
How much the subject currently owes.
What amount is past due.
Greatest amount of money that was owed in the past five years.
Number of delinquent payments in the past several years.
Credit rating of the subject.
Repossession of property for nonpayment.

While FCRA gives consumers access to their credit reports, it limits the rights of other individuals to examine these reports. A consumer can have his or her credit report withheld from anyone who does not have a legitimate business need for the information in it.

FCRA applies only to credit reporting agencies that gather information from such sources as county records, newspapers, creditors, and neighbors. Information that an employer supplies concerning actual experiences with the consumer is not a credit report and thus is not covered by the act. If an employer is questioned about the employment record of a former employee and reports only actual experiences, the information supplied by the employer is not subject to the act. But if the employer includes information from outside sources, the information is subject to the act. Similarly, an employer may check an applicant's personal references without becoming a consumer reporting agency.

Finally, FCRA does not apply to reports issued in connection with business purchases, such as commercial insurance or commercial credit. If a corporation applies for a life insurance policy on a key employee, the report submitted to the insurance company is for a business purpose and thus not covered by FCRA.

Under FCRA, consumers can sue for damages for negligent or willful violation of the act. In a successful willful violation suit, punitive damages as well as actual damages may be awarded and the plaintiff can collect attorneys' fees and court costs. The Federal Trade Commission is charged with administrative enforcement of FCRA.

Fair Credit Billing Act

In 1974 Congress amended the Truth in Lending Act with the *Fair Credit Billing Act* (FCBA). This act gives the consumer the right to (1) correct errors in billing and (2) withhold payments on disputed purchases. It gives merchants the right to offer discounts for cash purchases.

A consumer who feels that an error has been made on a bill, such as an incorrect amount or a charge for a transaction that never occurred, can send written notice of the error to the creditor within 60 days of the billing statement. The creditor then has 30 days to acknowledge the dispute. Within 90 days from the date of the consumer's original notice, the creditor must either correct the error or provide a written explanation to the consumer. The creditor may not notify a third party of the delinquent account without including a statement that the amount is in dispute.

An FCBA provision that has gone almost unnoticed by consumers is the right to withhold payments in certain circumstances. A holder of a credit card who has an unresolved dispute with a merchant in connection with a credit card purchase can withhold the disputed amount from the credit card issuer. In the past the card issuer, usually a bank, was a "holder in due course" of the debt. Under that doctrine, the card issuer was entitled to collect from cardholders who never received merchandise or who received unsatisfactory merchandise. FCBA takes this privilege away from the card issuer in certain circumstances.[2] The cardholder has a right to withhold payments if he or she made a good faith attempt to settle the dispute with the merchant, if the amount of the liability is more than $50, and if the transaction occurred either in the cardholder's home state or within 100 miles of the cardholder's current mailing address. The card issuer may not charge interest on the amount in question until the dispute has been settled.

Few cardholders have exercised the right to withhold payment. Cardholders seem to be unaware of this right even though it is stated in fine print on the reverse side of credit statements. In those situations in which cardholders have withheld payment, card issuers have generally settled the dispute by crediting the card-holder's account and charging the merchant's account. The merchant must then informally resolve the dispute with the cardholder or pursue legal remedies.

Previously, card issuers specified in their contract with merchants that the merchants could not offer a discount to induce customers to pay by cash or check. FCBA allows merchants to offer discounts of up to 5 percent for cash payments. These discounts represent the merchant's cost for offering credit.

Equal Credit Opportunities Act

In 1974 Congress passed the *Equal Credit Opportunities Act* (ECOA). This act prohibited discrimination in credit transactions on the basis of sex or marital status. Previously, women had been subject to unfair screening practices based on sex or marital status when they applied for loans, bank cards, or retail credit. ECOA was a natural extension of laws prohibiting discrimination in employment. As amended in 1976, it forbids discrimination in credit transactions on the basis of sex, marital status, age (assuming that the applicant has capacity to contract), race, color, religion, or national origin. It also forbids creditors from *discouraging* applications on the basis of these categories. Thus a married woman can open an account in her maiden name or open an account separate from that of her husband.

ECOA applies to all creditors that regularly extend credit, including banks, finance companies, retail stores, credit card companies, and credit unions. In evaluating an applicant's income, the creditor must consider consistently re-ceived alimony, child support, and separate maintenance payments and income from public assistance programs. Further, the creditor may not assume that a woman of childbearing age will stop work to have or raise children. It is illegal to ask about birth control practices.

In the past credit was denied to women who were divorced, widowed, or separated from their husbands, because they lacked an established record of credit in their own names. Creditors reported information about shared accounts in the husband's name only. ECOA attempts to solve this problem by requiring that information reported to credit bureaus on accounts shared by both spouses be reported in the names of both spouses.

ECOA provides remedies similar to those provided by other consumer legisla-tion. A plaintiff filing a private lawsuit against a creditor can recover actual damages, punitive damages of up to $10,000, court costs, and attorneys' fees. In a class action suit the total punitive damages are limited to $500,000 or 1 percent of the creditor's net worth. An aggrieved applicant can also file a complaint with the Federal Trade Commission, which enforces ECOA.

Real Estate Settlement Procedures Act

The purchase of a home is the most important single transaction that most people ever make. Many consumers are shocked to discover at "settlement time" that, in addition to the down payment, they must pay hundreds or even thousands of dollars for closing costs. Typical closing costs include attorneys' fees, brokers' commissions, loan origination fees, title insurance costs, and taxes. The purpose of the *Real Estate Settlement Procedures Act* (RESPA), as amended in 1976, is to provide home buyers and borrowers with advance information on the nature and costs of the settlement process and to prevent certain abusive practices. RESPA does not establish a maximum amount for closing costs. The advance information is a tool for shopping, so that the consumer can, in theory, compare the available options and thereby select the most favorable option. The act governs all federally related mortgage loans.

To accomplish its objective, RESPA requires that the lender provide the borrower with a "good faith estimate" of most of the settlement costs within three business days after the borrower's application for a loan. Table 15-5 illustrates a good faith estimate of the settlement costs for a $120,000 30-year loan with a fixed interest rate.

THE CONSUMER AND DEBTS

The emergence of easy credit brought with it harsh collection methods. The tactics of some credit sellers and collectors fanned public discontent and spurred Congress to pass legislation protecting the consumer as a debtor. This section focuses on laws that (1) control the collection of debts by garnishment, (2) protect holders of credit cards, (3) protect debtors against holder in due course claims, (4) control independent collection agencies, (5) discharge debtors from their debts, and (6) govern the content of warranties.

Garnishment

The legal proceeding by which an employer withholds a debtor's earnings for payment to a creditor is called **garnishment.** During the committee hearings on the Consumer Credit Protection Act, Congress discovered that unrestricted garnishment of wages led to (1) predatory extension of credit, (2) discharge of employees as a result of garnishment, and (3) variances in state laws that destroyed the effectiveness of uniform bankruptcy laws. The CCPA therefore restricted garnishment. The amount of garnished wages in a given week cannot exceed 25 percent of the disposable earnings (the amount after tax and social security deductions) for that week or the amount by which the disposable earnings for that week exceed 30 times the federal minimum hourly wage. These restrictions do not apply to the debtor's payments under an order by a bankruptcy court, support payments under a court order, or payments to a state or the federal government. The CCPA also prevents the employer from firing an employee because of one garnishment or because of more than one garnishment on the same debt.

Before the CCPA was enacted, each state already had laws governing garnishment. The CCPA allows legal proceedings to be governed by state law when state law is more favorable to the debtor than the CCPA. For example, Illinois courts are bound by the state garnishment law because it places a 15 percent limit on the amount that can be deducted from wage attachments. The Connecticut garnishment law prevents an employer from discharging an employee who is subject to no more than seven garnishments within one year. Since this law is more favorable to the debtor than the CCPA, it is applied.

Garnishment

the legal proceeding by which a debtor's earnings are withheld by an employer for payment to a creditor

TABLE 15–5   **Good Faith Estimate of Settlement Costs**

Pleasant Town Savings and Loan Association
Good Faith Estimate of Costs
of Mortgage Settlement Services

Loan application for $120,000
Loan Type: 30-year fixed rate

Sales Price	$150,000
Earnest money	$ 5,000
Mortgage amount	−$ 120,000
Total from line 10	+$ 5,160
Seller contributions	−$ 0
Estimated amount to close	$30,160.00

Applicant(s): Mr. and Mrs. John R. Brady

Closing Attorney: Frederick G. Marquer, Esquire   *Phone:* 565-0152

Settlement Service	Estimated Costs
1. Loan origination fee (1½%)	$ 1,800.00
2. Appraisal fee	$ 250.00
3. Credit report	$ 50.00
4. Attorney's fee	$ 900.00
5. Title insurance	$ 285.00
6. Recording fee	$ 15.00
7. (Intangible tax)	$ 360.00
8. Loan discount (1%)	$ 1,200.00
9. Survey	$ 300.00
10. *Total estimated costs*	$ 5,160.00

THIS FORM MAY NOT COVER ALL OF THE ITEMS YOU WILL BE REQUIRED TO PAY IN CASH AT CLOSING, THAT IS, PREPAID ITEMS SUCH AS DEPOSITS IN ESCROW FOR INSURANCE AND REAL ESTATE TAXES. ACTUAL CHARGES MAY BE HIGHER OR LOWER. THIS IS A GOOD FAITH ESTIMATE AND THE BEST FIGURE AVAILABLE TO US AT THIS TIME.

THIS STATEMENT DOES NOT
CONSTITUTE A LOAN COMMITMENT.

The purpose of this form is to provide an *estimate* of the costs you will be required to pay at closing (settlement). It may not cover all of the items applicable to your mortgage.

John R. Brady	By Robert T. Tullos
Borrower	Loan Officer/Loan Processor
Mary Beth Brady	*Date:* January 16, 1992
Coborrower	

BROWN LOSES HIS CREDIT CARD

Brown lost his wallet, which contained a Continental credit card, but he did not miss it until after the finder had made $1,200 in purchases with the credit card. He then reported the loss of the credit card to Continental. What is Brown's liability, if any, to Continental?

Hypothetical Case

Credit Cards

The mid-1960s boom in credit cards started when the major oil companies began issuing credit cards at no cost to their customers.[3] The oil companies reasoned that the cardholders would buy not only gas from the issuing company's stations but also oil and auto accessories. Major banks followed suit by issuing their own cards, such as MasterCharge and VISA.

The flood of "plastic credit" created problems. The cards often fell into the wrong hands. Companies mass-mailed credit cards, including duplicates for spouses, to anyone who asked for them and often to individuals who did not request them. Inevitably, credit cards were lost or stolen. A legal controversy arose concerning the liability for unauthorized credit card purchases. Congress responded to the problem in CCPA provisions, one of which forbids the issuance of credit cards to individuals who have not applied for them.

In addition, if a credit card is lost or stolen, the maximum liability of cardholders for its unauthorized use is $50. The cardholder is not liable for any use of the card after he or she has reported its loss or theft. If $35 is charged against a lost or stolen credit card before the cardholder has given notice of its loss or theft, the cardholder is responsible for only $35.

The process of issuing credit cards is controlled by a series of agreements. First, the issuer bank becomes a member of a credit card association such as VISA or MasterCard[4] and agrees to abide by the association's rules concerning the collection of credit card charges among its members. The second agreement arises when an individual applies to the issuer bank for a card. This agreement details the responsibilities of the bank and the cardholder with regard to billing, payment, and interest rates. In a third agreement, between a merchant and the issuer bank, the merchant agrees to sell goods or services to any qualified cardholder who presents the card. A qualified cardholder is generally one who lawfully owns an unrevoked card. The sales agreement between the cardholder and the merchant is primarily controlled by Article 2 of the Uniform Commercial Code, which was discussed in Chapters 8 and 9.

After having made a sale to the cardholder, the merchant tenders a copy of the receipt for goods or services to the issuer bank. The bank pays the merchant the amount due, less a percentage for handling the credit transaction and assuming the risk of nonpayment. The discount percentage is typically 3-6 percent of the sales price.

Figure 15-1 illustrates the agreements of the credit card process.

Holder in Due Course

In the past consumers who purchased defective goods or services on credit were frustrated by the **holder in due course rule.** Generally, a holder in due course is a transferee who has given value for negotiable commercial paper (for example, a check or a promissory note) in good faith and has acquired it before the obligation of the paper is overdue. Under the UCC, the holder in due course is granted a favored status. The purchaser of a negotiable instrument who qualifies as a holder in due course takes the instrument free of most of the defenses that can be asserted against the original seller of the instrument.

A typical problem occurred when a person bought a used car from a dealer and gave the dealer a promissory note, agreeing to make monthly payments on the note. Immediately after the sale, the dealer would negotiate, or "discount," the note to a finance company, which usually qualified as a holder in due course. If the car was defective or even if it was not delivered, the buyer had to make payments on the note to the finance company. If the seller is unscrupulous, the buyer is unlikely to obtain a satisfactory result without taking legal action, because the buyer cannot withhold payments from the seller.

The holder in due course rule remained in effect for all buyers until 1976, when the Federal Trade Commission abolished it for *consumer transactions.* Specifi-

---

FIGURE 15–1　　**The Credit Card Agreements**

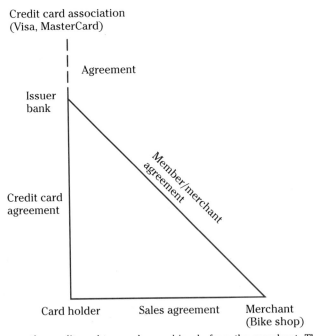

The cardholder uses the credit card to purchase a bicycle from the merchant. The merchant then sends the charges to the issuer bank, generally through the credit card association. The issuer bank pays the merchant the amount of the charge, less the percentage for handling the credit transaction, and then bills the customer according to the terms of the credit card agreement.

cally, a sale or lease of consumer goods that includes a promissory note must contain boldface notice stating that any person who takes the note is subject to all of the claims and defenses that the debtor can assert against the seller. Thus the consumer is assured that any of his or her defenses against the seller are also available against a third person.

Before abolishing the holder in due course rule for consumer credit transactions, the Federal Trade Commission considered a four-year study that reported that the rule forced tens of thousands of credit buyers annually to keep paying for shoddy goods and services. The change instituted by the FTC applies only to consumer credit. Commercial buyers may still be subject to the holder in due course rule. Figure 15-2 illustrates this rule.

COLLECTING AN OVERDUE DEBT

Hypothetical Case

Mrs. Jones, a 60-year-old widow with high blood pressure and epilepsy, received medical treatment at a hospital but failed to pay the hospital for the entire cost of the treatment. A year after her treatment was completed, a representative of Collection Accounts Terminal phoned Mrs. Jones and informed her that she owed $561 to the hospital that had treated her. When she denied this, the representative replied, "You owe it, you don't want to pay, so we're going to have to do something about it." One month later Mrs. Jones received this letter from Collection Accounts Terminal:

An Example of the Holder In Due Course Rule

FIGURE 15–2

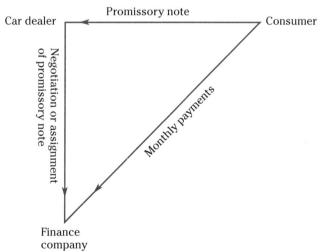

The consumer purchased a car from the car dealer and signed a promissory note (a written promise to pay a designated party). The car dealer negotiated or assigned the note to the finance company, so the consumer must now send her monthly payments to the finance company. Before the FTC abolished the holder in due course rule for consumer credit transactions, the finance company became a holder in due course. Thus, if the car dealer breached a warranty made to the customer, the consumer could not use that breach as a reason for refusing to pay the finance company. Now, however, the finance company is subject to all of the claims and defenses that the consumer can assert against the car dealer.

You have shown that you are unwilling to work out a friendly settlement with us to clear the above debt. Our field investigator has now been instructed to make an investigation in your neighborhood and to personally call on your employer. The immediate payment of the full amount or a personal visit to this office will spare you this embarrassment.

The envelope containing the letter bore a return address that included the full name of Collection Accounts Terminal. Did Collection Accounts Terminal violate any laws? Why? What advice would you give Mrs. Jones? Explain.

Fair Debt Collection Practices Act

The phenomenal growth of consumer credit resulted in a number of defaults by consumers. Quite often the creditors turned the debts over to collection agencies. There are about 5,000 such agencies, and each year they attempt to collect over $5 billion in unpaid debts. They recover about one third of the money owed, and their fees range up to 50 percent of the amount they collect. Some agencies, however, used harsh, abusive tactics in collecting debts, such as threats of violence, harassing telephone calls, and general embarrassment before neighbors and employers. In 1978 Congress, spurred by complaints, passed the *Fair Debt Collection Practices Act* (FDCPA).

This act regulates the practices of any person who regularly does any type of collection work that involves consumer debts owed to someone else. Thus the act covers collection agencies, the Internal Revenue Service, and attorneys who collect consumer debts for their clients, but not creditors who attempt to collect their own debts. Moreover, it covers consumer debts, but not debts contracted for a business purpose. Before the enactment of FDCPA, about three fourths of the states had already enacted statutes regulating debt collection. Some of these statutes regulate collection practices of creditors as well as collection agencies. FDCPA does not preempt the state statutes that give the consumer greater protection than it does.

The first task of the collector may be to find the debtor. To accomplish this, it is usually necessary to contact neighbors, relatives, and friends. The collector is allowed to contact third persons, but only once. The information that the collector may obtain from third persons is limited to the debtor's address and telephone number, but the collector cannot indicate that a debt is owed. If the collector is aware that the debtor is represented by an attorney, the collector may communicate only with the attorney.

After the debtor has been located, FDCPA restricts the collector's direct contact with the debtor. Communications with the debtor, including telephone calls, can be made only at reasonable hours, usually defined as the hours between 8 A.M. and 9 P.M. Debt collectors are prohibited from using these abusive techniques:

1. Threats of violence.
2. Abusive language.
3. Harassing telephone calls.
4. Impersonation of government officials, policemen, or attorneys.
5. Misrepresentation of the consumer's legal rights.
6. Publication of "shame lists."

The FDCPA further provides that the debtor's employer cannot be contacted without the debtor's permission, except to verify employment or obtain location information from a former employer. A catchall provision of FDCPA prohibits the collector from using "unfair or unconscionable means" to collect debts that the act does not specifically spell out.

The collector may be prevented from using even lawful means to contact the debtor. The collector must cease further communication with the debtor if the debtor makes a written request that this be done. Afterward the collector is limited to notifying the debtor that other collection remedies will be utilized.

Ordinarily, the collector will then bring legal proceedings against the debtor. The lawsuit must be filed in a court convenient to the debtor. If it involves real property, it must be brought in the district where the real property is located. In other cases it must be filed either where the consumer signed the contract or where the consumer lives at the time it is filed. Previously, some collection agencies purposely filed suit in a forum remote from the debtor, so that a default would be likely.

A debtor may sue any collector who fails to comply with FDCPA and may collect actual damages, such as loss of a job, punitive damages of up to $1,000 for deliberate noncompliance, court costs, and reasonable attorneys' fees. The Federal Trade Commission is charged with administrative enforcement of FDCPA.

Credit laws are very complex. If a company is engaged in consumer credit transactions, it should retain legal counsel for guidance on how to deal with them.

Bankruptcy

A consumer who is overwhelmed by debts may choose the option of bankruptcy. Article I, Section 8 of the U.S. Constitution provides that "the Congress shall have Power . . . to establish . . . uniform Laws on the subject of Bankruptcies throughout the United States." Thus bankruptcy is federal law; the states have no power to enact bankruptcy laws.

The first bankruptcy law was enacted in 1800. In 1978 Congress, prompted by the consumer movement, completely revised the bankruptcy laws. Bankruptcy law today is quite different from its earliest forms. Previously, the major purpose of bankruptcy law was to assure a fair distribution of the debtor's property among the creditors so that one creditor was not preferred over another. Present bankruptcy law seeks to discharge debtors from their debts and provide them with a fresh start.

At one time bankrupt debtors were stigmatized, but today they are no longer social outcasts. There are approximately 600,000 bankruptcy filings each year in the United States, about 95 percent of which are for liquidation proceedings that provide a "fresh start" discharge of all debts. Moreover, because certain property is exempt from bankruptcy proceedings, quite often little change in lifestyle results from them. However, the credit rating of the former bankrupt debtor is usually affected. As noted, bankruptcies can be reported by credit bureaus for 10 years. Many lenders will not extend credit to former bankrupt debtors, even though these persons cannot file for bankruptcy again for six years.

The bankruptcy law today makes three primary types of bankruptcy proceedings available to individuals and businesses: (1) liquidation under Chapter 7, (2) reorganization under Chapter 11, and (3) adjustment of debts of individuals with regular income under Chapter 13.

Insolvency

the financial condition of a debtor whose debts are greater than the fair market value of his or her assets

A liquidation proceeding is the most common type of bankruptcy declared by consumers. The case is commenced when a debtor files a voluntary petition or when the debtor's creditors file an involuntary petition. The debtors subject to liquidation proceedings include not only individuals but also corporations and partnerships. In a voluntary bankruptcy case, the debtor need not be insolvent, but insolvency is ordinarily the reason that debtors file the petition for voluntary bankruptcy. **Insolvency** is defined by the federal bankruptcy act as the financial condition of a debtor whose debts are greater than the fair market value of his or her assets.

In an involuntary bankruptcy case, the petition is filed by one or more of the creditors. The total unsecured claims of the creditors must amount to at least $5,000.

Within a short time the debtor's creditors meet and elect a trustee who takes possession of the debtor's property and has it appraised. In both voluntary and involuntary cases, the trustee ultimately sells the debtor's tangible and intangible property, including such property as accounts receivable, patent rights, consumer goods, and inventory. The proceeds from the sale are used to pay off the creditors' claims on a pro rata basis. It is very common for creditors to receive less than five cents for each of the dollars they claim.

Secured debts (those backed by an interest in property) are satisfied first. Thus the holder of a lien on the debtor's car is not affected by the bankruptcy proceedings. The lien can be exercised directly against the car in satisfaction of the debt before or during the bankruptcy proceedings. The remaining assets are divided among the unsecured creditors according to an order of priority.

The bankruptcy act divides claims into classes, each of which must be fully satisfied before the next class is entitled to anything. Payment of unsecured debts is made according to the following order of priority:

1. Administrative expenses.
2. For involuntary cases, debts incurred in the ordinary course of the debtor's business after the bankruptcy petition was filed but before the trustee was appointed.
3. Unsecured claims of up to $2,000 for wages, salaries, or commissions earned by an individual within 90 days before the filing of the bankruptcy petition or the cessation of the debtor's business, whichever occurred first.
4. Unsecured claims for contributions to employee benefit plans, such as pension plans and health or life insurance plans, arising from service performed within 180 days before the bankruptcy petition was filed or the debtor stopped doing business (but the limit is $2,000 per employee).
5. Unsecured claims, up to $2,000, of grain farmers and American fishermen against debtors who own or operate grain or fish storage facilities.
6. Unsecured claims for deposits of up to $900 for the purchase of consumer goods or services that were not received.
7. Taxes.

After all the priority claims and expenses have been satisfied, any money left over is paid on a pro rata basis to other unsecured creditors who have filed a proof of their claims.

Not all the property of an individual debtor may be sold. In keeping with the "fresh start" philosophy of the bankruptcy act, certain property is exempt and cannot be collected and sold by the trustee. Because of the consumer movement the act provides much greater exemptions than did previous bankruptcy acts.

Under the new bankruptcy act, the debtor can choose the exemptions listed in the federal act or the exemptions listed by state law, whichever is more favorable, but may not select a mixture of the two. However, states may limit a debtor's exemptions to those provided by state law, and most of the states have chosen this option.

The goal of the individual bankrupt debtor is to receive a discharge from liability for debt. If the court grants a **discharge,** the debtor is released from most of his or her debts at the end of the court proceedings. However, a debtor may not receive a discharge if the court finds that the debtor has concealed assets, destroyed financial records, failed to explain the loss of assets, refused to obey a court order, or been discharged from bankruptcy within the previous six years.

A discharge in bankruptcy does not relieve the debtor of all obligations. The debtor will continue to be liable on **nondischargeable debts,** such as certain taxes, claims arising out of money or property obtained by fraud or embezzlement, intentional torts, alimony and child support, debts not listed in the bankruptcy case, and student loans that became due within five years before the bankruptcy petition.

Although corporations and partnerships may not be discharged from their debts, they may use Chapter 11 bankruptcy to reorganize themselves. The purpose of such reorganization is to restructure the finances of the business so that it may continue to operate and thus pay its creditors, provide employment, and produce dividends for stockholders. Many businesses with major financial problems perceive Chapter 11 as a means of solving their difficulties while preserving the business. However, reorganization under Chapter 11 is an expensive and risky procedure. Federal court officials estimate that only 1 in 10 companies that file for Chapter 11 bankruptcy actually survive.

For an individual with regular income, an alternative to liquidation, or straight bankruptcy, is **adjustment of the debts** under Chapter 13 of the bankruptcy act. This special procedure enables such individuals to pay their debts under court protection over an extended period of time. The court adjusts the debts by arranging a repayment schedule. Commonly called the "wage earner's plan," the procedure is limited to individuals whose income is derived primarily from salary, wages, or commissions. This plan is voluntarily initiated by debtors; creditors cannot initiate it. Most debtors prefer liquidation, which discharges them from nearly all of their obligations.

The present bankruptcy act went into effect in October 1979, and since 1980 the number of personal bankruptcy filings has doubled, to about one-half million each year. One reason for the growth in the number of such filings is that debtors no longer need to show financial distress in order to file bankruptcy. Another reason is the proliferation of advertising by attorneys. Bankruptcy is a profitable legal procedure, requiring relatively little time, and ads in newspapers and on radios, buses, and trains stress the ease of filing for bankruptcy.

Some observers maintain that personal bankruptcy filings are caused by conditions beyond the individual's control, such as unemployment, recession, and inflation, as well as personal problems for which the individual may bear no responsibility, such as divorce, death in the family, and high medical bills. These observers contend that the sweeping changes of the 1978 bankruptcy act were necessary. They note that the extension of time credit has continued to increase despite predictions of a reduction because of the act.

Discharge

an order by a bankruptcy court that releases the debtor from most of his or her debts

Nondischargeable debt

a type of debt for which the debtor continues to be liable after bankruptcy

Adjustment of debts

a method by which debtors with regular income can pay their debts over an extended period of time

LAW ABROAD

Germany

In bankruptcy proceedings, all of the debtor's assets may be seized, including assets located abroad. However, the effect of a claim raised in a German bankruptcy proceeding on assets located in foreign countries may vary. The bankruptcy of the German branch of a corporation whose main residence is in a foreign country will affect only that branch.

After bankruptcy proceedings have begun, the court appoints a trustee and a provisional committee of creditors. In a case of involuntary bankruptcy, the creditors' petitions, in addition to stating their claims, must establish the insolvency of the bankrupt party. The court will examine all of these claims. The petitioning creditors must offer security for court costs.

Bankruptcy proceedings do not wipe the slate clean for debtors, who remain liable for unsatisfied debts whether or not those debts were included in the bankruptcy proceedings.

Workers whose employer is unable to meet the payroll because of insolvency or bankruptcy can be compensated by the government for their lost wages and salaries. Company pensions are partially protected against the bankruptcy of an employer by a pension security fund that employers are required to pay into. Deposits in private banks are also protected by insurance.

Japan

Bankruptcy proceedings are initiated by petition to the district court having jurisdiction over the debtor's legal residence or principal place of business. The petition may be made by the creditors or the debtor, but it is usually made by the creditors. If the court finds the debtor to be bankrupt, it appoints a receiver (who has power to administer and dispose of the bankrupt debtor's estate), orders a report of claims, and requires a creditors' meeting. All of the bankrupt debtor's obligations to third parties become due upon adjudication of bankruptcy.

A person who has been adjudicated bankrupt may lose certain rights, such as the right to practice law or hold public office. These rights may be reacquired by repayment of the debt or the passage of time.

Bankruptcy procedures are applied uniformly to Japanese citizens and foreigners, provided the foreigners come from countries whose law affords reciprocity to Japanese citizens.

Federal Law on Warranties

Historically, a primary problem of the U.S. marketplace was the confusion surrounding warranties. Vague wording and technical language in warranties made it difficult for consumers to tell whether they were buying a product with a worthwhile warranty. Highly legalistic language appeared to extend full warranties, but qualifying clauses in fine print eliminated or severely limited them. In 1975 Congress, recognizing that consumers needed protection, passed the *Magnuson-Moss Warranty Act*, which prevents deception in warranties by making them easier to understand. Under this act, the terms of a warranty must be written in language clear enough for the average person to understand its protections and limitations. The provisions of the act apply only to written warranties for purchases of consumer goods costing $15 or more.

Magnuson-Moss does not require that a warranty be provided, but it states that when a warranty *is* provided, the warranty must comply with the provisions of the act. Warranties on consumer products costing $10 or more must be labeled as "full" or "limited." For consumer products covered by a **full warranty,** the warrantor must assume such duties as the following:

Full warranty
a warranty that must meet certain requirements set by federal law

1. The warrantor must agree to repair or replace the defective product within a reasonable time and without charge.

2. If the warrantor cannot repair or replace the defective product within a reasonable time, the warrantor must give the consumer the choice of a cash refund or replacement without charge.

A **limited warranty** is one that fails to meet any of the requirements of a full warranty. The limitation must be conspicuously stated.

Limited warranty
a warranty that fails to meet any of the requirements of a full warranty

In the past consumers often had little knowledge of what the warranty provided or did not know that there was a warranty until after the sale. Magnuson-Moss requires that the warranty be made available to the consumer prior to the sale. Now the warranty is generally printed on the product box or displayed on the floor sample.

Since Magnuson-Moss covers only written warranties, it does not affect the implied warranties of merchantability and fitness provided by the Uniform Commercial Code. However, a manufacturer's express warranty cannot relieve a retailer from its implied warranty, except that the effective period of implied warranties may be limited to the *duration* of the written warranty or to a reasonable period of time. Magnuson-Moss empowers the Federal Trade Commission to set standards for express warranties.

THE CONSUMER AND INFORMATION

Most of the information that consumers obtain about goods and services comes from the sellers and producers of these goods and services. Quite naturally, the sellers and producers place their goods and services in the most favorable light possible. At one time, only the common law protected consumers from misinformation on goods and services. In the early part of this century, state legislatures recognized that the common law was tilted toward producers and sellers and away from the rights of consumers. State statutes to protect consumers from misinformation on goods and services were passed but were generally ineffective. There arose a call for federal action. Congress responded by creating the Federal Trade Commission and authorizing it to prohibit unfair or deceptive acts or practices in commerce. This section discusses how consumers are protected from misleading information in advertising and selling.

Federal Trade Commission

The first major federal legislation protecting consumers was the Federal Trade Commission Act, passed in 1914, which created the Federal Trade Commission (FTC). The act authorized the FTC to prohibit **unfair methods of competition in commerce.** It could prohibit certain commercial practices if they injured a competing business, but it had no authority to protect consumers. In 1938 Congress passed the Wheeler-Lea Amendment to the Federal Trade Commission Act, which

Unfair method of competition in commerce
a commercial practice that the law prohibits because its use by a business unfairly injures a competing business

**Unfair or deceptive
act or practice
in commerce**

a commercial practice by
a business that the law
prohibits because its use
by a business unfairly injures consumers

expanded the FTC's jurisdiction to prohibit **unfair or deceptive acts or practices in commerce.** Previously, the FTC could protect the consumer only indirectly by promoting competition. But this added power enabled it to focus its attention on the direct protection of the consumer. For example, it could now declare certain advertisements to be unfair or deceptive acts or practices in commerce.

Unfair or Deceptive Business Practices

The FTC may hold that advertisements are deceptive even though they only tend to mislead. The capacity to mislead is sufficient to sustain such a holding; actual deception of a consumer is not necessary. Similarly, advertisers cannot use as a defense their lack of knowledge that an advertisement was false or their lack of intention to deceive. The interest of the consumer is paramount; the FTC's primary concern is focused on whether the advertisement is likely to mislead a consumer acting reasonably under the circumstances.

In the case that follows, the federal court of appeals in Washington, D.C., considered whether to uphold an FTC order restricting the advertising of a topical pain reliever.

THOMPSON MEDICAL CO., INC. v. FTC
U.S. COURT OF APPEALS, DISTRICT OF COLUMBIA CIRCUIT
791 F.2d 189 (1985)

Thompson Medical Company, Inc. sold an over-the-counter analgesic cream known as Aspercreme. Aspercreme was said to relieve minor arthritic pain as well as other minor pains. It was supposed to be rubbed onto the affected area. It contained no aspirin; its active ingredient was a chemical relative of aspirin. Thompson's advertising, however, strongly suggested that Aspercreme and aspirin were related. In addition, Thompson claimed that the efficacy of Aspercreme had been scientifically established.

An Aspercreme television ad contained the following monologue:

> When you suffer from arthritis, imagine putting the strong relief of aspirin right where you hurt. Aspercreme is an odorless rub which concentrates the relief of aspirin. When you take regular aspirin, it goes throughout your body like this. But, in seconds, Aspercreme starts concentrating all the temporary relief of two aspirin directly at the point of minor arthritis pain. . . . [*Voice over:*] Aspercreme. The strong relief of aspirin right where you hurt.

In this and other ads, the speaker was shown holding aspirin tablets at the beginning of the monologue. As he spoke, the aspirin was replaced by a tube of Aspercreme.

In February 1981 the FTC issued an administrative complaint against Thompson, charging it with having violated sections of the Federal Trade Commission Act that prohibited false advertising to induce the purchase of drugs. After a hearing before an administrative law judge and an appeal to the commission, the FTC issued a final order against Thompson. The order prohibited Thompson from using the name Aspercreme unless its advertising and packaging made clear that the product did not contain aspirin. The order further prohibited Thompson from representing that Aspercreme "involves a new scientific principle" and from misrepresenting Aspercreme's ingredients or testing. Thompson petitioned the federal court of appeals in Washington, D.C., for review.

MIKVA, CIRCUIT JUDGE

Thompson contends that the FTC erred in requiring two clinical studies as a prerequisite for any future representation that Aspercreme is an effective analgesic. Thompson correctly acknowledges that in general an advertisement is considered deceptive if the advertiser lacks a "reasonable basis" to support the claims made in it. The controversy here concerns what constitutes such a basis. Thompson is unhappy with the Commission's requirement of two clinical studies. Thompson asserts that neither case law nor scientific wisdom justifies the imposition of this requirement, and that it has never before been imposed.

The Commission's opinion contains a thorough discussion of the framework traditionally used by the FTC in deciding when ads are properly supported by a reasonable basis and why the order issued here contained the term it did. We think the Commission has properly employed the framework established by its precedents in concluding that there was no reasonable basis shown here and in requiring two clinical studies before any representations can be made about Aspercreme's efficacy.

We pause briefly to respond to Thompson's repeated expressions of horror at the alleged effect of the FTC's order. Thompson asserts that the Commission's decision will destroy its business, and is tantamount to an order to cease selling Aspercreme. Two responses to Thompson's bleatings are appropriate. First, they are simply not true. The FTC's order did not bar the sale of Aspercreme forever and under all circumstances. Indeed, the sale of Aspercreme was not barred at all. Only misleading advertising was prohibited. If Thompson does come up with new clinical studies or if the FDA reclassifies trolamine salicylate, Thompson would be free to continue to make efficacy claims in its Aspercreme ads. In the interim, Thompson is free to advertise Aspercreme so long as it does not make false or misleading representations. Second, although the effect of the order on Thompson's business may well be severe, we see no reason that Thompson should be able to make advertising claims if they are not true. The FTC has a mandate to assure that advertising is not false and misleading. Allowing firms to continue such advertising because to stop would hurt the firms' economic interests is obviously not part of the calculus of interests Congress intended the FTC to consider. Thompson has no right to stay in business if the only way it can do so is to engage in false and misleading advertising.

Thompson also challenges the portion of the FTC order requiring it to disclose in all advertising and labeling that Aspercreme does not contain aspirin. This part of Thompson's argument borders on the frivolous. Thompson argues that no misrepresentation occurred, that it is not material to consumers whether Aspercreme contains aspirin or not, that Aspercreme is merely a trademark and does not convey any information about the product's content, and that in any event Aspercreme labeling has always indicated that Aspercreme does not contain aspirin. (One wonders why Thompson is upset about being ordered to disclose that its product does not contain aspirin if no one cares and everyone has always known anyway.)

The issue of what message was reasonably likely to be conveyed to consumers by Aspercreme's advertising was extensively addressed by expert testimony. The FTC's summation of the law in this area is accurate and succinct.

> Advertising representations will be condemned if they are likely to deceive; actual deception need not be shown. The tendency of a particular advertisement to deceive is determined by the net impression it is likely to make upon the viewing public. Consequently, literally true statements may nonetheless be found deceptive, and advertisements reasonably capable of being interpreted in a misleading way are unlawful even though other, nonmisleading interpretations may also be possible.

The FTC adequately considered a large mass of technical evidence and concluded that Thompson had engaged in deceptive advertising with respect to Aspercreme. We cannot find fault in the Commission's conclusions or in the remedial measures it imposed. Indeed, in all respects we find the FTC Order and Opinion clear and logical. If and when Thompson comes up with evidence that Aspercreme is effective, it will be free to again make efficacy claims in its advertising. Until that time it should not say what it cannot prove. The FTC's requirement of aspirin-content disclaimers also is entirely appropriate; Aspercreme does not contain any aspirin, and its makers should not imply that it does. Accord-

ingly, Thompson's petition for review of the FTC's order is
Denied.

Legal Issues

1. Does the FTC need to show actual deception before condemning advertising?

2. Suppose that following the FTC's order would destroy Thompson's business. Would the court consider this justification for overturning the order? Why?

Ethical Issues

1. Thompson Medical Company charged that the FTC's order would destroy its business because, by barring it from using the name Aspercreme unless its advertising and packaging made clear that Aspercreme did not contain aspirin, the order was tantamount to a directive that it cease selling Aspercreme. What ethical standard was Thompson relying on when it made that charge? What ethical standard could be used to support the FTC's order? Discuss.

2. Thompson Medical Company argues that under the circumstances it was inappropriate for the FTC to require two clinical tests of Aspercreme's effectiveness before Aspercreme could make any representations as to Aspercreme's effect on minor arthritic pain. Would an advocate of situation ethics view this argument as ethically acceptable? Why?

Statements of opinion by the seller are not illegal. The seller's exaggerations of the product's value and qualities are viewed as "sales talk" or "puffery" and cannot form the basis of a lawsuit. Puffery is a statement of opinion, not a representation of fact. "Blatz is Milwaukee's finest beer" and "You meet the nicest people on a Honda" are examples of puffery.

The FTC does not require advertisers to "tell all," but it may view *nondisclosure* of certain information as deceptive. If certain facts would influence the consumer's purchasing decision, advertisements must disclose those facts. For example, the advertising of Geritol was found to be false and misleading because it created the impression that tiredness is caused by a problem that Geritol can solve. The makers of Geritol were ordered to state in future Geritol ads that most people are not tired and rundown because of an iron or vitamin deficiency.

"Bait and switch" advertising is prohibited. In this sales tactic a product is advertised at a very low price as bait to lure the consumer to the store. At the store the salesclerk discourages the customer from purchasing the advertised product by emphasizing its defects and then switches the customer's attention to a higher-priced product that the advertiser really wants to sell. Sellers may, however, employ a selling technique known as "trading-up." The seller can legally convince the customer to purchase a higher-priced product, provided there is a sufficient stock of the advertised product and no attempt is made to disparage or refuse to sell it.

Deceptive price advertising, which may take several forms, has been traditionally attacked by the FTC. Price comparisons with former prices must not be based on fictitious former prices. A seller that tried to increase the sales of an item by reducing its price must base the reduction on a genuine former price. Some retailers have deliberately fabricated former selling prices to create savings offers. This practice is prohibited. For example, an advertisement that states "Brand Z toaster, was $17.95, now $9.95" is illegal if the former price is not bona fide. The standard for the genuineness of a former selling price is whether that price was used for a reasonable time in the recent course of business. Price comparisons of products must refer to products that are of like grade and quality in all material aspects.

Offers of free goods and "two for one" sales may be deceptive trade practices if the seller is not in fact offering anything free. In attempting to compete with large paint companies, Mary Carter Paint Company offered two cans of paint for the price of one. But since the company had never sold a single can of paint at any price, the second can was not "free."

In dealing with a deceptive trade practice, the action that the FTC usually takes is to issue a cease and desist order. Such an order prohibits the illegal practice but generally does not penalize the company for its past conduct. Recently, the FTC has gone further and ordered *corrective advertising.* A corrective advertising order usually requires that future ads disclose that former ads were false or deceptive and also provide the necessary information needed to correct the erroneous impression created by the former ads. The basis for issuing such orders is that the lingering effect of the false or deceptive advertising claims continues to influence purchasing decisions.

In one case the court received evidence of studies revealing that Warner-Lambert advertising had created the impression that Listerine mouthwash was effective in preventing and curing sore throats and colds. Expert testimony revealed that Listerine would neither cure nor prevent sore throats and colds. Warner-Lambert was then required to include this corrective message in its Listerine ads for two years: "Listerine will not help prevent colds or sore throats or lessen their severity." In other cases the corrective advertising required was a message stating that the FTC had questioned the accuracy of the former ads or that a settlement had been reached with the FTC concerning inaccurate former ads.

"Little FTC laws" have been enacted by 49 states and the District of Columbia to prevent deceptive and unfair trade practices. Although these laws were patterned on the Federal Trade Commission Act, their administrative enforcement is generally less vigorous than that of the federal government.

The following case concerns an Illinois statute that was patterned on the Federal Trade Commission Act.

PERKINS v. COLLETTE

APPELLATE COURT OF ILLINOIS, SECOND DISTRICT
534 N.E.2d 1312 (1989)

The plaintiffs, Thomas and Eileen Perkins, alleged as follows: On or about September 26, 1981, they met with James Collette, a real estate agent for Century 21 Realty, at the Century 21 Plaza office in Villa Park, Illinois. The Perkinses told Collette that they wanted to purchase a vacant lot and build a home on the lot. Collette showed them a vacant parcel of land owned by himself and his wife, Adele. He informed the plaintiffs that the land was a suitable place to build a house. On October 3, 1981, a sales contract was executed in which the plaintiffs agreed to pay $14,000 for the lot. Subsequently, articles of agreement for the deed were executed and the Perkinses paid an additional $5,216.

After the closing Thomas Perkins requested an application for a building permit from the Du Page County supervisor of zoning enforcement. He was told that Collette had submitted an application for a building permit, which had been denied, and that the Perkinses' application would be denied as well.

The Perkinses brought action for the rescission of the sales contract and misrepresentation against James and Adele Collette, as vendors of the land, and against Century 21 Realty, for which, they alleged, Collette had been acting as an agent. The trial court dismissed the plaintiffs' complaint on the basis that any misrepresentations made by Collette were misrepresentations of law upon which the plaintiffs were not entitled to rely. The plaintiffs appealed.

DUNN, JUSTICE

Two counts of plaintiffs' amended complaint allege violations of Section 2 of the Illinois Consumer Fraud and Deceptive Business Practices Act. Section 2 of the Act applies to intentional misrepresentations made by real estate brokers to prospective purchasers. The broker must have knowledge of the false, misleading, or deceptive nature of the information he conveys. Plaintiffs have clearly alleged facts establishing that James Collette, a real estate broker and agent of Century 21 Plaza, made misrepresentations to them and had knowledge that the information he was communicating to them was false.

Defendants assert, however, that the Act only applies to misrepresentations of material fact and that the alleged misrepresentations of James Collette were ones of law, not fact. Defendants rely largely upon the decision of this court in *Hamming v. Murphy* (1980), 83 Ill.App.3d 1130.

In *Hamming,* one of the sellers advised a buyer of certain real estate that all of the zoning "red tape" had been taken care of so as to permit the construction of apartments on the subject property. The court held that this could not constitute a fraudulent misrepresentation because it was a representation of law. The court stated that a party to a transaction is not generally entitled to rely upon a representation of law because both parties are presumed to be equally capable of knowing and interpreting the law.

The primary factor which distinguishes *Hamming* is whether the seller's misrepresentation could have been discovered merely by reviewing applicable zoning or building ordinances.

Considering only the facts alleged in the amended complaint, as we are required to do, we cannot determine whether plaintiffs could have discovered the alleged misrepresentations of James Collette merely by reviewing applicable zoning and building ordinances. The amended complaint alleged that James Collette told plaintiffs that the vacant lot was a suitable location for a home, even though Collette himself had been denied a building permit for the lot. It further alleged that plaintiffs subsequently discovered that they would be unable to obtain a building permit for the lot. The amended complaint contained no facts, however, which would conclusively indicate that plaintiffs could have discovered the alleged misrepresentations by merely reviewing local zoning or building ordinances or that plaintiffs, as a matter of law, were not entitled to rely upon Collette's misrepresentations for any other reasons. The trial court therefore erred by dismissing the two counts based upon the Act.

Accordingly, the judgment of the circuit court of Du Page County is reversed and the cause remanded for further proceedings.

Reversed and remanded.

Legal Issues

1. According to the court, would Collette have violated the Illinois Consumer Fraud and Deceptive Business Practice Act if he had inadvertently misled the Perkins? Why?

2. What were the defendants' assertions regarding the misrepresentations, and how did the court deal with those assertions? Explain.

Ethical Issues

1. The defendant contended that the plaintiff was not entitled to relief because of an error of law. The court rejected this contention on the ground that the complaint did not contain any facts that would conclusively indicate that the plaintiff could have discovered the alleged misrepresentations by merely reviewing the law, such as local zoning or building ordinances. Is this an example of a court's use of pragmatic ethics to arrive at a result? Why?

2. What ethical standards obviously served as Collette's view of how business should be conducted? Why?

---

1. Many persons resent the "intrusion" of government regulation into their affairs, particularly in the area of consumer protection. Can you think of arguments for and against consumer protection?

REVIEW QUESTIONS & PROBLEMS

2. What was the intent of Congress in passing the Consumer Credit Protection Act in 1968? Explain.

3. Charles of the Ritz, a corporation engaged in the manufacture and distribution of cosmetics, advertised that "a vital organic ingredient" in its Charles of the Ritz Rejuvenescence Cream "restores natural moisture . . . and is constantly active in keeping your skin clear, radiant, and young-looking." The Federal Trade Commission issued a complaint charging that this constituted deceptive advertising. Charles of the Ritz claimed that the advertisement was not misleading since no straight-thinking person would believe that the cream could actually rejuvenate skin. Do you agree? Explain.

4. After moving from Washington, D.C., to St. Louis to begin a new job, Millstone applied for a new automobile insurance policy. He was told that a background investigation would be conducted in connection with the application. One week later he was notified that the policy would not be granted because of a report that the insurance company had received from Investigative Reports, a credit bureau. After repeated efforts Millstone was informed by Investigative Reports that his former neighbors in Washington considered him a "hippie," a drug user, and a possible political dissident. Millstone maintained that the information was inaccurate, but Investigative Reports refused to discuss the matter further. Has Investigative Reports fulfilled its obligations to Millstone? Explain. If the insurance company had denied the policy based on its own investigation, would Millstone have been entitled to receive the results of the investigation and to demand an explanation for alleged inaccuracies? Explain.

5. ABC Company utilized a computerized system to evaluate credit card applications. One of the factors that ABC used was a value that it assigned to the applicant's zip code based on its delinquency experience in the area comprised by that zip code. The plaintiff, whose zip code was rated 1, the least desirable rating on a scale of 1 to 5, challenged ABC under the Equal Credit Opportunities Act. She introduced evidence showing (1) that a correlation existed between ABC's rejection rate in a zip code area and the percentage of the nonwhite population in that area and (2) that if she had lived in an area rated 3 or higher, her application would have been approved. How should the court rule? Discuss.

6. Brown went through a stop sign while driving his car and hit Smith's automobile, causing Smith to suffer personal injuries and property damage. Smith obtained a judgment against Brown, but when she tried to enforce the judgment, Brown informed her that since he had recently been discharged in bankruptcy, the judgment was unenforceable. Did the discharge in bankruptcy relieve Brown of the obligation to satisfy Smith's judgment? Discuss.

ENDNOTES

1. There is no statute of limitations for the reporting of adverse information when the consumer applies for (1) a loan of $50,000 or more, (2) life insurance of $50,000 or more, or (3) a job with an annual salary of $20,000 or more. In practice, however, most credit bureaus apply the same statute of limitations for adverse information regardless of the size of the transaction.

2. Additional limitations on the holder in due course doctrine are discussed in a later section.

3. Credit cards were first used in 1915, when Western Union and a few railroads, hotels, and department stores issued them to preferred customers.

4. VISA and MasterCard charges comprise 53 percent of the credit card purchases in the United States.

CHAPTER

16

Environmental Regulation

A half century ago few laws dealt with protection of the environment and little money was spent to shield humankind's habitat from damage and destruction. Since then, there has been a growing awareness of the fact that unless action—at times even drastic action—is taken, people will no longer be able to enjoy an acceptable quality of life. That awareness has led to the enactment of a variety of federal, state, and local laws designed to regulate conduct that poses a threat to the environment. It is expected that by the year 2000 about 2 percent of the U.S. gross national product will be devoted to controlling pollution and cleaning up the environment. Many countries are already parties to multinational agreements that restrict or outlaw behavior harmful to the planet. New regional and worldwide efforts to expand the scope of such agreements are in the wings.

This chapter considers measures that the federal government and state and local governments have taken to preserve and enhance the environment as well as constitutional and other legal principles that restrict governmental action in this area. It also considers treaties regarding environmental matters.

COMMON CAUSES OF INJURY TO THE ENVIRONMENT

Broadly defined, environment includes the entire ambience of humankind. This includes not only geographic features of our surroundings, such as oceans, beaches, rivers, lakes, streams, wetlands, groundwater, soil, air, rainfall, the atmosphere, and the ozone layer that envelops the earth, but also wildlife species, plants, forests, open spaces, historic sites, landmarks, noise level, and aesthetic qualities. One or more of these environmental components can be injured in various ways. For instance, an oil spill, such as the seepage of oil from the tanker *Exxon Valdez* into Alaskan waters in 1989, pollutes water and also destroys wildlife.

The discharge of some chemicals into the air may result in smog and acid rain. The acid rain, in turn, may destroy forests, lakes, and animals. Burning trash fills the air with dust and gases, and the ash of burned trash may contain lead and cadmium, harmful to both human beings and marine life, which may find their way into the water supply. Uncontrolled automobile emissions pollute the air with substances that are especially harmful to persons with respiratory illnesses. Chlorofluorocarbons (CFCs), which are used in such products as air conditioners, refrigerators, and aerosol cans, deplete the ozone layer that surrounds the earth. Depletion of the ozone layer poses severe health threats, including increases in some forms of cancer.

These are but a few examples of the factors that have increased concern about the environment and given rise to demands for legal restrictions to protect and improve it.

In 1991, during Operation Desert Storm, in which a coalition of nations sought to carry out United Nations resolutions that called for the removal of Iraq's armed forces from conquered Kuwait, Iraq used environmental terrorism as a weapon of war. To stymie the coalition's efforts to drive its armed forces from Kuwait, Iraq discharged huge quantities of crude oil into the Persian Gulf. As with the *Exxon Valdez* oil spill, it will be a long time before the environmental damage caused by Iraq's action can be completely assessed. Future negotiations among nations may focus on outlawing environmental despoliation as a weapon of war.

A DISTURBING RESPONSE TO A QUEST FOR INEXPENSIVE ENERGY

To avoid purchasing electricity, Lang built a windmill on his property, just 10 feet from Hane's house. The nerve-racking noise produced by the windmill's blades made it difficult for Hane to sleep. She brought a lawsuit to enjoin Lang from operating the windmill. Lang asked the court to dismiss the suit on the grounds that the windmill was on his property, that use of the windmill reduced the amount of oil used by the local utility to generate electricity, and that if Hane's home were properly insulated, the noise level inside it would be no higher than the noise level produced by her TV set. What judgment? Why? Which ethical standard or standards of conduct would support a decision allowing Lang to use the windmill if it did not exceed a noise level set by the court? Discuss.

Hypothetical Case

PRIVATE AND PUBLIC NUISANCES

Nuisance law prohibits landowners from *unreasonably* using their land so as to interfere with others' reasonable use and enjoyment of property or so as to cause injury to the public. A nuisance may be a private nuisance, a public nuisance, or a mixed nuisance—that is, both a private nuisance and a public nuisance.

Private Nuisance

A **private nuisance** is a landowner's conduct that substantially and unreasonably interferes with another landowner's use or enjoyment of his or her land or is injurious to another landowner's physical or mental well-being. Such conduct is a tort. Reasonableness is determined on the basis of simple tastes, not luxurious habits, and on the basis of the social value of what is or is not done when weighed against the harm that is caused. Account is taken of such factors as alternative ways in which the landowner can achieve comparable satisfaction; the nature, frequency, duration, and time of day of the conduct in question; the location of the parties' properties; and the demands of modern life. In light of these criteria, it can be concluded that a homeowner's operation of an air conditioner in a strictly residential neighborhood is a private nuisance if the air conditioner produces an exceptionally loud outside noise 24 hours a day, interfering with the sleep of nearby residents and with their everyday activities, such as speaking on the telephone, reading, and engaging in family conversations.

A party injured by a private nuisance may bring a lawsuit for damages as well as **abatement of the nuisance,** that is, a court grant of injunctive relief that orders the defendant to end the objectionable conduct.

Public Nuisance

What occurs on one's land is a **public nuisance** if it occurs continuously or repeatedly; creates a condition that is a substantial inconvenience or extremely troublesome or poses a significant threat to public health, safety, or morals; and affects the rights of the public at large, not merely the rights of a particular person or several persons. For objectionable conduct to be classified as a public nuisance, it must have an impact on a considerable number of persons or a substantial part of the community.

Many jurisdictions view a public nuisance as a *crime* rather than as a tort. Generally, only governmental authorities or other representatives of the general public can bring suit to challenge a public nuisance. However, a private party who is caused "special damage" by a public nuisance, that is, injury *distinct* from the harm that the nuisance causes to the public at large, may bring a suit to abate the nuisance or recover damages, or to be granted both types of relief.

NATIONAL ENVIRONMENTAL POLICY ACT

The National Environmental Policy Act (NEPA), adopted by Congress in 1969, establishes a national environmental policy, creates a Council on Environmental Quality, declares the federal government's responsibilities in environmental mat-

---

Nuisance law
legal principles concerning misuse of one's land

Private nuisance
a landowner's use of property that substantially and unreasonably harms one or more persons

Abatement of a nuisance
injunctive relief directing that a nuisance be stopped

Public nuisance
the repeated or continuous misuse of land to the substantial detriment of the public at large

ters, and requires federal agencies to prepare and take into account an "environmental impact statement" when conducting their affairs.

NEPA Policy

NEPA establishes a national commitment to protect and enhance the environment. It calls for efforts to prevent and eliminate damage to the environment and the biosphere and to stimulate the health and welfare of human beings. NEPA recognizes "the profound impact of man's activity on the interrelations of all components of the natural environment." It calls for the federal government, in cooperation with state and local governments and other concerned organizations, public and private, "to use all practicable means and measures to foster and promote the general welfare, to create and maintain conditions under which" people and "nature can exist in productive harmony, and [to] fulfill the social, economic, and other requirements of present and future generations of Americans."

Federal Government's Responsibilities

NEPA makes the federal government responsible for using "all practicable means, consistent with other essential considerations of national policy, to improve and coordinate Federal plans, functions, programs, and resources to the end that the Nation may (1) fulfill the responsibilities to each generation as trustee of the environment for succeeding generations; (2) assure for all Americans safe, healthful, productive, and esthetically and culturally pleasing surroundings; (3) attain the widest range of beneficial uses of the environment without degradation, risk to health or safety, or other undesirable and unintended consequences; (4) preserve important historic, cultural, and natural aspects of our national heritage, and maintain, wherever possible, an environment which supports diversity and variety of individual choice; (5) achieve a balance between population and resource use which will permit high standards of living and a wide sharing of life's amenities; and (6) enhance the quality of renewal resources and approach the maximum attainable recycling of depletable resources." NEPA asserts "that each person should enjoy a healthful environment and" that everyone "has a responsibility to contribute to the preservation and enhancement of the environment."

Environmental Impact Statement

NEPA directs that for every recommendation, report on proposals, or other major federal action significantly affecting the quality of the environment a detailed **environmental impact statement** be prepared that includes information on "(i) the environmental impact of the proposed action, (ii) any adverse environmental effects which cannot be avoided should the proposal be implemented, (iii) alternatives to the proposed action, (iv) the relationship between local short-term uses" of the "environment and the maintenance and enhancement of long-term productivity, and (v) any irreversible and irretrievable commitments of resources which would be involved in the proposed action should it be implemented." Copies of statements together with "the comments and views of the appropriate Federal, State, and local agencies, which are authorized to develop and enforce environmental standards," must "accompany the proposal through the existing

Environmental impact statement
a report that specifies the effects of a proposed action on the environment

agency review process." In those cases in which an agency proposal "involves unresolved conflicts concerning alternative uses of available resources," the agency is obliged to "study, develop, and describe appropriate alternatives to [the] recommended courses of action."

Protection of Human Health

In *Metropolitan Edison Co. v. People Against Nuclear Energy,*[1] the U.S. Supreme Court was asked to declare that one of the demands that NEPA places on federal agencies is to take human health into account in the preparation of an environmental impact statement.

Metropolitan Edison Company operated two licensed nuclear plants at Three Mile Island, near Harrisburg, Pennsylvania. When one of them, TMI-1 was shut down for refueling, the other, TMI-2, suffered a serious accident that damaged its nuclear reactor and caused widespread concern about the danger that the accident posed to human health. The Nuclear Regulatory Commission (NRC) held a hearing to consider whether to allow TMI-1 to resume operations. At the hearing the NRC refused to listen to evidence that restarting TMI-1 would cause severe damage to the psychological health of persons who lived near the plant.

The Supreme Court identified concern for human health, expressed in NEPA, as one of the *ends* that Congress sought to accomplish through the *means* it selected, that is, protecting the physical environment. The Court's distinction between ends (human health) and means (protection of the environment) led to its conclusion that NRC was obliged to listen to evidence regarding the effect that reopening TMI-1 would have on the physical environment but that it was not required to listen to evidence regarding the effect that reopening TMI-1 would have on the psychological health of persons who lived near it.

International Cooperation

NEPA directs that agencies "recognize the worldwide and long-range character of environmental problems and, where consistent with the foreign policy of the United States, lend appropriate support to initiatives, resolutions, and programs designed to maximize international cooperation in anticipating and preventing a decline in [the] quality of mankind's world environment."

Council on Environmental Quality

NEPA establishes a three-member Council on Environmental Quality within the Executive Office of the President. "Each member" is required to "be a person who, as a result of his training, experience, and attainments," is "exceptionally well qualified to analyze and interpret environmental trends; to appraise programs and activities of the Federal Government in the light of the [act's] policy [and] to be conscious of and responsive to the scientific, economic, social, esthetic, and cultural needs and interests of the Nation." Among the tasks assigned to the council are the following: "to formulate and recommend national policies to promote the improvement of the quality of the environment"; to "assist and advise the President" in the preparation of an annual presidential Environmental Quality Report; "to develop and recommend to the President national policies to foster and promote the improvement of environmental quality to meet the conservation, social, economic, health, and other requirements and goals of the Nation"; and "to report at least once each year to the President on the state and condition of the environment."

ENVIRONMENTAL PROTECTION AGENCY

In 1970, on the heels of NEPA's proclamation of a national environmental policy, the president exercised the authority given to him by Congress to restructure federal agencies as necessary to promote better execution of the laws and to increase the efficiency of government by establishing the Environmental Protection Agency (EPA). The president noted that without the new agency the national government was "not structured to make a coordinated attack on the pollutants which debase the air we breathe, the water we drink, and the land that grows our food."

As directed by the president, "the principal roles and functions of EPA include:

- The establishment and enforcement of environmental standards consistent with national environmental goals.
- The conduct of research on the adverse effects of pollution and on methods and equipment for controlling it, the gathering of information on pollution, and the use of this information in strengthening environmental protection programs and recommending policy changes.
- Assisting others, through grants, technical assistance, and other means, in arresting pollution of the environment.
- Assisting the Council on Environmental Quality in developing and recommending to the President new policies for the protection of the enviroment."

The relationship "between EPA and the Council on Environmental Quality" is described in the following terms. The "Council is a top-level advisory group (which might be compared with the Council of Economic Advisers), while EPA would be an operating, 'line' organization. The Council is concerned with all aspects of environmental quality—wildlife preservation, parklands, land use, and population growth, as well as pollution." The task of EPA is to "protect the environment by abating pollution. In short, the Council focuses on what our broad policies in the environmental field should be; EPA" is to "focus on setting and enforcing pollution control standards. The two are not competing, but complementary—and taken together, they should give us the means to mount an effectively coordinated campaign against environmental degradation in all of its many forms."

Figure 16-1 (page 480) shows EPA's present structure and the extensive breadth of its activities.

FEDERAL ENVIRONMENTAL STATUTES

The following are the popularly used names of the most significant federal environmental statutes, each of which indicates the aspect of the environment at which the statute is directed: Clean Air Act; Coastal Zone Management Act; Endangered Species Act; Federal Water Pollution Control Act; Federal Insecticide,

Fungicide, and Rodenticide Act; Noise Control Act; Nuclear Waste Disposal Act; Ocean Dumping Act; Resources Conservation and Recovery Act; Safe Drinking Water Act; Submerged Lands Act; Surface Mining and Reclamation Act; Toxic Substances Control Act; and Uranium Mill Tailings Radiation Control Act.

Although different environmental risks are covered by distinct federal environmental laws, most of these laws have the same general format. The laws each (*a*)

FIGURE 16–1   **Environmental Protection Agency**

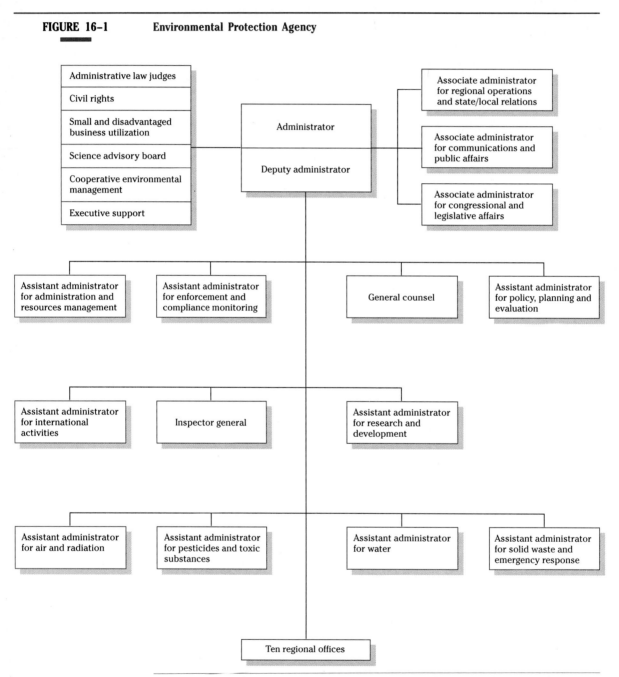

Source: Office of the Federal Register, National Archives and Records Administration, *The United States Government Manual, 1990/91* (Washington, D.C. U.S. Government Printing Office, July 1, 1990), p. 543.

establish a national policy; (*b*) assign particular tasks to a specified federal administrative agency, generally EPA, so that the policy established in the law can be put into effect; (*c*) authorize the agency to establish rules promoting the policy; (*d*) invest the agency with power to adjudicate disputes that arise under the law or under the agency's rules; (*e*) provide for judicial review of the agency's actions; (*f*) invite the states to take part in the established program; (*g*) make federal money available to fund one or more aspects of the program; (*h*) specify the sanctions that may be imposed on those who violate the law or one or more rules of the agency and (*i*) when the problem dealt with by the law is not confined to the United States, call for an exploration of the feasibility of working together with other nations to curtail or eliminate it. Some federal environmental laws also authorize private citizens to bring suit to enforce the law against those who violate it.

SECTOR-DIRECTED FEDERAL AGENCIES

In addition to EPA, the following are among the federal bodies in the network of federal environmental regulatory agencies.

Agency for Toxic Substances and Disease Registry

This agency's duties include carrying out the health-related responsibilities of the Comprehensive Environmental Response, Compensation, and Liability Act of 1980; the Resource Conservation and Recovery Act; provisions of the Solid Waste Disposal Act that relate to waste disposal sites and substances found at those sites; and legislation directed at the release of various toxic substances into the environment.

Department of the Interior

Environmental programs with which the Department of the Interior is involved include the development, conservation, and utilization of fish, wildlife, recreational areas, historic sites, and national parks.

Land and Natural Resources Division of the Department of Justice

This division represents the United States in litigation regarding such matters as public lands and natural resources, environmental quality, and wildlife resources. It is responsible for civil and criminal enforcement of environmental statutes. Among the laws for which it may bring suit to enforce legislative policy and standards are those that concern the control of toxic substances, risks posed by hazardous chemical wastes, and air and water pollution.

National Institute of Environmental Health Sciences

This institute conducts and supports fundamental research concerned with defining, measuring, and understanding the effects of chemical, biological, and physical factors in the environment on human health and well-being.

National Oceanic and Atmospheric Administration

Among the tasks assigned to this agency are the following: to explore and chart the global ocean and its living resources and to manage, use, and conserve those resources; to conduct an integrated program of management, research, and services related to the protection and rational use of living marine resources and their habitats; to carry on research and development aimed at providing alternatives to ocean dumping; and to develop sound national policy in the areas of ocean mining and energy.

U.S. Army Corps of Engineers

The Rivers and Harbors Act of 1899 makes it unlawful for anyone to discharge any sort of refuse, except for liquid materials that flow from streets or sewers, into any navigable waters of the United States or into any tributary of such waters. The secretary of the army may grant an applicant a permit to deposit refuse otherwise barred by the act when in the judgment of the chief of engineers of the U.S. Army Corps of Engineers the refuse will not injure anchorage or navigation; will satisfy the demands of NEPA and other federal legislation, such as the Federal Water Pollution Control Act; and will meet the standards established by the secretary of the army.

CLEAN AIR LEGISLATION

1955 and 1970 Acts

In 1955 Congress enacted the first of a series of statutes on air pollution. This statute states that "in recognition of the dangers to public health and welfare, injury to agricultural crops and livestock, damage to and deterioration of property, and hazards to air and ground transportation from air pollution, it is declared that it is the policy of Congress to preserve and protect the primary responsibilities and rights of the states and local governments in controlling air pollution, to support and aid technical research to devise and develop methods of abating such pollution, and to provide Federal technical services and financial aid to State and local government air pollution control agencies and other public or private agencies and institutions in the formulation and execution of their air pollution abatement research programs." In the Clean Air Act of 1970, Congress imposed an array of restrictions on the discharge of various pollutants into the air. From time to time, this act has been amended to further curb air pollution.

The 1970 Act charges EPA with the administration of a federal-state program to control air pollution. EPA is required to set limits—known as National Ambient Air Quality Standards (NAAQSs)—on atmospheric concentrations of various air pollutants that may endanger public health and welfare. There are two types of NAAQSs, primary and secondary. The primary NAAQSs are intended to allow an adequate margin of safety for the protection of public health; the secondary NAAQSs are intended to protect the public welfare from known or anticipated adverse effects associated with air pollutants. Under the 1970 Act, EPA sets standards for specified pollutants, including lead, sulfur dioxide, particulate matter, hydrocarbon compounds, carbon monoxide, and nitrogen dioxide and other nitrogen oxides that reduce the ozone in the stratosphere.

The 1970 Act requires every state to have an EPA-approved State Implementation Plan (SIP) to implement, maintain, and enforce the NAAQSs. A SIP must conform to the criteria set forth in the 1970 Act and must be likely to achieve and maintain the prescribed NAAQSs.

Citizen Suits Any person may commence a civil suit for injunctive relief against anyone, including the United States or a state, for a violation of a statutory standard, an EPA order, or a SIP, or may sue the EPA administrator if he or she fails to perform any nondiscretionary act or duty called for by the 1970 Act. Federal district courts have jurisdiction, regardless of the amount of money in controversy or the citizenship of the parties, to enforce emission standards or limitations or to order the EPA administrator to perform a mandatory act or duty.

A citizen suit may not be commenced if EPA or a state has brought a civil suit to require compliance and is diligently prosecuting that litigation. Prior to commencing a lawsuit, the complainant must give 60 days' notice of the violation to the EPA administrator, the state where the violation occurs, and the violator. Such notice allows government agencies to take responsibility for enforcing environmental regulations and gives an alleged violator an opportunity to take corrective action. If either is done, a citizen suit is unnecessary.

A citizen suit may not be brought to force a state to attain an NAAQS or to modify a SIP so that it conforms to an individual's notion of proper environmental policy. However, a citizen may sue a state for its failure to enforce a SIP standard or limitation. While courts are not empowered to directly enforce a SIP's overall goals or an NAAQS, they can enforce specific SIP provisions.

BUNKER RESOURCE RECYCLING AND RECLAMATION, INC. v. MEHAN
SUPREME COURT OF MISSOURI
782 S.W.2d 381 (1990)

In May 1987, before Bunker began to operate its incinerator for solid infectious waste material at its Missouri solid waste disposal facility, it obtained a clean air permit from the Missouri Department of Natural Resources (DNR). At that time state law did not require Bunker to have a permit to operate either the incinerator or the solid waste disposal facility. In July, 1987, however, the Missouri legislature enacted a law that barred the operation of a solid waste disposal facility without a DNR solid waste disposal facility permit. DNR promptly notified all infectious waste handlers, including Bunker, that until it adopted regulations to carry out the law, they could continue to operate their solid waste disposal facilities under their clean air permits. The chief of DNR's solid waste section instructed the DNR officer for the region in which Bunker's facility was located that so long as Bunker complied with its clean air permit, it could continue to operate its facility until the regulations were adopted.

A citizens group brought suit against Bunker in which it charged that Bunker was operating its facility in violation of Missouri law and asked the court to permanently enjoin it from continuing to do so. The court granted the injunction because Bunker did not have a DNR solid waste disposal facility permit. The judgment was affirmed on appeal.

In September 1987 Bunker brought a suit in which it asked the court to direct DNR to issue the firm a solid waste disposal facility permit. In May 1988, while Bunker's suit was pending, the Missouri legislature enacted a statute that barred DNR from issuing such a permit to any recipient of a clean air permit in 1987 that had thereafter operated an incinerator to burn infectious waste without applying for and obtaining a DNR solid waste disposal facility permit. Only Bunker could be denied a permit under this statute. DNR asked the court to rule that the statute made Bunker ineligible to receive a solid waste disposal facility permit.

The trial court held that the 1988 statute was a legitimate exercise of the state's power to regulate the handling and disposal of solid infectious waste and entered a judgment in favor of DNR. Bunker appealed.

HOLSTEIN, JUDGE

[T]he Missouri Constitution provides:

> The [state legislature] shall not pass any special law where a general law can be made applicable.

A statute is invalid as a "special law" if members of a stated class are omitted from the statute's coverage whose relationship to the subject matter cannot by reason be distinguished from that of those included. Worded differently, "[a] law may not include less than all who are similarly situated."

[T]he [1988] statute imposes its sanction only against those who received clean air permits in 1987. Others similarly situated, that is, who performed the identical acts as [Bunker] but who either never held a clean air permit or received a clean air permit in a year other than 1987, are excluded from the statutory classification. An entity like Bunker in all respects, but for its failure to receive a clean air permit in 1987, has no special characteristics justifying its exclusion from the statutory class. No reasonable basis exists for the differential treatment of one who disposed of infectious waste by incineration in 1987. [The 1988 Act] is a prohibited special law under the Missouri Constitution. However, there is an equally compelling reason for declaring the statute unconstitutional.

Art. I, Sec. 10 of the U.S. Constitution prohibits any state from passing a bill of attainder. [This Court has] defined bills of attainder as "legislative acts, no matter what their form, that apply either to named individuals or to easily ascertainable members of a group in such a way as to inflict punishment on them without a judicial trial."

The best available evidence, [regarding] the writings of the architects of our constitutional system, indicates that the Bill of Attainder Clause was intended, not as a narrow, technical (and therefore soon to be outmoded) prohibition, but rather as an implementation of the separation of powers, a general safeguard against legislative exercise of the judicial function, or more simply—trial by legislature.

Two elements identify a legislative act as a bill of attainder. The first is that the statute singles out a "specifically designated person or group," and the second element is that the act inflicts punishment on that person or group.

In the statute under consideration, Bunker is not referred to by name. However, it is difficult, if not impossible, to describe [the firm] with more specificity short of uttering the corporate title. The statute applies only to those persons or entities who (1) received a clean air permit in 1987, (2) thereafter operated a facility for the treatment of infectious waste, (3) used incineration as the method for the treatment of infectious waste, and (4) did not apply for and receive a solid waste permit pursuant to [the state 1987 legislation]. Given the nature of the multiple conditions essential to membership in the class, the only rational conclusion is that the legislature intended the statute to affect Bunker alone.

[L]egislation directed at and burdensome to only a single individual or group does not by itself violate the Bill of Attainder Clause if there is a rational, nonpunitive basis for the legislation. The question becomes whether the legislation imposes a constitutionally forbidden punishment.

[A] statute [unavoidably] barring Bunker from engaging in a lawful enterprise is punishment.

Generally, legislation intended to prevent further danger, rather than to punish past action, is not an unconstitutional bill of attainder. However, if the function of the statute does not advance the intended purpose and the statute operates only as a punishment of specific persons or a class, the act is a bill of attainder.

[T]he statutory class of which Bunker is the sole member is not reasonably related to any proper legislative purpose and serves only to punish [Bunker].

In holding [the statute] unconstitutional, we do not say that the legislature cannot weed out those who through persistent or intentional violation of the environmental laws have demonstrated some degree of moral or legal culpability which would make them unfit or unworthy to operate infectious waste disposal facilities. If the [state legislature] chooses to accomplish that purpose, it must do so by rules of general applicability and cannot specify the people upon whom its sanction is to be levied.

The judgment of the [trial court] is reversed and the cause remanded with directions to [order] DNR to perform those acts required upon the filing of the application for a solid waste processing permit as provided [in the 1987 statute] and to enter judgment against DNR.

Legal Issues

1. A state statute established a commission that was charged with the task of identifying specific homes and buildings as historic sites. The commission then had to follow a set procedure to designate a structure as a historic site. A property owner had to be notified of the commission's planned action and given an opportunity to present evidence showing that the structure should not be designated as a historic site. Once a site was so designated, the designation could not be altered without the commission's approval. Is the statute a bill of attainder? Why?

2. A state statute declared a species of wildlife an endangered species and banned the killing of this species and the sale of its skins. Lauretta Lee, one of but two persons in the United States who dealt in the skins of this species, had done so for more than 25 years. The day before the statute took effect, she sold the remainder of her skin inventory and closed her shop. She then brought a lawsuit against the state in which she requested compensation for having been forced out of business. What judgment? Why?

Ethical Issues

1. When, if ever, would it be ethical for an administrative agency, without

first holding a quasi-judicial trial, to bar a party from continuing to carry on a business activity that is believed to be causing environmental damage in violation of law? Discuss.

2. What concerns should a code of ethics require an official of an environmental protection agency to take into account before granting an applicant an exemption from a general statutory ban on the discharge of toxic substances into the air? Discuss.

1990 Act

Thirty-five years after the passage of the first federal law on air pollution, in response to the public's concern over the state of the environment and its demands to further improve air quality, Congress passed the 1990 Clean Air Act, which made sweeping changes in existing federal clean air law.

Further Curtailment of Pollutants   The 1990 Act requires a 90 percent reduction by the year 2003 of 189 toxic and cancer-causing chemical compounds that are discharged into the air. Many of the act's antipollution standards are to be phased in over a 15-year period. Among the more demanding restrictions that the act imposes are strict limits on the emission of industrial pollutants, such as sulfur dioxide and nitrogen oxides, which cause acid rain; cessation by the year 2000 of the use of chlorofluorocarbons and most of the other pollutants that threaten the ozone layer; a reduction in the release of toxic and cancer-causing chemicals by manufacturers and utilities; a lowering of the amount of nitrogen oxides and hydrocarbons emitted from most cars in the 1994 model year and from all other cars in the 1995 model year; and the production of cleaner-burning types of gasoline that by 1995 would be the only types sold in the country's nine smoggiest cities.

The 1990 Act will affect both large and small businesses. To satisfy its demands, utility power plants will have to burn low-sulfur coal or use costly scrubbers to remove banned pollutants caused by burning high-sulfur coal. Although coke ovens emit cancer-causing pollutants, the steel industry may continue to use them until the year 2020, so long as it takes action to reduce such emissions. Such small businesses as neighborhood bakers, auto-repair shops, and dry cleaners will have to purchase equipment that reduces their discharge of toxic air pollutants.

Permit Program   The 1990 Act requires that a permit program be in place by 1994. A firm that discharges certain pollutants into the air must obtain a permit to do so. The permit must specify the maximum amount of pollutants that the firm may discharge. So long as the firm satisfies the terms of the permit, it has a defense to the charge that it has violated the act.

Citizen Suits   Under the 1990 Act, courts may award civil penalties in citizen suits brought against violators of the 1990 Act. Citizen suits may also be brought to challenge the propriety of issuing a permit or the legality of a permit's provisions.

EPA Imposition of Administrative Penalties   The 1990 Act authorizes EPA to impose penalties of $25,000 a day, up to $200,000, for various violations of the act.

FEDERAL WATER POLLUTION CONTROL ACT

In 1948 Congress passed the Water Pollution Control Act, a significant step toward extensive federal involvement in the control and abatement of water pollution. The act states that it is "the policy of Congress to recognize, preserve, and protect the primary responsibilities and rights of the States in controlling water pollution; to support and aid technical research to devise and perfect methods of treatment of industrial wastes which are not susceptible to known effective methods of treatment; and to provide Federal technical services to State and interstate agencies and to industries, and financial aid to State and interstate agencies and to municipalities, in the formulation and execution of their stream pollution abatement programs." Numerous amendments to the 1948 Act, which is now commonly referred to as the Federal Water Pollution Control Act, have expanded its scope considerably and have also expanded the role of state and local governments in containing water pollution.

The Federal Water Pollution Control Act is now administered by the administrator of EPA, who is charged with the preparation and development "of comprehensive programs for preventing, reducing, or eliminating the pollution of the navigable waters and groundwaters and improving the sanitary conditions of surface and underground waters." Such programs must take into account what is "necessary to conserve" water "for the protection and propagation of fish and aquatic life and wildlife, recreational purposes, and the withdrawal of" water "for public water supply, agricultural, industrial, and other purposes."

The act makes it unlawful to discharge any pollutant into surface waters or groundwaters except as authorized by the act or EPA regulations. EPA sets the standards that must be met for the pretreatment and discharge of effluents into these waters. To be effective, state water standards must satisfy the requirements of the act and be approved by EPA.

Permits for Discharge of Pollutants

Within the limits set by the Federal Water Pollution Control Act, EPA may issue National Pollution Discharge Elimination System (NPDES) permits that allow the discharge of pollutants into navigable waters in accordance with specified conditions. Illustrative of the joint federal and state involvement in the control of water pollution is the fact that when a state establishes a program that conforms to federal guidelines and is approved by EPA, the state, rather than EPA, issues permits for discharges into the navigable waters within its jurisdiction.

Citizen Suits

The Federal Water Pollution Control Act empowers any citizen to bring a civil action to enforce it. This empowerment includes the right to bring suit against NPDES holders. Such a suit is aside from any action that federal or state agencies may take on the same issues.

Penalties Imposed on NPDES Permit Holders

The Federal Water Pollution Control Act authorizes the imposition of a civil penalty on an NPDES permit holder of not more than $25,000 a day for each statutory or permit violation. This means that a $25,000 penalty can be imposed for each unlawful discharge of effluent (waste material) during a single day. For example, if there are four unlawful discharges during a single day, the maximum penalty is $100,000. A polluter guilty of a single violation on each of 30 days may be fined $750,000.

WASTE DISPOSAL LEGISLATION

Congress has been extensively involved with waste disposal legislation for more than a quarter of a century. Because of the ever-increasing quantity of waste that is generated and because of the difficulty of coping with the threats that waste materials, especially hazardous wastes, pose to the environment, this sphere of environmental regulation has attracted and continues to attract intensive examination and action by government officials.

Solid Waste Disposal Act

In 1965 Congress passed the Solid Waste Disposal Act. This act directed that the Bureau of Solid Waste Management provide technical and financial assistance to state and local governments in planning and developing resource recovery and solid waste disposal programs.

Resources Recovery Act

The Resources Recovery Act of 1970 amended the 1965 act so as to include as part of the national solid waste disposal program the promulgation of guidelines for solid waste collection, transport, recovery, and disposal systems and the promotion, demonstration, construction, and application of solid waste management and resource recovery systems that preserve and enhance the quality of air, water, and land resources.

Resources Conservation and Recovery Act

In 1976 Congress passed the Resources Conservation and Recovery Act (RCRA). This act was designed to deal with the general problems posed by the disposal of wastes and with the particular problems associated with the disposal of hazardous waste. A key objective of the act is to preserve and enhance the quality of air, water, and land resources. To attain this objective, as well as other objectives, Congress included in the act provisions that (1) establish an Office of Solid Waste within EPA; (2) detail a federal procedure, to be used in the absence of a state program, for regulating hazardous waste from its inception to its elimination; (3) encourage the states to establish solid waste control plans that include provisions for closing hazardous waste disposal dumps; and (4) expand the federal government's role in the development of means for dealing with solid waste.

RCRA requires EPA to set minimum federal standards for those who generate, transport, treat, store, or dispose of hazardous waste. For the purposes of the act, "hazardous waste" means nonradioactive hazardous waste, but it includes solid wastes "which because of their quantity, concentration, or physical, chemical, or infectious characteristics may—(1) cause, or significantly contribute to, an increase in mortality, or an increase in serious irreversible or incapacitating reversible illness; or (2) pose a substantial present or potential hazard to human health or the environment when improperly treated, stored, transported, or disposed of, or otherwise managed."

RCRA offers financial aid and technical assistance to state solid waste management programs. States are ineligible for such assistance if they do not develop or implement solid waste management plans for their municipal waste that meet the act's criteria. If a state assumes responsibility for solid waste disposal within its boundaries, its minimum standards must not be less demanding than those imposed under the act. However, if a state chooses to do so, it may set requirements more rigorous than those set by the federal government.

Toxic Substances Control Act

In 1976 Congress enacted the Toxic Substances Control Act. This act was designed to protect the public and the environment from exposure to hazardous chemicals.

Comprehensive Environmental Response, Compensation, and Liability Act

The Comprehensive Environmental Response, Compensation, and Liability Act (CERCLA) was passed in 1980 as part of an effort to eliminate unsafe hazardous waste sites. CERCLA authorizes EPA to arrange the cleanup of leaking hazardous waste sites or to effect a cleanup if there is a threat of leakage at such sites.

Superfund Amendments and Reauthorization Act of 1986   CERCLA was amended by the Superfund Amendments and Reauthorization Act of 1986 (SARA). SARA established a Hazardous Substance Superfund for the cleanup of hazardous waste sites that are leaking or that threaten to leak. The Superfund is financed by appropriations, industry taxes, and judgments received through legal actions to recover response costs from those responsible for the leakage of hazardous wastes or the threat of their leakage.

The two primary purposes for which Superfund money may be spent are (1) to finance governmental responses and (2) to pay claims. A governmental response may be either short-term cleanup and remedial action or the achievement of a permanent solution to a particular waste problem. Claims are demands for reimbursement from the Superfund. There are two types of claims. One type is a demand by private persons for the costs they incur under the national contingency plan in cleaning up hazardous wastes for which they are not responsible.[2] The Superfund may reimburse such individuals only to the extent that the federal government expressly authorizes their cleanup activities. The other type is a demand by the federal government or a state government for compensation for damages to natural resources belonging to it. Superfund money may not be used to pay for injuries to persons or property caused by hazardous wastes.

CERCLA Liability for the Costs of Cleaning Up Hazardous Substances CERCLA imposes ultimate responsibility for the costs incurred in cleaning up hazardous substances as they are defined in the act on the following classes of persons: (1) the owners and operators of vessels or facilities where hazardous substances are found, such as buildings, pipelines, motor vehicles, and sites for the deposit, storage, or disposal of such substances; (2) any person who at the time of disposal of hazardous substances owned or operated a facility at which those substances were disposed of; (3) any person who by contract, agreement, or otherwise arranged for disposal or treatment, or arranged with a transporter for transport for disposal or treatment, of hazardous substances owned or possessed by that person, by any other party or entity, at any facility or incineration vessel owned or operated by another party or entity and containing those hazardous substances; and (4) any person who accepts or accepted any hazardous substances for transport to disposal or treatment facilities, incineration vessels, or sites selected by that person, from which there is a release, or a threatened release, of a hazardous substance that causes the incurrence of response costs.

These four classes of persons are liable for (1) all costs incurred by the United States, a state, or an Indian tribe that are not inconsistent with the national contingency plan provided for by CERCLA; (2) any other necessary costs of response consistent with the national contingency plan incurred by any other person; (3) damages for injury to, destruction of, or loss of natural resources, including the reasonable costs of assessing such injury, destruction, or loss; and (4) the costs of any health assessment or health effects study carried out under the provisions of CERCLA.

A person who would otherwise be liable for cleanup costs is excused from such liability only if by a preponderance of the evidence it is shown that the release of a hazardous substance and the damages that resulted were caused solely by (1) an act of God; (2) an act of war; (3) an act or omission of a third party other than an employee or agent of the defendant, or than one whose act or omission occurred in connection with a contractual relationship, existing directly or indirectly, with the defendant, if by a preponderance of the evidence the defendant establishes that he or she (*a*) exercised due care with respect to the hazardous substance concerned, taking into consideration the characteristics of that hazardous substance, in light of all the relevant facts and circumstances, and (*b*) took precautions against foreseeable acts or omissions of any such third party and the consequences that could foreseeably result from such acts or omissions; or (4) any combination of the events set forth in (1), (2), and (3).

State Involvement with Cleanup Programs under CERCLA Each state is obliged to submit to the president its priorities for remedial action among known releases and potential releases in that state based on the criteria contained in CERCLA. The president is charged with promulgating regulations that provide for each state's substantial involvement in the initiation, development, and selection of remedial actions that are to be undertaken in that state.

CERCLA allows the federal government to negotiate cooperative cleanup agreements with site owners. These owners in turn may recover cleanup costs from the responsible parties. The act authorizes the president to enter into cleanup agreements with those states that meet SARA's requirements regarding state hazardous waste disposal programs.

EPA Action under CERCLA   CERCLA authorizes EPA to identify hazardous wastes, to promulgate standards for transporters of hazardous wastes and operators of hazardous waste disposal facilities, and to issue permits for the operation of hazardous waste disposal facilities. In addition, EPA may bring suit if the past or present handling, storage, treatment, transportation, or disposal of any solid waste or hazardous waste may present a substantial imminent endangerment to health or the environment. Suit may be brought against any person who has contributed or is contributing to such handling, storage, treatment, transportation, or disposal to restrain that person or to order that person to take whatever other action may be necessary, or to secure both forms of relief.

Hazardous Waste and Solid Waste Amendments to CERCLA   The Hazardous and Solid Waste Amendments to CERCLA, enacted in 1984, introduced a comprehensive program to regulate the land disposal of hazardous wastes. The statute is intended to ensure that land disposal for such wastes is used only if it can be reasonably anticipated that this procedure will protect human health and the environment in the very long term, even if there are no alternatives. The statute authorizes EPA to prohibit land disposal of specified hazardous wastes because Congress believes that land disposal is the least desirable way to manage the disposal of those wastes. In May 1985 a nationwide ban was placed on burying liquids in hazardous waste landfills.

NATIONAL SOLID WASTES MANAGEMENT ASSOCIATION v. ALABAMA DEPARTMENT OF ENVIRONMENTAL MANAGEMENT

U.S. DISTRICT COURT, NORTHERN DISTRICT OF ALABAMA
729 F. Supp. 792 (1990)

In 1973 EPA listed Alabama's Sumter County as a good place for hazardous waste disposal because it sits on a thick layer of chalk. Several years later Chemical Waste Management, Inc., one of the plaintiffs, opened its Emelle site for the burial of hazardous waste in Sumter County. Between 1978 and 1989, the amount of waste shipped annually to the Emelle site increased tremendously, from 200 million pounds to an estimated 1.6 billion pounds.

In 1989 the Alabama state legislature, in response to increased use of the Emelle site, enacted the so-called Holley Bill. Among the bill's stated purposes is the prohibition in Alabama of commercial hazardous waste treatment or disposal facilities that accept hazardous wastes generated in a state that refuses to comply with the CERCLA requirement that each state adequately treat and dispose of all hazardous wastes reasonably expected to be generated within it over the next 20 years by establishing a hazardous waste treatment or disposal facility within the state or by using a hazardous waste treatment or disposal facility outside the state in accordance with an interstate agreement or a regional agreement or authority. The bill makes it unlawful for a commercial hazardous waste treatment or disposal facility within Alabama to dispose of or treat any hazardous wastes generated in such a state.

The plaintiffs, Chemical Waste Management, Inc. and an association of solid waste disposal operators, brought suit. They challenged the constitutionality of the Holley Bill on the grounds that it violated the Constitution's Commerce Clause and that it was preempted by the Resource Conservation and Recovery Act and CERCLA.

GUNN, DISTRICT JUDGE

During the last four decades the United States has had to reevaluate its attitude toward conservation of its natural resources and protection of the environment. As public awareness has increased, numerous laws to protect the health and welfare of the people and to protect the environment have been enacted. [Between 1950 and 1990, Congress enacted the Solid Waste Disposal Act of 1965; the Resource Recovery Act of 1970; the Resource Conservation and Recovery Act of 1976; the Toxic Substances Control Act of 1976; the Comprehensive Environmental Response, Compensation, and Liability Act of 1980; the Hazardous and Solid Waste Amendments of 1984; and the Superfund Amendments and Reauthorization Act of 1986.]

While [a section of an early] *draft* [emphasis added] of [the Resource Conservation and Recovery Act of 1976 (RCRA)] was entitled "Preemption of State Law," when the legislation was *enacted* (italics supplied [by court]), the section was entitled "Retention of State Authority," indicating it was not the intention of Congress for RCRA to preempt [that is, bar] state laws [on the subject of the disposal of hazardous waste]. The most clear-cut reference to preemption in the House report is the following statement: "At this time federal preemption is undesirable, inefficient, and damaging to local initiative." Nor was federal preemption championed by EPA.

Pertinent to the case at bar is [that section of CERCLA] which reads as follows:

[T]he President shall not provide any remedial actions [permitted by the statute, such as authorizing the removal of a hazardous substance, pollutant, or contaminant] unless the State in which the release occurs first enters into a contract or cooperative agreement with the President providing assurances deemed adequate by the President that the State will assure the availability of hazardous waste treatment or disposal facilities which [satisfy CERLA].

Plaintiffs contend the Holley Bill is violative of the Constitution because it places restrictions on waste moving in interstate commerce. In order to withstand this attack, the state statute must require a legitimate local public interest in the regulation.

[W]here the statute regulates evenhandedly to effectuate a legitimate local public interest, and its effects on interstate commerce are only incidental, it will be upheld unless the burden imposed on such commerce is clearly excessive in relation to the putative local benefits. If a legitimate local purpose is found, then the question becomes one of degree. And the extent of the burden that will be tolerated will of course depend on the nature of the local interest involved, and on whether it could be promoted as well with a lesser impact on interstate activities.

Not only must the court scrutinize the Holley Bill for commerce clause violations, it must determine whether the federal law has preempted the field.

Under the [Constitution's] Supremacy Clause, the enforcement of a state regulation may be preempted by federal law in several circumstances: first, when Congress, in enacting a federal statute, has expressed a clear intent to preempt state law; second, when it is clear, despite the absence of explicit preemptive language, that Congress had intended, by legislating comprehensively, to occupy an entire field of regulation and has thereby "left no room for the States to supplement" federal law; and, finally, when compliance with both state and federal law is impossible, or when the state law "stands as an obstacle to the accomplishment and execution of the full purposes and objectives of Congress."

Having scrutinized the Alabama statute, the court is of the opinion that the law is directed toward a legitimate state concern: an effort to comply with the 20-year CERCLA capacity assurance directive and, more importantly, to assure that all hazardous waste buried in Alabama is treated and disposed of in the most environmentally protective manner, as is the hazardous waste generated in-state. It is not an effort to isolate Alabama from the national economy. Alabama's statute does not close its borders to all out-of-state waste, only to out-of-state waste from states that are not in compliance with federal law. As soon as they are in compliance, the borders will be opened to them.

Nor is the court of the opinion that the Holley Bill imposes "a significant burden on out-of-state economic interests." The Court holds there is not significant discrimination against out-of-state economic interests sufficient to warrant striking the Holley Bill as unconstitutional.

Alabama's act does not prohibit importation of all solid waste. It does not have the effect of closing its borders to all out-of-state waste. The ban is directed toward protection of the health and welfare of the people and preservation of the environment while encouraging compliance with federal legislation. Its aim is to prevent Alabama from becoming the dumping ground for those states that refuse to "clean up their act." Its impact on interstate commerce is incidental and not excessive in relation to local benefits.

Alabama has not closed its borders to all waste from other states, but has only limited its available landfills to those states that are cooperating in an effort to control the environment and protect the health and safety of citizens of all states pursuant to Congress's plan.

For the above-stated reasons the court holds that the Holley Bill does not violate the Commerce Clause of the Constitution.

Nor does the Holley Bill violate the Supremacy Clause of the Constitution. None of the environmental legislation enacted expresses a clear intent to preempt state law. Case law and legislative history indicate there was no such intent. Absent any intention to preempt the field, and there is no conflict between the Alabama statute and federal legislation which would make compliance with both a physical impossibility, the court holds that the Alabama statute does not violate the supremacy clause of the Constitution.

For the reasons set forth in this opinion, the court grants summary judgment in favor of the defendants.

Legal Issues

1. A state statute barred the importation of solid waste for disposal at privately operated dump sites located in the state. Under this statute, similar solid waste that originated *in* the state could be disposed of at these dump sites. The constitutionality of the statute was challenged on these grounds: (1) neither the legislative history of the statute nor the statute itself offered any reason why out-of-state waste should be treated differently from waste that originated in the state; and (2) the statute accorded the state's residents preferential access to dump

sites in the state. What judgment? Why?

2. A committee of the state legislature found that a severe shortage of cement made it impossible for the state to deal effectively with a number of environmental problems. Shortly thereafter the state legislature enacted a law under which all of the cement produced in the state could be sold only to state residents when state environmental needs could not be satisfied because of a cement shortage. An out-of-state firm that was barred from purchasing cement under the terms of the statute challenged the constitutionality of the statute on the ground that it discriminated against interstate commerce. What judgment? Why?

Ethical Issues

1. Which view or views of ethics would you include in a statement supporting the contention that it was ethical for the Alabama legislature to enact the Holley Bill? Discuss.

2. When, if ever, would it be ethical for a state to use general state personal and business income tax money to store in overseas dump sites hazardous wastes resulting from in-state business activities? Why? Would your answer differ if the storage were funded by a tax imposed on the enterprises that generated the hazardous wastes? Why?

EMINENT DOMAIN AND ENVIRONMENTAL REGULATION

Eminent Domain and Police Power Distinguished

As noted in Chapter 10, the Fifth Amendment to the U.S. Constitution recognizes that the federal government has the power of *eminent domain*. This power allows it to *take* private property for *public use*, but it must *justly compensate* those whom it deprives of their property. The 14th Amendment obliges state and local governments to likewise compensate those from whom they *take* property by exercising their powers of *eminent domain*.

Eminent domain is a means for attaining socially desirable ends. Under the Constitution, the legislature judges what constitutes a public use and a court's power to review such a judgment is extremely narrow. A court must respect the legislature's judgment unless it is shown that what is to be done cannot possibly be viewed as a public purpose.

Chapter 10 also examined the government's *police power*. There we saw that the guarantees of just compensation in the 5th and 14th amendments do not assure persons complete freedom from government restraints on what they do with their property. The police power allows government to *regulate* how persons use their property if regulation is necessary to *protect the health, safety, morals, or well-being of society*. When government exercises its police power to achieve any of these purposes, neither the 5th Amendment nor the 14th Amendment requires that the affected property owners be compensated for injuries that result from what government has done. Although every regulation necessarily involves a prohibition, for constitutional purposes not every prohibition is treated as an exercise of eminent domain. For example, there is *no* taking when the government acts to eliminate a public nuisance or a serious threat to public health. Such action is treated as an exercise of the *police power.*

When Regulation Is a Taking

Whether an environmental regulation that bars property owners from using their property in a particular way entitles them to just compensation depends on whether such governmental interference is classified as an exercise of the police power or as equivalent to a taking. There is no clear-cut formula for distinguishing between a regulation that is merely an exercise of the police power and a regulation that is to be treated as a taking. Whether a regulation calls for compensation is determined by the particular circumstances of each case.

Governmental action that amounts to a physical invasion of a person's property is easily classified as a taking. For example, building an entrance road to a highway on someone's land is clearly a taking and calls for just compensation. On the other hand, there is no taking when a zoning regulation bars a property owner from converting a residential building into a commercial structure and thereby earning more profit.

NOLLAN v. CALIFORNIA COASTAL COMMISSION
SUPREME COURT OF THE UNITED STATES
483 U.S. 825 (1987)

The Nollans bought a small bungalow located on a beachfront lot. In order to replace the bungalow with a three-bedroom home, they were required to obtain a redevelopment permit from the California Coastal Commission.

There was a public beach 1,800 feet south of the lot and an oceanside public park with a public beach and recreation area a quarter of a mile north of the lot. A concrete seawall approximately 8 feet high separated the beach portion of the Nollan property from the rest of their lot.

The commission found that the new house would increase blockage of the ocean view, contributing to "a 'wall' of residential structures" that would prevent the public "psychologically from realizing a stretch of coastline exists nearby that they have a right to visit." It said that construction of the house, along with other development in the area, would cumulatively "burden the public's ability to traverse to and along the shorefront." It informed the Nollans that it would issue them a permit only if they granted the public a permanent easement (permission to pass across a portion of their property).

The Nollans brought suit, challenging the commission's decision. They charged that in conditioning the issuance of a permit on the grant of a public easement, the state was taking property without making just compensation, and thus in violation of the 14th Amendment. A judgment was entered in their favor. The appellate court reversed. The Nollans appealed.

JUSTICE SCALIA
Delivered the Opinion of the Court

Had California simply required the Nollans to make an easement across their beachfront available to the public on a permanent basis in order to increase public access to the beach, rather than conditioning their permit to rebuild their house on their agreement to do so, we have no doubt there would have been a taking. To say that the appropriation of a public easement across a landowner's premises does not constitute the taking of a property interest but rather (as Justice Brennan [in his dissenting opinion] contends) "a mere restriction on its use," is to use words in a manner that deprives them of all their ordinary meaning. We have repeatedly held that, as to property reserved by its owner for private use, "the right to exclude [others is] 'one of the most essential sticks in the bundle of rights that are commonly characterized as property.'"

"[O]ur cases uniformly have found a taking to the extent of [a permanent physical] occupation, without regard to whether the action achieves an important public benefit or has only minimal economic impact on the owner." We think a "permanent occupation" has occurred, for purposes of that rule, where individuals are given a permanent and continuous right to pass to and fro, so that the real property may continuously be traversed, even though no particular individual is permitted to station himself permanently upon the premises.

We have long recognized that land-use regulation does not effect a taking if it "substantially advance[s] legitimate state interests" and does not "den[y] an owner economically viable use of his land." ("[A] use restriction may constitute a 'taking' if not reasonably necessary to the effectuation of a substantial governmental purpose.")

The Commission argues that among these permissible purposes are protecting the public's ability to see the beach, assisting the public in overcoming the "psychological barrier" to using the beach created by a developed shorefront, and preventing congestion on the public beaches.

[I]f the Commission attached to the permit some condition that would have protected the public's ability to see the beach notwithstanding construction of the new house—for example, a height limitation, a width restriction, or a ban on fences—so long as the Commission could have exercised its police power (as we assumed it could) to forbid construction of the house altogether, imposition of the condition would also be constitutional.

[Here, the purpose is] quite simply [to obtain] an easement to serve some valid government purpose, but without payment of compensation. Whatever may be the outer limits of "legitimate state interests" in the taking and land-use context, this is not one of them.

It is quite impossible to understand how a requirement that people already on the public beaches be able to walk across Nollans' property reduces any obstacles to viewing the beach created by the new house. It is also impossible to understand how it lowers any "psychological barrier" to using the public beaches, or how it helps to remedy any additional congestion on them caused by construction of the Nollans' new house. We therefore find that the Commission's imposition of the permit condition cannot be treated as an exercise of its land-use power.

[The Commission also seeks to justify the condition on the ground that the] access required as a condition of this permit is part of a comprehensive program to provide continuous public access along [the beach] as the lots undergo development or redevelopment.

That is simply an expression of the Commission's belief that the public interest will be served by a continuous strip of publicly accessible beach along the coast. The Commission may well be right that it is a good idea, but that does not establish that the Nollans (and other coastal residents) alone can be compelled to contribute to its realization. Rather, California is free to [attain its stated objective] by using its power of eminent domain for this "public purpose," but if it wants an easement across the Nollans' property, it must pay for it.

Reversed.

Legal Issues

1. In a dissenting opinion in *Nollan v. California Coastal Commission,* Justice Brennan objected to the majority's conclusion that the commission acted irrationally in seeking to preserve *lateral* access to the coastline when the Nollans' development blocked *visual* access. He insisted that the commission was in a better position than the Court to solve the perplexing problem of how to assure public access. He favored affirming the commission's action because it was not clearly arbitrary and unreasonable. Do you agree with Justice Brennan? Why?

2. Justice Blackmun, who also delivered a dissenting opinion in the *Nollan* case, observed: "The land-use problems this country faces require creative solutions. These are not advanced by an 'eye for an eye' mentality. The close nexus between benefits and burdens that the Court now imposes on permit conditions creates an anomaly in the ordinary requirement that a State's exercise of its police power need be no more than rationally based. In my view, the easement exacted [from the Nollans] and the problems their development created are adequately related to the governmental interest in providing public access to the beach." Do you agree with Justice Blackmun's point of view? Why?

Ethical Issues

1. Is the position taken by the majority in *Nollan* consistent with utilitarian ethics? Why? Is it consistent with ethical egoism? Why?

2. Are the statements of Justices Brennan and Blackmun consistent with the ethical concepts of fairness? Discuss.

BALANCING THE PRESERVATION OF AN ENDANGERED SPECIES AGAINST THE LOSS OF JOBS AND BUSINESS OPPORTUNITIES

Hypothetical Case

Exercising the power granted by the Endangered Species Act, the U.S. Fish and Wildlife Service classified the northern spotted owl, native to the western part of the United States, as an endangered species and proposed adoption of a plan to prevent its disappearance. The plan called for the barring of logging operations on 3 million acres of federally owned forestlands. The 25 eminent biologists who prepared the plan insisted that unless it were approved, the northern spotted owl would soon disappear. Under the plan, the annual harvest of trees in the affected areas would be reduced by about 40 percent, several lumber mills would close, about 30,000 jobs would be eliminated, and hundreds of millions of dollars in taxes, profits, salaries, and wages would be lost.

Avid environmentalists heartily approved the plan not only because it would preserve the northern spotted owl but also because it would spare forests from destruction. A number of timber firms opposed the plan, insisting that more than enough owls of other species could be found elsewhere in the nation, that the plan barred logging in areas without northern spotted owls, that vast forestlands were already closed to logging, and that timber firms were reforesting to replace harvested trees. WITA (Wait, Investigate, and Then Act), a group of concerned citizens, recommended that a panel of officials from federal and state agencies and representatives of environmentalist groups explore alternative courses of action, including the permission of logging in areas inhabited by the northern spotted owl when this would be in the best interests of the state economy or local economies. Which point of view do you favor? Why?

ETHICS AND THE ENVIRONMENT

Congress, state legislatures, and local governments across the nation have enacted a broad spectrum of environmental statutes, but law alone is incapable of effectively dealing with environmental problems. Unless environmental concerns are integrated into individual and business ethics, a time may come when Earth is no longer a fit home for humankind.

Irresponsible personal behavior can result in enormous damage to the environment. The likely consequences of an individual's indifference to the disposal of unused materials after completing the repair and maintenance of his or her automobile is illustrative. Such hazardous materials as paint, drained coolant, contaminated gasoline, replaced oil, brake and transmission fluids, and the acid in a spent battery will probably be left over. If not thoughtfully disposed of, these materials are likely to find their way into surface water or groundwater. Persons who are determined to do the right thing will take the action necessary to avoid such havoc to the environment.

Indifferent business conduct can cause inestimable damage to the environment. Ethical concerns require firms to integrate environmental considerations into their everyday decision-making processes. Executives must be aware of the environmental damage that results from inattentive behavior and must aggressively seek environment-neutral or, better yet, environment-enhancing means for doing the firm's work.

Ideally, a company's commitment to environmental protection would not be based on the belief that its actions are ethical if it behaves lawfully. If businesses apply this view of ethics to their environment-related conduct, an ever-increasing amount of lawmaking and costly enforcement programs will be needed to protect the environment from avoidable business-caused damage. A "do only what the law requires" standard of company behavior is certain to cause a company to do far less than it should do to protect and improve the environment. A company that adopts this standard may also uphold as ethical forceful efforts by the company to block the enactment of environmental legislation that would dictate changes in the way it does business and thus increase its operational costs and reduce its profits.

A firm's code of ethical conduct should insist that research and development programs include the study of the possible environmental damage that new products are likely to cause. It should recognize that protecting the environment will at times require forgoing profits. A firm that acknowledges its ethical obligation to sell only environmentally safe products may properly seek to persuade potential customers to deal with it even if those products cost more than substitutes that are injurious to the environment.

INTERNATIONAL COOPERATION

Certain types of environmental damage can be prevented by the independent action of a single nation. For instance, the United States can protect an endangered species that is found only within its boundaries. Other types of environmental damage can be curtailed or eliminated by the joint action of several nations. Acid rain, in one, two, or three nations, for example, can be significantly reduced through the cooperation of several neighboring nations. However, certain types of environmental damage cannot be curtailed or eliminated without the cooperation of a large number of nations. For instance, 1, 2, or even 20 nations cannot effectively deal with the irresponsible dumping of hazardous wastes into the world's oceans. An agreement of some nations to ban such dumping is likely to give companies in the nations that are not parties to the agreement a competitive advantage over companies in the nations that are parties to the agreement. Thus, the ban would probably be unsuccessful.

In 1990 the 64 nations that are parties to the London Dumping Convention, which include the United States, Great Britain, Germany, France, the Soviet Union, Japan, Denmark, Finland, Norway, Sweden, Spain, Brazil, and most of the world's other industrialized nations, agreed to a global ban on ocean dumping of industrial wastes. Under the agreement, such dumping will come to an end in 1995.

The United Nations Environmental Program was established at a 1972 conference held in Stockholm. The conference also issued a declaration that recognized the responsibility of nations to assure that activities within their borders or in areas under their control do not damage the environment elsewhere.

In the 1980s many nations became parties to the so-called Montreal protocol, which curbs the use of chlorofluorocarbons and the manufacture of other chemicals that damage the ozone layer surrounding the Earth. In 1990, at a London conference, almost 60 nations agreed to a far more ambitious plan than that of the Montreal protocol. This plan provides for the near elimination by the year 2000 of the production of chlorofluorocarbons and certain other chemicals that damage the ozone layer. It also provides for a complete end to the production of two ozone-destructive chemicals—carbon tetrachloride, by the year 2000, and methyl chloroform, by the year 2005. Under the plan, a fund will be established to assist poor nations in obtaining substitutes for products that contain chlorofluorocarbons.

Multinational agreements on environmental protection are certain to become more important in the future. Global warming and deforestation are two matters that certainly require further worldwide cooperation. Until there is broad-based international agreement on how to deal with these matters, individual nations are unlikely to cope with them effectively.

REVIEW QUESTIONS & PROBLEMS

1. Thomas Dodd, a chemist, embarked on an experiment that he estimated would take five years. He worked on this experiment evenings, weekends, and holidays in MyLab, a small structure that he built on his property. MyLab was located about 100 feet from Leddy Lee's home, which was on a 2-acre lot adjacent to Dodd's property. Dodd's experiment resulted in the emission of nauseating odors that blanketed the area surrounding MyLab. Those odors prevented Lee from working, sleeping, or enjoying her home leisure activities. When she asked Dodd to stop whatever he was doing, he said: "Why don't you wear a gas mask like I do. Look, take mine and I'll get another one." Lee brought suit against Dodd in which she asked for a judgment enjoining him from doing any work in MyLab that caused emission of nauseating odors. What judgment? Why?

2. To use a highly efficient new manufacturing process, your firm would have to discharge effluents into a nearby river. Under the provisions of the Federal Water Pollution Act, which federal agency would the firm have to contact in order to obtain a permit authorizing it to do so? Under what circumstances would the firm have to obtain a permit from a state agency? Discuss.

3. In 1972 Barb Corporation entered into an agreement with Neutro Organic Chemical Company under which Barb leased a 4-acre site to Neutro. The lease permitted Neutro to store raw materials and finished products in a large warehouse that was located on the site. In the mid-1970s Neutro expanded its business to include the transportation and storage of hazardous wastes generated by third parties. It used the warehouse to store such wastes until they could be transported to a nearby disposal facility. In 1976 Neutro's owners organized a subsidiary, State Recycling and Disposal, Inc., which assumed Neutro's waste-handling business. Barb thereafter accepted rental payments from State Recycling. Between 1976 and 1980, State Recycling haphazardly stored more than 7,000 55-gallon drums of hazardous wastes on the leased site. The drums gradually rotted, and their contents leaked into the ground. The hazardous wastes commingled with incompatible chemicals that had escaped from containers stored by Neutro, generating noxious fumes, fires, and explosions. Thereafter the federal and state governments notified Barb that under CERCLA it was potentially responsible for the costs of cleaning up of the site. The state, using money it received from the federal Superfund and an equal amount of state money, cleaned up the site. The federal and state governments then brought suit under CERCLA against Barb to recover the cleanup costs. Barb asked the trial court to dismiss the suit on the ground that it was an innocent absentee landlord. The trial court, finding that Barb owned the site when the hazardous substances were deposited there, granted summary judgment in favor of the plaintiffs. Barb Corporation appealed. What judgment? Why?

4. Acting under the city's landmark preservation law, the local landmarks preservation commission designated as a landmark the four-story railroad terminal owned and operated by the plaintiff. As a result the plaintiff was required to keep the terminal in good repair and to obtain commission approval before making any exterior alterations. Several months later the plaintiff entered into a lease arrangement with a firm that agreed to pay it several million dollars a year in rent for permission to build and operate a multistory office building

over the terminal. When the commission refused to approve the alterations to the terminal that would be necessary to build the new structure, the plaintiff brought suit against the commission. It asked the court to declare that the commission's actions constituted a taking for which the plaintiff was entitled to receive just compensation. In support of its contention, the plaintiff noted that it had been deprived of the profits it would have made if the terminal had not been designated as a landmark. The commission asked the court to dismiss the suit, pointing out that the plaintiff was still free to use the terminal for the purposes for which it had been built and continued to reap profits from its terminal operations. What judgment? Why?

5. Art Hawthorne brought a citizen suit against Rako, Inc. under the Resource Conservation and Recovery Act, which permits citizens to bring suits in a federal district court to enforce EPA waste regulations promulgated under the act. The Resource Conservation and Recovery Act requires that a plaintiff notify the alleged violator, the state, and EPA at least 60 days before commencing such a suit. Rako, Inc.'s attorney asked the court to dismiss the case because the plaintiff had failed to satisfy this requirement. The plaintiff asked the court to give the requirement a flexible, pragmatic construction and to stay prosecution of the suit so that the plaintiff could comply with the notice requirement. What judgment? Why?

ENDNOTES

1. Metropolitan Edison Co. v. People Against Nuclear Energy, 460 U.S. 766 (1983).

2. The national contingency plan, prepared by the president, provides for the removal of oil and hazardous substances. In a section known as "the national hazardous substances response plan," it establishes procedures and standards for responding to releases of hazardous substances, pollutants, and contaminants. This plan includes methods for discovering and investigating facilities at which hazardous substances are disposed of or located; methods for evaluating (including analyses of relative cost) and remedying releases or threats of releases from facilities that pose substantial danger to the public health or the environment; methods and criteria for determining the appropriate extent of removal, remedy, and other measures authorized by CERCLA; and appropriate roles and responsibilities for the federal government, state governments, local governments, and interstate and nongovernmental entities in effectuating the plan.

PART

8

SECURITIES LAW AND ANTITRUST POLICY

In the 1980s many investors could not resist deals that might bring them unusually high profits. "Junk bonds," bonds promising unusually high rates of return for extraordinarily risky investments, were highly touted and in great demand. It has been estimated that between 1986 and 1990 investors purchased more than $113 billion worth of these bonds. By 1990 many junk bonds had substantially depreciated in value, and more than $42 billion of them were in default. Another $45 billion of them were expected to be in default by the end of 1992. In 1987 the value of other types of investments in publicly held U.S. firms plummeted abruptly. Since then there have been repeated ups and downs in the value of numerous publicly held securities, bonds, and other types of investments.

In addition to losing money because the value of their investments declined, investors suffered financial losses because swindlers engaged in such activities as rigging securities prices or using material nonpublic information to gain an unfair advantage when they bought or sold securities.

This chapter considers federal laws that are intended to provide current and potential investors with information about the firms in which they have invested or plan to invest and to curb a variety of the abuses that have plagued the securities business. It also considers some features of the state laws that are intended to protect investors.

Equity security

an instrument that represents an ownership interest in a firm

Bondholder

a creditor of a firm who owns a bond, a document that represents a debt of the firm

Issuer

a firm that distributes an instrument representing ownership in the firm or a debt of the firm

Investment contract

an agreement that represents ownership in a firm or an understanding regarding a firm's indebtedness

Preorganization certificate

a document that a promoter issues to an investor

Underwriter

a person who purchases a firm's securities for later resale or who undertakes to market them to investors

Public offering

an offer to sell securities that is extended to the public at large

Private placement

an offer to sell securities that is extended only to certain persons

Dealer

a person who offers or buys an issuer's securities or in some other way participates in their distribution

Broker

a person who buys or sells securities at an investor's request

THE INVESTMENT PROCESS

Generally, an investor decides whether to buy or sell a security on the basis of information provided by persons who stand to profit if he or she buys or sells the security. These persons include issuers, underwriters, brokers, dealers, and investment advisers.

Issuers

Investors who purchase an **equity security** take an ownership position in such enterprises as a corporation or a limited partnership. Although said to be "owners," they have *no* direct say in the management of these enterprises. A **bondholder** or debenture holder is an investor who assumes a creditor-debtor relationship with an enterprise. An enterprise that issues or proposes to issue an equity security or a bond is referred to as an **issuer.** The arrangement between an issuer and an investor is evidenced by an oral or written **investment contract.** A stock certificate, for example, which represents ownership in an enterprise, is an investment contract.

A promoter who enters into a contract with an investor before a company is established may provide the investor with a **preorganization certificate.** This document contains the contract between the parties. In such cases the promoter is referred to as an "issuer" because the certificate is a form of security.

Underwriters, Brokers, and Dealers

Generally, an issuer's securities are *not* sold by the issuer but by one or more **underwriters.** These underwriters may purchase the securities for resale or may simply undertake to sell them either to anyone who wishes to buy them, in a so-called **public offering,** or only to particular persons, in what is known as a **private placement.**

An underwriter may resell securities to one or more dealers. A **dealer** offers or buys an issuer's securities or in some other way participates in their distribution. A **broker,** on the other hand, is an investor's agent who responds to the investor's order to buy or sell particular securities.

Commonly, investors buy securities from a **broker-dealer.** A broker-dealer combines the functions of the broker and the dealer, both soliciting investors to purchase securities and executing investors' buy or sell orders. Securities laws treat underwriters, dealers, and broker-dealers differently from brokers. They regard underwriters, dealers, and broker-dealers, but not brokers, as participants in the distribution process.

Investment Adviser

Someone who wants help in deciding whether to make an investment may employ the services of a person who is in the business of offering investment advice. Such a person is known as an **investment adviser.**

SECURITIES ACT OF 1933

The first federal statute expressly designed to regulate the sale of securities was the Securities Act of 1933, which has frequently been referred to as the Truth in Securities Act. This act has been described as the response of Congress to demands that the federal government protect uninformed, ignorant, gullible, and naive investors from reckless, speculative, and fraudulent schemes involving the sale of newly issued securities. Courts view the act as the legislature's way of assuring that the securities business is conducted in an ethical, honest, and fair manner. The act is based on the power of Congress to regulate interstate commerce. Accordingly, it is not applicable to securities transactions that are in no way related to interstate commerce. Standards established under the act are applicable to interstate offers or sales of securities. The act is administered by the Securities and Exchange Commission (SEC), which engages in rulemaking, adjudication, and enforcement activities. Figure 17-1 (page 508) provides a diagram of the overall structure of the SEC.

Caveat Emptor

The Securities Act of 1933 modifies the ancient rule of **_caveat emptor_** (let the buyer beware) by requiring full, fair, and truthful disclosure to potential investors on a variety of matters. The SEC neither evaluates the worth of securities nor advises investors on the purchase of securities.

REGISTRATION

The 1933 Act requires that a "registration statement" be filed with the SEC before an issuer, underwriter, or dealer _makes an initial offer to sell_ or _sells_ an issue of a security unless the security is "exempt" from this requirement because of its nature or because of the manner in which it is sold. The registration statement is open to the public.

The registration statement is intended to assure investors of access to adequate, honest, and complete material information when deciding whether to buy a security. This document has two parts. One is the **registration statement** (its name is the same as that used for the complete document), and the other is the **prospectus.** The registration statement is far more detailed than the prospectus.

Statutory Definition of a Security

Among the documents that the 1933 Act defines as a **security** for the purpose of the act are any note, stock, treasury stock, bond, debenture, evidence of indebtedness, investment contract, and generally any interest or instrument that is commonly known as a "security." A security is generally thought of as an agreement in which a person invests his or her money along with that of others _in order to make a profit solely from the efforts of others._ To determine whether what an investor purchased is a "security," a court must consider the total circumstances,

---

Broker-dealer
a person who solicits investors to purchase securities and executes investors' orders to buy or sell securities

Investment adviser
a person who is in the business of offering investment advice

Caveat emptor
the rule that requires investors to look after their own interests when engaging in securities transactions

Registration statement
a document filed with the SEC that includes extensive information about a firm

Prospectus
a part of the registration statement; a document delivered to investors that contains a condensation of the information found in a registration statement

Security
an instrument that contains the agreement between an investor and a firm

FIGURE 17–1   Securities and Exchange Commission

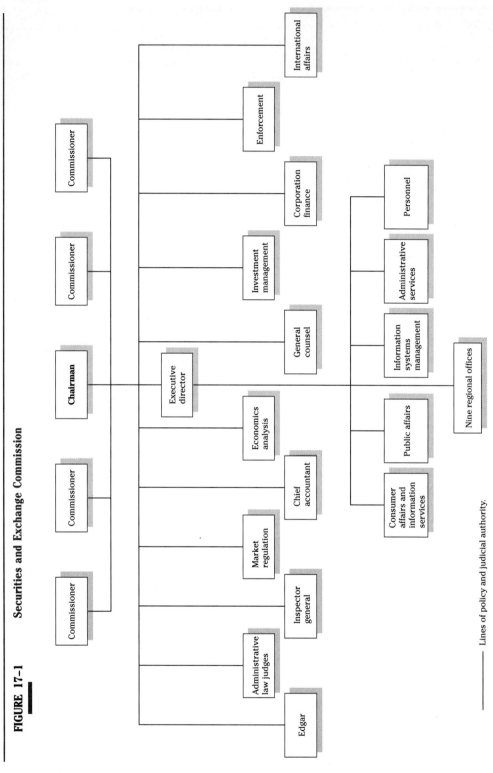

Source: Federal Register, National Archives and Records Administration, *The United States Government Manual, 1990/91* (Washington, D.C.: U.S. Government Printing Office, July 1, 1990), p. 698.

including how the transaction was marketed. The *substance* of the arrangement, not its *form,* determines whether it comes within the act's definition of a security.

A contract between general partners is not a security, because the partners can participate in the management of the firm. They do not seek to profit solely from the efforts of others. A limited partnership agreement is a securitiy because limited partners have no say in managing the firm. They intend to profit solely from the efforts of the firm's one or more general partners.

Exempt Securities and Transactions

A security may be *exempt* from the 1933 Act's usual registration statement and prospectus requirements either because the *security is itself exempt* or because of the way in which the security is *transferred.*

Exempt Securities

Because of their nature certain types of securities are expressly exempted from the act. These are known as **exempt securities.**

Ordinarily, insurance agreements, endowment policies, and annuity contracts issued by corporations that are subject to the supervision of certain government agencies are exempt from the act. These agreements do not meet the usual definition of a security, because the issuer agrees to make specified payments regardless of the firm's profitability. However, an insurance product that includes a significant security dimension is not exempt from the act. For example, a *variable* annuity contract is a security for the purposes of the act, rather than an insurance agreement, since the amount of the payments that the beneficiary will receive depends in part on the profitability of the insurer's operations.

Among other securities excluded from the provisions of the act are (1) commercial paper, such as a promissory note, if it originates out of a current business arrangement or if its proceeds have been or are to be used for current transactions, if it has a maturity date of not more than nine months after its date of issue, and if it is *not sold* to the public as an *investment;* (2) securities guaranteed by the United States, a state, or one of a state's political subdivisions; (3) securities issued by banks or savings and loan associations that are supervised by a federal or state agency; (4) securities issued by a corporation exclusively to its current security holders for which no commission or other remuneration is paid, in exchange for other securities that they hold in the corporation, as in the case of a stock split; (5) securities issued by an organization that is operated, not for the purpose of pecuniary profit, but exclusively for religious, educational, charitable, or benevolent purposes and no part of whose net earnings is payable to any person or private stockholder; and (6) certificates issued with a court's approval by a receiver or trustee of a firm in Chapter 11 bankruptcy proceedings.

Exempt Transactions

Certain securities are exempt from the act because of the manner in which they are sold. The following are examples of **exempt transactions.**

Small Issue The act authorizes the SEC to establish regulations that exempt from the usual registration and prospectus requirements issues that do not exceed $5 million when the agency finds these requirements unnecessary to protect investors

Exempt securities

securities excluded from the 1933 Act's registration and prospectus requirements

Exempt transaction

a method of selling securities that excludes them from the 1933 Act's registration and prospectus requirements

and the public interest because of the small amount involved or the limited nature of the offering.

Regulation A. An issuer may file an offering statement and an offering circular with the SEC instead of the usual registration statement and prospectus if the total offering price of the issue does not exceed $1.5 million if the securities are offered or sold by or on behalf of the issuer, or by the estate of a decedent who owned the securities at death if the securities are offered within two years after the decedent's death, or by an affiliate of the issuer (a person controlling, controlled by, or under common control with the issuer) so long as the offering price of the securities offered or sold by or on behalf of the affiliate (other than an estate) does not exceed $100,000. Issues of up to $100,000, as well as issues of up to $300,000, that satisfy other Regulation A criteria are also exempt from the usual registration statement and prospectus requirements. The offering circular must describe the securities and contain financial information about the firm. Investors must be provided with a copy of the circular at least 48 hours before the sale of the securities is confirmed. A corporate issuer may use Regulation A only if it is incorporated in the United States and its principal operations are carried on in the United States or Canada. An individual issuer must be a resident of the United States or Canada.

Regulation D. An issuer may file a notice of sale with the SEC instead of the usual registration statement and prospectus if the total offering price of a new class of securities to be issued within a 12-month period does not exceed $5 million. During the 12-month period the securities may be issued to an unlimited number of accredited investors and the issuer must reasonably believe that there are not more than 35 other investors. Among those whom the SEC classifies as accredited investors are banks, savings and loan associations, regulated brokers and dealers, the issuer's directors, individuals whose net worth at the time of the purchase exceeds $1 million, and individuals whose income has been in excess of $200,000 in each of the two most recent years or couples whose joint income has been in excess of $300,000 in each of the two most recent years and, in the case of both the individuals and the couples who have a reasonable expectation of exceeding these respective amounts in the current year. Investors who are not accredited investors must themselves, or together with their representatives, have such knowledge and experience in financial and business matters that they are capable of evaluating the merits and risks of the prospective investment or the issuer must reasonably believe immediately prior to making the sale that they are so qualified.

Private offering

an offer to sell securities that is made to persons who meet certain qualifications

Private Offering   If an offer to sell securities is directed only to particular persons, it is a **private offering.** For a private offering to qualify as an exempt transaction, the offer must be directed to persons who are capable of shifting for themselves, who are sophisticated enough to intelligently assess the risks of purchasing the securities and competent to decide whether to purchase them. Such persons do not need the protection offered by the act's registration and prospectus process. There is no neat mechanical standard by which to determine whether an offer is private. However, there is general agreement that the following facts should be taken into account: (1) the relationship among the investors themselves and between the investors and the issuer, (2) the number of offerees, (3) the number of units offered, and (4) the size of the offering.

Intrastate Offering Intrastate offerings and sales of securities are outside the act's requirements under the **intrastate offering** exemption. For an offering to qualify for this exemption, the issuer's principal place of business must be in the same state in which it conducts substantially all of its business, all of the securities issued in the transaction must be offered and sold to bona fide residents of that state, and the issuer must intend to use substantially all of the net proceeds that it obtains from the sale of these securities in connection with its *in-state operations*. The issuer must take reasonable steps to preclude any resale of the securities to nonresidents within nine months after the sale of the last of the securities involved in the transaction has been completed. To satisfy this requirement, the issuer may place a statement on the security document reciting the nine-month restriction and informing the party charged with handling the transfer of the securities that they may not be resold sooner than nine minths after the issuer has sold all of the securities offered. The intrastate offering exemption is available even if the mails, interstate commerce, interstate transportation, or interstate means of communication are used to distribute the securities.

Intrastate offering
an offering to sell securities that is made solely to residents of the state in which a firm is located and does substantially all of its business, with substantially all of the proceeds of the sale to be used locally

Merger or Combination The issuance of securities as part of the reorganization of an enterprise, such as a merger or a combination, is an exempt transaction if it falls within one of the exempt transaction categories.

DISCLOSURE OF PERSONAL RESERVATIONS

Hypothetical Case

Andrew Ennis, a prominent computer engineer, obtained a patent on a device for substantially reducing the cost of manufacturing laptop computers. He organized AA Computer, Inc. and transferred the patent to it in return for 51 percent of its shares. The firm would raise the $15 million it required to take full advantage of the patent by a public sale of the remaining shares. Ennis viewed the AA Computer venture as "somewhat risky" because at any time someone else might obtain a patent on a device that would even further reduce the cost of manufacturing laptop computers.

Ennis asked Donald Platt, a well-known adviser to newly organized companies, whether AA Computer should point out to potential investors that at some future time it might run into stiff competition from the holder of an even more cost-efficient manufacturing process. Platt cautioned Ennis to think very carefully before he did this, pointing out that such information could needlessly turn off potential investors. He stressed the present value of Ennis's patent and the high profits that AA Computer could make by quickly putting the patent to use. "Remember," Platt said, "everyone knows that nothing lasts forever."

Would it be ethical for AA Computer not to clearly inform potential purchasers of AA Computer stock of Ennis's expectation of stiff competition if a more cost-efficient process for making laptop computers were invented? Discuss should securities law require AA Computer to call attention to the harm that its stockholders might suffer if this happened? Why?

Registration Statement

The registration statement must include the names and addresses of the issuer's chief executive, financial officers, and directors; the general nature of its business; the risks associated with its securities; its capitalization; the amount of its debt; a description of the securities being offered or sold; a statement of how the proceeds of their sale will be used; the amounts paid, or an estimate of the amounts that will be paid, for the past year and the next year to the issuer's directors and officers; a profit and loss statement showing earnings and income, together with a balance sheet for the current year as of no later than 90 days prior to the filing, prepared by an independent CPA on the basis of an audit conducted in accordance with generally accepted accounting principles; and the names of all the persons who owned more than 10 percent of any class of stock or more than 10 percent of all the outstanding stock within 20 days prior to the filing.

A registration statement filed by a corporate issuer must be signed by the principal executive, financial, and accounting officers of the issuer and by at least a majority of its board of directors. If the issuer is not a corporation, the registration statement must be signed by its managers.

Effective Registration Statement

The time between the filing of a registration statement with the SEC and the effectiveness of the registration statement is known as the **waiting period.** During this time it is unlawful for an issuer, underwriter, or dealer to *sell* a nonexempt security through interstate facilities or the mails. The ban on sales during the waiting period does not apply to *oral offers to sell* the security even if such offers are made by interstate telephone. If the SEC does not object to the registration statement, it becomes *effective* 20 days after it is filed. It is then known as an **effective registration statement.** If the SEC concludes that a registration statement contains a material misstatement or that there has been a material omission from a registration statement, it may prevent the registration statement from becoming effective. It may communicate its objections informally or state them in a formal communication known as a **letter of comment.** If the issuer files amendments to the original registration statement that are satisfactory to the SEC, the amended registration statement becomes effective 20 days after the amendments are filed unless the SEC authorizes it to be effective before that time. If the issuer does not respond in a manner acceptable to the SEC, the SEC may issue a **stop order.** This prevents the registration statement from taking effect. The issuer may then challenge the legality of the stop order in a quasi-judicial proceeding.

The SEC may also issue a stop order if it determines that a registration already in effect contains a material misstatement or is incomplete. This suspends the effectiveness of the registration. The stop order is terminated if the issuer files the requested amendments. The issuer may challenge the legality of such a stop order in the same manner that it may challenge the legality of a stop order issued before a registration becomes effective.

Shelf Registration

To make sure that investors have current material information, a registration statement can ordinarily be filed only shortly before a security is offered for sale or sold. **Shelf registration** gives issuers more flexibility in scheduling an offer or sale by allowing them to satisfy the basic registration requirement long before the offer or sale is made. At the time of a shelf registration, the issuer must have a bona fide intention to offer or sell a security within two years. The shelf registration need not specify the security. However, before the security is offered for sale or sold, the registration must be amended to identify the security and to include any material events that occurred after the filing of the shelf registration.

When the issuer uses shelf registration, it must exercise due diligence to assure that the prospectus includes information about any fundamental changes that occurred after the filing.

False Registration Statement

A registration statement is false if it misrepresents or omits a fact that is of such significance as to be **material**—to have an effect on a reasonable investor. An objective standard is used to determine whether a fact or omission does have such an effect. A misrepresentation or omission is material if, taking a *realistic view,* there is a *substantial likelihood* that a reasonable investor would have acted differently were it not for the misrepresentation or omission.

> **Material statement**
> a misrepresentation or omission of fact that renders a registration statement false

Persons Liable for a False Registration Statement

If a registration statement became effective when any part of it misrepresented or omitted a material fact, any person who acquired the security described in the registration statement and did not know about the misrepresentation or omission may bring suit against a number of persons for legal or equitable relief. These persons include everyone who signed the registration statement; directors of the issuer, or persons who performed similar functions, or partners in the issuer when the registration was filed; persons who consented to be named in the registration statement as being or about to become directors, or to perform functions similar to those of a director, or partners; accountants, lawyers, engineers, appraisers, or any other persons whose profession gave authority to his or her statement in the registration statement or who consented to being named as having prepared or certified any report or valuation in the registration statement or any report or valuation used in connection with the registration statement; and every underwriter involved in the distribution of the security.

Establishing Liability

To recover damages attributable to a defective registration statement, the purchaser of the security described in the registration statement need *not* have dealt *directly* with the defendant (in other words, **privity** is not required) or establish that the defendant was negligent or guilty of fraud. Unless the security was purchased when the issuer's earnings statement for a 12-month period after the registration became effective was generally available, the purchaser need not show reliance on the statement in order to recover damages. However, to recover a judgment when the 12-month exception is applicable, the purchaser must prove that he or she relied on untrue information contained in the registration statement or was misled by the absence of a material fact in the statement of which he or she was unaware.

> **Privity**
> a securities transaction in which the issuer and investor deal directly with each other

Defenses

Three defenses are available to a person who is sued because of a faulty registration statement. (1) Before the registration statement became effective, the defendant resigned from his or her position with the issuer and so notified the SEC and the issuer in writing, stating that he or she was not responsible for specified parts of the registration statement. (2) Upon discovering that the registration statement had become effective, the defendant promptly (*a*) notified the SEC that he or she had been unaware that the statement had become effective and (*b*) then took reasonable steps to notify the public of the parts of the statement about which he or she had had no knowledge when it became effective. (3) Except for an issuer, a signatory to a faulty registration statement is excused from liability if he or she acted with *due dilligence* and was not guilty of fraud. The due diligence defense may *not* be used by issuers, because they are *liable without fault.*

Due Diligence

Whether a party acted with due diligence depends on the character of that part of the registration statement on which the plaintiff's claim is based.

A party acts with due diligence with regard to any part of a registration statement *not purporting to be based* on the *authority* of an *expert,* or an *expert's report* or *evaluation,* or a *public official document* or *statement,* if after conducting a reasonable investigation, he or she had reasonable ground to believe, and did believe, when that part of the registration statement became effective, that the part was true and that no material fact has been omitted from it. An investigation or a ground for belief is reasonable if it is at least equal to the standard of care that a prudent person would exercise to reasonably manage his or her own property.

A party acts with due diligence with regard to any part of a registration statement *based* on the *authority* of an *expert other than himself or herself,* or an *expert's report* or *valuation,* if he or she had no reasonable ground to believe, and did not believe, when that part of the registration statement became effective, that the part was untrue, or that a material fact had been omitted from it, or that it failed to fairly represent the expert's report or was not a fair copy of or extract from that report.

A party acts with due diligence with regard to any part of a registration purporting to be based on his or her authority as an expert, or represented as a copy of or extract from his or her report or valuation as an expert, if after conducting a reasonable investigation, he or she had reasonable ground to believe, and did believe, when that part of the registration statement became effective, that the part was true and that no material fact had been omitted from it, or that it fairly represented his or her statement as an expert or was a fair copy of or extract from his or her report or valuation as an expert.

A party acts with due diligence regarding any part of a registration statement purporting to be a statement made by an official person, or a copy of or extract from a public official document, if he or she had no reasonable ground to believe and did not believe at the time that part of the registration statement became effective that the part was untrue, or that a material fact had been omitted from it, or that it failed to fairly represent the public official's statement or was not a fair copy or extract from that statement.

Damages

A party is liable only for injury caused by defects in the portion of the registration statement for which he or she is accountable. Damages are limited to the difference between what the plaintiff paid for the security, up to its publicly offered price, and either (1) its value when the lawsuit was brought or (2) its selling price if it was disposed of before the lawsuit was brought. If the security was sold after the lawsuit was brought, but before judgment was entered, and the security's value declined during that time, the plaintiff may recover the difference between what he or she paid for the security, up to the price at which the security was publicly offered for sale, and its value when the suit was brought. A judgment in favor of the plaintiff may never be for more than the price at which the security was offered to the public.

Generally, an underwriter is not liable for damages in excess of the sales price of the securities that he or she underwrote and distributed to the public.

In a lawsuit in which the plaintiff's claim is based on an alleged false registration statement, the successful party may recover reasonable attorney's fees and expenses if the other party's claim or defense lacked merit. This is so if that party acted in bad faith, if his or her conduct bordered on the frivolous, or if the suit was maliciously brought.

Contribution

A party who has paid a judgment based on a violation of the Securities Act of 1933 has a right to recover from others who similarly violated the act a pro rata share of the amount paid. This right is known as **contribution.** Contribution is not available to such a party if the judgment was based on a fraudulent misrepresentation and the other parties were not guilty of fraud.

Contribution
the right of a person who has paid a judgment to recover a portion of what was paid from other persons guilty of like misconduct

PROSPECTUS

A prospectus is a written announcement that contains an offer to sell a security or a written confirmation of such a sale. A written offer to sell a nonexempt security made by mail or by the use of any interstate means or instrument of transportation or communication must comply with the prospectus standards of the 1933 Act and be filed with the SEC before the offer is made.

Prospectus Content and Delivery

A prospectus, which, as we have seen, is part of the two-part registration statement filed with the SEC, contains a condensation of the registration statement. It must not contain any materially false or misleading information, and it must include any material changes of fact that occurred after the registration statement was filed. A purchaser of the security described in a prospectus must be provided with the prospectus no later than when the security is delivered.

Dissemination of Information during the Waiting Period

Before the registration statement becomes effective, a "red herring prospectus" or a "tombstone advertisement" may be used to provide information about the security described in the registration statement.

Red Herring Prospectus

A preliminary prospectus, commonly referred to as a **red herring prospectus,** must have across its cover a *red line* and a *statement,* also in *red,* that it is a *preliminary* prospectus. Such a prospectus contains essentially the same information as the

Red herring prospectus
a document that takes the place of a prospectus during the waiting period

standard prospectus. It must include an announcement that any not yet available information required by law to be included in a prospectus will be found in the prospectus that will be distributed after the registration statement takes effect. Mention must also be made of the fact that the registration statement is not yet effective and that only after it is effective may the security described in the red herring prospectus be offered for sale.

Tombstone Advertisement

Investors may be informed of the future availability of a security by a **tombstone advertisement.** This is a notice, circular, advertisement, letter, or other communication that identifies the security and states how a prospectus may be obtained, what the security costs, who will execute purchase orders, and whatever other information the SEC requires to protect investors and the public interest.

Liability for Defective Prospectus

If a person sold, or offered to sell, a security by the use of any means or instrument of transportation or communication in interstate commerce, or by mail, by means of a prospectus that included an untrue statement of a material fact or omitted a material fact, and the person knew, or in the exercise of reasonable care could have known, of the untruth or omission, that person is liable to a purchaser who was unaware of the untruth or omission.

Control Persons   Anyone who for whatever reason controls any person who comes within the provisions of the 1933 Act is called a **control person.** Such persons are liable along with the controlled person for the filing of a false registration statement or prospectus unless they had no knowledge of the facts that gave rise to the liability of the controlled person or no reasonable grounds for being aware of those facts.

Remedies for Prospectus Violation

If the prospectus requirements have not been satisfied, the purchaser may seek legal or equitable relief in a court. The purchaser may rescind the transaction. In that case the damages are the amount of the consideration paid for the security, together with interest, less any income that the purchaser received while he or she owned the security. If the purchaser no longer owns the security, he or she may sue for damages caused by the deficient prospectus or oral offer. Generally, such damages are the difference between the purchase price of the security and its actual value, less any income that the purchaser received as the owner of the security.

Fraud

The antifraud section of the Securities Act of 1933 applies to securities *whether or not* they are covered by the act's registration statement and prospectus provisions. It is unlawful to directly or indirectly use any means of interstate commerce, such as the mails or an instrument of transportation or communication, (1) to offer to sell or to sell securities by using any untrue statement of a material fact or by failing to state a material fact; or (2) to enage in any transaction, practice, or course of business that operates, or would operate, as a fraud or deceit on the purchaser; or (3) to employ any device, scheme, or artifice to defraud.

Arbitrability of Claims

Any condition, stipulation, or provision to waive compliance with the 1933 Act or any oral or written disclaimer of liability under the act is unenforceable. However, an agreement between the parties to a securities transaction providing for the resolution by arbitration of any dispute that may later arise between them, including a dispute over an alleged violation of the act's antifraud provisions, is enforceable.

SEC Enforcement Powers

The SEC is authorized to investigate what appear to be past, present, or possible future violations of the 1933 Act or SEC rules. If it concludes that a violation is taking place or is about to occur, it may bring suit in any federal district court to enjoin the violation and the court may grant a preliminary or permanent injunction to bar the violation. Upon application of the SEC, a federal court may issue a **writ of mandamus,** a court order commanding that the named person or persons comply with the act or an SEC order.

Writ of mandamus
a court order that directs one or more named persons to obey the law

The SEC may transmit evidence of misconduct to the attorney general of the United States, who may take the action necessary to initiate a criminal proceeding.

State Jurisdiction

Concurrent Federal and State Jurisdiction   State courts have concurrent jurisdiction to enforce any liability or duty created by the 1933 Act or SEC rules. A lawsuit brought in a state court to enforce the act or an SEC rule cannot be removed to a federal court.

Action by State Securities Agencies   The 1933 Act specifically provides that it does not deprive any state securities commission from taking any action in regard to any security or from regulating sales of securities or offers to sell them. Under the act, a state is free to require those who wish to sell securities in the state to first obtain from the state a permit authorizing them to do so.

SECURITIES EXCHANGE ACT OF 1934

The Securities Exchange Act of 1934 is intended to promote fairness and honesty in securities transactions. Unlike the 1933 Act, it regulates securities transactions that take place *after* securities have been issued. In addition, it deals with such matters as the operation of securities exchanges and the over-the-counter market; the way in which underwriters, dealers, and brokers do business; the registration of securities exempt from the registration provisions of the 1933 Act; the protection of investors from deceptive and fraudulent practices in securities trading; the prohibition of some kinds of securities transactions; and the curbing of certain types of behavior by officers and directors of the firms that issue securities and by the principal holders of a firm's securities.

Exempt Securities

Among the securities exempt from the 1934 Act are U.S. obligations; obligations guaranteed by the federal government; obligations of state governments; securities issued by federally chartered savings and loans associations; industrial development bonds; and securities of religious, educational, benevolent, fraternal, and charitable organizations that do not distribute any part of their earnings to private shareholders.

Securities Markets

Exchange
an association whose members engage in securities transactions with one another

Listed security
a security that may be regularly bought or sold through a particular exchange

Over-the-counter market
an informal means used by brokers and dealers to trade securities

Securities are publicly traded through exchanges or the over-the-counter market. An **exchange** is an association of broker-dealers who generally use the exchange's facilities to trade **listed securities,** that is, securities regularly bought and sold through the exchange. An exchange's rules of eligibility for membership and listing are intended to protect investors and to promote public confidence in the exchange and its members. The 1934 Act and SEC rules and regulations set the criteria that an exchange must meet to qualify as a national or regional exchange. The New York Stock Exchange and the American Stock Exchange are the largest national exchanges, while the Boston, Philadelphia, Midwest, and Pacific exchanges are the largest regional exchanges.

Securities not sold through an exchange are traded in the **over-the-counter market** (OTC). Unlike an exchange, this market is not a formal association of a limited number of broker-dealers but consists of all the brokers and dealers who buy and sell securities. The operational standards they must follow are set by the National Association of Securities Dealers (NASD), which must comply with the 1934 Act, register with the SEC, and satisfy the SEC's rules and regulations.

Brokers and Dealers

Registration   Unless they engage solely in intrastate transactions *and* do not use the facilities of a registered national securities exchange, brokers and dealers may not use the mails or any means or instrumentality of interstate commerce to effect a securities transaction or to induce the purchase or sale of a security without first registering with the SEC.

Fraudulent Broker and Dealer Practices   The 1934 Act bars brokers and dealers who use the mails or any means or instrumentality of interstate commerce from employing any manipulative, deceptive, or other fraudulent device or contrivance, as defined by the SEC, to induce the purchase or sale of a security.

Broker and Dealer Structure and Solvency   The 1934 Act authorizes the SEC to regulate the way brokers and dealers operate and to establish financial standards for detecting their insolvency.

Margin
the use of a loan to finance part of the cost of a securities purchase

Margin   When a buyer obtains a loan to finance part of the purchase price of securities, the securities are said to be bought on **margin.** To prevent excessive use of credit, the 1934 Act authorizes the Board of Governors of the Federal

Reserve System to set the maximum amount of credit that a lender may extend for the purchase of securities. This is known as the **initial level.** It is enforceable by the SEC.

Broker and Dealer Obligations   Brokers and dealers have obligations aside from those laid down by the 1934 Act and the SEC. For example, brokers who lead their clients to believe that they are experts have a duty to exercise a higher level of care than they would have had to exercise if they had not represented themselves as experts. They are expected to know material facts about the securities they recommend, and those facts must reasonably support their recommendations.

The New York Stock Exchange's **know thy customer rule** requires that a broker make reasonable inquiries to a customer about matters relevant to the customer's financial status and investment plans before recommending the purchase or sale of a security. The recommendation must be based on the facts that the customer provides, including the customer's investment objectives, financial situation, and needs, and there must be reasonable grounds to believe that it is appropriate in view of those facts.

NASD requires that member brokers who recommend the purchase or sale of a security have reasonable grounds to believe that on the basis of the facts that the customer provides about his or her investment portfolio, financial situation, and needs, the recommendation made is suitable for that customer. This requirement is known as the **suitability rule.**

A broker who has been granted discretionary power to control a customer's account by buying and selling securities on the customer's behalf may not engage in overtrading simply to earn commissions at the customer's expense. This practice, known as **churning,** violates SEC Rule 10b-5, which is discussed below.

SEC Sanctions   After a quasi-judicial hearing the SEC may impose such penalties on brokers or dealers as censure, restriction of their business activities, suspension from trading for not more than 12 months, or revocation of their registration. The penalties are imposed if the brokers or dealers, or any persons associated with them, (1) were found guilty of willfully submitting a false registration application or required report with the SEC; or (2) within 10 years prior to filing a registration application with the SEC or at any time thereafter were convicted of a crime relating to the purchase or sale of a security, the taking of a false oath, the filing of a false report, bribery, burglary, or conspiracy to commit any of these offenses; or (3) fraudulently converted or misappropriated funds or securities.

Securities Investor Protection Act   Brokers and dealers commonly hold the cash and securities of investors. To afford investors some protection in the event of a broker's or dealer's insolvency when the investor's cash or securities are not segregated from the assets of the broker or dealer, Congress enacted the Securities Investor Protection Act (1970), which established the Securities Investor Protection Corporation (SIPC).

All registered brokers and dealers must be SIPC members and must pay assessed amounts of money into SIPC's treasury. If these assessments do not yield enough money to pay investors' claims, the SEC may raise additional funds by imposing charges on all securities transactions made through securities exchanges or the over-the-counter market. The maximum amount that an investor may recover under the Securities Investor Protection Act is $500,000, of which not more than $100,000 may be for lost cash.

Initial level

the maximum amount of credit that may be used to fund a securities transaction

Know thy customer rule

the requirement that brokers and dealers have sufficient information about a customer's financial status before offering investment advice

Suitability rule

the requirement that a broker's recommendation on the security be suitable for the given client

Churning

overtrading by a broker on a client's investment account so as to generate commissions

Securities Registration

Registered Securities   The 1934 Act requires that any security for which a registration statement has not been filed with the SEC under the 1933 Act must be registered if the security is not exempt from the 1934 Act. The 1934 Act also requires registration for any class of equity securities owned by 500 or more persons that is publicly traded over-the-counter if the issuer is engaged in interstate commerce or in a business affecting interstate commerce, or if any of the issuer's securities are traded by use of the mails or any means of interstate commerce, and the issuer has more than $5 million in assets. A security that must be registered under the 1934 Act or for which a registration statement must be filed under the 1933 Act is called a **registered security.**

To register a security under the 1934 Act, a registration statement is filed with the SEC. This statement must contain certain information about the issuer, including its capital structure; the nature of its outstanding securities; the names of its directors, officers, and underwriters and of the persons who hold more than 10 percent of any class of its equity securities; and certified balance sheets and profit and loss statements for the past three years of its operations.

Reporting Requirements

Periodic Company Reports   An issuer with registered securities must file various reports with the SEC. Among these reports are a **Form 10-K,** an annual report, which must be filed within 90 days after the end of a firm's fiscal year and includes audited financial data that update the firm's registration statement; a **Form 10-Q,** a quarterly report which is submitted for each of a firm's first three fiscal quarters; and a **Form 8-K,** commonly referred to as a "current report," which is filed within 10 days after particular types of extraordinary events take place, such as the acquisition or sale of a significant amount of a firm's assets, a change in the persons who control a firm, or the initiation of bankruptcy proceedings.

Beneficial Ownership Report   A person is the **beneficial owner** of a registered equity security when he or she is named as the owner of the security; or his or her spouse, minor child, or a person living in the same household is named as the owner; or he or she is a beneficiary of a trust that holds the security. The 1934 Act requires that within 10 days after a person becomes the beneficial owner of more than 5 percent of any class of a firm's registered securities, he or she must file a report with the SEC, the issuer, and the national exchange on which the security is traded. The report must state the origin of the funds used to buy the securities and whether the person plans to buy more of them, to change the firm's structure or business, or to gain control of the firm.

Transaction Report   The 1934 Act establishes a reporting requirement for transactions engaged in by corporate officers, corporate directors, and persons who are the beneficial owners of more than 10 percent of any class of a firm's equity securities (other than exempt securities) that is listed and registered on a national securities exchange. These persons must inform both the SEC and any exchange on which the firm's equity securities are listed of the extent of any change in his or her equity security holdings in the firm. Not more than 10 days after the end of the calendar month in which these persons buy or sell any of the firm's equity

Registered security

a security that must be registered with the SEC or for which a registration statement must be filed with the SEC

Form 10-K

an annual report that a firm with registered securities must file with the SEC

Form 10-Q

a quarterly report that a firm with registered securities must file with the SEC

Form 8-K

a report that a firm with registered securities must file with the SEC within 10 days after certain types of unusual events have taken place

Beneficial owner

a person who is treated as the owner of a security because of his or her relationship with the person who has title to the security

securities, they must advise the SEC and the appropriate exchange of such purchases or sales.

Liability for a False or Misleading Filing

Anyone who files an application, report, or document that is false or misleading with respect to any material fact is liable to any person who was unaware that the application, report, or document was false or misleading, relied on it, and bought or sold a security at a price that was affected by it. However, there is no liability if the party who filed the application, report, or document acted in good faith without knowledge that it was false or misleading.

Manipulative or Deceptive Conduct

Section 10(b) of the 1934 Act makes it unlawful for anyone, directly or indirectly, by any means or instrumentality of interstate commerce or by use of the mails or any facility of a national exchange, to employ any manipulative or deceptive device or contrivance or to engage in deceptive conduct in connection with the purchase or sale of a security, *whether or not* the security is registered on a national exchange, if such conduct violates Section 10(b) or an SEC rule or regulation that the SEC promulgates to implement Section 10(b).

Section 10(b) sets legislative policy. SEC Rule 10b-5 implements the legislative mandate of Section 10(b). Rule 10b-5 is applicable only when the mails, means or instrumentality of interstate commerce, or a facility of a national exchange is used to carry out a securities transaction. It prohibits any behavior in connection with the purchase or sale of a security that defrauds or deceives a buyer or seller by (1) using any device, scheme, or artifice designed to defraud or (2) making any untrue statement of a material fact or failing to state a material fact. It also prohibits any practice, or course of business, that operates, or would operate, as a fraud or deceit on a party to a securities transaction.

Neither Section 10(b) nor Rule 10b-5 is violated unless the party who engaged in a form of conduct prohibited by Section 10(b) or Rule 10b-5 acted with **scienter.** A party acts with scienter when he or she behaves either intentionally or recklessly. Reckless behavior is far more irresponsible than negligence (a failure to exercise ordinary care). A party is reckless in connection with Section 10(b) or Rule 10b-5 when he or she *knew,* or it was so *obvious* that he or she *must have known* that his or her conduct presented a danger of misleading a buyer or seller.

Scienter
the intentional or reckless carrying out of an act

Liability for Manipulative or Deceptive Conduct

Neither Section 10(b) nor Rule 10b-5 *expressly* creates a civil remedy. Through *judicial construction,* however, both have been found to *impliedly* create civil liability.

Establishing Liability   To recover damages for a Section 10(b) or Rule 10b-5 violation, a plaintiff must prove (1) that the defendant acted with scienter when he or she misrepresented or omitted a material fact or engaged in a scheme to defraud in connection with a securities transaction; (2) that the plaintiff was caused injury by relying on the defendant's misconduct, because the misconduct affected the price of the security; and (3) that despite due diligence the plaintiff could not have discovered the truth.

Out-of-pocket loss

the difference between the value of securities and what the buyer or seller paid or received for them

Benefit of the bargain

the right of a party to recover the profit lost in a securities deal as a result of the wrongdoer's misconduct

Measure of Damages   Generally, the damages of a securities buyer are the buyer's **out-of-pocket loss,** that is, the difference between the amount that the buyer paid for the securities and the value of those securities at a reasonable time after the buyer learned of the defendant's wrongdoing. Some courts use the **benefit of the bargain** rule. This entitles the plaintiff buyer to recover whatever profit he or she may have lost because of the defendant's wrongdoing.

Arbitrability of Section 10(b) and Rule 10b–5 Claims   Although the 1934 Act declares void any condition, stipulation, or provision to waive compliance with the act, claims arising under Section 10(b) and Rule 10b–5 are arbitrable.

INSIDER TRADING

Insider

Insider

a party whose position in a firm or relationship with a firm affords lawful access to material non-public information about the firm

An **insider** includes an issuer; or a firm's officers or directors; or a person who controls or is controlled by an issuer; or a person, such as an underwriter, investment banker, accountant, lawyer, or consultant, who because of a past or present full-time or part-time relationship with an issuer knows a material fact about the issuer or its securities that is not available to the public. Securities law limits insiders from trading in the securities of a firm to prevent them from profiting by the use of material nonpublic information about the firm.

Short-Swing Profits

Short-swing profit

profit earned by owners of more than 10 percent of any class of registered nonexempt securities or an issuer's directors or officers due to trades in a firm's equity securities that are completed within less than six months

The 1934 Act's "short-swing profit rule" prevents beneficial owners of more than 10 percent of any class of registered nonexempt equity securities, as well as an issuer's directors and officers, from unfairly profiting by the use of nonpublic information about a firm's *equity securities* that are *not exempt* from the act's registration requirements. This rule entitles a firm to recover what is called a **short-swing profit**—a profit that results when such a person, within less than six months, buys and sells, or sell and buys, any securities of the firm of which he or she was the beneficial owner. The profit must be surrendered to the firm even if the securities were bought with the intent to hold them for more than six months or were sold without any intent to make a later purchase. The short-swing profit rule does *not* apply to securities acquired in good faith in connection with a debt under a contract made *before* any securities were bought or sold.

The firm may sue to recover short-swing profits. If it fails to bring a lawsuit, or does not sue within 60 days after having been asked to do so, or fails to diligently prosecute a pending suit, any owner of its securities may sue on its behalf. To calculate the amount of the judgment, the number of shares bought at the lowest price are matched against the same number sold at the highest price, the number bought at the next highest price are then matched against the same number sold at the next lowest price, and so on. This is known as the "highest out, lowest in" principle. It is intended to assure that the firm recovers all of the short-swing profits that may have been made.

Wrongful Insider Trading

Insiders who have material nonpublic information about a firm may not buy or sell the firm's securities without first disclosing that information. This is known as the

disclose or abstain principle. When disclosure of material nonpublic information by an insider would be improper or inappropriate in light of the interests of the firm and its shareholders and inconsistent with the insider's status as a fiduciary vis-à-vis the firm and its shareholders, the insider is *not free* to reveal the information. In such instances the insider may not trade in the firm's securities with someone who does not have the same information. Nondisclosure by an insider of nonpublic material information is equivalent to the use of a manipulative or deceptive device or contrivance in violation of Section 10(b) and to the use of a device, scheme, or artifice to defraud in violation of Rule 10b-5.

Tipper and Tippee

An insider who gives material nonpublic information about a firm to a person who does not have access to that information is a **tipper.** The recipient of the information is a **tippee.** Unlike a tipper, a tippee may not have a fiduciary obligation to either the firm or its shareholders not to disclose material nonpublic information about the firm. This is the case, for example, with a tippee who is not affiliated with the firm. However, a tippee not affiliated with the firm does have a duty to reveal such information before dealing in a firm's securities if the tipper passed the information along for the tipper's direct or indirect gain and the tippee knew or should have known that the tipper's behavior was a breach of the tipper's fiduciary duty to the firm or its shareholders. The tippee's duty to disclose or abstain is derived from the tipper's fiduciary obligation not to exploit his or her relationship with the firm. Even if the tippee is not affiliated with the firm, the tippee assumes a fiduciary duty to the firm's shareholders upon participating in a tipper's breach of his or her fiduciary obligation. For the purposes of Section 10(b) and Rule 10b-5, such a tippee is no different from an insider. Broadly put, a tippee must abide by the disclose or abstain principle when aware that the tipper's disclosure is for an improper purpose. A tippee who does not owe a fiduciary duty to either the firm or its stockholders is not bound by the disclose or abstain principle.

Insider Trading and Securities Fraud Act

The Insider Trading and Securities Fraud Act (1988) limits the amount of damages that a party may recover because he or she was injured by trading in securities at the same time that a buyer or seller who, while in possession of material nonpublic information, in violation of the 1934 Act or an SEC Rule, traded in the same class of securities. The injured party may not recover from the party who violated the act or rule more than the profit that party gained or the loss that party avoided by carrying out the unlawful transaction.

Disclose or abstain
the requirement that an insider who has material nonpublic information about a firm may not trade in the firm's securities without first publicly disclosing that information

Tipper
an insider who wrongfully shares material nonpublic information about a firm

Tippee
a person who wrongfully obtains from an insider material nonpublic information about a firm

---

BATEMAN EICHLER, HILL RICHARDS, INC. v. BERNER
SUPREME COURT OF THE UNITED STATES
472 U.S. 299 (1986)

The plaintiffs (investors), seeking compensatory and punitive damages, charged that they were victims of a conspiracy between Lazarro, a registered securities broker who was employed by the defendant, Bateman Eichler, Hill Richards, Inc., a broker-dealer, and Nadeau, the president of T.O.N.M. Oil & Gas Exploration Corporation (TONM). Lazarro and Nadeau allegedly persuaded them to buy large quantities of TONM stock through the defendant broker-dealer by giving them materially false and incomplete information about TONM on the pretext that it was accurate inside information. They were told that TONM had options to buy property on which vast amounts of gold had been discovered and was negotiating with other companies to mine the gold and that TONM stock, then selling at between $1.50 and $3 a share, would climb to perhaps $100 a share once this information was made public. After the plaintiffs bought TONM stock, the mining venture fell through and the price of a share of TONM stock declined to substantially below what they had paid.

Concluding that the plaintiffs were tippees who possessed material nonpublic information when they purchased the TONM stock, and had therefore violated Rule 10b-5, the federal district court dismissed the complaint on the basis of the *in pari delicto* doctrine, which bars a party from recovering damages for a wrongful act in which he or she participated. The court of appeals reversed, ruling that "securities professionals and corporate officers who have allegedly engaged in fraud should not be permitted to invoke the *in pari delicto* principle to shield themselves from the consequences of their fraudulent misrepresentation." The Supreme Court granted the plaintiffs' petition for certiorari.

JUSTICE BRENNAN
Delivered the Opinion of the Court

The common law defense [of *in pari delicto*] is grounded on two premises: first, that courts should not lend their good offices to mediating disputes among wrongdoers; and second, that denying judicial relief to an admitted wrongdoer is an effective means of deterring illegality. [T]he public policy considerations that [undergird the refusal to allow a defendant to use the *in pari delicto* doctrine as a defense] even where the plaintiff [bears] substantial fault for his injury [is based on the view that this is necessary to support] "public interests or public policy, however reprehensible the [plaintiff's behavior] may be."

[The] implied private [right to sue for a Rule 10b-5 violation provides] "a most effective weapon in the enforcement" of the securities laws and [is] "a necessary supplement to [SEC] action." Accordingly, a private action for damages [for a Rule 10b-5 violation] may be barred on the grounds of the plaintiff's own culpability only where (1) as a direct result of his own actions, the plaintiff bears at least substantially equal responsibility for the violation he seeks to redress and (2) preclusion of suit would not significantly interfere with the effective enforcement of the securities laws and protection of the investing public.

[F]or purposes of resolving the issue before us [we accept the district court's and court of appeals'] assumption that the [plaintiffs have violated] Section 10(b) and Rule 10b-5.

Notwithstanding the broad reach of Section 10(b) and Rule 10b-5, there are important distinctions between the relative culpability of tippers, securities professionals, and tippees. The Court has made it clear that a tippee's use of material nonpublic information does not violate Section 10(b) and Rule 10b-5 unless the tippee owes a corresponding duty to disclose the information [prior to trading in the firm's securities]. "[T]he tippee's obligation [to disclose or refrain from dealing in the securities] has been viewed as arising from his role as a participant after the fact in the insider's breach of a fiduciary duty" toward corporate shareholders. In the context of insider trading, we do not believe that a person whose liability is solely derived [that is, not based on a direct obligation to the firm's shareholders] can be said to be as culpable as one whose breach of duty gave rise to that liability in the first place.

Moreover, insiders and broker-dealers who selectively disclose material nonpublic information commit a potentially broader range of violations than do tippees who trade on the basis of that information. [I]n cases where the tipper intentionally conveys false or materially incomplete information to the tippee, the tipper is not only in violation of securities law, [but is guilty of] an additional violation: fraud against the tippee. Such conduct is particularly egregious [that is, strikingly bad,] when committed by a securities professional, who owes a duty of honesty and fair dealing toward his clients. Absent other culpable actions by a tippee that can fairly be said to outweigh these violations by insiders and broker-dealers, we do not believe that the tippee properly can be characterized as being of substantially equal culpability as his tippers.

We also believe that denying the [application of the] *in pari delicto* defense in [these] circumstances will promote the primary objective of the federal securities laws—protection of the investing public and the national economy through the promotion of "a high standard of *business ethics* [emphasis supplied] in every facet of the securities industry."

[I]t is particularly important to permit "litigation among guilty parties [that will serve] to expose their unlawful conduct and render them more easily subject to appropriate civil, administrative, and criminal penalties." Moreover, we believe the deterrence of insider trading most frequently will be maximized by bringing enforcement pressures to bear on the sources of such information—corporate insiders and broker-dealers. In addition, corporate insiders and broker-dealers will in many instances be more responsive to the deterrent pressure of potential sanctions; they are more likely than ordinary investors to be advised by counsel and thereby informed fully of the "allowable limits on their conduct."

We therefore conclude that the public interest will most frequently be advanced if defrauded tippees are permitted to bring suit and to expose illegal practices by corporate insiders and broker-dealers. [T]here is no warrant to give corporate insiders and broker-dealers "a license to defraud the investing public with little fear of prosecution."

Affirmed.

Legal Issues

1. A state statute required that brokers doing business in the state register with the State Security Commission. Talton Ross, a broker employed by Wilson & Associates Company, a broker-dealer, did not register with the commission, and Wilson & Associates was aware of this fact. Gig Mart had an account with Wilson & Associates. In his dealings with Ross, through behavior that violated Section 10(b) and Rule 10b–5, Mart caused Wilson & Associates $500,000 in damages. When Wilson & Associates brought a lawsuit to recover the $500,000, Mart asked the court to dismiss the suit on the ground that Wilson & Associates was aware that Ross had failed to register with the State Security Commission. What judgment, and why?

2. Frank, a promoter, offered to sell Victor $300,000 worth of stock in a firm that was about to be organized. In his presentation to Victor, Frank violated Section 10(b) and Rule

10b-5. After Victor bought the stock, Frank said that the whole idea would have to be dropped unless he could sell an additional $200,000 worth of the firm's stock to other investors. Victor convinced five other persons to each invest $40,000 in the firm. Within months the firm was bankrupt. Victor brought suit against Frank to recover damages for the Section 10(b) and Rule 10b-5 violations. When Victor bought the firm's stock and convinced the five other persons to do so, he knew that the stock was not registered with the SEC as required by federal securities law. Is the *in pari delicto* defense applicable? Why?

Ethical Issues

1. Which ethical standard or standards would you most closely identify with Justice Brennan's view, expressed in *Bateman Eichler, Hills Richard, Inc.*, as to when a defendant may invoke the *in pari delicto* defense? Why?

2. Under what circumstances, if any, would an advocate of utilitarian ethics regard *in pari delicto* as an ethically acceptable defense? Why?

PROXIES

Proxies, described in detail in Chapter 11, are used by shareholders to authorize someone else to vote their stock. The format, content, and solicitation of proxies used to vote stocks registered under the Securities Exchange Act of 1934 are regulated by the act and SEC rules.

Proxy Format and Content

A proxy must indicate in bold print whether it is being solicited on behalf of the firm's board of directors, contain spaces for the shareholder's signature and the shareholder's insertion of the signature date, clearly and impartially state the subject or subjects on which the shareholder's stock may be voted, and permit the shareholder to specify whether and how his or her stock should be voted on a particular subject. Proxies used in elections of directors must allow shareholders to designate their choices, or to authorize one or more named persons to decide how to vote their stock, or to indicate the candidates for whom their votes cannot be cast.

Proxy Solicitation

Proxy statement
a written explanation, including relevant material information, of the purposes for which a solicited proxy will be used

A *proxy solicitation* may ask a shareholder to supply his or her proxy, or to deny anyone else a proxy, or to revoke an earlier proxy. A proxy solicitation must be accompanied by a written **proxy statement.** This statement must include all of the material information concerning the matters for which the proxy can be used. A person who solicits proxies to challenge management's slate of directors has a limited right to the firm's assistance in his or her proxy solicitation. The firm can fulfill this obligation, at the challenger's expense, either by providing the challenger with the names and addresses of the firm's shareholders or by itself distributing the challenger's materials.

At least 10 days before the proxy, the proxy statement, and other proxy solicitation materials are distributed, copies of these materials must be filed with the SEC and the exchange on which the stock is traded. Shareholders injured because a proxy statement contains a false or misleading material statement or because it omits material information, can recover damages together with reasonable attorney's fees. When the proxy or proxy solicitation requirements have not been satisfied, a court may bar or set aside a vote.

INFORMING INVESTORS OF A PLANNED CORPORATE TAKEOVER?

Hypothetical Case

Over the course of several decades, Carlton, Inc., through internal expansion and a number of acquisitions, grew from a small family-owned and -operated enterprise into a multi-billion-dollar publicly held corporation. Carlton's acquisitions committee, made up of the chief executive officer, two vice presidents, a lawyer, and a certified public accountant, had an outstanding record of correctly deciding which companies warranted in-depth analysis with a view toward acquisition. After such an analysis of Wide-Right Corporation, the committee decided that Carlton, Inc. should acquire all of Wide-Right's 1 million shares of stock. At what point should Carlton be required to make public its plan to acquire Wide-Right? What information must Carlton reveal to Wide-Right's shareholders when offering to purchase their stock? Should Wide-Right's management be *allowed* to distribute to Wide-Right's shareholders a statement of its opinion as to whether they would be wise to accept or reject Carlton's offer? Why? Should such a statement be *required*? Why?

TENDER OFFERS

Individuals, groups of persons, or corporations that desire to acquire a substantial portion or all of the equity securities of a publicly held corporation may do so by inviting all the current owners of these securities to offer to sell them some or all of their shares. Such a proposal is known as a **tender offer** because the shareholders are asked to tender their shares, that is, make the shares available for purchase by the offeror. The corporation whose equity securities are to be bought is referred to as the **target company.**

Tender offer
an offer extended to a firm's shareholders to buy their equity securities

Target company
the firm whose shares are the subject of a tender offer

Williams Act

The Williams Act (1968), which amended the Securities Exchange Act of 1934, regulates public tender offers, whether they are "friendly" (approved by management) or "hostile" (opposed by management). It applies to offers made to shareholders through the direct or indirect use of the mails, or any instrumentality or means of interstate commerce, or any facility of a national exchange, that (1) propose to buy at a specified price (2) during a stated period of time (3) an equity security registered under the 1934 Act or the Investment Company Act of 1940, or an equity security of an insurance company whose shares would have had to be registered if they had not been expressly exempted from registration by the 1934 Act, (4) if after such an offer has been accepted, the offeror would be a beneficial owner of more than 5 percent of the class of the security covered by the offer.

Compulsory Disclosure and Procedure

The purposes of the Williams Act are to assure (1) that shareholders are provided with enough information to decide whether to tender their shares and (2) that the way a tender offer is carried out is fair to investors and consistent with the public interest.

When a tender offer is published or given to securities holders, the offeror must provide the SEC with certain information, including (1) the name of the target company, (2) the terms of the offer, (3) the amount and source of the money or other consideration that is to be paid for the securities, (4) a description of any prior dealings between the offeror and the target company or its management, (5) whether the offeror was convicted of a crime during the past five years, and (6) whether the offeror intends to control, liquidate, or merge the target company or to make any change in its structure or operation. The same information must be given to the target company.

Fraudulent Tender Offers

Whether or not the securities are registered with the SEC, it is unlawful for the party who tenders securities to misrepresent or omit a material fact or for the party who makes the tender offer, or who favors or opposes it, to engage in any fraudulent, deceptive, or manipulative act or practice in connection with the offer.

Duration of Tender Offer

Unless withdrawn, a tender offer must remain open until the expiration of at least 20 business days from its commencement and at least 10 business days from the date of any notice of an increase or decrease in the percentage of the class of securities being bought or the amount of the consideration promised for them. Tendered securities may be withdrawn while the tender offer remains open. If the purchase price is raised while a tender offer is still in effect, all shareholders are entitled to the higher price. Unless the tender offer calls for the purchase of all tendered shares, these shares must be purchased on a pro rata basis.

SEC rules, rather than the Williams Act, specify what information must be filed with the SEC, what disclosures must be made, and what procedures must be followed when the issuer itself offers to repurchase its outstanding shares from stockholders.

Management's Response

Within 10 days after a tender offer has been made, the target company's management must inform the shareholders of its stand, if any, on the tender offer. The shareholders may be advised that management expresses no opinion and is nonpartisan, or is unable to take a position to evaluate the offer, or recommends that the offer be accepted or rejected. The explanation that management presents in support of its position is subject to the same antifraud standards that are applicable to all other aspects of the tender offer process.

Enforcement

The SEC may obtain appropriate equitable relief when the provisions of the Williams Act or SEC rules to implement the act are violated. When this happens, private persons are also entitled to suitable equitable relief, which may call for such action as the return of their shares or the cancellation of the tender offer and the return of all the parties to the state of affairs that existed prior to the tender offer.

CRIMINAL SANCTIONS FOR SECURITIES ACT VIOLATIONS

Criminal sanctions for violations of the Securities Act of 1933 and the Securities Exchange Act of 1934 are found in Table 17-1.

INVESTMENT COMPANY ACT OF 1940

An investment company is primarily engaged in the business of investing and reinvesting in the securities of other companies. Investment companies enable persons to invest in a pool of securities, which diversifies risk. These companies generally deal in what are commonly referred to as "mutual funds." If they use the mails or any form of interstate facilities, they must comply with the registration requirements of the Investment Company Act of 1940, which resemble the registration requirements of the Securities Act of 1933 and the Securities Exchange Act of 1934. The Investment Company Act makes those who advise a registered

Criminal Sanctions for Securities Act Violations   **TABLE 17-1**

Securities Act of 1933	A willful violation of the act, or of an SEC rule or regulation promulgated under the act, or a willful misrepresentation or omission of a material fact is punishable by a fine of not more than $10,000, or imprisonment of not more than five years, or both.
Securities Exchange Act of 1934	A willful violation of the act (other than a violation of that portion of the act concerning the corruption of a foreign official, a foreign political party, or a candidate for a foreign political office), or a willful violation of any rule promulgated under the act that is unlawful, or willfully and knowingly making, or causing to be made, any statement in any application, report, or document required to be filed under the act, or any rule promulgated under the act, that is false or misleading with respect to any material fact, is punishable in the case of a natural person by a fine of not more than $1 million, or imprisonment of not more than 10 years, or both. However, a person who violated a rule promulgated under the act may not be imprisoned unless he or she acted with knowledge of the rule or regulation. When the violator is not a natural person, the fine may not exceed $2.5 million.
	An issuer that violates one of the act's bans having to do with the corruption of a foreign official, or a foreign political party, or a candidate for a foreign political office may not be fined more than $2 million. Any officer, director, or stockholder of an issuer who, acting on behalf of the issuer, violates the act's bans having to do with the corruption of a foreign official, or a foreign political party, or a candidate for a foreign political office may be punished by a fine of not more than $10,000, or imprisonment of not more than five years, or both.

investment company fiduciaries in regard to their compensation for their advisory services. Under the act, the NASD may by rule prohibit its members from offering mutual fund shares at a price that includes an excessive sales load. At the same time the act recognizes that sales personnel, broker-dealers, and underwriters are entitled to receive reasonable compensation for their services.

INVESTMENT ADVISERS ACT OF 1940

The Investment Advisers Act of 1940 regulates investment advisers. For the purposes of the act, an investment adviser is a person who, for compensation, is in the business of advising others, either directly or through publications or writings, as to the value of securities or as to the desirability of buying, selling, or investing in securities. Exempt from the act's provisions are banks; publishers of bona fide newspapers, newsmagazines, or business or financial publications of general and regular circulation; persons whose advice is limited to securities issued or guaranteed by the federal government; brokers or dealers whose investment advice is only incidental to the conduct of their business; and lawyers, accountants, engineers, and teachers whose investment advice is incidental to the practice of their profession.

Investment advisers who fall within the terms of the act must register with the SEC and periodically file reports with it. The registration document must include certain information about the adviser, such as the adviser's principal business, the nature of that business, the scope of the adviser's authority to act on the client's behalf, fee arrangements, the adviser's educational and business history, a description of the adviser's other businesses, and any criminal activity by the adviser akin to the sort of misconduct that may result in the imposition of SEC sanctions on a broker-dealer.

The Investment Advisers Act requires investment advisers to disclose any conflict of interest between them and their clients. It prohibits them from engaging in any conduct that operates as a fraud or deceit on a client or a prospective client or in misleading advertising, excessive trading, or fraudulent, deceptive, or manipulative acts or practices as SEC rules define these terms.

Although the adviser's fee may be based on the value of the investor's principal at a specified time, it may not be based on the appreciation of the investor's capital or on any gain that results from following the adviser's suggestions.

SECURITIES ENFORCEMENT REMEDIES REFORM ACT OF 1990

During the decade of the 1980s, fraud, stock manipulation, and other illegal activities in securities transactions climbed to unprecedented levels. At the same time the number of securities firms increased by more than 90 percent, the number of investment companies increased by more than 145 percent, the number of investment advisers more than tripled, the number of registration statements filed annually with the SEC doubled, and the number of tender offers filed with the SEC increased by 670 percent. The Securities Enforcement Remedies Reform Act of 1990 makes new remedies available to the SEC and the courts.

These remedies are intended to deter unlawful conduct, curb recidivism, that is, persons repeatedly violating federal securities laws, make injunctive relief against illegal behavior more readily available, and expand the range of punishment for violations of federal securities laws. Table 17-2 summarizes the act's key provisions.

Securities Enforcement Remedies Reform Act of 1990	**TABLE 17-2**

SEC cease and desist proceedings	*Cease and desist order:* If after a hearing the SEC finds that a person is violating, has violated, or is about to violate a provision of the Securities Act of 1933, the Securities Exchange Act of 1934, the Investment Company Act of 1940, or the Investment Advisers Act of 1940, or any rule or regulation promulgated under these acts, it may order that person to cease and desist from violating the act, rule, or regulation and to temporarily or permanently take appropriate action assuring future compliance with the act, rule, or regulation. In addition, the SEC may require the person to account for illegally made profits and to surrender them together with reasonable interest.
	Temporary order issued during a cease and desist proceeding: If prior to the completion of a cease and desist proceeding the SEC determines that the violation on which the proceeding is based is likely to result in significant dissipation or theft of assets, significant harm to investors, or substantial harm to the public interest, such as losses to the Securities Investor Protection Corporation, it may, after notice and a hearing, enter a temporary order that the accused cease and desist from the violation or threatened violation and take appropriate action to prevent dissipation or theft of assets, significant harm to investors, or substantial harm to the public interest. A temporary order may be entered without notice and a hearing if the SEC determines that notice and a hearing would be impracticable or contrary to the public interest.
SEC-imposed civil remedies	If after notice and an opportunity for a hearing the SEC finds that a person has willfully violated the Securities Act of 1933, the Securities Exchange Act of 1934, the Investment Company Act of 1940, or the Investmment Advisers Act of 1940, or rules or regulations promulgated under any of these acts, and that the imposition of a penalty is in the public interest, it may impose a penalty in accordance with the following three-tier standard: (1) not more than $5,000 for a natural person or $50,000 for any other person for any such violation; (2) not more than $50,000 for a natural person or $250,000 for any other person if the violation involved fraud, deceit, manipulation, or deliberate or reckless disregard of a regulatory requirement; (3) not more than $100,000 for a natural person or $500,000 for any other person if the violation involved fraud, deceit, manipulation, or deliberate or reckless disregard of a regulatory requirement and it directly or indirectly resulted in substantial losses, or created a significant risk of substantial losses to other persons, or resulted in substantial pecuniary gain to the guilty party.
Civil proceedings brought by SEC in federal district court to impose a penalty	When it appears to the SEC that any person has violated any provision of the Securities Act of 1933, or the Securities Exchange Act of 1934, or any rule or regulation promulgated under either act, or an SEC cease and desist order, other than for insider trading, the SEC may bring suit in a U.S. district court to have the court impose a penalty on that person. The court is to use the same three-tier

TABLE 17–2   *Continued*

	standard as the SEC itself would use (described above) to arrive at the penalty.
Court ban on a person acting as a corporate officer or director	In a suit brought by the SEC in a U.S. district court to enjoin a violation of the Securities Act of 1933, or any rule or regulation promulgated under the act, the court may temporarily or permanently, conditionally or unconditionally, bar any person guilty of violating the act's antifraud provisions from acting as an officer or a director of any issuer that either has a class of securities registered with the SEC or must file reports with the SEC if that person's conduct demonstrates substantial unfitness to serve as an officer or a director of such an issuer. In a proceeding brought by the SEC to obtain an injunction for a violation of the Securities Exchange Act of 1934, or any rule or regulation promulgated under the act, the court may temporarily or permanently, conditionally or unconditionally, bar any person who violated Section 10(b) of the act from acting as an officer or a director of any issuer that has a class of securities registered with the SEC or is required to file reports with the SEC if that person's conduct demonstrates substantial unfitness to so serve.

STATE BLUE-SKY LAWS

Blue-sky laws
state statutes that regulate securities transactions

State statutes designed to regulate securities transactions are commonly referred to as **blue-sky laws.** In 1911 Kansas enacted the first blue-sky law, a statute to regulate the sale and distribution of securities. A reason given for the enactment of this statute was to protect state residents from speculative schemes that had no more basis than "so many feet of blue sky." Numerous other states adopted securities regulation statutes before Congress passed the Securities Act of 1933.

Like federal securities legislation, the state blue-sky laws outlaw fraud in the sale or purchase of securities. However, federal securities legislation differs fundamentally from most of the state blue-sky laws in the manner in which it seeks to protect investors from being victimized by blue-sky schemes. The Securities Act of 1933 and the Securities Exchange Act of 1934 are based on the premise that the task of government is to enable investors to arrive at an informed decision as to whether to purchase a security. The state blue-sky laws, on the other hand, usually allow a security to be offered for sale in a state only after a state agency determines that the quality of the security is adequate. Such laws generally require that an issuer file an effective registration statement with the designated state agency before distributing securities in the state.

CTS CORP. v. DYNAMICS CORPORATION OF AMERICA
SUPREME COURT OF THE UNITED STATES
481 U.S. 69 (1987)

The Indiana Control Share Acquisitions Act provided that before an entity could acquire stock that would give it control of 20 percent or 33⅓ percent or 50 percent of the voting stock of certain Indiana corporations, a majority of such a corporation's shareholders who were in no way involved with the acquisition would have to approve the acquisition at a specially called or regularly scheduled shareholders' meeting. The act specified that it was applicable only to corporations whose boards of directors voted to be bound by its provisions.

After the board of directors of CTS Corp. voted that the act should govern acquisitions of CTS stock, Dynamics Corporation, which already owned 9.6 percent of CTS's common stock, announced a tender offer that, if successful, would have increased its share of CTS stock to 27.5 percent. Dynamics sued CTS in federal district court. In part it charged that the Williams Act preempted the Indiana statute. The district court agreed and ruled in favor of Dynamics. The court of appeals affirmed. CTS appealed.

JUSTICE POWELL
Delivered the Opinion of the Court

[A]bsent an explicit indication by Congress of an intent to preempt state law, a state statute is preempted only

> "where compliance with both federal and state regulations is a physical impossibility," or where the state "law stands as an obstacle to the accomplishment and execution of the full purposes and objectives of Congress."

Because it is entirely possible for entities to comply with both the Williams Act and the Indiana Act, the [Indiana] statute can be preempted only if it frustrates the purposes of the federal law.

[In *Edgar v. MITE Corp.* (1982)] this Court struck down an Illinois statute which established a 20-day precommencement period in the case of tender offers. In addition, the law provided for a hearing to determine whether the offeror could proceed with the tender offer. Because it set no date for the hearing, [a corporation's] management could indefinitely stymie a takeover. The Illinois Secretary of State was authorized to review the tender offer to determine whether it was fair. Justice White, who wrote the Court's opinion in *Mite* but spoke only for himself and three other Justices on the question of whether the Illinois law was preempted by the Williams Act, concluded that the Illinois law did conflict with the Williams Act and therefore was preempted by the federal statute.

[T]he statute [now] before the Court protects the independent shareholders against the contending parties. Thus the Act furthers a basic purpose of the Williams Act, [placing] "investors on an equal footing with the takeover bidder."

The Indiana Act operates on the assumption, implicit in the Williams Act, that independent shareholders faced with tender offers often are at a disadvantage. By allowing such shareholders to vote as a group [at a stockholders' meeting], the [Indiana] Act protects them from the coercive aspects of some tender offers.

The [Indiana] Act does not impose an indefinite delay on tender offers. Nor does the Act allow state government [as in *MITE*] to impose its views of fairness between willing buyers and sellers of shares of the target company. Rather, the Act allows shareholders to evaluate the fairness of the offer collectively.

Even assuming that the Indiana Act imposes some additional delay, nothing in *MITE* suggested that *any* [italics supplied] delay imposed by state regulation, however short, would conflict with the Williams Act. [In MITE Justice White] argued only that the offer should "be free to go forward without unreasonable delay."

[T]he possibility that the Indiana Act will delay some tender offers is insufficient to require a conclusion that the Williams Act preempts the Act. The long-standing prevalence of state regulation in this area suggests that if Congress had intended to preempt all state laws that delay the acquisition of voting control following a tender offer, it would have said so explicitly. The regulatory conditions that the Act places on tender offers are consistent with the text and the purposes of the Williams Act. [T]he Williams Act does not preempt the Indiana Act.

[W]e reverse the judgment of the Court of Appeals.

It is so ordered.

Legal Issues

1. Would a state statute that provides that any person, partnership, association, or corporation that owned more than 10 percent of the equity securities of any corporation organized under the laws of the state at the time of a hostile tender offer must turn over to the firm any profits such persons or organizations made from a sale of the shares within 18 months after the tender offer be preempted by the Williams Act? Why?

2. A state statute bars stockholders who own more than 20 percent of a corporation's shares from voting their shares without the prior approval of all the other stockholders at a stockholders' meeting held to decide whether to approve a *hostile* takeover. Is this statute preempted by the Williams Act? Discuss.

Ethical Issues

1. Following a lawfully made tender offer initiated by a three-person investment group that was seeking to acquire all of the outstanding equity securities of Big Fellows, the group's attorney asked Allison, the president of Big Fellows, to meet with the investment group so that it could thoroughly explore the financial status of Big Fellows and ward off a possible tender offer by any other investment group. Compare Allison's ethical obligations to Big Fellows and its stockholders with her ethical obligations to the three-person investment group and any other groups that might seek to acquire the stock of Big Fellows.

2. At what point, if any, in the course of a *hostile* takeover does a corporate officer's ethical obligations to his or her firm and its stockholders outweigh the corporate officer's ethical obligations to an outside investor who wishes to acquire the firm? To what extent should a firm's attorney's ethical obligations to the firm be influenced by the interests of the firm's minority stockholders? Discuss.

LAW ABROAD

Germany

Neither Germany's federal government nor its state governments have a separate, comprehensive body of laws regarding securities transactions. For the most part, guaranties of investors' rights and restrictions on the purchase or sale of securities are found in Germany's general corporation law; a national statute that limits the liability of investors; the federal Stock Corporation Act, which mainly concerns judicial examination into charges by shareholders that they have been deprived of one or more of the rights guaranteed to them by statute; rules set by the nation's stock exchanges, all of which are privately operated; and the Stock Exchange Act, which requires that the *prices* of securities listed on exchanges *be representative of their fair market value.*

Neither at the federal level nor the state level is there an agency like the U.S. Securities and Exchange Commission or state securities agencies. Equity securities may be issued without the approval of any sector of the German government. Commonly, banks underwrite and market newly issued securities. There is no federal or state legislation on the subject of tender offers, but representatives of the German stock exchanges have set suggested tender offer guidelines.

REVIEW QUESTIONS & PROBLEMS

1. Four investors, all of whom were Oklahoma residents, established a Delaware corporation that would conduct all of its business in Oklahoma. To raise sufficient capital, the corporation would issue $5 million worth of equity securities. Each of the four investors would purchase 10 percent of the issue, and the rest of the issue would be distributed through an underwriter who dealt with Oklahoma broker-dealers. When would the four investors qualify as accredited investors under Regulation D?

2. What action may the SEC take if it concludes that a registration statement is deficient?

3. Falter Financial Services, Inc. sells a variety of insurance products, including variable annuity contracts issued by Great Benefits Corporation. Instead of simply providing for set monthly payments to the insured, these contracts allow the insured to share in the profits that Great Benefits earns from its investment portfolio, which includes securities and real estate. Does Falter Financial Services have to satisfy the broker-dealer registration requirements of the Securities Exchange Act of 1934? Why?

4. Mary Wills, general counsel of Vari, Inc., signed an incomplete registration statement at the request of the firm's president. Without her knowledge the firm's president inserted false and misleading material information in the statement before filing it with the SEC. Shortly after the sale of the entire issue covered by the registration statement, Vari became insolvent. The purchasers of the issue sued Vari, Inc., as well as Wills and everyone else whose signature was on the registration statement. Wills's attorney asked the court to dismiss the suit against her because she was not aware that the registration statement contained false and misleading material information when it was filed with the SEC. Should the request be granted? Why?

5. May a tombstone advertisement and a red herring prospectus serve as a substitute for the usual prospectus requirement? Explain your answer.

CHAPTER

18

Restraints of Trade and Monopoly

Competition can be suppressed or destroyed in many ways. For example, a manufacturer may refuse to deal with retailers who resell its products below a price that the manufacturer suggests; a person who sells an ongoing business may promise the buyer not to engage in the same kind of business; a manufacturer of a product may control the market price at which its competitors sell like products; at the request of several of its retailer customers, a manufacturer may agree not to do business with one of their competitors; firms selling the same kind of product may agree that each of them will do business only in a specific geographical area; and business executives may persuade state legislators to enact legislation that severely limits the number of new competitors in their industries.

This chapter considers two legislative policies that are intended to protect and promote competition. These policies are embodied in laws that bar restraints of trade and monopolization. The chapter also considers exemptions from those laws. In addition, it examines the civil remedies with which the government and private persons can combat restraints of trade and monopolization and the criminal penalties that can be imposed for engaging in these activities.

ORIGIN OF ANTITRUST POLICY

American resentment toward anticompetitive behavior and toward the domination of an industry by just one, two, or three firms can be traced to centuries-old English legal thought and to the American colonists' views about how business should be done. Early in the 15th century an English court ruled that an agreement between individuals not to compete with one another was invalid. To raise revenue, England's monarchs granted individuals and companies "letters patent," which gave each holder exclusive power to trade in a particular product. In the early 17th century an English court ruled illegal a letters patent that gave the holder exclusive control over the making and trading of playing cards in England. Soon afterward Parliament enacted the Statute of Monopolies. This statute curbed the power of those who held letters patent and allowed only Parliament to grant future monopolies.

Shortly before the American Revolution the English government granted the British East India Company a monopoly that allowed it to control the importation and sale of tea in the American colonies. In 1773, in what has ever since been called the Boston Tea Party, a group of radical colonists stormed East India Company ships at anchor in Boston harbor and cast their cargo of tea overboard. Many colonial merchants approved of this blow against monopolization.

The Declaration of Independence was signed in 1776, and in the same year Adam Smith's well-known economic treatise, *The Wealth of Nations,* was published. The former upheld the rights of individuals and denounced the abuses of government; the latter extolled the blessings of competition in the marketplace. Both the Declaration and *The Wealth of Nations* gave expression to the views of many of the American colonists.

From the time that the United States was founded through the beginning of the Civil War, small business dominated the nation's economic order. After the Civil War large companies led by "captains of industry" gained ever greater power over American business. Some of these business leaders believed that competition should be curtailed, if not destroyed, whenever and however possible. They arranged to have their firms jointly set prices, restrict production, or combine with one another. Congress enacted the Sherman Antitrust Act in response to widespread fears that unless steps were taken to protect competition, a handful of persons would curtail, perhaps even eliminate the benefits of competition and exercise increasing control over the nation's political affairs. Sometimes referred to as the Second Constitution of the United States, the Sherman Act became law on July 2, 1890. Section 1 of the act outlaws certain restraints of trade; Section 2 deals with monopolization.

SECTION 1 OF THE SHERMAN ACT

Section 1 of the Sherman Act provides that "every contact, combination in the form of trust or otherwise, or conspiracy, in restraint of trade or commerce" in either interstate or foreign trade or commerce is illegal. The act does not define those terms. Courts have the ultimate authority to decide what each means. In doing so, however, they generally take into account the points of view voiced by administrative agencies, economists, and business experts.

Definition of Terms

Every

In *United States v. Trans-Missouri Freight Association,*[1] the first case in which the U.S. Supreme Court construed Section 1 of the Sherman Act, the Court was asked to rule that an agreement in which competitors fixed the prices that they would charge for their services was necessarily unlawful. The defendants insisted that the agreement was not unlawful, because the prices set were reasonable. In a 5–4 decision the Court ruled that the agreement was a contract in restraint of trade and therefore a violation of Section 1. The majority held that Section 1 made "every" contract in restraint of trade unlawful. The minority insisted that when Congress used the word *every,* it meant to ban only *unreasonable* restraints of trade.

In time the Supreme Court opted for a split interpretation of "every." Under this construction, some restraints of trade are regarded as detrimental to competition because their unavoidable consequence is the destruction of competition. Such "unreasonable" restraints are **illegal per se,** that is, always unlawful. However, the **rule of reason** recognizes that other restraints may or may not dampen or eliminate competition. Such restraints are evaluated on a case-by-case basis to determine their effect on competition. If a restraint of this kind has no effect or a beneficial effect on competition, it is reasonable and therefore does not violate Section 1. If it limits or destroys competition, it is unreasonable and therefore illegal. Later in this chapter we will examine the kinds of restraints that are tested by the illegal per se standard and the kinds that are tested by the rule of reason.

Illegal per se

a restraint of trade that is always unlawful

Rule of reason

a restraint of trade is evaluated on a case-by-case basis to decide whether its effect on competition makes it illegal

Contract

As noted in Chapter 8, a "contract" is an agreement voluntarily entered into between two or more parties. The kind of restriction imposed by a contract that restrains trade or commerce determines which criterion—the illegal per se standard or the rule of reason—will be applied to the contract.

Obviously, the effects of an agreement not to compete are not limited to the parties themselves. Section 1 bans certain restraints of trade because they are against the public interest. Even if freely agreed to, they are unlawful because Section 1 places the protection of competition ahead of the freedom of individuals to enter into a contract that is prohibited by either the illegal per se standard or the rule of reason.

Combination

Combination

a union of independent firms

Under Section 1, a **combination** exists when independent firms join together to pursue a particular objective, such as the construction and sale of a building or the manufacture and sale of a product; or when independent firms abandon their independence by consolidating into a single firm.

Company officers, company employees, and a corporation and its wholly owned subsidiaries and divisions share a "unity of purpose." Thus, their joint activity is not a combination under Section 1.

In the Form of Trust

Trust

a form of business organization in which the shareholders of two or more corporations transfer their stock to a trustee or a board of trustees but retain the right to earnings

The trust was a means used in the 1880s to suppress or eliminate competition. To create a **trust,** the shareholders of two or more corporations transferred their stock to a trustee or a board of trustees. In return they received trust certificates, which entitled them to receive the corporations' dividends after they were distributed to the trustee or board. The trustee or board selected the corporations' boards of directors, which in turn chose the corporations' officers. The directors and officers saw to it that the corporations acted in concert with one another.

Or Otherwise

Congress included the catchall phrase "or otherwise" after the word *trust* to outlaw arrangements that could fairly be viewed as a means of attaining a result banned by Section 1.

Or Conspiracy

A scheme that requires two or more persons to use lawful or unlawful means to accomplish an illegal objective is a **conspiracy.**

In Restraint of Trade or Commerce

Trade involves dealing in something, such as exchanging commodities by barter, or buying and selling commodities for money, or providing services for a fee. **Commerce** involves the exchange of any kind of goods, products, property, or services for money. There is a **restraint** of trade or commerce under Section 1 when an independent business unit surrenders its *liberty to choose* how it will conduct its affairs. For example, an agreement between manufacturers not to deal with certain buyers or to deal with buyers only on certain terms is such a restraint of trade because the agreement deprives the manufacturers of their freedom to choose how they will do business.

Interstate and Foreign Trade and Commerce

Section 1 applies to interstate as well as foreign trade and commerce. This means that it is applicable to all trade and commerce that the Constitution allows Congress to regulate. Because the courts narrowly interpreted the meaning of "interstate trade or commerce" so as to include only those activities that have a *direct* relation to trade or commerce between states when the Sherman Act was adopted, and did so for a long time thereafter, for some time the act was not applicable to manufacturing, farming, mining, and insurance. These types of businesses were said to involve but a single state. As we have seen in Chapter 10, the meaning of the term *interstate* has been expanded to include conduct carried on in one state that *affects* trade or commerce in another state. Under the current interpretation, the Sherman Act applies to the four mentioned types of businesses and to any other type of business that takes place in one state but has an indirect or accidental impact on interstate trade or commerce or poses potential harm to such trade or commerce.

Just as the courts at one time narrowly interpreted the meaning of "interstate," they also narrowly interpreted the meaning of "trade or commerce." This meant, for example, that lawyers, doctors, dentists, and other professional persons were not covered by the Sherman Act, because it was said that they were not involved in trade or commerce. This is no longer so.

PER SE VIOLATIONS OF SECTION 1

The following restraints are illegal per se under Section 1.

Conspiracy
the joining of two or more persons to attain an illegal objective

Trade
dealing in goods or services

Commerce
the exchange of property or services for money

Restraint
an independent business unit's surrender of its freedom to do business as it pleases

Naked Restraint

Naked restraint
a restraint whose sole purpose is to eliminate competition

An agreement between two potential or actual competitors that has no other purpose than to assure that they will not compete with each other is a **naked restraint.** It is illegal per se.

Price-Fixing

Horizontal price-fixing
an agreement between competitors on the price they will charge for their goods or services

Vertical price-fixing
an agreement between a manufacturer and those who purchase its goods for resale as to the resale price of the goods

Resale price maintenance
an agreement between a manufacturer and a retailer that sets the resale price of the manufacturer's goods

An agreement between competitors as to the price they will charge for their goods or services is known as **horizontal price-fixing.** An agreement between a manufacturer and those to whom it sells its goods for resale that sets the price at which they may resell the goods is known as **vertical price-fixing.** Commonly, such an agreement between a manufacturer and a retailer is referred to as **resale price maintenance.** Whether a price-fixing agreement is horizontal or vertical, it necessarily restrains trade in the marketplace because it deprives one or both parties to the agreement of the freedom to charge whatever they wish for the goods or services they offer for sale. *Generally,* a horizontal or vertical agreement that sets the maximum or minimum price at which goods or services may be sold is illegal per se.

Conscious Parallelism

Conscious parallelism
the independent decision of a firm to behave in the same way as one or more of its competitors

Firms may *independently* decide to behave in the same way as one or more of their competitors. Such behavior is known as **conscious parallelism.** It is lawful because the firms are simply exercising their freedom to conduct their businesses as they see fit. For example, firms are free to single-handedly seek out information about the prices their competitors charge for certain products or services and to use that information as a guide in setting their own prices.

In a lawsuit in which it is shown that firms are selling identical products at the same price, it is a question of fact, based on the evidence whether their behavior results from independently made pricing decisions or from a price-fixing agreement.

Group Boycott

Group boycott
an agreement between manufacturers, between a manufacturer and a distributor, or between a manufacturer and retailers not to deal with a particular competing retailer

Agreements between manufacturers that they will not deal with a particular retailer, between a manufacturer and a distributor that they will not deal with a particular retailer, and between a manufacturer and two or more retailers that the manufacturer will not deal with a particular competing retailer are **group boycotts.** An agreement between a *single* manufacturer and a *single* retailer that the manufacturer will not deal with a particular retailer is *not* a group boycott.[2]

Hypothetical Case

NO, THANK YOU, WE DO NOT WANT YOUR BUSINESS

Arkin Corporation's board of directors decided that Arkin's operations would produce significantly more profits if Arkin convinced consumers that its new AL&B Court products were "the in thing" with wealthy, powerful, and demanding food connoisseurs and if it sold those products exclusively to grocers with a reputation for dealing in exotic and expensive foods.

Arkin's director of marketing informed Arkin customers who operated discount grocery stores that Arkin would not sell them AL&B Court products because their reputations as discounters would not promote the "top of the line" image that Arkin wanted for its AL&B Court products. However, it offered to continue to sell them its other products.

Is Arkin's refusal to sell the discounters AL&B Court products a violation of Section 1 of the Sherman Act? Which ethical standard or standards of behavior support Arkin's policy? Which ethical standard or standards do not support Arkin's policy? Why?

Refusal to Deal

The *Colgate* doctrine, which originated in *United States v. Colgate Co.,*[3] decided by the U.S. Supreme Court in 1919, recognizes the manufacturer's right to choose the customers with whom it will do business. This freedom to deal or not to deal allows a manufacturer to announce in advance the resale price that it expects its customers to charge for its product and to refuse to deal with any customer who fails to charge that price.

It is not price-fixing for a retailer to *independently* decide to charge a manufacturer's announced price, even if the retailer does this to obtain the manufacturer's product. The *Colgate* doctrine does not exempt a firm from Sherman Act liability if its refusal to do business is part of a scheme to acquire a monopoly.

Distribution and Output Restrictions

Agreements between two or more competitors that restrict where they will do business, or specify with whom they will deal, or limit the amount of goods they will buy or sell, have no purpose other than to restrain trade. For this reason they are illegal per se.

Tying Agreements

Sellers may exploit their control over a product or service by *forcing* a buyer to purchase or not to purchase another product or service through a **tying agreement.** Generally, such an arrangement requires the buyer to purchase from the seller a product or service that he or she would not otherwise purchase so as to procure the product or service that he or she actually wants. The desired product or service is called the **tying product,** and the product or service that is forced on the buyer is called the **tied product.** At times the tying agreement conditions the sale of a product or service on the agreement of the buyer not to purchase a product or service from anyone else. A tying agreement is suspect because it may damage competition in the market for the tied product. Depending on the circumstances, such an agreement may be illegal per se or tested by the rule of reason.

A tying agreement is illegal per se when its effect on competition is so detrimental and it is so completely without any redeeming virtue that it is fair to presume that it is an unreasonable restraint of trade. The illegal per se standard is used only when the seller has **forcing power,** that is, the seller is capable of coercing a buyer to purchase a product or service that the buyer does not want.

A seller who possesses **economic power** is presumed to have forcing power. Economic power means that the seller is dominant in the market for the tying product. That dominance may be due to a patent, copyright, a monopoly, or the uniqueness of the tying product. Because of the seller's dominance in the market for the tying product, it is presumed that the seller has the economic power to

Tying agreement
an agreement a seller forces on a buyer to purchase or not to purchase a product or service so as to obtain the product or service the buyer wants

Tying product
a product or service that the buyer wants and that the seller uses to force the buyer to purchase an unwanted product or service

Tied product
a product or service that a buyer must purchase so as to obtain a desired product or service

Forcing power
the ability of a seller to coerce a buyer to purchase unwanted products or services

Economic power
a situation in which a seller is dominant in the market for a tying product

force buyers to purchase the tied product. The requirement that there be an adverse effect on an appreciable amount of competition in the tied product is satisfied when a tying agreement forecloses a substantial volume of business in the market for the tied product.

RULE OF REASON UNDER SECTION 1

In the *Standard Oil Company of New Jersey* case,[4] decided in 1911, the U.S. Supreme Court reconsidered what Congress meant by the word *every* in the context of the Sherman Act. The Court concluded that despite its use of the word *every,* Congress did not intend to establish a mechanical standard outlawing all restraints of trade. Rather, the Court found, Congress established a standard that calls on courts to use their judgment to decide whether some sorts of restraints are unlawful. This standard is known as the "rule of reason," which has already been mentioned.

To decide whether a restraint is lawful under the rule of reason, a court must determine the effect of the restraint on competition. Shortly after *Standard Oil Company of New Jersey* the Supreme Court offered the following statement as a guide to decisions on whether a restraint is reasonable:

> [T]he court must ordinarily consider the facts peculiar to the business to which the restraint is applied; its condition before and after the restraint was imposed; the nature of the restraint and its effect, actual or probable; the history of the restraint; the evil [that the restraint was supposed to address]; the reason for adopting the particular [restraint]; and the purpose or end sought to be attained [by the restraint], are all relevant facts [to be taken into account in deciding whether a restraint is reasonable]. This is not because a good intention will save an otherwise objectionable regulation or the reverse, but because knowledge of intent may help the court to interpret the facts and to predict consequences.[5]

Ancillary Restraints

Ancillary restraint
a restraint that supplements a lawful agreement

Unlike a naked restraint, an **ancillary restraint** supplements an otherwise lawful agreement. Its prime purpose is to assure that the beneficiary of the restraint is not deprived of some other benefit that he or she is in fairness entitled to receive. The legality of an ancillary restraint is tested by the rule of reason.

Restrictive covenant
an agreement not to compete within a designated area for a set period of time

Restrictive Covenant in a Sale Agreement   Part of the purchase price that a buyer pays to acquire a firm is for the firm's *goodwill,* that is, its current reputation and the likelihood that those who currently deal with it will continue to do so. To allow the buyer to reap the full benefit of purchasing the firm, the seller commonly agrees not to compete with the buyer within a certain geographic area for a stated period of time. The agreement is an ancillary restraint because it is *supplemental* to the underlying agreement—the sale of the firm. Such an agreement is commonly called a **restrictive covenant.** Although the agreement restrains trade, the restraint is lawful so long as it is reasonable. To decide whether the restraint is reasonable, a court takes into account such facts as the nature of the business, the duration of the ban on competition, the length of time that customers are likely to favorably remember the firm's prior owner, the quality of the firm's goods and services when the seller operated it, the benefits that will accrue to the buyer if the ban is enforced, and the distance between the seller's possible new place of business and the one sold.

Restrictive Covenant in an Employment Agreement An employment contract may contain a restrictive covenant. Such an ancillary agreement provides that for a stated period of time after the employee leaves the firm, he or she will not, within a specified territory, compete with the employer or work for someone who does. To determine whether the restraint is reasonable, the length of time that the former employee is barred from competing with the employer, the span of the territory in which he or she may not compete, and the economic value to the employer of the employee's absence from the market are taken into account.

Location and Resale Restraints

A manufacturer may seek to enhance its profits by requiring those who purchase its goods for resale to sell them only at a particular location or only to a particular class of customers. For example, a microcomputer manufacturer may refuse to deal with any retailer who does not agree to offer its products for sale solely at a specified location. A perfume manufacturer that is intent on creating and maintaining a particular image for its products may sell them only to distributors who agree to resell them solely to retailers catering to affluent clienteles. At one time such vertical restrictive arrangements were treated in the same manner as vertical price-fixing agreements. They were illegal per se. At present the legality of a vertical nonprice restriction between a manufacturer and a distributor is tested by the rule of reason.

Tying Agreements

The rule of reason is used to determine the legality of tying agreements that are not illegal per se. In such cases the court inquires into the actual adverse effect of the tie on competition in the market for the tied product or service.

Exchange of Information

We have seen that neither independently gathering information on the prices charged by a competitor nor independently deciding to behave in the same fashion as a competitor is a restraint of trade.

The exchange of price information among competitors is not itself a violation of Section 1. But if the exchange is done to interfere with prices being set by free market forces, then the exchange is an unreasonable restraint. For example, the exchange of information is an unreasonable restraint in a concentrated industry if it tends to stabilize prices so that sellers cut prices either simultaneously or not at all when that market should be characterized by competitive pricing.

Joint Research and Development Venture

The National Cooperative Research Act (1984) directs that in any action brought under either federal antitrust laws, or any state laws similar to federal antitrust laws, the legality of a "joint research and development venture" is to be judged by the rule of reason. To decide whether the challenged joint conduct is unlawful under the rule of reason the court is to take into account all relevant factors affecting competition, including the effects of the venture on competition in relevant research and development markets.

The act defines a joint research and development venture as a group activity carried on for the purpose of (a) theoretical analysis, experimentation, or systematic study of phenomena or observable facts, (b) the development or testing of basic engineering techniques, (c) the collection, exchange, and analysis of research information, and (d) the extension of investigative findings or theory of a scientific or technical nature into practical application for experimental and demonstration purposes, including the experimental production and testing of models, prototypes, equipment, materials, and processes. Such activities can include establishing and operating facilities to conduct research, pursuing applications for patents, and granting licenses to make use of the results of the joint research and development venture.

Horizontal Price-Tampering

The U.S. Supreme Court has concluded that the unique nature of an industry may require that likely competitors partake in some types of mutually agreed-upon arrangements. When this is so, the Court has rejected the mechanical application of the illegal per se standard to horizontal price-tampering. Instead, it has used the rule of reason to test the legality of such behavior.

□□□□

The National Collegiate Athletic Association (NCAA) and its member colleges and universities established rules under which NCAA members could compete in football games. One NCAA rule set the price that its members must charge to allow television broadcasters to televise games in which they played. Another NCAA rule limited output, that is, the number of games that each member could agree to have televised. The U.S. Supreme Court observed that an agreement setting price or output is ordinarily illegal per se. However, because college football contests may require a degree of joint behavior, the Court evaluated the NCAA price-setting and output-setting arrangements under the rule of reason. Finding them to be anticompetitive, it declared that they were unreasonable and therefore violated Section 1.[6]

□□□□

Franchisor

a firm that authorizes another firm to use its trade name, trademark, or service mark

Franchisee

a firm that is licensed to use a franchisor's trade name, trademark, or service mark

FRANCHISE ARRANGEMENTS

A franchise is a license granted by a **franchisor** to a **franchisee.** The franchisee, an independent firm, may be allowed to use the franchisor's trade name, trademark, or service mark; or to sell the franchisor's products; or to provide the services for which the franchisor is known; or to do all of these things.

Operational Franchise

An **operational franchise** is a franchise in which the agreement between the franchisor and the franchisee grants the franchisor significant control over how the franchisee conducts its affairs. Ordinarily, the franchisee pays the franchisor a specified amount of money for the franchise as well as a **royalty.** The royalty is likely to be a percentage of the franchisee's earnings during a designated period. The franchisor may sell the franchisee products that are unobtainable elsewhere. The franchisee is allowed to buy and use comparable products that are obtainable elsewhere only if they satisfy the franchisor's quality standards and do not endanger the reputation of the franchisor or its products.

Fast-food franchises are an excellent example of how operational franchises generally work. The premises and operations of franchisees are indistinguishable from one another. Customers of a fast-food franchisee expect a particular quality and assortment of food and a particular level of service and cleanliness. Fast-food franchisors view the uniform appearance and operation of their franchisees as means of assuring acceptable profitability and of protecting goodwill.

Operational franchise
a franchise in which the franchisor is granted extensive power over how the franchisee conducts its business

Royalty
a franchisee's periodic payment to a franchisor

Product Franchise

In a **product franchise** the franchisee sells products or offers services that are identified by the franchisor's name. Automobile dealers are an example of product franchisees.

Product franchisee
a franchise in which the franchisee sells products or offers services identified as those of the franchisor

Franchise Restrictions

The Sherman Act does not require a franchisor to grant anyone a franchise. A price-fixing agreement between a franchisor and a franchisee is treated under Section 1 in the same way as any other price-fixing agreement. The rule of reason is used to test the legality of requiring a franchisee to conduct its business solely at one or more specified locations, of stipulating the manner in which a franchisee conducts its business, and other nonprice vertical restraints.

BUSINESS ELECTRONICS CORPORATION v. SHARP ELECTRONICS CORPORATION

SUPREME COURT OF THE UNITED STATES
485 U.S. 717 (1988)

In 1968 Business Electronics Corporation (petitioner) became the only retail dealer in Houston, Texas, to sell calculators made by Sharp Electronics Corporation (respondent). In 1972 Hartwell became the second Houston retail dealer to sell the respondent's calculators. Petitioner often sold the respondent's calculators at discount prices; Hartwell did not. In 1973 Hartwell told the respondent that it would no longer sell the respondent's calculators unless the respondent canceled the petitioner's dealership. The respondent promptly did so.

The petitioner brought a lawsuit in which it charged that the respondent and Hartwell were guilty of a per se violation of Section 1 of the Sherman Act because they had conspired to end its dealership. In response to a liability interrogatory, the jury found that "there was an agreement or understanding between" the respondent and Hartwell to terminate the petitioner as a dealer because of the petitioner's price-cutting. The trial judge instructed the jury that: if a dealer demands that a manufacturer terminate a price-cutting dealer and the manufacturer agrees to do so, the agreement is illegal per se if the manufacturer's purpose is to eliminate the price-cutting.

After the jury awarded the petitioner $600,000 in damages, a judgment was entered for $1.8 million (three times the amount of the actual damages) plus attorney's fees. The court of appeals reversed and remanded for a new trial, holding that an agreement between a manufacturer and one of its dealers that calls for the manufacturer to no longer deal with another dealer is not illegal per se *unless* the dealer "expressly or impliedly" agrees to set its prices at some level, though not a specific one. If the surviving dealer retains "complete freedom to set whatever price it chooses" the refusal of the manufacturer to any longer deal with the discounter is not illegal per se. The Supreme Court granted the petitioner's request for certiorari.

JUSTICE SCALIA
Delivered the Opinion of the Court

Since the earliest decisions of this Court interpreting [Section 1], we have recognized that it was intended to prohibit only unreasonable restraints of trade. Ordinarily, whether particular concerted action violates Section 1 is determined through case-by-case application of the so-called rule of reason—that is, "the fact finder weighs all of the circumstances of a case in deciding whether a restrictive practice should be prohibited as imposing an unreasonable restraint on competition." Certain categories of agreement, however, have been held to be per se illegal, dispensing with the need for case-by-case evaluation. We have said that per se rules are appropriate only for "conduct that is manifestly anticompetitive," that is, conduct "that would almost always tend to restrict competition and decrease output."

Although vertical agreements on resale prices have been illegal per se since [1911], we have recognized that the scope of the per se illegality should be narrow in the context of vertical restraints. [We have] refused to extend per se illegality to vertical nonprice restraints. [E]specially in the vertical restraint context "departure from the rule-of-reason standard must be based on demonstrable economic effect rather than upon formalistic line drawing." [V]ertical nonprice restraints [have] not been shown to have such a "pernicious effect on competition" and to be so "lack[ing in] redeeming value" as to justify per se illegality. [T]hey [have] real potential to stimulate *inter*brand [italics added] competition, "the primary concern of antitrust law."

Moreover, a rule of per se illegality for vertical nonprice restraints [is] not needed or effective to protect *intra*brand competition. First, so long as *inter*brand [italics added] competition [exists, it] provide[s] a "significant check" on any attempt to exploit *intra*brand [italics added] market power. In fact, in order to meet that *inter*brand [italics added] competition, a manufacturer's dominant incentive is to lower resale prices. Second, the per se illegality of vertical restraints would create a perverse incentive for manufacturers to integrate vertically into distribution, an outcome hardly conducive to fostering the creation and maintenance of small businesses.

[There is] support for the proposition that vertical price restraints reduce *inter*brand price competition because they "facilitate cartelizing." Similar support for the cartel-facilitating effect of vertical nonprice restraints was and remains lacking.

The District Court's rule on the scope of per se illegality for vertical restraints would threaten to dismantle [this Court's use of the rule of reason to test the legality of vertical nonprice restraints]. Any agreement between a manufacturer and a dealer to terminate another dealer who happens to have charged lower prices can be alleged to have been directed against the terminated dealer's "price-cutting." In the vast majority of cases, it would be extremely difficult for the manufacturer to convince a jury that its motivation was to ensure adequate services since price-cutting and some measure of service cutting usually go hand in hand. Manufacturers would be likely to forgo legitimate and competitively useful conduct rather than risk treble damages and perhaps even criminal penalties.

We cannot avoid this difficulty by invalidating as illegal per se only those arrangements imposing vertical restraints that contain the word "price," or that affect the "prices" charged by dealers. Such formalism [has been] explicitly rejected [by this Court]. [A]ll vertical restraints have the potential to allow dealers to increase "prices" [but at the same time may bring about such benefits as ensuring that they will] earn "sufficient profit to pay for programs such as hiring and training additional salesmen or demonstrating the technical features of the product [or providing better service and repair facilities] and will want to see that 'free-riders' [that is, discounters] do not interfere."

[W]e do not agree with petitioner's contention that an agreement on the remaining dealer's price or price levels will so often follow from terminating another dealer "because of [its] price-cutting" that prophylaxis against resale price maintenance warrants the District Court's per se rule. Petitioner has provided no support for the proposition that vertical price agreements generally underlie agreements to terminate a price cutter. That proposition is simply incompatible with the conclusion of [this Court in past cases] that manufacturers are often motivated by a legitimate desire to have dealers provide services, combined with the reality that price-cutting is frequently made possible by "free riding" [that is, discounters having customers rely] on the services provided by other dealers [who do not engage in price-cutting]. The District Court's per se rule would therefore discourage conduct recognized by [the Court in prior cases] as beneficial to consumers.

In the present case no agreement on resale price or price level was found by the jury.

[A] vertical restraint is not illegal per se unless it includes some agreement on price or price levels. Accordingly, the judgment of the Fifth Circuit is
Affirmed.

Legal Issues

1. Why did the Court not treat the agreement between Sharp and Hartwell as a group boycott, illegal per se under Section 1?

2. Would it be proper to classify Sharp's agreement to terminate the

dealership of Business Electronics as an ancillary agreement? Why?

Ethical Issues

1. Does Justice Scalia's discussion of the benefits that consumers are likely to enjoy through the elimination of a discounter indicate that pragmatic and utilitarian ethics influenced his view as to the acceptability of the arrangement between Sharp and Hartwell? Explain your answer.

2. Which standards of ethics are consistent with the stance taken by Hartwell? Why?

TRADE ASSOCIATIONS

Trade association

an organization whose members are firms engaged in the same kind of business

The National Association of Manufacturers and the numerous other entities whose membership include firms and individuals engaged in the same type of business are commonly spoken of as **trade associations.** Although such groups may tend to promote like thinking among competitors, they are not unlawful unless they are used as devices to suppress or destroy competition. For example, if all the members of a trade association band together to fix prices or allocate markets, they are guilty of a per se violation of Section 1.

SECTION 2 OF THE SHERMAN ACT

Section 2 of the Sherman Act provides that "every person who shall monopolize, or attempt to monopolize, or combine or conspire with any other person or persons, to monopolize any part of" interstate or foreign trade or commerce is guilty of a crime. As we have seen, an independently acting individual or firm cannot violate Section 1. That section's prohibitions are directed solely at joint behavior. This is not so with Section 2, which bans particular types of both independent and joint behavior. As is the case with Section 1, the key terms used in Section 2 are not defined in the Sherman Act. Each calls for special attention.

Definition of Terms

Every

The word *every* has not been interpreted to mean "every" in the context of Section 2. A rule of reason is used to determine whether what is done violates Section 2.

Person

A natural person as well as a partnership, a corporation, or any other type of organization is a person for the purposes of Section 2.

Monopolize

In the absence of congressionally established guidelines as to the meaning of "monopolize," courts could have chosen to decide whether a monopoly exists for the purposes of Section 2 by relying in each trial on the opinions offered by experts on how business is done and on the effects of certain business practices in the context of the market structure. Instead, they selected a relatively simple yardstick to determine whether a person possesses a **monopoly.** Under this yardstick, "monopoly" is defined as the *power to control prices* or *exclude competitors* in the manufacture or distribution of a particular product or service in the market in which a company does business. As we will see, courts determine whether a company has such power on the basis of its *market share.*

The mere possession of monopoly power is not unlawful under Section 2 because the Sherman Act does not outlaw success. Section 2 is violated only if that power was *willfully* acquired or *willfully* maintained. Thus a firm's monopoly power is unlawful if it results from willful anticompetitive behavior but not if it is *passively* acquired, perhaps because other firms chose not to enter the firm's market or because the firm produced a superior product, possessed superior business acumen, or profited from a historic accident. "Willful conduct" in the context of Section 2 means that a party purposely carried out the act or acts that brought about or perpetuated its monopoly. It does not mean that the party carried out the act or acts with a specific intent to accomplish what Section 2 forbids.

Predatory pricing is a form of willful conduct whose purpose is to destroy competition so as to acquire or maintain a monopoly. A company is guilty of predatory pricing when it lowers the price it charges for a product or service even to a price below its cost, in order to drive out competitors and then to increase the price to a level that allows it to make more than normal profits. Predatory pricing is sometimes described as a means of acquiring the power to charge monopoly prices and reap monopoly profits. Other forms of willful conduct that may be used to acquire or retain monopoly power are coercing the suppliers of a competitor so that they will not deal with the competitor, leasing rather than selling products, using exclusive buying arrangements in order to lock out competitors, and expanding product capacity beyond current or likely future needs or purchasing larger quantities of materials than are needed in order to eliminate competitors or scare off potential competitors.

Geographic and Product Markets   Whether a firm has a monopoly can be determined only by taking into account the *geographic region in which the firm does business* and the *product or service in which it deals.* Only after these factors have been considered can it be decided whether a firm has the power to control either price or market access. It is far simpler to ascertain a firm's geographic market than its product or service market. The former is simply the geographic region in which the firm competes for customers. For example, the geographic market of a hotel chain is New York City if it owns and operates only three hotels, all of which are located in that city.

Ascertaining a firm's product or service market requires a detailed examination of what the firm offers. Obviously, a hotel that charges $600 a night for a room and $45 for breakfast is not in the same product market as one that charges $45 a night for a room and $3.95 for breakfast. A person in search of the sort of hotel that charges $600 a night is not attracted to or influenced by the offerings of a hotel that charges $45 a night.

In *United States v. E. I. du Pont de Nemours & Co.,*[7] one of the leading cases on the question of what constitutes a product market, the U.S. Supreme Court had to decide whether cellophane was a distinct product or but one of several types of flexible wrapping materials. The defendant produced 75 percent of the cellophane sold in the United States. The Court concluded that flexible wrapping, not

Monopoly
the power of a firm to control prices or exclude competitors

Predatory pricing
the setting of prices so as to destroy competitors and thereafter earn more than normal profits

**Cross-elasticity of
demand**

a situation in which products or services are alike enough to be used in place of one another

cellophane, was the product market. It found that a **cross-elasticity of demand** existed between cellophane and other flexible wrapping materials because cellophane and other flexible wrapping materials were functionally interchangeable. Although cellophane did have some distinct characteristics, it was interchangeable with other types of flexible wrapping. The Court was convinced that customers would probably turn to some other type of flexible wrapping once the price of cellophane went beyond a certain point. Consequently, it concluded that the defendant competed not only with firms that sold cellophane but also with firms that sold other types of flexible wrapping. Thus the defendant did not control 75 percent of a product market but 75 percent of a material that accounted for only 17.9 percent of the flexible wrapping product market.

Monopolistic Market Share   A firm's market share for a product or service within the geographic market in which it competes for customers determines whether it has a monopoly. Although there is no established percentage at which a firm's market share is equivalent to a monopoly, a firm whose market share hovers around the 90 percent mark is regarded as a monopoly. Once a firm acquires a market share of more than 70 percent, a court is likely to give serious attention to the claim that it has power to control price or market entry. In the Du Pont case the government charged that the defendant had a monopoly because of its 75 percent share of the market for cellophane. This charge was rejected once the Supreme Court concluded that the product market was flexible wrapping, not cellophane. Since cellophane accounted for just 17.9 percent of that product market, the defendant's market share clearly fell far short of a monopoly.

Hypothetical Case

TRYING TO CONTROL IT ALL

In 1988 Westco, Inc., an advertising firm that did business in the two New Jersey counties situated closest to New York City, held a 4 percent market share and had annual billings that exceeded $5 million. Martha Signet, Westco's president, decided that it was time for Westco "to take control." Westco instituted a reduced fee schedule and initiated free consulting services for its customers. As a result, within two years four of Westco's competitors went out of business and several of Westco's other competitors were "hurting." By March 1991 Westco's two-county market share had climbed to 9 percent and its annual billings had neared the $8 million mark.

Thomas Winslow, the chief operating officer of Best Advertising Company, telephoned Signet and told her that unless Westco immediately stopped its ruinous practices, he would inform the U.S. attorney of Westco's attempt to monopolize the market. Signet insisted that Winslow was "off base." She said, "We do business in the same market as advertising firms with offices in New York City. I bet that the combined billings of both of our firms are a drop in the bucket compared with the billings of any of the 10 top New York City firms." "Listen Martha," Winslow replied, "don't try to confuse me. Our firms do business in just two New Jersey counties. I know that New York advertising firms are among our competitors, but we're still big players in New Jersey. And anyway, what Westco is doing is just plain unethical."

Should Westco's conduct be regarded as an attempt to monopolize in violation of Section 2 of the Sherman Act? Why? Do you agree with Winslow that Westco's behavior is unethical? Why?

Attempt to Monopolize

A mere intent to monopolize or an intent to monopolize coupled with the sort of behavior that might lead to monopolization is insufficient to violate the Sherman Act's ban on an attempt to monopolize. The act is violated only when *all* of the following elements are present.

Specific Intent   As we have seen, monopolization that violates Section 2 involves the deliberate performance of the act or acts that led to the creation of a monopoly or made it possible to maintain a lawfully acquired monopoly. The intent necessary to make the creation or maintenance of a monopoly unlawful is known as a **general intent.** Such an intent is present when one deliberately—that is, consciously—did what was done. This means that monopolization can violate Section 2 even if the act or acts that led to the creation or maintenance of a monopoly were not carried out with that purpose in mind. A general intent is *not* sufficient to prove an *attempt* to monopolize. To prove an attempt to monopolize, it must be shown that anticompetitive action was carried out with the **specific intent** of securing a monopoly. For example, a specific intent is present when for the purpose of achieving a monopoly a firm prevents competitors from doing business or takes action that enables it to control the price it charges for its goods or services.

> **Specific intent**
> the aim of performing an act so as to attain a particular result

> **General intent**
> the aim of performing a particular act

Predatory or Anticompetitive Behavior   Predatory or anticompetitive behavior must be shown to establish an attempt to monopolize. An example of such behavior is setting prices at an unprofitable level in order to curb or eliminate competition with the intent to raise prices and garner extraordinary profits once that goal has been accomplished. Such behavior is a far cry from lowering prices in order to remain competitive or to increase overall profits.

Dangerous Probability of Success   To establish an attempt to monopolize, it must be shown that the firm charged with such an attempt has sufficient economic power to create a dangerous probability that its efforts to obtain a monopoly will be successful. A firm with a 5 percent market share that intends to monopolize and engages in predatory pricing or other sorts of anticompetitive practices in order to destroy competition is not guilty of an attempt to monopolize, because its *present* market share is so small that there is no dangerous probability that it will attain its objective.

A Combination or Conspiracy to Monopolize

To establish a combination or conspiracy to monopolize, it must be shown that two or more firms, acting in concert, engaged in overt acts with the specific intent to further their combination or conspiracy to monopolize.

Any Part of Trade or Commerce

This portion of Section 2 requires that the challenged conduct affect an *appreciable amount* of interstate trade or commerce. An activity that has a **de minimis** effect—that is, an insignificant effect—on such trade or commerce does not violate Section 2. For example, if a company is the only supplier of handmade nails in a three-state area because its anticompetitive practices destroyed its

> **De minimis**
> an act whose effect is insufficient to warrant the law's attention

competitors, but it grosses less than $5,000 a year, the company is not guilty of a Sherman Act violation. Section 2 is inapplicable because the trivial amount of the company's business has an insignificant impact on interstate commerce.

EXEMPT RESTRAINTS AND MONOPOLIES

Agency Regulation

The Sherman Act does not apply to price-fixing or other regulatory measures dictated by federal agencies.

Labor Unions

Labor unions have a monopoly when they are the sole representative of company employees. They are parties to price-fixing and other restraints when they enter into collective bargaining agreements that set wages and working conditions. However, labor unions are exempt from the Sherman Act when they engage in genuine union activities.

Simply because a group of persons is called a "labor union" does not mean that it is exempt from the Sherman Act. For example, an association that claims to be a labor union, but whose members are private entrepreneurs, is not exempt from the Sherman Act when it sets the prices that its members charge for their services and designates how and with whom they may do business. Such an association is simply a group of businesspersons, and thus subject to the provisions of the Sherman Act.

Learned Professions

Generally, professional persons are subject to the same prohibitions that the Sherman Act imposes on nonprofessional persons. For example, the legality of a price-fixing agreement among lawyers, doctors, or engineers is tested in the same way as a price-fixing agreement among persons who are not members of a profession. However, the U.S. Supreme Court has cautioned that because of the *public service dimension* of a profession, there may be instances in which the conduct of professional persons would not violate the Sherman Act, while like conduct on the part of nonprofessional persons would violate the act.

Noerr-Pennington Doctrine

The Noerr-Pennington doctrine is a defense to conduct of a person or a company that would otherwise violate the Sherman Act. This doctrine is based on the premise that the act is not intended to interfere with efforts by businesspersons or businesses to exercise their constitutional rights to communicate their wishes to legislators or to persons in the executive branch of government, or to deprive businesspersons or businesses of their constitutional rights of access to courts and administrative agencies, *even if* their *motives are selfish* and their actions are *intended* to restrain trade or commerce or to monopolize.

The Noerr-Pennington doctrine allows companies and representatives of companies to speak out in favor of a state or local law that will suppress or destroy competition or lead to a monopoly, or seek to have state or local legislators vote for such a law, or persuade state or local officials to approve such a law. Companies may bring a lawsuit or initiate an agency proceeding, or defend themselves against a lawsuit or an agency proceeding, even though doing this injures or eliminates competition as well as competitors.

The "sham exception" bars the use of the Noerr-Pennington doctrine as a defense to a charge of a Sherman Act violation if the *process,* whether it involved lobbying or judicial or agency action, was used only to *directly* interfere with competition and not to achieve an anticompetitive *result* by obtaining the passage or approval of a law or by successfully pursuing or defending against a lawsuit or an agency proceeding. For example, if a lawsuit or an agency proceeding is pursued in *bad faith,* such as by knowingly bringing a groundless claim, or relying on a ficticious or worthless defense, or presenting false evidence simply to delay, suppress, or destroy competition, such action is a "sham" because it is not a genuine exercise of a constitutionally protected right. It is simply a cloak for unlawful behavior. Conduct of this kind is not excused by the Noerr-Pennington doctrine.

State Action Exemption

In *Parker v. Brown,*[8] the U.S. Supreme Court established the principle that the Sherman Act does not apply to anticompetitive restraints imposed by states "as an act of government." This principle is known as the "state action exemption." It exempts from the Sherman Act anticompetitive behavior that would otherwise violate the act when a state clearly articulates its determination to exempt such behavior and actively supervises the behavior.

The state action exemption also applies to anticompetitive conduct exempted by the action of a political subdivision of a state, such as a municipality, so long as that subdivision is authorized by state law to impose the anti-competitive restraint and the subdivision actively supervises such anticompetitive conduct. For example, if state law authorizes a municipality to establish zoning regulations and the zoning regulations (supervised by the municipality) result in a restraint of trade that enables a company to acquire a monopoly of the municipality's billboard business, both the municipality and the company can invoke the state action exemption to avoid Sherman Act liability.

Local Government and Official Immunity

In instances in which the state action exemption is unavailable to them, political subdivisions, school and sanitary districts, and other governmental entities established by a state may invoke the Local Government Antitrust Act of 1984 to avoid liability for damages, costs, or attorney's fees for Sherman Act violations. This act also excuses from the same kinds of civil liability officials or employees of any of these entities who violated the Sherman Act in the course of their official duties.

Agricultural Product Producers Associations

Farmers, planters, ranchers, nut or fruit growers, and others engaged in the production of agricultural products may band together in an association, commonly called a "cooperative," and collectively market their products in interstate commerce without violating the Sherman Act if (1) the association is operated for the mutual benefit of its members, (2) only those eligible for membership are affiliated with the association, (3) the value of the agricultural products of non-members that the association markets does not exceed the value of the agricultural products of association members, (4) each member has no more than one vote in the association or the association's dividends do not exceed 8 percent a year, and (5) the activities of the association do not unduly enhance the prices of the agricultural products that it markets.

Patents and Copyrights

The lawful monopoly granted by a patent or a copyright may not be used to otherwise restrain or monopolize trade or commerce. Patent holders may not join together to fix the prices that they will each charge for the products on which they hold patents.

A price-fixing agreement among copyright holders that is nothing more than a *naked restraint* of trade (has no purpose except to stifle competition) is illegal per se. However, a marketing arrangement reasonably necessary to effect the copyright holders' legal rights is *not* illegal per se. For example, the rule of reason is used to test a copyright holders' agreement that is designed to integrate the sale of copyrighted materials, to monitor their use to assure that royalties are paid, and to detect any unauthorized use although such an agreement does affect the prices charged for the use of the copyrighted materials.

Business of Insurance

Except for conduct that amounts to a boycott or involves coercion or intimidation, the business of insurance is exempt from federal antitrust law to the extent that it is regulated by state law. The expression "business of insurance" includes conduct that transfers or spreads policyholder risk, concerns the insurance policy relationship between the insurer and the insured, or involves entities exclusively engaged in the insurance business.

Professional Sports

When the restraints contained in employment contracts between baseball players and the owners of professional baseball teams were first challenged under the Sherman Act, the U.S. Supreme Court concluded that professional baseball was neither a trade nor commerce, and to this day professional baseball remains exempt from the act. However, the Court has refused to recognize a similar exemption for any other professional sport. In 1961 Congress enacted a statute that permits professional baseball, football, basketball, and hockey leagues to sell the exclusive rights to telecast league games and to restrict the telecasting of a team's home games.

GLOBAL CONCERNS

Cooperative Research Centers

The secretary of commerce is authorized to advance technological innovation in the United States by providing assistance in the creation of Cooperative Research Centers. Among the purposes of these centers are to enable individuals from industry and universities to cooperate in conducting research supportive of technological and industrial innovation; to help individuals and small businesses to generate, evaluate, and develop technological ideas supportive of industrial innovation and the establishment of new business ventures; and to provide technical assistance and advisory services to business, particularly small business.

At one time the secretary of commerce was authorized to request the attorney general's opinion as to whether particular joint research projects would violate antitrust law. Repeal of the portion of the law that authorized such inquiries suggest that congressional interest in how best to promote U.S. competitiveness in world markets outranks its interest in antitrust policy.

Foreign Trade

The Sherman Act does *not* apply to anticompetitive behavior affecting trade or commerce with foreign nations (unrelated to import trade or commerce) *unless* such behavior has a direct, substantial, and reasonably foreseeable effect (1) on trade or commerce that is not trade or commerce with foreign nations; or (2) on import trade or commerce with foreign nations; or (3) on export trade or export commerce with foreign nations that injures export business in the United States.

Export Trade Associations

An association that is organized solely to carry on export trade and actually engages only in export trade is exempt from the Sherman Act so long as (1) neither its acts nor its agreements are in restraint of trade within the United States or in restraint of the export trade of any U.S. competitor and (2) its conduct does not (*a*) artificially or intentionally raise or lower the prices charged in the United States for the kinds of commodities that it exports or (*b*) substantially lessen competition or otherwise restrain trade in the United States.

CIVIL REMEDIES FOR SHERMAN ACT VIOLATIONS

Private Suits

The Sherman Act makes no mention of civil relief to compensate anyone injured because of a violation of the act. Nor does it provide for equitable relief, such as a court directing a defendant not to engage in behavior that is illegal under the act. These remedies became available under the Clayton Act. Section 4 of the Clayton Act authorizes a variety of monetary damages to be awarded to persons injured in their business or property by reason of anything forbidden in the antitrust laws. Section 16, discussed below, specifies when courts may grant private persons equitable relief.

Antitrust injury

damage to business or
property resulting from
an antitrust violation that
injured competition

Money Damages

Persons who suffer **antitrust injury** in their business or property may sue for damages. "Antitrust injury" means that the injury for which damages are sought is (1) of the type that antitrust law is intended to prevent and (2) flows from conduct that is unlawful under antitrust law.

The purpose of antitrust law is to protect *competition,* not *competitors.* Thus a price reduction designed to increase a firm's market share that causes competitors to reduce their prices, and as a result to lose profits, or even to go out of business, does not cause antitrust injury unless the price reduction *also injures competition.*

A lawsuit to recover damages under Section 4 may be brought in any federal district court in the district in which the defendant resides, is found, or has an agent, *regardless of the amount of money* involved in the suit. If successful, the plaintiff is entitled to recover *three times* the damages that he or she sustained, together with the cost of the lawsuit and reasonable attorney's fees. In addition, a court may award simple interest on the actual damages for the period between the date that the summons and complaint were served on the defendant and the date of the judgment. If in the court's opinion the circumstances make it just to do so, the court may award interest for a shorter period. To decide whether interest should be awarded, the court should consider only whether either party, or the party's attorneys, (1) asserted claims or defenses so lacking in merit as to show that they were intentionally used to delay the proceeding or were offered in bad faith; (2) violated any statute, rule, or court order designed to expedite the proceeding; or (3) took steps primarily for the purpose of delaying or increasing the cost of the lawsuit.

Pass-On Doctrine   A plaintiff who paid the defendant more than he would otherwise have paid because the defendant was a party to a price-fixing agreement can recover damages under Section 4 of the Clayton Act even though the plaintiff passed the excess cost on to his customers. This is known as the "pass-on doctrine." For example, because the defendant manufacturer was a party to a price-fixing agreement with other manufacturers, it overcharged the plaintiff $100,000 for the goods it sold him. The plaintiff retrieved the $100,000 by raising the resale price of the goods. Since the passing on of costs is not a defense, the plaintiff can still recover $100,000 from the defendant.

Indirect Purchasers   In *Illinois Brick Co. v. Illinois*[9] the U.S. Supreme Court ruled that only a person who dealt *directly* with the party guilty of price-fixing can recover damages under Section 4 of the Clayton Act. For instance, a retailer paid a wholesaler more than he would otherwise have been charged because the wholesaler passed on to him part of the excess price he had to pay the manufacturer that was a party to a price-fixing agreement. As an *indirect* purchaser, the retailer cannot recover damages against the manufacturer. The retailer has no claim against the wholesaler, because the wholesaler was not guilty of price-fixing.

Contribution.   When two or more persons are participants in a Sherman Act violation and a judgment is entered against all of them, a defendant who pays part or all of the judgment is not entitled to contribution from any of the codefendants even if they too violated the Sherman Act.

Lawsuits by the United States

The U.S. attorney in each of the federal districts, acting under the direction of the attorney general of the United States, may institute a proceeding in equity to prevent or restrain a violation of the Sherman Act. In a lawsuit of this kind, the court may enjoin or grant such other relief as may be appropriate to enforce the act.

Whenever the United States is injured in its business or property because of anything forbidden by the antitrust laws, it may bring a lawsuit to recover three times the damages that it suffered plus the cost of the lawsuit. To decide whether it may also be awarded simple interest on the treble damages for the period between the day the summons and complaint in the suit were served and the day judgment was entered, the court must (1) determine whether this is necessary to adequately compensate the United States for the injuries it has sustained and (2) consider the same factors as would be considered if a private person were seeking the payment of such interest.

Parens Patriae Action

The Hart-Scott-Rodino Antitrust Improvement Act of 1976 authorizes the attorney general of any state to bring a lawsuit in the state's name on behalf of natural persons who reside in that state to recover damages for injuries they suffered because of a violation of the Sherman Act. Such a lawsuit is known as a ***parens patriae* action.** The judgment in such a suit may include only the claims of natural persons. No amount may be awarded for injuries suffered by a business. Since the pass-on doctrine is applicable to a *parens patriae* action, a court can award damages for injuries suffered by consumers only against those with whom the consumers did business directly.

Parens patriae **action**
a lawsuit brought by the attorney general of a state on behalf of the state's citizens

Equitable Relief

Section 16 of the Clayton Act authorizes a court to grant persons equitable relief to prevent threatened loss or damage because of a violation of any antitrust law if such relief is necessary to prevent antitrust injury and equitable relief would be granted in another kind of case. For instance, an injunction may direct that a planned combination not take place, or that a firm be dissolved, or that a company divest itself of one or more of its subsidiaries.

Consent Judgment

Generally, when parties to a lawsuit resolve their dispute by agreement between themselves, they may put their agreement in the form of a **consent judgment.** This arrangement, also known as a "consent decree," has the same effect as a judgment arrived at by a court. In an antitrust lawsuit brought by or on behalf of the United States, a consent judgment may not take effect without court approval.

Consent judgment
a judgment in a lawsuit arrived at by the parties themselves

Judgment Prima Facie Evidence of Guilt

In any lawsuit brought by a party *other* than the United States in which the plaintiff charges the defendant with an antitrust violation, a final judgment or decree

Prima facie evidence
a finding of guilt in a prior case on the basis of which liability in a subsequent lawsuit is presumed

entered against that defendant in a prior *civil* or *criminal* case *brought by or on behalf of the United States* under antitrust law is **prima facie evidence** of presumed guilt of all of the actions for which the defendant was held accountable in the prior case. Because the earlier judgment or decree is *not* a *conclusive* presumption of guilt, but only a *rebuttable* one, the defendant may offer evidence to refute the presumption of guilt. If the defendant's evidence is sufficient to convince the trier of the fact that he or she did not commit the alleged unlawful act or acts, the presumption of guilt is rebutted. The plaintiff, of course, is free to offer other evidence to establish the defendant's liability.

Whether a consent judgment or decree is prima facie evidence of guilt in a later case depends on the stage at which the earlier case came to an end. If the judgment or decree was entered before any testimony was taken, the prima facie evidence rule does not apply.

Statute of Limitations

A civil antitrust lawsuit to enforce the Sherman Act must be commenced within four years after the violation occurred. However, when the United States brings a civil or criminal proceeding to prevent, restrain, or punish a violation of any antitrust law (except a suit in which the United States is the injured party), the statute of limitations is suspended for a private lawsuit or a lawsuit of a state that is based in whole or in part on anything charged in the action brought by the United States. The suspension is in force while the case brought by the United States is pending and for one additional year. When the statute of limitations is suspended, a lawsuit may be brought no later than during the suspension period or within four years after the violation occurred.

CRIMINAL SANCTIONS

It is a crime to violate either Section 1 or Section 2 of the Sherman Act.

Imprisonment and/or Fine

Concurrent sentence
a sentence in a criminal case in which the terms of imprisonment imposed for different crimes are served at the same time

Consecutive sentences
sentences in a criminal case in which the terms of imprisonment imposed for different crimes are served independently

It is a felony to violate either Section 1 or Section 2 of the Sherman Act. A corporation may be fined up to $10 million for each violation of the act. The possible punishment for each violation committed by an individual is a fine of not more than $350,000 or imprisonment for up to three years, or both, in the discretion of the court.

A court that imposes imprisonment on a defendant who in the same case is convicted of two or more Sherman Act violations may direct that the sentences be served concurrently or consecutively. In a **concurrent sentence** the prison terms for all of the sentences are served simultaneously. In **consecutive sentences,** the prison term for each of the sentences is served independently. For example, a defendant sentenced to three concurrent three-year sentences can be imprisoned for three years at most. A defendant sentenced to three consecutive three-year sentences can be imprisoned for nine years.

Nolo Contendere Plea

In a criminal case brought under the Sherman Act, the defendant may enter a ***nolo contendere* plea.** This means that he or she neither admits guilt nor proclaims innocence, but simply *does not contest* the accusation. The court is free to impose the same sentence on an accused who pleads *nolo contendere* as it would impose on an accused who admits guilt or is found guilty after a trial. However, a *nolo contendere* plea to a charge may *not* be used as evidence of guilt in any later civil proceeding based on the same accusation of wrongdoing that was made in the criminal proceeding.

Nolo contendere **plea**
a plea in which the defendant in a criminal case does not contest the charge

GLOBAL CONCERNS

Generally, a foreign nation that is injured in its business or property because of a Sherman Act violation can recover a judgment for not more than the amount of the damages it actually sustained, together with the cost of the lawsuit and a reasonable attorney's fee. However, it may recover damages to the same extent as a private person who suffered a like antitrust injury if (1) its claim relates to a commercial activity or act for which it could be sued in the United States, (2) it waives all of the defenses that it might use in the lawsuit because it is a foreign state, (3) it engages primarily in commercial activities, and (4) when it carried on the commercial activity or act that is the basis of its lawsuit, it was not functioning as a procurement entity for itself or for any other foreign state.

STATE ANTITRUST LAWS

States generally have what are commonly referred to as "little Sherman Acts." These acts apply to behavior in *intra*state trade or commerce that would be unlawful under the Sherman Act if it took place in *inter*state or foreign trade or commerce.

CALIFORNIA v. ARC AMERICA CORPORATION
SUPREME COURT OF THE UNITED STATES
490 U.S. 93 (1989)

Lawsuits were brought in federal district courts by the states of Alabama, Arizona, California, and Minnesota on behalf of each of these states and of classes of state and local government entities within each of these states. The plaintiffs' claims were based on direct and indirect purchases of cement. The plaintiffs sought to recover damages for the defendants' violations of Section 1 of the Sherman Act and for their violations of the states' little Sherman Acts, which expressly allowed indirect purchasers to recover damages.

The federal district court to which the cases were transferred denied the indirect purchasers relief under the little Sherman Acts. It ruled that these state statutes were "clear attempts to frustrate the purposes and objectives of Congress as interpreted by the Supreme Court in *Illinois Brick,* and accordingly, are preempted by federal law." After the court of appeals affirmed the district court's decision, the plaintiffs appealed.

JUSTICE WHITE
Delivered the Opinion of the Court

Under *federal* [italics supplied] law, no indirect purchaser is entitled to sue for damages for a Sherman Act violation, and there is no claim here that state law could provide a remedy for the *federal* [italics supplied] violation that federal law forbids. Had these cases gone to trial and a Sherman Act violation been proved, only direct purchasers would have been entitled to damages for that violation.

It is accepted that Congress has the authority [when it enacts a statute within its constitutional authority] to preempt state law. In the absence of an express statement by Congress that state law is preempted, there are two other bases for finding preemption. First, when Congress intends that federal law occupy a given field, state law in that field is preempted. Second, even if Congress has not occupied the field, state law is nevertheless preempted to the extent it actually conflicts with federal law, that is, when compliance with both state and federal law is impossible, or when the state law "stands as an obstacle to the accomplishment and execution of the full purposes and objectives of Congress."

In this case, in addition, the appellees must overcome the presumption against finding preemption of state law in areas traditionally regulated by the States. When Congress legislates in a field traditionally occupied by the States, "we start with the assumption that the historic police powers of the States were not to be superseded by the Federal Act unless that was the clear and manifest purpose of Congress." Given the long history of state common law and statutory remedies against monopolies and unfair business practices, it is plain that this is an area traditionally regulated by the States.

[T]he Court of Appeals erred in holding that the state indirect purchaser statutes are preempted. There is no claim that the federal antitrust laws expressly preempt state laws permitting indirect purchaser recovery. Moreover, appellees concede that Congress has not preempted the field of antitrust laws. Congress intended the federal antitrust laws to supplement, not displace, state antitrust remedies.

As we made clear in *Illinois Brick,* the issue before the Court [in that case] was strictly a question of statutory construction—what was the proper construction of Section 4 of the Clayton Act.

It is one thing to consider the congressional policies identified in *Illinois Brick* in defining what sort of recovery federal antitrust law authorizes; it is something altogether different to consider [*Illinois Brick*] as defining what federal law allows States to do under their own antitrust law. We construed Section 4 [of the Clayton Act] in *Illinois Brick* as not authorizing indirect purchasers to recover under federal law because that would be contrary to the purposes of Congress. But nothing in *Illinois Brick* suggests that it would be contrary to the congressional purposes for States to allow indirect purchasers to recover under their own antitrust laws.

[T]he Court of Appeals concluded that state indirect purchaser claims might subject antitrust defendants to multiple liability, in contravention of the "express federal policy" condemning multiple liability [as mentioned in *Illinois Brick*]. But *Illinois Brick,* as well as [the other cases decided by this Court that the Court of Appeals relied on to support its conclusion] were all cases construing Section 4 of the Clayton Act; in none of those cases did [this] Court identify a federal policy against States imposing liability in addition to that imposed by federal law. Ordinarily, state causes of action are not preempted solely because they impose liability over and above that authorized by federal law, and no clear purpose of Congress indicated that we should decide otherwise in this case.

When viewed properly, *Illinois Brick* was a decision construing the federal antitrust laws, not a decision defining the interrelationship between the federal and state antitrust laws. The congressional purposes on which *Illinois Brick* was based provide no support for a finding that state indirect purchaser statutes are preempted by federal law. The judgment of the Court of Appeals is therefore reversed.

Legal Issues

1. In a lawsuit brought under a state antitrust statute that allows an indirect purchaser to recover treble damages from a manufacturer guilty of price-fixing, what weight, if any, should be given to the fact that the manufacturer has already paid a treble damages judgment entered against it in a lawsuit brought under federal antitrust law for that aspect of the same price-fixing scheme that involved interstate commerce? Why?

2. What argument or arguments might a lobbyist use to persuade members of Congress to vote to amend Section 4 of the Clayton Act so that it would preempt state antitrust law in regard to the right of indirect purchasers to recover damages?

Ethical Issues

1. Which ethical standard calls for an exception to *Illinois Brick* that would allow indirect purchasers to recover the damages that they suffered from an unlawful price-fixing scheme because they dealt with the direct purchaser on a cost-plus basis? Discuss.

2. Which ethical standard, if any, supports the distinction drawn in *Illinois Brick* between the rights of direct and indirect purchasers to sue a manufacturer for the damages they suffered because the manufacturer was guilty of price-fixing in violation of the Sherman Act? Why?

LAW ABROAD

Japan

Prior to World War II a significant amount of private Japanese business was conducted through the **zaibatsu.** These combinations of independent firms are commonly compared with trusts or cartels. A cartel is a combination of independent firms that together may set prices, limit production, and market products. Generally, the members of a zaibatsu belonged to the same family. To assure that member firms had access to capital, a zaibatsu would include a bank. After World War II, when American forces occupied Japan, the zaibatsu were outlawed.

Zaibatsu

a combination of independent Japanese firms generally headed by members of the same family

Keiretsu
an alliance of Japanese
firms

The **keiretsu** has replaced the zaibatsu as a means to promote cooperation among Japanese businesses. A keiretsu is a horizontal and/or vertical alignment (alliance) of Japanese firms that includes among its members a dominant Japanese firm. Cooperatively, member firms seek to promote their interests in a variety of ways, such as by exchanging technological information, assembling capital, and when doing business favoring a fellow keiretsu member over outsiders.

Japan's Antimonopoly Law of 1947 is intended to protect and promote competition. In some respects it resembles American antitrust law. Price-fixing agreements and agreements that limit output are illegal per se. Criminal sanctions may be imposed on those who violate the law. Like Section 2 of the Sherman Act, the Antimonopoly Law bars "private monopolization," which is defined as the control or exclusion of others from a business activity. Unlike the Sherman Act, it expressly exempts some types of cartels.

The Japanese view of the relationship between business and government is an important factor in the content of Japan's antitrust law. Government and business are expected to cooperate with each other. Officials are expected to provide guidance for private enterprise. Consistent with these ideas, designated ministries of the Japanese government are charged with the supervision of particular industries. One of the tasks of such a ministry is to formulate an industrial policy that will promote the well-being of the sector or sectors of the Japanese economy for which it is responsible. For example, the Ministry of International Trade and Industry (MITI) oversees commerce, manufacturing, and mining. At times MITI is more likely to establish industrial policy through cooperation between industry and government than to encourage competition.

The Japanese Fair Trade Commission (FTC), an independent regulatory agency, is responsible for the enforcement of the Antimonopoly Law. Its task is complicated by the desire of the ministries to have their industrial policies succeed, even if this requires that competition give way to cooperation.

European Community

European Community law is aimed at maintaining effective competition within the EC. To do so, it prohibits some types of restrictive trade practices that American antitrust law would speak of as "restraints of trade." It bans agreements between firms that may prevent, restrict, or distort competition within the EC. Among such agreements are those that directly or indirectly fix purchase or sales prices or any other trading conditions; or limit or control production, markets, technical development, or investment; or share markets or sources of supply.

EC law does not bar monopolization. However, it does prohibit a firm or an association of firms that has a dominant position within the EC market, or in a substantial part of that market, from engaging in *abuses* that are incompatible with that market and affect trade between EC member nations. Dominance is present when a firm, or an association of firms, because of its market share, taken together with its technical knowledge, raw materials, or capital, has the power to determine prices or to control the production or distribution of a significant part of the trade affected by the abuses.

Among the types of conduct regarded as abusive are actions that directly or indirectly impose unfair purchase or sales prices; or directly or indirectly create some other type of unfair trading condition; or limit production, markets, or technical development to the prejudice of consumers.

The European Commission, which is charged with enforcement of the segment of EC law that is intended to prevent the distortion of competition, is authorized to grant individual exemptions from the law's ban on restrictive practices. Ordinarily, an exemption may be granted if all of the following conditions are met: the restriction will improve the production or distribution of goods or promote technical or economic progress; consumers will gain a fair share of the benefit that will result from the exemption; the exemption is essential to the achievement of the desired objective; and competition is still a possibility.

The commission is not authorized to grant an exemption from the law's ban on abuses by dominant firms or associations of firms.

REVIEW QUESTIONS & PROBLEMS

1. Stress Corporation granted individuals franchises to do business under the name Stress Control Center. The franchises were issued for 25 years, but Stress could terminate them at any time "for good cause." The franchise agreement required the franchisee to pay Stress a $50,000 issuance fee and royalty of 8 percent of gross annual profits, specified the location of the franchisee's center, and stated how the center must be operated. "For goodwill purposes" the agreement suggested that "franchisees charge customers the fees found in Stress Corporation's weekly newsletter." Do any of these arrangements violate the Sherman Act? Why?

2. During a three-month "price war" among the operators of 14 retail gasoline stations located in a suburban area, whenever one station operator lowered the price of a gallon of gasoline by one cent or more, all of the other station operators quickly did the same. The price war ended after the 14 station operators held a closed meeting. The price of a gallon of all grades of gasoline had then declined by 18 cents. After the closed meeting, whenever one station operator raised the price of a gallon of gasoline by one cent or more, all of the others promptly did the same. Within a month the price of a gallon of all grades of gasoline had increased by 19 cents. What legal principles would a court use to decide whether the 14 station operators were guilty of price-fixing? Discuss.

3. Because in their opinion chiropractic was not based on "scientific principles," all of the 200 physicians who practiced medicine in a county agreed not to refer any of their patients to chiropractors, or to share information about their patients with chiropractors, or to treat patients at a hospital that made its facilities available to chiropractors. Six chiropractors brought suit against the physicians, charging that they were guilty of violating Section 1 of the Sherman Act. What judgment? Why?

4. When Taylor Corporation, located in Dover, New Hampshire, hired Wiggins, a research chemist, he was required to sign a "Noncompetition Contract." The contract provided that for two years after leaving Taylor, which manufactured adhesive materials, he would not work for any firm that manufactured the same products anywhere in the United States. Wiggins was not promoted during the five years that he worked for Taylor, but he did receive token salary increases. When Ad-Hes, Inc., a German firm that was opening an adhesive manufacturing plant in California, offered Wiggins an executive position at twice the salary that Taylor paid him, he left Taylor and went to work for Ad-Hes. Under what circumstances, if any, would Taylor be entitled to an injunction barring Wiggins from working for Ad-Hes? Discuss.

5. In its weekly *Newsletter to Members,* Glass Makers of America, Inc., a trade association of the nation's leading glass manufacturers, published a list of the average prices that its members had charged during the preceding week for 20 types of glass products. The list divided the nation into 25 "sectors." Over the course of a year, the listed prices remained essentially the same in each sector for only short periods of time. When price changes occurred, in almost every instance the price went up. Are Glass Makers of America, Inc. and the subscribers to its weekly *Newsletter to Members* who took the published information into account to make pricing decisions guilty of violating the Sherman Act? Why?

ENDNOTES

1. 166 U.S. 290 (1897).
2. *Business Electronics Corp. v. Sharp Electronics Corp.,* 485 U.S. 717 (1988).
3. 250 U.S. 300 (1919).
4. *Standard Oil Company of New Jersey v. United States,* 221 U.S. 1 (1911).
5. *Board of Trade v. United States,* 246 U.S. 231 (1918).
6. *National Collegiate Athletic Association v. Board of Regents,* 468 U.S. 85 (1984).
7. 351 U.S. 377 (1956).
8. 317 U.S. 341 (1943).
9. 431 U.S. 720 (1977).

CHAPTER

19

Mergers and Other Anticompetitive Practices

A corporation with billions of dollars in annual gross receipts invades a new geographic market by acquiring a firm that is well established in that market. Two of the corporations on whose board of directors a person serves become competitors, but the person continues to serve on both boards. To retain the business of its two largest customers, a manufacturer sells them its products at lower prices than it charges its other customers. What is done in each of these cases may injure competition and even lead to monopolization.

This chapter considers how the legality of such actions is tested under federal laws that are intended to protect competition and prevent monopolization. These laws include the Clayton Act and the Robinson-Patman Act. The chapter also examines the Federal Trade Commission Act, which outlaws unfair methods of competition and unfair and deceptive acts or practices.

CLAYTON ACT

The Clayton Act, passed in 1914, was designed to fill gaps in federal antitrust policy. We have already seen that Sections 4 and 16 of the Clayton Act establish civil remedies for Sherman Act violations. Sections 3, 7, and 8 supplement and overlap the Sherman Act.

Section 3

Section 3 of the Clayton Act makes it unlawful for persons engaged in commerce to lease, sell, or contract to sell patented or unpatented goods or any type of merchandise, or to fix, discount, or rebate a part of the price that is charged for such items, on the condition, agreement, or understanding that the purchaser or lessee will not use or deal in the goods or other commodities of one or more of the seller's or lessor's competitors, when the effect of such an arrangement may be to substantially lessen competition or tend to create a monopoly in any line of commerce.

Unlike Section 1 of the Sherman Act, which applies to tying arrangements that involve either products or services, Section 3 is directed *only* at tying arrangements that involve *products.* The lawfulness of a tying arrangement under Section 3 is judged in the same way as the lawfulness of such an arrangement under Section 1 of the Sherman Act.

Section 7

Mergers and Acquisitions

Merger
a combination of two or more firms

Two independent firms may become one through a **merger,** which means that they combine, or through an **acquisition,** which means that one firm acquires the stock or assets of the other. If the two firms were engaged in the same type of business, a **horizontal merger** has taken place. The acquisition of a firm that operates 11 motels by a firm that operates 30 motels catering to the same type of guests is a horizontal merger. If the two firms transacted business at different levels of distribution, so that there was a seller-buyer relationship between them, a **vertical merger** has taken place. An electrical appliance manufacturer's acquisition of a firm that operates a number of retail electrical appliance shops is a vertical merger.

Acquisition
a situation in which one firm comes into possession of the stock or assets of another firm

The joining together of firms that deal in complementary products is known as a **product extension merger.** The merger of a firm that sells concrete for building foundations with a firm that sells metal rods used to reinforce concrete foundations is such a merger. In a **conglomerate merger** the firms are engaged in unrelated businesses. The merger of a firm that manufactures automobile parts with a firm that provides individuals with investment advice is a conglomerate merger.

Horizontal merger
a combination of firms engaged in the same type of business

Vertical merger
a combination of firms that conduct business at different distribution levels

Product extension merger
a combination of firms whose products complement each other

Conglomerate merger
a combination of firms that deal in unrelated products or services

The Original Section 7

In 1914, when the Clayton Act was passed, Section 1 of the Sherman Act had not yet been interpreted to cover mergers or acquisitions of firms, although the Sherman Act specifically bars *combinations* in restraint of trade. So, in its quest to protect competition and curb monopoly, Congress, in Section 7 of the Clayton Act, barred a corporation engaged in commerce from acquiring, "directly or indirectly," any portion or all "of the stock or other share capital of another corporation" that was also "engaged in commerce, where the effect of such acquisition may be to substantially lessen competition between the corporation whose stock" was "acquired and the" acquiring corporation, "or to restrain such commerce in any section or community, or tend to create a monopoly of any line of commerce."

Judicial Construction   In 1926 the U.S. Supreme Court ruled that Section 7 does not apply to a merger by acquisition of another firm's stock when the acquiring corporation then liquidates the other firm and takes over its assets. The purpose of Section 7, in the Court's opinion, was to prevent a corporation from *continuing to hold* the acquired stock of another corporation. This construction of Section 7 severely limited the significance of the Clayton Act, because it enabled competing firms to merge without violating the act. A firm could take over a competitor either by directly acquiring the competitor's assets or by acquiring its stock and then taking over its assets.

The Amended Section 7

Displeasure with the large number of mergers that took place during World War II led to the passage of the Anti-Merger Act of 1950, popularly known as the Celler-Kefauver Act. This act amended Section 7. Its advocates insisted that Congress had to sweep away the 1926 Supreme Court decision in order to check the rising tide of economic concentration. They were convinced that unless mergers that probably posed a threat to competition or would probably lead to monopoly were stopped, the nation's economy would be injured and the nation would be deprived of the political and social benefits generated by the diffusion of economic power and the domination of markets by locally controlled businesses.

As amended by the Celler-Kefauver Act, Section 7 prohibits a corporation that is "subject to the jurisdiction of the Federal Trade Commission" and is "engaged in commerce" from "directly or indirectly" acquiring any part or all of the stock or other share capital, or any part or all of the assets of another corporation that is also engaged in commerce, "where in any line of commerce in any section of the country, the effect of such acquisition may be substantially to lessen competition, or to tend to create a monopoly." Thus, a firm could no longer evade Section 7 by simply acquiring another firm's stock and then taking control of its assets. Furthermore, in its new form, Section 7 no longer speaks of the effect of an acquisition on competition between the acquiring corporation and the acquired corporation "in any section or community." Instead, it speaks of the effect "in any line of commerce, in any section of the country."

Definition of Terms

Section of the Country   Neither in its original nor its amended form does Section 7 state what constitutes a "section of the country," that is, the geographic area in which effective competition may be lessened or a tendency to monopolization is probable because of a merger. A "functional" standard is used to determine the boundaries of such an area. This is a pragmatic standard, not a formalistic standard. Commercial realities—the boundaries within which competing firms can effectively vie with one another for customers—determine what a section of the country is. Depending on the nature of the commerce that is involved, a section of the country may comprise the entire nation or be confined to a particular metropolitan area or even a segment of a city.

Line of Commerce The product market affected by a merger is spoken of as a "line of commerce." Section 7 does not specify how the boundaries of this market are to be determined. As with "section of the country," a "functional" standard is used to judge what items a particular product market comprises. This standard includes in a product market all of the items that may be used interchangeably— all of the items for which there is a cross-elasticity of demand.

One or more "submarkets" may exist within a broad product market. For purposes of Section 7, a submarket is a distinct line of commerce. Its boundaries are determined on the basis of such practical considerations as recognition of the submarket as a separate economic entity by an industry or the public, the product's peculiar characteristics and uses, unique production facilities, distinct customers, distinct prices, and specialized sellers. For example, to determine whether Section 7 was violated by a merger of two shoe companies, both of which manufactured shoes and operated retail shoe outlets, the U.S. Supreme Court found that men's, women's, and children's shoes were distinct submarkets of the shoe business. The public recognizes them as different products; they are manufactured in separate plants; their particular characteristics generally make them noncompetitive with one another; and they are sold to three distinct classes of customers.

Predicting the Effect of a Merger Because Section 7 outlaws mergers that *may* substantially lessen competition or *tend* to create a monopoly, it is usually necessary for the decision maker to predict whether either of these objectionable results will occur at some later date. Only a transaction that will *probably* lead to one or both of these results violates Section 7. This probability standard is often expressed as follows: If it is simply *possible* that the objectionable result will happen, Section 7 is not violated, yet the objectionable result need not *certainly* happen for Section 7 to be violated. Section 7 is violated if the objectionable result is *likely* to happen.

Section 7 does not prescribe whether a quantitative test (such as the amount of the merged firms' sales, or assets, or market shares) or a qualitative test (that is, the worth of the merged firms as compared to that of other firms) should be used to determine whether a merger may "substantially lessen competition" or head the market toward monopolization. As with the other provisions of Section 7, a "functional" test is used to foretell the consequences of a merger. In the case of a *horizontal merger,* this test requires that attention be given to such factors as the history of any leaning toward concentration in the given industry, whether there has been a recent trend in the industry toward domination by a few firms, whether the industry is fragmented or concentrated; the market shares of the postmerger firm and the industry leaders; probable future trends in the industry; the ease with which a new firm may gain entry into the industry; and the degree of difficulty experienced by those who seek to do business with firms in the industry.

In view of the fact that Section 7 is intended to thwart increased concentration in an industry, it is not surprising that in general the larger the market share of the surviving firm and the larger the market share enjoyed by the industry's leading firms, the greater is the likelihood that a court will rule that a merger violates Section 7.

An acquisition that would ordinarily be viewed as too small to have an anticompetitive effect may violate Section 7 if the industry in which the acquisition occurs is *highly fragmented,* that is, if the industry consists of many firms, each of which has but a small market share. In such an industry the control of what would ordinarily be regarded as an insubstantial market share may have a significant impact on competition. For instance, in an extremely fragmented market for retail electrical applicances, a firm with a 6 percent market share would be in a far better position than firms with a market share of 0.05 percent to 1 percent. With a 6 percent share, the firm might be able to insulate particular outlets from the vagaries of competition by reducing the prices of certain items at those outlets. This practice would probably injure competition because it would place very small independent retailers at a disadvantage when they vie with those outlets for customers.

In a *vertical* merger the likelihood of injury to competition is commonly due to the acquisition of a formerly independent firm that buys and sells one or more products sold by the acquiring firm. Now part of a firm that can provide it with merchandise for resale, the formerly independent firm is likely to satisfy its needs by dealing with the acquiring firm rather than one of that firm's rivals.

The legality of *product extension* and *conglomerate* mergers is tested in the same manner as that of horizontal and vertical mergers. What is the merger's likely effect on competition? Will the merger tend to advance the new firm down the road toward monopolization?

DOES A MERGER THAT INJURES COMPETITORS INJURE COMPETITION?

Hypothetical Case

In 1990 High Quality, Inc. manufactured 12 percent of all the logic boards used in personal computers sold in the United States. At a strategy session the firm's top executives agreed that unless High Quality quickly increased its market share to at least 20 percent, it would be unable to compete effectively with the top three firms in its industry, whose combined market share was 65 percent. Walter Write, High Quality's chief executive officer, rejected the idea that the firm should seek to expand its market share by increasing its capital and debt and then proceed by way of internal expansion. He insisted that acquisition of one or two smaller firms was the best route to follow. After a brief discussion Write's plan was approved. Minor Tech Corporation was identified as the best merger candidate. Although it had only a 2 percent market share, it had an excellent research and sales staff. High Quality's attractive offer to acquire Minor Tech was quickly approved by Minor Tech's board of directors. All of Minor Tech's shareholders promptly approved the merger. Logico Corporation, one of High Quality's competitors, brought suit to enjoin the merger. The evidence established that the merger would significantly "heat up the competition" in the logic board industry and would probably drive Logico out of business within a year. What judgment? Why?

Injury to Competition Section 7 of the Clayton Act, like Sections 1 and 2 of the Sherman Act, is intended to protect *competition,* not *competitors.* Its purpose is not to safeguard competitors from the dislocations and losses that normally result from competition. A merger is not unlawful simply because it will intensify competition and thus drive one or more firms out of business. Since the purpose of Section 7 is to prevent injury to competition, not to assure the welfare of competitors, the impact of a merger on competitors has no bearing on whether the merger violates Section 7. Because Section 7 is intended to protect competition and not competitors, a competitor is *not* entitled to injunctive relief under Section 16 of the Clayton Act on the ground that a merger will enhance *competition* and thus probably force the *competitor* to shut down. Injunctive relief can be granted only if a competitor shows a threat of loss or damage due to antitrust injury.

Potential Competition   When a firm enters a market in which it has not previously done business, it is known as a "*de novo* entrant," a newcomer. Generally, its entry is likely to enhance competition. For example, if a respected company doing business in several midwestern states enters the Oregon market, where it is already well-known for the high quality of its products and service, competition in the Oregon market is likely to increase.

Instead of starting afresh in a new market under its own name, an established firm may choose to acquire a firm that is already doing business in that market. Such a merger violates Section 7 if it would probably eliminate either *perceived* or *actual* potential competition.

Perceived potential competition is eliminated when (1) the "target market," that is, the market in which the acquired firm is already doing business is highly concentrated; (2) because of the economic incentives to enter the target market, and the acquiring firm's characteristics and capabilities, the firms already in that market picture the acquiring firm as a potential independent entrant; and (3) the existing firms in the target market kept their power to affect the market within bounds because of their concern about what action the acquiring firm might take in regard to the market while it remained on the fringe of the market. The behavior of the firms in the market that was attributable to their fear of what the acquiring firm might do, so long as they saw that firm as a potential *de novo* entrant, and the likelihood that they did not seek to reap the profits that they might have sought if they had taken full advantage of their dominance in the market are referred to as the "wings effect" or the "edge effect." A merger that eliminates the wings effect injures competition.

Actual potential competition is eliminated when a merger puts an end to the prospect that long-term deconcentration in an oligopolistic target market might result if the acquiring firm entered either as a *de novo* entrant or through the acquisition of a small present competitor, a so-called foothold or toehold acquisition. To estabish that a merger eliminates actual potential competition, it must be shown that the relevant market is oligopolistic; that if the merger did not take place, the acquiring firm would probably have entered the market in the near future either as a *de novo* entrant or through a toehold acquisition; and that such an entry would probably have brought about deconcentration in the target market or would probably have had other significant procompetitive effects.

Statute of Limitations

The usual four-year statute of limitations that applies to lawsuits brought for violations of antitrust law also applies to lawsuits brought for unlawful mergers. In the case of a merger, however, the four-year time period does not begin to run until the merger causes an antitrust injury. For instance, if an acquisition occurs in 1982, but the acquiring firm does not resort to destroying competition until a year later, perhaps by forcing firms from which it purchases products to now purchase certain goods only from the acquired company, the statute of limitations starts to run in 1983.

Section 7 and Joint Ventures

As noted in Chapter 11, a "joint venture" is a form of partnership that is undertaken for a limited purpose or a single transaction. Section 7 applies to a joint venture that may substantially lessen competition or tend to create a monopoly. To establish that a joint venture violates Section 7, it need not be shown that all of the participants would probably have independently entered into the business conducted by the joint venture. It only has to be shown that it was reasonably probable that one of the participants would have entered into the same business, while one or more of the other participants would have remained a significant potential competitor.

When the parties to a joint venture do not band together so as to eliminate competition and there is no evidence of a restrictive agreement that eliminates competition among them, the following are among the factors that are taken into account to assess the probability that the joint venture will substantially lessen competition: the number and power of the competitors in the relevant market, the previous growth of the participants in the joint venture, the power of the participants in the markets in which they ordinarily compete for business, the relationship between the lines of commerce in which the participants are ordinarily involved, the competition that exists between the participants, each participant's power when dealing with competitors of the other participants, the setting in which the joint venture was created, the reasons for creating the joint venture, the line of commerce in which the joint venture is involved and the relationship between that line of commerce and the lines of commerce of its participants, the ease with which the joint venture may engage in anticompetitive practices, the potential power of the joint venture in the relevant market, and what the level of competition in the relevant market would have been if one of the participants had entered it alone.

Reciprocity

A company that sells a firm goods or services may in turn buy the goods or services sold by that firm so as to keep the firm as a customer. Such cross-dealing is known as **reciprocity.** When a buyer requires a seller to buy what the buyer sells, regardless of the price, quality, or type of service offered by competitors, reciprocity is especially likely to injure competition. When it is probable that a merger will result in reciprocal dealing that will substantially lessen competition, the merger violates Section 7.

Reciprocity
a situation in which a firm buys the products or services it needs from the firms to which it sells its own products or services

Lawful Increase in Market Share

Three doctrines exempt a merger from Section 7 even though the merger increases the acquiring firm's market share.

Failing Company Doctrine   Under the *failing company doctrine*, a merger does not violate Section 7 if the acquired company's resources are so depleted and its prospects for rehabilitation are so remote that it faces the grave probability of failure and if the acquired company has been unable to find some other company with which to merge despite having taken reasonable steps to do so. The rationale for this doctrine is that a merger is the lesser of two evils. With or without the merger the acquired company would not survive as an independent enterprise. Although the acquisition of the frail company by the healthy one may pose a threat to competition because the healthy company will now control a larger share of the market, this result is preferable to the more debilitating impact on competition and the other economic and social losses that would probably result if the merger were not allowed to take place and the frail company were forced to go out of business.

Merger of Minor Players A merger of two small competing companies is not treated as anticompetitive under Section 7 if it is likely that the company resulting from the merger will be in a better position to compete with sizable enterprises than are the two competing companies.

De Minimis Market Share Section 7 does not apply to a merger of firms whose share of the market is so trivial that their merger will have an insignificant impact on competition. This principle is commonly referred to as the *"de minimis exclusion."* For example, as we have seen, any injury to competition likely to be caused by a vertical merger is primarily attributable to the fact that firms that competed with the supplier division of one of the merged firms are now likely to have limited, if any, access to the buyer division of the combined firm. However, if only a trifling share of the market is foreclosed by a vertical merger, Section 7 is not violated, because the acquisition is too small to substantially lessen competition or tend to create a monopoly.

Investment and Organizational Exemptions

Section 7 does not apply to the acquisition of stock solely for investment purposes so long as the stock is not used to bring about or attempt to bring about the substantial lessening of competition. Also, because there is a total unity of interest between a corporation and a wholly owned subsidiary, when a corporation acquires all the assets or stock of such a subsidiary, Section 7 is not violated since there is no joining together of independent companies.

HART-SCOTT-RODINO ANTITRUST IMPROVEMENT ACT

The Hart-Scott-Rodino Antitrust Improvement Act (1976) requires that the Federal Trade Commission and the assistant attorney general in charge of the Antitrust Division of the Justice Department be notified before the completion of certain types of acquisitions when either the acquiring person or firm, or the firm whose voting securities or assets are being acquired, is engaged in interstate commerce or in an activity that affects interstate commerce. Such a notification must contain sufficient information for the FTC and the assistant attorney general to determine whether completion of the acquisition will violate antitrust laws.

The notification process must be followed when (1) the voting securities or assets being acquired are those of a firm engaged in manufacturing that has annual net sales or total assets of $10 million or more and the acquiring party has total assets or annual net sales of $100 million or more, or (2) the firm whose voting securities or assets are being acquired is not engaged in manufacturing but has total assets of $10 million or more and the acquiring party has total assets or annual net sales of $100 million or more, or (3) a person or firm with total assets or annual net sales of $10 million or more is acquiring any voting securities or assets of a firm with annual net sales or total assets of $100 million or more, *and*

(4) as a result of *any one of these three types of acquisitions,* the acquiring party would hold at least *15 percent* of the voting securities or assets of the firm whose voting securities or assets are being acquired *or* more than *$15 million* worth of that firm's voting securities or assets.

Among the types of acquisitions that are exempt from the notification requirement are acquisitions of goods or realty transferred in the ordinary course of business, acquisitions specifically exempted from the antitrust laws, and acquisitions of voting securities solely for the purpose of investment if as a result of obtaining the securities the acquirer's holdings do not exceed 10 percent of the issuer's outstanding voting securities.

There is a *30-day waiting period* (in the case of a *cash tender offer* a *15-day waiting period*) following the filing of the notification. During this period the acquisition may not take place. In individual cases the FTC and the assistant attorney general may shorten the waiting period. When either the FTC or the assistant attorney general needs additional information to decide whether to challenge the acquisition, the waiting period may be extended for up to an additional 20 days. If the FTC or the assistant attorney general concludes that the acquisition will violate antitrust law, a lawsuit may be brought in which the court is asked to bar the parties from proceeding with the transaction.

A civil penalty of not more than $10,000 may be imposed on any person, firm officer, director, or partner for each day that the notification requirement is not satisfied. In addition, at the request of either the FTC or the assistant attorney general, a federal district court may order compliance with the notification requirement, extend the waiting period until the notification requirement has been satisfied, and grant other necessary or appropriate relief.

FEDERAL TRADE COMMISSION v. ELDERS GRAIN, INC.

U.S. COURT OF APPEALS, SEVENTH CIRCUIT
868 F.2d 901 (1989)

Illinois Cereal Mills (ICM), which operated plants in Illinois and Indiana, was the nation's second-largest manufacturer of industrial dry corn, a type of processed corn sold to makers of cornflakes, corn bread, doughnuts, and other food products. It bought Lincoln Grain Company, the nation's fifth-largest manufacturer of industrial dry corn, from Elders Grain, Inc. Lincoln's mill was located in Kansas. The acquisition made ICM the nation's largest manufacturer of industrial dry corn, with a market share of 32 percent (up from 23 percent before the acquisition). Nearly all of the remaining industrial dry corn made in the United States was produced by four other firms.

The Federal Trade Commission learned of the acquisition five days before it was to occur. Four days before the acquisition was to occur, it gave ICM and Elders written notice of its intention to challenge and seek rescission of the acquisition if the acquisition occurred before it could obtain an injunction. On a Sunday, two days before the acquisition was originally supposed to occur, ICM and Lincoln merged. On the following day the FTC filed suit.

After an evidentiary hearing the district court issued a preliminary injunction that ordered the rescission of the acquisition until the FTC concluded its administrative proceedings to determine whether the acquisition violated Section 7. The district court stayed the injunction pending appeal, but left in place its order forbidding ICM to alter the operations at Lincon's Kansas mill. ICM and Elders appealed.

POSNER, CIRCUIT JUDGE

[T]he decision to grant or deny a preliminary injunction would turn on the likelihood that the acquisition really does violate section 7.

If the market were correctly defined as the sale of industrial dry corn throughout the nation, there can be little doubt that the district judge was correct in finding that the Commission is likely to prevail on the merits. The supply of industrial dry corn was already highly concentrated before the acquisition, with only six firms of any significance [in the market]. The acquisition has reduced that number to five. This will make it easier for leading members of the industry to collude on price and output without committing a detectable violation of section 1 of the Sherman Act or section 5 of the [Federal Trade Commission Act, which bars unfair competition]. [Both acts] forbid price-fixing. [I]f conditions are ripe, sellers may not have to communicate or otherwise collude overtly in order to coordinate their price and output decisions; at least they may not have to collude in a readily detectable manner. Since there are no close substitutes for industrial dry corn, its sellers can raise prices above competitive levels (i.e., above cost, which economists define as including a reasonable profit) without immediately losing all or most of their sales to the makers of other products. The varieties of industrial corn (such as brewers' grits, cornmeal, and flaking grits) appear to be largely standardized and homogeneous, making it easier for sellers to agree on a common price to charge for them, if they are so minded. And since entry into the industry is slow—it takes three to nine years to design, build, and start operating a new mill—colluding sellers need not fear that any attempt to restrict output in order to drive up price will be promptly nullified by new production. It comes as no surprise that there is a history of efforts to fix prices in the industry—a history that predates the market structure even more prone to collusion that the challenged acquisition created.

Section 7 forbids mergers and other acquisitions the effect of which "may" be to lessen competition. A certainty, even a high probability, need not be shown. Of course, the word "may" should not be taken literally, for if it were, every acquisition would be unlawful. But the statute requires a prediction, and doubts are to be resolved against the transaction. The theory of competition and monopoly that has been used to give concrete meaning to section 7 teaches that an acquisition which reduces the number of significant sellers in a market already highly concentrated and prone to collusion by reason of its history and circumstances is unlawful in the absence of special circumstances.

But all this assumes a properly defined market. The defendants point out that shipping costs are substantial, that their plants are in different parts of the country (ICM's is east of the Mississippi and Lincoln's west—and there is a surcharge for rail shipments that cross the river), and that they tend to sell different varieties of industrial dry corn to different customers. These points are not impressive. All of the nation's industrial dry corn mills are in a belt of states running from Indiana on the east to Kansas and Nebraska on the west.

All of these mills, it appears, ship industrial dry corn into the nation's largest states, which include New York, Pennsylvania, Florida, and California. Lincoln's plant, located in Atchison, Kansas, ships to both the east and west coasts and to the southeastern tip of the country (Florida), while ICM's plant in Indiana ships its products more than 2,000 miles to California. It is true that there is a surcharge for shipping by rail across the Mississippi, but it is small and subject to negotiation and, despite it, Lincoln ships anywhere from 9 to 19 percent of its output east of the Mississippi, and ICM about 30 percent of its output west of the Mississippi. The defendants, valiantly striving to establish two markets, one east of the Mississippi and one west (so that ICM and Lincoln are not even competitors), have explanations for each and every shipment that has crossed the river—a special deal here, an emergency there—but the district judge was not required to believe this special pleading. The defendants and everyone else in their industry ship industrial dry corn all over the United States. If shipping costs were as high as the defendants say they are relative to price and profit, there would be mills closer to major customers in California, Florida, and New York. The existence of excess capacity, by reducing the incremental cost of production to variable cost, enables mills to absorb substantial freight costs, and they do.

A market is the set of sellers to which a set of buyers can turn for supplies at existing or slightly higher prices. The size of the market is a function of price; other things remaining the same, a rise in price will expand the market by enabling more sellers to sell profitably to the customers in it. Buyers of industrial dry corn already scout the whole country for sources of supply; they would do so more avidly if sellers colluded. The challenged acquisition has eliminated an independent source of supply—a plant capable of selling anywhere in the country—to which customers might turn for succor if the other sellers tried to jack prices above the competitive level.

The argument that ICM and Lincoln are not in the same market because most of their customers are different and because the two firms don't sell the same product mix is based on a misunderstanding of competition. No market fits the economist's model of perfect competition—implying an infinite number of sellers having identical costs, a perfectly homogeneous product, and perfectly informed buyers—although some agricultural markets come close. In a normal market, sellers establish relations of mutual trust and advantage with particular customers, and the result is that at a given moment different sellers may have different customers. That doesn't mean the sellers are not competing. Customers aren't locked into these relationships; they can be lured away by a better offer. The possibility of such offers keeps the existing relationships from becoming exploitive.

The last issue is remedy. Apparently, a district court has never ordered rescission in a proceeding [brought for a preliminary injunction]. But the defendants concede, as they must, that the statutory grant of the power to issue a preliminary injunction carries with it the power to issue whatever ancillary equitable relief is necessary to the effective exercise of the granted power. The circumstances of the present case show how strange it would be to suppose that Congress meant to deny the district courts the power to rescind a transaction as a form of preliminary equitable relief. The Hart-Scott-Rodino Act requires a firm the size of ICM to file a premerger notification of any acquisition of stock or assets for more than $15 million [of the acquired enterprise]; after the notification there is a waiting period, during which the acquisition cannot be completed, to give the antitrust enforcement agencies a chance to determine the lawfulness of the transaction. To avoid having to file a premerger notification and observe the statutory waiting period, ICM and Elders, which had initially negotiated on the basis of a purchase price of $20 million or more for all the assets of Lincoln Grain Company, split Lincoln into two parts—the dry corn mill itself (and some associated assets) and the grain elevator attached to the mill to store the corn for milling. ICM paid $14 million for the mill and acquired an option to buy the grain elevator at any time in the next five years for $6 million. Having stolen one march on the Commission, the defendants stole another by accelerating the closing date for their deal in order to prevent the Commission from getting into court in time to seek a temporary restraining order. To reward these tactics by holding that a district court has no power to rescind a consummated transaction would go far toward rendering the statute a dead letter. Some statutes are born dead, opponents having succeeded in blocking the enactment of a viable statute. There is no indication that this statute was meant to be a stillbirth. The judgment of the district court is

Affirmed.

Legal Issues

1. Are the defendants in *FTC v. Elders Grain, Inc.* liable for the payment of a civil penalty of $10,000 a day because of the manner in which the merger was carried out? Why?

2. Courts generally use what is called a "sliding scale" approach to decide whether to grant a preliminary injunction, which is also known as an "injunction *pendente lite.*" Such an injunction bars a merger from taking place until a lawsuit has been completed. It is granted to protect the public interest. In deciding whether to grant a preliminary injunction, the court must take into account (1) which party is likely to succeed after a full trial or an administrative proceeding and (2) the injuries that are likely to result if a preliminary injunction is denied. In deciding whether to grant a preliminary injunction, should the court give greater weight to the public interest or to the firm's pecuniary interest? Discuss. Should the court give attention to the likely effect of a merger on competitors if a preliminary injunction is not granted? Why?

Ethical Issues

1. Would it be ethical for an attorney, after having been told that the FTC had learned of the acquisition in *FTC v. Elders Grain, Inc.,* to advise Elders and ICM to stymie the FTC's efforts to delay the acquisition by completing the acquisition at an earlier date than the date originally scheduled? Why?

2. What ethical standard or standards would best describe the apparent core of values that influenced the behavior of Elders and ICM when they structured the acquisition to avoid the Hart-Scott-Rodino Act's $15 million notification threshold? Discuss.

DEPARTMENT OF JUSTICE MERGER GUIDELINES

In 1984 the Department of Justice (DOJ) issued Revised Merger Guidelines for Horizontal and Non-Horizontal Mergers. These Guidelines contain the analytical framework used by DOJ decision makers in deciding whether to contest a merger. A statement that accompanies the Guidelines notes that most mergers do not threaten competition and are in fact procompetitive and of benefit to consumers. The statement says that the Guidelines are not intended to interfere with mergers that promote efficiency, or to impede efforts by American firms to compete *internationally,* or to deprive consumers of the benefits that mergers produce. It mentions the need to take into account the significance of *foreign competition* and *world markets.*

Among the factors defined and discussed in the Guidelines that the DOJ is to consider in deciding whether to challenge a horizontal merger are product market, geographic area, market power, cross-elasticity of demand, market concentration, market share, efficiency, and acquisition of a failing company or a failing division of a healthy company.

The Herfindahl-Hirschman Index (HHI) is the linchpin in the DOJ's analytical scheme for judging whether a horizontal merger should be contested. The HHI is the sum of the squares of the market shares of all the firms in a market. For example, assume that there are five firms in a market, each with a 20 percent market share. To arrive at the market's HHI, the number 20 is squared. This yields 400. Since five firms have a 20 percent share, the number 400 is multiplied by 5 to arrive at the market's HHI. In this instance it is 2,000. When there are but two firms in a market, each with a 50 percent share the number 50 is squared to calculate each firm's HHI points. The product, 2,500, is then multiplied by 2 to arrive at the market's HHI. It is 5,000. When a firm controls 100 percent of a market, the market's HHI is 10,000, the square of 100.

The DOJ uses HHI figures to judge the change in concentration in a market as a result of a merger, the market share of the merged firms, and the acceptability of concentration in the market after the merger.

Except in extraordinary circumstances the DOJ will not challenge a horizontal postmerger HHI of less than 1,000. For instance, assume that 25 firms each have a 4 percent market share. The squared figure for each firm is 16, yielding a market HHI of 400. Assume that 2 of the 25 firms merge. This gives the merged firm an 8 percent market share. Squaring 8 yields 64 HHI points. There are now 24 firms in the market, 23 with 16 HHI points and 1 with 64 HHI points. The market's HHI is calculated by adding 64 to the 16 HHI points of each of the other 23 firms. This yields an HHI of 432. Absent exceptional circumstances this merger will not be challenged.

When a merger results in an HHI of between 1,000 and 1,800, the DOJ is unlikely to challenge the merger if the increase in the HHI is less than 100 points. It is likely to challenge a merger in this category that produces an HHI increase of more than 100 points unless it concludes that it should not do so because the merger is not likely to substantially lessen competition because of the postmerger HHI, the increase in the HHI, and a variety of other factors such as the probable future competitive significance of one or more firms in the market, changes in concentration and the market shares of firms, ease of entry into the market, the likely effect of the merger on the exercise of market power, and the likelihood that the merger will achieve significant net efficiencies.

A post-merger market above 1800 is generally considered to be "highly concentrated." Still DOJ is unlikely to challenge a merger in such a market that produces an increase in the HHI of less than 50. The Department is likely to challenge mergers in this category that produce an increase of more than 50 points unless it concludes it should not do so on the basis of the same factors taken into account to decide whether to challenge a merger that results in a post-merger HHI in the 1,000 to 1,800 range. However, if the increase in the HHI exceeds 100 and the postmerger HHI substantially exceeds 1800, only in extraordinary cases will the merger not be challenged because of other factors.

One segment of the Guidelines is devoted to what the Guidelines call "nonhorizontal mergers." Such mergers are defined as combinations involving firms that do not operate in the same market. Mergers of this kind are said not to immediately change the concentration level in any relevant market, to be less likely to create competitive problems than horizontal mergers, and to be harmless almost always. In some instances the DOJ is likely to challenge a nonhorizontal merger, such as when the merger effectively removes the acquiring firm from the edge of the market and thereby eliminates a significant competitive threat that constrains the behavior of firms already in the market, or when the merger will destroy actual potential competition by eliminating the possibility of entry by the acquiring firm in a more procompetitive manner, or when the merger could result in a lost opportunity for improvement in market performance through the addition of a significant competitor or through a more procompetitive aternative than the one taken.

Although courts generally do not regard the Guidelines as binding, they *may* take them into account in deciding whether a merger is legal.

Policy Choices

The authors of the Guidelines apparently did not share the view of antitrust policy that had been held by the sponsors of the Celler-Kefauver Act. Today, unlike in 1950, the United States is not the world's key economic giant. Collectively, American enterprise is now but one of a number of major players in the world economy. It has to compete with mighty foreign companies in domestic and foreign markets. Acquisitions of influential American firms by foreign companies, the appearance of large firms in the United States that are owned by foreign companies, the banding together of 12 West European economies into the European Community, the economic power of the Pacific Rim nations, and the establishment of significant regional trading blocs are among the factors that have led to important changes in the federal government's attitude toward antitrust policy.

Currently, antitrust law is not generally viewed by federal officials as an important means of protecting and promoting cherished social and political values or of assuring the appearance and success of small businesses. Antitrust policy is now directed primarily against mergers that are likely to significantly injure competition through excessive concentration in a realistically defined market. The Guidelines are intended to assure an acceptable level of competition, promote efficiency, improve goods and services, prevent undue transfers of wealth from consumers to businesses by way of artificially inflated prices, bar vertical mergers that are likely to lead to horizontal collusion, and prevent cartelization. Within this framework, so far as the U.S. government is concerned, businesses are free to effect mergers, some of which, tested by earlier standards, would be unlawful.

Remedies for Section 7 Violations

Under Section 4 of the Clayton Act, private persons may recover damages for antitrust injury caused by a Section 7 violation. Equitable relief is available under Section 16 to prevent antitrust injury. The U.S. attorney general in each federal district may obtain equitable relief to bar or rescind an unlawful merger.

LAW ABROAD

Germany

The Cartel Authority must be notified of a planned merger before it can take place if the sales of *one* or more of the parties to the merger during the prior fiscal year were 2 billion marks or more or if the previous fiscal year's sales of *two* or more of the parties involved in the merger totaled at least 1 billion marks. The Cartel Authority will approve or reject the merger on the basis of its finding as to the effect of the merger on competition.

England

The Competition Act of 1980 authorizes the director general of fair trading to investigate what appear to be anticompetitive practices. A merger can be such a practice. The director general may investigate a merger in which at least one of the parties is an English firm and either the resulting firm will have a market share of more than 25 percent or there will be an acquisition of assets worth more than 5 million pounds. His or her finding as to whether the merger is an anticompetitive practice is submitted to the Monopolies and Mergers Commission.

The commission's task is to conduct an investigation to determine whether the merger wil have an anticompetitive effect that can be expected to work against the public interest. If the commission concludes that the merger will have such an effect, its report must state what should be done to prevent or remedy the effect.

The commission's report is forwarded to the secretary of state. If the secretary of state concludes that the merger will be adverse to the public interest, he or she may request the director general of fair trading to secure an agreement from the parties involved in the merger to take the steps needed to protect the public interest. If the director general is unable to obtain a satisfactory agreement, the secretary of state will forbid the merger.

SECTION 8 OF THE CLAYTON ACT

Section 8 of the Clayton Act is aimed an any person who simultaneously serves as a director **(interlocking directorate)** or officer of two firms of at least the size specified in the act that are in competition with each other as the term *competition* is defined in Section 8. The purpose of Section 8 is to strengthen the Sherman

Interlocking directorate

a situation in which an individual simultaneously serves as a director of two or more corporations

Act by nipping early on the possibility that directors or officers will promote policies that stifle or eliminate competition between the firms they serve.

Section 8 prohibits a person from simultaneously serving as a director or officer of any two corporations (other than banks, banking associations, and trust companies) if (1) the corporations are partially or entirely engaged in commerce, (2) the corporations are competitors because of the nature and location of their businesses, (3) elimination of competition by an agreement between the corporations would violate antitrust law; and (4) each of the corporations has capital, surplus, and undivided profits that together total more than $10 million (adjusted as described below).

Simultaneous service as a director or officer of two corporations is not prohibited by Section 8 if the competitive sales of *either* corporation are less than $1 million (as adjusted); or the competitive sales of *either* corporation are less than 2 percent of *that* corporation's total sales; or if the competitive sales of *each* corporation are less than 4 percent of that corporation's total sales.

"Competitive sales" is defined as the gross revenue for all products and services sold by one corporation in competition with the other. The amount of such revenue is determined on the basis of the annual gross income from the sale of those products and services during the corporation's last completed fiscal year. "Total sales" are the gross revenues for all products and services sold by one corporation during its last complete fiscal year.

For each fiscal year begining after September 30, 1990, the $10 million and $1 million thresholds are to be increased (or decreased) as of October 1 by an amount equal to the percentage increase (or decrease) in the gross national product, as determined by the Department of Commerce, for the year then ended over the level established for the year ending September 30, 1989. By October 30 of each year, the Federal Trade Commission must publish the adjusted amounts.

A person who is chosen as a director or officer of a second firm at a time when this does not violate Section 8 may continue to serve both firms for one year beyond the time when doing so becomes unlawful. After the one-year grace period expires, the director or officer may no longer serve both firms.

A lawsuit may be brought to compel a director or officer to resign so that he or she is no longer in violation of Section 8. To recover treble damages in a lawsuit based on a Section 8 violation, a plaintiff must prove that he or she suffered actual damage because of the injury that the unlawful interlock caused to competition.

ROBINSON-PATMAN ACT

Objective

To secure and retain the business of a large buyer or to retain the business of a longtime customer, a manufacturer may be willing to charge such a buyer a lower price than the price it demands of those who buy identical goods in small quantities or are newcomers to the market. The price differential gives the favored buyer a distinct marketplace advantage over its competitors. Furthermore, it may injure competition.

Initially, Section 2 of the Clayton Act made it unlawful for a seller "to discriminate in price between different purchasers of commodities where the effect of such discrimination may be substantially to lessen competition or tend to create a monopoly in any line of commerce." However, a seller could discriminate in the price it charged different buyers who bought the same type of goods if the discrimination was "on account of differences in the quantity of the commodity sold or [the discrimination was] made in good faith to meet competition." Those who purchased goods in large quantities could fare well under Section 2.

In 1936 Congress enacted the Robinson-Patman Act, which amended Section 2. This act outlaws discrimination based *solely* on a difference in the amount of identical goods purchased by different buyers if such discrimination is likely to injure competition. The Robinson-Patman Act also bars sellers from offering those who purchase goods in large quantities services or facilities that are denied to those who purchase like goods in smaller quantities.

Prohibited Price Discrimination

Section 2(a) of the Robinson-Patman Act makes it unlawful for any person when engaged in commerce to discriminate, either directly or indirectly, in the price charged to buyers who purchase commodities of like grade and quality, if either or any of the items involved in such discrimination are in commerce, when one or more of the items are sold for use, consumption, or resale within the United States, or any U.S. territory or insular possession, or the District of Columbia or any other place that is under the jurisdiction of the United States, if the effect of such discrimination may be to substantially lessen competition or tends to create a monopoly in any line of commerce, or to injure, destroy, or prevent competition with any person who either grants or knowingly receives the benefit of such discrimination or with customers of either of them.

Interstate Commerce

Section 2(a), which speaks of *commerce,* applies only to *interstate* transactions. This means that goods of like grade and quality must be sold to at least two different buyers, *one* of whom does business *out* of state.

Competitive Injury and Predatory Conduct

Price discrimination does not violate Section 2(a) unless there is a reasonable probability that it will cause **competitive injury.** There is competitive injury when a banned form of discrimination is likely to result in the substantial lessening of competition or tend to create a monopoly.

Competitive injury may be shown in various ways. For example, there is presumption of competitive injury when over a period of time a seller is guilty of substantial price discrimination between competing purchasers. Unless there is direct evidence of displaced sales, the presumption is overcome by proof that the price differential did not cause the victim of the discrimination to lose sales or profits.

Another way to show competitive injury is by **market analysis.** Market analysis considers how price discrimination has affected the favored purchaser's market

Competitive injury

a substantial lessening of competition or a tendency toward monopolization that is caused by discriminatory behavior

Market analysis

an examination of market share to determine whether there is competitive injury

share. For example, market analysis may show that because of the price advantage granted the favored purchaser, that purchaser's market share increased significantly at the expense of competitors who paid the seller more for the same goods. Market analysis may also show competitive injury by revealing that discrimination was followed by a decline of competition in the market where the goods were resold or by a drastic collapse in the prices that the victims of price discrimination charged their customers. There is no competitive injury when, despite price discrimination, purchasers who paid more for the goods retained or increased their market share.

Predatory intent

the intent of destroying competition by underpricing so as to later earn monopoly profits

Predatory intent may also be used to establish competitive injury. A seller acts with predatory intent when it prices goods to drive out one or more rivals and thus to acquire the power to raise future prices so as to recover past losses and reap monopoly profits. Continuously suffering losses by pricing products below their average variable costs and granting radical price discounts that undercut competitors' prices are evidence of predatory intent.

Indirect Price Discrimination

To prevent a seller from using some roundabout way to achieve a result barred by the Robinson-Patman Act, the act prohibits indirect price discrimination. A seller, for example, is guilty of unlawful price discrimination if it does not charge a large corporate buyer for every 50th case of mineral water but requires all other buyers to pay for every case they get.

Bona Fide Cost Differences

A seller is not barred from charging a buyer a lower price than the price it charges other buyers for goods of like grade and quality when the price discount is merely a due allowance for the seller's lower transaction costs. For example, a price discount may be due to a difference in the quantities or methods that the seller uses to manufacture or sell or transport the goods delivered to the buyer who pays less than other buyers for identical merchandise.

The Federal Trade Commission, after an investigation and a hearing, may establish quantity limits if it finds that the buyers who purchase larger quantities are so few in number as to make differentials based on the amount of the goods bought unjustly discriminatory and promotive of monopoly in any line of commerce. When the FTC establishes quantity limits, a seller may not vary the price charged for large-volume purchases beyond the set amount.

Change in Market Conditions

Section 2(a) allows a seller to lower the price of a product in response to changes in conditions that affect either the product's market or its marketability. For example, a seller may charge less than it previously charged for goods of like grade and quality when the goods are perishable and are deteriorating or will soon deteriorate; or when the goods are seasonal and are about to become obsolescent; or when the goods are being sold under a court order; or when the seller is about to discontinue dealing in the goods and the price reduction is made in good faith.

CONSUMER PERCEPTION OF PRODUCT SUPERIORITY

Hypothetical Case

Mid Seas Clothing Company manufactured and marketed men's leisure-time clothing directly to retailers in 35 states. Regardless of the price it charged its customers for sweaters, jackets, shirts, and pants, Mid Seas used the same process to produce these items and made them of the same materials. Less than half of the Mid Seas output in each of its product lines carried the Mid Seas label and the Mid Seas emblem, a sea lion holding an anchor. The rest carried whatever label and emblem, if any, a retailer requested.

Rodnow, Inc., a national retail chain that did business in 22 states, annually purchased about $2 million in merchandise from Mid Seas. Instead of the Mid Seas label and emblem, that merchandise carried Rodnow's trademark and the word "Him." When Rodnow's sales fell drastically, Carolyn Want, Rodnow's purchasing agent, called on Daniel Dill, the president of Mid Seas. She told him that unless the prices Mid Seas charged Rodnow for the Him items were immediately reduced by 25 percent Rodnow would seek another supplier. Dill agreed to the reduction.

Five retailers who sold goods with the Mid Seas label and emblem and were in competition with Rodnow brought a lawsuit against Mid Seas. They alleged that by charging Rodnow 25 percent less for identical goods, Mid Seas was guilty of discriminatory pricing. Mid Seas insisted that the Him clothing was not the same as clothing with the Mid Seas label and emblem. Consumers universally regarded Mid Seas products as of significantly higher quality than products that carried Rodnow's trademark and the word "Him." Retailers who sold products with the Mid Seas label and emblem marketed them as "top of the line," and their customers generally earned far in excess of $100,000 a year. Him products were sold primarily to customers whose annual income was between $25,000 and $35,000. Is Mid Seas correct? Why?

Goods of Like Grade and Quality

For purposes of Section 2(a), regardless of the price charged for goods, or how they are marketed, or of how consumers perceive them, they are of like grade and quality if they have the same physical or chemical characteristics. This principle is significant in regard to **private label** goods. Such goods are basically *identical* with other goods made and sold by the manufacturer, but they do not bear the manufacturer's label or emblem. Instead, they bear some other label or emblem and the purchaser markets them as distinct products. They may be represented as goods of especially high quality or as excellent goods sold at money-saving prices.

> **Private label**
> a distinct label used to distinguish the seller's goods from like goods made by the same manufacturer and resold as a different product

The sale of private label goods by a manufacturer for less than the price the manufacturer charges for goods of like grade and quality sold under the manufacturer's own label or some other label does not raise a question of a Robinson-Patman violation unless the effect of such price discrimination has an effect barred by the act.

Price Allowances and Discounts

Section 2(c) bars a seller from avoiding the Robinson-Patman Act's ban on price discrimination by simply calling a price reduction a commission or a brokerage fee. It is also unlawful to reduce the price charged particular buyers by granting them an allowance or a discount for services that they supposedly provide.

However, the price of goods may be reduced to *compensate* the buyers for services that they *actually* render in connection with their sales or purchases. Discrimination in violation of this section, unlike a violation of Section 2(a), is unlawful even if it is not shown that such discrimination is likely to adversely affect competition.

Functional Discount

Section 2(c) does not bar sellers from granting a discount to buyers who perform some *function* in the seller's marketing process that is not performed by buyers who do not receive the discount. Such a discount is known as a **functional discount.** For instance, wholesalers may lawfully pay less for items than retailers. They operate at a level of distribution different from that of retailers, and they help in the distribution of the seller's product. Similarly, a functional discount may be extended to retailers who perform services for the seller that other retailers do not provide. The retailers who receive this discount do not gain any price advantage, because the discount is merely compensation for services not made available by the retailers who do not receive it.

Functional discount

a discount that is granted to buyers in return for the services they provide in the seller's marketing process

Discrimination in Benefits, Services, or Facilities

Price differentials are not the only form of discrimination that can give one buyer a competitive advantage over other buyers. When a seller, without charge, provides certain buyers with services or facilities that it does not provide to other buyers, the buyers who receive the services or facilities plainly gain a competitive edge. To prevent the injury to competition that may result from such discrimination, Section 2(d) of the Robinson-Patman Act makes it unlawful for a seller to pay, or agree to pay, for anything of value to, or for the benefit of, a buyer, or to furnish a buyer, without charge, any services or facilities in connection with the processing, handling, sale, or offering for sale of any product or commodities manufactured, sold, or offered for sale by the buyer, unless like arrangements are made available on proportionately equal terms to all other buyers who compete with the favored buyer at the same level of distribution.

Meeting Competitor's Conduct

Prima facie case

a case in which misconduct is presumed because the seller has charged different customers different prices for the same product

Section 2(b) of the Robinson-Patman Act provides that a complainant establishes a **prime facie case,** that is, a presumption that the act has been violated, by showing that a seller discriminated in the price it charged a particular customer or in the services or facilities it provided to a particular customer. This means that the seller has the **burden of proof,** the task of refuting the presumption that the discrimination was unlawful. This can be done by proving that it was justified. In addition to other justifications open to the seller under the act, Section 2(b) recognizes the so-called **good faith defense.** To establish this defense, the seller must show that it charged the lower price so as to honestly meet the equally low price of a competitor or that it provided the additional services or facilities so as to honestly meet the services or facilities provided by a competitor.

Burden of proof

the task of proving a fact or refuting evidence

Good faith defense

an excuse for engaging in a discriminatory selling practice

A seller acts in good faith when, in view of the facts surrounding the sale to the favored buyer, a reasonable and prudent person would believe that the sale to *that* buyer could be made, despite a competitor's offer, *only if* the buyer were charged the lower price or provided with the additional services or facilities. The good faith defense is *not* satisfied by showing that a seller's competitor is charging *some buyers* a lower price or providing them with certain services or facilities.

The good faith defense permits a seller to meet a competitor's offer to a particular potential buyer by charging that buyer a lower price for goods than it charges other buyers, or by providing that buyer with services or facilities that it does not provide to other buyers, or by granting that buyer all three advantages. A seller that matches a competitor's offer is not required to either raise or lower the price it charges other buyers of goods of like grade or quality. The same is true in regard to any services or facilities that the seller provides to the favored buyer.

Purchaser-Provoked Discrimination

Obviously, a buyer who prods a seller to offer a discriminatory price gains the same advantage over competitors as would be gained if the seller initiated the price discrimination. Section 2(f) of the Robinson-Patman Act prohibits a buyer from knowingly inducing or receiving a discrimination in price that is unlawful under section 2(a). Section 2(c) makes it unlawful for a buyer to accept anything of value as a discount or allowance except as payment for services rendered in connection with the sale.

Civil Liability

To recover a judgment based on a Robinson-Patman violation, a plaintiff must establish that the defendant's violation caused competitive injury, which has already been discussed, as well as **personal injury,** that is, personal damages. When both of these elements are proved, the plaintiff is entitled to recover three times the amount of the personal damages he or she was caused by the defendant's violation of the act, reasonable attorney's fees, court costs, and, when appropriate, equitable relief. Personal damages include any losses that the plaintiff suffered because of the diversion of sales as well as profits that the plaintiff lost because the lower prices competitors charged were made possible by the seller's discriminatory pricing practices or because the seller provided competitors with services and facilities that were not made available to the plaintiff. Competitive injury alone does not entitle a plaintiff to recover automatic damages, such as the difference between the price that he or she was charged and what the favored buyer paid, or the cost of the services or facilities that he or she was denied.

Personal injury
the damages suffered by a buyer as a result of a seller's unlawful discriminatory behavior

Criminal Liability

It is a crime for any person while engaged in commerce (1) to partake or assist in a sales contract or a sales transaction that he or she knows discriminates against the buyer's competitors because of any discount, rebate, allowance, or advertising service charge that is granted to that buyer over and above any discount, rebate, allowance, or advertising charge made available at the time of that sales transaction to any of the buyer's competitors in respect to a sale of goods of like grade, quality, and quantity; or (2) to sell, or contract to sell, goods in any part of the United States at prices lower than the prices charged elsewhere in the nation for the purpose of destroying competition or eliminating a competitor in that part of the nation; or (3) to sell, or contract to sell, goods at unreasonably low prices for the purpose of destroying competition or eliminating a competitor.

A person who is found guilty of any of these outlawed acts may be fined not more than $5,000, or be imprisoned for not more than a year, or be punished by both a fine and imprisonment.

HASBROUCK v. TEXACO, INC.

U.S. COURT OF APPEALS, NINTH CIRCUIT
842 F.2d 1034 (1988)

Hasbrouck purchased gasoline directly from Texaco. Texaco supplied gasoline to Dompier Oil Company and Gull Oil Company at a price that at various times was between 2.5 cents and 5.75 cents per gallon less than the price that Hasbrouck paid. Dompier resold the gasoline to independent retailers who resold it under the Texaco trademark. Gull marketed the gasoline to independent service stations that resold it under private brand names.

Hasbrouck brought suit against Texaco for treble damages, charging that it had violated Section 2(a) of the Robinson-Patman Act. The jury returned a verdict for Hasbrouck in the amount of $449,900. The court trebled that amount and judgment was entered for $1,349,700. After its motions for a judgment notwithstanding the verdict or for a new trial were denied, Texaco appealed.

REINHARDT, CIRCUIT JUDGE

Texaco challenges the jury's finding of liability under section 2(a) on two grounds, (1) that the price differential was justified and (2) that, in any event, the differential did not affect competition.

Manufacturers are permitted to use price differentials, commonly known as wholesale or functional discounts, to compensate classes of buyers for the distributional services they perform. However, the discount Texaco provided here does not qualify as a functional or wholesale discount. Moreover, Texaco is simply incorrect when it argues that it is absolved from Robinson-Patman if it can show that a particular discount was available to all wholesalers.

That all wholesalers were offered the same discount would be an appropriate defense in a case where the plaintiff and the other customers of the defendant were all wholesalers performing at the same level in the chain of distribution. Here, however, only the other customers are wholesalers; the plaintiffs are retailers who are further down the chain of distribution. The injury occurs at the latter level and results from the receipt by wholesalers of a functional discount in excess of the value of the services they perform, all or a portion of which they then pass on to the retailers they supply.

There may be a Robinson-Patman violation even if the favored and disfavored buyers do not compete, so long as the customers of the favored buyer compete with the disfavored buyer or its customers. Despite the fact that Dompier and Gull did not compete directly with Hasbrouck, a section 2(a) violation may occur if (1) the discount they received was not cost-based and (2) all or a portion of it was passed on by them to customers of theirs who competed with Hasbrouck.

Hausbrouck presented ample evidence to demonstrate that both conditions were met. [A]s the district court put it, Texaco made "no serious attempt" to provide a quantitative justification for its functional discount, instead "merely identifying some of the functions" that Dompier and Gull were said to have performed. In the face of Hasbrouck's evidence challenging the cost basis of the discount, Texaco's showing was clearly inadequate.

Hasbrouck also presented sufficient evidence to support a finding that the 2.5 cents to 5.75 cents per gallon discount received by Gull and Dompier was passed on, at least in part, to retail competitors of Hasbrouck.

We recognize that, generally, selling at different prices to customers who are at different levels of distribution will not constitute a violation of the Robinson-Patman Act.

Texaco also attacks the finding of section 2(a) liability by arguing that Hasbrouck failed to prove that the price discrimination resulted in injury to competition and instead presented evidence reflecting only injury to [the plaintiff itself] as [a competitor]. We disagree. The purpose of drawing a distinction between harm to competition and harm to competitors is to point out that not all acts that harm competitors harm competition. However, the converse is *not* true. Injury to competition necessarily entails injury to at least some competitors. Competition does not exist in a vacuum; it consists of rivalry among competitors. Clearly, injury to competitors may be probative of harm to competition.

With respect to price discrimination claims, the significance of proof of harm to competitors is particularly clear. Section 2(a) of the Robinson-Patman Act is a prophylactic statute, designed to prevent the occurrence of price discrimination rather than to provide a remedy for its effects. The section is violated upon a showing that "the effect of such discrimination *may* be substantially to lessen competition." [A plaintiff need] show only "a reasonable possibility that a price differential may harm competition." [It is] permissible to infer harm to competition from evidence of harm to competitors.

> [F]or the purpose of section 2(a), injury to competition is established prima facie by proof of a substantial price discrimination between competing purchasers over time. In the absence of direct evidence of displaced sales, this inference may be overcome by evidence breaking the causal connection between a price differential and lost sales or profits.

Thus, in order for a plaintiff to prove competitive injury under Robinson-Patman, he need only show that a substantial price discrimination existed as between himself and his competitors over a period of time.

It is undisputed that a price differential existed between the rate Texaco charged Hasbrouck and the rate it charged Dompier and Gull. Furthermore, there was evidence that the price differential was substantial and that it was in effect for several years. There can be little doubt that Texaco's pricing policy constituted price discrimination that was unlawful unless it could be justified under the Act. [T]here was sufficient evidence to permit the jury to conclude that competition may have been harmed, i.e., that there was "a reasonable possibility" that a competitive injury had occurred.

Texaco also challenges the jury's damages award, contending that Hasbrouck failed to present sufficient proof of the amount of damages. Damages resulting from illegal price discrimination may not be measured merely by determining the overcharge to the favored buyer, i.e., the excess paid by

[the] disfavored buyer for the goods it purchased.

There is no evidence that the jury based its damages award on an overcharge theory. In an attempt to estimate lost sales resulting from Texaco's price differentials, Hasbrouck's expert presented a market analysis that compared Hasbrouck's actual prices, volume, and profits and its estimated amounts had the price discrimination not occurred. The expert arrived at the estimated figures using six economic projections based on different underlying assumptions, some of which assumed that Texaco eliminated the differential by raising its price to Dompier and Gull, while others assumed that Texaco lowered its price to Hasbrouck.

None of the projections estimated Hasbrouck's damages by measuring the amount of the overcharge.

Texaco argues that Hasbrouck's damages theory was speculative and internally inconsistent. The burden of proving damages in an antitrust case is, as a matter of necessity, not "unduly rigorous," because "[t]he vagaries of the marketplace usually deny us sure knowledge of what plaintiff's situation would have been in the absence of the defendant's antitrust violation." Accordingly, the plaintiff's burden of proving antitrust damages is "to some extent lightened" once a violation is established and the jury is allowed to approximate the amount of damages.

In this case, Hasbrouck submitted a market analysis which estimated lost profits six different ways. Hasbrouck's evidence was sufficient to support the jury's damage award.

Affirmed.

Legal Issues

1. If Texaco charged Dompier and Gull lower prices so that Dompier's and Gull's customers could meet the lower prices of *their* competitors, would Texaco have been guilty of a Section 2(a) violation? Why?

2. Which method other than market analysis may retailers use to establish competitive injury?

Ethical Issues

1. Is it ethical for a manufacturer to emphasize in its advertisements the unique qualities of a product that bears its distinct label and is sold only in exclusive shops while selling the same product to discounters at a lower price under a variety of private labels? Discuss.

2. Is it ethical for a retailer to sell a product that bears the manufacturer's label and is represented by the retailer to be of "premium quality" for a higher price than the price it charges for the same product when it markets the product under its own label and represents it to be "solid but inexpensive"? Why?

LAW ABROAD

European Community

European Community law bars a business concern from entering into agreements that in some way favor particular firms over other firms with which it does business if all of the business concern's transactions with these firms are otherwise alike and the discrimination will give the favored firms a competitive advantage. For example, a manufacturer that sells retailers like goods for the same price may not agree to provide a few of them with storage facilities and a variety of services free of charge. This cost savings enables the favored firms to draw customers away from the firms that must pay for such storage facilities and services by charging less for the goods without reducing their earnings.

In Chapter 18, we saw that EC law does not bar monopolization but does forbid dominant firms to engage in what is referred to as "abuse." When all of the firms with which a dominant firm deals are involved in the same sort of transaction, it is an abuse for the dominant firm to favor particular firms with preferred treatment if the preferred treatment gives the favored firms a competitive edge over the other firms. For instance, it is an abuse for a dominant firm to allow one or more buyers to pay for their purchases 180 days after goods are delivered, while competitors of those buyers must pay on receipt.

FEDERAL TRADE COMMISSION ACT

Congress enacted the Federal Trade Commission Act in 1914. The act established the Federal Trade Commission (FTC), which is composed of five members, one of whom is chosen by the president to serve as chairperson. Section 5 of the act declares that unfair methods of competition in or affecting interstate commerce and unfair or deceptive acts or practices in or affecting interstate commerce are unlawful. The FTC is empowered to prevent persons, partnerships, and corporations, except banks, savings and loan associations, most common carriers, and several other specified types of enterprises engaged in domestic activities, from engaging in unfair methods of competition and unfair or deceptive acts or practices in or affecting interstate commerce.

Global Concern

The FTC has the power to prevent unfair methods of competition in foreign commerce when those methods have a direct, substantial, and reasonably foreseeable effect on (1) domestic commerce or (2) import commerce with foreign nations or (3) export commerce with foreign nations if it is conducted by a person engaged in such commerce in the United States and the unfair methods injure export business in the United States.

Unfair or Deceptive Behavior

Neither the expression "unfair method of competition" nor the expression "unfair or deceptive act or practice" is defined in the Federal Trade Commission Act. The FTC is empowered to promulgate rules and regulations specifying the sort of conduct that the act bans.

Unfair Method of Competition In addition to conduct barred by an FTC regulation, anticompetitive conduct unlawful under either the Sherman or Clayton acts, as well as any other conduct that if not halted will injure competition, is an unfair method of competition.

Unfair or Deceptive Act or Practice An act or practice that causes substantial injury to consumers, competition, or another company may under certain circumstances be an unfair act or trade practice even though it is not expressly barred by a specific FTC regulation. Among such acts or practices is conduct that is against public policy as established by court decision or statute, or violates a judicial or statutory standard or objective, or is immoral, unethical, or unscrupulous. Even though it is not specifically prohibited by an FTC rule, an act or practice is deceptive if it is likely to deceive a potential customer. Conduct may be deceptive even if there is no intent to mislead, no damage is caused, and the other party is not in fact deceived.

Enforcement

Responsibility for the enforcement of the Federal Trade Commission Act is vested primarily in the FTC. The role of the U.S. attorney general in the area covered by the act is limited. Private persons are *not* entitled to seek any form of relief for a violation of the act.

REVIEW QUESTIONS & PROBLEMS

1. Lavto Products, Inc., a computer chip manufacturer with gross annual sales of over $10 million, entered into an agreement with Incop, Ltd. under which Incop would acquire all of Lavto's outstanding shares. Incop, a manufacturer of portable computers, had never previously done business with Lavto, having satisfied its needs for computer chips through purchases from other firms. Although Incop had only a 2 percent share of the personal computer market persons well acquainted with the computer chip industry predicted that its share was likely to increase quickly because of several newly acquired patents. Under what circumstances, if any, would the FTC have to be notified of the planned merger? What factors should the FTC take into account in deciding whether to oppose the merger?

2. Marmar Corporation, a manufacturer, had been in the automobile replacement parts business for more than half a century and had a 15 percent share of the relevant market. Wilson, Inc. and Edmonds Corporation, Marmar's two leading competitors, shared 25 percent of the relevant market. When Marmar learned that Wilson and Edmonds were about to merge, it brought suit against the two firms. It asked the court to enjoin the merger because if Wilson and Edmonds did merge, the new firm would probably intensify competition by cutting its prices. This would reduce Marmar's market share and was likely to injure the profit margins of other competitors, so that one or more of them would probably have to go out of business. Wilson and Edmonds asked the court to dismiss the suit on the ground that Marmar's allegations did not state a basis on which the court could grant the requested relief. What judgment, and why?

3. Felte Corporation had a 4 percent share of the relevant market. Although Felte held three very valuable patents that gave it an advantage over its competitors, it suffered mounting losses while its more efficient competitors gained market share. Swiftly Shift, Inc., with a 35 percent share of the market, entered into an agreement to acquire all of Felte's outstanding stock. What factors should the DOJ take into account to decide whether to challenge the merger? If the merger

were challenged, what would Felte and Swiftly Shift have to show to have the case dismissed on the ground of the failing company doctrine? Discuss.

4. When may a manufacturer grant a particular buyer a discount without violating the Robinson-Patman Act? Discuss.

5. When, if ever, may the FTC challenge the legality of a merger under Section 5 of the Federal Trade Commission Act?

6. "An administrative law judge may not find that conduct is unethical and therefore violates Section 5 of the Federal Trade Commission Act unless such conduct violates a statute, a court decision, or an agency regulation." Do you agree with this statement? Discuss.

PART
9

INTERNATIONAL BUSINESS

20. Transnational Trade

Nations generally seek ways to make exports exceed imports and thus to achieve a balance of trade in their favor. When imports exceed exports, and no compensatory factors soften the shortfall, nations seek means of stemming imports and increasing exports. They may impose tariffs or duties on imports, set import quotas, completely bar the importation of certain products, subsidize exports, or promote policies under which domestically produced goods are sold abroad at less than their fair market value.

Legal questions concerning import and export control are important to those who engage in transnational trade, but so are numerous other legal questions. For example, how can a domestic firm that sells goods to a foreign firm assure that it will be paid? If a domestic firm fails to meet its obligations to a foreign firm, may the foreign firm sue the domestic firm in a foreign court? When is a judgment of one nation's courts enforceable in another nation?

This chapter considers legal principles relating to the questions mentioned above, as well as other important principles having to do with transnational trade. It also considers U.S. policies intended to prevent foreign products from gaining undue competitive advantages in U.S. markets. In addition, the chapter examines the roles that federal courts, agencies, and officials play in the regulation of transnational trade.

TRANSNATIONAL SALES

An American firm that is about to enter into a sales contract with a firm located abroad must recognize that it should handle some features of the transaction differently than it would handle them if both firms were headquartered in the United States. For example, the American firm should consider the question of what legal principles would be used to resolve disputes that might arise under the contract. It should take special care to assure timely payment especially if the firm located abroad has no assets in the United States. It should make sure that the contract clearly provides which nation's currency the buyer must use. It should also consider what will be expected of each party in the event of changes in national trade policy that affect the transaction.

Sales Law

In all of the states except Louisiana, unless the parties agree otherwise, the state's Uniform Commercial Code is used to determine the rights and obligations of the parties to a sales contract that bears an appropriate relation to the state.

Historically, the effect of the terms in a sales contract between firms located in different nations has been governed by the legal principles followed by the courts of the nation that has jurisdiction over the parties. The Convention of Contracts for the International Sale of Goods (CISG), which was drawn up by the United Nations Commission on International Trade Law, was ratified by the United States in 1988. Unless the parties to a lawsuit that involves an international sale of goods have chosen not to be bound by CISG, if suit is brought in a nation that is a signatory to CISG, the court is required to follow CISG if the parties' places of business are located in two nations that have ratified CISG. When the dual-nation standard is not met, unless the law of a foreign nation or another state is applicable, U.S. courts will follow state sales law. Except in Louisiana, as noted, this is the Uniform Commercial Code.

Documentary Sale

A U.S. firm that is about to ship goods to a foreign purchaser is faced with such possibilities as buyer insolvency or deception. On the other hand, the foreign purchaser is faced with the risk that it may make payment but not receive the goods specified in the sales contract. To resolve these seller's and buyer's concerns, the transaction is likely to be in the form of what is commonly referred to as a **documentary sale.** Such a sale involves several documents, including a bill of lading, commonly referred to as a "document of title"; a letter of credit; and an inspection certificate.

Documentary sale

a sale in which documents are used to protect the seller's and buyer's interests

Bill of Lading

The written receipt issued to the seller (shipper) by the carrier who is hired to transport the goods to the buyer is known as a **bill of lading.** It identifies the goods; states the number, weight, condition, perhaps the value, and any identifying markings of the items received; gives the names of the shipper, the carrier, and the consignee (the person to whom the goods are to be delivered); specifies the amount of the shipping charges; and tells where the goods are to be delivered.

Bill of lading

a carrier's receipt for shipped goods

Because a bill of lading is also the contract between the shipper and the carrier, it sets forth their respective rights and duties.

A bill of lading may call for the goods to be delivered to a specified person or to bearer or a person's order. A bill that specifies the person who is to receive the goods, commonly referred to as a **straight bill,** is nonnegotiable. A bill that calls for the goods to be delivered to a bearer or person's order is a **negotiable bill of lading.** The person named in a negotiable bill of lading can transfer ownership of the bill by affixing his or her signature to the instrument and delivering it to the new owner. The signature is known as an **indorsement.** The delivery of an **indorsed bill of lading**—a negotiable bill of lading signed by the person named in the instrument—to another party entitles that party to take delivery of the goods or to determine who is to receive them. By paying for the bill of lading and taking possession of the bill, the buyer (transferee) becomes the owner of the bill and of the goods it represents. Because ownership of a bill of lading is equivalent to owning the goods for which it is issued, a bill of lading is referred to as a **document of title.**

Absent a valid agreement to the contrary, the issuer of a bill of lading is responsible for releasing the goods only to the party who presents the bill of lading and demands them. If the carrier delivers the goods to someone other than the authorized holder of the bill of lading, the carrier is responsible for any loss caused by their misdelivery.

The Uniform Commercial Code governs the rights and duties of the parties to a bill of lading for goods that are to be transported solely within a single state. A bill of lading that involves an interstate or international shipment is governed by the Pomerene Act, which is also known as the Federal Bill of Lading Act. The rights and duties of the parties to a bill of lading or a similar document of title that is used in transporting goods by sea to or from U.S. ports in foreign trade are governed by a federal statute. This statute is commonly referred to as the Carriage of Goods by Sea Act (COGSA).

Absent an agreement between the nations in which the parties to a bill of lading are located, or a multinational arrangement subscribed to by those nations, the meaning of the terms contained in a bill of lading is determined under the law of the nation in which the court with jurisdiction to determine the parties' rights and duties is located.

Letter of Credit

A document that specifies the circumstances under which the issuer, ordinarily a bank, will pay the beneficiary (creditor) a specified sum of money is known as a **letter of credit.** In a documentary sale a letter of credit is used to assure that the seller (the beneficiary of the letter of credit) is paid for goods shipped to the buyer. When the buyer is located in a foreign nation, a U.S. seller generally wishes to receive a letter of credit issued by a U.S. bank. To have a letter of credit issued to the seller, the foreign buyer either requests a bank in his or her country to make arrangements with a U.S. bank to issue a letter of credit in favor of the seller or the buyer personally makes such an arrangement with a U.S. bank. If the letter of credit is issued at the request of a foreign bank, the U.S. bank relies on the foreign bank for payment. If the U.S. bank deals directly with the buyer, it relies on the buyer's credit for payment. An issuer can cancel a **revocable letter of credit** at any time. An **irrevocable letter of credit** cannot be revoked. Obviously, to best

Straight bill
a bill of lading that identifies the person to whom the carrier should deliver goods

Negotiable bill of lading
a bill of lading that requires the carrier to deliver goods as ordered by the owner of the instrument

Indorsement
the signature of the person named in a negotiable bill of lading

Indorsed bill of lading
a negotiable bill of lading with the signature of the person named in the instrument

Document of title
a receipt for goods that confers their ownership on whoever owns the instrument

Letter of credit
a document in which a promisor (the issuer) agrees to satisfy a debtor's obligation to a creditor

Revocable letter of credit
a letter of credit that can be canceled at the issuer's discretion

Irrevocable letter of credit
a letter of credit that cannot be invalidated by the issuer

protect his or her interests, a U.S. seller would demand that the sales contract call for an *irrevocable* letter of credit. The issuer is obliged to honor its obligations to the seller so long as the seller satisfies the conditions contained in the letter of credit.

Inspection Certificate

When a letter of credit is used to assure that the seller in an international sales transaction is paid for shipped goods, aside from any other conditions that the seller must satisfy, the letter of credit will require that the seller deliver to the issuing bank a properly indorsed negotiable bill of lading acknowledging that the carrier has received the goods called for by the sales contract. In addition, the letter of credit is likely to require that the seller deliver to the issuing bank an **inspection certificate** from a source identified in the letter. The certificate must attest to the quality and quantity of the goods. Upon receipt of a bill of lading and an inspection certificate that meet the standards required by the letter of credit, the issuer is obliged to pay the seller the amount of money specified in the letter of credit. The bank will see that the properly indorsed bill of lading and the certificate of inspection are delivered to the buyer. In turn, the buyer will gain possession of the goods by delivering the bill of lading to the carrier.

Inspection certificate

a document that verifies the actual quality and quantity of goods available for delivery

Separate Agreements

The sales contract, the bill of lading, the letter of credit, and the agreement between the foreign bank or foreign buyer and the American bank that issues the letter of credit are independent contracts. This means that the *failure* of a party to one of these contracts to carry out its terms does *not* necessarily excuse the victim of the default from meeting his or her obligations under the other contracts.

TO MATCH OR NOT TO MATCH THE ETHICAL STANDARDS OF OVERSEAS COMPETITORS?

Hypothetical Case

Ted Topp, sales vice president of the Global Division of Waylock, Inc., learned that an East European nation was about to purchase several million dollars' worth of the sort of metal pipe made by Waylock. He immediately arranged a meeting with the nation's minister of purchasing. The minister told him: "We are a poor country. We not only need quality suppliers; we also need suppliers who will make it possible for our officials to be reasonably compensated. Unofficially, our officials are expected to supplement their salaries by receiving an enhancement allowance from those who do business with us. My decision on whether to buy several million dollars' worth of metal pipe from Waylock would be objective. My country must receive the best quality for the lowest price. My enhancement allowance would be the going rate, 2 percent of the purchase price. Because the enhancement allowance is technically unlawful, it must be paid in cash. You can check around and see whether or not I am telling you the truth when I say that regardless of who sells us the pipe, an enhancement allowance will be paid. I must have all the particulars of your proposal, including how the enhancement allowance will be handled, within 10 days." After making a number of inquiries, Topp concluded that the minister's statements about the enhancement allowance were "on the money."

To meet the 10-day deadline, Topp immediately returned to the United States to discuss Waylock's offer and the enhancement allowance with Waylock's president, Jim Jarr, and Waylock's corporate counsel, Barbara Carroll. Jarr told Topp: "Go for it. I am behind you, and so is the board of directors. We need the order. Management's survival is at stake. Our sales have been sliding." Carroll, indignant, said: "Our firm has a code of ethics. Rule 1 is that we do not give bribes. Rule 2 is that we do not cheat. Let's not kid ourselves—we all know what the so-called enhancement allowance is. Sure we can use the business, but being ethical means being willing to make sacrifices. I say let's look for business elsewhere." After thinking a moment, Topp said: "I agree with Jarr. If we don't pay the enhancement allowance, someone else will. Losing the sale will only mean that someone else will make money. That official will still be paid. What harm does it do to pay a bribe when that is the way business is done?"

Do you agree with the stance taken by Jarr and Topp or with the one taken by Carroll? Why?

FOREIGN CORRUPT PRACTICES ACT

The Foreign Corrupt Practices Act, passed in 1977 and amended in 1988, establishes standards of acceptable business behavior for American firms that do business abroad. The act prohibits an American firm or any officers, directors, employees, agents, or stockholders who act on its behalf, from using the mails or any means or instrumentality of interstate commerce to *corruptly* offer to pay, promise to pay, pay, or authorize to pay any money, or to offer to give, promise to give, give, or authorize to give anything of value to any foreign official in order to influence how that official performs his or her official duties, or to induce that official to violate the law or to use his or her position with a foreign government, or any of its instrumentalities, to affect or influence any act or decision of the government or government instrumentality in order to help the firm to *obtain* or *retain* business.

The act imposes a like ban on *corrupt* dealings of a firm with any foreign political party, or party official, or any candidate for foreign political office, for the purpose of influencing any act or decision regarding how the party conducts its affairs or how the individual goes about his or her official duties or pursues his or her quest for public office, or to induce a political party, official, or candidate to behave unlawfully, or to induce a party official or candidate to use his or her influence with a foreign government or government instrumentality to affect or influence any of its acts or decisions in order to help the firm to *obtain* or *retain* business.

Grease Payments

The Foreign Corrupt Practices Act does not outlaw payments made to a foreign official, political party, or party official so as to *expedite* or *secure* the performance of a routine governmental action by a foreign official, political party, or party official. Such a payment is known as a **grease payment.** Routine governmental action includes such things as issuing permits, licenses, or other official documents to qualify a person to do business in a foreign country; processing governmental papers, such as visas and work orders; providing police protection, mail pickup, or inspections related to the transportation of goods across a country; providing phone service, power, and water; loading and unloading cargo; or protecting perishable products from deterioration.

Grease payments
a payment that is made to hasten or assure the performance of an official act

The act is not violated if it is shown that a payment, gift, offer, or promise to give anything of value to a foreign official, political party, party official, or candidate was lawful under the written laws and regulations applicable to that foreign official, political party, party official, or candidate, or that a payment, gift offer, or promise to give anything of value was a reasonable and bona fide expenditure, such as travel and lodging expenses incurred by or on behalf of the foreign official, political party, party official, or candidate, and was directly related to the promotion, demonstration, or explanation of products or services or the performance of a contract between the American firm and the foreign government or one of its agencies.

Enforcement

The attorney general of the United States, at his or her discretion, may bring a civil action in an appropriate federal district court to temporarily or permanently enjoin a *domestic concern* from engaging in any act or practice outlawed by the Foreign Corrupt Practices Act. The act defines a domestic concern as any individual who is a citizen, national, or resident of the United States or any corporation, partnership, association, joint-stock company, unincorporated association, or sole proprietorship that has its principal place of business in the United States or is organized under the laws of any state or of any U.S. territory, possession, or commonwealth. Injunctive relief may also be sought against officers, directors, employees, agents, or stockholders of a firm who seek to promote the firm's interests by engaging in, or being about to engage in, a form of behavior banned by the act.

If found guilty in an action brought by the attorney general for a violation of the act, a domestic firm may be fined not more than $2 million and be held liable for a civil penalty of not more than $10,000. Any officer or director of a domestic firm, or any stockholder who acts on its behalf, who willfully violates the act may be fined not more than $100,000 or imprisoned for not more than five years, or both. An employee or agent of a domestic firm who is a U.S. citizen, national, or resident, or is otherwise subject to the jurisdiction of the United States, but is not an officer, director, or stockholder of the firm, may be fined not more than $100,000 or imprisoned for not more than five years, or both, if he or she acts on the firm's behalf and willfully violates the act.

SELECTION OF APPLICABLE LAW

When a lawsuit concerns conduct that involves more than a single U.S. state, a court must decide which state's law should be used to rule on the parties' rights and duties. Similarly, when a lawsuit concerns conduct that involves two or more nations, a court must determine which nation's law should be followed.

Parties' Choice of Law

The parties to a contract that has ties to two or more nations may agree on which nation's law, or which political subdivision's law, is to be used to determine their respective rights and duties. For example, a contract between an Illinois firm and a German firm may provide that any dispute between them is to be resolved according to the law of Illinois or Germany. Should the two firms decide that the law of neither of these jurisdictions is acceptable, they may choose the law of another jurisdiction. Absent a compelling reason why the parties' choice is unacceptable, an American court will abide by their selection.

Conflict of Laws

U.S. courts generally use the *conflict of laws* substantial or significant contacts standard to determine which nation's substantive law should be used to decide the parties' rights and duties when the parties do not state their choice of law. Foreign nations have their own conflict of laws rules. Their courts may use a substantial or significant contacts standard, or the law of the nation in which a contract was made or a tort occurred, or the law of the nation in which a contract is to be performed, or simply the same law that is used to resolve a purely local dispute.

CHOICE OF FORUM

The geographic location of the court in which the plaintiff brings a lawsuit is known as the **forum.** Just as the parties to a transaction may by contract specify which jurisdiction's law is to determine their legal rights and duties, they may also specify the court that is to have jurisdiction to resolve their disputes. For instance, a contract between a California firm and a foreign firm may specify that any lawsuit regarding the contract is to be brought in a California court. Absent an overpowering reason not to do so, the California court will honor the parties' wishes. However, as is the case with an agreement as to which jurisdiction's law is to be used to determine the parties' rights and duties under a contract, there is no guarantee that the court will abide by the contract's forum provision if one of the parties to a lawsuit brings the suit in a court located outside California that has jurisdiction over the parties. For example, if one of the parties brings a lawsuit in the nation where the defendant has a place of business, the tribunal in that nation may choose to hear and resolve the controversy despite the parties' agreement that any lawsuit arising under the contract is to be brought in a California court. The foreign tribunal may conclude that because of the subject matter of the contract or because of the locale in which the parties entered into the contract, their choice need not be respected.

Forum
the place where a lawsuit
is brought

ARBITRATION

As mentioned in Chapter 5, parties to an international business transaction, like parties to a domestic transaction, may agree to have a present or future dispute resolved by arbitration. Their arbitration agreement should include the same kinds of provisions that are included in arbitration agreements that lack an international dimension. For instance, it should identify the arbitrator or the members of an arbitration panel, or it should simply state that the dispute is to be heard and decided in accordance with the rules of a designated body, such as the American Arbitration Association.

Aside from the United States, seventy-five nations are now parties to the United Nations Convention on the Recognition and Enforcement of Foreign Arbitral Awards. Under the convention, a foreign arbitral award made in a dispute regarding an international transaction that U.S. law views as commercial is enforceable in U.S. courts unless the arbitration process does not satisfy the convention's standards for enforceability.

RECOGNITION OF FOREIGN LAW

Comity

a doctrine that calls for nations to recognize and enforce one another's laws and official actions

Comity is a rule of private international law. Based on practice, conscience, or expediency, it is one nation's expression of its respect for the legislative, executive, and judicial acts of another nation. It is a way in which a nation demonstrates its regard both for its international obligations and for the convenience and rights of persons who are to be protected by their own nation's laws.

When an American court is asked to recognize or enforce the judgment of a foreign tribunal, comity requires the court to do so if it is convinced that the foreign tribunal had jurisdiction over the parties and treated them fairly under a system of law likely to secure the impartial administration of justice between the citizens of its nation and the citizens of other nations. Under comity, U.S. courts generally recognize only the final valid judgments of foreign tribunals.

Reciprocity doctrine

the doctrine that a court should enforce the judgments of courts in another country only if courts in that country will enforce its judgments

Courts disagree as to whether the **reciprocity doctrine**, which originated in a 19th-century U.S. Supreme Court decision, limits the enforceability of foreign judgments. Under this doctrine, comity does not require a U.S. court to enforce a judgment of a foreign court unless the courts of the nation in which the judgment was entered would accord recognition to such a judgment if it originated in a U.S. court.

Federal and state courts may take national and state public policy into account in deciding whether they should respect foreign law. When there is a conflict between domestic public policy and the law of another nation, that nation's law need not be treated as paramount to domestic policy. Comity allows a court to follow its own sense of justice and equity in deciding whether to respect foreign law.

Generally, a party who secures a foreign judgment and wishes to enforce it in the United States simply asks the court for money damages. But comity does not limit a U.S. court to awarding monetary relief. When it is appropriate to do so, a U.S. court may enforce a foreign judgment by granting injunctive relief. For instance, if a foreign judgment bars the performance of a certain act, an "enforcing judgment," that is, a U.S. court's judgment that enforces the foreign judgment, may grant the same relief if the U.S. court concludes that this remedy is necessary to suitably carry out the foreign judgment and that awarding such relief will neither unduly burden the court nor conflict with fundamental principles of justice and good morals.

Sovereign immunity

the doctrine that a nation is excused from having to answer for its actions in the courts of another nation

Absolute immunity

the doctrine that a nation is exempt from suit in a foreign court

Restrictive immunity

the doctrine that a nation is exempt from suit in a foreign court only for public or governmental acts

SOVEREIGN IMMUNITY

As a matter of comity, a nation grants other nations **sovereign immunity.** That is, excuses them from having to defend themselves within the framework of the nation's legal system. At one time the United States embraced the doctrine of **absolute immunity.** This doctrine completely excuses foreign nations from having to defend themselves in lawsuits brought against them in another nation regardless of why the plaintiff seeks relief. At present the United States does not follow this approach. Instead, it observes **restrictive immunity.** This narrower standard recognizes sovereign immunity as a defense only in cases in which a plaintiff's claim against a foreign nation arises from a *public* or *governmental* act. Restrictive immunity does *not* shield a foreign nation from liability for actions that relate to its involvement in commercial transactions, the operation of businesses, or the other pursuits that resemble the activities of private entrepreneurs rather than the traditional activities of governments.

ACT OF STATE DOCTRINE

The **act of state doctrine** bars one nation's courts from declaring invalid a *governmental act* of a foreign nation executed by that nation within its geographic limits. Under this doctrine, federal and state courts are bound by an act of a foreign nation that concerns matters normally dealt with by government. For instance, if a foreign nation decides who owns consumer goods, or a bank deposit, or a vessel, or an aircraft while such items are located within the nation's boundaries, U.S. courts would abide by that decision.

Act of state doctrine
the doctrine that bars the courts of one nation from invalidating governmental acts taken by another nation within its own boundaries

The act of state doctrine recognizes that judicial refusal to respect an act of a foreign nation could embarrass the executive branch of the U.S. government, which, under the Constitution, is charged with conducting the foreign affairs of the United States. This concern was forcefully voiced by the U.S. Supreme Court in *Banco National de Cuba v. Sabbatino*.[1] In *Sabbatino* the plaintiff, a U.S. firm, charged that the Cuban government had seized its property *contrary* to customary international law. The Court, invoking the act of state doctrine, insisted that U.S. courts could not overrule action taken by the Cuban government within Cuba *even if* that action violated customary international law. The Court cautioned that allowing U.S. courts to rule on the validity of action taken by a foreign nation within that nation's territory might hinder rather than further the pursuit of national goals and the goals of the community of nations.

Disturbed by the *Sabbatino* decision, Congress enacted the so-called Second Hickenlooper Amendment. The amendment directs that no U.S. court use the act of state doctrine to refuse to decide the validity of a claim of title to or other interest in property by anyone, including a foreign nation or a party claiming ownership through action taken by a foreign nation, when the claim of title or other interest is based on an act of a foreign government that is *contrary* to international law. This means, for example, that if a U.S. firm seeks to recover property in a lawsuit on the ground that the property was taken by a foreign nation in violation of international law, a U.S. court may *not* refuse to decide whether the foreign nation behaved in accordance with international law. If a U.S. court finds that the foreign nation's act did violate international law, the court may refuse to invoke the act of state doctrine to reach a decision.

To allow the executive branch of the U.S. government sufficient latitude to fulfill its responsibility for conducting U.S. foreign policy, the amendment provides that in any case in which the president decides that application of the act of state doctrine would promote U.S. foreign policy, he or she may suggest to the court in which the case is pending that the act of state doctrine should be invoked even though the foreign nation's action violated international law. It is the U.S. attorney general's task to apprise the court of the president's suggestion and foreign policy interests of the United States.

Apart from the Second Hickenlooper Amendment, it is generally agreed that the act of state doctrine does not require U.S. courts to recognize an act of a foreign nation that concerns a *purely commercial* activity. For instance, a foreign nation engaged in the tobacco business enters into an agreement with a U.S. firm under which the U.S. firm is to establish and operate a cigar factory in that nation. In return, the foreign nation is to give the U.S. firm 20 percent of the net annual profits earned from the sale of goods manufactured at the factory. After the factory has been in operation for a year and earned a substantial profit, the foreign nation refuses to abide by the profit sharing arrangement. If the U.S. firm were to bring a lawsuit in a U.S. federal or state court to recover 20 percent of the factory's net annual profits, the act of state doctrine would not bar the firm from recovering a judgment against the foreign nation, because the act of the foreign nation on which the firm's claim is based is of a purely commercial nature.

FOREIGN SOVEREIGN IMMUNITIES ACT

The Foreign Sovereign Immunities Act (FSIA), passed by Congress in 1976, is keyed to the restrictive theory of sovereign immunity. Under certain circumstances, FSIA bars foreign nations and their agencies from invoking the defense of sovereign immunity in a lawsuit brought in any court in the United States. A foreign nation is not immune from liability when it waives immunity, either expressly or by its behavior; or when, in violation of international law, it seized property that is in the United States or when it received property that is in the United States in exchange for property that it seized, and the property was connected with a commercial activity carried on in the United States. A foreign nation is also not immune from liability for acts based on a commercial activity that it carried on in the United States, or for acts that it performed in the United States in connection with a commercial activity that it carried on elsewhere, or for acts based on a commercial activity that it carried on outside the United States but that had a direct effect in the United States.

Under FSIA, U.S. courts have jurisdiction over a foreign nation and its agencies when that nation carries on a commercial activity in the United States that involves substantial contact with the United States. If the commercial activity lacks sufficient contact with the United States, U.S. courts do not have jurisdiction over the foreign nation or its agencies. For the purposes of FSIA, a foreign nation is involved in a commercial activity if it engages in either a course of commercial conduct or a particular commercial transaction or act. Whether an activity is commercial is determined by reference to the *nature* of the course of conduct or the particular transaction or act. Neither the *purpose* of a foreign country's involvement or the manner of *performance* of an act is taken into account to decide whether an activity is commercial for the purposes of FSIA.

MILLEN INDUSTRIES, INC. v. COORDINATION COUNCIL FOR NORTH AMERICAN AFFAIRS

U.S. COURT OF APPEALS, DISTRICT OF COLUMBIA
855 F.2d 879 (1988)

Millen Industries, Inc. brought suit for breach of contract and misrepresentation against the Coordination Council for North American Affairs (CCNAA), an instrumentality of the Taiwan government that acted as its public relations agent and broker to solicit U.S. citizens to establish commercial ventures in Taiwan. Millen charged that CCNAA had entered into a contract with it in which CCNAA represented and agreed that Millen could build and operate a factory in Taiwan, that it would receive easy access through Taiwan customs for imported machinery and equipment, that it could import raw materials duty-free if they were used to make shoe boxes for shoes made in Taiwan, and that it would enjoy the benefit of existing Taiwan law. When CCNAA entered into the contract, it knew that the cancellation of Taiwan's duty-free policy was being considered.

After obtaining the required approvals and licenses from Taiwan, Millen built a plant in Taiwan and put it into operation. From the beginning of this venture, Taiwan officials obstructed Millen's importation of machinery and raw materials. Shortly after Millen opened the plant, Taiwan ended its duty-free policy. When Millen closed the plant because it suffered losses on account of Taiwan's actions, the Taiwan government did not allow it to remove its machinery and raw materials.

The district court dismissed Millen's complaint, noting that Millen's contract claims against CCNAA related to uniquely sovereign import-export activity and thus were unenforceable under the act of state doctrine. Millen appealed.

SENTELLE, CIRCUIT JUDGE

[The lower court failed] to invoke the jurisdictional provisions of the Foreign Sovereign Immunities Act (FSIA). [W]e have previously recognized that a principal purpose of the FSIA was to settle responsibility in the courts rather than the Executive for determining the jurisdiction of United States courts over foreign sovereigns.

The District Court, rightly noting that the claims asserted by [the] plaintiff relate primarily to acts done in Taiwan by the Taiwanese government, dismissed a portion of the claims pursuant to [the act of state] doctrine. However, a further development of the jurisdictional facts may establish that neither the District Court nor this Court have jurisdiction under the FSIA to pass on Millen's claims at all.

The CCNAA is an "instrumentality" established by Taiwan. [S]hortly put, the CCNAA for purposes of this action, rather than being a subject or citizen of Taiwan, *is* Taiwan.

As all laws, including the FSIA, applicable to nations *also* [italics added] apply to Taiwan, CCNAA enjoys the same immunity under the FSIA as do other nations. [T]he FSIA is the exclusive means of exercising jurisdiction over foreign sovereigns.

The FSIA provides a general rule that "foreign state[s] [are] immune from the jurisdiction of the courts of the United States" subject to specified exceptions. The only exception at issue here is the so-called commercial activity exception.

> [T]he applicability of this exception is dependent upon the presence of "commercial activity." Commercial activity is defined as either a regular course of commercial conduct or a particular commercial transaction or act. The commercial character of an activity shall be determined by reference to the nature of the course of conduct or particular transaction or act, rather than by reference to its purpose.

While making it clear that the commercial or govermental character of an activity depends upon its nature and not its purpose, the FSIA does not further distinguish between the two, leaving it to the courts to refine the distinction. A useful inquiry in pursuing this refinement is whether the essence or central elements of an agreement made by a foreign state "might be made by a private person." It is this test that we must apply to the complaint before the District Court.

[W]hen a transaction partakes of both commercial and sovereign elements, jurisdiction under FSIA will turn on which element the cause of action is based on. Even if a transaction is partly commercial, jurisdiction will not obtain if the cause of action is based on a sovereign activity.

The transaction between Millen and CCNAA involved both sovereign and commercial elements. Promotion of investment is ordinarily a commercial activity; private parties commonly act as public relations agents. On the other hand, the "right to regulate imports and exports [is] a sovereign prerogative." Thus, to the extent that the causes of action are based on promises, breaches of promises, and other allegedly actionable conduct involving duty-free status and/or the benefit of Taiwanese law, there would plainly be sovereign aspects of the transaction over which we lack jurisdiction.

One allegation of the complaint, however, may be sufficient to create jurisdiction. Generously read, the allegation that defendant promised plaintiff that they "would receive easy access for imported machinery and equipment," could refer to not essentially governmental activities of customs agents but rather the commercial activity of a commercial "customs expediter." Therefore, the potential exists that claims based on the breach of that promise encompassed within the plaintiff's complaint for breach of contract fall within the commercial activity exception and, therefore, [the complaint] should not be dismissed on jurisdictional grounds. [T]he act of state doctrine should not be [considered] if this case is in fact beyond the proper jurisdiction of [the District] Court by reason of the FSIA. [W]e remand [the plaintiff's] claim [to the District Court] for further development of the jurisdictional facts.

Vacated and remanded.

Legal Issues

1. Which federal official or officials are authorized to attend to the interests of the United States once the question of the applicability of the act of state doctrine is at issue in a court proceeding?
2. If the United States severs diplomatic relations with another nation, does this necessarily mean that the act of state doctrine is inapplicable to all of the actions taken by that nation? Why?

Ethical Issues

1. Should a court consider a foreign nation's views on ethical behavior in certain relationships when it decides whether the activity in question in a lawsuit is commercial in nature under FSIA? Why?
2. When the chief executive officer of a U.S. corporation learned that a number of officials of a foreign nation planned to prevent her firm from carrying out the terms of its contract with that nation's import-export agency, she met with an individual who was highly respected by key political figures in the foreign nation. After she explained the importance of her firm's contract with the import-export agency, she gave him $500,000 "to do what you believe has to be done to put an end to any interference." Did her conduct violate the Foreign Corrupt Practices Act? Why?

JURISDICTION OF FOREIGN COURTS

When a firm that is organized under the laws of one nation maintains a place of business in a foreign nation, that nation's courts have jurisdiction over the firm's local activities and assets. The courts of a nation can obtain jurisdiction over a foreign firm that does not have a continuous presence in that nation under the same circumstances that a U.S. state court can obtain jurisdiction over an out-of-state firm.

SHOULD THE COURT DECLINE JURISDICTION?

Hypothetical Case

Dalin, Inc., a Delaware corporation with its home office in New York City, manufactured a variety of chemical substances. One of the by-products of its Pakistan plant generated a toxic gas that could injure or kill human beings. In 1984 a huge tank containing the toxic gas exploded. As a result 200 people were killed and over 15,000 were injured. The attorneys for the injured persons and the estates of the deceased persons brought a class suit for compensatory and punitive damages against Dalin, Inc. in the federal district court in New York City.

Dalin asked the court to dismiss the case on the following grounds: the injuries for which the plaintiffs sought relief occurred in Pakistan; Pakistan had an extensive and well-organized judicial system that commonly dealt with personal injury cases; almost all of the parties' prime witnesses resided in Pakistan; most of the documents that would probably be used as evidence were located in Pakistan; and it would be unfair to the parties to have an American court determine whether Dalin was liable for an event that took place in Pakistan. The plaintiffs' attorneys insisted that it was proper for the court to decide the case because the defendant corporation's home office was in New York City, a number of the plaintiffs resided in New York City, and the plaintiffs who did not reside in New York City were ready, willing, and able to appear before the court to offer evidence establishing Dalin's liability.

Should the court hear the case, or should it dismiss the lawsuit and thus require the plaintiffs to seek relief in a Pakistani court? Why?

FORUM NON CONVENIENS

A trial court may invoke the principle of ***forum non conveniens*** to dismiss a lawsuit in which it has jurisdiction over both the parties and the subject matter. This principle is invoked when the trial court, in the exercise of its sound discretion, concludes that it would be *just* to have the lawsuit heard in another jurisdiction. To decide whether *forum non conveniens* should be invoked, a court weighs and balances a variety of factors, such as the convenience of the parties and the witnesses, the location of the documentary evidence, the comparative ability to decide the case of the court in which the case is pending and of the alternative court that also has jurisdiction to hear the case, the relative familiarity with the legal principles likely to be used to decide the case of the court in which the case is pending and of the alternative court, the extent of the government's interest in the case in the nation in which the case is pending and in the

Forum non conveniens

the principle under which a court declines to hear a lawsuit because justice requires that the suit be tried in an alternative jurisdiction

alternative nation in which the case may also be heard, the administrative burden that the court would have to bear if the case were not dismissed, and the court-related expenses that the government would have to bear if the case were not dismissed.

Forum non conveniens may be invoked when the plaintiff and the defendant are residents of different U.S. states or of different nations. An American court is more likely to respect the choice of U.S. residents that a particular state court hear their case than it is to respect the choice of foreign residents that a particular American state court rather then a court in a foreign nation hear their case.

INTERNATIONAL TRADE AND THE NATIONAL INTEREST

Mercantilism
the view that a nation should enjoy a net gain from its trade with other nations

The promotion of the economic well-being of one nation at the expense of other nations long preceded the founding of the United States. During the period before the American Revolution, for example, Great Britain, like other European nations, sought to regulate its foreign trade in accordance with the tenets of **mercantilism**. Under this doctrine, nations seek to advance their interests by obtaining a favorable balance of trade. Similarly, for centuries European nations commonly regulated the trade of their colonies so as to make the colonies markets for their exports and sources of the raw materials they needed. Great Britain, for example, enacted laws designed to assure that it prospered at the expense of its North American colonies.

From the very beginning of its existence, the federal government of the United States enacted legislation to protect American business from foreign competition. A tariff statute was among the laws that the First Congress adopted.[2] To this day federal laws as well as treaties between the United States and other nations reflect a continuous effort to strike an acceptable balance between shielding American industries from what is regarded as unfair foreign competition and enabling the United States to enjoy the benefits of free trade among nations. The Buy American Act is an excellent example of the desire to insulate U.S. goods from foreign competition. For instance, within prescribed limits the act requires that federal agencies that buy articles for public use buy items whose contents are substantially all materials mined, produced, or made in the United States.

U.S. REGULATION OF INTERNATIONAL TRADE

A number of federal bodies are involved in the formulation and enforcement of the international trade policy of the United States.

U.S. International Trade Commission

In 1916 Congress established the U.S. Tariff Commission, an independent agency whose name was changed to the U.S. International Trade Commission (ITC) in 1975. An overview of some of ITC's tasks reveals the depth of congressional concern with the effect that imports may have on the well-being of the nation in general and on U.S. business in particular. Among the tasks assigned to ITC are to:

1. Investigate the administration and fiscal consequences of the nation's customs laws.

2. Study the relationship between duty rates on raw materials and duty rates on finished or partly finished products.

3. Examine the effects of specific duties.

4. Probe all questions that relate to the arrangement and classification of articles in customs law schedules.

5. Delve into the operation of the customs laws and into their effect on industries and labor.

6. Submit reports of its investigations to interested agencies.

7. Review tariff relations between the United States and foreign nations.

8. Take stock of commercial treaties.

9. Compare the volume of imports with the volume of domestic production and consumption.

10. Scrutinize the conditions, causes, and effects of imports, including the effects of dumping as they relate to competition between foreign industries and U.S. industries.

11. Participate in the process of deciding whether to initiate countervailing or antidumping duties.

12 Make available to the president, the House Ways and Means Committee, and the Senate Finance Committee all of the information at its command whenever requested to do so.

13. Provide reports requested by the president, the House Ways and Means Committee, the Senate Finance Committee, or either branch of Congress.

To fulfill its tasks, ITC engages in extensive research, conducts studies, and seeks to maintain a high level of expertise in matters that concern the nation's international trade policies.

In its capacity as a regulatory agency, ITC is empowered to adjudicate various questions, such as whether importation or the sale of imports is tainted by an unfair method of competition or an unfair act. Generally, it may not disclose any confidential business information that it receives in the course of an investigation unless the party who submitted the information had prior knowledge that this would be done or consents to the disclosure.

Trade Remedy Assistance Office

The Trade Remedy Assistance Office is a separate body housed in the U.S. International Trade Commission. This office is required to provide, upon request, full information to the public and, to the extent feasible, assistance and advice to interested parties concerning remedies and benefits available under trade laws that have to do with (1) injuries caused by import competition, (2) adjustment assistance for workers and firms, (3) relief from foreign import restrictions and export subsidies, (4) the imposition of countervailing duties and antidumping duties, (5) the safeguarding of national security, and (6) unfair practices in import trade.

U.S. Court of International Trade

The U.S. Court of International Trade (CIT) is a civil court with jurisdiction in almost any case brought against the United States that is based on a federal statute concerning imports. For example, CIT has exclusive jurisdiction to review U.S. International Trade Commission determinations that concern the impact of the subsidization of foreign goods and the dumping of foreign goods in the United States on American business. CIT hears protests from those who object to U.S. Customs Service decisions as to the value of imported articles or as to the amount of duty that is payable on imported merchandise. This court alone has the authority to hear suits brought against the United States to recover customs duties. It does not have jurisdiction over disputes concerning restrictions on imported merchandise in which public safety or health issues are involved.

Appeals from the U.S. Court of International Trade are heard by the Court of Appeals for the Federal Circuit. Further review by the U.S. Supreme Court may be available.

Office of the U.S. Trade Representative

The Office of the U.S. Trade Representative is headed by the U.S. trade representative, who is a cabinet official with the rank of ambassador. He or she is directly responsible to the president. Overall national trade policy is recommended and administered by the Office of the U.S. Trade Representative. The U.S. trade representative is the nation's chief delegate on matters that concern the General Agreement on Tariffs and Trade (GATT) and on negotiations with foreign nations that relate to direct investment by Americans abroad. He or she also plays a part in the initial decision-making process as to the imposition of countervailing duties on imports, the formulation of the nation's response to dumping, the monitoring of existing trade agreements, and the negotiation of trade arrangements between the United States and other nations.

U.S. Customs Service

Congress established the Bureau of Customs in 1789. In 1973 this agency, a division of the Department of the Treasury, was renamed the U.S. Customs Service. Among its many tasks are the evaluation and classification of imported merchandise; the collection of customs duties, fees, and penalties that are payable on imports; and the enforcement of customs laws, including restrictions on the importation of goods and limitations on the exportation of high-technology items. The U.S. Customs Serivce is also involved in the execution of antidumping orders and countervailing duty directives, the monitoring of quotas imposed on various imported items, and the observance of patent, copyright, and trademark laws as they relate to imported products.

International Trade Administration

The International Trade Administration (ITA) was established by the secretary of commerce in 1980. ITA is headed by the undersecretary for international trade. Among its tasks are promoting world trade, enhancing the nation's status in international trade and investment, and formulating and administering countervailing and antidumping duty orders. ITA works with the Office of the U.S. Trade Representative and other federal agencies that play a part in the formulation of international trade policies.

UNLAWFUL IMPORTATION PRACTICES

Congress has identified a number of ways in which foreign nations or firms can give their products an undeserved competitive advantage over products made by U.S. companies. It has enacted legislation designed to head off and penalize such conduct.

Tariff Act of 1930

Often amended, the Tariff Act of 1930 is a key component of the legislation enacted by Congress to promote the nation's economic well-being through trade regulation and to guard American business from injury attributable to unacceptable import practices. The act identifies various sorts of objectionable conduct and sets up remedies to deal with them.

Unfair Conduct

The Tariff Act prohibits unfair methods of competition and unfair acts in the importation of goods into the United States or in the sale of goods imported into the United States if the effect or tendency of such behavior is to destroy or substantially injure an industry in the United States, or to prevent the establishment of a U.S. industry, or to restrain or monopolize trade or commerce in the United States.

Infringement

It is unlawful to import articles, or to sell articles after they are imported, if such articles infringe on a valid and enforceable U.S. patent, or a valid and enforceable U.S. trademark registered under the Trademark Act of 1946, or to import a semiconductor chip product that infringes on a properly registered mask work, if a U.S. industry that deals in such patented, copyrighted, trademarked, or registered mask work exists or is in the process of being established.[3] For the purpose of this ban, an industry exists if there is significant investment in plant or equipment; or significant employment of labor or capital; or substantial investment in the exploitation of a product, including engineering, research and development, or licensing.

Enforcement of Prohibitions ITC is authorized to investigate possible infractions of the Tariff Act's ban on unfair methods of competition, unfair acts, or infringement. If it finds that the act has been violated, it may order the guilty party to cease and desist from engaging in the outlawed behavior or bar the guilty party from thereafter importing the kinds of articles in question. However, it will not impose either sanction if it finds this inadvisable in light of the public health and welfare, competitive conditions in the United States, the production of like or directly competitive articles in the United States or the interests of American consumers.

Subsidization of Foreign Goods

The Tariff Act permits a **countervailing duty** to be placed on imported articles that are subsidized by a foreign nation, a citizen or national of a foreign nation, or a foreign corporation, association, or other organization. Such a duty is intended to eradicate the adverse impact on the sale of U.S. merchandise caused by foreign subsidization of imported goods. The amount of this duty is equal to the amount of the subsidy. The duty is payable in addition to any other duty that may have to be paid on the imported articles. ITC plays an important role in the assessment of countervailing duties on imported goods.

Assessment of Duty   The criteria used to determine whether a countervailing duty should be assessed on subsidized merchandise are linked to the nature of the trade relationship between the United States and the nation from which the subsidized merchandise is exported. For example, when a foreign nation comes under the General Agreement on Tariffs and Trade (GATT) or when a foreign nation has assumed obligations to the United States that are substantially equivalent to those of a nation that does come under GATT, a countervailing duty can be imposed on merchandise imported from that nation when (1) that nation or a person who is a citizen or national of that nation, or a corporation, association, or other organization organized in that nation, (2) directly or indirectly provides a subsidy with respect to the manufacture, production, or exportation of the class or kind of merchandise that is imported or sold or is likely to be sold for importation into the United States and (3) ITC finds that an industry in the United States is materially injured or is threatened with material injury or that the establishment of an industry in the United States is materially retarded by reason of imports of that merchandise or by reason of sales or the likelihood of sales of that merchandise for importation.

   When merchandise is a product of a nation that is not under GATT or that has not assumed obligations to the United States substantially equivalent to those of a nation that does come under GATT, and such a nation or a person, partnership, association, cartel, or corporation pays or bestows directly or indirectly any bounty or grant on the manufacture or production or export of any merchandise manufactured or produced in that nation, a countervailing duty equal to the bounty or grant is to be levied on such merchandise when it is imported into the United States.

Dumping of Foreign Goods

Imported merchandise is "dumped" when it is being sold, or is likely to be sold, in the United States at less than its fair value. For dumping purposes a lease arrangement is treated as if it were a sale when it has the same effect as a sale. The Tariff Act provides for the assessment of an **antidumping duty** on dumped goods. Here too ITC plays a role in the assessment process.

Assessment of Duty   When merchandise is dumped or is likely to be dumped and ITC determines that an industry in the United States is materially injured or threatened with material injury, or that the establishment of an industry in the United States is materially retarded, by reason of imports of that merchandise or by reason of sales or the likelihood of sales of that merchandise for importation, an antidumping duty may be assessed to equalize competitive conditions between exporters and U.S. industry. The duty is equal to the amount by which the foreign market value of the merchandise exceeds its U.S. price. It is payable in addition to any other duty imposed on such merchandise.

Discrimination against U.S. Commerce

The Tariff Act authorizes the president, when he finds that the public interest will be served if this is done, to declare (1) new or additional duties on articles that are wholly or in part a growth or a product of a foreign nation or are imported in a vessel of a foreign nation (2) that directly or indirectly (3) imposes any unreasonable charge, exaction, regulation, or limitation (4) on the shipment from, transportation through, or reexportation from that nation (5) of any article wholly or in part the growth or a product of the United States and (6) the nation does not take equal action against comparable articles of every foreign country. The president may also declare new or additional duties on articles of a nation when he finds that the nation, directly or indirectly, discriminates against commerce of the United States by law, administrative regulation, or practice with respect to any customs, tonnage, port duty, fee, charge, exaction, or prohibition, so that the commerce of the United States is placed at a disadvantage in comparison with the commerce of any other foreign country.

If the president finds not only that a nation has discriminated against U.S. commerce but that after the imposition of new or additional duties by the United States it has maintained or increased the level of its discrimination against U.S. commerce, he may, if he believes this to be consistent with the interests of the United States, direct that products of that nation or articles imported in its vessels be excluded from the United States.

IMPORT LIMITS

Federal quota laws limit the amount of hundreds of types of foreign products that may be imported annually into the United States. Congress has authorized the president to restrict the importation of agricultural commodities and textiles or textile products into the United States.

IPSCO, INC. v. UNITED STATES
U.S. COURT OF INTERNATIONAL TRADE
715 F. SUPP. 1104 (1989)

The plaintiffs, Ipsco, Inc. and Ipsco Steel, Inc. (IPSCO), Canadian firms, requested an International Trade Administration (ITA) ruling that the steel pipes and hollow structural sections imported by IPSCO into the United States were not within the scope of the ITA antidumping and countervailing duty orders covering oil country tubular goods (OCTG). OCTG are hollow steel products intended for use in drilling for oil or gas. IPSCO claimed that its pipes and hollow sections, which it did not label as of OCTG grade, were supposed to be used to transmit water or construct foundations, not to drill for oil or gas. ITA rejected the plaintiffs' requests and ruled that IPSCO's pipes and hollow sections did come within the scope of ITA's antidumping and countervailing duty orders since they met the physical criteria for OCTG goods. The plaintiffs brought suit to have ITA's ruling reversed.

RESTAINI, JUDGE

The first issue before the court, simply stated, is whether ITA's scope ruling was an *expansion* [italics supplied] of the original scope determination or merely a *clarification* [italics supplied] of that determination. According to plaintiffs, "the scope determination being challenged establishes such a broad set of physical criteria for the identification of OCTG that it in fact encompasses types of pipe not intended for use in drilling for oil and gas." Plaintiffs specifically challenge what they perceive as ITA's "inclusion of [non-OCTG] within the OCTG orders."

It is well established, and undisputed, that [an ITA determination] may not expand the scope of [ITA's] antidumping and countervailing duty orders. ITA, however, does have the authority to *clarify and explain* [italics supplied] the scope of such orders.

At the center of this controversy is ITA's treatment of certain pipe which has been labeled [and stenciled] by the manufacturers as a non-OCTG grade of pipe which nonetheless meets the physical criteria selected by ITA to identify OCTG. Plaintiffs argue that such pipe is not lawfully within the scope of the orders. [Plaintiffs contend that]

> [t]he steel industry distinguishes different pipe products through stencils and other immutable markings on the pipe that attest to the industry-approved performance specifications which the pipe is designed to satisfy. A manufacturer intending to produce OCTG will seek to attain the chemical composition and molecular structure of an OCTG grade of

pipe, will test the product against various OCTG performance requirements to insure that it will survive the stresses that it will encounter in OCTG applications, will certify this fact, *and will stencil or otherwise indelibly mark the end product as such*.

Reasoning that it "would be illogical for a manufacturer that wished to market pipe as OCTG to label it as [a] generally less valuable line or standard pipe grade," plaintiffs argue that such stenciling or marking should be considered as conclusive evidence of the pipe's "intended use."

Defendant disagrees and argues that because the stenciling or marking of pipe "is a voluntary practice which is not required the labeling and marking of pipe as 'standard' or 'line' pipe are meaningless within the context of these orders."

The court is not persuaded that ITA acted improperly in rejecting plaintiffs' contention that a pipe's stenciling or marking should be regarded as conclusive evidence of the pipe's intended use when such stenciling or marking is a voluntary practice in the industry and when such pipe possesses all of the physical characteristics which would enable it to be used as OCTG. Although stenciling or marking may be strong evidence of what the manufacturer considers to be the product's intended use, such labeling does not necessarily reflect an importer['s] or end-user's view of the product's intended use, nor does it prevent the pipe from actually being used as OCTG. As indicated in the record, a knowledgeable engineer may use for drilling purposes any pipe that meets the minimum requirements for OCTG. Plaintiffs do not deny an overlap in physical characteristics between OCTG and other types of non-OCTG pipe or that pipe meeting the physical specifications for OCTG may be used as OCTG regardless of the stenciling or marking placed on the pipe. ITA, therefore, acted reasonably in rejecting plaintiffs' suggested approach, which would allow manufacturers and importers to evade imposition of duties by simply labeling OCTG pipe as non-OCTG pipe sharing the same physical characteristics.

Plaintiffs have also failed to convince the court that the physical criteria selected by ITA for identifying OCTG are in any way unreasonable or that the use of these criteria when combined with the end-use certification procedure results in an unlawful expansion of the scope of the antidumping and countervailing duty orders. In reaching this conclusion, the court notes the importance of the fact that ITA afforded plaintiffs full opportunity to assist the agency in selecting the relevant physical criteria.

While the court is sympathetic to plaintiffs' legitimate concern that pipe actually used in non-OCTG applications not be included within the scope of the orders, that concern appears to be adequately addressed through ITA's end-use certification procedure. [On its face, the procedure appears to be a reasonable means of ensuring that pipe which meets the physical criteria of OCTG but which is not actually used in OCTG application is excluded from the orders.] ITA's use of this sort of procedural safeguard has previously been upheld and is a reasonable extension of ITA's authority to clarify the scope of antidumping and countervailing duty orders.

For the foregoing reasons judgment is entered in favor of defendant.

Legal Issues

1. Should ITA be permitted to clarify and explain the scope of a countervailing or antidumping duty order so as to subject goods to a duty when for a long period of time they were universally regarded as outside the scope of either order? Discuss.
2. When determining whether imported articles are subject to a countervailing or antidumping duty order, why should the U.S. Court of International Trade not accept as conclusive the foreign manufacturer's intention as to the use of those articles in the United States? Discuss.

Ethical Issues

1. Would it have been fair for ITA not to notify IPSCO that it planned to review past countervailing or antidumping duty orders to see whether they applied to a new kind of pipe manufactured by IPSCO that IPSCO stenciled "for non-OCTG use only"? Why?
2. Was the court's refusal to abide by the classification stenciled on the pipe by IPSCO consistent with pragmatic ethics? Why?

ADJUSTMENT FOR IMPORT COMPETITION

The Trade Reform Act of 1974, which has been amended a number of times, established a program intended to assist American industry and workers to adjust to injury caused by competition from imports. Under the program, the U.S. International Trade Commission and the president are the key decision makers.

ITC Action

Under the Trade Reform Act, ITC is to initiate an investigation at the request of the president or the U.S. Trade Representative, or when called upon to do so by a resolution of the House Ways and Means Committee, or the Senate Finance Committee, or after it receives a petition from an organization representative of the industry in question, such as a trade association, a firm, a certified or recognized union, or a workers' group, that asks it to investigate whether an imported product is causing competitive damage. ITC must promptly send a copy of the petition to the Office of the U.S. Trade Representative and other concerned federal agencies. When the petitioner believes that there is competitive injury, the petition may include a proposed plan that would facilitate positive adjustment to such injury.

Aside from requesting an investigation, a firm, a certified or recognized union or group of workers in the industry, a local community, a trade association representing the industry, and any other persons or groups of persons may submit a statement to ITC on the commitment they intend to make to facilitate positive adjustment if ITC finds competitive injury. No form of proposed action is immune from the antitrust laws simply because it is part of a plan to facilitate positive adjustment to import competition.

ITC must determine whether an article is being imported into the United States in such increased quantities as to be a *substantial* cause—a cause that is important and not less than any other cause—of *serious* injury, or the threat of serious injury, to an industry that produces an article like or directly competitive with the imported article.

To judge whether substantial cause is present, ITC must take into account any increase in imports, either actual or relative to domestic production, and any decline in domestic producers' share of the domestic market.

To decide whether serious injury *is* present, ITC must take into account all of the economic factors that it believes to be relevant, including such events as the significant idling of U.S. productive facilities, the inability of a significant number of domestic firms to produce the article at a reasonable level of profit, and significant unemployment or underemployment in the affected industry. As for a *threat* of serious injury, ITC must give attention to such items as a decline in sales or market share; a higher and growing inventory, whether it is maintained by domestic producers, importers, wholesalers, or retailers; increasing unemployment in the industry or a downward trend in the industry's production, profits, wages, or employment; the extent to which U.S. firms are unable to generate adequate capital to finance the modernization of their domestic plants and equipment; and the industry's ability to maintain existing levels of expenditures for research and development.

If ITC finds that an article is being imported into the United States in such increased quantities as to be a substantial cause of serious injury, or the threat thereof, to a domestic industry producing an article directly competitive with the imported article, it is to recommend to the president the sort of action that should be taken to help the endangered industry to make a positive adjustment to the objectionable import competition. For example, ITC may propose a duty increase or the imposition of a duty, placement of a tariff-rate quota on the article, modification or imposition of a quantitative restriction on the importation of the article, or other appropriate measures, such as some form of trade adjustment assistance, or any combination of these actions. In addition, it may suggest that the president initiate negotiations to deal with the undesirable increase in imports, or to take other action authorized by law to facilitate a positive adjustment to the unacceptable state of import competition.

ITC forwards its findings and recommendations to the president.

President's Response

Following an affirmative finding by ITC that an article is being imported in such increased quantities as to be a substantial cause of serious injury, the president, as allowed by law, may take appropriate and feasible actions to facilitate efforts by U.S. industry and workers to make a positive adjustment to import competition and provide greater economic and social benefits than costs, taking into account such factors as the ITC report and its recommendations; the extent to which workers and firms in domestic industry are benefiting from adjustment assistance and other work force programs and are engaged in worker retraining efforts; matters that relate to the national economic interest, such as the economic and social costs that taxpayers, communities, and workers would incur if import relief were not provided; the effect that a particular action would have on domestic markets for the affected article; the impact on U.S. industries and firms that would result from U.S. international obligations should the president take a particular action; and the risk that particular action would pose to national security.

The actions that the president may take include proclaiming an increase or imposition of a duty on the imported article, a tariff-rate quota on the article, and a modification or imposition of a quantitative restriction on the importation of the article; implementing adjustment measures; negotiating, concluding, and carrying out orderly marketing agreements with foreign countries that limit their exports of the article and set a volume for the import of the article into the United States; and establishing procedures necessary to allocate by import licenses the quantity of the article that may be brought into the United States. The president may invite Congress to enact further legislation to assist U.S. industry to adjust to import competition, initiate negotiations to address the underlying causes of the increase in the importation of the article, and otherwise act to alleviate the injury or threat of injury.

The president must advise Congress of the action that he has chosen to take as well as his reasons for taking it. If what he does differs from what he previously told Congress he would do, the president must inform Congress of what was done and why.

Positive Adjustment

There is a positive adjustment to import competition when the domestic industry is able to successfully compete with imports because of action taken by the president or when the domestic industry experiences an orderly transfer of resources to other productive pursuits and dislocated workers in the industry experience an orderly transition to other productive pursuits. An industry may be considered to have made a positive adjustment to import competition even though its size and composition are not the same as they were when ITC began its investigation.

ENGLIGHTENED IMPORT REGULATION

Congress and the president recognize that one way to expand foreign markets for U.S. goods is to keep this goal in mind when they and governmental agencies formulate rules regarding the importation of foreign goods into the United States. To promote exports, attention must be paid not only to the development of foreign outlets for U.S. goods but also to the wishes of foreign nations regarding the exportation of their goods to the United States. Alert to the fact that mutuality of benefits between and among nations can promote U.S. exports, Congress has authorized the president, whenever he finds that existing U.S. import restrictions on any foreign nation are unduly burdensome or restrictive of that nation's trade with the United States, to modify those restrictions, within statutory limits.

GENERAL AGREEMENT ON TARIFFS AND TRADE

In 1947 President Harry S. Truman, through an "executive agreement" rather than a treaty, made the United States a party to the General Agreement on Tariffs and Trade (GATT). Unlike a treaty, an executive agreement does not require the approval of the U.S. Senate. The prime objective of GATT is to reduce restrictions on trade among the nations that come under it and to promote free trade across national boundaries. Presidents, seeking to further facilitate the business done abroad by U.S. companies, continue to seek the removal of limitations on international trade among GATT members. At present, 107 nations participate in GATT.

Although Congress has specifically disclaimed that it approves or disapproves of the executive agreement that made the United States a party to GATT, it has expressly acknowledged the power of the president to link the nation to GATT. This action indicates that Congress too views GATT as a means for increasing U.S. exports.

Most Favored Nation Status

Tariff laws have traditionally imposed dissimilar customs duties on imports from different nations. Patently, a foreign nation that is allowed to export its products to a country at a duty level not greater than that enjoyed by any other nation has a far better opportunity to do business in that country than do nations whose products are subject to a higher duty.

Most favored nation
a nation whose goods are subject to import duties no greater than the lowest duties placed on imports from other nations

A nation is said to enjoy **most favored nation** (MFN) treatment when the duty that another nation places on its goods is as low as the one that it places on the imports of the nations that pay the lowest duty on their goods. GATT provides that, except as authorized by its terms, each of its parties is to accord no less favorable treatment to the commerce of any party than it accords to any other party. This means that the nations that are parties to GATT automatically enjoy MFN treatment in their dealings with the United States. The United States, like the other nations that belong to GATT, is free to grant MFN treatment to nations that are not GATT members.

In addition to its MFN mandate, GATT does not allow a party to GATT to place a higher duty on any other party than is specified in the agreement. Except as authorized by GATT, a party to GATT may not impose any restriction on the imports of other parties beyond the import duties allowed by the agreement.

Escape Clauses

GATT recognizes that despite the harmful effects of subsidies on trade and production and a nation's firms marketing products abroad below their fair market value, governments do use subsidies to promote what they regard as important national policies and firms do market products abroad below their fair market value. To accommodate the clash of national interests to the prime objective of GATT, the agreement contains what is commonly referred to as **escape clauses**. These provisions excuse GATT members from the agreement's ban on the imposition of duties on imports aside from those specified in the agreement. For example, one escape clause allows a member to impose a countervailing duty when there is sufficient evidence that another member's exports are subsidized; that there is serious injury, as defined in GATT, to the member adversely affected by the subsidy; and that there is a causal link between the subsidized imports and the alleged injury. With GATT's prime objective in view, the escape clause calls on the importing member and the exporting member to engage in consultations with a view to avoiding the imposition of retaliatory duties through the negotiation of a mutually acceptable arrangement. It is the escape clause that allows the United States to impose countervailing duties on imports from nations that are parties to GATT.

Another escape clause directs that antidumping duties be applied in the face of dumping only if the dumping causes or threatens material injury to an established industry or materially retards the establishment of an industry. It also directs that antidumping duties be resorted to only as permitted by GATT and only after an investigation has been conducted in accordance with GATT's antidumping provisions. When two GATT members become involved in a dumping controversy, they are obliged to consult with each other to see whether retaliatory action can be avoided.

Escape clauses
GATT provisions that allow a GATT member to impose a duty on imports from another GATT member under certain circumstances

FOREIGN BOYCOTTS BY U.S. PERSONS

The Export Administration Act of 1979 declares it to be the policy of the United States to oppose boycotts fostered or imposed by foreign countries against countries friendly to the United States. The president is authorized to issue regulations prohibiting any U.S. person engaged in interstate or foreign commerce from taking part in, or knowingly agreeing to further, or supporting any boycott fostered or imposed by a foreign country against a country which is friendly to the U.S. if such a boycott is not called for by U.S. law.

A U.S. person is a U.S. resident or a U.S. national, including individuals, domestic concerns, or a foreign subsidiary of a domestic concern. Regulations issued under the act prohibit such persons from refusing, knowingly agreeing to refuse, requiring any other person to refuse, or knowingly agreeing to require any other person to refuse to do business with or in a boycotted country, or with any business concern organized under the laws of a boycotted country, or with any national or resident of a boycotted country, or with any other person when such refusal is pursuant to an agreement with the boycotting country, or is a requirement of the boycotting country, or is done in response to a request from or on behalf of the boycotting country.

The secretary of commerce may impose a civil penalty of up to $10,000 for each violation of the act or a regulation issued under the act. Anyone who knowingly violates or conspires to or attempts to violate the act or a regulation may be punished by a fine of not more than five times the value of the exports involved or $50,000, whichever is greater, or be imprisoned for not more than 5 years, or both, in the discretion of the court.

EUROPEAN COMMUNITY

The European Community (technically the European Communities), commonly referred to as EC or the Common Market, is a highly structured organization composed of 12 member nations. In time, additional nations are likely to join the EC. Unlike some regional organizations of nations, the EC has its own extensive legal system, with procedural and substantive rules of law, and two courts, the Court of First Instance and the Court of Justice. EC government includes the European Commission, an executive body that also helps to initiate and amend legislation; the European Parliament, a legislative body that makes recommendations to the European Commission; and the Council of Ministers, a group composed of ministers from the 12 member nations that makes important policy decisions and works closely with the European Parliament. The Committee of Permanent Representatives, composed of ambassadors from the EC member nations, sets the agenda for the Council of Ministers and interlocks the governments of EC members and the European Commission. Representatives of labor unions and professional groups make up the Economic and Social Committee, which advises the commission and council on policies and practices.

The EC is able to significantly influence the international trade of its member nations because of its authority to bind them to treaties with nonmember nations on such matters as tariffs, trade arrangements, exports, subsidies, and dumping. The EC is a party to GATT. There are a number of trading agreements between the EC and the United States, among which are agreements on the importation of some petroleum products and manufactured tobacco products. Responding to concerns of the sorts that have triggered action by the U.S. Congress, the EC has adopted regulations to curb what are regarded as unfair trade practices and improper commercial activities in transactions between EC members and other nations.

Some features of EC law that concern the protection of competition were noted in Chapters 18 and 19. Articles 85 and 86 of the European Economic Community Treaty (1957), commonly referred to as the Treaty of Rome, are the prime source of these features. Article 85, which among other things deals with price-fixing and the division of markets, resembles Section 1 of the Sherman Act. Article 86, which is directed at firms that dominate a particular market, shows that the EC's view of monopolization is markedly different from that of the United States. Section 2 of the Sherman Act makes monopolization illegal; the Treaty of Rome does not. Instead, as we have seen, EC law on competition prohibits firms that dominate a market from engaging in what the Treaty of Rome characterizes as abusive practices. Examples of such practices were discussed in Chapter 18. EC law designed to protect competition is binding on the EC member nations.

In the antitrust area the Council of Ministers establishes competition regulations under which the European Commission is authorized to call for information, make inquiries, conduct investigations, and decide whether EC antitrust law has been violated. A commission decision is reviewable by the Court of Justice. The court, relying on Articles 85 and 86, has sustained commission regulation of acquisitions and mergers.

The Single European Act (1986) further integrates the EC's member nations by practically doing away with trade barriers commonly associated with national boundaries, such as laws that regulate the importation and marketing of foreign goods. It is anticipated that for trading purposes EC members will be parties to but one economic market by the end of 1992. This structural change is likely to lead to new EC legal rules on how international trade and business are to be conducted within the EC. If such rules are introduced, they will significantly affect how American business is conducted in the Common Market.

REVIEW QUESTIONS & PROBLEMS

1. What documents are commonly used in an international sales transaction to assure that a U.S. seller of goods receives payment when the goods are shipped and that the foreign purchaser receives the quantity and quality of goods specified in the sales contract?

2. Does the Foreign Corrupt Practices Act bar a wholly owned foreign subsidiary of a U.S. corporation from making contributions to candidates for public office in a foreign nation who favor the relaxation of that nation's long-established stringent restrictions on the importation of U.S. goods and the lifting of its ban on U.S. investments? Explain your answer.

3. Covenant, Inc. a Florida corporation, obtained a judgment in a French court against Viestmort Company, a Belgian firm. When Covenant was unable to enforce the judgment in Belgium, it sought to enforce it in Nebraska, where Viestmort owned an extremely large farming operation. Under what circumstances, if any, should the Nebraska state court that Covenant asked to enforce the judgment refuse to do so?

4. The plaintiff, a U.S. firm, brought a lawsuit in a federal district court against the defendant, an agency of a foreign nation engaged in commercial activities in the United States. The plaintiff asked the court to direct the agency to deliver to the U.S. firm equipment that the foreign nation took from it while it was doing business in that nation and then transferred to the agency. The defendant asked the court to dismiss the lawsuit on the grounds of sovereign immunity and the act of state doctrine. What judgment? Why?

5. What are the roles of the U.S. International Trade Commission and the U.S. Court of International Trade?

6. Compare the underlying purpose of countervailing duties with the objective of antidumping duties.

ENDNOTES

1. 376 U.S. 398 (1964).

2. A tariff may be (1) fiscal, intended to raise revenue, or (2) protective, intended to insulate domestic business from foreign competition. Tariff schedules set customs duties,

that is, the amount of tax to be paid on identified imported goods. A customs duty may be in the form of (1) an ad valorem tax, which is calculated by multiplying the value of the gross volume of imported goods by a designated tax rate, or (2) a specific tax, which is a set amount that must be paid for each unit of an imported product.

3. The Semiconductor Chip Protection Act of 1984 views semiconductor chips and mask works as a unique form of intellectual property. It extends copyright protection to both. Semiconductor chips are used to operate such items as microwave ovens, cash registers, personal and business computers, TV sets, refrigerators, hi-fi equipment, automobile engine controls, automatic tool machines, robots, and X-ray imagery and scanning equipment. A photographic mask is used to etch, deposit layers on, or otherwise process a semiconductor chip.

APPENDIXES

APPENDIX

A

The Constitution of
the United States

PREAMBLE

We the People of the United States, in Order to form a more perfect Union, establish Justice, insure domestic Tranquility, provide for the common defence, promote the general Welfare, and secure the Blessings of Liberty to ourselves and our Posterity, do ordain and establish this Constitution for the United States of America.

ARTICLE 1

Section 1. All legislative Powers herein granted shall be vested in a Congress of the United States, which shall consist of a Senate and House of Representatives.

Section 2. [1] The House of Representatives shall be composed of Members chosen every second Year by the People of the several States, and the Electors in each State shall have the Qualifications requisite for Electors of the most numerous Branch of the State Legislature.

[2] No Person shall be a Representative who shall not have attained to the Age of twenty five Years, and been seven Years a Citizen of the United States, and who shall not, when elected, be an Inhabitant of that State in which he shall be chosen.

[3] Representatives and direct Taxes shall be apportioned among the several States which may be included within this Union, according to their respective Numbers, which shall be determined by adding to the whole Number of free Persons, including those bound to Service for a Term of Years, and excluding Indians not taxed, three fifths of all other Persons. The actual Enumeration shall be made within three Years after the first Meeting of the Congress of the United States, and within every subsequent Term of ten Years, in such Manner as they shall by Law direct. The Number of Representatives shall not exceed one for every thirty Thousand, but each State shall have at Least one Representative; and until such enumeration shall be made, the State of New Hampshire shall be entitled to chuse three, Massachusetts eight, Rhode Island and Providence Plantations one, Connecticut five, New York six, New Jersey four, Pennsylvania eight, Delaware one, Maryland six, Virginia ten, North Carolina five, South Carolina five, and Georgia three.

[4] When vacancies happen in the Representation from any State, the Executive Authority thereof shall issue Writs of Election to fill such Vacancies.

[5] The House of Representatives shall chuse their Speaker and other Officers; and shall have the sole Power of Impeachment.

Section 3. [1] The Senate of the United States shall be composed of two Senators from each State, chosen by the Legislature thereof, for six Years; and each Senator shall have one Vote.

[2] Immediately after they shall be assembled in Consequence of the first Election, they shall be divided as equally as may be into three Classes. The Seats of the Senators of the first Class shall be vacated at the Expiration of the Second Year, of the second Class at the Expiration of the fourth Year, and of the third Class at the Expiration of the sixth Year, so that one third may be chosen every second Year; and if Vacancies happen by Resignation, or otherwise, during the Recess of the Legislature of any State, the Executive thereof may make temporary Appoint-

ments until the next Meeting of the Legislature, which shall then fill such Vacancies.

[3] No Person shall be a Senator who shall not have attained to the Age of thirty Years, and been nine Years a Citizen of the United States, and who shall not, when elected, be an Inhabitant of that State for which he shall be chosen.

[4] The Vice President of the United States shall be President of the Senate, but shall have no Vote, unless they be equally divided.

[5] The Senate shall chuse their other Officers, and also a President pro tempore, in the Absence of the Vice President, or when he shall exercise the Office of President of the United States.

[6] The Senate shall have the sole Power to try all Impeachments. When sitting for that Purpose, they shall be on Oath or Affirmation. When the President of the United States is tried, the Chief Justice shall preside: And no Person shall be convicted without the Concurrence of two thirds of the Members present.

[7] Judgment in Cases of Impeachment shall not extend further than to removal from Office, and disqualification to hold and enjoy any Office of honor, Trust, or Profit under the United States: but the Party convicted shall nevertheless be liable and subject to Indictment, Trial, Judgment and Punishment, according to Law.

Section 4. [1] The Times, Places and Manner of holding elections for Senators and Representatives, shall be prescribed in each State by the Legislature thereof; but the Congress may at any time by Law make or alter such Regulations, except as to the Places of chusing Senators.

[2] The Congress shall assemble at least once in every Year, and such Meeting shall be on the first Monday in December, unless they shall by Law appoint a different Day.

Section 5. [1] Each House shall be the Judge of the Elections, Returns, and Qualifications of its own Members, and a Majority of each shall constitute a Quorum to do Business; but a smaller Number may adjourn from day to day, and may be authorized to compel the Attendance of absent Members, in such Manner, and under such Penalties as each House may provide.

[2] Each House may determine the Rules of its Proceedings, punish its Members for disorderly Behavior, and, with the Concurrence of two thirds, expel a Member.

[3] Each House shall keep a Journal of its Proceedings, and from time to time publish the same, excepting such Parts as may in their Judgment require Secrecy; and the Yeas and Nays of the Members of either House on any question shall, at the Desire of one fifth of those Present, be entered on the Journal.

[4] Neither House, during the Session of Congress, shall, without the Consent of the other, adjourn for more than three days, nor to any other Place than that in which the two Houses shall be sitting.

Section 6. [1] The Senators and Representatives shall receive a Compensation for their Services, to be ascertained by Law, and paid out of the Treasury of the United States. They shall in all Cases, except Treason, Felony and Breach of the Peace, be privileged from Arrest during their Attendance at the Session of their respective Houses, and in going to and returning from the same; and for any Speech or Debate in either House, they shall not be questioned in any other Place.

[2] No Senator or Representative shall, during the Time for which he was elected, be appointed to any civil Office under the Authority of the United States, which shall have been created, or the Emoluments whereof shall have been

increased during such time; and no Person holding any Office under the United States, shall be a Member of either House during his Continuance in Office.

Section 7. [1] All Bills for raising Revenue shall originate in the House of Representatives; but the Senate may propose or concur with Amendments as on other Bills.

[2] Every Bill which shall have passed the House of Representatives and the Senate, shall, before it becomes a Law, be presented to the President of the United States; If he approve he shall sign it, but if not he shall return it, with his Objections to the House in which it shall have originated, who shall enter the Objections at large on their Journal, and proceed to reconsider it. If after such Reconsideration two thirds of that House shall agree to pass the Bill, it shall be sent together with the Objections, to the other House, by which it shall likewise be reconsidered, and if approved by two thirds of that House, it shall become a Law. But in all such Cases the Votes of both Houses shall be determined by yeas and Nays, and the Names of the Persons voting for and against the Bill shall be entered on the Journal of each House respectively. If any Bill shall not be returned by the President within ten Days (Sundays excepted) after it shall have been presented to him, the Same shall be a Law, in like Manner as if he had signed it, unless the Congress by their Adjournment prevent its Return, in which Case it shall not be a Law.

[3] Every Order, Resolution, or Vote, to Which the Concurrence of the Senate and House of Representatives may be necessary (except on a question of Adjournment) shall be presented to the President of the United States; and before the Same shall take Effect, shall be approved by him, or being disapproved by him, shall be repassed by two thirds of the Senate and House of Representatives, according to the Rules and Limitations prescribed in the Case of a Bill.

Section 8. [1] The Congress shall have Power To lay and collect Taxes, Duties, Imposts and Excises, to pay the Debts and provide for the common Defence and general Welfare of the United States; but all Duties, Imposts and Excises shall be uniform throughout the United States;

[2] To borrow money on the credit of the United States;

[3] To regulate Commerce with foreign Nations, and among the several States, and with the Indian Tribes;

[4] To establish an uniform Rule of Naturalization, and uniform Laws on the subject of Bankruptcies throughout the United States;

[5] To coin Money, regulate the Value thereof, and of foreign Coin, and fix the Standard of Weights and Measures;

[6] To provide for the Punishment of counterfeiting the Securities and current Coin of the United States;

[7] To Establish Post Offices and Post Roads;

[8] To promote the Progress of Science and useful Arts, by securing for limited Times to Authors and Inventors the exclusive Right to their respective Writings and Discoveries;

[9] To constitute Tribunals inferior to the supreme Court;

[10] To define and punish Piracies and Felonies committed on the high Seas, and Offenses against the Law of Nations;

[11] To declare War, grant Letters of Marque and Reprisal, and make Rules concerning Captures on Land and Water;

[12] To raise and support Armies, but no Appropriation of Money to that Use shall be for a longer Term than two Years;

[13] To provide and maintain a Navy;

[14] To make Rules for the Government and Regulation of the land and naval Forces;

[15] To provide for calling forth the Militia to execute the Laws of the Union, suppress Insurrections and repel Invasions;

[16] To provide for organizing, arming, and disciplining, the Militia, and for governing such Part of them as may be employed in the Service of the United States, reserving to the States respectively, the Appointment of the Officers, and the Authority of training the Militia according to the discipline prescribed by Congress;

[17] To exercise exclusive Legislation in all Cases whatsoever, over such District (not exceeding ten Miles square) as may, by Cession of particular States, and the Acceptance of Congress, become the Seat of the Government of the United States, and to exercise like Authority over all Places purchased by the Consent of the Legislature of the State in which the Same shall be, for the Erection of Forts, Magazines, Arsenals, dock-Yards and other needful Buildings;—And

[18] To make all Laws which shall be necessary and proper for carrying into Execution the foregoing Powers, and all other Powers vested by this Constitution in the Government of the United States, or in any Department or Officer thereof.

Section 9. [1] The Migration or Importation of Such Persons as any of the States now existing shall think proper to admit, shall not be prohibited by the Congress prior to the Year one thousand eight hundred and eight, but a Tax or duty may be imposed on such Importation, not exceeding ten dollars for each Person.

[2] The privilege of the Writ of Habeas Corpus shall not be suspended, unless when in Cases of Rebellion or Invasion the public Safety may require it.

[3] No Bill of Attainder or ex post facto Law shall be passed.

[4] No Capitation, or other direct, Tax shall be laid, unless in Proportion to the Census or Enumeration herein before directed to be taken.

[5] No Tax or Duty shall be laid on Articles exported from any State.

[6] No Preference shall be given by any Regulation of Commerce or Revenue to the Ports of one State over those of another: nor shall Vessels bound to, or from, one State be obliged to enter, clear, or pay Duties in another.

[7] No money shall be drawn from the Treasury, but in Consequence of Appropriations made by Law; and a regular Statement and Account of the Receipts and Expenditures of all public Money shall be published from time to time.

[8] No Title of Nobility shall be granted by the United States: And no Person holding any Office of Profit or Trust under them, shall, without the Consent of the Congress, accept of any present, Emolument, Office, or Title, of any kind whatever, from any King, Prince, or foreign State.

Section 10. [1] No State shall enter into any Treaty, Alliance, or Confederation; grant Letters of Marque and Reprisal; coin Money; emit Bills of Credit; make any Thing but gold and silver Coin a Tender in Payment of Debts; pass any Bill of Attainder, ex post facto Law, or Law impairing the Obligation of Contracts, or grant any Title of Nobility.

[2] No State shall, without the Consent of the Congress, lay any Imposts or

Duties on Imports or Exports, except what may be absolutely necessary for executing it's inspection Laws: and the net Produce of all Duties and Imposts, laid by any State on Imports or Exports, shall be for the Use of the Treasury of the United States; and all such Laws shall be subject to the Revision and Control of the Congress.

[3] No State shall, without the Consent of Congress, lay any Duty of Tonnage, keep Troops, or Ships of War in time of Peace, enter into any Agreement or Compact with another State, or with a foreign Power, or engage in War, unless actually invaded, or in such imminent Danger as will not admit of delay.

ARTICLE II

Section 1. [1] The executive Power shall be vested in a President of the United States of America. He shall hold his Office during the Term of four Years, and, together with the Vice President, chosen for the same Term, be elected, as follows:

[2] Each State shall appoint, in such Manner as the Legislature thereof may direct, a Number of Electors, equal to the whole Number of Senators and Representatives to which the State may be entitled in the Congress; but no Senator or Representative, or Person holding an Office of Trust or Profit under the United States, shall be appointed an Elector.

[3] The Electors shall meet in their respective States, and vote by Ballot for two Persons, of whom one at least shall not be an Inhabitant of the same State with themselves. And they shall make a List of all the Persons voted for, and of the Number of Votes for each; which List they shall sign and certify, and transmit sealed to the Seat of the Government of the United States, directed to the President of the Senate. The President of the Senate shall, in the Presence of the Senate and House of Representatives, open all the Certificates, and the Votes shall then be counted. The Person having the greatest Number of Votes shall be the President, if such Number be a Majority of the whole Number of Electors appointed; and if there be more than one who have such Majority, and have an equal Number of Votes, then the House of Representatives shall immediately chuse by Ballot one of them for President; and if no Person have a Majority, then from the five highest on the List the said House shall in like Manner chuse the President. But in chusing the President, the Votes shall be taken by States, the Representation from each State having one Vote; A quorum for this Purpose shall consist of a Member of Members from two thirds of the States, and a Majority of all the States shall be necessary to a Choice. In every Case, after the Choice of the President, the Person having the greater Number of Votes of the Electors shall be the Vice President. But if there shall remain two or more who have equal Votes, the Senate shall chuse from them by Ballot the Vice President.

[4] The Congress may determine the Time of chusing the Electors, and the Day on which they shall give their Votes; which Day shall be the same throughout the United States.

[5] No person except a natural born Citizen, or a Citizen of the United States, at the time of the Adoption of this Constitution, shall be eligible to the Office of President; neither shall any Person be eligible to that Office who shall not have attained to the Age of thirty five Years, and been fourteen Years a Resident within the United States.

[6] In Case of the Removal of the President from Office, or of his Death, Resignation or Inability to discharge the Powers and Duties of the said Office, the Same shall devolve on the Vice President, and the Congress may by Law provide for the Case of Removal, Death, Resignation or Inability, both of the President and Vice President, declaring what Officer shall then act as President, and such Officer shall act accordingly, until the Disability be removed, or a President shall be elected.

[7] The President shall, at stated Times, receive for his Services, a Compensation, which shall neither be increased nor diminished during the Period for which he shall have been elected, and he shall not receive within that Period any other Emolument from the United States, or any of them.

[8] Before he enter on the Execution of his Office, he shall take the following Oath or Affirmation: "I do solemnly swear (or affirm) that I will faithfully execute the Office of President of the United States, and will to the best of my Ability, preserve, protect and defend the Constitution of the United States."

Section 2. [1] The President shall be Commander in Chief of the Army and Navy of the United States, and of the militia of the several States, when called into the actual Service of the United States; he may require the Opinion, in writing, of the principal Officer in each of the Executive Departments, upon any Subject relating to the Duties of their respective Offices, and he shall have Power to grant Reprieves and Pardons for Offenses against the United States, except in Cases of Impeachment.

[2] He shall have Power, by and with the Advice and Consent of the Senate to make Treaties, provided two thirds of the Senators present concur; and he shall nominate, and by and with the Advice and Consent of the Senate, shall appoint Ambassadors, other public Ministers and Consuls, Judges of the supreme Court, and all other Officers of the United States, whose Appointments are not herein otherwise provided for, and which shall be established by Law; but the Congress may by Law vest the Appointment of such inferior Officers, as they think proper, in the President alone, in the Courts of Law, or in the Heads of Departments.

[3] The President shall have Power to fill up all Vacancies that may happen during the Recess of the Senate, by granting Commissions which shall expire at the End of their next Session.

Section 3. He shall from time to time give to the Congress Information of the State of the Union, and recommend to their Consideration such Measures as he shall judge necessary and expedient; he may, on extraordinary Occasions, convene both Houses, or either of them, and in Case of Disagreement between them, with Respect to the Time of Adjournment, he may adjourn them to such Time as he shall think proper; he shall receive Ambassadors and other public Ministers; he shall take Care that the Laws be faithfully executed, and shall Commission all the Officers of the United States.

Section 4. The President, Vice President and all civil Officers of the United States, shall be removed from Office on Impeachment for, and Conviction of, Treason, Bribery, or other high Crimes and Misdemeanors.

ARTICLE III

Section 1: The judicial Power of the United States, shall be vested in one supreme Court, and in such inferior Courts as the Congress may from time to time ordain and establish. The Judges, both of the supreme and inferior Courts, shall hold their Offices during good Behaviour, and shall, at stated Times, receive for their Services a Compensation, which shall not be diminished during their Continuance in Office.

Section 2. [1] The judicial Power shall extend to all Cases, in Law and Equity, arising under this Constitution, the Laws of the United States, and Treaties made, or which shall be made, under their Authority;—to all Cases affecting Ambassadors, other public Ministers and Consuls;—to all Cases of admiralty and maritime Jurisdiction;—to Controversies to which the United States shall be a Party;—to Controversies between two or more States;—between a State and Citizens of another State;—between Citizens of different States;—between Citizens of the same State claiming Lands under the Grants of different States, and between a State, or the Citizens thereof, and foreign States, Citizens or Subjects.

[2] In all Cases affecting Ambassadors, other public Ministers and Consuls, and those in which a State shall be a Party, the supreme Court shall have original Jurisdiction. In all the other Cases before mentioned, the supreme Court shall have appellate Jurisdiction, both as to Law and Fact, with such Exceptions, and under such Regulations as the Congress shall make.

[3] The trial of all Crimes, except in Cases of Impeachment, shall be by Jury; and such Trial shall be held in the State where the said Crimes shall have been committed; but when not committed within any State, the Trial shall be at such Place or Places as the Congress may by Law have directed.

Section 3. [1] Treason against the United States, shall consist only in levying War against them, or, in adhering to their Enemies, giving them Aid and Comfort. No Person shall be convicted of Treason unless on the Testimony of two Witnesses to the same overt Act, or on Confession in open Court.

[2] The Congress shall have Power to declare the Punishment of Treason, but no Attainder of Treason shall work Corruption of Blood, or Forfeiture except during the Life of the Person attainted.

ARTICLE IV

Section 1. Full Faith and Credit shall be given in each State to the public Acts, Records, and judicial Proceedings of every other State. And the Congress may by general Laws prescribe the Manner in which such Acts, Records and Proceedings shall be proved, and the Effect thereof.

Section 2. [1] The Citizens of each State shall be entitled to all Privileges and Immunities of Citizens in the several States.

[2] A Person charged in any State with Treason, Felony, or other Crime, who shall flee from Justice, and be found in another State, shall on demand of the executive Authority of the State from which he fled, be delivered up, to be removed to the State having Jurisdiction of the Crime.

[3] No Person held to Service or Labour in one State, under the Laws thereof, escaping into another, shall, in Consequence of any Law or Regulation therein, be discharged from such Service or Labour, but shall be delivered up on Claim of the Party to whom such Service or Labour may be due.

Section 3. [1] New States may be admitted by the Congress into this Union; but no new State shall be formed or erected within the Jurisdiction of any other State; nor any State be formed by the Junction of two or more States, or Parts of States, without the Consent of the Legislatures of the States concerned as well as of the Congress.

[2] The Congress shall have Power to dispose of and make all needful Rules and Regulations respecting the Territory or other Property belonging to the United States; and nothing in this Constitution shall be so construed as to Prejudice any Claims of the United States, or of any particular State.

Section 4. The United States shall guarantee to every State in this Union a Republican Form of Government, and shall protect each of them against Invasion; and on Application of the Legislature, or of the Executive (when the Legislature cannot be convened) against domestic Violence.

ARTICLE V

The Congress, whenever two thirds of both Houses shall deem it necessary, shall propose Amendments to this Constitution, or, on the Application of the Legislatures of two thirds of the several States, shall call a Convention for proposing Amendments, which, in either case, shall be valid to all Intents and Purposes, as part of this Constitution, when ratified by the Legislatures of three fourths of the several States, or by Conventions in three fourths thereof, as the one or the other Mode of Ratification may be proposed by the Congress; Provided that no Amendment which may be made prior to the Year One thousand eight hundred and eight shall in any Manner affect the first and fourth Clauses in the Ninth Section of the first Article; and that no State, without its Consent, shall be deprived of its equal Suffrage in the Senate.

ARTICLE VI

[1] All Debts contracted and Engagements entered into, before the Adoption of this Constitution shall be as valid against the United States under this Constitution, as under the Confederation.

[2] This Constitution, and the Laws of the United States which shall be made in Pursuance thereof; and all Treaties made, or which shall be made, under the Authority of the United States, shall be the supreme Law of the Land; and the Judges in every State shall be bound thereby, any Thing in the Constitution or Laws of any State to the Contrary notwithstanding.

[3] The Senators and Representatives before mentioned, and the Members of the several State Legislatures, and all executive and judicial Officers, both of the United States and of the several States, shall be bound by Oath or Affirmation, to support this Constitution; but no religious Test shall ever be required as a Qualification to any Office or public Trust under the United States.

ARTICLE VII

The Ratification of the Conventions of nine States shall be sufficient for the Establishment of this Constitution between the States so ratifying the Same.

AMENDMENTS

Articles in addition to, and in amendment of, the Constitution of the United States of America, proposed by Congress, and ratified by the Legislatures of the several States pursuant to the Fifth Article of the original Constitution.

Amendment 1 [1791]

Congress shall make no law respecting an establishment of religion, or prohibiting the free exercise thereof; or abridging the freedom of speech, or of the press; or the right of the people peaceably to assemble, and to petition the Government for a redress of grievances.

Amendment 2 [1791]

A well regulated Militia, being necessary to the security of a free State, the right of the people to keep and bear Arms, shall not be infringed.

Amendment 3 [1791]

No Soldier shall, in time of peace be quartered in any house, without the consent of the Owner, nor in time of war, but in a manner to be prescribed by law.

Amendment 4 [1791]

The right of the people to be secure in their persons, houses, papers, and effects, against unreasonable searches and seizures, shall not be violated, and no Warrants shall issue, but upon probable cause, supported by Oath or affirmation, and particularly describing the place to be searched, and the persons or things to be seized.

Amendment 5 [1791]

No person shall be held to answer for a capital, or otherwise infamous crime, unless on a presentment or indictment of a Grand Jury, except in cases arising in the land or naval forces, or in the Militia, when in actual service in time of War or public danger; nor shall any person be subject for the same offence to be twice put in jeopardy of life or limb; nor shall be compelled in any criminal case to be a witness against himself, nor be deprived of life, liberty, or property, without due process of law; nor shall private property be taken for public use, without just compensation.

Amendment 6 [1791]

In all criminal prosecutions, the accused shall enjoy the right to a speedy and public trial, by an impartial jury of the State and district wherein the crime shall have been committed, which district shall have been previously ascertained by law, and to be informed of the nature and cause of the accusation; to be confronted with the witnesses against him; to have compulsory process for obtaining witnesses in his favor, and to have the Assistance of Counsel for his defence.

Amendment 7 [1791]

In Suits at common law, where the value in controversy shall exceed twenty dollars, the right of trial by jury shall be preserved, and no fact tried by jury, shall be otherwise re-examined in any Court of the United States, than according to the rules of common law.

Amendment 8 [1791]

Excessive bail shall not be required, nor excessive fines imposed, nor cruel and unusual punishments inflicted.

Amendment 9 [1791]

The enumeration in the Constitution, of certain rights, shall not be construed to deny or disparage others retained by the people.

Amendment 10 [1791]

The powers not delegated to the United States by the Constitution, nor prohibited by it to the States, are reserved to the States respectively, or to the people.

Amendment 11 [1798]

The Judicial power of the United States shall not be construed to extend to any suit in law or equity, commenced or prosecuted against one of the United States by Citizens of another State, or by Citizens or Subjects of any Foreign State.

Amendment 12 [1804]

The Electors shall meet in their respective states and vote by ballot for President and Vice-President, one of whom, at least, shall not be an inhabitant of the same state with themselves; they shall name in their ballots the person voted for as President, and in distinct ballots the person voted for as Vice-President, and they shall make distinct lists of all persons voted for as President, and of all persons voted for as Vice-President, and of the number of votes for each, which lists they shall sign and certify, and transmit sealed to the seat of the government of the United States, directed to the President of the Senate;—The President of the Senate shall, in the presence of the Senate and House of Representatives, open all the certificates and the votes shall then be counted;—The person having the greatest number of votes for President, shall be the President, if such number be a majority of the whole number of Electors appointed; and if no person have such majority, then from the persons having the highest numbers not exceeding three on the list of those voted for as President, the House of Representatives shall choose immediately, by ballot, the President. But in choosing the President, the votes shall be taken by states, the representation from each state having one vote;

a quorum for this purpose shall consist of a member or members from two-thirds of the states, and a majority of all states shall be necessary to a choice. And if the House of Representatives shall not choose a President whenever the right of choice shall devolve upon them before the fourth day of March next following, then the Vice-President shall act as President, as in the case of the death or other constitutional disability of the President.—The person having the greatest number of votes as Vice-President, shall be the Vice-President, if such number be a majority of the whole number of Electors appointed, and if no person have a majority, then from the two highest numbers on the list, the Senate shall choose the Vice-President; a quorum for the purpose shall consist of two-thirds of the whole number of Senators, and a majority of the whole number shall be necessary to a choice. But no person constitutionally ineligible to the office of President shall be eligible to that of Vice-President of the United States.

Amendment 13 [1865]

Section 1. Neither slavery nor involuntary servitude, except as a punishment for crime whereof the party shall have been duly convicted, shall exist within the United States, or any place subject to their jurisdiction.

Section 2. Congress shall have power to enforce this article by appropriate legislation.

Amendment 14 [1868]

Section 1. All persons born or naturalized in the United States, and subject to the jurisdiction thereof, are citizens of the United States and of the State wherein they reside. No State shall make or enforce any law which shall abridge the privileges or immunities of citizens of the United States; nor shall any State deprive any person of life, liberty, or property, without due process of law; nor deny to any person within its jurisdiction the equal protection of the laws.

Section 2. Representatives shall be apportioned among the several States according to their respective numbers, counting the whole number of persons in each State, excluding Indians not taxed. But when the right to vote at any election for the choice of electors for the President and Vice President of the United States, Representatives in Congress, the Executive and Judicial officers of a State, or the members of the Legislature thereof, is denied to any of the male inhabitants of such State, being twenty-one years of age, and citizens of the United States, or in any way abridged, except for participation in rebellion, or other crime, the basis of representation therein shall be reduced in the proportion which the number of such male citizens shall bear to the whole number of male citizens twenty-one years of age in such State.

Section 3. No person shall be a Senator or Representative in Congress, or elector of President and Vice President, or hold any office, civil or military, under the United States, or under any State, who having previously taken an oath, as a member of Congress, or as an officer of the United States, or as a member of any State legislature, or as an executive or judicial officer of any State, to support the Constitution of the United States, shall have engaged in insurrection or rebellion against the same, or given aid or comfort to the enemies thereof. But Congress may by a vote of two thirds of each House, remove such disability.

Section 4. The validity of the public debt of the United States, authorized by law, including debts incurred for payment of pensions and bounties for services in suppressing insurrection of rebellion, shall not be questioned. But neither the United States nor any State shall assume or pay any debt or obligation incurred in aid of insurrection or rebellion against the United States, or any claim for the loss or emancipation of any slave; but all such debts, obligations and claims shall be held illegal and void.

Section 5. The Congress shall have power to enforce, by appropriate legislation, the provisions of this article.

Amendment 15 [1870]

Section 1. The right of citizens of the United States to vote shall not be denied or abridged by the United States or by any State on account of race, color, or previous condition of servitude.

Section 2. The Congress shall have power to enforce this article by appropriate legislation.

Amendment 16 [1913]

The Congress shall have power to lay and collect taxes on incomes, from whatever source derived, without apportionment among the several States, and without regard to any census or enumeration.

Amendment 17 [1913]

[1] The Senate of the United States shall be composed of two Senators from each State, elected by the people thereof, for six years; and each Senator shall have one vote. The electors in each State shall have the qualifications requisite for electors of the most numerous branch of the State legislatures.

[2] When vacancies happen in the representation of any State in the Senate, the executive authority of such State shall issue writs of election to fill such vacancies: *Provided*, That the legislature of any State may empower the executive thereof to make temporary appointments until the people fill the vacancies by election as the legislature may direct.

[3] This amendment shall not be so construed as to affect the election or term of any Senator chosen before it becomes valid as part of the Constitution.

Amendment 18 [1919]

Section 1. After one year from the ratification of this article the manufacture, sale, or transportation of intoxicating liquors within, the importation thereof into, or the exportation thereof from the United States and all territory subject to the jurisdiction thereof for beverage purposes is hereby prohibited.

Section 2. The Congress and the several States shall have concurrent power to enforce this article by appropriate legislation.

Section 3. This article shall be inoperative unless it shall have been ratified as an amendment to the Constitution by the legislatures of the several States, as provided in the Constitution, within seven years from the date of the submission hereof to the States by the Congress.

Amendment 19 [1920]

[1] The right of citizens of the United States to vote shall not be denied or abridged by the United States or by any State on account of sex.

[2] Congress shall have power to enforce this article by appropriate legislation.

Amendment 20 [1933]

Section 1. The terms of the President and Vice-President shall end at noon on the 20th day of January, and the terms of Senators and Representatives at noon on the third day of January, of the years in which such terms would have ended if this article had not been ratified; and the terms of their successors shall then begin.

Section 2. The Congress shall assemble at least once in every year, and such meeting shall begin at noon on the third day of January, unless they shall by law appoint a different day.

Section 3. If, at the time fixed for the beginning of the term of the President, the President elect shall have died, the Vice-President elect shall become President. If the President shall not have been chosen before the time fixed for the beginning of his term, or if the President elect shall have failed to qualify, then the Vice-President elect shall act as President until a President shall have qualified; and the Congress may by law provide for the case wherein neither a President elect nor a Vice-President elect shall have qualified, declaring who shall then act as President, or the manner in which one who is to act shall be selected, and such person shall act accordingly until a President or Vice-President shall have qualified.

Section 4. The Congress may by law provide for the case of the death of any of the persons from whom the House of Representatives may choose a President whenever the right of choice shall have devolved upon them, and for the case of the death of any of the persons from whom the Senate may choose a Vice-President whenever the right of choice shall have devolved upon them.

Section 5. Sections 1 and 2 shall take effect on the 15th day of October following the ratification of this article.

Section 6. This article shall be inoperative unless it shall have been ratified as an amendment to the Constitution by the legislatures of three fourths of the several States within seven years from the date of its submission.

Amendment 21 [1933]

Section 1. The eighteenth article of amendment to the Constitution of the United States is hereby repealed.

Section 2. The transportation or importation into any State, Territory, or possession of the United States for delivery or use therein of intoxicating liquors, in violation of the laws thereof, is hereby prohibited.

Section 3. This article shall be inoperative unless it shall have been ratified as an amendment to the Constitution by conventions in the several States, as provided in the Constitution, within seven years from the date of the submission hereof to the States by the Congress.

Amendment 22 [1951]

Section 1. No person shall be elected to the office of the President more than twice, and no person who has held the office of President, or acted as President, for more than two years of a term to which some other person was elected President shall be elected to the office of President more than once. But this Article shall not apply to any person holding the office of President when this Article was proposed by the Congress, and shall not prevent any person who may be holding the office of President, or acting as President, during the term within which this Article becomes operative from holding the office of President or acting as President during the remainder of such term.

Section 2. This article shall be inoperative unless it shall have been ratified as an amendment to the Constitution by the legislatures of three fourths of the several States within seven years from the date of its submission to the States by the Congress.

Amendment 23 [1961]

Section 1. The District constituting the seat of Government of the United States shall appoint in such manner as the Congress may direct:

A number of electors of President and Vice-President equal to the whole number of Senators and Representatives in Congress to which the District would be entitled if it were a State, but in no event more than the least populous state; they shall be in addition to those appointed by the states, but they shall be considered, for the purposes of the election of President and Vice-President, to be electors appointed by a state; and they shall meet in the District and perform such duties as provided by the twelfth article of amendment.

Section 2. The Congress shall have power to enforce this article by appropriate legislation.

Amendment 24 [1964]

Section 1. The right of citizens of the United States to vote in any primary or other election for President or Vice-President, for electors for President or Vice-President, or for Senator or Representative in Congress, shall not be denied or abridged by the United States, or any State by reason of failure to pay any poll tax or other tax.

Section 2. The Congress shall have power to enforce this article by appropriate legislation.

Amendment 25 [1967]

Section 1. In case of the removal of the President from office or of his death or resignation, the Vice-President shall become President.

Section 2. Whenever there is a vacancy in the office of the Vice-President, the President shall nominate a Vice-President who shall take office upon confirmation by a majority vote of both Houses of Congress.

Section 3. Whenever the President transmits to the President pro tempore of the Senate and the Speaker of the House of Representatives his written declaration that he is unable to discharge the powers and duties of his office, and until he transmits to them a written declaration to the contrary, such powers and duties shall be discharged by the Vice-President as Acting President.

Section 4. Whenever the Vice-President and a majority of either the principal officers of the executive departments or of such other body as Congress may by law provide, transmit to the President pro tempore of the Senate and the Speaker of the House of Representatives their written declaration that the President is unable to discharge the powers and duties of his office, the Vice-President shall immediately assume the powers and duties of the office as Acting President.

Thereafter, when the President transmits to the President pro tempore of the Senate and the Speaker of the House of Representatives his written declaration that no inability exists, he shall resume the powers and duties of his office unless the Vice-President and a majority of either the principal officers of the executive department or of such other body as Congress may by law provide, transmit within four days to the President pro tempore of the Senate and the Speaker of the House of Representatives their written declaration that the President is unable to discharge the powers and duties of his office. Thereupon Congress shall decide the issue, assembling within forty-eight hours for that purpose if not in session. If the Congress, within twenty-one days after receipt of the latter written declaration, or, if Congress is not in session, within twenty-one days after Congress is required to assemble, determines by two-thirds vote of both Houses that the President is unable to discharge the powers and duties of his office, the Vice-President shall continue to discharge the same as Acting President; otherwise, the President shall resume the powers and duties of his office.

Amendment 26 [1971]

Section 1. The right of citizens of the United States, who are eighteen years of age or older, to vote shall not be denied or abridged by the United States or by any State on account of age.

Section 2. The Congress shall have power to enforce this article by appropriate legislation.

APPENDIX

B

Administrative Procedure (Excerpts)

[The Administrative Procedure Act, passed by Congress in 1946, established basic procedures for federal agencies. Although the act itself was repealed in 1966, its provisions were incorporated into Title 5 of the U.S. Code, "Government Organization and Employees." The retained provisions of the 1946 Act, as amended, are found under the subhead "Administrative Procedure."]

Section 551. Definitions

For the purpose of this subchapter—

(1) "agency" means each authority of the Government of the United States, whether or not it is within or subject to review by another agency, but does not include—

(A) the Congress;

(B) the courts of the United States;

(C) the governments of the territories or possessions of the United States;

(D) the government of the District of Columbia; . . .

(E) agencies composed of representatives of the parties or of representatives of organizations of the parties to the disputes determined by them;

(F) courts martial and military commissions;

(G) military authority exercised in the field in time of war or in occupied territory; . . .

. . .

(2) "person" includes an individual, partnership, corporation, association, or public or private organization other than an agency;

(3) "party" includes a person or agency named or admitted as a party, or properly seeking and entitled as of right to be admitted as a party, in an agency proceeding, and a person or agency admitted by an agency as a party for limited purposes;

(4) "rule" means the whole or a part of an agency statement of general or particular applicability and future effect designed to implement, interpret, or prescribe law or policy or describing the organization, procedure, or practice requirements of an agency and includes the approval or prescription for the future of rates, wages, corporate or financial structures or reorganizations thereof, prices, facilities, appliances, services or allowances therefor or of valuations, costs, or accounting, or practices bearing on any of the foregoing;

(5) "rule making" means agency process for formulating, amending, or repealing a rule;

(6) "order" means the whole or a part of a final disposition, whether affirmative, negative, injunctive, or declaratory in form, of an agency in a matter other than rule making but including licensing;

(7) "adjudication" means agency process for the formulation of an order;

(8) "license" includes the whole or part of an agency permit, certificate, approval, registration, charter, membership, statutory exemption or other form of permission;

(9) "licensing" includes agency process respecting the grant, renewal, denial, revocation, suspension, annulment, withdrawal, limitation, amendment, modification, or conditioning of a license;

(12) "agency proceeding" means an agency process as defined by paragraphs (5), (7), and (9) of this section;

(13) "agency action" includes the whole or a part of an agency rule, order, license, sanction, relief, or the equivalent or denial thereof, or failure to act; and

(14) "ex parte communication" means an oral or written communication not on the public record with respect to which reasonable prior notice to all parties is not given, but it shall not include requests for status reports on any matter or proceeding . . .

Section 553. Rule Making

(a) This section applies, according to the provisions thereof, except to the extent that there is involved—

(1) a military or foreign affairs function of the United States; or

(2) a matter relating to agency management or personnel or to public property, loans, grants, benefits, or contracts.

(b) General notice of proposed rule making shall be published in the Federal Register, unless persons subject thereto are named and either personally served or otherwise have actual notice thereof in accordance with law. The notice shall include—

(1) a statement of the time, place, and nature of public rule making proceedings;

(2) reference to the legal authority under which the rule is proposed; and

(3) either the terms or substance of the proposed rule or a description of the subjects and issues involved.

Except when notice or hearing is required by statute, this subsection does not apply—

(A) to interpretative rules, general statements of policy, or rules of agency organization, procedure, or practice; or

(B) when the agency for good cause finds (and incorporates the finding and a brief statement of reasons therefor in the rules issued) that notice and public procedure thereon are impracticable, unnecessary, or contrary to the public interest.

(c) After notice required by this section, the agency shall give interested persons an opportunity to participate in the rule making through submission of written data, views, or arguments with or without opportunity for oral presentation. After consideration of the relevant matter presented, the agency shall incorporate in the rules adopted a concise general statement of their basis and purpose. When rules are required by statute to be made on the record after opportunity for an agency hearing, sections 556 and 557 of this title apply instead of this subsection.

(d) The required publication or service of a substantive rule shall be made not less than 30 days before its effective date, except—

(1) a substantive rule which grants or recognizes an exemption or relieves a restriction;

(2) interpretative rules and statements of policy; or

(3) as otherwise provided by the agency for good cause found and published with the rule.

(e) Each agency shall give an interested person the right to petition for the issuance, amendment, or repeal of a rule.

Section 554. Adjudications

(a) This section applies, according to the provisions thereof, in every case of adjudication required by statute to be determined on the record after opportunity for an agency hearing, except to the extent that there is involved—

(1) a matter subject to a subsequent trial of the law and the facts de novo in a court;

(2) the selection or tenure of an employee, except an administrative law judge appointed under section 3105 of this title;

(3) proceedings in which decisions rest solely on inspections, tests, or elections;

(4) the conduct of military or foreign affairs functions;

(5) cases in which an agency is acting as an agent for a court; or

(6) the certification of worker representatives.

(b) Persons entitled to notice of an agency hearing shall be timely informed of—

(1) the time, place, and nature of the hearing;

(2) the legal authority and jurisdiction under which the hearing is to be held; and

(3) the matters of fact and law asserted.

When private persons are the moving parties, other parties to the proceeding shall give prompt notice of issues controverted in fact or law; and in other instances agencies may by rule require responsive pleading. In fixing the time and place for hearings, due regard shall be had for the convenience and necessity of the parties or their representatives.

(c) The agency shall give all interested parties opportunity for—

(1) the submission and consideration of facts, arguments, offers of settlement, or proposals of adjustment when time, the nature of the proceeding, and the public interest permit; and

(2) to the extent that the parties are unable so to determine a controversy by consent, hearing and decision on notice and in accordance with sections 556 and 557 of this title.

(d) The employee who presides at the reception of evidence pursuant to section 556 of this title shall make the recommended decision or initial decision required by section 557 of this title, unless he becomes unavailable to the agency. Except to the extent required for the disposition of ex parte matters as authorized by law, such an employee may not—

(1) consult a person or party on a fact in issue, unless on notice and opportunity for all parties to participate; or

(2) be responsible to or subject to the supervision or direction of an employee or agent engaged in the performance of investigative or prosecuting functions for an agency.

An employee or agent engaged in the performance of investigative or prosecuting functions for an agency in a case may not, in that or a factually related case, participate or advise in the decision, recommended decision, or agency review pursuant to section 557 of this title, except as witness or counsel in public proceedings. This subsection does not apply—

(A) in determining applications for initial licenses;

(B) to proceedings involving the validity or application of rates, facilities, or practices of public utilities or carriers; or

(C) to the agency or a member or members of the body comprising the agency.

(e) The agency, with like effect as in the case of other orders, and in its sound discretion, may issue a declaratory order to terminate a controversy or remove uncertainty.

Section 555. Ancillary Matters

. . .

(b) A person compelled to appear in person before an agency or representative thereof is entitled to be accompanied, represented, and advised by counsel or, if permitted by the agency, by other qualified representative. A party is entitled to appear in person or by or with counsel or other duly qualified representative in an agency proceeding. So far as the orderly conduct of public business permits, an interested person may appear before an agency or its responsible employees for the presentation, adjustment, or determination of an issue, request, or controversy in a proceeding, whether interlocutory, summary, or otherwise, or in connection with an agency function. With due regard for the convenience and necessity of the parties or their representatives and within a reasonable time, each agency shall proceed to conclude a matter presented to it. This subsection does not grant or deny a person who is not a lawyer the right to appear for or represent others before an agency or in an agency proceeding.

. . .

(d) Agency subpoenas authorized by law shall be issued to a party on request and, when required by rules of procedure, on a statement or showing of general relevance and reasonable scope of the evidence sought. On contest, the court shall sustain the subpoena or similar process or demand to the extent that it is found to be in accordance with law. In a proceeding for enforcement, the court shall issue an order requiring the appearance of the witness or the production of the evidence or data within a reasonable time under penalty of punishment for contempt in case of contumacious failure to comply.

. . .

Section 556. Hearings; Presiding Employees; Powers and Duties; Burden of Proof; Evidence; Record as Basis of Decision

(a) This section applies, according to the provisions thereof, to hearings required by section 553 or 554 of this title to be conducted in accordance with this section.

(b) There shall preside at the taking of evidence—

(1) the agency;

(2) one or more members of the body which comprises the agency; or

(3) one or more administrative law judges appointed under section 3105 of this title.

This subchapter does not supersede the conduct of specified classes of proceedings, in whole or in part, by or before boards or other employees specially provided for by or designated under statute. The functions of presiding employees and of employees participating in decisions in accordance with section 557 of this title shall be conducted in an impartial manner. A presiding or participating employee may at any time disqualify himself. On the filing in good faith of a timely and sufficient affidavit of personal bias or other disqualification of a presiding or participating employee, the agency shall determine the matter as a part of the record and decision in the case.

(c) Subject to published rules of the agency and within its powers, employees presiding at hearings may—

(1) administer oaths and affirmations;

(2) issue subpoenas authorized by law;

(3) rule on offers of proof and receive relevant evidence;

(4) take depositions or have depositions taken when the ends of justice would be served;

(5) regulate the course of the hearing;

(6) hold conferences for the settlement or simplification of the issues by consent of the parties;

(7) dispose of procedural requests or similar matters;

(8) make or recommend decisions in accordance with section 557 of this title; and

(9) take other action authorized by agency rule consistent with this subchapter.

(d) Except as otherwise provided by statute, the proponent of a rule or order has the burden of proof. Any oral or documentary evidence may be received, but the agency as a matter of policy shall provide for the exclusion of irrelevant, immaterial, or unduly repetitious evidence. A sanction may not be imposed or rule or order issued except on consideration of the whole record or those parts thereof cited by a party and supported by and in accordance with the reliable, probative, and substantial evidence. The agency may, to the extent consistent with the interests of justice and the policy of the underlying statutes administered by the agency, consider a violation of section 557(d) of this title sufficient grounds for a decision adverse to a party who has knowingly committed such violation or knowingly caused such violation to occur. A party is entitled to present his case or defense by oral or documentary evidence, to submit rebuttal evidence, and to conduct such cross-examination as may be required for a full and true disclosure of the facts. In rule making or determining claims for money or benefits or applications for initial licenses an agency may, when a party will not be prejudiced thereby, adopt procedures for the submission of all or part of the evidence in written form.

(e) The transcript of testimony and exhibits, together with all papers and requests filed in the proceeding, constitutes the exclusive record for decision in accordance with section 557 of this title and, on payment of lawfully prescribed costs, shall be made available to the parties. When an agency decision rests on official notice of a material fact not appearing in the evidence in the record, a party is entitled, on timely request, to an opportunity to show the contrary.

Section 557. Initial Decisions; Conclusiveness; Review by Agency; Submissions by Parties; Contents of Decisions; Record

(a) This section applies, according to the provisions thereof, when a hearing is required to be conducted in accordance with section 556 of this title.

(b) When the agency did not preside at the reception of the evidence, the presiding employee or . . . an employee qualified to preside at hearings pursuant to section 556 of this title, shall initially decide the case unless the agency requires, either in specific cases or by general rule, the entire record to be certified to it for decision. When the presiding employee makes an initial decision, that decision then becomes the decision of the agency without further proceedings unless there is an appeal to, or review on motion of, the agency within time provided by rule. On appeal from or review of the initial decision, the agency has all the powers which it would have in making the initial decision except as it may limit the issues on notice or by rule.

. . .

(c) Before a recommended, initial, or tentative decision, or a decision on agency review of the decision of subordinate employees, the parties are entitled to a reasonable opportunity to submit for the consideration of the employees participating in the decisions—

(1) proposed findings and conclusions; or

(2) exceptions to the decisions or recommended decisions of subordinate employees or to tentative agency decisions; and

(3) supporting reasons for the exceptions or proposed findings or conclusions. The record shall show the ruling on each finding, conclusion, or exception presented. All decisions, including initial, recommended, and tentative decisions, are a part of the record and shall include a statement of—

(A) findings and conclusions, and the reasons or basis therefor, on all the material issues of fact, law, or discretion presented on the record; and

(B) the appropriate rule, order, sanction, relief, or denial thereof.

(d)(1) In any agency proceeding which is subject to subsection (a) of this section, except to the extent required for the disposition of ex parte matters as authorized by law—

(A) no interested person outside the agency shall make or knowingly cause to be made to any member of the body comprising the agency, administrative law judge, or other employee who is or may reasonably be expected to be involved in the decisional process of the proceeding, an ex parte communication relevant to the merits of the proceeding;

(B) no member of the body comprising the agency, administrative law judge, or other employee who is or may reasonably be expected to be involved in the decisional process of the proceeding, shall make or knowingly cause to be made to any interested person outside the agency an ex parte communication relevant to the merits of the proceeding;

(C) a member of the body comprising the agency, administrative law judge, or other employee who is or may reasonably be expected to be involved in the decisional process of such proceeding who receives, or who makes or knowingly causes to be made, a communication prohibited by this subsection shall place on the public record of the proceeding:

(i) all such written communications;

(ii) memoranda stating the substance of all such oral communications; and

(iii) all written responses, and memoranda stating the substance of all oral responses to the materials described in clauses (i) and (ii) of this subparagraph;

(D) upon receipt of a communication knowingly made or knowingly caused to be made by a party in violation of this subsection, the agency, administrative law judge, or other employee presiding at the hearing may, to the extent consistent with the interests of justice and the policy of the underlying statutes, require the party to show cause why his claim or interest in the proceeding should not be dismissed, denied, disregarded, or otherwise adversely affected on account of such violation; and

(E) the prohibitions of this subsection shall apply beginning at such time as the agency may designate, but in no case shall they begin to apply later than the time at which a proceeding is noticed for hearing unless the person responsible for the communication has knowledge that it will be noticed, in which case the prohibitions shall apply beginning at the time of his acquisition of such knowledge.

(2) This subsection does not constitute authority to withhold information from Congress.

JUDICIAL REVIEW

Section 701. Application; Definitions

(a) This chapter applies, according to the provisions thereof, except to the extent that—

(1) statutes preclude judicial review; or

(2) agency action is committed to agency discretion by law.

(3) For the purpose of this chapter—

(1) "agency" means each authority of the Government of the United States, whether or not it is within or subject to review by another agency, but does not include—

(A) the Congress;

(B) the courts of the United States;

(C) the governments of the territories or possessions of the United States;

(D) the government of the District of Columbia;

(E) agencies composed of representatives of the parties or of representatives of organizations of the parties to the disputes determined by them;

(F) courts martial and military commissions;

(G) military authority exercised in the field in time of war or in occupied territory; . . .

. . .

Section 702. Right of Review

A person suffering legal wrong because of agency action, or adversely affected or aggrieved by agency action within the meaning of a relevant statute, is entitled to judicial review thereof. An action in a court of the United States seeking relief other than money damages and stating a claim that an agency or an officer or employee thereof acted or failed to act in an official capacity or under color of legal authority shall not be dismissed nor relief therein be denied on the ground that it is against the United States or that the United States is an indispensable party. The United States may be named as a defendant in any such action, and a judgment or decree may be entered against the United States: *Provided,* That any mandatory or injunctive decree shall specify the Federal officer or officers (by name or by title), and their successors in office, personally responsible for compliance. Nothing herein (1) affects other limitations on judicial review or the power or duty of the court to dismiss any action or deny relief on any other appropriate legal or equitable ground; or (2) confers authority to grant relief if any other statute that grants consent to suit expressly or impliedly forbids the relief which is sought.

Section 704. Actions Reviewable

Agency action made reviewable by statute and final agency action for which there is no other adequate remedy in a court are subject to judicial review. A preliminary, procedural, or intermediate agency action or ruling not directly reviewable is subject to review on the review of the final agency action. Except as otherwise expressly required by statute, agency action otherwise final is final for the purposes of this section whether or not there has been presented or determined an application for a declaratory order, for any form of reconsiderations, or, unless the agency otherwise requires by rule and provides that the action meanwhile is inoperative, for an appeal to superior agency authority.

Section 706. Scope of Review

To the extent necessary to decision and when presented, the reviewing court shall decide all relevant questions of law, interpret constitutional and statutory provisions, and determine the meaning or applicability of the terms of an agency action. The reviewing court shall—

(1) compel agency action unlawfully withheld or unreasonably delayed; and

(2) hold unlawful and set aside agency actions, findings, and conclusions found to be—

(A) arbitrary, capricious, an abuse of discretion, or otherwise not in accordance with law;

(B) contrary to constitutional right, power, privilege, or immunity;

(C) in excess of statutory jurisdiction, authority, or limitations, or short of statutory right;

(D) without observance of procedure required by law;

(E) unsupported by substantial evidence in a case subject to sections 556 and 557 of this title or otherwise reviewed on the record of an agency hearing provided by statute; or

(F) unwarranted by the facts to the extent that the facts are subject to trial de novo by the reviewing court.

In making the foregoing determinations, the court shall review the whole record or those parts of it cited by a party, and due account shall be taken of the rule of prejudicial error.

Section 1305. Administrative Law Judges

For the purpose of section 3105, 3344, . . . and 5372 of this title and the provisions of section 5335(a)(B) of this title that relate to administrative law judges, the Office of Personnel Management may, and for the purpose of section 7521 of this title, the Merit Systems Protection Board may investigate, require reports by agencies, issue reports, including an annual report to Congress, prescribe regulations, appoint advisory committees as necessary, recommend legislation, subpoena witnesses and records, and pay witness fees as established for the courts of the United States.

Section 3105. Appointment of Administrative Law Judges

Each agency shall appoint as many administrative law judges as are necessary for proceedings required to be conducted in accordance with sections 556 and 557 of this title. Administrative law judges shall be assigned to cases in rotation so far as practicable, and may not perform duties inconsistent with their duties and responsibilities as administrative law judges.

Section 3344. Details; Administrative Law Judges

An agency as defined by section 551 of this title which occasionally or temporarily is insufficiently staffed with administrative law judges appointed under section 3105 of this title may use administrative law judges selected by the Office of Personnel Management from and with the consent of other agencies.

❀

Section 5372. Administrative Law Judges

Administrative law judges appointed under section 3105 of this title are entitled to pay prescribed by the Office of Personnel Management independently of agency recommendations or ratings and in accordance with . . . this title.

Section 7521. Actions against Administrative Law Judges

(a) An action may be taken against an administrative law judge appointed under section 3105 of this title by the agency in which the administrative law judge is employed only for good cause established and determined by the Merit Systems Protection Board on the record after opportunity for hearing before the Board.

(b) The actions covered by this section are—

(1) a removal;

(2) a suspension;

(3) a reduction in grade;

(4) a reduction in pay; and

(5) a furlough of 30 days or less;

but do not include—

(A) a suspension or removal . . . or

(B) a reduction-in-force action . . .

APPENDIX

C

Sherman Act
(Excerpts)

Section 1

Every contract, combination in the form of trust or otherwise, or conspiracy, in restraint of trade or commerce among the several States, or with foreign nations, is hereby declared to be illegal. Every person who shall make any contract or engage in any combination or conspiracy hereby declared to be illegal shall be deemed guilty of a felony and, on conviction thereof, shall be punished by fine not exceeding $10,000,000 if a corporation, or, if any other person, $350,000, or by imprisonment not exceeding three years, or by both said punishments, in the discretion of the court.

Section 2

Every person who shall monopolize, or attempt to monopolize, or combine or conspire with any other person or persons, to monopolize any part of the trade or commerce among the several States, or with foreign nations, shall be deemed guilty of a felony, and, on conviction thereof, shall be punished by fine not exceeding $10,000,000 if a corporation, or, if any other person, $350,000, or by imprisonment not exceeding three years, or by both said punishments, in the discretion of the court.

Section 4

The several circuit courts of the United States are hereby invested with jurisdiction to prevent and restrain violations of this act; and it shall be the duty of the several district attorneys of the United States, in their respective districts, under the direction of the Attorney-General, to institute proceedings in equity to prevent and restrain such violations. Such proceedings may be by way of petition setting forth the case and praying that such violation shall be enjoined or otherwise prohibited. When the parties complained of shall have been duly notified of such petition the court shall proceed, as soon as may be, to the hearing and determination of the case; and pending such petition and before final decree, the court may at any time make such temporary restraining order or prohibition as shall be deemed just in the premises.

Section 5

Whenever it shall appear to the court before which any proceeding under section four of this act may be pending, that the ends of justice require that other parties should be brought before the court, the court may cause them to be summoned, whether they reside in the district in which the court is held or not; and subpoenas to that end may be served in any district by the marshal thereof.

Section 6

Any property owned under any contract or by any combination, or pursuant to any conspiracy (and being the subject thereof) mentioned in section one of this act, and being in the course of transportation from one State to another, or to a foreign country, shall be forfeited to the United States, and may be seized and condemned by like proceedings as those provided by law for the forfeiture, seizure, and condemnation of property imported into the United States contrary to law.

Section 7

This Act shall not apply to conduct involving trade or commerce (other than import trade or import commerce) with foreign nations unless—

(1) such conduct has a direct, substantial, and reasonably foreseeable effect—

(A) on trade or commerce which is not trade or commerce with foreign nations, or on import trade or import commerce with foreign nations; or

(B) on export trade or export commerce with foreign nations, of a person engaged in such trade or commerce in the United States; and

(2) such effect gives rise to a claim under the provisions of this Act, other than this section. If this Act applies to such conduct only because of the operation of paragraph (1)(B), then this Act shall apply to such conduct only for injury to export business in the United States.

Section 8

That the word "person," or "persons," wherever used in this Act shall be deemed to include corporations and associations existing under or authorized by the laws of either the United States, the laws of any of the Territories, the laws of any State, or the laws of any foreign country.

APPENDIX

D

Clayton Act
(Excerpts)

Section 1

(a) "Antitrust laws," as used herein, includes the [Sherman Act]. . . .

"Commerce," as used herein, means trade or commerce among the several States and with foreign nations, or between the District of Columbia or any Territory of the United States and any State, Territory, or foreign nation, or between any insular possessions or other places under the jurisdiction of the United States, or between any such possession or place and any State or Territory of the United States or the District of Columbia or any foreign nation, or within the District of Columbia or any Territory or any insular possession or other place under the jurisdiction of the United States . . .

The word "person" or "persons" wherever used in this Act shall be deemed to include corporations and associations existing under or authorized by the laws of either the United States, the laws of any of the Territories, the laws of any State, or the laws of any foreign country.

Section 2

[See Robinson-Patman Act.]

Section 3

That it shall be unlawful for any person engaged in commerce, in the course of such commerce, to lease or make a sale or contract for sale of goods, wares, merchandise, machinery, supplies or other commodities, whether patented or unpatented, for use, consumption or resale within the United States or any Territory thereof or the District of Columbia or any insular possession or other place under the jurisdiction of the United States, or fix a price charged therefor, or discount from, or rebate upon, such price, on the condition, agreement or understanding that the lessee or purchaser thereof shall not use or deal in the goods, wares, merchandise, machinery, supplies or other commodities of a competitor or competitors of the lessor or seller, where the effect of such lease, sale, or contract for sale or such condition, agreement or understanding may be to substantially lessen competition or tend to create a monopoly in any line of commerce.

Section 4

(a) Except as provided in subsection (b), any person who shall be injured in his business or property by reason of anything forbidden in the antitrust laws may sue therefor in any district court of the United States in the district in which the defendant resides or is found or has an agent, without respect to the amount in controversy, and shall recover threefold the damages by him sustained, and the cost of suit, including a reasonable attorney's fee. The court may award under this section, pursuant to a motion by such person promptly made, simple interest on actual damages for the period beginning on the date of service of such person's pleading setting forth a claim under the antitrust laws and ending on the date of judgment, or for any shorter period therein, if the court finds that the award of such interest for such period is just in the circumstances. In determining whether an award of interest under this section for any period is just in the circumstances, the court shall consider only—

(1) whether such person or the opposing party, or either party's representative, made motions or asserted claims or defenses so lacking in merit as to show that such party or representative acted intentionally for delay, or otherwise acted in bad faith;

(2) whether, in the course of the action involved, such person or the opposing party, or either party's representative, violated any applicable rule, statute, or court order providing for sanctions for dilatory behavior or otherwise providing for expeditious proceedings; and

(3) whether such person or the opposing party, or either party's representative, engaged in conduct primarily for the purpose of delaying the litigation or increasing the cost thereof.

(b)(1) Except as provided in paragraph (2), any person who is a foreign state may not recover under subsection (a) an amount in excess of the actual damages sustained by it and the cost of suit, including a reasonable attorney's fee.

(2) Paragraph (1) shall not apply to a foreign state if—

(A) such foreign state would be denied . . . immunity [under the Foreign Sovereign Immunities Act] in a case in which the action is based upon a commercial activity, or an act, that is the subject matter of its claim under this section.

(B) such foreign state waives all defenses based upon or arising out of its status as a foreign state, to any claims brought against it in the same action;

(C) such foreign state engages primarily in commercial activities; and

(D) such foreign state does not function, with respect to the commercial activity, or the act, that is the subject matter of its claim under this section as a procurement entity for itself or for another foreign state.

(c) For purposes of this section—

(1) the term "commercial activity" [means that a party is involved either in a regular course of commercial conduct or in a particular commercial transaction or act].

(2) the term "foreign state" [means a foreign nation, or one of its political subdivisions, agencies or instrumenalities].

Section 4A

Whenever the United States is hereafter injured in its business or property by reason of anything forbidden in the antitrust laws it may sue therefor in the United States district court for the district in which the defendant resides or is found or has an agent, without respect to the amount in controversy, and shall recover threefold the damages by it sustained and the cost of suit. The court may award under this section, pursuant to a motion by the United States promptly made, simple interest on threefold the damages for the period beginning on the date of service of the pleading of the United States setting forth a claim under the antitrust laws and ending on the date of judgment, or for any shorter period therein, if the court finds that the award of such interest for such period is just in the circumstances. In determining whether an award of interest under this section for any period is just in the circumstances, the court shall consider only—

(1) whether the United States or the opposing party, or either party's representative, made motions or asserted claims or defenses so lacking in merit as to show that such party or representative acted intentionally for delay or otherwise acted in bad faith;

(2) whether, in the course of the action involved, the United States or the opposing party, or either party's representative, violated any applicable rule,

statute, or court order providing for sanctions for dilatory behavior or otherwise providing for expeditious proceedings;

(3) whether the United States or the opposing party, or either party's representative, engaged in conduct primarily for the purpose of delaying the litigation or increasing the cost thereof; and

(4) whether the award of such interest is necessary to compensate the United States adequately for the injury sustained by the United States.

Section 4B

Any action to enforce any cause of action under section 4, 4A, or 4C shall be forever barred unless commenced within four years after the cause of action accrued. . . .

Section 4C

(a)(1) Any attorney general of a State may bring a civil action in the name of such State, as parens patriae on behalf of natural persons residing in such State, in any district court of the United States having jurisdiction of the defendant, to secure monetary relief as provided in this section for injury sustained by such natural persons to their property by reason of any violation of the Sherman Act. The court shall exclude from the amount of monetary relief awarded in such action any amount of monetary relief (A) which duplicates amounts which have been awarded for the same injury, or (B) which is properly allocable to (i) natural persons who have excluded their claims pursuant to subsection (b)(2) of this section, and (ii) any business entity.

(2) The court shall award the State as monetary relief threefold the total damage sustained as described in paragraph (1) of this subsection, and the cost of suit, including a reasonable attorney's fee. The court may award under this paragraph, pursuant to a motion by such State promptly made, simple interest on the total damage for the period beginning on the date of service of such State's pleading setting forth a claim under the antitrust laws and ending on the date of judgment, or for any shorter period therein, if the court finds that the award of such interest for such period is just in the circumstances. In determining whether an award of interest under this paragraph for any period is just in the circumstances, the court shall consider only—

(A) whether such State or the opposing party, or either party's representative, made motions or asserted claims or defenses so lacking in merit as to show that such party or representative acted intentionally for delay or otherwise acted in bad faith;

(B) whether, in the course of the action involved, such State or the opposing party, or either party's representative, violated any applicable rule, statute, or court order providing for sanctions for dilatory behavior or otherwise providing for expeditious proceedings; and

(C) whether such State or the opposing party, or either party's representative, engaged in conduct primarily for the purpose of delaying the litigation or increasing the cost thereof.

(b)(1) In any action brought under subsection (a)(1) of this section, the State attorney general shall, at such times, in such manner, and with such content as the court may direct, cause notice thereof to be given by publication. If the court finds that notice given solely by publication would deny due process of law to any person or persons, the court may direct further notice to such person or persons according to the circumstances of the case.

(2) Any person on whose behalf an action is brought under subsection (a)(1) may elect to exclude from adjudication the portion of the State claim for monetary relief attributable to him by filing notice of such election with the court within such time as specified in the notice given pursuant to paragraph (1) of this subsection.

(3) The final judgment in an action under subsection (a)(1) shall be res judicata as to any claim under section 4 of this Act by any person on behalf of whom such action was brought and who fails to give such notice within the period specified in the notice given pursuant to paragraph (1) of this subsection.

(c) An action under subsection (a)(1) shall not be dismissed or compromised without the approval of the court, and notice of any proposed dismissal or compromise shall be given in such manner as the court directs.

(d) In any action under subsection (a)—

(1) the amount of the plaintiff's attorney's fee, if any, shall be determined by the court; and

(2) the court may, in its discretion, award a reasonable attorney's fee to a prevailing defendant upon a finding that the State attorney general has acted in bad faith, vexatiously, wantonly, or for oppressive reasons.

Section 4D

In any action under section 4C(a)(1), in which there has been a determination that a defendant agreed to fix prices in violation of the Sherman Act, damages may be proved and assessed in the aggregate by statistical or sampling methods, by the computation of illegal overcharges, or by such other reasonable system of estimating aggregate damages as the court in its discretion may permit without the necessity of separately proving the individual claim of, or amount of damage to, persons on whose behalf the suit was brought.

Section 4E

Monetary relief recovered in an action under section 4C(a)(1) shall—

(1) be distributed in such manner as the district court in its discretion may authorize; or

(2) be deemed a civil penalty by the court and deposited with the State as general revenues; subject in either case to the requirement that any distribution procedure adopted afford each person a reasonable opportunity to secure his appropriate portion of the net monetary relief.

Section 4F

(a) Whenever the Attorney General of the United States has brought an action under the antitrust laws, and he has reason to believe that any State attorney general would be entitled to bring an action under this Act based substantially on the same alleged violation of the antitrust laws, he shall promptly give written notification thereof to such State attorney general.

(b) To assist a State attorney general in evaluating the notice or in bringing any action under this Act, the Attorney General of the United States shall, upon request by such State attorney general, make available to him, to the extent permitted by law, any investigative files or other materials which are or may be relevant or material to the actual or potential cause of action under this Act.

Section 4G

For the purposes of sections 4C, 4D, 4E, and 4F of this Act:

(1) The term "State attorney general" means the chief legal officer of a State, or any other person authorized by State law to bring actions under section 4C of this Act, and includes the Corporation Counsel of the District of Columbia, except that such term does not include any person employed or retained on—

(A) a contingency fee based on a percentage of the monetary relief awarded under this section; or

(B) any other contingency fee basis, unless the amount of the award of a reasonable attorney's fee to a prevailing plaintiff is determined by the court under section 4C(d)(1).

(2) The term "State" means a State, the District of Columbia, the Commonwealth of Puerto Rico, and any other territory or possession of the United States.

(3) The term "natural persons" does not include proprietorships or partnerships.

Section 4H

Sections 4C, 4D, 4E, 4F, and 4G shall apply in any State, unless such State provides by law for its nonapplicability in such State.

Section 5

(a) A final judgment or decree heretofore or hereafter rendered in any civil or criminal proceeding brought by or on behalf of the United States under the antitrust laws to the effect that a defendant has violated said laws shall be prima facie evidence against such defendant in any action or proceeding brought by any other party against such defendant under said laws as to all matters respecting which said judgment or decree would be an estoppel as between the parties thereto: *Provided,* That this section shall not apply to consent judgments or decrees entered before any testimony has been taken. . . .

(i) Whenever any civil or criminal proceeding is instituted by the United States to prevent, restrain, or punish violations of any of the antitrust laws, but not including an action under section 4A, the running of the statute of limitations in respect of every private or State right of action arising under said laws and based in whole or in part on any matter complained of in said proceeding shall be suspended during the pendency thereof and for one year thereafter: *Provided, however,* That whenever the running of the statute of limitations in respect of a cause of action arising under section 4 or 4C is suspended hereunder, any action to enforce such cause of action shall be forever barred unless commenced either within the period of suspension or within four years after the cause of action accrued.

Section 6

That the labor of a human being is not a commodity or article of commerce. Nothing contained in the antitrust laws shall be construed to forbid the existence and operation of labor, agricultural, or horticultural organizations, instituted for the purposes of mutual help, and not having capital stock or conducted for profit, or to forbid or restrain individual members of such organizations from lawfully carrying out the legitimate objects thereof; nor shall such organizations, or the members thereof, be held or construed to be illegal combinations or conspiracies in restraint of trade, under the antitrust laws.

Section 7

That no person engaged in commerce or in any activity affecting commerce shall acquire, directly or indirectly, the whole or any part of the stock or other share capital and no person subject to the jurisdiction of the Federal Trade Commission shall acquire the whole or any part of the assets of another person engaged also in commerce or in any activity affecting commerce, where in any line of commerce or in any activity affecting commerce in any section of the country, the effect of such acquisition may be substantially to lessen competition, or to tend to create a monopoly.

No person shall acquire, directly or indirectly, the whole or any part of the stock or other share capital and no person subject to the jurisdiction of the Federal Trade Commission shall acquire the whole or any part of the assets of one or more persons engaged in commerce or in any activity affecting commerce, where in any line of commerce or in any activity affecting commerce in any section of the country, the effect of such acquisition, of such stocks or assets, or of the use of such stock by the voting or granting of proxies or otherwise, may be substantially to lessen competition, or to tend to create a monopoly.

This section shall not apply to persons purchasing such stock solely for investment and not using the same by voting or otherwise to bring about, or in attempting to bring about, the substantial lessening of competition. Nor shall anything contained in this section prevent a corporation engaged in commerce or in any activity affecting commerce from causing the formation of subsidiary corporations for the actual carrying on of their immediate lawful business, or the natural and legitimate branches or extensions thereof, or from owning and holding all or a part of the stock of such subsidiary corporations, when the effect of such formation is not to substantially lessen competition.

Section 8

(a)(1) No person shall, at the same time, serve as a director or officer in any two corporations (other than banks, banking associations, and trust companies) that are—

(A) engaged in whole or in part in commerce; and

(B) by virtue of their business and location of operation, competitors, so that the elimination of competition by agreement between them would constitute a violation of any of the antitrust laws;

if each of the corporations has capital, surplus, and undivided profits aggregating more than $10,000,000, as adjusted pursuant to paragraph (5) of this subsection.

(2) Notwithstanding the provisions of paragraph (1), simultaneous service as a director or officer in any two corporations shall not be prohibited by this section if—

(A) the competitive sales of either corporation are less than $1,000,000, as adjusted pursuant to paragraph (5) of this subsection;

(B) the competitive sales of either corporation are less than 2 per centum of that corporation's total sales; or

(C) the competitive sales of each corporation are less than 4 per centum of that corporation's total sales.

For purposes of this paragraph, "competitive sales" means the gross revenues for all products and services sold by one corporation in competition with the other, determined on the basis of annual gross revenues for such products and services in that corporation's last completed fiscal year. For the purposes of this paragraph, "total sales" means the gross revenues for all products and services sold by one corporation over that corporation's last completed fiscal year.

(3) The eligibility of a director or officer under the provisions of paragraph (1) shall be determined by the capital, surplus, and undivided profits, exclusive of dividends declared but not paid to stockholders, of each corporation at the end of that corporation's last completed fiscal year.

(4) For purposes of this section, the term "officer" means an officer elected or chosen by the Board of Directors.

(5) For each fiscal year commencing after September 30, 1990, the $10,000,000 and $1,000,000 thresholds in this subsection shall be increased (or decreased) as of October 1 each year by an amount equal to the percentage increase (or decrease) in the gross national product, as determined by the Department of Commerce or its successor, for the year then ended over the level so established for the year ending September 30, 1989. As soon as practicable, but not later than October 30 of each year, the Federal Trade Commission shall publish the adjusted amounts required by this paragraph.

(b) When any person elected or chosen as a director or officer of any corporation subject to the provisions hereof is eligible at the time of his election or selection to act for such corporation in such capacity, his eligibility to act in such capacity shall not be affected by any of the provisions hereof by reason of any change in the capital, surplus and undivided profits, or affairs of such corporation from whatever cause, until the expiration of one year from the date on which the event causing ineligibility occurred.

Section 14

That whenever a corporation shall violate any of the penal provisions of the antitrust laws, such violation shall be deemed to be also that of the individual directors, officers, or agents of such corporation who shall have authorized, ordered, or done any of the acts constituting in whole or in part such violation, and such violation shall be deemed a misdemeanor, and upon conviction therefor of any such director, officer, or agent he shall be punished by a fine of not exceeding $5,000 or by imprisonment for not exceeding one year, or by both, in the discretion of the court.

Section 15

That the several district courts of the United States are hereby invested with jurisdiction to prevent and restrain violations of this Act, and it shall be the duty of the several district attorneys of the United States, in their respective districts, under the direction of the Attorney General, to institute proceedings in equity to prevent and restrain such violations. Such proceedings may be by way of petition setting forth the case and praying that such violation shall be enjoined or otherwise prohibited. When the parties complained of shall have been duly notified of such petition, the court shall proceed, as soon as may be, to the hearing and determination of the case; and pending such petition, and before final decree, the court may at any time make such temporary restraining order or prohibition as shall be deemed just in the premises. Whenever it shall appear to the court before which any such proceeding may be pending that the ends of justice require that other parties should be brought before the court, the court may cause them to be summoned, whether they reside in the district in which the court is held or not, and subpoenas to that end may be served in any district by the marshal thereof.

Section 16

That any person, firm, corporation, or association shall be entitled to sue for and have injunctive relief, in any court of the United States having jurisdiction over the parties, against threatened loss or damage by a violation of the antitrust laws, including sections two, three, seven, and eight of this Act, when and under the same conditions and principles as injunctive relief against threatened conduct that will cause loss or damage is granted by courts of equity, under the rules governing such proceedings, and upon the execution of proper bond against damages for an injunction improvidently granted and a showing that the danger of irreparable loss or damage is immediate, a preliminary injunction may issue.

APPENDIX

E

Robinson-Patman Act (Excerpts)

[The following provisions of the Robinson-Patman Act were enacted as amendments to the Clayton Act and appear in the Clayton Act as sections 2(a)–2(f).]

Section 2

(a) That it shall be unlawful for any person engaged in commerce, in the course of such commerce, either directly or indirectly, to discriminate in price between different purchasers of commodities of like grade and quality, where either or any of the purchases involved in such discrimination are in commerce, where such commodities are sold for use, consumption, or resale within the United States or any Territory thereof or the District of Columbia or any insular possession or other place under the jurisdiction of the United States, and where the effect of such discrimination may be substantially to lessen competition or tend to create a monopoly in any line of commerce, or to injure, destroy, or prevent competition with any person who either grants or knowingly receives the benefit of such discrimination, or with customers of either of them: Provided, That nothing herein contained shall prevent differentials which make only due allowance for differences in the cost of manufacture, sale, or delivery resulting from the differing methods or quantities in which such commodities are to such purchasers sold or delivered: Provided, however, That the Federal Trade Commission may, after due investigation and hearing to all interested parties, fix and establish quantity limits, and revise the same as it finds necessary, as to particular commodities or classes of commodities, where it finds that available purchasers in greater quantities are so few as to render differentials on account thereof unjustly discriminatory or promotive of monopoly in any line of commerce; and the foregoing shall then not be construed to permit differentials based on differences in quantities greater than those so fixed and established: And provided further, That nothing herein contained shall prevent persons engaged in selling goods, wares, or merchandise in commerce from selecting their own customers in bona fide transactions and not in restraint of trade: And provided further, That nothing herein contained shall prevent price changes from time to time where in response to changing conditions affecting the market for or the marketability of the goods concerned, such as but not limited to actual or imminent deterioration of perishable goods, obsolescence of seasonal goods, distress sales under court process, or sales in good faith in discontinuance of business in the goods concerned.

(b) Upon proof being made, at any hearing on a complaint under this section, that there has been discrimination in price or services or facilities furnished, the burden of rebutting the prima-facie case thus made by showing justification shall be upon the person charged with a violation of this section, and unless justification shall be affirmatively shown, the Commission is authorized to issue an order terminating the discrimination: Provided, however, That nothing herein contained shall prevent a seller rebutting the prima-facie case thus made by showing that his lower price or the furnishing of services or facilities to any purchaser or purchasers was made in good faith to meet an equally low price of a competitor, or the services or facilities furnished by a competitor.

(c) That it shall be unlawful for any person engaged in commerce, in the course of such commerce, to pay or grant, or to receive or accept, anything of value as a commission, brokerage, or other compensation, or any allowance or discount in lieu thereof, except for services rendered in connection with the sale or purchase of goods, wares, or merchandise, either to the other party to such transaction or to an agent, representative, or other intermediary therein where such intermediary is acting in fact for or in behalf, or is subject to the direct or indirect control, of any party to such transaction other than the person by whom such compensation is so granted or paid.

(d) That it shall be unlawful for any person engaged in commerce to pay or contract for the payment of anything of value to or for the benefit of a customer of such person in the course of such commerce as compensation or in consideration for any services or facilities furnished by or through such customer in connection with the processing, handling, sale, or offering for sale of any products or commodities manufactured, sold, or offered for sale by such person, unless such payment or consideration is available on proportionally equal terms to all other customers competing in the distribution of such products or commodities.

(e) That it shall be unlawful for any person to discriminate in favor of one purchaser against another purchaser or purchasers of a commodity bought for resale, with or without processing, by contracting to furnish or furnishing, or by contributing to the furnishing of, any services or facilities connected with the processing, handling, sale, or offering for sale of such commodity so purchased upon terms not accorded to all purchases on proportionally equal terms.

(f) That it shall be unlawful for any person engaged in commerce, in the course of such commerce, knowingly to induce or receive a discrimination in price which is prohibited by this section.

[The following section of the Robinson-Patman Act (Section 3) is not part of the Clayton Act.]

Section 3

It shall be unlawful for any person engaged in commerce, in the course of such commerce, to be a party to, or assist in, any transaction of sale, or contract to sell, which discriminates to his knowledge against competitors of the purchaser, in that, any discount, rebate, allowance, or advertising service charge is granted to the purchaser over and above any discount, rebate, allowance, or advertising service charge available at the time of such transaction to said competitors in respect of a sale of goods of like grade, quality, and quantity; to sell, or contract to sell, goods in any part of the United States at prices lower than those exacted by said person elsewhere in the United States for the purpose of destroying competition, or eliminating a competitor in such part of the United States; or, to sell, or contract to sell, goods at unreasonably low prices for the purpose of destroying competition or eliminating a competitor.

Any person violating any of the provisions of this section shall, upon conviction thereof, be fined not more than $5,000 or imprisoned not more than one year, or both.

APPENDIX

F

Federal Trade
Commission Act
(Excerpts)

Section 1

. . . a commission is hereby created and established, to be known as the Federal Trade Commission (hereinafter referred to as the Commission). . .

Section 4

The words defined in this section shall have the following meaning when found in this Act, to wit:

"Commerce" means commerce among the several states or with foreign nations, or in any territory of the United States or in the District of Columbia, or between any such territory and another, or between any such territory and any state or foreign nation, or between the District of Columbia and any state or territory or foreign nation.

"Corporation" shall be deemed to include any company, trust, so-called Massachusetts trust, or association, incorporated or unincorporated, which is organized to carry on business for its own profit or that of its members, and has shares of capital or capital stock or certificates of interest, and any company, trust, so-called Massachusetts trust, or association, incorporated or unincorporated, without shares of capital or capital stock or certificates of interest, except partnerships, which is organized to carry on business for its own profit or that of its members.

Section 5

(a) (1) Unfair methods of competition in or affecting commerce, and unfair or deceptive acts or practices in or affecting commerce, are hereby declared unlawful.

(2) The Commission is hereby empowered and directed to prevent persons, partnerships, or corporations, except banks, savings and loan institutions described in section 18(f)(3), Federal credit unions described in section 18(f)(4), common carriers subject to the Acts to regulate commerce, air carriers and foreign air carriers subject to the Federal Aviation Act of 1958, and persons, partnerships, or corporations insofar as they are subject to the Packers and Stockyards Act, 1921, as amended, except as provided in section 406(b) of said Act, from using unfair methods of competition in or affecting commerce and unfair or deceptive acts or practices in or affecting commerce.

(3) This subsection shall not apply to unfair methods of competition involving commerce with foreign nations (other than import commerce) unless—

(A) such methods of competition have a direct, substantial, and reasonably foreseeable effect—

(i) on commerce which is not commerce with foreign nations, or on import commerce with foreign nations; or

(ii) on export commerce with foreign nations, of a person engaged in such commerce in the United States; and

(B) such effect gives rise to a claim under the provisions of this subsection, other than this paragraph.

If this subsection applies to such methods of competition only because of the operation of subparagraph (A)(ii), this subsection shall apply to such conduct only for injury to export business in the United States.

APPENDIX

G

Title VII of the Civil Rights Act of 1964 (Excerpts)

Section 701. Definitions

(j) The term "religion" includes all aspects of religious observance and practice, as well as belief, unless an employer demonstrates that he is unable to reasonably accommodate to an employee's or prospective employee's religious observance or practice without undue hardship on the conduct of the employer's business.

(k) The terms "because of sex" or "on the basis of sex" include, but are not limited to, because of or on the basis of pregnancy, childbirth, or related medical conditions; and women affected by pregnancy, childbirth, or related medical conditions shall be treated the same for all employment-related purposes, including receipt of benefits under fringe benefit programs, as other persons not so affected but similar in their ability or inability to work, and nothing in Section 703(h) of this title shall be interpreted to permit otherwise. This subsection shall not require an employer to pay for health insurance benefits for abortion, except where the life of the mother would be endangered if the fetus were carried to term, or except where medical complications have arisen from an abortion: *Provided,* That nothing herein shall preclude an employer from providing abortion benefits or otherwise affect bargaining agreements in regard to abortion.

Section 703. Discrimination because of Race, Color, Religion, Sex, or National Origin

(a) It shall be an unlawful employment practice for an employer—

(1) to fail or refuse to hire or to discharge any individual, or otherwise to discriminate against any individual with respect to his compensation, terms, conditions, or privileges of employment, because of such individual's race, color, religion, sex, or national origin; or

(2) limit, segregate, or classify his employees or applicants for employment in any way which would deprive or tend to deprive any individual of employment opportunities or otherwise adversely affect his status as an employee, because of such individual's race, color, religion, sex, or national origin.

(b) It shall be an unlawful employment practice for an employment agency to fail or refuse to refer for employment, or otherwise to discriminate against, an individual because of his race, color, religion, sex, or national origin, or to classify or refer for employment any individual on the basis of his race, color, religion, sex, or national origin.

(c) It shall be an unlawful employment practice for a labor organization—

(1) to exclude or to expel from its membership, or otherwise to discriminate against, any individual because of his race, color, religion, sex, or national origin;

(2) to limit, segregate, or classify its membership or applicants for membership or to classify or fail or refuse to refer for employment any individual, in any way which would deprive or tend to deprive any individual of employment opportunities, or would limit such employment opportunities or otherwise adversely affect his status as an employee or as an applicant for employment, because of such individual's race, color, religion, sex, or national origin; or

(3) to cause or attempt to cause an employer to discriminate against an individual in violation of this section.

(d) It shall be an unlawful employment practice for any employer, labor organization, or joint labor-management committee controlling apprenticeship or other training or retraining, including on-the-job training programs, to discriminate against any individual because of his race, color, religion, sex, or national origin in admission to, or employment in, any program established to provide apprenticeship or other training.

(e) Notwithstanding any other provision of this title, (1) it shall not be an unlawful employment practice for an employer to hire and employ employees, for an employment agency to classify, or refer for employment any individual, or for any employer, labor organization, or joint labor-management committee controlling apprenticeship or other training or retraining programs to admit or employ any individual in any such program, on the basis of his religion, sex, or national origin in those certain instances where religion, sex, or national origin is a bona fide occupational qualification reasonably necessary to the normal operation of that particular business or enterprise, and (2) it shall not be an unlawful employment practice for a school, college, university, or other educational institution or institution of learning to hire and employ employees of a particular religion if such school, college, university, or other educational institution or institution of learning is, in whole or in substantial part, owned, supported, controlled, or managed by a particular religion or by a particular religious corporation, association, or society, or if the curriculum of such school, college, university, or other educational institution or institution of learning is directed toward the propagation of a particular religion.

(f) As used in this title, the phrase "unlawful employment practice" shall not be deemed to include any action or measure taken by an employer, labor organization, joint labor-management committee, or employment agency with respect to an individual who is a member of the Communist Party of the United States or of any other organization required to register as a Communist-action or Communist-front organization by final order of the Subversive Activities Control Act of 1950.

(g) Notwithstanding any other provision of this title, it shall not be an unlawful employment practice for an employer to fail or refuse to hire and employ any individual for any position, for an employer to discharge an individual from any position, or for an employment agency to fail or refuse to refer any individual for employment in any position, or for a labor organization to fail or refuse any individual for employment in any position, if—

(l) the occupancy of such position, or access to the premises in or upon which any part of the duties of such position is performed or is to be performed, is subject to any requirement imposed in the interest of the national security of the United States under any security program in effect pursuant to or administered under any statute of the United States or any Executive order of the President; and

(2) such individual has not fulfilled or has ceased to fulfill that requirement.

(h) Notwithstanding any other provision of this title, it shall not be an unlawful employment practice for an employer to apply different standards of compensation, or different terms, conditions, or privileges of employment pursuant to a bona fide seniority or merit system, or a system which measures earnings by quantity or quality of production or to employees who work in different locations, provided that such differences are not the result of an intention to discriminate because of race, color, religion, sex, or national origin; nor shall it be an unlawful employment practice for an employer to give and to act upon the results of any professionally developed ability test provided that such test, its administration or action upon the results is not designed, intended, or used to discriminate because of race, color, religion, sex, or national origin. It shall not be an unlawful employment practice under this title for any employer to differentiate upon the basis of sex in determining the amount of wages or compensation paid or to be paid to employees of such employer if such differentiation is authorized by the provisions of Section 6(d) of the Fair Labor Standards Act of 1938 as amended (29 U.S.C. 206(d)).

(i) Nothing contained in this title shall apply to any business or enterprise on or near an Indian reservation with respect to any publicly announced employment practice of such business or enterprise under which a preferential treatment is given to any individual because he is an Indian living on or near a reservation.

(j) Nothing contained in this title shall be interpreted to require any employer, employment agency, labor organization, or joint labor-management committee subject to this title to grant preferential treatment to any individual or to any group because of the race, color, religion, sex, or national origin of such individual or group on account of an imbalance which may exist with respect to the total number or percentage of persons of any race, color, religion, sex, or national origin employed by any employer, referred or classified for employment by any employment agency or labor organization, admitted to membership or classified by any labor organization, or admitted to, or employed in, any apprenticeship or other training program, in comparison with the total number or percentage of persons of such race, color, religion, sex, or national origin in any community, State, section, or other area, or in the available work force in any community, State, section, or other area.

Section 704. Other Unlawful Employment Practices

(a) It shall be an unlawful employment practice for an employer to discriminate against any of his employees or applicants for employment, for an employment agency, or joint labor-management committee controlling apprenticeship or other training or retraining, including on-the-job training programs, to discriminate against any individual, or for a labor organization to discriminate against any member thereof or applicant for membership, because he has opposed any practice, made an unlawful employment practice by this title, or because he has made a charge, testified, assisted, or participated in any manner in an investigation, proceeding, or hearing under this title.

(b) It shall be an unlawful employment practice for an employer, labor organization, employment agency, or joint labor-management committee controlling apprenticeship or other training or retraining, including on-the-job training programs, to print or cause to be printed or published any notice or advertisement relating to employment by such an employer or membership in or any classification or referral for employment by such a labor organization, or relating to any classification or referral for employment by such an employment agency, or relating to admission to, or employment in, any program established to provide apprenticeship or other training by such a joint labor-management committee, indicating any preference, limitation, specification, or discrimination, based on race, color, religion, sex or national origin, except that such a notice or advertisement may indicate a preference, limitation, specification, or discrimination based on religion, sex, or national origin when religion, sex, or national origin is a bona fide occupational qualification for employment.

APPENDIX

H

National Labor Relations Act (Excerpts)

Section 2. Definitions

When used in this Act—

(2) The term "employer" includes any person acting as an agent of an employer, directly or indirectly, but shall not include the United States or any wholly owned Government corporation, or any Federal Reserve Bank, or any State or political subdivision thereof, or any person subject to the Railway Labor Act, as amended from time to time, or any labor organization (other than when acting as an employer), or anyone acting in the capacity of officer or agent of such labor organization.

(3) The term "employee" shall include any employee, and shall not be limited to the employees of a particular employer, unless the Act explicitly states otherwise, and shall include any individual whose work has ceased as a consequence of, or in connection with, any current labor dispute or because of any unfair labor practice, and who has not obtained any other regular and substantially equivalent employment, but shall not include any individual employed as an agricultural laborer, or in the domestic service of any family or person at his home, or any individual employed by his parent or spouse, or any individual having the status of an independent contractor, or any individual employed as a supervisor, or any individual employed by an employer subject to the Railway Labor Act, as amended from time to time, or by any other person who is not an employer as herein defined.

(11) The term "supervisor" means any individual having authority, in the interest of the employer, to hire, transfer, suspend, lay off, recall, promote, discharge, assign, reward, or discipline other employees, or responsibly to direct them, or to adjust their grievances, or effectively to recommend such action, if in connection with the foregoing the exercise of such authority is not of a merely routine or clerical nature, but requires the use of independent judgment.

(12) The term "professional employee" means—

(a) any employee engaged in work (i) predominantly intellectual and varied in character as opposed to routine mental, manual, mechanical, or physical work; (ii) involving the consistent exercise of discretion and judgment in its performance; (iii) of such a character that the output produced or the result accomplished cannot be standardized in relation to a given period of time; (iv) requiring knowledge of an advanced type in a field of science or learning customarily acquired by a prolonged course of specialized intellectual instruction and study in an institution of higher learning or a hospital, as distinguished from a general academic education or from an apprenticeship or from training in the performance of routine mental, manual, or physical processes; or

(b) any employee who (i) has completed the courses of specialized intellectual instruction and study described in clause (iv) of paragraph (a), and (ii) is performing related work under the supervision of a professional person to qualify himself to become a professional employee as defined in paragraph (a).

Section 7. Rights of Employees

Employees shall have the right to self-organization, to form, join, or assist labor organizations, to bargain collectively through representatives of their own choosing, and to engage in other concerted activities for the purpose of collective bargaining or other mutual aid or protection, and shall also have the right to refrain from any or all of such activities except to the extent that such right may be affected by an agreement requiring membership in a labor organization as a condition of employment as authorized in section 8(a)(3).

Section 8. Unfair Labor Practices

(a) It shall be an unfair labor practice for an employer—

(1) to interfere with, restrain, or coerce employees in the exercise of the rights guaranteed in section 7;

(2) to dominate or interfere with the formation or administration of any labor organization or contribute financial or other support to it: *Provided,* That subject to rules and regulations made and published by the Board pursuant to section 6, an employer shall not be prohibited from permitting employees to confer with him during working hours without loss of time or pay;

(3) by discrimination in regard to hire or tenure of employment or any term or condition of employment to encourage or discourage membership in any labor organization: *Provided,* That nothing in this Act, or in any other statute of the United States, shall preclude an employer from making an agreement with a labor organization (not established, maintained, or assisted by any action defined in section 8(a) of this Act as an unfair labor practice) to require as a condition of employment membership therein on or after the thirtieth day following the beginning of such employment or the effective date of such agreement, whichever is the later, (i) if such labor organization is the representative of the employees as provided in section 9(a), in the appropriate collective-bargaining unit covered by such agreement when made, and (ii) unless following an election held as provided in section 9(e) within one year preceding the effective date of such agreement, the Board shall have certified that at least a majority of the employees eligible to vote in such election have voted to rescind the authority of such labor organization to make such an agreement: *Provided further,* That no employer shall justify any discrimination against an employee for nonmembership in a labor organization (A) if he has reasonable grounds for believing that such membership was not available to the employee on the same terms and conditions generally applicable to other members, or (B) if he has reasonable grounds for believing that membership was denied or terminated for reasons other than the failure of the employee to tender the periodic dues and the initiation fees uniformly required as a condition of acquiring or retaining membership;

(4) to discharge or otherwise discriminate against an employee because he has filed charges or given testimony under this Act;

(5) to refuse to bargain collectively with the representatives of his employees, subject to the provisions of section 9(a).

(b) It shall be an unfair labor practice for a labor organization or its agents—

(1) to restrain or coerce (A) employees in the exercise of the rights guaranteed in section 7: *Provided,* That this paragraph shall not impair the right of a labor organization to prescribe its own rules with respect to the acquisition or retention of membership therein; or (B) an employer in the selection of his representatives for the purposes of collective bargaining or the adjustment of grievances;

(2) to cause or attempt to cause an employer to discriminate against an employee in violation of subsection (a)(3) or to discriminate against an employee with respect to whom membership in such organization has been denied or terminated on some ground other than his failure to tender the periodic dues and

the initiation fees uniformly required as a condition of acquiring or retaining membership;

(3) to refuse to bargain collectively with an employer, provided it is the representative of his employees subject to the provisions of section 9(a);

(4) (i) to engage in, or to induce or encourage any individual employed by any person engaged in commerce or in an industry affecting commerce to engage in, a strike or a refusal in the course of his employment to use, manufacture, process, transport, or otherwise handle or work on any goods, articles, materials, or commodities or to perform any services; or (ii) to threaten, coerce, or restrain any person engaged in commerce or in an industry affecting commerce, where in either case an object thereof is—

    (A) forcing or requiring any employer or self-employed person to join any labor or employer organization or to enter into any agreement which is prohibited by section 8(e);

    (B) forcing or requiring any person to cease using, selling, handling, transporting, or otherwise dealing in the products of any other producer, processor, or manufacturer, or to cease doing business with any other person, or forcing or requiring any other employer to recognize or bargain with a labor organization as the representative of his employees unless such labor organization has been certified as the representative of such employees under the provisions of section 9: *Provided,* that nothing contained in this clause (B) shall be construed to make unlawful, where not otherwise unlawful, any primary strike or primary picketing;

    (C) forcing or requiring any employer to recognize or bargain with a particular labor organization as the representative of his employees if another labor organization has been certified as the representative of such employees under the provisions of section 9;

    (D) forcing or requiring any employer to assign particular work to employees in a particular labor organization or in a particular trade, craft, or class rather than to employees in another labor organization or in another trade, craft, or class, unless such employer is failing to conform to an order or certification of the Board determining the bargaining representative for employees performing such work:

Provided, That nothing contained in this subsection (b) shall be construed to make unlawful a refusal by any person to enter upon the premises of any employer (other than his own employer), if the employees of such employer are engaged in a strike ratified or approved by a representative of such employees whom such employer is required to recognize under this Act: *Provided further*, That for the purposes of this paragraph (4) only, nothing contained in such paragraph shall be construed to prohibit publicity, other than picketing, for the purpose of truthfully advising the public, including consumers and members of a labor organization, that a product or products are produced by an employer with whom the labor organization has a primary dispute and are distributed by another employer, as long as such publicity does not have an effect of inducing any individual employed by any person other than the primary employer in the course of his employment to refuse to pick up, deliver, or transport any goods, or not to perform any services, at the establishment of the employer engaged in such distribution;

(5) to require of employees covered by an agreement authorized under subsection (a)(3) the payment, as a condition precedent to becoming a member of such organization, of a fee in an amount which the Board finds excessive or discrimi-

natory under all the circumstances. In making such a finding, the Board shall consider, among other relevant factors, the practices and customs of labor organizations in the particular industry, and the wages currently paid to the employees affected;

(6) to cause or attempt to cause an employer to pay or deliver or agree to pay or deliver any money or other thing of value, in the nature of an exaction, for services which are not performed or not to be performed; and

(7) To picket or cause to be picketed, or threaten to picket or cause to be picketed, any employer where an object thereof is forcing or requiring an employer to recognize or bargain with a labor organization as the representative of his employees, or forcing or requiring the employees of an employer to accept or select such labor organization as their collective bargaining representative, unless such labor organization is currently certified as the representative of such employees:

(A) where the employer has lawfully recognized in accordance with this Act any other labor organization and a question concerning representation may not appropriately be raised under section 9(c) of this Act;

(B) where within the preceding twelve months a valid election under section 9(c) of this Act has been conducted, or

(C) where such picketing has been conducted without a petition under section 9(c) being filed within a reasonable period of time not to exceed thirty days from the commencement of such picketing; *Provided,* That when such a petition has been filed the Board shall forthwith, without regard to the provisions of section 9(c)(1) or the absence of a showing of a substantial interest on the part of the labor organization, direct an election in such unit as the Board finds to be appropriate and shall certify the results thereof: *Provided further,* That nothing in this subparagraph (C) shall be construed to prohibit any picketing or other publicity for the purpose of truthfully advising the public (including consumers) that an employer does not employ members of, or have a contract with, a labor organization, unless an effect of such picketing is to induce any individual employed by any other person in the course of his employment, not to pick up, deliver, or transport any goods or not to perform any services.

Nothing in this paragraph (7) shall be construed to permit any act which would otherwise be an unfair labor practice under this section 8(b).

(c) The expressing of any views, argument, or opinion, or the dissemination thereof, whether in written, printed, graphic, or visual form, shall not constitute or be evidence of an unfair labor practice under any of the provisions of this Act, if such expression contains no threat of reprisal or force or promise of benefit.

(d) For the purposes of this section, to bargain collectively in the performance of the mutual obligation of the employer and the representative of the employees to meet at reasonable times and confer in good faith with respect to wages, hours, and other terms and conditions of employment, or the negotiation of an agreement, or any question arising thereunder, and the execution of a written contract incorporating any agreement reached if requested by either party, but such obligation does not compel either party to agree to a proposal or require the making of a concession: *Provided,* That where there is in effect a collective-bargaining contract covering employees in an industry affecting commerce, the duty to bargain collectively shall also mean that no party to such contract shall terminate or modify such contract, unless the party desiring such termination or modification.—

(1) serves a written notice upon the other party to the contract of the proposed termination or modification sixty days prior to the expiration date thereof, or in the event such contract contains no expiration date, sixty days prior to the time it is proposed to make such termination or modification;

(2) offers to meet and confer with the other party for the purpose of negotiating a new contract or a contract containing the proposed modifications;

(3) notifies the Federal Mediation and Conciliation Service within thirty days after such notice of the existence of a dispute, and simultaneously therewith notifies any State or Territorial agency established to mediate and conciliate disputes within the State or Territory where the dispute occurred, provided no agreement has been reached by that time; and

(4) continues in full force and effect, without resorting to strike or lockout, all the terms and conditions of the existing contract for a period of sixty days after such notice is given or until the expiration date of such contract, whichever occurs later.

The duties imposed upon employers, employees, and labor organizations by paragraphs (2), (3), and (4) shall become inapplicable upon an intervening certification of the Board, under which the labor organization or individual, which is a party to the contract, has been superseded as or ceased to be the representative of the employees subject to the provisions of section 9(a), and the duties so imposed shall not be construed as requiring either party to discuss or agree to any modification of the terms and conditions contained in a contract for a fixed period, if such modification is to become effective before such terms and conditions can be reopened under the provisions of the contract. Any employee who engages in a strike within any notice periods specified in this subsection, or who engages in any strike within the appropriate period specified in subsection (g) of this section, shall lose his status as an employee of the employer engaged in the particular labor dispute, for the purposes of sections 8, 9, and 10 of this Act, but such loss of status for such employee shall terminate if and when he is re-employed by such employer. Whenever the collective bargaining involves employees of a health care institution, the provisions of this section 8(d) shall be modified as follows:

(A) The notice of section 8(d)(1) shall be ninety days; the notice of section 8(d)(3) shall be sixty days; and the contract period of section 8(d)(4) shall be ninety days.

(B) Where the bargaining is for an initial agreement following certification or recognition, at least thirty days' notice of the existence of a dispute shall be given by the labor organization to the agencies set forth in section 8(d)(3).

(C) After notice is given to the Federal Mediation and Conciliation Service under either clause (A) or (B) of this sentence, the Service shall promptly communicate with the parties and use its best efforts, by mediation and conciliation, to bring them to agreement. The parties shall participate fully and promptly in such meetings as may be undertaken by the Service for the purpose of aiding in a settlement of the dispute.

(e) It shall be an unfair labor practice for any labor organization and any employer to enter into any contract or agreement, express or implied, whereby such employer ceases or refrains or agrees to cease or refrain from handling, using, selling, transporting, or otherwise dealing in any of the products of any other employer, or to cease doing business with any other person, and any contract or agreement entered into heretofore or hereafter containing such an agreement shall be to such extent unenforceable and void: *Provided,* That nothing in this subsection (e) shall apply to an agreement between a labor organization and an employer in the construction industry relating to the contracting or subcontracting of work to be done at the site of the construction, alteration, painting, or repair of a building, structure, or other work: *Provided further*, That for the purposes of this subsection (e) and section 8(b)(4)(B) the terms 'any employer,' 'any person engaged in commerce or any industry affecting commerce,' and 'any person' when used in relation to the terms 'any other producer, processor, or manufacturer,' 'any other employer,' or 'any other person' shall not include persons in the relation of a jobber, manufacturer, contractor, or subcontractor working on the goods or premises of the jobber or manufacturer or performing parts of an integrated process of production in the apparel and clothing industry: *Provided further,* That nothing in this Act shall prohibit the enforcement of any agreement which is within the foregoing exception.

(f) It shall not be an unfair labor practice under subsections (a) and (b) of this section for an employer engaged primarily in the building and construction industry to make an agreement covering employees engaged (or who, upon their employment, will be engaged) in the building and construction industry with a labor organization of which building and construction employees are members (not established, maintained, or assisted by any action defined in section 8(a) of this Act as an unfair labor practice) because (1) the majority status of such labor organizations has not been established under the provisions of section 9 of this Act prior to the making of such agreement, or (2) such agreement requires as a condition of employment, membership in such labor organization after the seventh day following the beginning of such employment or the effective date of the agreement, whichever is later, or (3) such agreement requires the employer to notify such labor organization of opportunities for employment with such employer, or gives such labor organization an opportunity to refer qualified applicants for such employment, or (4) such agreement specifies minimum training or experience qualifications for employment or provides for priority in opportunities for employment based upon length of service with such employer, in the industry or in the particular geographical area: *Provided*, That nothing in this subsection shall set aside the final proviso to section 8(a)(3) of this Act: *Provided further*, That any agreement which would be invalid, but for clause (1) of this subsection, shall not be a bar to a petition filed pursuant to section 9(c) or 9(e).

(g) A labor organization before engaging in any strike, picketing, or other concerted refusal to work at any health care institution shall, not less than ten days prior to such action, notify the institution in writing and the Federal Mediation and Conciliation Service of that intention, except that in the case of bargaining for an initial agreement following certification or recognition the notice required by this subsection shall not be given until the expiration of the period specified in clause (b) of the last sentence of section 8(d) of this Act. The notice shall state the date and time that such action will commence. The notice, once given, may be extended by the written agreement of both parties.

Section 9. Representatives and Elections

(a) Representatives designated or selected for the purposes of collective bargaining by the majority of the employees in a unit appropriate for such purposes, shall be the exclusive representatives of all the employees in such unit for the purposes of collective bargaining in respect to rates of pay, wages, hours of employment, or other conditions of employment: *Provided,* That any individual employee or a group of employees shall have the right at any time to present grievances to their employer and to have such grievances adjusted, without the intervention of the bargaining representative, as long as the adjustment is not inconsistent with the terms of a collective-bargaining contract or agreement then in effect: *Provided further,* That the bargaining representative has been given opportunity to be present at such adjustment.

(b) The Board shall decide in each case whether, in order to assure to employees the fullest freedom in exercising the rights guaranteed by this Act, the unit appropriate for the purposes of collective bargaining shall be the employer unit, craft unit, plant unit, or subdivision thereof: *Provided,* That the Board shall not (1) decide that any unit is appropriate for such purposes if such unit includes both professional employees and employees who are not professional employees unless a majority of such professional employees vote for inclusion in such unit; or (2) decide that any craft unit is inappropriate for such purposes on the ground that a different unit has been established by a prior Board determination, unless a majority of the employees in the proposed craft unit vote against separate representation or (3) decide that any unit is appropriate for such purposes if it includes, together with other employees, any individual employed as a guard to enforce against employees and other persons rules to protect property of the employer or to protect the safety of persons on the employer's premises; but no later organization shall be certified as the representative of employees in a bargaining unit of guards if such organization admits to membership, or is affiliated directly or indirectly with an organization which admits to membership, employees other than guards.

(c)(1) Whenever a petition shall have been filed, in accordance with such regulations as may be prescribed by the Board—

    (A) by an employee or group of employees or an individual or labor organization acting in their behalf alleging that a substantial number of employees (i) wish to be represented for collective bargaining and that their employer declines to recognize their representative as the representative defined in section 9(a), or (ii) assert that the individual or labor organization, which has been certified or is being currently recognized by their employer as the bargaining representative, is no longer a representative as defined in section 9(a); or

    (B) by an employer, alleging that one or more individuals or labor organizations have presented to him a claim to be recognized as the representative defined in section 9(a); the Board shall investigate such petition and if it has reasonable cause to believe that a question of representation affecting commerce exists shall provide for an appropriate hearing upon due notice. Such hearing may be conducted by an officer or employee of the regional office, who shall not make any recommendations with respect thereto. If the Board finds upon the record of such hearing that such a question of representation exists, it shall direct an election by secret ballot and shall certify the results thereof.

(2) In determining whether or not a question of representation affecting commerce exists, the same regulations and rules of decision shall apply irrespective of the identity of the persons filing the petition or the kind of relief sought and in no case shall the Board deny a labor organization a place on the ballot by reason of an order with respect to such labor organization or its predecessor not issued in conformity with section 10(c).

(3) No election shall be directed in any bargaining unit or any subdivision

within which, in the preceding twelve-month period, a valid election shall have been held. Employees engaged in an economic strike who are not entitled to reinstatement shall be eligible to vote under such regulations as the Board shall find are consistent with the purposes and provisions of this Act in any election conducted within twelve months after the commencement of the strike. In any election where none of the choices on the ballot receives a majority, a run-off shall be conducted, the ballot providing for a selection between the two choices receiving the largest and second largest number of valid votes cast in the election.

(4) Nothing in this section shall be construed to prohibit the waiving of hearings by stipulation for the purpose of a consent election in conformity with regulations and rules of decision of the Board.

(5) In determining whether a unit is appropriate for the purposes specified in subsection (b), the extent to which the employees have organized shall not be controlling.

(d) Whenever an order of the Board made pursuant to section 10(c) is based in whole or in part upon facts certified following an investigation pursuant to subsection (c) of this section and there is a petition for the enforcement or review of such order, such certification and the record of such investigation shall be included in the transcript of the entire record required to be filed under section 10(e) or 10(f), and thereupon the decree of the court enforcing, modifying, or setting aside in whole or in part the order of the Board shall be made and entered upon the pleadings, testimony, and proceedings set forth in such transcript.

(e)(1) Upon the filing with the Board, by 30 per centum or more of the employees in a bargaining unit covered by an agreement between their employer and a labor organization made pursuant to section 8(a)(3), of a petition alleging they desire that such authority be rescinded, the Board shall take a secret ballot of the employees in such unit, and shall certify the results thereof to such labor organization and to the employer,

(2) No election shall be conducted pursuant to this subsection in any bargaining unit or any subdivision within which, in the preceding twelve-month period, a valid election shall have been held.

Section 14. Execution of Agreements Requiring Membership

(b) Nothing in this Act shall be construed as authorizing the execution or application of agreements requiring membership in a labor organization as a condition of employment in any State or Territory in which such execution or application is prohibited by State or Territorial law.

APPENDIX

I

Securities Act of 1933 (Excerpts)

Section 5. Prohibitions Relating to Interstate Commerce and the Mails

(a) Sale or Delivery after Sale of Unregistered Securities

Unless a registration statement is in effect as to a security, it shall be unlawful for any person, directly or indirectly—

(1) to make use of any means or instruments of transportation or communication in interstate commerce or of the mails to sell such security through the use or medium of any prospectus or otherwise; or

(2) to carry or cause to be carried through the mails or in interstate commerce, by any means or instruments of transportation, any such security for the purpose of sale or for delivery after sale.

(b) Necessity of Prospectus Meeting Requirements of This [Act]

It shall be unlawful for any person, directly or indirectly—

(1) to make use of any means or instruments of transportation or communication in interstate commerce or of the mails to carry or transmit any prospectus relating to any security with respect to which a registration statement has been filed under this subchapter, unless such prospectus meets the requirements of . . . this [Act]; or

(2) to carry or cause to be carried through the mails or in interstate commerce any such security for the purpose of sale or for delivery after sale, unless accompanied or preceded by a prospectus that meets the requirements of . . . [this Act].

(c) Necessity of Filing Registration Statement

It shall be unlawful for any person, directly or indirectly, to make use of any means or instruments of transportation or communication in interstate commerce or of the mails to offer to sell or offer to buy through the use or medium of any prospectus or otherwise any security, unless a registration statement has been filed as to such security, or while the registration statement is the subject of a refusal order or stop order or (prior to the effective date of the registration statement) any public proceeding or examination under this [Act].

Section 11. Civil Liabilities on Account of False Registration Statement

(a) Persons Possessing Cause of Action; Persons Liable

In case any part of the registration statement, when such part became effective, contained an untrue statement of a material fact or omitted to state a material fact required to be stated therein or necessary to make the statements therein not misleading, any person acquiring such security (unless it is proved that at the time of such acquisition he knew of such untruth or omission) may, either at law or in equity, in any court of competent jurisdiction, sue—

(1) every person who signed the registration statement;

(2) every person who was a director of (or person performing similar functions) or partner in the issuer at the time of the filing of the part of the registration statement with respect to which his liability is asserted;

(3) every person who, with his consent, is named in the registration statement as being or about to become a director, person performing similar functions, or partner;

(4) every accountant, engineer, or appraiser, or any person whose profession gives authority to a statement made by him, who has with his consent been named

as having prepared or certified any part of the registration statement, or as having prepared or certified any report or valuation which is used in connection with the registration statement, with respect to the statement in such registration statement, report, or valuation, which purports to have been prepared or certified by him;

(5) every underwriter with respect to such security.

If such person acquired the security after the issuer has made generally available to its security holders an earnings statement covering a period of at least twelve months beginning after the effective date of the registration statement, then the right of recovery under this subsection shall be conditioned on proof that such person acquired the security relying upon such untrue statement in the registration statement or relying upon the registration statement and not knowing of such omission, but such reliance may be established without proof of the reading of the registration statement by such person.

(b) Persons Exempt from Liability upon Proof of Issues

Notwithstanding the provisions of (a) [above] no person, other than the issuer, shall be liable as provided therein who shall sustain the burden of proof—

(1) that before the effective date of the part of the registration statement with respect to which his liability is asserted (A) he had resigned from or had taken such steps as are permitted by law to resign from, or ceased or refused to act in, every office, capacity, or relationship in which he was described in the registration statement as acting or agreeing to act, and (b) he had advised the Commission and the issuer in writing that he had taken such action and that he would not be responsible for such part of the registration statement; or

(2) that if such part of the registration statement became effective without his knowledge, upon becoming aware of such fact he forthwith acted and advised the Commission, in accordance with paragraph (1) of this subsection, and, in addition, gave reasonable public notice that such part of the registration statement had become effective without his knowledge; or

(3) that (A) as regards any part of the registration statement not purporting to be made on the authority of an expert, and not purporting to be a copy of or extract from a report or valuation of an expert, and not purporting to be made on the authority of a public official document or statement, he had, after reasonable investigation, reasonable ground to believe and did believe, at the time such part of the registration statement became effective, that the statements therein were true and that there was no omission to state a material fact required to be stated therein or necessary to make the statements therein not misleading; and (B) as regards any part of the registration statement purporting to be made upon his authority as an expert or purporting to be a copy of or extract from a report or valuation of himself as an expert, (i) he had, after reasonable investigation, reasonable ground to believe and did believe, at the time such part of the registration statement became effective, that the statements therein were true and that there was no omission to state a material fact required to be stated therein or necessary to make the statements therein not misleading, or (ii) such part of the registration statement did not fairly represent his statement as an expert or was not a fair copy of or extract from his report or valuation as an expert; and (C) as regards any part of the registration statement purporting to be made on the authority of an expert (other than himself) or purporting to be a copy of or extract

from a report or valuation of an expert (other than himself), he had no reasonable ground to believe and did not believe, at the time such part of the registration statement became effective, that the statements therein were untrue or that there was an omission to state a material fact required to be stated therein or necessary to make the statements therein not misleading, or that such part of the registration statement did not fairly represent the statement of the expert or was not a fair copy of or extract from the report or valuation of the expert; and (D) as regards any part of the registration statement purporting to be a statement made by an official person or purporting to be a copy of or extract from a public official document, he had no reasonable ground to believe and did not believe, at the time such part of the registration statement became effective, that the statements therein were untrue, or that there was an omission to state a material fact required to be stated therein or necessary to make the statements therein not misleading, or that such part of the registration statement did not fairly represent the statement made by the official person or was not a fair copy of or extract from the public official document.

(c) Standard of Reasonableness

In determining, for the purpose of paragraph (3) of . . . (b) [above] what constitutes reasonable investigation and reasonable ground for belief, the standard of reasonableness shall be that required of a prudent man in the management of his own property.

(d) Effective Date of Registration Statement with Regard to Underwriters

If any person becomes an underwriter with respect to the security after the part of the registration statement with respect to which his liability is asserted has become effective, then for the purposes of paragraph (3) of . . .

(b) [above] such part of the registration statement shall be considered as having become effective with respect to such person as of the time when he became an underwriter.

(e) Measure of Damages; Undertaking for Payment of Costs

The suit authorized under subsection (a) of this section may be to recover such damages as shall represent the difference between the amount paid for the security (not exceeding the price at which the security was offered to the public) and (1) the value thereof as of the time such suit was brought, or (2) the price at which such security shall have been disposed of in the market before suit, or (3) the price at which such security shall have been disposed of after suit but before judgment if such damages shall be less than the damages representing the difference between the amount paid for the security (not exceeding the price at which the security was offered to the public) and the value thereof as of the time such suit was brought: *Provided*, That if the defendant proves that any portion or all of such damages represents other than the depreciation in value of such security resulting from such part of the registration statement, with respect to which his liability is asserted, not being true or omitting to state a material fact required to be stated therein or necessary to make the statements therein not misleading, such portion of or all such damages shall not be recoverable. In no event shall any underwriter (unless such underwriter shall have knowingly received from the issuer for acting as an underwriter some benefit, directly or indirectly, in which all other underwriters similarly situated did not share in proportion to their respective interests in the underwriting) be liable in any suit or as a consequence of suits authorized under subsection (a) of this section for damages in excess of the total price at which the securities underwritten by him and distributed to the public were offered to the public. In any suit under this or any other section of this subchapter the court may, in its discretion, require an undertaking for the payment of the costs of such suit, including reasonable attorney's fees, and if judgment shall be rendered against a party litigant, upon the motion of the other party litigant, such costs may be assessed in favor of such party litigant (whether or not such undertaking has been required) if the court believes the suit or the defense to have been without merit, in an amount sufficient to reimburse him for the reasonable expenses incurred by him, in connection with such suit, such costs to be taxed in the manner usually provided for taxing of costs in the court in which the suit was heard.

(f) Joint and Several Liability

All or any one or more of the persons specified in . . . (a) [above] shall be jointly and severally liable, and every person who becomes liable to make any payment under this section may recover contribution as in cases of contract from any person who, if sued separately, would have been liable to make the same payment, unless the person who has become liable was, and the other was not, guilty of fraudulent misrepresentation.

(g) Offering Price to Public as Maximum Amount Recoverable

In no case shall the amount recoverable under this section exceed the price at which the security was offered to the public.

Section 12. Civil Liabilities Arising in Connection with Prospectuses and Communication

Any person who—
   (1) offers or sells a security in violation of . . . this [Act], or,
   (2) offers or sells a security (whether or not exempted by the provisions of . . . this [Act] by the use of any means or instruments of transportation or communication in interstate commerce or of the mails, by means of a prospectus or oral communication, which includes an untrue statement of a material fact or omits to state a material fact necessary in order to make the statements, in the light of the circumstances under which they were made, not misleading (the purchaser not knowing of such untruth or omission), and who shall not sustain the burden of proof that he did not know, and in the exercise of reasonable care could not have known, of such untruth or omission, shall be liable to the person purchasing such security from him, who may sue either at law or in equity in any court of competent jurisdiction, to recover the consideration paid for such security with interest thereon, less the amount of any income received thereon, upon the tender of such security, or for damages if he no longer owns the security.

APPENDIX

J

Securities Exchange Act of 1934 (Excerpts)

Section 9. Manipulation of Security Prices

(a) Transactions Relating to Purchase or Sale of Security

It shall be unlawful for any person, directly or indirectly, by the use of the mails or any means or instrumentality of interstate commerce, or of any facility of any national securities exchange, or for any member of a national securities exchange—

(1) For the purpose of creating a false or misleading appearance of active trading in any security registered on a national securities exchange, or a false or misleading appearance with respect to the market for any such security, (A) to effect any transaction in such security which involves no change in the beneficial ownership thereof, or (B) to enter an order or orders for the purchase of such security with the knowledge that an order or orders of substantially the same size, at substantially the same time, and at substantially the same price, for the sale of any such security, has been or will be entered by or for the same or different parties, or (C) to enter any order or orders for the sale of any such security with the knowledge that an order or orders of substantially the same size, at substantially the same time, and at substantially the same price, for the purchase of such security, has been or will be entered by or for the same or different parties.

(2) To effect, alone or with one or more other persons, a series of transactions in any security registered on a national securities exchange creating actual or apparent active trading in such security or raising or depressing the price of such security, for the purpose of inducing the purchase or sale of such security by others.

(3) If a dealer or broker, or other person selling or offering for sale or purchasing or offering to purchase the security, to induce the purchase or sale of any security registered on a national securities exchange by the circulation or dissemination in the ordinary course of business of information to the effect that the price of any such security will or is likely to rise or fall because of market operations of any one or more persons conducted for the purpose of raising or depressing the prices of such security.

(4) If a dealer or broker, or other person selling or offering for sale or purchasing or offering to purchase the security, to make, regarding any security registered on a national securities exchange, for the purpose of inducing the purchase or sale of such security, any statement which was at the time and in the light of the circumstances under which it was made, false or misleading with respect to any material fact, and which he knew or had reasonable ground to believe was so false or misleading.

(5) For a consideration, received directly or indirectly from a dealer or broker, or other person selling or offering for sale or purchasing or offering to purchase the security, to induce the purchase or sale of any security registered on a national securities exchange by the circulation or dissemination of information to the effect that the price of any such security will or is likely to rise or fall because of the market operations of any one or more persons conducted for the purpose of raising or depressing the price of such security.

(6) To effect either alone or with one or more other persons any series of transactions for the purchase and/or sale of any security registered on a national securities exchange for the purpose of pegging, fixing, or stabilizing the price of such security in contravention of such rules and regulations as the Commission

may prescribe as necessary or appropriate in the public interest or for the protection of investors.

(e) Persons Liable; Suits at Law or in Equity

Any person who willfully participates in any act or transaction in violation of . . . this section, shall be liable to any person who shall purchase or sell any security at a price which was affected by such act or transaction, and the person so injured may sue in law or in equity in any court of competent jurisdiction to recover damages sustained as a result of any such act or transaction.

(f) Subsection (a) Not Applicable to Exempted Securities

The provisions of subsection (a) of this section shall not apply to an exempted security.

Section 10. Manipulative and Deceptive Devices

It shall be unlawful for any person, directly or indirectly, by the use of any means or instrumentality of interstate commerce or of the mails, or of any facility of any national securities exchange—

(a) To effect a short sale, or to use or employ any stop-loss order in connection with the purchase or sale, of any security registered on a national securities exchange, in contravention of such rules and regulations as the Commission may prescribe as necessary or appropriate in the public interest or for the protection of investors.

(b) To use or employ, in connection with the purchase or sale of any security registered on a national securities exchange or any security not so registered, any manipulative or deceptive device or contrivance in contravention of such rules and regulations as the Commission may prescribe as necessary or appropriate in the public interest or for the protection of investors.

Glossary

Abatement of a nuisance

Injunctive relief directing that a nuisance be stopped.

Abdication

A legislative body's unconstitutional surrender of its authority to enact law by transferring that authority elsewhere.

Absolute immunity

The doctrine that a nation is completely exempt from suit in the courts of another nation; the exemption of government officials from liability for any wrongful conduct that occurs while they are acting within the scope of their official duties.

Acceptance

The offeree's assent to the terms of the offer.

Accord

Agreement by both parties to a contract that performance different from the performance specified in the contract will terminate the contract.

Acquisition

A situation in which one firm comes into possession of the stock or assets of another firm.

Act of state doctrine

The doctrine that bars the courts of one nation from invalidating governmental or public acts taken by another nation within its own boundaries.

Actual authority

The authority that the principal, expressly or implicitly, intentionally grants or delegates to the agent.

Actual damages

The money awarded by a court to an injured party for the actual financial loss resulting from a breach of contract.

Actus rea

A criminal act.

Ad hoc

A method of proceeding in which the questions posed in lawsuits are decided on a case-by-case basis, with no attention being paid to how those questions were resolved in previous court decisions.

Adjudication

The process by which an administrative agency determines an individual's rights and duties.

Adjustment of debts

A method by which individual debtors with regular income can pay their debts over an extended period of time; partnerships and corporations are not eligible for this type of bankruptcy proceeding.

Administrative agency

A branch of the government that regulates certain types of conduct and/or administers particular government policies.

Administrative hearing

A proceeding of an administrative agency that is similar to a court trial but lacks one or more of its key features.

Affirm

The outcome of an appeal in which the higher court sustains the lower court's judgment.

Affirmative action program

A program that imposes a duty on employers to correct past discrimination by giving preference to minorities and women in the employment process.

Affirmative defense

The allegation of new matter in the defendant's answer that acts as a bar to the plaintiff's recovery.

Agency

The relationship in which one person, called the "agent," is authorized to act for the benefit of and under the control of another person, called the "principal."

Agency shop

A provision in the collective bargaining agreement under which employees who do not join the union are required to pay an amount equivalent to union dues.

Agent

A person who is authorized to act for the benefit of and under the control of another person, called the "principal."

Agreement

A contract that is formed when one party makes an offer that the other party accepts; the language in which parties commit themselves to their obligations under a contract.

Ally doctrine

The doctrine that because of an alliance between a primary and a secondary employer, a striking union is permitted to picket a secondary employer whose employees are doing work that in the absence of a strike would have been done by the strikers.

Analytical jurisprudence

The view that legal principles are to be painstakingly identified and applied.

Ancillary restraint (antitrust policy)

A restraint of trade agreement that is an addition to an underlying legitimate contract.

Answer

A written statement in which the defendant denies or admits each allegation in the plaintiff's complaint.

Anticipatory breach

One party's indication of nonperformance to the other party before the time for performance has arrived. This entitles the nonbreaching party to immediately sue for damages.

Antidumping duty

A duty on imported goods equal to the amount by which their foreign market value exceeds their price in the nation to which they are exported.

Antitrust injury

Damage to business or property resulting from an antitrust violation that injured competition.

Apparent authority

The authority that the principal, by words or acts, has led a third party to reasonably believe the agent possesses even though the agent has no express or implied authority.

Appellant

The party in a lawsuit who makes the appeal.

Appellate court

A court that hears appeals from the judgments of lower courts.

Appellee

The party in a lawsuit against whom the appeal is made.

A priori ethics

Views behavior that satisfies established standards of conduct as ethical.

Arbitration

A process in which an individual or a panel is empowered to impose a binding solution on the parties to a dispute.

Arbitrational due process

The procedures that the law requires be used in the arbitration process to assure the fair treatment of the parties.

Arbitration clause

A contract provision that calls for arbitration of disputes arising under the contract.

Arbitration contract

An agreement to resolve disputes by arbitration.

Articles of incorporation

The legal document, filed with a state official, that establishes the legal existence of a corporation; also referred to as a charter.

Assignee

The party to whom a legal right is transferred.

Assignment

The transfer of a legal right from one party to another party.

Assignor

The party who transfers a legal right to another party.

Association

A collection of persons who voluntarily joined together to achieve a common objective.

Assumption of risk (products liability)

A defense to a charge of negligence in which the defendant shows that the plaintiff knew the risks or defects of a product but nevertheless chose to use it.

Attorney-client privilege

The concept that allows the client to prevent the attorney from testifying concerning matters that the client told the attorney in confidence while seeking legal advice.

Award

An arbitrator's written decision.

Bench trial

A case in which the judge makes the decision.

Beneficial owner (securities)

A person who is treated as the owner of a security because of his or her relationship with the person who has title to the security.

Benefit of the bargain

The right of a party to recover the profits made by a wrongdoer because of his or her misconduct in the purchase or sale of securities.

Beyond a reasonable doubt

The burden of proof required of the prosecution in a criminal trial.

Bicameral

A lawmaking body made up of two distinct groups, each of which is commonly known as a "house."

Bilateral contract

An agreement in which both parties make promises.

Bill

A proposed law that has been presented to a lawmaking body.

Bill of lading

A carrier's receipt for a shipper's goods.

Bill of Rights

The first 10 amendments to the Constitution, which protect the liberties of citizens from actions of the federal government. Through a series of cases, the Supreme Court has interpreted the due process clause of the 14th Amendment to make the protection of the first 10 amendments applicable to actions by state governments.

Blacklist

List of employees involved in union activities that was circulated among employers to prevent these employees from finding new employment in the same trade.

Blue-sky laws

State statutes that regulate securities transactions.

Bona fide occupational qualification

A job-related qualification, reasonably necessary to the normal operation of a particular business, that allows an employer to discriminate with regard to an employee's religion, sex, national origin, or age.

Bond

A document that represents a company debt.

Bondholder

A creditor of a firm who owns a bond issued by the firm.

Bottom-line ethics

The view that behavior is acceptable only if it contributes to a company's profits.

Bribery

Illegally offering or promising to offer anything of value to influence a person's exercise of an official duty or responsibility.

Broker (securities)

A person who buys or sells securities at an investor's request.

Broker-dealer (securities)

A person who solicits investors to purchase securities and executes investors' orders to buy or sell securities.

Bundestag

The elected national assembly of Germany.

Burden of proof

The obligation of a party at a trial to go forward with the evidence and prove the facts alleged.

Business judgment rule

The doctrine holding that the directors and officers of a corporation are not liable for good faith errors in judgment.

Business torts

Wrongful interference with the business rights of others.

By a preponderance of the evidence

The burden of proof required for plaintiffs in a civil trial.

Bylaws

The rules governing the internal affairs of a corporation.

Capacity to contract
The legal ability to enter into a contract.

Cause of action
A set of facts that entitle a person to judicial relief.

Caveat emptor (let the buyer beware)
A principle of law that requires buyers to look after their own interests when engaging in sales transactions and to be aware of defects in the property that they are buying. This principle of law has been weakened by court decisions and statutes.

Certification
A NLRB declaration that a union is the exclusive bargaining representative of the employees in a bargaining unit.

Challenge for cause
The elimination of potential jurors because they may not be impartial.

Change of venue
A change in the geographic location of a trial.

Checks and balances
Constitutional restraints that prevent any branch of the federal government from becoming too powerful by having each branch check and balance the powers of the other two branches.

Chief justice
The term that designates the presiding judge of the U.S. Supreme Court and of the state supreme courts.

Churning
Overtrading by a broker on a client's investment account so as to generate commissions rather than to benefit the client.

Circuit
A division of an area of a state or of the United States where different judges serve.

Civil law
Law rooted in Roman law, such as the law of West European nations.

Civil suits
Lawsuits over private wrongs committed between individuals.

Closed shop
A provision in the collective bargaining agreement that requires the employer to hire individuals who are members of the contracting union.

Code of ethics
A statement of standards of valuable conduct.

Code of Federal Regulations
An annual publication of the federal government that contains current federal agency rules and regulations.

Collective bargaining
The process in which the employer and the union meet at reasonable times and discuss in good faith wages, hours, and other terms and conditions of employment.

Combination (antitrust policy)
A union of independent firms.

Comity
A doctrine that calls for nations to recognize and enforce one another's laws and official actions.

Commerce
The exchange of property or services for money.

Commercial arbitration
Arbitration of a business-related dispute.

Commercial bribery
Offering or promising to offer a company employee something of value in order to influence the exercise of the authority that the company has conferred on the employee.

Commercial impracticability
The doctrine under which nonperformance is excused if unforeseeable events make performance highly impracticable or unreasonably expensive.

Commercial speech
Speech that advertises a product or service for business purposes. Such speech is not given the same degree of protection as other forms of speech.

Common law
Law of England; unwritten or judge-made law.

Common law trademark
An effective unregistered trademark that is acquired by the first firm to employ it.

Communication of the offer
The offeror's transmission of an offer to the offeree by which the offeror indicates an intent to enter into a contractual relationship with the offeree.

Company union
A union established and controlled by an employer.

Comparable worth

The doctrine that requires employers to provide equal pay for work of comparable value.

Comparative negligence

The doctrine under which, in an accident caused by the negligent behavior of both the plaintiff and the defendant, the negligence of the defendant and the negligence of the plaintiff are compared and damages are divided on the basis of their respective percentages of fault.

Competitive injury

A substantial lessening of competition or a tendency toward monopolization that is caused by behavior barred by antitrust law.

Complete performance

The duties that both parties to a contract must perform in full and as agreed in order to discharge their obligations under the contract.

Compulsory arbitration

Arbitration required by a statute.

Concurrent conditions

The requirement that both parties to a contract perform their duties at the same time.

Concurrent jurisdiction

Cases that both the federal and state courts are empowered to hear.

Concurrent sentence

A sentence in which the terms of imprisonment that the court imposes on the defendant for having committed different crimes are served simultaneously.

Concurring opinion

A judge's explanation of why he or she agrees with the decision made by one or more other members of the court.

Condition

A clause in a contract that makes a party's duty to perform contingent on the happening of an event that may or may not occur.

Condition precedent

A future event that must take place before a party is obligated to perform contractual obligations.

Condition subsequent

A future event whose occurrence discharges a duty to perform contractual obligations.

Conflict of laws

The body of legal rules that determine which jurisdiction's law a court should follow to decide the litigants' rights and duties.

Conglomerate merger

A combination of firms that deal in unrelated products or services.

Conscious parallelism (antitrust policy)

The independent decision of firms to behave in the same way as one or more of their competitors.

Consecutive sentences

Sentences in which the terms of imprisonment that the court imposes on the defendant for having committed different crimes are served independently.

Consent judgment

A judgment in a lawsuit that is reached by the parties themselves and has the same effect as a judgment after a trial.

Consequential damages

The money awarded by a court to an injured party for losses that are not the automatic result of a contract breach, but result from special circumstances.

Consideration

Something of value given to the promisor in exchange for the promisor's act or promise; the price that makes a promise legally enforceable.

Conspiracy (antitrust policy)

The joining together of two or more persons to attain an unlawful objective by lawful or unlawful means.

Construct validity

Proof that a test is actually able to measure a psychological trait necessary for a job.

Content validity

Proof that a test samples a real job function.

Contract

A legally enforceable promise or group of promises.

Contract Clause

The clause in the Constitution that prohibits states from passing statutes that unduly interfere with existing contracts.

Contracts in restraint of trade

Contracts that restrict competition.

Contribution

The legal principle that allows a person who has paid a judgment to recover a portion of the amount paid from other persons guilty of the misconduct for which the judgment was awarded.

Contributory negligence

The doctrine under which recovery by the plaintiff is barred if the accident was caused by the negligent behavior of both the plaintiff and the defendant.

Contributory pension plan

A retirement plan that is financed by contributions from both the employer and the employee.

Control person (securities)

A person whose liability under federal securities law is based on his or her power to influence the conduct of a person guilty of securities law violations.

Cooperative association

An association owned by its members and operated for their benefit.

Co-owners

Joint owners of a business, with each owner having a voice in management and a share of the profits.

Copyright

A government grant that gives the copyright holder the exclusive right to control the copying and distribution of a literary or artistic work for the life of the author or creator plus an additional 50 years.

Corporate opportunity

The doctrine that prohibits a corporate officer or director from taking advantage of a business opportunity that belongs to the corporation.

Corporation

An artificial being that is created through a charter granted by a state and has the right to do business in accordance with the terms of its charter. It has a legal existence separate and apart from that of its owners.

Counterclaim

The assertion in the defendant's answer of the defendant's own claim against the plaintiff, asking that the plaintiff be required to pay the defendant money damages.

Countervailing duty

A duty on imported goods that is equal to the amount that the goods are subsidized by a foreign grant or bounty.

Court-annexed arbitration

A form of arbitration that is required as part of a lawsuit.

Court of appeals

A court that hears appeals from the judgments of lower courts.

Court of original jurisdiction

The trial court in which cases are initially brought and tried.

Court of record

A court that is required to keep a record of its proceedings.

Court record

A written account of a court proceeding.

Creditor beneficiary

A creditor who has rights in a contract entered into by the debtor (promisee) and a third party for the express purpose of benefiting the creditor. The creditor beneficiary may recover from either the promisee (debtor) or the third party.

Crime

An offense against society that is prosecuted by the government. The offense involves a breach of a duty owed to society.

Criminal lawsuits

Lawsuits over wrongs committed against the state.

Criterion validity

The existence of a statistical correlation between test performance and job performance.

Cross-elasticity of demand

A situation in which products or services are alike enough to be used in place of one another.

Cross-examination

Questioning by the attorney who did not call the witness.

Cultural relativism

The view that varying standards of conduct among societies must be considered in evaluating behavior.

Cumulative voting

A system of voting in which each share of common stock is entitled to one vote for each director that is to be elected.

Dealer (securities)

A person who offers or buys an issuer's securities or in some other way participates in their distribution.

Decertification

An NLRB declaration that a union is no longer the bargaining representative of the employees in a bargaining unit.

Defamation

False statements made by one person that damage the reputation of another person.

Default judgment

A judgment taken against the defendant if the defendant fails to respond to the plaintiff's complaint.

Defendant

The party who is being sued.

Definite offer

An offer whose terms are clearly stated.

Delegation

The transfer by a legislature, such as Congress, of a portion of its lawmaking power to another body, ordinarily an administrative agency.

Delegation of duties

The act by which a person transfers his or her contractual duties to another person. The person who transfers the duties remains secondarily liable for their performance.

De minimis (antitrust policy)

An act whose effect is insufficient to warrant the law's attention.

De novo

A method of proceeding in which the court pays no attention to prior decisions that relate to the case at hand, dealing with that case as if no governmental body had ever dealt with the case.

Dependent agency

An administrative agency that is lodged within some sector of government.

Deposited acceptance rule

The effectiveness of the acceptance of an offer when sent provided the means of communication are reasonable.

Deposition

The testimony, recorded by a court reporter, that a witness gives out of court under oath and subject to cross-examination.

Derogation of the common law

The purpose of the statute is to change a judge-made rule of law.

Directed verdict

A verdict that the judge tells the jury to render because the evidence presented is so insufficient that a reasonable person could not possibly decide the case for the plaintiff.

Direct examination

Questioning by the attorney who called the witness.

Discharge

An order by a bankruptcy court that releases the debtor from most of his or her debts; the completion of all the obligations of the parties under a contract.

Disclosed principal

Contracting between the agent and a third party in which the third party knows of the agency relationship and the identity of the principal.

Disclose or abstain (securities)

The requirement that an insider who has material non-public information about a firm may not trade in the firm's securities without first publicly disclosing that information.

Discrimination against interstate commerce

The doctrine that state laws unreasonably favoring intrastate business activity over interstate business activity are invalid.

Disparagement of reputation

Communication of false statements about the business practices of a person or a company that tends to damage the person or company in the eyes of the public.

Disparate impact

A situation in which seemingly neutral employment criteria impair the employment opportunities of a protected group.

Disparate treatment

Intentional discrimination by an employer against an employee or a potential employee based on race, sex, religion, or national origin.

Distributive jurisprudence

Views law as a means for controlling the distribution of wealth.

Diversity of citizenship cases

Cases in which the plaintiff and the defendant are

citizens of different states and the amount of damages claimed in good faith is over $50,000.

Documentary sale

A sale in which the transfer of ownership of goods and the payment of the sales price are effected through the use of documents designed to protect the seller's and buyer's interests.

Document of title

A receipt for goods that confers their ownership on whoever owns the instrument.

Domestic relations court

A court that hears family matters such as divorce and custody proceedings.

Donee beneficiary

A person who, because the promisee intends to provide that person with a gift, benefits from a contract set up and performed by others.

Draft (of a bill)

The initial form of a proposed law.

Dual sovereignty

Rule by two types of government.

Economic power (to force a tying agreement)

The seller's dominance in the market for the tying product. This enables the seller to compel a buyer of the tying product to buy a tied product.

Economic strike

A work stoppage to obtain financial concessions from an employer.

Effective registration statement (securities law)

A registration statement that is in force, so that the securities covered by the registration statement may be offered for sale or sold in the same manner in which securities are commonly offered for sale or sold under federal securities law.

Egalitarian jurisprudence

A legal philosophy that advocates the use of legal principles that treat people alike unless there is a legitimate reason not to do so.

Embezzlement

The wrongful deprivation of another's property by a person entrusted with authority to handle or manage it.

Eminent domain

The government's power to take private property for public use by paying the property owner a fair price. Property owners are protected by this clause of the Fifth

Amendment to the Constitution: "nor shall private property be taken for public use, without just compensation."

Employment at will doctrine

The doctrine under which the employee is hired for an indefinite amount of time and either the employer or the employee can terminate the employment at any time for any reason or for no reason.

Environmental impact statement

A report that specifies the effects of a proposed action on the environment.

Equal protection clause

The clause in the 14th Amendment to the Constitution that prevents state laws from establishing unreasonable classifications (categories) of persons to justify treating persons unfairly.

Equitable remedy

A legal action in which a court of equity uses its power to serve justice because the legal remedy of damages is not sufficient to fully compensate the injured party.

Equity security

An instrument that represents an ownership interest in a firm.

Escape clauses

Provisions in the General Agreement on Tariffs and Trade (GATT) that allow a GATT member to impose an antidumping duty and/or a countervailing duty on imports from another GATT member under certain circumstances.

Establishment clause

A clause in the First Amendment to the Constitution that prohibits the government from establishing a state-supported church or an official state religion.

Estoppel

A legal bar to alleging or denying a fact because of one's previous statements or actions to the contrary where another person's position has materially changed to that person's detriment because he or she relied on the statements or actions.

Ethics

Standards of worthy behavior.

Ethical egoism

Views behavior motivated by self-interest as ethical.

Ethical relativism

Views conduct anticipated by other group members as ethical.

Ethics of fairness
Views upright behavior as ethical.

Evidentiary hearing
A proceeding of an administrative agency that closely resembles a court trial.

Exchange (securities)
An association whose members engage in securities transactions with one another.

Executive order
A presidential order that has the force of law.

Executive power
The authority of a government official or agency to enforce the law.

Exempt securities
Securities excluded from the federal securities law registration and prospectus requirements.

Exempt transaction (securities)
A method of selling securities that excludes them from the federal securities law registration and prospectus requirements.

Exhaustion of administrative remedies
The requirement that before seeking judicial relief to correct an error supposedly made by an administrative agency, the affected party must make complete use of all the agency procedures available to correct the error.

Existentialist jurisprudence
A legal philosophy that favors the adoption and utilization of legal standards that serve the interests of otherwise helpless persons.

Ex parte contact
The decision-maker's communication with one party to a judicial or quasi-judicial proceeding in the absence of the other party.

Ex parte hearing
A hearing at which one of the parties to a judicial, quasi-judicial, or arbitration proceeding offers evidence to the decision maker in the absence of the other party.

Expectancy ethics
Views action that satisfies commonly held expectations as ethical.

Experience rating
The employer's record of layoffs, a factor in determining the amount of the employer's unemployment compensation taxes.

Expert witness
A witness who has specialized knowledge in a particular field.

Express contract
An agreement whose intentions and terms are stated in clear, definite, and explicit words, either orally or in writing.

Express warranty
The guarantee created by a seller's factual statement or promise concerning an item.

External dependencies
Persons who do business with a firm or are in some way affected by what it does.

Extradition
The process by which a state or country voluntarily turns the criminal defendant over to the requesting state or country for trial.

Fact finder
Determines what did or did not occur.

Fairness jurisprudence
Views the purpose of legal standards as the promotion of decent behavior.

Featherbedding
The hiring of more workers than are actually needed to perform a task.

Federal question cases
Cases based on the U.S. Constitution, a federal law, or a treaty of the United States.

Federal Register
A daily journal published by the federal government that reports federal agency processes, actions, and decisions.

Felony
A serious crime whose maximum punishment is death or confinement for more than one year in a federal or state prison.

Fiduciary duty of loyalty
The obligation that arises from being entrusted to act for the benefit of another; the undivided loyalty that directors and officers owe to the corporation.

Finality
The completion of an agency's involvement in a proceeding.

Firm offer

A merchant's written offer to buy or sell goods in which it is stated that the offer will be held open for a specified period of time. The offer becomes irrevocable for the time specified up to a maximum of three months.

Fixed schedule

A schedule listing the amount of compensation to be paid to workers for particular losses or disabilities.

Forcing power (antitrust policy)

The ability of a seller to coerce a buyer to purchase unwanted goods or services.

Foreign commerce

Trade with foreign nations consisting of imports and exports.

Formal rulemaking

A structured, exacting method used by an administrative agency to create rules or regulations.

Form 8-K

A report that a firm with registered securities must file with the SEC within 10 days after certain types of unusual events have taken place.

Form 10-K

An annual report that a firm with registered securities must file with the SEC.

Form 10-Q

A quarterly report form that a firm with registered securities must file with the SEC.

Forum

The place where a lawsuit is brought.

Forum non conveniens

The principle under which a court declines to hear a lawsuit because it finds that justice requires that the suit be tried in an alternative jurisdiction.

Four-fifths rule

The rule that an employment test has an adverse impact if its selection rate for one race, sex, religion, or national origin is less than four fifths of its selection rate for the majority group.

Franchisee

A firm that is licensed to use a franchisor's trade name, trademark, or service mark.

Franchising

Granting an individual or a group (the franchisee) the right to market the products or services of another firm (the franchisor).

Franchisor

A firm that authorizes another firm to use its trade name, trademark, or service mark.

Fraud

The intentional misrepresentation of a material fact that causes a party to enter into a transaction and thereby suffer a monetary loss.

Freedom of religion clause

A clause in the First Amendment of the Constitution that limits the power of Congress to advance or inhibit any religion. The purpose of this clause is to separate church and state.

Freedom of speech clause

A clause in the First Amendment to the Constitution that limits the power of Congress to prohibit the free expression of ideas.

Free exercise clause

A clause in the First Amendment to the Constitution that prohibits governmental interference with the practices of any religion unless the practices are injurious to the members of the religion or others.

Full Faith and Credit Clause

The clause in the Constitution that requires the courts in one state to recognize and enforce the final judgments of the courts in other states.

Full warranty

A warranty that must meet certain requirements set by federal law.

Functional discount (antitrust policy)

A discount that is granted to buyers in return for the services they provide in the seller's marketing process.

Garnishment

A judge's order that allows the plaintiff to satisfy a judgment by reaching the defendant's wages, bank accounts, or accounts receivable.

General intent (antitrust policy)

The aim of performing a particular act.

General trial court

A court of general jurisdiction that has the power to hear most types of cases.

Good faith bargaining

A duty of the employer and the union to meet at reasonable times and in good faith with respect to wages, hours, and other conditions of employment.

Good faith defense (antitrust policy)

An excuse for engaging in a discriminatory selling practice.

Goods

Tangible property that is movable.

Grease payment

A payment that is made to hasten or assure the performance of routine governmental action.

Grievance procedure

An orderly way of handling complaints by union workers.

Group boycott (antitrust policy)

An agreement between manufacturers, between a manufacturer and a distributor, or between a manufacturer and retailers not to deal with a particular retailer.

Guaranty contract

A third party's promise to fulfill the obligation of an original party to the contract if the original party fails to perform.

Hired judge

A person, usually knowledgeable in law, whom the parties to a dispute pay to rule on their claims.

Historical jurisprudence

The view that standards of lawful behavior embody the will or spirit of a people.

Holder in due course rule

A holder in due course is more likely than any assignee to collect payment on an instrument since he or she takes it free of most defenses.

Horizontal merger

A combination of firms engaged in the same type of business.

Horizontal price-fixing

An agreement between competitors on the price they will charge for their goods or services.

Hot cargo contract

An illegal agreement between an employer and a union in which the employer promises not to do business with certain persons or businesses.

House counsel

An attorney who is a full-time company employee.

Illegal contract

A contract whose formation calls for the performance of an illegal act.

Illegal per se (antitrust policy)

A restraint of trade that is always unlawful.

Illegal strike

A work stoppage that is conducted for an unlawful purpose or that uses unlawful means to accomplish a lawful purpose.

Impeach

Demonstrating that a witness at trial is untruthful.

Implied contract

An agreement whose intentions and terms are indicated by the actions of the parties and the surrounding circumstances.

Incidental beneficiary

A person who benefits indirectly or accidentally from a contract set up and performed by others. The incidental beneficiary has no right to sue under the contract for nonperformance.

Indemnification (principal-agent)

Reimbursement for losses to agent sustained while following the principal's instructions when the agent is not at fault.

Independent agency

A regulatory and/or administrative body that is separate from any other unit of government.

Independent contractor

A person who contracts to do a piece of work for a fixed fee in accordance with his or her own judgment and methods.

Indorsed negotiable bill of lading

A negotiable bill of lading that has the signature of the person authorized by the bill to determine who is to receive the goods identified in the bill.

Indorsement (bill of lading)

The signature of the person authorized by a negotiable bill of lading to determine who is to receive the goods identified in the bill.

Informal rulemaking

A loose, unexacting method used by an administrative agency to create rules or regulations.

Initial decision

The ruling of the administrative law judge in an adjudication.

Initial level (securities)

The maximum amount of credit that federal law allows to be used to finance a securities transaction.

Injunction

A court order commanding a person to do a specific act or to refrain from doing a specific act that threatens irreparable harm to others.

In personam jurisdiction

Jurisdiction over the defendant that is obtained by arrest in a criminal suit and by service of process in a civil suit.

In rem jurisdiction

Jurisdiction of the court over the property that is the subject of the dispute.

Insider (securities)

A party whose position in a firm or relationship with a firm affords lawful access to material nonpublic information about the firm.

Insolvency

In bankruptcy, the financial condition of a debtor whose debts are greater than the fair market value of his or her assets.

Inspection certificate (documentary sale)

A document that verifies the actual quality and quantity of goods available for delivery under a bill of lading.

Instructions

The directions that the judge gives the jury about the rules of law it is to apply to the facts of the case.

Intent to contract

A state of mind that is measured by the conduct of the parties, using the objective standard of whether a reasonable person would be justified in believing that a contract has been made.

Interlocking directorate

A situation in which an individual simultaneously serves as a director of two or more corporations.

Internal dependencies

A firm's officers and employees.

Interpretative rule

An agency rule that contains the agency's definition of a statutory term or provision.

Interrogatories

Written questions that one party in a lawsuit sends to the other party to obtain sworn written answers.

Interstate commerce

Business activity that takes place in or affects more than one state.

Intrastate commerce

Business activity that is confined to a single state.

Intrastate offering (securities)

An offering to sell securities that is made solely to residents of the state in which a firm is located and does substantially all of its business, with substantially all of the proceeds of the sale to be used locally.

Introduction of a bill

The submission of a proposed statute for consideration by a legislative body.

Intuitive ethics

Uses personal perceptions of right and wrong in deciding whether behavior is ethical.

Investment adviser

A person who is engaged in the business of offering investment advice.

Investment contract

An agreement that represents ownership in a firm or an understanding regarding a firm's indebtedness.

Irrevocable letter of credit

A letter of credit that cannot be invalidated by the issuer.

Issuer (securities)

A firm that distributes an instrument representing ownership in the firm or a debt of the firm.

Joint venture

A business association created for a limited purpose or a single transaction.

Judgment

The final decision that a trial court gives when a dispute in that court has terminated.

Judgment notwithstanding the verdict

A judgment rendered after the verdict that sets aside the jury's decision in favor of the other party.

Judicial activist

A judge who is not unwilling, when this is called for, to abandon precedent and create new law.

Judicial legislation

The creation of legal principles by courts.

Judicial review

A court's examination and assessment of the legality of the action taken by an administrative agency; the power of the judiciary to declare acts of the legislative and executive branches unconstitutional.

Judicial self-restraint

The reluctance of judges to initiate changes in the law.

Jurisdiction
The authority of a court to hear a case.

Justices
The term that designates judges of the U.S. Supreme Court and of the state supreme courts.

Justifiable reliance
The reasonable belief of an injured party that a misrepresentation is true.

Kieretsu
An alliance of Japanese firms.

Know thy customer rule (securities)
The requirement that brokers and dealers have sufficient information about a customer's status before offering the customer investment advice.

Labor arbitration
Arbitration of a dispute between an employer and a union or an employee who is represented by a union.

Larceny
The taking of another's property with the intent to deprive the owner of it.

Lay witness
A witness who does not qualify as an expert witness.

Legal detriment
In exchange for the promisor's promise, the doing or promising to do that which one has no legal obligation to do or the refraining from doing or promising to refrain from doing that which one has a legal right to do.

Legal impossibility
The doctrine under which a promisor's contractual duties are discharged because circumstances have made it impossible for the promisor to fulfill them.

Legal philosophy
A view of law.

Legislative committee
A group of legislators who have been chosen to evaluate proposed laws.

Legislative history
The circumstances in which a statute was enacted.

Letter of comment (securities)
A formal statement of the SEC's objections to a registration statement.

Letter of credit
A document in which a promisor (the issuer) agrees to

make payment to a creditor to satisfy a debtor's obligation.

Libel
A defamation that is communicated in writing; published words or pictures, representations to the eye, that injure a person's reputation or character.

Liberal construction
Loose definition of a term in a statute.

Limited partnership
A partnership in which the liability of some partners is limited to the capital they contributed. These limited partners do not take part in the management of the business.

Limited warranty
A warranty that fails to meet any of the requirements of a full warranty.

Liquidated damages
A specified amount of damages that is payable in the event of a breach of contract.

Listed security
A security that may be regularly bought or sold through a particular exchange.

Lockout
The closing of a business by an employer to bring economic pressure on its employees.

Long-arm statute
A state statute that allows service of process beyond the borders of the state, provided the defendant has sufficient minimum contacts with the forum state to satisfy due process requirements.

Majority opinion
Presents the position taken by most of the court's judges.

Margin (securities)
The use of a loan to finance part of the cost of a securities purchase.

Market analysis (antitrust law)
An examination of market share to determine whether there is competitive injury.

Markup (of a bill)
The process of wording a bill in its final form.

Material breach
A substantial breach by one party to a contract that permits the other party to suspend the performance of its obligations under the contract.

Material fact

An act or event that induces a party to enter into a contract.

Material misstatement (securities)

A misrepresentation or omission of fact that renders a registration statement false.

Mediation

A process in which a third party's help is used to resolve a dispute.

Memorandum

An informal record or account.

Mens rea

A criminal intent.

Mercantilism

The view that a nation should enjoy a net gain from its trade with other nations.

Merchant

A professional businessperson who deals in the class of goods involved in a transaction.

Merger

A combination of two or more firms.

Minitrial

A privately sponsored hearing that resembles a court trial.

Minor court

A court of limited jurisdiction.

Minority opinion

Presents the position taken by the judge or judges who disagree with most of the court's members.

Misdemeanor

A crime less serious than a felony whose maximum punishment is usually a fine or confinement for no more than one year in a local jail.

Misrepresentation

The innocent misstatement of a material fact or a manifestation of an untrue material fact by conduct that causes a party to enter into a contract and thereby suffer a monetary loss.

Misuse (products liability)

A defense in which the defendant shows that the plaintiff deliberately used a product in a manner neither intended nor foreseeable by the manufacturer.

Mixed motive case

A situation in which employment decisions are based on both nondiscriminatory and discriminatory reasons.

Mock jury trial

A "trial" in which a number of persons listen to the disputants' claims and behave as if they were jurors in an actual lawsuit.

Modification of sales contracts rule

A UCC rule under which changes in the terms of sales contracts are enforceable without consideration.

Monopoly (antitrust policy)

The power of a firm to control the price of a product or service or to exclude competitors from the market for a product or service.

Most favored nation

A nation whose goods are subject to import duties no greater than the lowest duties placed on imports from other nations.

Naked restraint (antitrust policy)

A restraint whose sole purpose is to eliminate competition.

Natural law

The view that laws exist that are paramount to any of the laws made by humankind.

Negligence

The failure to exercise the degree of reasonable care that a person of ordinary prudence would employ.

Negligence per se

Negligence as a matter of law; usually occurs because the defendant has violated a law.

Negotiable bill of lading

A bill of lading that requires the carrier to deliver goods as ordered by the owner of the instrument.

Negotiation

A give-and-take process in which the parties to a controversy resolve their dispute by themselves.

Noise (environment)

An unwanted sound.

Nolo contendere **plea** (antitrust policy)

A plea in which a defendant accused of a violation of the Sherman Act does not contest the criminal charge but pleads neither guilty nor not guilty.

Nominal damages

A very small award of damages, such as $1, where a technical breach of a contract has occurred but no actual loss has been suffered.

Noncontributory pension plan

A retirement plan that is financed solely by contributions from the employer.

Nondischargeable debt

A type of debt for which the debtor continues to be liable after bankruptcy.

Novation

The substitution of a new contract for an old one by mutual agreement.

Nuisance law

Legal principles concerning the misuse of one's land.

Obiter dictum

A legal principle, mentioned in a past court decision, that had no bearing on the issues before the court or the outcome of the case.

Obligor

A party to a contract who owes a duty to another party to the contract.

Occupational disease

A job-related disease caused by exposure to harmful conditions that are present to a greater extent in a particular job than in jobs generally.

Offer

A proposal in which one party (the offeror) promises to give something in return for a promise or act by the other party (the offeree).

Official notice

The authority of the decision maker in a quasi-judicial proceeding of an administrative agency to treat something not beyond reasonable doubt as true, despite the absence of evidence, because it is commonly believed to be true and to take it into account in arriving at a judgment.

Ombudsperson

An individual whose job is to informally facilitate the resolution of disputes that ordinarily involve challenges to the actions of government or company officials.

Opening statement

A statement in which an attorney gives a preview of the case and of the type of evidence that the attorney plans to introduce.

Operational franchise

A franchise in which the franchisor is granted extensive power over how the franchisee conducts its business.

Opinion

A judge's explanation of why the court decided a lawsuit in the manner that it did.

Opinion of the court

The opinion of most of the judges.

Option contract

An agreement in which one party gives something of value to the other party to hold the offer open for a stated period of time, thereby making the offer irrevocable.

Order

A directive that an administrative agency issues at the end of an adjudication in which the agency states its decision and specifies the action it requires.

Order for relief

A ruling by a bankruptcy court that requires selling the debtor's assets, paying off the creditors, and discharging the debtor from legal liability for his or her debts.

Ordinance

A written standard of legal or illegal behavior established by a local unit of government whose function is to enact law.

Out-of-pocket loss

The difference between the value of securities and what the buyer or seller paid or received for them.

Over-the-counter market

An informal means used by brokers and dealers to trade securities.

Parens patriae action (antitrust policy)

A lawsuit brought by the attorney general of a state on behalf of the state's citizens.

Parliament

The legislative body that makes England's statutory law.

Parol evidence rule

The rule that a written contract cannot be changed by evidence of prior or concurrent oral agreements.

Partnership

An association of two or more persons to carry on as co-owners of a business for profit.

Past consideration

The doctrine that the promise of something that has already been given is not consideration.

Patent

A government grant that gives an inventor the exclusive right to manufacture, use, and sell an invention for 17 years.

Patent infringement

The use or sale of a patented invention without authorization from the patent holder during the term of the patent.

Per curiam

A court opinion for which no judge is identified as the author.

Peremptory challenge

The elimination of prospective jurors without giving a cause.

Permanent injunction

A court directive that prohibits a party from ever engaging in specified conduct.

Personal injury (price discrimination)

The damages suffered by a buyer as a result of a seller's unlawful discriminatory behavior.

Personal jurisdiction

The power of the court over the person of the plaintiff and the defendant.

Personal property

Property that can be moved from place to place.

Personal service

A form of service of process in which the summons is personally handed to the defendant.

Petition to confirm an award

A request that a court convert an arbitrator's award into a judgment.

Petty offense

A minor violation of the law (such as speeding or illegal parking) whose primary punishment is a fine.

Philosophy

A point of view on a particular subject.

Plaintiff

The party who initiates a lawsuit.

Pleadings

The initial written statements that the parties to a civil suit present to the trial court; create the basic issues of the dispute.

Pocket veto

The president's failure to sign a bill; treated in the same way as the president's express rejection of a bill through a veto.

Police power

The power of the state or local government to enact laws that protect the health, safety, morals, or general welfare of its citizens.

Political action committee

An association that channels money to elect particular persons to public office.

Political question doctrine

The doctrine that the U.S. Supreme Court will not review the constitutionality of political matters.

Positivist jurisprudence

A legal philosophy that views law as a body of commands that courts are to use in arriving at decisions.

Pragmatic ethics

Views behavior that produces desired results as ethical.

Pragmatic jurisprudence

A legal philosophy that views law as made up of rules and decisions that courts should use to arrive at workable results.

Preamble

An introductory statement found at the beginning of a statute.

Precedent

Prior court decisions that are relevant to the case now before the court.

Predatory intent

The intent to destroy competition.

Predatory pricing

The setting of prices so as to destroy competitors and thereafter earn more than normal profits.

Preemption doctrine

The doctrine that the states may not pass laws conflicting with the laws passed by Congress in the same subject area.

Preexisting duty rule

The rule that promising to do that which one already has a legal duty to do is not consideration.

Preorganization certificate (securities)

A document that a promoter issues to an investor.

Pretrial conference

A meeting of the opposing attorneys and the judge to determine what issues and facts of the case are still in controversy.

Preventive ethics

Views action taken to shield others from harm as ethical.

Prima facie case (price discrimination)

A case in which misconduct is presumed because a seller has charged different customers different prices for the same product.

Prima facie evidence (antitrust policy)

An admission of guilt or a finding of guilt of an antitrust violation in a prior proceeding brought by the United States on the basis of which the defendant is presumed guilty of such a violation in a later civil antitrust suit brought by a private party.

Primary boycott

A union's use of a strike, picketing, or other pressure against an employer with which the union has a dispute.

Primary jurisdiction

The doctrine that a party's claim must be dealt with by the appropriate administrative agency before it may come before a court.

Primary liability

The liability of the party to the contract who is absolutely required to perform.

Primary promise

A third party's promise to fulfill the obligation of an original party to the contract whether or not that party performs.

Principal

A person who hires another person, called the "agent," to act for him or her.

Prior restraint of speech

The prohibition of speech by the government before it has been seen or heard.

Private label (antitrust policy)

A distinct label used to distinguish the seller's goods from like goods made by the same manufacturer and sold by others.

Private nuisance

A landowner's use of property that substantially and unreasonably harms one or more persons.

Private offering (securities)

An offer to sell securities that is made only to persons who meet certain federally set qualifications.

Private placement (securities)

An offer to sell securities that is extended only to certain persons.

Privilege

The concept that allows a witness to refuse to testify or allows a person to prevent a witness from testifying.

Privileges and Immunities Clause

The clause in the Constitution that prevents a state from denying the citizens of other states the basic rights that it extends to its own citizens.

Privity (securities)

A transaction in which the issuer and the investor deal directly with each other.

Privity of contract

Those persons who are the actual parties to a contract.

Probate court

A court that hears disputes over the validity of wills, administers estates, and oversees the distribution of the assets of deceased persons.

Procedural due process

The requirement, based on the due process clauses of the 5th and 14th Amendments, that governmental proceedings affecting life, liberty, or property be fair and not arbitrary.

Procedural law

Rules of law that the parties to a lawsuit must follow to enforce their rights and to protect themselves from uncalled for liability.

Procedural rule

An operational standard established by an agency that specifies how the agency is to perform its tasks.

Product extension merger

A combination of firms whose products complement each other.

Product franchise

A franchise in which the franchisee sells products or offers services identified as those of the franchisor.

Products liability

The liability of the manufacturer and seller for injuries caused by defective products.

Promissory estoppel

The doctrine that an offer that the offeror reasonably expects the offeree to rely upon becomes irrevocable for a reasonable period of time; the doctrine that a promise is enforceable without consideration if the promisee reasonably relied on the promise and injustice can be avoided only by enforcing the promise.

Promoter

The individual or legal entity that plays a part in the creation and capitalization of a firm and does the legal groundwork for incorporation.

Promulgate

An administrative agency's adoption of a rule or regulation that establishes a standard of required conduct.

Prospectus (securities)

A document delivered to investors that contains a condensation of information found in a registration statement.

Proxy

A written authorization directing the person holding it to vote the shares of the named shareholder; also the person with the authority to vote the shares.

Proxy statement

A written explanation, including relevant material information, of the purposes for which a solicited proxy will be used.

Psychological realism

Views action in one's best interest as ethical if it is acceptable to other group members.

Public issue management

A firm's involvement with interest groups that favor the promotion, modification, or defeat of proposed public programs.

Public nuisance

The repeated or continuous misuse of land to the substantial detriment of the public at large.

Public offering

An offer to sell securities that is extended to the public at large.

Public policy

Conduct that is currently considered in the best interest of society.

Punitive damages

Compensation in excess of actual damages that serves as a punishment in tort law; not usually available in contracts cases.

Qualified immunity

The exemption of government officials under certain circumstances from legal liability for wrongful conduct that occurs while they are acting within the scope of their official duties.

Qualified privilege (employer-employee)

The right of a former employer to give another employer information about an employee's work habits and abilities. Even if the information given is incorrect, no suit may be brought unless malice is shown.

Quasi contract

An agreement created by the courts to offset the unjust enrichment of one party at the expense of the other party; also called an "implied-in-law contract."

Quorum

The number of shareholders' votes required to be present to transact business at a shareholders' meeting.

Ratification

Subsequent approval by the principal of an agent's act that was unauthorized when the agent committed it.

Rational basis review

A test used by courts to determine whether state or federal laws violate equal protection under the U.S. Constitution by creating unreasonable classifications; specifically, to determine whether they satisfy the requirement that the classifications in state and federal laws be reasonably related to a legitimate governmental objective.

Reasonable person

An imaginary person who views the facts of a particular situation.

Reciprocity (antitrust policy)

A situation in which a firm buys the products or services it needs from the firms to which it sells its own products or services.

Reciprocity doctrine (foreign nations)

The doctrine that a court should enforce the judgments of courts in another country only if courts in that country will enforce its judgments.

Recusal

A judge's refusal to take part in a judicial or quasi-judicial proceeding.

Red herring prospectus

A document that may be used to offer securities for sale (in lieu of the usual prospectus) during the waiting period, that is, between the time when a registration statement is filed as required by federal securities law and the time when the registration statement takes effect.

Registered security

A security that must be registered with the SEC or for which a registration statement must be filed with the SEC.

Registration statement

A document (containing extensive information about a firm) that must be filed with the SEC before that firm may sell or offer to sell its securities.

Remedial statute

A law that is intended to improve upon a legal principle that it replaces.

Reply

A pleading by the plaintiff in response to the defendant's answer that specifically admits or denies each allegation of fact in that answer.

Request for admissions

Written request served on one party by the other party asking that party to admit the truth of certain disputed matters of fact or the genuineness of a relevant document.

Resale price maintenance

An arrangement between a manufacturer and a retailer that sets the resale price of the manufacturer's goods.

Res ipsa loquitur

A situation in which it is obvious that an accident could not have occurred unless the defendant was negligent; literally, "the thing speaks for itself."

Respondeat superior

The doctrine that the principal is liable for the wrongful acts that the agent committed within the scope of his or her employment.

Restraint (antitrust policy)

An independent business unit's surrender of its freedom to do business as it pleases.

Restrictive covenant

An agreement in which one party agrees not to compete with the other party within a designated geographic area for a set period of time.

Restrictive immunity (foreign nations)

The doctrine that a nation is exempt from suit in the courts of another nation only for its public or governmental acts.

Reverse

The outcome of an appeal in which the higher court sets aside the lower court's judgment and enters its own.

Reverse and remand

The outcome of an appeal in which the higher court sets aside the lower court's judgment and sends the case back for a new trial.

Revocable letter of credit

A letter of credit that can be canceled at the issuer's discretion.

Revocation of the offer

The offeror's cancellation of the legal effect of an offer.

Right-to-work laws

State laws that prohibit union shop and agency shop agreements.

Ripe for review

The doctrine that an agency must rule on the legal issues in question before a court will consider them to spare distress to the affected party.

Royalty

A franchisee's periodic payment to a franchisor.

Rule (administrative law)

A standard of conduct set by an agency through the exercise of its power to legislate.

Rulemaking

The process by which an agency establishes a standard of behavior.

Rule of reason (antitrust policy)

A restraint of trade that is evaluated on a case-by-case basis to decide whether its effect on competition makes it illegal.

Satisfaction

The actual substitution of a performance different from the performance that terminated the obligations under the original contract.

Scabs

Workers hired to replace workers on strike.

Scalping (securities)

An investment adviser's failure to inform a client that the adviser stands to profit should the client follow the offered advice.

School of jurisprudence

A particular view of law.

Scienter (securities)

The performance of an act with the intent to deceive or with reckless disregard of whether anyone would be deceived.

Scope of employment

The time in which the employee was furthering the employer's interest.

Secondary boycott

A union's use of a strike, picketing, or other pressure against an employer that deals with the employer with which the union has a dispute.

Secondary liability

The liability of the party to the contract who is required to perform only if the party with primary liability fails to perform.

Secondary meaning

The public's association of a trademark with a particular manufacturer and with the quality of a product.

Security

An instrument that contains the agreement between an investor and a firm.

Seller's exemption

A state statute exempting retailers, wholesalers, and other nonmanufacturer dealers from strict liability on the products they handle.

Seniority system

A set of rules that bases many personnel decisions on the length of time that employees have worked for an employer.

Service mark

Artwork, symbol, or design intended to identify the services provided by a company as well as the company.

Service of process

The communication of a summons to a defendant, usually with a copy of the complaint.

Sex-plus discrimination

The unequal treatment of employees on the basis of sex plus a supposedly neutral requirement.

Sexual harassment

Unwelcome sexual advances, requests for sexual favors, and other verbal and physical conduct of a sexual nature.

Shelf registration (securities)

A procedure that eliminates the waiting period after the filing of a registration statement with the SEC.

Short-swing profit (securities)

Profit earned by beneficial owners of more than 10% of any class of registered nonexempt equity securities, as well as an issuer's directors and officers due to trades in a firm's equity securites in which both the purchase and sale (or sale and purchase) of the securities are completed in less than six months.

Silence of the offeree

Not an acceptance of the offer unless there is a duty to speak.

Situation ethics

Considers circumstances in determining whether one's conduct is ethical.

Slander

A defamation that is communicated orally; gestures or spoken words, representations to the ear, that injure a person's reputation or character.

Small claims court

A court that handles cases involving small amounts of money and is conducted with less formality than other courts.

Social audit

A procedure used to identify and report on a firm's contributions to society.

Social engineering

The view that law is a means of promoting selected social goals.

Sociological jurisprudence

The view that legal principles should reflect and promote contemporary needs and values.

Sole proprietorship

A business owned and operated by one person; the simplest form of business ownership.

Sovereign immunity

The doctrine that a nation is excused from having to answer for its actions in the courts of another nation; the exemption of the federal government and state governments from legal liability for any harm they may cause.

Special intent (antitrust policy)

The aim of performing an act so as to attain a particular result.

Specific performance

A court order requiring the party who breached a contract to do precisely what he or she promised to do under the contract; granted when the unique subject matter of a contract makes an award of money damages an inadequate remedy.

Standing

The personal effects that give an individual the right to seek relief in a judicial or quasi-judicial proceeding.

Stare decisis

The principle that a court should follow the law established in prior court decisions in that jurisdiction.

Statute

A written standard of legal or illegal behavior established by a body that has been specifically assigned the task of making law, such as Congress or a state legislature.

Statute of frauds

A statute providing that certain types of contracts will not be enforceable unless they are in writing.

Statute of limitations

A state or federal law limiting the time in which a lawsuit on a claim may be brought. After the expiration of that time, no lawsuit on the claim may be brought.

Statute of repose

A state statute limiting the time in which a plaintiff may bring a products liability lawsuit.

Statutory construction

The process by which a court arrives at the meaning of a provision in a statute.

Statutory law

Legal rules established by a body especially chosen to formally do so.

Stipulation of settlement

A written statement of a compromise agreed upon by the parties to a lawsuit.

Stop order (securities)

An SEC action that prevents a registration statement from becoming effective.

Straight bill

A bill of lading that identifies the person to whom the carrier should deliver shipped goods.

Strict constructionist

A judge who narrowly interprets the wording of the Constitution and closely follows past court decisions as to the meaning of its provisions.

Strict scrutiny review

A test used by courts to determine whether state or federal laws violate equal protection under the U.S. Constitution by creating unreasonable classifications; specifically, to determine whether they satisfy the requirement that the classifications in state and federal laws based on a fundamental constitutional right or that a suspect class be necessary to promote some compelling governmental purpose.

Strict statutory construction

Narrowly defining a term in a statute.

Substantial evidence in the record

The presentation before an administrative agency of sufficient proof for a reasonable person to reach the same conclusion as that reached by the agency.

Substantial performance

Less than perfect performance that conforms to the contract in all major aspects. Given substantial performance, the promisor can recover the contract price less any damage suffered by the promisee due to defective performance.

Substantive due process

The requirement, based on the due process clauses of the 5th and 14th amendments of the Constitution, that the provisions of the laws enacted by the federal government and state governments be fair and not arbitrary.

Substantive law

Rules of law that courts use to decide the parties' rights and duties.

Substantive rule

An agency rule that expands on the terms or provisions of a statute.

Substituted service

The form of service of process in which the summons is handed to a member of the defendant's household who is above a specified age, with a copy of the summons usually being mailed to the defendant's home.

Suitability (securities)

The requirement that a broker's recommendation to a client on the purchase or sale of a security be suitable for that client.

Summary judgment

A motion to dismiss a case prior to trial on the basis that no genuine issue of fact exists.

Summons

A notice to the defendant to appear in court and answer the plaintiff's allegations within a certain time or risk losing the case by default.

Sunday laws

Statutes that prohibit the formation or performance of certain contracts on Sunday.

Suspect class

A statutory classification based on race, religion, national origin, alienage, or sex. For a statute containing such a classification to be upheld as constitutional, the statute must be needed to promote some compelling state purpose.

Sweetheart contract

A collective bargaining agreement in which the union meets the employer's wishes rather than representing the best interests of its members.

Symbolic speech

Conduct designed to convey a message.

Syndicate

An association of individuals or companies to finance a particular project.

Tangible property

Property that can be touched.

Target company (securities)

The firm whose shares are the subject of a tender offer.

Temporary stay

A court order that bars a party from engaging in specified behavior for a limited period of time.

Tender offer

An offer extended to a firm's shareholders to buy their equity securities.

Theory

The use of a philosophy to predict, judge, or explain.

Third-party beneficiary

A person who benefits from a contract set up and performed by others.

Tied product

A product or service that a buyer must purchase so as to obtain a desired product or service (the tying product).

Tippee

A person who obtains from an insider material nonpublic information about a firm.

Tipper

An insider who wrongfully shares material nonpublic information about a firm with a person who has no legitimate need for that information.

Tombstone advertisement

A written advertisement of a securities offering that makes known the availability of a prospectus; used only during the waiting period, that is, between the time when a registration statement is filed as required by federal securities law and the time when the registration statement takes effect.

Tort

A private or civil wrong against an individual that involves the breach of a legal duty.

Trade (antitrust policy)

Dealing in goods or services.

Trade associations

An organization whose members are firms engaged in the same line of business.

Trademark

Artwork, symbol, or design placed on a product to identify its manufacturer.

Trademark infringement

The accidental or intentional use of a trademark so similar to a previously established trademark of another firm that its use is likely to confuse the public.

Trust (antitrust policy)

Shareholders of two or more corporations transfer their stock to one or more persons who vote the stock but retain the right to receive the dividends paid on the stock.

Tying agreement

An agreement in which, in return for providing a buyer with a product or service that the buyer wants, a seller forces the buyer to either agree to purchase another product or service from the seller or not to purchase another product or service from another seller.

Tying product

A product or service that a buyer wants and that a seller refuses to sell the buyer unless the buyer also purchases a product or service that the buyer might not have purchased otherwise.

Ultra vires

Action beyond the scope of an administrative agency's statutory authority.

Unconscionable contract

A contract so unfair that the courts will not enforce it; a contract in which the bargaining power of the two parties is so one-sided that the terms of the contract are oppressive to the party with less bargaining power.

Underwriter (securities)

A person who purchases a firm's securities for later resale or who undertakes to market them to investors.

Undisclosed principal

Contracting between the agent and a third party in which the third party does not know of the agency relationship or of the identity of the principal.

Undue burden on interstate commerce

The doctrine that state laws impeding interstate business activity are invalid.

Unenforceable contract

An agreement that meets the requirements of a contract—agreement, consideration, competent parties, and legality of purpose—but is not legally enforceable because a defense to the agreement exists.

Unfair labor practice

Conduct by an employer or a union that is prohibited by federal law.

Unfair labor practice strike

A work stoppage to protest an employer's unfair labor practice.

Unfair or deceptive act or practice in commerce

A commercial practice that the law prohibits because its use by a business unfairly injures consumers.

Unforeseeable difficulties rule

The rule that modification of a contract without consideration because of unforseeable difficulties is enforceable.

Unicameral

A single-unit lawmaking body.

Uniform Commercial Code

A comprehensive body of commercial law.

Unilateral contract

An agreement in which one party makes a promise in exchange for an act by the other party.

Union shop

A provision in the collective bargaining agreement that requires employees to join the union after a probationary period.

Unreasonable searches and seizures clause

A clause in the Fourth Amendment to the Constitution that prohibits government searches and seizures of persons or property without a search warrant issued by a court upon a showing of probable cause.

Usury

The lending of money at an illegal rate of interest.

Usury laws

Statutes that limit the interest that can be charged in contracts to borrow money.

Utilitarian ethics

Views conduct that brings the greatest happiness to the greatest number of persons as ethical.

Utilitarian jurisprudence

The view that a rule of law should benefit most persons.

Valid contract

An agreement that meets the requirements of a contract—agreement, consideration, competent parties, and legality of purpose—and is legally enforceable.

Venue

The geographic area in which a case should be tried.

Verdict

The jury's decision.

Vertical merger

A combination of firms that conduct business at different distribution levels.

Vertical price-fixing (antitrust policy)

An agreement between a manufacturer and those who purchase its goods for resale as to the price that the purchasers will charge for the resold goods.

Vesting

The legal right that an employee acquires in a retirement plan after completing a required length of service.

Veto

The rejection by a government's chief executive officer, such as the president or a governor, of a bill passed by the legislature.

Voidable contract

An agreement that can be rescinded by one or both of the parties but is legally enforceable unless one of the parties chooses to rescind it.

Void contract

An agreement that is without legal effect because it lacks one or more of the requirements of a contract.

Voir dire

The questioning by the attorneys and the judge to determine that those chosen to serve as jurors will be impartial.

Voting pool

An agreement among shareholders to vote their combined stock in accordance with a plan.

Waiting period (securities)

The period of time that must pass before a registration statement takes effect so that the securities covered by the registration statement may be offered for sale, or be sold, in the manner in which securities are generally offered for sale, or sold, under federal securities law.

Waiver of defense clause

A clause inserted in a contract for the transfer of legal rights from an assignor to an assignee that states that the assignee voluntarily gives up the right to assert any defenses against the assignor.

Warranty of fitness

The implied promise that goods are fit for the purpose for which they are sold.

Warranty of merchantability

The implied promise in a sale of goods by a merchant seller that the goods are fit for the purpose for which they are sold.

Winding up

A state just prior to dissolution, in which a corporation stops taking on new business and gradually closes out its accounts. The assets of the corporation are liquidated.

Writ

A legal document that is issued by a court.

Writ of certiorari

An order of a higher court used in the appeal process requiring a lower court to forward to it the records and proceedings of a particular case.

Writ of execution

A court's order directing the sheriff to seize enough of the defendant's nonexempt real and personal property to satisfy a judgment by selling the property at public auction.

Writ of mandamus

A court order that directs one or more named persons to obey the law.

Written confirmation

A writing sufficient to indicate that a contract of sale was made between a merchant seller and a merchant buyer.

Yellow-dog contract

An employment contract in which as a condition of employment the employee promises not to join a union.

Zaibatsu

A combination of independent Japanese firms generally headed by members of the same Japanese family.

Case Index

Subject Index